Incineration of Municipal Waste

Specialized Seminars on

Incinerator Emissions of Heavy
Metals and Particulates,
Copenhagen, 18–19 September 1985

and

Emission of Trace Organics from
Municipal Solid Waste Incinerators,
Copenhagen, 20–22 January 1987

edited by

ROBERT B. DEAN

Reprinted from Waste Management &
Research, Volume 4, Number 1, 1986 and
Volume 5, Number 3 1987

Published for the International Solid
Wastes and Public Cleansing Association
(ISWA) by Academic Press

ACADEMIC PRESS

Harcourt Brace Jovanovich, Publishers

London   San Diego   New York
Boston   Sydney   Tokyo   Toronto

ACADEMIC PRESS LIMITED
24/28 Oval Road
London NW1
(Registered Office)

US edition published by
ACADEMIC PRESS INC.
San Diego
CA 92101

© 1988 ISWA
ISBN 0 12 207690 7

Printed in Great Britain by
Richard Clay Ltd, Bungay Suffolk

PREFACE

The present volume includes the edited proceedings of two specialized seminars dealing with emissions from modern municipal waste incinerators. The first dealt with toxic metals, the second with organics such as Dioxin. In both cases it was shown that the use of modern stack gas cleaning equipment can reduce the emission of toxic substances, whether metallic or organic, by at least an order of magnitude below conventional equipment of a decade ago. The low emissions obtainable would lead to air quality changes that are well within normal background fluctuations arising from other sources.

The limiting factor, as always, is cost. Fortunately the techniques necessary for good control of mercury, cadmium and other heavy metals are the same as those that are needed to reduce Dioxin and other trace organics.

The levels of trace emissions available in favourable examples lie well within what has been accepted as safe for humans and the environment. The question, therefore, shifts to an evaluation of the calculated risk from an emission. This is an area of toxicology that has far greater inherent uncertainty than even analytical measurements of the isomers of Dioxin or other trace substances. To counteract this uncertainty, various and multiple safety factors have been applied with little or no justification. Further work in the evaluation of risks from traces of toxic substances is urgently needed.

Both seminars were organized by ISWA and its Danish member society, DAKOFA. The Dioxin seminar was also sponsored by the WHO, Regional Office for Europe. The Chairman and prime organizer of both seminars was Professor Jens Aage Hansen of Aalborg University, Department of Environmental Engineering. All contributions have been refereed and edited and numerous editorial cross references to other papers in the symposium supplement the references provided by the authors. The original pagination is given in a footnote on the first page of each paper to eliminate confusing bibliographic references.

This publication of the two specialized issues of *Waste Management & Research* as a separate volume should provide a handy source of information for all persons concerned with the control of emissions from incineration.

Terminology. Most of the papers in the second seminar on trace organics dealt with only one group of the highly toxic substances commonly referred to as Dioxin. This term is an abbreviation for polychlorinated dibenzo-*p*-dioxin (PCDD) of which there are 75 isomers. The most toxic isomer is one of the tetrachloro isomers (TCDD or TeCDD) with chlorine in the 2, 3, 7 and 8 positions. Other isomers of concern are the penta (PeCDD), hexa (HxCDD), hepta (HpCDD) and octa (OCDD) isomers. A very similar set of isomers of polychlorinated dibenzofurans. (PCDF) are also found along with Dioxins and have similar toxicities. Various methods have been developed to estimate the toxicity of mixtures of Dioxins usually in terms of 2, 3, 7, 8-TCDD, equivalents.

Robert B. Dean
Editor

TABLE OF CONTENTS

MONITORING OF HEAVY METALS BY ENERGY DISPERSIVE X-RAY FLUORESCENCE SPECTROMETRY*

Karl E. Lorber†

(*Received 7 Sept 1985, revised 28 October 1985*)

Fundamentals and salient features of a projected heavy metals monitoring system are discussed. Determination of mass concentrations is achieved by using a new dust emission monitor, consisting of a "Zero Pressure Probe" for isokinetic sampling, which is connected to a "Longitudinally Oscillating Band" mass detector. The thin dust layer, precipitated on the surface of heat resistant filter tapes could be analysed nondestructively by energy-dispersive X-ray fluorescence (EDXRF). Using a small portable EDXRF-system with radioisotope-excitation, quasi-continuous monitoring of particulate heavy metals (Cd, Hg, Pb, Cu, Sb, Zn, Sn) suspended in incinerator stack gases is expected to be feasible. Another application of EDXRF-analysis is the reported investigation of electrostatic precipitator ash (ESP-fly ash). Using the "Linear Multi-Elemental-Standard Addition Method" as a fast and simple routine technique, results are reported for the concentrations of Pb, Cd, Cu and Zn in fly ash samples which had been collected in different fields (hoppers) of the electrostatic precipitator.

Key Words—Waste incineration, precipitator ash, EDXRF analysis, particulate heavy metals, stack gas analysis.

1. Introduction

Waste incinerators may be considered as variable emission sources which are prone to frequent fluctuations and rapid changes in stack gas concentrations. To meet the practical requirements of monitoring heavy metals emitted by the combustion of waste, a fast and reliable analytical method has to be applied in combination with a continuous or quasi-continuous stack gas sampling system. Out of various analytical methods taken into consideration, energy-dispersive X-ray fluorescence (EDXRF) spectrometry offers the advantages of non-destructive, simultaneous multi-element analysis with a high degree of automatization.

Recently, an R&D project has been started at the Technical University in Berlin, dealing with the monitoring of particulate heavy metals suspended in incinerator stack gases. In this paper, principles and salient features of the projected Heavy Metals Monitoring System are discussed and a simple and fast method is reported for the determination of heavy metals in flyash which was collected in different fields of an electrostatic precipitator (ESP).

2. Principles of a new heavy metals monitoring system

For quasi-continuous monitoring of particulate heavy metals suspended in incinerator

---

*Presented at the ISWA Specialized Seminar *Incinerator Emissions of Heavy Metals and Particulates*, Copenhagen, 18–19 September 1985.

†Department of Air Chemistry—KF 3, Institute for Environmental Protection (ITU), Technical University Berlin, D–1000, Berlin 12, F.R.G.

Waste Management & Research (1986) **4**, 3–13

stack gases, the following approach is suggested, using an integrated system which contains a newly developed dust concentration measuring instrument (Gast & Kramm 1984), on-line connected to a modified EDXRF spectrometer. The dust measuring instrument used in the R&D project had been developed at the Institut für Meß- und Regelungstechnik, Technical University Berlin. It consists of an isokinetic stackgas sampling device (Zero Pressure Probe) and a Longitudinally Oscillating Band mass detector.

2.1. *Isokinetic stackgas sampling with the "Zero-Pressure-Probe"*

The basic principles of the "Zero-Pressure-Probe" (Nulldrucksonde) are demonstrated in Fig. 1. The probe works with an isokinetic flow divider, based on measurements of the pressure difference between a sensor channel (a) and the main channel (b).

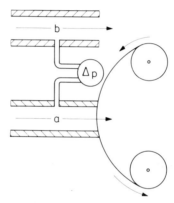

Fig. 1. Operating fundamentals of the Zero Pressure Probe for isokinetic stack gas sampling. a, Sensor channel; b, main channel.

Parallel to flow direction, sensor channel (a) and main channel (b) are placed in the stack gas stream. At the inside wall of the open main channel (b), the static pressure P_{stat} occurs. Suppose that sensor channel (a) is closed on the right-hand side, the inside wall pressure will be the sum of the static pressure P_{stat} and the dynamic pressure P_{dyn}. Thus, according to the Bernoulli equation, the pressure difference between (a) and (b) becomes: $\Delta P = P_{dyn}$. If the sensor-channel (a) is closed with a permeable filter tape as in Fig. 1, isokinetic sampling is achieved as soon as the pressure difference ΔP becomes zero. As the flow resistance increases with the thickness of the dust layer collected on the filter tape, the revolution (r m^{-1}) of the pump is regulated accordingly by an electrical signal from the pressure difference transmitter. Thus, isokinetic sampling is continuously controlled by keeping the pressure difference ΔP at zero and any change in the stack gas velocity is immediately accounted for.

This automatically controlled Zero Pressure Probe system offers some crucial advantages compared to conventional stack gas sampling devices. Using a Pitot tube or Prandtl-Staurohr arrangement like the standard VDI 2066 (VDI, 1979) provided by the Association of German Engineers, the requirements on trained manpower will be much higher and the accuracy of isokinetic sampling will be significantly lower. A schematic drawing of the integrated Zero Pressure Probe is shown in Fig. 2.

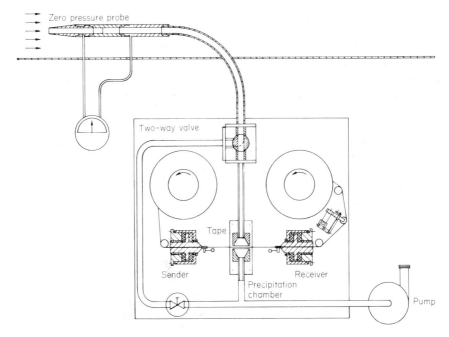

Fig. 2. Dust emission monitor with integrated Zero Pressure Probe and Longitudinally Oscillating Band mass detector. (Courtesy of Th. Gast and U. Kramm, Technical University, Berlin, F.R.G.).

2.2. *Dust concentration measurement by means of a longitudinally oscillating filter tape*

The fundamentals of the Longitudinally Oscillating Band mass detector are shown in Fig. 2. Using the integrated Zero Pressure Probe, a representative partial flow is sucked out of the stack gas. Via the two-way valve, the sampled gas is pumped to the precipitation chamber where the suspended particulate matter (dust) is mechanically deposited on the surface of a filter tape. Alternatively, electrostatic precipitation of the charged particles is possible too. In case of incinerator stack gas sampling, the gas temperature (about 250–230 °C in the stack) is cooled down to 140 °C and heat resistant Teflon (PTFE) type membrane filter tapes are used for dust collection. Mass detection of the precipitated dust is achieved quasi-continuously by measuring the change in the resonant frequency of the longitudinally oscillating filter tape.

According to the following equation (1), the piezo-electrically exited filter tape will change its resonant frequency when the precipitated dust mass participates in oscillation:

$$M = m \left(\frac{f_0^2}{f_m^2} - 1 \right),$$ (1)

where M = precipitated dust mass, m = filter band mass (before precipitation), f_o = resonant frequency of filter band (before precipitation), f_m = decreased resonant frequency of filter band (after precipitation). The voltage applied to the piezo-electrical sender will cause longitudinal oscillation of the filter tape. As already mentioned, the change in the resonant frequency of the oscillating band is a function of the precipitated dust mass.

For detection, the piezo-electrical receiver transfers the force of oscillation into voltage again. Finally, the input voltage of the sender and the output voltage of the receiver are displayed on the oscillograph. In the automatic operation mode of the instrument, it is fully controlled by a HP 85 calculator which converts the output signal of the resonant frequency into the mass of the precipitated dust. This new quasi-continuously operating dust emission monitor has some essential advantages compared to conventional measuring instruments. As the output signal does not depend on the chemical composition or the physical properties of the dust particles collected, no empirical conversion factors are necessary for calculating the mass. This is not true for radiometric or optical dust monitors, where the measured extinction values have to be converted into mass units by using an empirical factor between gravimetric determination and the indirect method used. The correlation coefficient may vary between 0.47 and 0.83 (Müller 1983). This new dust emission monitor, which recently became commercially available, has obtained a proven reliability in the mean time when it was used in the field. For a glass fibre filter tape, the observed sensitivity is 35 Hz mg^{-1}. A minimum detection limit of 0.1 mg or less seems to be possible by optimizing the system. The filter collection efficiency can be determined by the device used for testing high load sampling systems (Søby & Mosbaek 1983).

2.3. Photometric determination of the "average" particle size

In collaboration between the Technical University Berlin and the Nuclear Research Centre Karlsruhe, a modified version of the reported dust emission monitor has been developed (Kernforschungszentrum Karlsruhe 1985). Using the mass concentration extinction size analyser (MESA) instrument, simultaneously the "average"-particle size of the dust can be determined by measuring the Lambert–Beer extinction factor,

$$E = \ln\frac{I_0}{I}, \tag{2}$$

with the attached photometer.
From the equation

$$d_{em} = \frac{3 \times l \times C_m}{E \times \rho}, \tag{3}$$

where I_0 and I are the intensities of the transmitted light before and after absorbance, respectively, the so-called "average" particle size of the suspended dust particles can be calculated, when the mass concentration, C_m, and the extinction, E, is measured, and the path length of the transmitted light, l, and the density of the particulate matter, ρ, are known. The reported working-range of the photometer for C_m is between 10^{-3} and 1.0 gm^{-3}, and the particle size detection range is between 0.3 and 10.0 μm.

2.4. Quantitative multi-elemental analysis by X-ray fluorescence spectrometry

For the quasi-continuous monitoring of particulate heavy metals suspended in incinerator stack gases, it is suggested that an EDXRF system is connected on-line to the MESA instrument reported above. In Fig. 3, the non-destructive, simultaneous multi-elemental analysis of the fine dust layer collected on the filter tape is schematically shown.

X-Ray fluorescence (XRF) analysis of fine dust layers collected on the surface of membrane filters is advantageous, as long as the precipitated mass is in the range of 1–10 mg dust cm^{-2} filter surface (Lorber et al. 1978). In this case, the sample can be considered as a "thin film" which does not show any serious matrix effects. If the surface is smooth

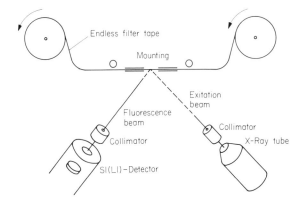

Fig. 3. Suggested approach for the quasi-continuous monitoring of heavy metals (R&D project, Technical University, Berlin, F.R.G.): on-line analysis of the collected dust by means of energy dispersive. X-ray fluorescence.

enough, no particle effect will occur, and the measured fluorescence intensities of the elements will be a linear function of their concentrations. Thus, no sample preparation seems to be necessary when appropriate membrane filter tapes (e.g. "fluoropore") are used. (In our experience, glass fibre filter materials are not adequate because of the rough surface and the relatively high blank values due to contamination.)

Another problem to solve is the calibration of the analysis system. In principle, two different ways might be taken into consideration: the application of synthetic "thin-film" standards (Billiet *et al.* 1980) or the re-calibration of the XRF system by atomic absorption spectrometry (AAS) analysis of the non-destructively investigated filter tape samples. At present, a series of filters are analysed by AAS after they had been measured by the EDXRF system.

Early results indicate that the minimum detection limits (MDL) for heavy metals are in the range between 1–10 μg cm^{-2}. Using the Totally Reflecting Sample Holders technique (Ketelsen & Knöchel 1983) or by improving the geometry of the sample chamber, lower minimum detection limits and higher sensitivities are achievable.

In a first approach, a TRACOR NORTHERN TN 2000-EDXRF-system is being modified for the automatic analysis of filter tapes which are supplied by the dust emission monitor developed at the Institut für Meß- und Regelungstechnik in Berlin. For this purpose, the filter tape has to be fitted into a conventional sample chamber where on-line analysis is not possible.

The final goal of the R & D project reported is the development of a quasi-continuous heavy metals monitor with on-line analysis of the endless filter tape. To meet these expectations, we have the intention to use a small portable EDXRF system with radio-isotope (γ-source) excitation and a simple detector system with a limited number of fixed channels. This type of analysis system is supposed to be fully compatible with the already existing dust emission monitor.

Based on the observed minimum detection limits between 1 and 10 μg cm^{-2}, the necessary amounts (mg) of dust, which have to be precipitated on the tape for EDXRF detection of different heavy metals are estimated in Table 1. It can be seen from Table 1, that EDXRF monitoring of Cd, Hg, Pb, Cu, Sb, Zn and Sn is expected to be feasible, due to sufficient concentrations of these elements in the emitted fine incinerator dust. For Ni, Cr, As and V, EDXRF detection is questionable and monitoring could be possibly done only after extended sampling times. Monitoring of Tl will not be possible at all.

TABLE 1

Average concentrations of heavy metals in emitted fine dust from incinerators (Vogg 1984; Lorber 1984) and estimated necessary amounts of dust collected on the tape for energy dispersive X-ray fluorescence detection

Element	Mass-fraction in emitted fine dust ($\mu g\ g^{-1}$)	Precipitated dust mass necessary for EDXRF-detection (mg)	
		MDI*: 10 $\mu g\ cm^{-2}$	MDI*: 1 $\mu g\ cm^{-2}$
Cd†	1500–2000	7–5	0.7–0.5
Hg†	1000–2000	10–5	1–0.5
Tl‡	1	10,000	1000
Ni§	100	100	10
Cr§	200–300	50–30	5–3
As§	100	100	10
Pb†	30,000	0.3	0.03
Cu†	3000	3	0.3
Sb†	3000	3	0.3
V§	100	100	10
Zn†	80,000	0.1	0.01
Sm†	4000	2.5	0.25

*MDL = Minimum detection limit.
†Sufficient sensitivity for monitoring.
‡Monitoring not possible.
§Monitoring questionable.

3. Determination of heavy metals in ESP-collected fly ash

Another application of EDXRF multi-elemental analysis is the determination of heavy metals in fly ash. The most common methods currently used for fly ash analysis are AAS or wet chemistry methods defined in ASTM-C311 (American Society for Testing and Materials 1981). However, the requirements in time and trained manpower are rather high compared to X-ray fluorescence spectrometry. For EDXRF analysis of heavy metals in fly ash, different techniques of sample preparations are commonly used, as follows.

(1) *Borate fusion technique:* by using $Li_2\ B_4\ O_7$ as a fluxing agent, the sample is converted into a borate-glass pellet. To avoid matrix-effects of the "non-infinitely-thick" samples, a heavy absorber (such as MoO_3) is added to the flux. Calibration is achieved by a set of synthetic borate glass standards (Lorber *et al.* 1978).

(2) *Pressed pellet technique:* the finely ground fly ash is mixed with a briquetting agent (like cellulose-powder) and pressed to "infinitely thick" pellets. Quantification is preferentially done by the linear multi-elemental standard addition technique.

(3) *Loose powder technique:* A loose powder of finely ground fly ash (about 3 g, passing through a 106 μm sieve) is filled into a Mylar cup. Excitation of the "infinitely-thick" layer of powder takes place through a thin polycarbonate foil on the bottom of the cup. Quantification is accomplished by the linear multi-elemental standard addition technique. In case of matrix effects—which result in non-linear response curves—the powdered sample can be diluted with SiO_2 to reduce concentrations.

A comparison of the three sample preparation methods mentioned above revealed that the most simple Loose Powder technique enables fast routine analyses of fly ash. As the agreement of the results obtained with different methods was satisfactory, this technique has been used for the following investigation of fly ash, precipitated in different sections (first and second field) of the ESP.

3.1. *Linear multi-elemental standard addition method*

Using an agate mortar or a tungsten carbide mill, the original fly ash sample is ground to a fine powder which is divided into four equal portions. One portion remains as it is, but the other portions are "doped" with known amounts of a multi-elemental standard which can be added in powder form. After carefully grinding and mixing, the four partial samples are filled into Mylar-cups and measured by EDXRF.

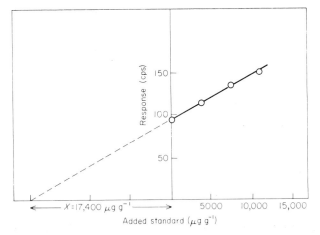

Fig. 4. Linear multi-elemental Standard Addition Technique: determination of lead in the fly ash sample R 1.4. (Ash collected in the hopper of the second field of electrostatic precipitator investigated. – – –, Extrapolation of line. Correlation coefficient, $r^2 = 0.9983$.

As shown in Fig. 4, linear extrapolation is possible, as long as the following criteria are met:

(1) The powdered sample must be homogeneous in respect of composition and particle size.
(2) For the excitation- and fluorescence radiation, the analysed layer of loose powder must be "infinitely thick".
(3) The bulk density of the four partial samples should be the same.
(4) The concentrations of the elements investigated and standard added should not be to high (less than about 2–5%), or powder dilution techniques should be applied.

3.2. Results

Using the same scale for display, the EDXRF-spectra of three different fly ash samples are shown in Figs 5–6 (Cd, which has been analysed at higher tube voltage, is not visible on this display). A comparison of the EDXRF spectra reveals the well known fact, that the concentration of heavy metals in incinerator fly ash is significantly higher than in fly ash from coal fired power stations.

When an ESP is used with two electrical fields in flow direction, the major portion of

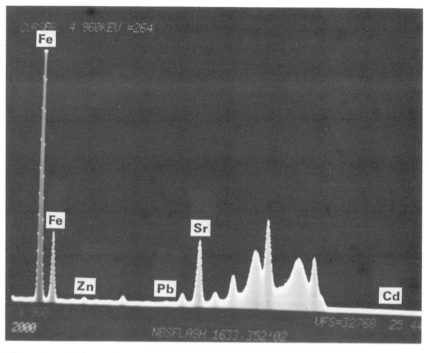

Fig. 5. Energy dispersive X-ray fluorescence spectrum of NBS fly ash SRM 1633 from coal fired power stations.

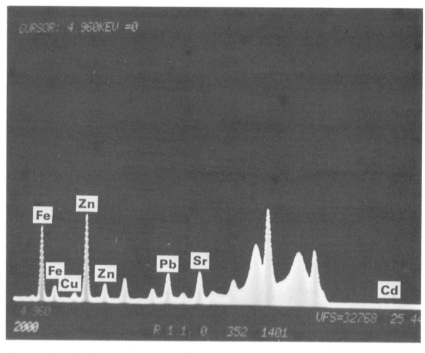

Fig. 6. Energy dispersive X-ray fluorescence spectrum of incinerator fly ash from Berlin (collected from the hopper of the first field of the investigated electrostatic precipitator).

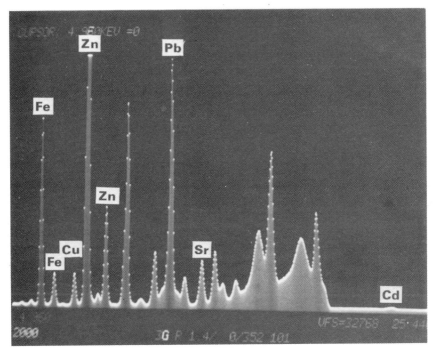

Fig. 7. Energy dispersive X-ray fluorescence spectrum of incinerator fly ash from Berlin (collected from the hopper of the second field of the investigated electrostatic precipitator.

fly ash is precipitated in the first field and only a rather small portion is collected in the hoppers of the second field. But due to the well known prevalence of heavy metals on the surface of small particles (Lorber 1980), the concentration of these elements (Pb, Cd, Cu, Zn, etc.) is significantly higher in the fly ash sample collected in the hopper of ESP field 2.

The results discussed above are quantitatively presented in Table 2.

TABLE 2

Quantitative results for different fly ash samples, using the energy dispersive X-ray fluorescence detection Linear Multi-Elemental-Standard Addition technique. The NBS-SRM 1633* was used for verification. (Confidence limit = 95%, number of determinations = 7)

| | Mass fraction in fly ash ($\mu g\ g^{-1}$) | | | |
| | NBS-SRM 1633 | | Pre-Filter Ash | Post-Filter Ash |
Element	Certified	Found	(ESP field 1)*	(ESP field 2)*
Cd	1.45±0.06	—	168±12	654±31
Pb	70±4	81±12	2480±89	18850±662
Cu	128 ±5	125±15	500+47	2570+253
Zn	210±20	223±27	5830±492	23970±1181

*Standard reference material, from U.S. National Bureau of Standards.

4. Conclusions

Energy dispersive X-ray fluorescence spectrometry offers the advantages of fast and simple multi-elemental analyses, which are needed for monitoring of heavy metals mobilized by incineration of waste. Using a newly developed dust emission monitor system, which contains a Zero Pressure Probe connected to a Longitudinally Oscillating Band mass detector, fine dust from stack gas can be collected on a filter tape. The results of EDXRF analysis of filter tapes indicate that for heavy metals the minimum detection limits are in the range of 1–10 $\mu g\ cm^{-2}$. Based on known stack gas concentrations, the minimum amounts of fine dust required for stack gas monitoring of heavy metals are estimated. It is expected, that for Cd, Hg, Pb, Cu, Sb, Zn and Sn the sensitivity of the EDXRF analysis system, connected on-line to the dust emission monitor, is sufficient.

Using the simple Loose Powder Standard Addition technique, fly ash can be quickly analysed for heavy metals. When filter ash from different fields of the ESP was investigated, it was shown that the concentrations of Cd, Pb, Cu and Zn are significantly higher in the post-filter ash of ESP-field 2 compared to the pre-filter ash of ESP-field 1.

References

American Society for Testing and Materials (1981), *Annual Book of ASTM-Standards*, Part 14. ASTM Philadelphia, U.S.A.

Billiet, J., Dams, R. & Hoste, J. (1980), Multielement thin film standards for XRF analysis, *X-Ray Spectrometry*, 9(4).

Gast, Th. & Kramm, U. (1984), Abschlußbericht zum Forschungsvorhaben Kraftwerksemissionsmessungen. Bundesministerium für Forschung und Technologie (BMFT) (Final report: Measurement of emissions from power stations. Ministry of Research & Technology) *Reference No. 1-ET 1141 A*. Ministry of Research and Technology, F.R.G.

Kernforschungszentrum Karlsruhe (1985), Koordinationsstelle Technologietransfer (Nuclear research centre Karlsruhe, coordination bureau for technology transfer), personal communications.

Ketelsen, P. & Knöchel A. (1983), *Multielementanalyse von Aerosolen mit Hilfe der Röntgenfluoreszenzanalyse mit totalreflektierendem Probenträger (TRFA)*. (Multi-element analysis of aerosols by XRF with totally reflecting sample holder). Publication of the Institut für Anorganische und Angewandte Chemie, Universität Hamburg, F.R.G.

Lorber, K. E., Wegscheider, W., Spitzy, H., Heinrich, K. F. J. & Pella, P. A. (1978), Development of EDXRF-Techniques for the Quantitative Multielement Analysis of Environmental Samples, *Mikrochim. Acta, I*.

Lorber, K. E. (1980), Müllverbrennung und Schwermetallemission (Waste incineration and emission of heavy metals), *Müll und Abfall, 6*.

Lorber, K. E. (1985), Incineration of RDF and incineration of total waste—comparison of emissions. In *Sorting of Household Waste and Thermal Treatment of Waste, Commission of the European Communities* (Ferranti & Ferrero, Eds). Elsevier Applied Science Publishers, London and New York.

Müller, J. (1983), Test of sampling instruments for suspended particulate matter in ambient air. Umweltbundesamt, Frankfurt/Main. Contribution to the poster-session during the *Seminar: Aerosols in Science, Medicine and Technology*, 14–16 September 1983, München, F.R.G.

Søby F. & Mosbaek, H. (1983), Assessment of stack gas emitted trace metals from incineration: determination of filter collection efficiency by condensational enlargement of penetrating submicron particles, *Waste Management & Research 1*, 255–266.

VDI (1979) *Verein Deutscher Ingenieure: VDI 2066. Messen von Partikeln. Staubmessungen in strömenden Gasen. Gravimetrische Bestimmung der Staubbeladung* (Assoziation of German Engineers, VDI-guidelines: Measurement of particles. Measurement of dust in moving gases. Gravimetrical determination of the dust load). VDI-Kommission Reinhaltung der Luft, VDI-Verlag GmbH, Düsseldorf, F.R.G.

Vogg, H. (1984), Verhalten von (Schwer)-Metallen bei der Verbrennung kommunaler Abfälle (Behavior of heavy metals during incineration of municipal refuse), *Chem.-Ing.-Techn.*, *56*.

HEAVY METALS FROM "ENERGY FROM WASTE" PLANTS— COMPARISON OF GAS CLEANING SYSTEMS

Kurt Carlsson†

(*Received 30 August 1985*)

Municipal waste incinerators produce more heavy metals calculated per usable energy unit (g MWh^{-1}) than other solid fuel fired plants, e.g. coal, peat and wood waste. This paper presents a comparison of some modern proven gas cleaning methods including an electrostatic precipitator (ESP) followed by a scrubber with condensation or an electrostatic scrubber, and a dry scrubbing systems using slurry injection followed by ESP or powder injection followed by fabric filter. The comparison shows that the system with fabric filter has a lower emission of many heavy metals than the other methods.

Key Words—Waste incineration, energy from waste, electrostatic precipitator, scrubber with condensation, electrostatic scrubber, dry scrubbing, slurry injection, powder injection, fabric filter, mercury, cadmium, lead.

1. Introduction

Waste which is burnt in normal waste incinerators is usually collected from households (apartments, individual houses), city districts (shops, supermarkets, services industries, hotels) and light business areas (distribution centres, light industries). The waste components contain varying quantities of metals and acid forming elements.

2. Metal distribution from incinerators

A normal waste incinerator produces 20–30% (by weight) bottom ash of the original waste (by volume, 5–10%). This ash contains most of the heavy metals, e.g. Zn, Pb, Cu, Ni, but mercury is almost completely evaporated at the common combustion temperature of 800–1000°C.

The amount of cadmium evaporated varies widely in different incinerators. In a study of the Avesta incinerator (Lundquist 1984a), about 15% of the Cd was found to stay in the bottom ash, but in the Uppsala incinerator the value was 50% (Lundquist 1984b), and Linköping, 80% (Lundquist 1984c). The concentrations of some heavy metals in the flue gas from waste incinerators are shown in Table 1, (the SYSAV data was reported by Bergström & Lundquist 1983).

Many efforts have been made to measure the particle size distribution of this dust with impactors but not many have succeeded mainly due to problems with low increase of weight on each stage and absorption of HCl, SO$_2$, HF, etc., by the particles and the filter. The content of the heavy metals in the different dusts is enriched towards the stack as shown in Table 2. These concentrations are on the same level as the ones reported by

*Presented at the ISWA Specialized Seminar *Incinerator Emissions of Heavy Metals and Particulates*, Copenhagen, 18–19 September 1985
†Fläkt Industri AB, S-351 87, Växjö, Sweden.
Waste Management & Research (1986) **4**, 15–20

K. Carlsson

TABLE 1

Concentrations (mg m^{-3} norm dry gas 10% CO_2) of heavy metals in flue gas from waste incinerators before gas cleaning

Element	Plant				
	SYSAV	Linköping	Uppsala	Avesta	Estimated range
Zn	20–50	52	60	100	20–100
Pb	6–15	14	24	40	6–40
Cd	0.3–0.6	1	0.6	1	0.3–1.0
Hg		0.4	0.3	0.4	0.2–0.5
Total dust	3500	1400–2000		c. 1500	1500–5000
	− 5000				
Dust > 10 μm	2000				
	− 3000				
Dust < 10 μm	c. 1500				

TABLE 2

Content of heavy metals (mg g^{-1}) in ashes and dust

	Linköping				Avesta			
	Pb	Cd	Zn	Hg	Pb	Cd	Zn	Hg
Bottom ash	1.5	0.05	6	0.001	4	0.06	7	Low
ESP* dust	6.5	0.40	24	0.006	13	0.40	23	0.007
Emitted dust	25.0	1.50	80	1.000	30	0.80	140	0.020

*ESP = Electrostatic precipitator.

Brunner & Zobrist (1983), who also give a good summary of other measurements (see also Brunner & Mönch (1986).

3. Gas cleaning systems

The development of gas cleaning is today concentrated on increasing the cleaning efficiency, decreasing the consumption of costly chemicals and the amount of residues which now have to be taken to a controlled landfill, and increasing the heat recovery. As the municipal incinerators contribute to the contamination of the atmosphere, especially with heavy metals, it is interesting to compare some approved gas cleaning systems on their efficiency in collecting of heavy metals.

3.1. Gas cleaning with saturated gas

3.1.1. Electrostatic precipitators (ESP) and electrostatic scrubbers

A normal low pressure adiabatic wet scrubber has a rather low efficiency with regard to submicron dust. As the heavy metals are concentrated in this submicron dust results of two new scrubber types are presented as representatives of the first category, viz. electrostatic scrubber and scrubber with condensation.

An electrostatic scrubber is installed after an ESP in MVA, Lausanne, Switzerland (Vicard & Knocke 1984); Table 3 shows the results that have been reported using a train of five impingers as specified in the Swiss guidelines but without a filter upstream of the impingers.

TABLE 3

Emissions from electrostatic precipitator + electrostatic scrubber at MVA, Lausanne, Switzerland

Pollutant	Number of measurements	Outlet loading (mg m^{-3}) norm dry 11% O_2
Particulates + gaseous	10	34
Cl$^-$	10	< 50
F$^-$	10	< 0.01
Pb	10	0.9
Zn	10	1.8
Pb + Zn	10	2.7
Cd	10	0.04
Hg	2	0.12

TABLE 4

Loads (g h^{-1}) and concentrations (mg m^{-3}) of dust and heavy metals in norm dry gas before and after a scrubber with condensation installed downstream of an electrostatic precipitator at Avesta, Sweden (unpublished)

Test No.	Total dust				Cadmium particulates (conc.)		Lead particulates (conc.)		Zinc particulates (conc.)		Mercury, particulate plus gaseous (conc.)	
	Inlet		Outlet		Inlet	Outlet	Inlet	Outlet	Inlet	Outlet	Inlet	Outlet
	Load	Conc.	Load	Conc.								
1	5.7	58	2.3	23								
2	6.0	50	4.3	43	0.05	0.04	1	0.9	2.3	2.0	0.3	0.01
3	6.4	58	4.4	33	0.05	0.03	0.8	0.6	2.5	1.6	0.2	0.03
4	6.3	63	3.7	37	0.03	0.02	1.4	1.0	3.7	2.5	0.3	0.01
5	6.0	19	2.5	8	0.02	0.005	0.4	0.2	1.0	0.3	0.1	0.06
Average scrubber efficiency (%)		44				40		40		40		80

3.1.2. *Scrubbers with internal cooling*

Scrubbers with internal cooling followed by condensation of water have been used for a long time, especially after ESP in flue gases at pulp mill recovery boilers. The water produced is hot enough (60 °C) to be used directly for washing the pulp. Many measurements have indicated very good efficiency for fine particles, mainly due to the effect of condensation.

At municipal incinerators the first, and only, test has been made on a small pilot plant following the existing ESP at a 3–4 ton h^{-1} incinerator for municipal waste belonging to Avesta Energiverk, Avesta, Sweden. The tests were partly financed by the "Värmeforsk" Foundation, and a report of the measurements will be published by this foundation. An abstract of the results with respect to heavy metals is given in Table 4.

3.2. *Gas cleaning without saturation*

3.2.1. *Dry scrubber with slurry injection*

Wet-dry systems with ESP for dust collection are rather common. One of the first units in operation was the Fläkt-Gadelius System with a ball bed reactor called Fläkt-Nateko.

TABLE 5

Concentrations (mg m³ norm, dry gas, 11% O_2 of different impurities in the gas at MVA, Munich Nord, F.R.G. (slurry injection + electrostatic precipitator)

Contaminant	Concentrations		Collection efficiency (%)
	Raw gas	Treated gas	
HCl	600–1500	50–100 ⎫	Dependent on the
SO$_2$	200–500	100–150 ⎭	lime feed
HF	5–15	<1	
NO	205	160	
NO$_2$	16	10	
Total particulates	2000–5000	<25	
Cd + Tl + Hg	1.3	0.02	
As + Co + Ni + Se + Te	4.1	0.15	
Sb + Pb + Cr + Cu + Mn + V	32.5	0.60	
Particulates			
Cd	1.29	0.02	98.45
Pb	21.1	0.24	98.8
Zn	74.3	1.3	98.3
Hg	Low	Low	
(Gaseous) Hg	0.08–0.45	0.05–0.2	50

TABLE 6

Emission levels (mg m^{-3} norm dry 11% O_2) from dry powder injection + fabric filter at SYSAV, Malmö, Sweden, and MVE, Kempton

Element	SYSAV plant (160 °C)			Kempton plant (220 °C)		
		Clean gas			Clean gas	
	Raw gas	Particulates	Gas	Raw gas	Particulates	Gas
Cd	0.57	0	0.0001		0.00004	
Pb	11.9	0.01	0.002		0.0004	
Zn	49.1	0.075	0.015			
Hg	0.06–0.50	0	0.012–0.065			0.2–0.6
	4000	<20		3000	4	

The first commercial unit was started in 1978 and now 19 plants are operating, all in Japan. Hydrated lime slurry is fed to the ball bed for binding the acidic gases of hydrochloric acid and sulphur dioxide.

In Japan, much of the heavy metals are sorted out from the waste before incineration. The emission levels are therefore low and not comparable to the European and North American conditions. For that reason, we choose a European installation as an example of a dry scrubber with slurry injection. There are only limited results published of the combination of wet-dry reactor plus fabric filter (FF) but more results are available for this type of reactor with ESP, e.g. from Düsseldorf and Munich.

The installation in Munich is equipped with a new ESP giving a low emission of particulates. Table 5 shows the performance of unit 5 at that plant as an example of what

TABLE 7

Emission levels (μg m^{-3} norm dry gas) and total removal efficiencies (%) for different gas cleaning systems*

Emission	ESP + ESS		ESP + CS		Spray tower + ESP		Dry injection + FF	
	Emission	Removal	Emission	Removal	Emission	Removal	Emission	Removal
Cadmium								
Particulate			30	97	20	98.5	0.04	
Gas							0.1	
Total	40	96					0.14	99.98
Mercury								
Particulate					0		0	
Gas					150	50.0	50	
Total	120	70	50	80			50	85.0
Lead								
Particulates			700	95	240	98.8	10	
Gas							2	
Total	900	95					12	99.9
Zinc								
Particulates			2000	96	1300	98.3	75	
Gas							15	
Total	1800	96					90	99.8
Dust	34000		35000	99.1	<25000	99.5	<20000	99.5

*ESP, electrostatic precipitator; ESS, electrostatic scrubber; CS, scrubber with condensation; FF, fabric filter.

a wet–dry reactor plus ESP can achieve (figures from Horch 1984, in a VDI report. The gas temperature in ESP is about 150 °C.

3.2.2. *Dry scrubber with powder injection*

It is advantageous to operate dry scrubbers at a low temperature. The SYSAV plant in Malmö, Sweden, is our example of a plant with dry powder injection at a rather low temperature. The gas cleaning plant, after the 2 × 12 ton waste h^{-1} furnaces, consists mainly of cyclones (collected dust is mixed with bottom ash), reactors with injection of hydrated lime and a common fabric filter. Table 6 presents the results from the SYSAV plant which operates at about 160 °C (Bergström & Lundquist 1983, 1985). As a comparison, some results from an identical type of plant in Kempten, Germany are also given. The Kempten plant operates at about 220 °C (Knorr 1985).

4. Comparison of gas cleaning systems

Table 7 presents a summary of emission levels and estimated efficiencies for different gas cleaning systems for the waste incinerators detailed in Tables 3 to 6.

5. Conclusion

Energy from waste plants produce more heavy metals per usable energy unit than other solid fuel fired plants (coal, peat, wood waste, etc.). Therefore these incinerators have to be equipped with the best available technology for fine dust collection and for removal of gaseous mercury, the main part of mercury at the usual gas temperatures (150–280°C). The fabric filter has an outstanding characteristic for collection of submicron dust and as, in combination with dry scrubbing, it also has a high efficiency for gaseous mercury, it seems that just a fabric filter in combination with dry injection or a downstream scrubber is the optimal solution of the gas cleaning problem for waste incinerators.

References

Bergström, J. & Lundquist, J. (1983), Driftstudie av SYSAV's avfallsvärmeverk i Malmö (SYSAV Waste Incinerator in Malmö—Studies of Operations), *SNV PM 1667*. SNV, Sweden.

Bergström, J. & Lundquist, J. (1985), Kvicksilveravskiljning or rökgaser från SYSAV's avfalls- värmeverk i Malmö (Collection of Mercury from SYSAV Waste Incinerator), *SNV PM 1887*. SNV, Sweden.

Brunner, P. H. & Zobrist, J. (1983), Die Müllverbrennung als Quelle von Metallen in der Umwelt (Waste Incinerators as a source of Metals in the Environment), *Müll und Abfall 9/83*.

Brunner, P. H. & Mönch, H. (1986), The flux of metals through municipal solid waste incinerators, *Waste Management & Research, 4*, 105–119.

Horch, K. (1984), Stand der Rauchgasreinigung in Müllverbrennungsanlagen—Möglichkeiten und Grenzen (Gas Cleaning from Waste Incinerators—Possibilities and Limits—State of the Art). VDI, Berichte.

Lundquist, J. (1984a), Driftstudie av Avesta Avfallsvärmeverk (Avesta Waste Incinerator—Studies of Operation), *SNV PM 1794*. SNV, Sweden.

Lundquist, J. (1984b), Driftstudie av UKAB's avfallsvärmeverk i Uppsala (Uppsala (UKAB) Waste Incinerator—Studies of Operation), *SNV PM 1875*.

Lundquist, J. (1984c), Driftstudie av Linköpings avfallsvärmeverk (Linköping Waste Incinerator— Studies of Operations), *SNV PM 1885*. SNV, Sweden.

Knorr, W. (1985), Entsorgungssicher—Emissionsmessungen an zwei Abfallverbrennungsanlagen mit nachgeschaltetem Gewebefilte (Emission measurents at two Waste Incinerators Equipped with Fabric Filters), *Entsorgungspraxis, 4/85*.

Vicard, J. F. & Knocke, M. (1984), *Operation of the Gas Cleaning Facilities at the Lausanne Incineration Plant*, pp. 95–100, Recycling International Berlin.

MERCURY FROM HÖGDALEN INCINERATION PLANT IN STOCKHOLM, 1972–1985*

Bengt Westergård†

(*Received 30 August 1985*)

Summary

Measurements of mercury in flue gases from the Högdalen incinerator (which burns most of the garbage in Stockholm), taken before the electrostatic precipitator (ESP), provide some information on the contents of this metal in the municipal garbage. Total mercury increased from about 1 to nearly 5 g tonne^{-1} of refuse from 1972 to 1982. At this time a campaign to collect mercury batteries in Sweden was started and approximately half of the mercury sold in batteries has been accounted for in collections.

Since the compaign started, the mercury content of flue gases has dropped to about 2 g tonne^{-1} as shown in Table 1. Over the same period particulate cadmium averaged 3.2 g tonne^{-1} and particulate lead 80 g tonne^{-1}. Maximum fluctuations of single measurements have been from 0.5 to 2 times the average.

Key Words—Mercury, incineration of municipal waste, Sweden.

TABLE 1

Mercury in flue gases (before ESP) from incineration of municipal solid waste, Högdalen, Stockholm

Year	Number of samples	Total mercury (g tonne^{-1} waste)
1972	3	1.0
1974	15	0.5
1980	2	3.1
1982	2	4.9
1983	1	3.8
1984	1	2.0
1985	5	2.0

*Presented at the ISWA Specialized Seminar *Incinerator Emissions of Heavy Metals and Particulates*, Copenhagen, 18–19 September 1985.

†Stockholm Energy, Box 39101, S-100054, Stockholm, Sweden.

Waste Management & Research (1986) **4**, 21

PERFORMANCE OF ELECTROSTATIC PRECIPITATORS*

H. Høgh Petersen†

(Received 29 August 1985)

Pontyposl

The large majority of municipal refuse incinerators utilize electrostatic precipitators for control of particulate emission. Precipitator performance is determined by the detailed chemical and physical properties of the fly ash and the gas in which it is suspended. Variations in the composition of the refuse burnt, of seasonal or other nature, as well as variations in the operation of the incinerator installation have a pronounced effect on precipitator exit emissions. Large temporal variations in the particulate emissions, not related to normally registered variations in refuse composition and plant operation, occur, as illustrated by measurements at a large Danish incinerator plant. Such variations, resulting from the variability of the process parameters, should be taken into account for the sizing and design of precipitators for new incinerator installations, and also when evaluating emission data from existing incinerator plants.

Key Words—Electrostatic precipitator, (ESP), incinerator, variability, refuse, resistivity, operation, performance, Denmark.

1. Introduction

Incineration of municipal waste has been practised successfully for more than 30 years and is increasingly becoming the preferred method for hygienic and economic elimination of more than 90% of its volume, leaving an inert, solid residue or slag. Further, in modern refuse incinerators the generated heat is usually recovered and utilized.

The incineration process produces substantial quantities of particulate and gaseous pollutants which must be effectively extracted from the combustion gases to meet increasingly stricter emission standards. In West Germany, for instance, the TALuft 1974/83 Regulations (Jost 1985) for incinerators burning more than 750 kg refuse h^{-1} (1650 lb h^{-1}) required particulate emissions of max. 100 mg per normal cubic meter of wet gas, referred to 11% O_2. West German incinerator installations built after 1974 are further required to control gaseous emissions of HCl and HF to 100 mg (measured as Cl^-) and 5 mg (measured as F^-), respectively, per normal cubic meter of wet gas referred to 11% O_2. A tightening of the limits for particulate emissions from 100 to 50 mg per normal cubic meter is being discussed.

The large majority of refuse incinerators utilize electrostatic precipitators (ESP), for control of particulate emission. Today electrostatic precipitation for this special application is a well-proven method, which with certainty and with high reliability can continuously meet the strictest emission standards when the precipitator is properly sized and designed for the characteristics of the process. A considerable amount of experience in the application of precipitators to incinerators for municipal waste has been accumulated through the years (Petersen 1984b). Further, a high level of research activity through the

---

*Presented at the ISWA Specialized Seminar *Incinerator Emissions of Heavy Metals and Particulates,* Copenhagen, 18–19 September 1985.

†F. L. Smidth & Co., 77 Vigersler Allé, DK-2500, Copenhagen, Denmark.

Waste Management & Research (1986) **4**, 23–33

past decade has increased our understanding of the precipitation process and has led to the emergence of new, promising techniques, aiming at solving the problems encountered in collection of fine particulate and reducing precipitator size and costs in general (Petersen 1984a).

This paper reviews basic physics and principles of ESP and describes some theoretical and practical advances of recent years. Against this background the application of precipitators for incinerators burning municipal waste is discussed. The occurrence of considerable temporal variations in precipitator emission with little or no correlation to registered plant data is illustrated.

2. Precipitator fundamentals

Electrostatic precipitation is based on three basic steps: (1) electric charging of the dust particles, (2) collection of the charged particles in an electric field, and (3) removal of the precipitated dust from the collecting plates.

2.1. Principle of operation

The ESP consists of discharge electrodes connected to a negative polarity high voltage DC source, which together with grounded collecting plates creates electric fields through which the dust-laden gas passes. The discharge electrodes can be wires, serrated tapes or rigid members having protrusions with a small radius of curvature. Because of the small radius of curvature the electric field in the immediate vicinity of the discharge electrode becomes so concentrated that the electrical breakdown strength of the gas is exceeded. Local electrical breakdowns in the form of corona discharge occur and ionize the gas, creating positive ions and free electrons (see Fig. 1).

The positive ions are captured by the negative discharge electrode, while the electrons, which initially are propelled towards the collecting plate, quickly become absorbed by electronegative gas molecules, particularly H_2O, O_2 and SO_2, contained in the gas. The negative ions created by this electron-attachment process have low mobilities compared to the free electrons, and they drift towards the collecting plate forming an ionic space charge, which stabilizes and determines the current flow in the precipitator.

In this flow of negative ions between discharge electrode and collecting plate, the suspended dust particles will acquire an electric charge by two distinct processes further

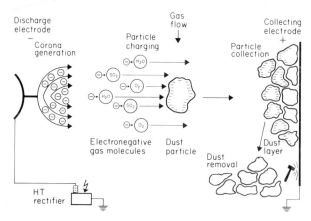

Fig. 1. Principle of operation of electrostatic precipitation.

described in the following. Under the influence of the electric field and hydrodynamic forces, the negatively charged particles migrate towards the grounded collecting plate. When the charged dust particles reach the collecting plate, they adhere to it while giving off their charge, forming a dust layer. The deposited dust is periodically dislodged by rapping and falls into the precipitator bottom hopper, from where it is removed continuously or periodically by suitable dust extraction equipment.

2.2. *Particle charging*

Two distinct charging mechanisms, usually identified as field charging and diffusion charging, are simultaneously active in the region between discharge electrode and collecting plate.

In field charging the ions, moving under the influence of the applied electric field along field lines intersecting the particle, impinge upon the particle and charge it (see Fig. 2). Field charging takes place very rapidly and ceases when the particle has acquired sufficient charge to repel additional ions. The saturation charge is determined by field

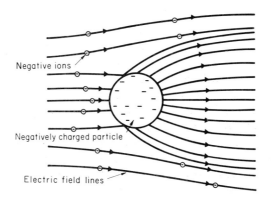

Fig. 2. Field charging of dust particle.

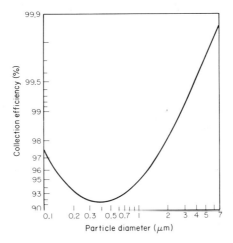

Fig. 3. Particle collection efficiency as function of particle size. Precipitator efficiency = 99.6%.

strength, particle diameter, and the dielectric constant of the particle. Field charging is the major charging process for particles larger than 1 or 2 μm diameter.

In the diffusion charging mechanism the random thermal motion of the ions results in their collision with and attachment to the particle even in the absence of an applied electric field. The charging rate is determined by the ion density, the mean thermal velocity of the ions, gas temperature, particle diameter and charge already acquired by the particle. Diffusion charging continues indefinitely with time without any saturation charge. The charging rate, however, becomes negligible after some time. Diffusion charging is particularly effective for submicron particles with diameters less than 0.2 μm.

The net result of the combined effects of field charging and thermal diffusion charging on the size band of particles is a minimum particle collection efficiency at a particle size around 0.4 μm, see Fig. 3 (White 1977).

2.3. Electrical conditions

The electrical conditions in the precipitator, i.e. field strengths and collecting plate current densities, are determined by the precipitator design and the properties of the gas and the dust. Gas composition, temperature and pressure determine ion mobility and electrical breakdown strength and have thereby a strong direct influence on precipitator current–voltage relationships. Particularly the moisture content of the gas can play a major role (see Fig. 4), which shows how precipitator current voltage characteristics are influenced by increasing degrees of cooling of the gas by injection and evaporation of atomized water.

A useful parameter for precipitator energization, and thereby for precipitator utilization, is the power density P/A (W m^{-2}) defined as the ratio of applied corona power (precipitator voltage × precipitator current) to collecting plate area.

2.4. Dust space charge

Dust concentration and particle size distribution also influence current voltage relation-

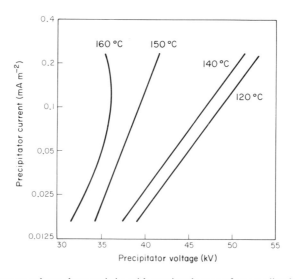

Fig. 4. Precipitator current voltage characteristics with varying degrees of gas cooling by H$_2$O conditioning.

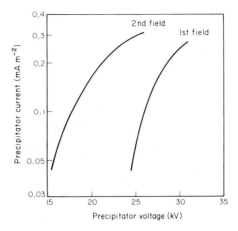

Fig. 5. Current voltage characteristics for first and second fields of precipitator for incinerator.

ships. The space charge of the suspended charged dust particles will partially shield the discharge electrodes from the electrical field lines emanating from the collecting plates. One effect of this is an increase in the electric field strength at the collecting plate surface which is beneficial for the collection efficiency. Another effect is the displacement of the current voltage characteristics for a precipitator inlet field with its higher dust concentration towards higher voltages (see Fig. 5).

2.5. *Resisitivity and back ionization*

The specific electrical resistance, or resistivity, of the dust layer precipitated on the collecting plate is an important parameter in electrostatic precipitation. The resistivity is determined by the chemical and physical properties of the dust particles and the surrounding gas. Gas temperature, and moisture and acid content of the gas play major roles (see Fig. 6).

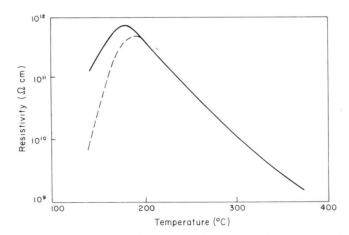

Fig. 6. Resistivity curves for fly ash with varying H_2O and SO_3 content of gas. ——, 5% H_2O, 4 ppm SO_2; ---, 10% H_2O, 8 ppm SO_3.

The precipitator operating voltage is strongly influenced by the dust resistivity, if this exceeds a critical value of about 10^{11} Ω cm. The reason for this is explained in the following two paragraphs.

The flow of corona current from the discharge electrode through the layer of dust deposited on the collecting plate builds up an electric field in the layer in accordance with Ohm's law. If the field strength exceeds the electric breakdown strength of the dust layer, discharges occur in the layer, and large quantities of positive ions are emitted into the space between the electrodes. The positive ions reduce the negative charging of the dust particles and reduce the precipitator operating voltage by increasing the conductivity of the gas.

This phenomenon, which manifests itself in very steep or even bent back current voltage characteristics, is known as "back corona" and results in rapid deterioration of precipitator performance as the resistivity exceeds 10^{11} Ω cm. Effective precipitation of high resisitivity dust therefore requires very large precipitators or use of special technology as for example pulse energization.

3. Precipitator efficiency

The Deutsch model or equation is commonly used to describe the precipitation process and to calculate precipitator performance (White 1963). It is expressed as

$$\frac{1}{1-\eta} = e^{wA/Q}, \tag{1}$$

where η is the particulate removal efficiency of the precipitator, w is the particle migration velocity, and A/Q is the ratio of collecting plate area to gas flow. A/Q is generally termed the specific collecting electrode area, or SCA. The Deutsch model assumes that turbulent mixing maintains a uniform particle concentration across the width of the collecting electrode duct as the gas passes through the precipitator.

The particle migration velocity w primarily depends on the strength of the electric fields for particle charging and collection, and on particle diameter. The migration velocity can be considered roughly proportional to the precipitator voltage raised to the second power, and to the particle diameter. The precipitator voltage thus plays a major role in precipitator efficiency. A reduction of precipitator voltage, e.g. by 5%, may increase the precipitator exit emission by 30%. Because the migration velocity is proportional to the particle diameter, the Deutsch equation can be directly applied only for a dust with uniform particle size.

For an industrial dust of non-uniform particle size the following empirical modification of the Deutsch equation is often applied:

$$\frac{1}{1-\eta} = e^{(w_k A/Q)^k}, \tag{2}$$

where w_k can be considered as the equivalent of the migration velocity w, whereas k is a constant, equalling approximately 0.5.

The Deutsch equation is based on some rather shaky assumptions. However, it has nevertheless been widely used for many years, mainly because nothing better has existed until recently.

4. Performance models

The U.S. Environmental Protection Agency has sponsored development of a sophisticated mathematical model for prediction of precipitator performance (Faulkner *et al.* 1984). The large computer programme of the model generates theoretical current voltage curves and calculates particle charging and precipitation for different particle size bands, increment for increment through the length of the precipitator. It includes effects of particle space charge, gas sneakage around the electrode systems, reentrainment and non-uniform gas distribution. The model, which is being continuously improved and refined, presently utilizes the Deutsch concept of precipitation combined with empirical adjustment factors.

The Deutsch model or equation, discussed earlier, does not in general predict precipitator performance accurately. In particular, it does not account adequately for observed dependence of the effective migration velocity on precipitator gas velocity and duct width.

Researchers in several countries are presently engaged in the development of models giving a more accurate description of the precipitation process. The Deutsch equation is based on the incorrect assumption that infinite turbulent mixing of the gas creates a uniform particle concentration across the width of the duct. The new models (Larsen *et al.* 1984) operate with variable levels of turbulence induced by the baffles on the collecting plates, the discharge electrodes and the electric wind generated by the corona discharge. They further take into account the effect on precipitator performance of the more or less orderly secondary gas flows created by the interaction of the electric winds and the mainflow of gas.

When fully developed, the new models can be expected to give more accurate predictions of precipitator efficiency. Further, they may eventually lead to new methods of improving precipitator performance by control of the turbulence and the corona induced flows in the precipitator.

5. Computer control

As discussed earlier, the precipitator voltage has a very strong influence on particle migration velocity, and thereby on precipitator collection efficiency. Therefore, microprocessor-based controllers for the precipitator high voltage power supplies have in recent years become general standard. These programmable, fast reacting, digital controllers can implement sophisticated control strategies, including differentiation of reactions according to type of spark in the precipitator, arc quenching, fast voltage recovery after sparking without re-ignition of the spark, and operation at, or near, the "knee" of the current voltage curve under back ionization conditions. They continuously control flashover rate and power input to the precipitator for optimum performance. Other microprocessor-based controllers are used for the rapping systems and the hopper evacuation systems.

One great asset of this new breed of controllers is their ability to communicate with a central computer dedicated to management and recording of the precipitator functions (Little *et al.* 1983). Such central computers are of particular advantage on large precipitator installations.

A central computer communicating with the individual microprocessor controllers, continuously receiving data from an opacity meter together with incinerator and boiler operation data, can be used for maintaining a desired opacity level with minimum use of power. Besides such energy management, the central computer would perform a score of other duties, including the following:

(1) Start up and shut down of the precipitator system on command.
(2) Adjustment of precipitator operation for irregular incinerator conditions.

(3) Depicting the status of the entire precipitator system.

(4) Gathering and processing of precipitator operation data, and presentation of the data in organized and condensed form on visual display unit or as hard copy.

6. Precipitators applied to incinerators

Economic and successful application of ESP to municipal refuse incinerators, with emission standards being met continuously without unscheduled outages, requires that the singular characteristics of the process be taken properly into account when sizing and designing the precipitator. One of the key factors here is the variability of the process parameters.

The composition of the refuse burnt, the design of the incinerator and the way in which it is operated all have a pronounced effect on the emission from the incinerator to the precipitator. The refuse is often a mixture of municipal and industrial waste, and large variations (seasonal as well as of other natures) in quantity, composition, moisture content and heating value of the refuse can occur.

Table 1 shows typical values for some of the parameters of importance for the sizing and design of a precipitator for an incinerator burning municipal waste. The two

TABLE 1

Typical design parameters for precipitators for incinerators for mass burning of municipal waste

Waste	
Moisture	30–40%
Non-combustibles	25–35%
Combustibles	30–40%
Heating value	1200–2500 kcal kg^{-1}
Solid residue	
Slag	250–300 kg per ton of refuse
Fly ash	10–40 kg per ton of refuse
Gas	
Specific gas flow	4.5–6 normal m^3 kg^{-1} of refuse
Moisture content	10–15% by volume
Grain loading	2.5–7.5 g m^{-3} (normal)

parameters of particular importance for precipitator design are particle size distribution and electrical resistivity of the fly ash. Figure 7 shows particle size distribution curves for fly ash from four different plants A, B, C and D. As seen large variations in mass median particle diameter from plant to plant occur. Though the fly ash measured by median particle size is usually rather coarse, it can also, depending on the type of refuse burnt, contain significant amounts of very fine particles. A high content of fine particles increases the necessary treatment time of the gas in the precipitator due to the lower migration velocities of fine particles than of coarse particles under the influence of the electric fields in the electrode systems. A high content of very coarse particles, often consisting mainly of silica, increases the risk of excessive abrasion and, therefore, requires limitation of the gas velocity in the precipitator.

As discussed earlier, the electrical resistivity of the fly ash is determined by the physical and chemical properties of the ash and gas surrounding it. The resistivity should ideally be in the range 10^6 to 10^{10} Ω cm. Too low a resistivity may cause dust already deposited on the collecting plates of a precipitator to be reentrained into the gas stream. If the resistivity becomes too high, i.e. above approximately 10^{11} Ω cm, the electrical conditions in the precipitator are upset and precipitator performance deteriorates.

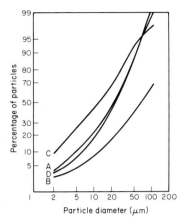

Fig. 7. Particle size distribution of fly ash from plants A, B, C and D. Percentage of particles indicates that percentage by mass of particles which is less than a certain diameter.

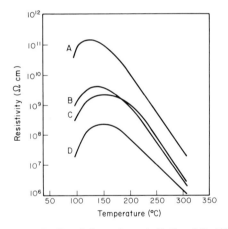

Fig. 8. Resistivity curves for fly ash from plants A, B, C and D. 12% H_2O by volume.

Figure 8 shows resistivity curves for fly ash from plants A, B, C and D. The curves exhibit a maximum around 125–150 °C, and have a rather steep back. As seen there may be considerable variation in the resistivity level of fly ash from different plants. In the temperature range 200–300 °C, which usually applies to precipitators for incinerators for municipal waste, the resistivity of the fly ash does not as a rule present any difficulties for electrostatic precipitation.

In spite of the efforts by the incinerator designer to ensure complete combustion, the fly ash always contains smaller or larger quantities of unburnt combustible particles. Such particles with a high carbon content have a low electrical resistivity and, therefore, after precipitation on to the collecting electrode, quickly lose their electrical charge. This reduces the electrical forces with which the particles are held on to the collecting plate until rapping, and the combustible particles are therefore exposed to re-entrainment into the gas stream, necessitating the use of moderate gas velocities in the precipitator. Typically, gas velocities in the range 0.6–0.9 m s^{-1} are chosen.

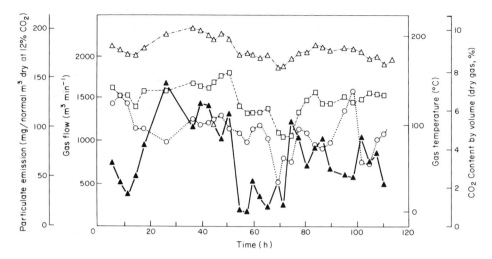

Fig. 9. Particulate emission and gas data following the precipitator over a period of 5 days at plant B.
▲, Particulate emission; □, gas flow; △, gas temperature; ○, gas CO_2 content.

Figure 9 shows the results of 32 particulate emission measurements made around the clock over a period of 5 days (120 h) after the precipitator at plant B (Jensen *et al.* 1982) with the incinerator burning a mixture of two parts municipal waste and one part industrial waste at a rate of 8.5 ton h^{-1}. Each of the emission measurements covers a period of approximately 2 h with a net sampling time of 90 min at 12 measuring points evenly distributed over the cross-section of the duct after the precipitator. The dust measuring apparatus utilizes an "in stack" filter.

The particulate emission exhibits extremely large variations, and these have little or no correlation with the measured gas data, or with other recorded plant data, for that matter. The occurrence of such large temporal variations in the emission, not related to any registered variations in fuel composition and plant operation, must be taken duly into account in the sizing of precipitators for municipal refuse incinerators in order to achieve satisfactory precipitator performance year in and year out over the lifetime of the installation. In this connection, of course, it is important to know whether the prescribed particulate emission limits are defined as a 2 h average as in some countries, or as monthly average, as in others.

7. Conclusions and recommendations

Precipitators are used for the large majority of incinerators for municipal waste. They are here capable of meeting the strictest emission requirements when properly sized and designed for the characteristics of the incineration process.

Emissions from incinerators with precipitator are determined by a large number of parameters in complex interaction. However, the specific collecting plate area A/Q, i.e. the ratio of collecting plate area to gas flow, provides a simple measure for installed precipitator capacity in relation to gas flow while the power density P/A, i.e. the ratio of applied corona power to collecting plate area, provides a simple but meaningful indication of how well the installed precipitator capacity is utilized. These two parameters can be combined into a useful, single key indicator for precipitator performance, termed specific corona power $P/Q = A/Q \times P/A$ (White 1977).

It is recommended that these few key indicators for precipitator performance be recorded in connection with emission measurements, and that they be used in the evaluation of measurements, where they may help to explain and reduce data scatter. Systematic use of these indicators on the large accumulation of emission measurement data that is continuously being created and expanded, could give useful additional knowledge about the factors actually affecting emission levels from incinerators. Such knowledge could lead to better utilization of the existing dedusting installations, and thereby to a reduction in total emission from incinerators.

References

Faulkner, M. G. & DuBard, J. L. (1984), *A Mathematical Model of Electrostatic Precipitation (Revision 3)*. Order No. PB 84-212 679 and Order No. PB 84-212 687, U.S. Environmental Protection Agency, National Technical Information Service, Springfield, VA, U.S.A.

Jensen, F. T. & Andersen, F. (1982), *Report on Particulate Emission Measurements at Incinerator*. Aalborg University Center, Denmark.

Jost, D. (1985), *Die neue TA-Luft. Aktuelle immissionsschutz-rechtliche Anforderungen an den Anlagenbetreiber*. (The new TA Luft. Demands on Plant Management of the Legal Requirements for Ambient Air Quality). WEKA-Verlag, Kissing, Federal Republic of Germany.

Larsen, P. S. & Soerensen, S. K. (1984), Effect of secondary flows and turbulence on electrostatic precipitator efficiency, *Atmospheric Environment*, *18*, 1963–1967.

Little, L. L., Randall, J. H. & Little, E. (1983), The role of the computer in electrostatic precipitator operation and maintenance. *76th Annual Meeting of the Air Pollution Control Association*, Atlanta, Georgia, June 1983.

Petersen, H. H. (1984*a*), Advanced technology in electrostatic precipitation for fine particulate. *APCA-Quebec Section Symposium*, Montreal, May 1984.

Petersen, H. H. (1984*b*), Electrostatic precipitators for resource recovery plants. *National Waste Processing Conference*, Orlando, Florida, June 1984.

White, H. J. (1963), *Industrial Electrostatic Precipitation*, Chapter 6. Addison-Wesley, Reading, MA, U.S.A.

White, H. J. (1977), Electrostatic precipitation of fly ash—precipitator design, *The Journal of the Air Pollution Control Association*, *27*, 214.

FLUXES OF MERCURY IN THE SWEDISH ENVIRONMENT: CONTRIBUTIONS FROM WASTE INCINERATION*

Oliver Lindqvist†

(*Received 30 August 1985*)

The environmental fluxes of mercury are viewed and emissions of mercury compounds from combustion processes are discussed. Waste incineration is becoming one of the major sources of mercury releases to the atmosphere in many industrialized countries. A review of some recent studies of mercury distribution in flue gases in waste heat boilers shows that a large part of the mercury can be retained on fly ash from electrostatic precipitators or fabric filters. About 20–80% of the mercury is retained, depending on the temperature over the filter, and the time of residence of the flue gases in the temperature range below 600 °C before the filter. Preliminary tempering and leaching tests indicate that most of the filter-removed mercury is suitable for deposition.

Key Words—Mercury, environmental damage, mercury chemistry, mercury concentrations, waste incineration, emissions, deposition, Sweden.

1. Introduction

The main environmental problem connected with mercury emissions in the industrialized countries in the northern hemisphere is that certain fresh water fish accumulate mercury to such amounts that it cannot be used unrestrictedly as food. The effects of high exposure to methyl mercury, which is the mercury form that accumulates in fish, is that the development of the brain in the foetal stage is inhibited causing mental retardation and retardation of the motor development. The retardation in the foetal stage will lead to certain degrees of impaired functions in the adult individual.

In order to quantify the occurrence and turnover of mercury in the environment, the National Swedish Environmental Protection Board and certain branches of Swedish industry have initiated a research programme for 1984–1989 (Lindqvist *et al.* 1985a).

The project objective is to describe and quantify those mercury fluxes in air, soil and water which are most important for the accumulation of mercury in food chains. Those factors which have a direct environmental impact are to be studied, and the results will serve as a basis for strategy aimed at decreasing the mercury content in lakewater fish. This means that basic research, such as studies of mechanisms, will be dealt with to a limited extent.

Research will be conducted in the following fields: emissions, atmospheric transport and transformation, deposition, turnover in aquatic and terrestrial systems, and bioaccumulation.

The aim of the present paper is first to summarize basic knowledge about the environmental mercury cycle, which has been described more extensively in two SNV reports

---

*Presented at the ISWA Specialized Seminar *Incinerator Emissions of Heavy Metals and Particulates*, Copenhagen, 18–19 September 1985.

†Department of Inorganic Chemistry, Chalmers University of Technology and University of Göteborg, S-412 96 Göteborg, Sweden.

Waste Management & Research (1986) **4**, (35–44)

Lindqvist et al. 1984; Lindqvist et al. 1985a) and in a review of cycling and deposition of atmospheric mercury (Lindqvist & Rodhe 1985). With this background, questions more specific to combustion and waste incineration will be discussed (see also Bergström 1986).

2. Fluxes of mercury in the environment

The mercury fluxes in the environment have been summarized comprehensively in the research programme SNV PM 1912 (Lindqvist et al. 1985a). This summary is cited here with the addition of some data and illustrations.

TABLE 1

Concentration of mercury in natural systems from background values in remote areas to normal levels in industrialized areas. Much higher values may occur near point sources of mercury

System	Mercury concentration
Air*	1–4 ng m^{-3}
Precipitation*	1–50 ng l^{-1}
Rivers and lakes†	1–10 ng l^{-1}
Open ocean*	1–3 ng l^{-1}
Coastal sea water*	3–15 ng l^{-1}
Different soils*‡	20–550 μg kg^{-1}
Humus layers§	150–500 μg kg^{-1}
Lake sediments*	100–500 μg kg^{-1}
Oceanic sediments*‡	20–100 μg kg^{-1}
Coastal sediments*	50–1200 μg kg^{-1}
Zooplankton¶	50–200 μg kg^{-1}
Roach¶	100–400 μg kg^{-1}
Pike*	200–2000 μg kg^{-1}

‡Variation mainly due to geological factors.
*From Lindqvist et al. 1984 and references therein.
†Å. Iverfeldt pers. comm. 1985.
§A. Andersson pers. comm. 1985.
¶B. Hasselroth & H. Hultberg pers. comm. 1985.

TABLE 2

Estimates of fluxes to and from the global atmosphere, the atmosphere of Europe (outside U.S.S.R.) and Sweden (cited from Lindqvist & Rodhe 1985 and references therein) (units: tonnes year^{-1})

Process	Global	Europe	Sweden
Present anthropogenic emissions	2000–17,000	300–1000	5
Present background emissions	<15,000	<150	<15
Total present emissions	2000–17,000	300–1200	5–20
Wet deposition	2000–10,000	50–200	2–10
Dry deposition	<7000	<150	2–10
Total present deposition	2000–17,000	50–350	4–20
Pre-industrial deposition (and emission)	2000–10,000	50–100	<10

The SNV PM 1816 report surveys the occurrence of mercury in natural systems (air, precipitation, surface waters, soils, sediment and biota), (cf. Table 1) the fluxes between these reservoirs, and transformation processes between different chemical modes of occurrence. The report also includes efforts at estimating budgets for the global

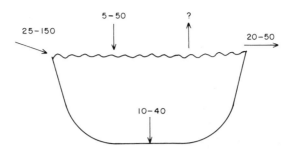

Fig. 1. Estimation of the flow of mercury (g year^{-1}) in a hypothetical oligothropic lake of 1 km² in the southern part of Sweden (from Lindqvist *et al.* 1984).

atmosphere, for the atmosphere over Europe, (cf. Table 2) and for a typical oligotrophic (nutrient-poor) Scandinavian lake (cf. Fig. 1).

The following points can be made.

(1) The present anthropogenic emissions to the atmosphere (cf. Table 3) seem to be of the same order of magnitude as natural (pre-historic) emissions. However, the present background fluxes are probably significantly elevated as a result of earlier anthropogenic emissions.

TABLE 3

Estimates of present anthropogenic emissions (tonnes year^{-1}) of total mercury to air, water and land (from Lindqvist & Rodhe 1985)

	Sweden*			U.S.A.†			Global†			
	Air	Water	Land	Air	Water	Land	Air	Water	Land	Total
Mining and smelting	1.2	0.5		70	3	4				} 2400
Industrial processes	1.5	0.3		40	20	310				
Fossil fuel combustion	0.4	0.0		120	0	10				450
Consumption‡	1.0	0.2		240	60	750				4650
Total	4.1	1.0		470	80	1070	2400	300	4800	7500
Sweden§	4.8	2.5	28							

*For the year 1977/78 (SNV 1981).
†For the year 1975 (Watson 1979). Figures rounded up.
‡Including waste incineration.
§Total for the year 1982 (Project KHM 1983).

(2) Most (>90%) of the mercury in the atmosphere consists of a relatively volatile component, probably elementary mercury, Hg°. Its residence time in the atmosphere is at least 2 months, maybe 1–2 years, and it is fairly homogeneously distributed in the troposphere (1–2 ng m^{-3}),

(3) The relatively sparingly soluble mercury form Hg⁰ is oxidized in the atmosphere to unknown forms which are readily soluble and can be washed out with precipitation, or dry-deposited on the ground or water surfaces. The oxidation processes are not known,

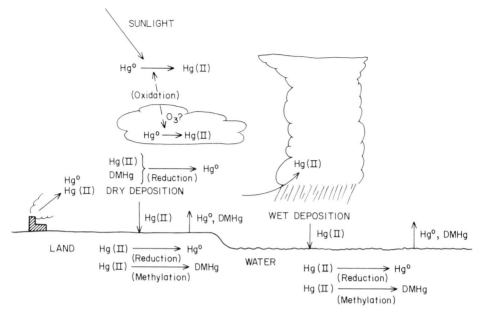

Fig. 2. A schematic description of the mercury cycle (from Lindqvist & Rodhe 1985).

but photochemical oxidants, including ozone, are probably important. The residence time of soluble forms in the atmosphere ranges from several days to several weeks, which corresponds to a transportation distance of up to several thousand kilometres, (cf. Fig. 2).

(4) Most of the mercury emitted by a point source, such a chlor-alkali plant, is dispersed regionally or globally, whereas less than 10% is deposited locally. Even so increases in deposition by a factor of 10–100 background have been recorded several kilometres from such plants. About 10–50 km away from the plant, deposition usually approaches normal values (Lodenius & Tulisalo, 1984).

(5) Measurements of mercury in lake sediments and peat-bogs show that the deposition of mercury in southern Scandinavia over the last 100 years has multiplied 5–10 times, while the increase in northern Scandinavia has been much smaller. The increase has probably been caused by anthropogenic emissions to the atmosphere in Europe, (cf. Fig. 3).

(6) The mercury load on a forest lake depends both on the deposition from the air to the lake surface and to the flux of mercury with surface flow from the catchment area of the lake (cf. Fig. 1). There are hardly any data on mercury levels of surface waters, but measurements in sediment and fish (methyl mercury) indicate a correlation between high mercury levels and regions where anthropogenic emissions have been high during the last few decades (cf. Fig. 4). There is also a relationship between the mercury content in fish, on one hand, and acidification, on the other. The mercury content in pike is generally high (> 1 mg kg^{-1}) at low pH values (> 5.5). Thus the ongoing acidification contributes to the high mercury content in pike.

(7) The relatively high mercury content in pike from Swedish lakes that are not exposed to emissions from local pollution sources calls for a better understanding of the turnover of mercury in the environment. This is particularly valid for the atmospheric

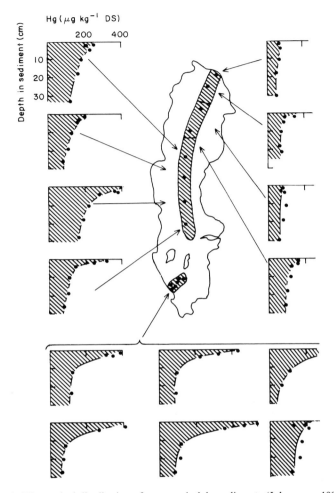

Fig. 3. The vertical distribution of mercury in lake sediments (Johansson, 1985).

dispersion of mercury whose importance is accentuated by the fact that higher emissions of mercury are anticipated in connection with coal firing and waste incineration.

(8) As a major part of airborne mercury is of natural origin, or a result of earlier anthropogenic deposition, the effects of increased or decreased anthropogenic emissions are not at all obvious. From the environmental point of view, the turnover of mercury is also probably adversely affected by acidification and oxidizing air pollutants (cf. Fig. 2).

3. Mercury chemistry in combustion processes

Solid fossil fuels, e.g. coal and peat, contain various mercury compounds, probably bound to sulphur in one way or another, usually amounting to 0.1–0.3 mg Hg kg^{-1}. The mercury content in municipal waste usually lies in the range 0.5–3.0 mg Hg kg^{-1} and has a higher content of elemental or amalgamated mercury than fossil fuels.

It is reasonable to assume that all mercury compounds are transformed to elemental

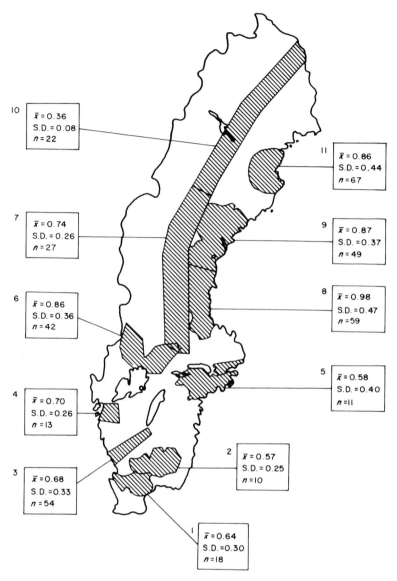

Fig. 4. Mercury concentrations in 1-k pike in Swedish forest lakes. The average values are given in mg kg^{-1} wet weight: n, number of lakes; $\bar{x}$, mean concentration; S.D., standard deviation from the mean in the investigated areas (from Lindqvist *et al.* 1984).

mercury during the combustion process since heating mercury compounds to temperatures above 700 °C leads to thermal decomposition giving elemental mercury. It is also probable that divalent mercury is reduced to elemental mercury on the reducing surface of a burning particle, for example

$$HgS + O_2 \xrightarrow{>700 \text{ °C}} Hg^0 + SO_2,$$

$$HgO + C \rightarrow Hg^0 + CO, \text{ etc.}$$

When the combustion gases are cooled down on heat exchangers, etc., it seems likely that a certain fraction of the mercury is oxidized as demonstrated in some recent reports (Bergström & Lundqvist 1985; Lindqvist *et al.* 1985). However, the oxidation processes are not known in a flue gas. The direct oxidation $Hg^0 + \frac{1}{2}O_2 \rightarrow HgO$ occurs readily in the temperature interval 350–600 °C, but the kinetics are not known. Some chlorinated compounds, HBr, NO_2 and H_2Se are reported to react at room temperature, while HCl only above 200 °C in air. Pyrolytic decomposition of organomercuric compounds according to $HgR_2 \rightarrow RHg + R \rightarrow Hg^0 + 2R$ occur during combustion conditions (Aylett 1973). Whether or not a corresponding recombination and formation or organomercuric compounds occurs under flue gas conditions remains unclear at this stage. Evidently, time of flue gas residence, temperature and chemical composition in the flue gas are key factors for the formation of oxidized mercury compounds in a combustor. Kinetic studies at relevant conditions are needed for a better understanding of these oxidation processes.

The importance of the oxidation processes in the temperature interval *c.* 100–600 °C is twofold:

(1) the oxidized forms of mercury are much more hazardous to the local environment if released to the atmosphere (cf. previous section).

(2) the possibility to retain the oxidized forms in filters or other flue gas cleaning systems is much better than for elemental mercury.

These two factors are working in different directions, i.e. if a combustion plant has low cleaning capacity it is desirable to have a low oxidation degree. On the other hand, having highly effective filters or scrubber systems it might be desirable to have a high oxidation factor to reduce the total emissions of mercury.

When the flue gases reach a filter, the operating temperatures are usually 120–240 °C depending on the type of combustor systems employed. The contact time within the filters and the temperature are important parameters for the degree of capture for different oxidized mercury compounds, e.g. the vapour pressure for halides may be too high for efficient retention. These parameters are also important for the transformation between oxidized mercury forms. Tempering and leaching studies (Bergström & Lundqvist 1985; Lindqvist 1984) indicate that most of the mercury has been transformed to very stable forms in the filter ash. This is also of great importance for the disposal of the filter ashes.

Again, research is needed to understand which stable forms are produced and the chemical kinetics for such processes.

4. Analytical problems

Analysis of mercury contents in coal, peat and filter ash is readily performed, using for example Cold Vapour Atomic Absorption (CVAA) analysis after $SnCl_2$ or $NaBH_4$ reduction of a digested sample. It is necessary to digest the ash samples in a sealed bomb with a mineral acid at an elevated temperature, e.g. with conc. HNO_3 at 150 °C for 1 h (Uhrberg 1982). Digestion with mineral acids at room temperature in open or closed systems at atmospheric pressure gives low values for the mercury concentration (Lindqvist *et al.* 1985*b*).

Analysis of mercury in the flue gases is more crucial. Methods used for sampling of total mercury are generally reliable. Such methods involve the use of filter + gold film or filter + sodium carbonate solution + potassium permanganate solution. The latter method has also been designed to separate water soluble mercury compounds, trapped in the Na_2CO_3 solution, from elemental mercury, oxidized and adsorbed in the $KMnO_4$ solution (Bergström & Lundqvist 1985). However, SO_2 reduction of mercuric compounds and other problems make it difficult to obtain reliable separations. Other methods using solutions with appropriate ligands for mercury(II) stabilization are needed for such separations. An effective method for on-line monitoring of total mercury in flue gases has recently become available. (Y. Iwasaki, pers-comm., Tokyo Metropolitan Research Institute for Environmental Protection).

Sampling and analysis leading to a complete determination of the various mercury compounds that may occur in flue gases, in ash samples or in scrubber slurries, will be a large task, and the development of such techniques must focus on compounds considered most important. Examples of work going on to improve mercury analysis are determination of organomercuric compounds in "sub-ppb" concentrations in water samples (Y.-H. Lee, pers. comm. 1985) and speciation of flue gas samples using potentiometric stripping analysis (G. Eklund pers. comm. 1985).

5. Mercury emissions from waste incineration

A recent study of the mercury distribution in the flue gas cleaning system at Malmö Avfalls värmeverk (Bergström & Lundqvist 1985) has shown a mercury flow of 2 g ton^{-1} waste. A rough estimate from this figure indicates that a total of about 5000 kg of mercury is processed per year in Sweden from municipal waste (0.5 g per capita per year). If all this mercury were to be released to the atmosphere it would dominate the anthropogenic emissions (cf. Table 3). Separation of mercury from waste before incineration and flue gas cleaning is therefore an important task in waste treatment. The Malmö study showed that 80–90% of the mercury can be bound in fly ash and lime and removed in the electrostatic precipitator (ESP) and the fabric filter. Mercury removed with the fly ash and lime is strongly bound and does not evaporate to any appreciable amount during handling and transport (Bergström & Lundqvist 1985). About 80% of the total mercury flow was removed in the ESP, c.10% in the fabric filter and c.10% was released to the atmosphere. The temperature over the ESP was c.170 °C and the mercury concentration in the ESP ash was 94 μg g^{-1} in a sample integrated over 2 days. Another recent study of mercury concentrations in ESP ash from Sävenäs Afvallsvämeverk, Göteborg (Lindqvist et al. 1985b) has given 48 μg g^{-1} in one of the boilers (No. 2). This is a mean value of samples covering the whole period February–June 1985, and would probably correspond to a removal of 40–60% of the total mercury flow. The temperature over this ESP was c.230 °C, which is probably the main explanation for the lower retention compared to the Malmö plant.

In another boiler (No. 1) in the Sävenäs plant, the corresponding concentration was only c.20 μg g^{-1} in the ESP ash, with a probable removal of 20–30%. The temperature over this filter was also c.230 °C, indicating that other factors besides the temperature over the filter are of importance for the removal of mercury.

The temperature over the filter is of course an important parameter for the degree of mercury retention in electrostatic precipitators and fabric filters, since the temperature directly influences the volatility of the mercury compounds formed initially. This was demonstrated by a failure at the Sävenäs boiler No. 1, causing the temperature to rise to c.290 °C, with a mercury capture of only c.5 μg g^{-1} instead of c.20 μg g^{-1} at c.230 °C.

Leaching studies of the filter ash from the Malmö plant indicate that most of the mercury compounds captured are, or have been, transformed to insoluble compounds. An investigation of leaching of mercury from peat ash showed that very stable forms of mercury are formed. Tempering and leaching data indicated that compounds as stable as HgS must be present in the ash (Lindqvist 1984). This is of course very favourable for deposition of filter ash, since HgS would be stable in aerated soil and would not be dissolved from landfills or lake bottom deposits.

6. Conclusions

Anthropogenic mercury emissions have caused severe environmental effects in large areas of the Northern Hemisphere. The problems are of long term character and consists of mercury accumulation in humic layers and lake sediments, leading to high mercury concentration in certain kinds of fish.

Waste incineration is presently responsible for increasing mercury emissions to air and may become a dominant source in many industrialized countries if not restricted. In the treatment of waste, mercury-containing articles should, when possible, be removed and processed separately before waste incineration.

Water soluble mercury compounds are, when released to the atmosphere, much more hazardous to the local environment than elemental mercury. Operational studies on waste incineration plants in operation have shown that it is possible to retain a major part of the waste content of mercury in filter ash or scrubber slurries. Preliminary studies have indicated that mercury may be bound in stable forms in filter ash, meaning that such ash could be deposited without serious environmental effects with respect to mercury.

Research is needed to understand the chemical reactions, and their kinetics, which determine how mercury compounds are formed in flue gases. Such research must also include development of improved analytical techniques for accurate determination of the dominating mercury compounds in flue gas, filter ash and scrubber slurries.

References

Aylett, B. J. (1973), Mercury. In *Comprehensive Inorganic Chemistry*, pp. 275–328. Pergamon Press, Elmsford, New York, U.S.A.

Bergström, J. G. T. & Lundqvist, J. (1985), Kvicksilveravskiljning ur rökgaser från SYSAV:s avfallsvärmeverk i Malmö (Mercury Removal from Flue Gases from SYSAV:s Waste Heat Boiler Plant in Malmö, with Extended Abstract in English). *Report DRAV Nr 20*, January 1985. Distributed by National Swedish Environmental Protection Board, Box 1302, S-171 25 Solna, Sweden.

Bergström, J. G. T. (1986), Mercury behaviour in flue gases, *Waste Management and Research, 4*, 57–64.

Johansson, K. (1985), Mercury in sediment in Swedish forest lakes, Verhandlungen der Internationalen Vereinigung für theoretische und angewandte Limnologie, *22*, 2359–2363.

Lindqvist, O. (1984), Kvicksilver i torvaskor (Mercury in ash from peat combustion). *THM Project Nr 276 184–1*, Statens Energiverk, 5–11787 Stockholm.

Lindqvist, O. & Rodhe, H. (1985), Atmospheric mercury, *Tellus*, 37B, 136–159.

Lindqvist, O., Jernelöv, A., Johansson, K. & Rodhe, H. (1984), Mercury in the Swedish Environment; Global and Local Sources. *Report SNV PM 1816*. Distributed by National Swedish Environmental Protection Board, Box 1302, S-171 25 Solna, Sweden.

Lindqvist, O., Johansson, K., Timm, B. & Hovsenius, G. (1985a), Mercury Research Programme 1984–1989. Occurrence and Turnover of Mercury in the Environment. *Report SNV PM 1912E*. Distributed by National Swedish Environmental Board, Box 1302, S-171 25 Solna, Sweden.

Lindqvist, O., Puromäki, K. & Werthén, M. (1985b), Analys av kvicksilverhalter i elfilteraska från Sävenäs avfallsvärmeverk under 1:a halvåret 1985 (Analysis of Mercury Concentrations in Electrostatic Precipitator Ash from Sävenäs Waste Heat Boiler Plant During the First Half of 1985). *Report No. 00K-85009*, Dept of Inorganic Chemistry, S-41296 Göteborg.

Lodenius, M. & Tulisalo, E. (1984), Environmental mercury contamination around a chlor-alkali plant, *Bulletin of Environmental Contamination and Technology, 32*, 439–444.

Project KHM (1983), *Kol, Hälsa och Miljö* (Coal, Health and the Environment), Final Report April 1983. The Swedish State Power Board, S-162 87 Vällingby, Sweden.

SNV (1981), *Utsläpp av tungmetaller i Sverige* (Emissions of heavy metals in Sweden). National Swedish Environmental Protection Board, Box 1302, S-171 25 Solna, Sweden.

Uhrberg, R. (1982), Acid digestion bomb for biological samples, *Analytical Chemistry, 54,* 1906–1908.

Watson, W. D. (1979), Economic considerations in controlling mercury pollution. In *The Biogeochemistry of Mercury in the Environment*, (J. O. Nriagu, Ed.). Elsevier/North-Holland Biomedical Press, Amsterdam.

MERCURY OUTPUT FROM GARBAGE INCINERATION*

Dieter O. Reimann†

(*Received 28 August 1985, revised 19 September 1985*)

Domestic garbage normally contains 3–4 g Hg tonne^{-1}. Slag and filter dust from garbage incineration contain only small quantities of mercury, which are difficult to leach. About 80–90% of the mercury in the flue gas can be bound in the washings at condensation temperatures of 60–70 °C from a wet scrubber operated at pH 0.5–1.0 in the presence of surplus chloride. In the following neutralization of the flue gas washings with lime *c.* 30–40% of the mercury can be bound as oxide; the degree of Hg precipitation can be increased to 99% or more by adding small quantities of the precipitating agent trimercapto-s-triazine—TMT 15.

The Bamberg Model for controlled deposition of residual materials containing concentrated pollutants consists of mixing the filter dust with neutralization sludge to produce a solid and only slightly permeable product.

The usual concentrations of mercury in garbage incineration plants do not present a danger for the operating personnel. The mercury concentration in the residual material and emission is clearly dependent upon the percentage of used batteries, which can account for over 50% of the total mercury.

Key Words—Mercury limits in Germany, waste water, sewage sludge, workplace, emission, incineration, flue gas purification mercury emission, mercury gas, mercury dust, trimercapto-s-triazine/TMT 15, Bamberg Model, mercury in batteries, mercury in domestic garbage.

1. General information on mercury

Highly varying quantities of mercury and its compounds occur in the combustion product during garbage incineration. A large number of different mercury compounds can be formed and decomposed again due to the continuously changing composition of the flue gas as well as the increasing and decreasing temperatures during the combustion process.

Mercury and its compounds must be detected in solid, liquid and gaseous form. Aqua regia solution can be used for solid samples. Oxidation with sulphuric or nitric acid and potassium peroxodisulphate ($K_2S_2O_8$) in sealed vials has proved very effective for determining the total content of mercury in liquid samples and from the gas phase (Welz 1984). After analysis, the mercury is present in a dissolved state as bivalent compounds. Quantitative analysis of the mercury is accomplished according to the cold vapour technique described in DIN 38406 (1983) using atomic absorption spectrometry (AAS).

Organic mercury compounds can be expected only in extremely low concentrations in garbage incineration—if at all. The compounds are thermally unstable and decompose generally at 300–400 °C.

*Presented at the ISWA Specialized Seminar *Incinerator Emissions of Heavy Metals and Particulates*, Copenhagen, 18–19 September 1985.

†Director, Garbage Incineration and Power Heating Plant, City and County of Bamberg, Rheinstr. 6, D-8600 Bamberg, F.R.G.

Waste Management & Research (1986) **4**, 45–56

2. Establishment of mercury limits for the environment

In the Federal Republic of Germany the laws, regulations, pollution codes and restrictions regarding mercury and its compounds in waste water and sewage sludge, as well as workplace pollution and emission, prescribe extremely low limits.

2.1. *Mercury in waste water*

The Community Waste Water Contamination Codes based on the presently valid regulatory work A 115 of the Technical Waste Water Union (Regelwerk der Abwassertechnischen Vereinigung, ATV 1983) do not allow concentrations higher than 0.05 mg l^{-1} for mercury. Cadmium is classified in second place for problematic heavy metals, with 0.5 mg l^{-1}, and the permissible concentrations are therefore 10 times as high.

The Federal Republic of Germany Waste Water Tax Code (AbwAG January 1978) also emphasizes the danger of mercury to such an extent that, under maintenance of the permissible pollution values, introduction or disposal of mercury per year into a recipient is calculated at 50 pollution units—equal to DM 2.000 per kilogram of mercury. By comparison the market price for 1 kg of Hg is between DM150 and DM400, depending upon the purity. In second place, the dangerous heavy metal cadmium is listed with 10 pollution units per kilogram.

2.2. *Mercury in sewage sludge*

The Sewage Sludge Regulation (AbfKlärV April 1983) allows a mercury concentration of 25 mg (kg dry mass)$^{-1}$ for agricultural use of the sludge from sewage plants. By comparison the cadmium concentration is slightly lower at 20 mg (kg dry mass)$^{-1}$.

2.3. *Mercury pollution at workplaces*

In order to avoid the possible danger presented for humans by mercury, limits are established for mercury in the Federal Republic of Germany as follows:

(1) *Upper standard limit:* definition according to DFG (1981) as a value, which is not exceeded by 95% of the average population; 5 μg Hg l^{-1} in blood or 5 μg Hg g^{-1} creatinine in urine (Schaller *et al.* 1983).

(2) *Biological material tolerance value (BMT-value):* established according to DFG (1981); up to this tolerance no negative influences to health are to be expected even for exposures during an 8 h day or 40 h week; 50 μg Hg l^{-1} in blood and 200 μg Hg l^{-1} in urine.

(3) *A maximum workplace concentration (MWC)* of 0.1 mg Hg m^{-3} has been fixed by the Deutsche Forschungsgesellschaft (1981):

> At concentrations of <0.1 mg m^{-3} no objective damage resulting from mercury has been reported, with the exception of subjective complaints as well as biological changes without any proven disease value. In comparison with the limits discussed on the basis of dosage effect relationships, these concentrations provide a sufficient safety range up to manifest mercury poisoning.

2.4. *Mercury emissions*

The draft for the Technical Codes for Air Pollution 2/85 presently being prepared as an executive order to the Federal Emission Protection Law (TA Luft 1985) classifies the heavy metals mercury, cadmium and thalium in the material class I as particularly dangerous. The expected limitation of the permissible emissions in dust form for these three heavy metals is 0.2 mg m^{-3} at 11% O_2. However, the further stipulations of these codes (paragraph 3.1.4, TA Luft 1985) reportedly state that special precaution of preventing the emissions are required when significant percentages of these materials are present in vapour or gaseous form.

These regulations apply particularly for mercury. In the Federal Republic of Germany a maximum permissible concentration of 0.2 mg m^{-3} can be expected in the future for heavy metals in class I in gas and dust form. In comparison the Swiss codes for emission (Swiss Federal Department of the Interior 1982), legally prescribe a limit of 0.1 mg m^{-3} at 11% O_2 for the total quantity of mercury in gas and dust form.

In consideration of the MWC value of 0.1 mg m^{-3}, limitation of the emission value to 0.1 or 0.2 mg Hg m^{-3} at 11% O_2 appears justified. During garbage incineration, emissions become ambient air concentrations with dilution factors of 1×10^5 to 1×10^6: thus, concentrations will be so far below the MWC values that a threat to health, resulting from mercury, can be excluded according to present knowledge, in spite of possible concentration in the soil and in the nutrient cycle. In my opinion the very strong appearing mercury limitation is fundamentally sound.

If the mercury emissions in the form of gas and dust, which are the most difficult to detect within the scope of flue gas purification, are bound or reduced then, by analogy, binding or reduction has occurred for all the other heavy metals specified in the technical directions for air pollution, because these metals are easier to remove than mercury. As a leading metal, mercury could become an indicator for the removal of all heavy metals.

3. Garbage incineration plant and associated mercury pollutants

Figure 1 is a flow diagram showing a garbage incineration plant with flue gas wet scrubber

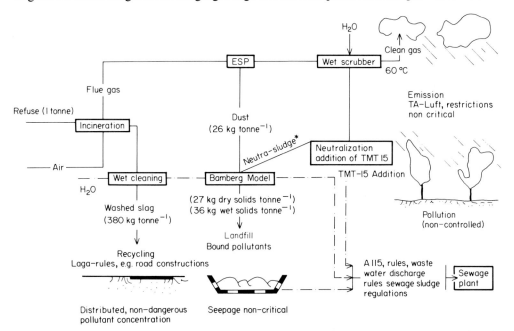

Fig. 1. Refuse incineration and residues—Bamberg wet system. All data refer to an input of 1 tonne of refuse
*1 kg dry substance (Reimann 1984c.)

and residual product quantities. In addition to the heated flue gases with dust concentrations resulting from the prescribed combustion temperature of at least 800 °C in the afterburner zone, pollutants and heavy metals released by the combustion are also present.

Flue gas purification therefore has three primary objectives: utilization of the free energy in the flue gas, collection of the dust particles; elimination of the pollutants and heavy metals; and for the gaseous heavy metals and compounds, particularly for mercury, the flue gas purification must achieve the greatest possible temperature reduction in the flue gas (saturation temperature c. 60–70 °C).

3.1. Specific mercury distribution for garbage incineration

A thermal treatment such as garbage incineration offers a method for determination of the mercury quantity in the garbage. The residual materials such as sludges, filter dusts, waste water from flue gas purification and sludge washing, and sorption residuals, as well as the pure gases, can be collected and analysed for mercury content as relatively homogeneous products much more easily than the initial product, garbage. The pollutant distribution shown in Figure 2 for mercury in garbage incineration with flue gas washing is based on the precisely collected quantitative data for individual pollutants over a longer period of time, (Figure 3) and extensive measurements of mercury concentrations (Table 1).

3.2. Effect of digested sludge upon the mercury balance

If garbage and digested sludge are incinerated together, this can be practiced without problems with an addition of up to 10–15% of dewatered digested sludge per ton of garbage. The mercury contents in the incineration product garbage + sewage sludge increases by c. 1 g mercury per 100 kg of dewatered sludge (Reimann 1984a).

3.3. Mercury in slag and filter dust

Only very low concentrations of mercury are present in the slag, which may be used as a construction material as well as in the slag washing water (Reimann 1984b). This results from the high temperature, to which the incineration material is subjected. If, in exceptional cases, higher concentrations are bound in these materials, this is due to insufficient incineration.

The percentage of mercury in the furnace and filter dust is also very low, because with the flue gas purification procedure the electrostatic precipitator (ESP) temperature varies between 200–300 °C and the condensation temperature of mercury compounds is in this range. Condensed mercury compounds are already present as solid material in the form of microparticles, which can only be separated in the ESP to a limited degree. The flue gas wet scrubber captures fine particles in the aqueous phase.

If the temperature for removal of the dust in the flue gas is lowered to c. 150 °C, as is common in the semi-dry procedure, the mercury content in the occuring sorption material increases greatly. However, in addition to temperature reduction and the associated condensation of mercury and its compounds in these flue gas cleaning processes, the addition of lime, for example, with its large surface plays a significant role in binding the acidic pollutants and removing mercury. Assuming a dry flue gas quantity of 5000–6000 m³ tonne^{-1} garbage following the ESP, a quantity of c. 0.5–0.6 results if

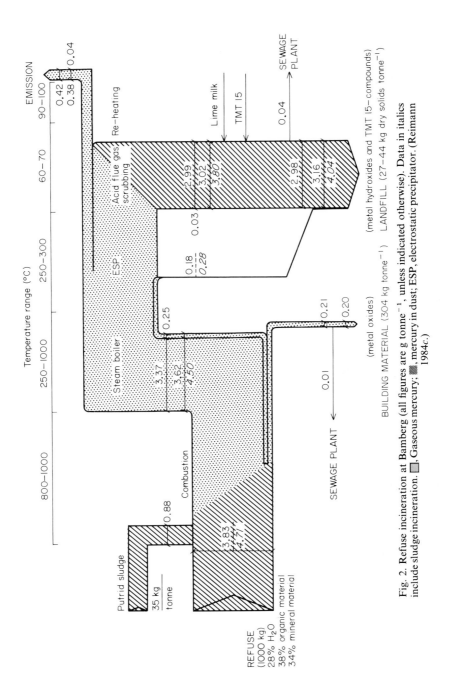

Fig. 2. Refuse incineration at Bamberg (all figures are g tonne^{-1}, unless indicated otherwise). Data in italics include sludge incineration. ▨, Gaseous mercury; ▨, mercury in dust; ESP, electrostatic precipitator. (Reimann 1984c.)

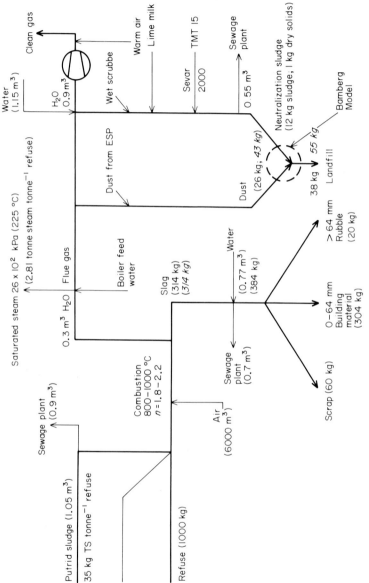

Fig. 3. Specific mercury distribution at the Bamberg refuse-fired power station with TMT 15 precipitation and with/without sludge incineration. Data in italics include sludge incineration; all data refer to an input of 1 tonne of refuse. (Reimann 1984c.)

TABLE 1

Specific mercury output of the refuse-fired power station, without sludge incineration, at Bamberg (Reimann 1984c.)*

Occurrence	Transport medium	Other	Units	Mercury quantities — Concentration Range	Average	Further treatment or discharge — Place	Adm. concentration	Specific quantity of transport medium per tonne of refuse	Mercury level in refuse (mg tonne^{-1})	% of total mercury
Wet ash extractor	Waste water	—	mg l^{-1}	0.007–0.1	0.009	Sewage plant	0.05 mg l^{-1}	700 l	0.006	0.2
Electrostatic precipitator	Dust	—	mg kg^{-1}	1.4–18.9	7.1	Landfill	—	26 kg	0.184	4.7
	Solution	—	mg l^{-1}	<0.001	—	Sewage plant	0.05 mg l^{-1}			
Slag treatment	Slag	—	mg kg^{-1}	0.46–1.80	0.70	Constr. mat.	—	304 kg	0.213	5.7
	Solution	—	mg l^{-1}	<0.0005	—	Sewage plant	0.05 mg l^{-1}			
Flue gas (scrubber) after neutralization	Waste water { w/o TMT 15		mg l^{-1}	0.47–8.00	2.47	Sewage plant	0.05 mg l^{-1}	(850 l)	(2.084)	(54.4)
	w TMT 15		mg l^{-1}	0.003–0.094	0.048			550 l	0.026	0.7
	Sludge { w/o TMT 15		mg kg^{-1}	—	927	Landfill	—	(1 kg)	(0.927)	(24.2)
	w TMT 15		mg kg^{-1}	1790–3400	2985			1 kg	2.985	77.9
	Solution	—	mg l^{-1}	<0.005	—	Sewage plant	0.05 mg l^{-1}			
Stack	Clean gas { Dusty		μg[m³f]$^{-1}$ 11%O	1.4–10.8	6.2	Emission	Probably 200 μg[m³f]$^{-1}$	6000 m³	0.037	1.0
	Gaseous		μg[m³f]$^{-1}$	48.6–76.8	62.8			6000 m³	0.377	9.8
Total mercury output (g tonne^{-1} refuse)									3.828	100.0

*Abbreviations: w = with, w/o = without; Constr. mat. = construction material, Adm. = admitted, m³f = m³ wet, m³ = m³ gas (at 273 K, 1012 kPa).

digested sludge is not included. This high mercury emission value is frequently still mentioned today for generalized comparison of the purity of energy obtained from garbage and from other primary energy sources, although it applies only for plants without further flue gas purification. Opponents of garbage incineration occasionally use this erroneous information to create prejudice and fear among ecologically minded citizens who are against garbage incineration plants.

With the flue gas purification using the dry and semi-dry procedures total gaseous mercury quantities of 0.04–0.57 mg m^{-3} are present in the purified gas (Knorr 1985; Mosch & Pfeiffer 1984; Cleve 1985). The salts from flue gas purification have considerably higher mercury concentrations compared to the wet washing of flue gases. The large range of variation for the specified emissions is certainly accountable to the lower condensation effect with these methods in comparison with wet washing as well as with the various concentrations in the initial material. Dust removal processes in the unpurified gas should be accomplished above the dew point, in order to prevent clogging, formation of lumps and incrustation in the dust removal equipment, whereby a differentiation must be made between the acid and water dew point.

3.4. *Mercury in the flue gas washings*

In the following description wet washing is emphasized, because it is presently the method by which the most efficient elimination of mercury can be achieved (Erbach *et al.* 1984; Reimann 1984). Figure 2 and Table 1 show the washing effect with the usual pH value of 0.5–1.0 in the flue gas washing water. This low pH value results from washing out the acidic pollutant in the flue gas and therefore provides ideal conditions for keeping heavy metal salts in solution. Not taking into consideration digested sludge, *c.* 3 g Hg tonne^{-1} of garbage, can be removed with this flue gas purification step.

3.4.1. *Theories on mercury binding via flue gas washing*

Among specialists, various opinions still exist regarding the exact relationships for washing mercury out of the flue gas. A few aspects are briefly mentioned below.

(a) For all theories agreement exists that the mercury condensation can be influenced decisively by the greatest possible temperature reduction.

(b) The efficient removal of mercury by acidic flue gas washing is not questioned on the basis of the achieved and measured mercury concentrations.

(c) A high degree of uncertainty exists as to whether mercury is present in the flue gas washing water in metallic form or in the form of dissolved salts or oxides; however, the possibility of the presence of metallic mercury in the flue gas is classified as slight by experts.

(d) There is still no clear opinion as to whether the very stable and easily soluble Hg (II) chloro complex $H_2(HgCl_4)$ is formed at a flue gas washing water temperature of 70 °C and in the presence of sulphuric acid with high surplus chloride (Ullmans 1980).

3.4.2. *Removal of the mercury in the flue gas washing water*

In addition to an average chloride content of 10–20 g l^{-1}, the acidic waste water from flue gas washing (in Bamberg, *c.* 0.5 m^3 tonne^{-1} garbage) contains an average mercury content of 3–4 mg l^{-1}, which can increase to over 15 mg l^{-1}. High concentrations in previous reports is attributable less to the differences in the pollution contained in the garbage than to the dilution or concentrating effect resulting from addition of various processing water quantities to the flue gas washings. The flue gas washing water quantities can vary between 0.3 to over 1.0 m^3 tonne^{-1} garbage, depending upon the operational procedure, the water and wastewater requirements as well as the costs.

Within the scope of final neutralization, for example with milk of lime (Ca (OH)$_2$), most of the problematic heavy metals are precipitated by > 80–90% to far below the permissible discharge concentrations in the form of hydroxides. For cadmium and nickel, the achievable precipitation degrees of c. 70% are sufficient to satisfy the discharge conditions applicable today. Problems result in elimination of the mercury. With neutralization using milk of lime, the reaction from H$_2$(HgCl$_4$) to Hg (II) oxide is incomplete due to the high excess of chloride (Reimann 1984d). Long-term tests in Bamberg on the achievable mercury precipitation results through neutralization alone showed precipitation degrees of 30–40% (Reimann 1984c). In this case the residual concentration of mercury was c. 2.5 mg l^{-1}, or higher, and exceeded the permissible discharge value by several times. Precipitation of mercury by trimercapto-s-triazine (C$_3$N$_3$S$_3$)$^{3-}$, TMT 15 (produced by Degussa, Frankfurt, West Germany), or SEVAR 2000 as a combined mercury precipitation and flocculation agent is available today for improvement of the mercury binding. Addition of small quantities of these precipitation agents (c. 50–100 ml m^{-3} flue gas wastewater) gives rise to capital and operating costs which, depending upon the quantity of mercury to be precipitated, amount to c. 0.25–0.50 DM tonne^{-1} garbage (Reimann 1984c). The degree of mercury precipitation can be increased to 99% or more by this method. The Hg (II)–TMT compound is very difficult to dissolve, resistant to acids and high temperature, and therefore has hardly measurable leaching characteristics. The degree of precipitation for cadmium and nickel is increased highly as a side effect by TMT treatment.

3.4.3. *The Bamberg Model*

The hydroxide and TMT sludge, with its low salt content due to the washing effect (Reimann 1984d), occurs in quantities of c. 1 kg tonne^{-1} (dry matter). The sedimented sludge contains approx. 5–6% dry matter. A compact, thick sludge with c. 20% dry matter can be created by mechanical dehydration.

Since depositing of this compact, however still mushy neutralization sludge presents problems, a material was required for solidifying this oxide hydrate sludge. Dust from the electrostatic precipitator, a product which had to be prepared by mixing with water to produce a dust-free substance before disposal, was found to be suitable as a solidifier.

A new, compactable and only slightly permeable mixed product, which was difficult to leach (Fichtel *et al.* 1983), resulted from forced mixing of the hydroxide sludge from the flue gas washings and the filter dust. This procedure is called the *Bamberg Model* (Reimann 1985). The product created in this manner offers an optimum sealing layer for domestic garbage depots in thicknesses of 1 m and greater.

Long-term leaching tests on the mixed product at the Bamberg incineration plant, with pH 4 and 7, have confirmed the previous experience that mercury can only be leached to an extremely low degree in an acidic environment. This applies even after decomposition of the alkaline buffer effect of the mixed product, which forms as a result of the alkaline ESP dust and the neutral sludge. Mercury in the seepage water from the residual materials from garbage incineration does not lead to a problem at domestic garbage landfills, because it is far below the permissible concentrations in the waste water.

3.5. *Mercury emissions from the smokestack*

The pollutants remaining in the purified gas can be in the form of dust or gases. When analysing the total mercury emissions particular attention must be paid to the gaseous constituents. Good results for the gaseous mercury constituents can be achieved with the Impinger procedure (VDI 2452; Swiss BfU 1983). Care must be taken in selecting the proper, representative sampling location, taking the samples over a number of hours with a sufficient quantity of gas and good filtration of fine dust. The finest particles can penetrate through the filter under unfavourable conditions and lead to erroneous results with excessively high gaseous pollutant constituent. The test results for several plants with unobjectionable filtration are listed in relationship to the flue gas purification procedure (Table 2).

TABLE 2

Mercury emissions (mg m^{-3}) as a function of flue gas cleaning procedures

Cleaning procedure	Mercury in dust	Gaseous mercury
Dry procedure with subsequent cloth filter*	0.4×10^{-4}	0.22–0.57
	2.3×10^{-4}	0.12–0.26
	4.3×10^{-4}	0.15–0.21
Semi-dry procedure with cyclone and ESP†	$< 10^{-5}$	0.05–0.20
Wet method following ESP‡	4×10^{-4}	0.05–0.08
	6×10^{-3}	

*Data from Knorr (1985).
†ESP = electrostatic precipitator. Data from Horch (1984).
‡Data from Reimann (1984*b*), Knorn & Fürmaier (1984), Vogg (1985) and Vicard & Knoche (1985).

Depending upon the selected flue gas purification procedure selected, the ratio of gaseous mercury to mercury in dust form in the purified gas is 1×10^{-1} to 1×10^{-4}. The gas phase is pre-eminent to such a degree that only its percentage is of significance in the emissions. Further reduction of the mercury in dust form by additional dust removal systems does not lead to any improvement of the emission value.

Good binding of the gaseous percentage of mercury in the wet procedure is attributable to the condensation connected with temperature reduction. The comparably favourable emission value for mercury using the semi-dry procedure may be explained by the cooling effect—and the connected condensation effect—resulting from the addition of milk of lime. The gaseous mercury can be bound by the lime due to the evaporation of the milk of lime sprayed in and the simultaneous availability of a very large condensation and absorption surface. The deposition of gaseous mercury on the precoat layer of the cloth filter attributed to the dry procedure does not appear to be confirmed.

4. Endangerment of employees at garbage incineration power plants from mercury

It can be stated that employees at garbage incineration plants are not endangered any more than the average population by contact with materials and gases containing mercury in the permitted concentrations. In this respect, examinations were performed on employees during two subsequent years, by blood and urine tests, which showed that the mercury levels were found to be *c.* 5–50% of the upper standard limit (see Section 2.3).

The median for the entire group of garbage incineration employees was 20% of the upper standard limit, which was slightly higher than the median value for the control population group not subjected to the mercury exposure possible in a garbage incineration plant (Reimann & Bloedner 1985).

5. Mercury reduction in garbage for emission reduction

Mercury content in the incoming garbage is a determinant of mercury concentration in the various residual materials and emissions. In addition to the only slightly controllable mercury content of vegetables in domestic garbage, the use of industrial products is responsible for a major percentage of mercury pollution. Examples of applications containing mercury are fungicides in paints, thermometers, electronic components and fluorescent tubes (Lorber 1985). More than 50% of the total mercury content in garbage is attributable to used batteries. The high degree of pollution is not attributable primarily to mercury oxide batteries but rather to alkaline manganese batteries, which are only separated today in the rarest cases (Genest & Reimann 1985). The most effective method to reduce the quantity of mercury in untreated garbage would be to focus on collecting used batteries separately.

References

AbfKlärV (April 1983), *Klärschlammverordnung*, vom 1 April 1983 (Sewage Sludge Regulations, from 1 April 1983), Bonn.

AbwAG (January 1978), *Abwasserabgabengesetz*, vom 1 January 1978 (Sewage Emission Law, from 1 January 1978), Bundestag, Bonn.

ATV (1983), *Hinweise für das Einleiten von Abwasser in eine öffentliche Abwasseranlage* (Guidelines for the Passage of Sewage Waters in a Public Sewage System), Worksheet A 115, vom January 1983. Report of Abwassertechnischen Vereinigung, St. Augustin.

Cleve, V. (1985), AFA-Verfahren zur trockenen Reinigung von Rauchgasen aus Müllverbrennungsanlagen (AFA Procedure for dry purification of flue gas from garbage incineration facilities), Technical Report, published by Vulkanverlag: *Müllverbrennungsanlagen, 5*, pp. 236–241.

Deutsche Forschungsgesellschaft (1981), *Quecksilber—Toxikologisch—arbeitsmedizinische Begründungen von MAK-Werten* (Mercury—Toxicological—Explanations for Industrial Medicine from MAK Plants). Verlag Chemie, Weinheim, 8, F.R.G.

DFG (1981), *Aufstellung von Grenzwerten im biologischen Material* (Recording Limit Values in Biological Material). *Deutsche Forschungsgesellschaft, Senatskommission.* Zentralinstitut für Arbeitsmedizin, Hamburg, F.R.G.

DIN 38406 (1983), (German Industrial Standard). Beuthe Verlag, Berlin.

Erbach, G., Schöner, P. & Maurer, P. (1984). Schwermetallgehalt im Rauchgas hinter der sauren Wäsche (Heavy metal content in flue gas after acidic washing). *VGB-Heft, 204,* 140–164.

Fichtel, Beck, W. & Giglberger, J. (1983), *Auslaugverhalten von Rückständen von Abfallverbrennungsanlagen—Rückstandsdeponie Großmehring* (Leaching Properties and Residues of Garbage Incineration Facilities—Großmehring Landfill), vol. 55. Schriftenreihe des Bay, Landesamtes für Umweltschutz, F.R.G.

Genest, W. & Reimann, D. (1985), Abfallproblematik von Altbatterien (Garbage problems from used batteries), *Müll und Abfall, 7,* 217–224.

Horch, K. (1984), Rauchgasreinigung für die MVA München-Nord (Flue gas purification for the MVA Munich-North). *VGB-Heft, 204,* 181–198.

Knorn, Ch. & Fürmaier, B. (1984), Ergebnisse von Emissions messungen an Abfallverbrennungsanlagen (Results of emission measurements in garbage incineration facilities). In *Müllverbrennung und Rauchgasreinigung* (Garbage Incineration and Flue Gas Purification) (J. Thomé Kosmiensky, Ed.). *Technik, Wirtschaft, Umweltschutz,* vol. 7 (Müll und Abfall) pp. 29–36.

Knorr, W. (1985), Ergebnisse von Emmissionsmessungen an den Müllheizkraftwerken Kempten und Würzburg (Results of emission measurements performed at garbage incineration plants in Kempten and Würzburg). In Abfallwirtschaftliches Fachkolloquium KABV, Saarbrücken, 5, F.R.G., 25–26 April 1985, pp. 1–3.

Lorber, K. (1983), Die Zusammensetzung des Mülls und die durch Müllverbrennungsanlagen emittierten Schadstoffe (The Composition of Garbage and the Harmful Substances Emitted by Garbage Incineration Facilities). In *Müllverbrennung und Rauchgasreinigung* (Garbage Incineration and Flue Gas Purification), (J. Thomé-Kosmiensky, Ed.). *Technik, Wirtschaft, Umweltschutz*, vol. 7, pp. 559–594.

Mosch, H. & Pfeiffer, K. (1984), Trockene Rauchgasreinigung in Müllverbrennungsanlagen (Dry flue gas purification in garbage incineration facilities). In *VGB-Heft*, vol. 204, pp. 165–182.

Reimann, D. (1984a), Belastung von Kläranlagen durch MVAs und/oder thermische Schlamm-konditionierung (Burdening of sewage treatment plants by MVAs and/or thermal sludge conditioning), *Kommunalwirtschaft*, 5, 155–161.

Reimann, D. (1984b), Quecksilber bei der Müllverbrennung (Mercury in garbage incineration), *Umweltmagazin*, 6, 48–54.

Reimann, D. (1984c), Reinigung von Rauchgaswaschwässern im MHKW Bamberg mit Schwerpunkt auf Quecksilbereliminierung durch TMT 15-Zugabe (Purification of flue gas washing water in the MHKW Bamberg with an emphasis on the elimination of mercury through the addition of TMT 15), *VGB Kraftwerkstechnik*, 3, 230–235.

Reimann, D. (1984d), Chlorverbindungen im Müll und in der Müllverbrennung—einfluß des Kunststoffes PVC (Chlorine compounds in garbage and in garbage incineration—effects of the plastic PVC), *Müll und Abfall*, 6, 169–176.

Reimann, D. (1985), Gemeinsame umweltschonende Beseitigung von Filterstäuben und Neutralisationsschlämmen aus der Rauchgaswäsche—Bamberger Modell (Joint environmental protection elimination of filter dust and neutralization sludges from flue gas washing—Bamberg model). *VGB-Heft*, vol. 204, KABV Saarbrücken s., Abfallwirtschaftliches Fachkolloquium 25–26 April 1985. Technische Mitteilungen H.d.T., Vulkanverlag *Müllverbrennungsanlagen*, 5, 268–272.

Reimann, D. & Bloedner, Cl.-D. (1985), Keine erhöhten Schwermetallgehalte (Pb, Hg, Cd) im Blut des Betriebspersonals eines Müllheizkraftwerkes (No raised heavy-metal contents (Pb, Hg, Cd) in the blood of company personnel of a garbage incineration plant), *Müll und Abfall*, 3, 72–76.

Schaller, K., Triebig, G. & Valentin, G. (1983), Praktische Hinweise für die Durchführung arbeitsmedizinisch-toxikologischer Untersuchungen (Practical guidelines for the conducting of toxicological experiments in industrial medicine), In *Arbeitsmedizin Aktuell*, pp. 55–69. Gustav Fischer Verlag, Stuttgart.

Swiss Federal Department of the Interior (1982), *Schweizerische Richtlinien Über die Luftreinhaltung beim Verbrennen von Siedlungsabfällen* (Swiss guidelines for keeping the air clean in the incineration of residential area garbage). Eidgenössisches Department des Inneren, 18 February 1982, Bern.

Swiss BFU (1983), *Empfehlungen Über die Emissionsmessungen von Luftfremdstoffen bei stationären Anlagen* (Recommendations for the emission measurements of air foreign particles in stationary facilities), supplements 14 & 25. Bundesamt für Umweltschutz, Switzerland.

TA-Luft (1985), *Technische Anleitung zur Reinhaltung der Luft* (Technical manual for keeping the air clean). Stand 28 February 1983, Referenzentwurf Stand 15 February 1985, Bundesimmissionsschutzgesetz (BImSchG), vom 15 March 1974 to 4 March 1982.

Ullmanns (1980), *Enzyklopädie der technischen Chemie* (Encyclopedia of Chemical Engineering), vol. 19, 4th Edn, pp. 643–671. Verlag Chemie, Weinheim.

VDI 2452 (1983), VDI Verlag, Düsseldorf.

Vicard, J. F. & Knoche, M. (1985), Die nasse Rauchgasreinigung hinter Müllverbrennungsanlagen (Wet flue gas purification facilities following garbage incineration). Vortrag s. Abfallwirtschaftliches Fachkolloquium, Saarbrücken, F–26 April 1985, pp. 1–10.

Vogg, H. (1985), Emissionen aus Müllverbrennungsanlagen) (Emissions from Garbage Incineration Facilities), *VDI-Seminar BW 433201*, VDI Verlag, Düsseldorf.

Welz, M. (1984), Picotrace Determination of Mercury Using the Amalgation Technique, *Atomic Spectroscopy*, 5, p. 38.

MERCURY BEHAVIOUR IN FLUE GASES*

Jan G. T. Bergström†

(*Received 30 August 1985*)

Mercury in the flue gas from waste incineration is predominantly in the vapour phase at temperatures down to 140 °C. Only a small portion of the mercury is metallic Hg°, most of it is oxidized, which has a high vapour pressure at these gas temperatures.

Oxidized mercury is absorbed by fly ash and will be captured on fabric filters. By injecting fly ash and lime before a fabric filter a high degree of collection can be achieved, both for hydrochloric acid and for mercury.

Up to 90% of the mercury can become attached to the dust. By optimizing the operation and with efficient dust removal it is therefore possible to limit mercury emissions to less than 0.3 g ton^{-1} of incinerated waste.

Key Words—Waste incineration, mercury emissions, flue gases.

1. Introduction

A wide range of concentrations of mercury in air has been reported during the last few years. These data indicate a background level of about 2 ng m^{-3} over Europe. Elemental mercury seems to be the dominant form in the atmosphere, however, there is also a water soluble fraction present. That fraction is found to constitute, on average, 5–10% of the total gaseous mercury during the winter and less during the summer. Mercury associated with particles in the atmosphere normally makes up only a small fraction of the total airborn mercury (Lindqvist *et al.* 1984). The anthropogenic emissions have increased during the last century and present activities are resulting in mercury mobilization and the emission of mercury to land, water and air (see also Lindqvist 1986).

Very little information is available about the species of mercury compounds in the emissions. It has generally been assumed that most of the mercury in emissions to air is metallic mercury vapour.

In an evaluation of the environmental consequences of increased coal combustion in Sweden (Project KHM, Coal–Health–Environment 1983) special interest was attached to the mercury problem. Measurements of mercury in coal- and oil-fired boilers then indicated that more than 50% occurred in a water soluble form. Most of the remainder was probably mercury vapour (Hg⁰) (Bergström 1983*a,b*).

From theoretical calculations of equilibrium and mass transfer data it has been concluded that when burning solid fuels in a furnace, mercury initially exists as mercury vapour (Hg⁰) (Moberg *et al.* 1983). During the cooling of the combustion gases in increasing fraction reacts to form HgCl$_2$. At 150 °C all mercury will be HgCl$_2$ vapour at equilibrium.

From the mercury mass balances in coal-fired boilers there are strong indications that the mercury sorption mechanism is influenced by the operation parameters and fly ash properties. It takes many hours to reach a mercury equilibrium in a plant after changing the mercury content of the fuel (Bergström 1983*b*).

*Presented at the ISWA Specialized Seminar *Incinerator Emissions of Heavy Metals and Particulates,* Copenhagen, 18–19 September 1985.

†Environmental Consultants at Studsvik AB, S-611 82, Nykoping, Sweden.

Waste Management & Research (1986) **4**, 57–64

2. Mercury and solid waste incineration

Since the beginning of the 1970s, mercury emissions from waste incineration have increased in Sweden. This is due to an increased mercury content in the products which are sent to the incineration plants. One example is mercury batteries. Waste incineration in Sweden is now responsible for mercury emissions in the flue gas of about 2 g per ton of waste. Efforts in the last few years have reduced this. These efforts comprise the collection of material containing mercury so that it does not reach the waste incinerators, and also flue gas cleaning. Thus mercury emissions from incinerators have been kept to less than 0.3 g per ton of waste. (See also Westergård 1986.)

Waste results in much higher concentrations of mercury in the flue gas than is the case for solid fuel. Despite this it is difficult to make measurements. The variations in the mercury concentrations mean that extended measurement series are necessary to ensure reliable mercury mass balances for a plant incinerating waste.

By interrupting the incineration of waste in a plant, and continuing with the combustion of wood, we have been able to determine that as much as 24 h are necessary for the mercury content in the fly ash and flue gas to attain the lower equilibrium concentration corresponding to the mercury concentration in the wood.

We have studied the mercury distribution and emission during the incineration of waste at a number of plants, and will report our experience in this paper.

Our involvement in the project "Operation Studies of Solid Waste Treatment" (DRAV) has been of great importance for our knowhow. The DRAV project is being undertaken by the Swedish Association of Public Cleansing and Solid Waste Management in close co-operation with the National Swedish Environment Protection Board. We have made operation studies of four incinerator plants and among other things performed measurements and evaluation of the mercury distribution in the plants (Bergström & Lundqvist 1983, 1985; Lundqvist 1984*a,b,c*; Lindqvist 1986).

3. Sampling and analysis

The species of mercury present and their reactions in the flue gas are not known. Therefore the sampling method used for mercury is of primary importance and has a considerable effect on the results.

Almost all the mercury in the flue gas is in the vapour phase after the boiler. During sampling some of the mercury becomes attached to particles in the sampling equipment. The proportion depends on, amongst other things, the particle concentration, filtration temperature, sampling time and the form in which the mercury is present in the flue gas. A standardized sampling method simplifies considerably interpretation of the analyses.

The sampling train is presented in Fig. 1. It is a particulate sampling train with additional wash bottles for the absorption of mercury vapour.

The dust sampling was performed by isokinetic sampling of between 20 and 40 $l\,min^{-1}$ of the flue gas from the cross section of the duct. The particles were collected on flat quartz fibre filters. The probe and the filter house were heated and temperature controlled.

The ordinary temperature was 160 or 200 °C. The gas was cooled and dried after passing through the filter. The extracted gas flow rate and volume were determined using a rotameter and gasometer.

A partial flow rate of 2–3 $l\,min^{-1}$ was sucked direct from the heated filter house through three wash bottles connected in series. The first bottle contained a 10% (by weight) solution of soda (Na_2CO_3), and the two other bottles contained a solution of

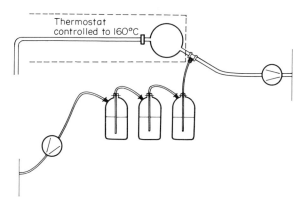

Fig. 1. Sampling train.

potassium permanganate acidified with sulphuric acid (6 g l^{-1} in 10%, by volume, H_2SO_4). Mercury soluble in water is absorbed in the soda solution, and metallic mercury is absorbed in the permanganate solution.

The gas was dried after passing through the wash bottles. The dry gas flow rate and volume were determined using a rotameter and gasometer.

Tests using this type of sampling equipment and metallic mercury have shown that Hg^0 is not noticeably absorbed in the soda solution. Hg^0 is however normally absorbed to more than 98% in the first wash bottle containing permanganate solution. The second bottle only provides a safety and control unit (see also Shendrikar & Ensor (1986).

The wash bottles were closed with ground-glass stoppers immediately after sampling, and were transported to the laboratory for analysis. The quantity of mercury which had attached itself during dust sampling was determined by fusing part of the particulate and filter material. The entire particulate and filter material in the filter holder was ground to a homogeneous powder prior to analysis. Ash samples from the plants were also fused. Carefully weighed samples were heat treated at 160 °C for 1 h with 50 ml H_2O and 5 ml conc. HNO_3 contained in a closed reaction vessel. The amounts of mercury in the solutions after fusing the solid material, and in the absorption solutions from the gaseous sampling, were determined using flameless atomic absorption. The mercury was driven out of the solutions using nitrogen after reduction with boron hydride (BH_4^-). The mercury in the flue gas was reported as three fractions:

Hg_s is the mercury attached to dust during sampling.

Hg_{aq} is the soluble mercury absorbed in the soda solution.

Hg^+ is the calculated sum of Hg_s and Hg_{aq}. It is a measure of the amount of reactive mercury in the flue gas, probably as $HgCl_2$.

Hg^0 is the mercury vapour absorbed in the permanganate solution.

Hg_t is the sum of Hg^0 and Hg^+ in the flue gas and is a measure of how much mercury that is transported by the flue gas, even it is distributed differently between the plant and the sample as a result of reactions which occur.

The flow rate of mercury from the furnace varies continuously since the waste being burnt contains different quantities of mercury. We have therefore tried to take samples at two points simultaneously, thus enabling differences in the analysis results to be used to assess the uncertainty inherent to the sampling and analysis methods.

The differences between two samples taken at different times can only illustrate the combined variation resulting from the uncertainty of the sampling and analyses and the different flow rates of mercury from the boiler.

4. Results and discussion

The results and discussion presented in this paper are a summary of work which has been reported elsewhere. In this paper only the average values of the mercury concentration or flow rate are quoted. In the fuller reports the standard deviation is given also, and the uncertainty in determining the mercury distribution in the flow trains is discussed. The coefficients of variation, $s\bar{x}^{-1}$, are between 0.3 and 1.0 and the distribution appears to be log-normal. Measurements carried out at the combined incineration and heating plant in Malmö (Bergström 1985a), and in a pilot plant at Gärstadverket in Linköping (Bergström 1985b) have provided the most illustrative results, and are reported here.

4.1. *Sampling effects*

Waste incinerators with electrostatic precipitators (ESP) for flue gas cleaning have not been shown to produce any marked removal of mercury from the flue gases, although sampling the flue gases before the ESP shows that there is a significant amount of mercury present in the fly ash coming from the sampling train. Table 7 presents the results of a test lasting a few hours. Sampling at points before and after the ESP was performed simultaneously, and the mercury content in fly ash samples collected from the ESP was low. In this example, analyses of an average sample of fly ash gave 9.5 μg g^{-1}. The figures given in the example correspond to 1 m^3 standard dry gas from the boiler.

Before the ESP, where the dust concentration in the flue gas is high, 170 or 245 μg mercury in the oxidized form was collected on the filter in the sampling train. In the sample taken after the ESP, where the dust content is very low, only 25 of 240 μg oxidized mercury was collected on the sampling filter. The fly ash removed from the ESP verifies that the mercury in the flue gas is not attached to the ash. The distribution of Hg$^+$ between the filter (Hg$_s$) and the carbonate solution (Hg$_{aq}$) is a result of the sampling procedure.

We have investigated what effect the fly ash has on the distribution of Hg$^+$ during sampling and with the filtration temperation. A large excess of fly ash from the electrostatic filter was distributed over the surface of a silica filter prior to sampling. Nine grams

TABLE 1

Mercury distribution: sampling in the waste incineration plant

	Sampling point		
	Before ESP*†	ESP Ash	Final emissions†
Fly ash (mg)	1500	1480	20
Mercury sample (μg)			
Hg$_s$	170		25
Hg$_{aq}$	75		215
Hg$^+$ ‡	245		240
Hg^0	45		30
Total mercury	290	14	270

*ESP = Electrostatic precipitator.
†Flue gas temperature = 250 °C.
‡Hg$^+$ = Hg$_s$ + Hg$_{aq}$.

TABLE 2
Mercury distribution in the sampling train

Mercury form*	Fly ash from boiler alone (%)	Additional fly ash from EP (%)
Hg_s	27	70
Hg_{aq}	59	22
Hg^+	86	92
Hg^0	14	8
Total mercury	100	100

*$Hg^+ = Hg_s + Hg_{aq}$. Hg^0 Determined by difference between 100% and Hg^+.

TABLE 3
Mercury distribution (% of total) at different sampling temperatures

Mercury form*	Sampling temperature (°C)			
	120	160	200	240
Hg_s	92	68	70	68
Hg_{aq}	1	22	22	29
Hg^+	93	90	92	97
Hg^0	7	10	8	3
Total mercury	100	100	100	100

*See Table 2 footnote.

of dust were added whilst the quantity of dust collected during sampling was 0.8 g. The change in the mercury distribution in the presence of an excess of dust is shown in Table 2. The filtration temperature was 200 °C and the flue gas temperature was 250 °C. Fly ash has a significant adsorption capacity, and binds a large proportion of the oxidized mercury in the flue gas.

The same test was carried at a few different temperatures in the filter house during sampling. The results are presented in Table 3. From this data it can be concluded that temperature has no significant influence on the mercury distribution when sampling at temperatures above the dew point of this system. At 120 °C the fly ash and silica filter are wet as a result of acid condensation.

4.2. Pilot plant tests

Fläkt Industri AB has installed pilot plant equipment for Tekniska Verken in Linköping AB (TV) in their waste incinerator plant Gärstadverket.

The pilot plant is being used to provide design information for a full scale flue gas cleaning system, in accordance with TV's requirements for HCl and mercury removal. The pilot plant is designed for a flue gas flow rate of 650 m³ h⁻¹. Its design is presented in Fig. 2, in which the sampling points are also indicated.

A large number of tests were run with clean flue gas taken from the duct behind the ESP. The dust content in the flue gas was not higher than 50 mg m⁻³. Hydrated lime was fed to the flue gas after cooling in the economiser.

Fly ash particles, lime and calcium chloride were then removed from the flue gas in the fabric filter. Although there was good efficiency for HCl-removal, almost no change could be found in the mercury present in the flue gas. The most recent results are presented

J. G. T. Bergström

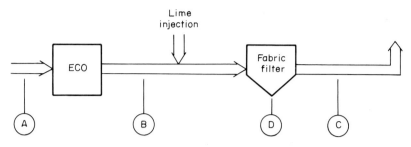

Fig. 2. Pilot plant sampling points (see Tables 4 and 5).

TABLE 4

Mercury flow (mg h^{-1}) in the pilot plant: flue gas containing relatively small amounts of fly ash (see Fig. 2)

	Sampling point			
Mercury	A Before economizer	B After economiser	C After fabric filter	D Ash from fabric filter
Hg$^+$	76	70	73	
Hg^0	18	16	14	
Total mercury	94	86	87	4

TABLE 5

Mercury flow in the pilot plant: flue gas containing considerable amounts of fly ash from the boiler (see Fig. 2)

	Sampling point					
	A Before economizer		C After fabric filter		D Ash from fabric filter	
Mercury	mg h^{-1}	%	mg h^{-1}	%	mg h^{-1}	%
Hg$^+$	84	92	11	12		
Hg^0	7	8	2	2		
Total mercury	91	100	13	14	83	91

in Table 4. Lime feed rate and temperature does not result in any significant change in the mercury flow or distribution.

In another run, flue gas containing fly ash from the boiler was led into the pilot plant and lime was added as before. The mesurements showed that under these conditions mercury is attached to the fly ash and separated in the fabric filter. An example of the mercury distribution in the plant under these conditions is shown in Table 5. The mercury balance in the example given here shows that 14% of the mercury entering the pilot plant is emitted, whilst 91% is removed with the dust in the suppression filter. The mass balance for mercury has a deficit of 5%. According to measurements on samples from the flue gas 87% of the reactive mercury entering the pilot plant is removed.

All the tests carried out under these conditions in the pilot plant show, as can be seen in Table 5, that even the Hg^0 content is reduced by reactions in the pilot plant. This result is however not statistically significant.

4.3. *Mercury distribution in the Malmö plant*

Since 1981 a dry flue gas cleaning system, designed and delivered by Fläkt Industri AB, has been in operation at Malmö.

From the boilers, the flue gas (at approximately 290 °C) is directed to the flue gas cleaning system which consists basically of four different parts. The flue gas is first directed to precollectors, cyclones, where the course dust particles are removed. More than 1000 mg m^{-3} is still present in the flue gases. The temperature in the flue gas is then reduced in a waste heat boiler to about 180 °C. The gas is further led to the reactors where lime is mixed with it.

To increase the mixing, the reactors have a special internal design, and the top of the reactor is formed as an axial cyclone in which coarse particles are collected and returned to the point of injection. The lime reacts with acidic compounds, mainly hydrogen chloride, and forms solid reaction products which are collected in the ESP and fabric filter. After the fabric filter there is another waste heat boiler which lowers the flue gas temperature to about 110 °C.

Several tests in this flue gas cleaning system have been presented. Our test results support what was found in the pilot plant. The oxidized mercury is bound to the fly ash particles, and mercury is removed from the flue gas in the dust collectors. From the boiler a small fraction of Hg^0 leaves with the flue gas. That fraction of the mercury is not effected. In this plant our test shows that there is the same mercury concentration on particles from the ESP as there is from the fabric filter. This result would appear to be due to good mixing and recirculation of fly ash in the reactors. Because of the long retention time and good contact, the mercury salts have already been attached to the fly ash particles before entering the fabric filter.

Separation efficiencies of mercury in the flue gas cleaning system of up to 89% have been measured.

The mercury transported from the plant with the dust is strongly attached to the particles. Evaporation during handling and transport is of little significance. Measurements show that evaporation from the dust collected in the fabric filter is measurable in laboratory experiments, but this is not the case for the mercury collected with the dust in the ESP. Over a period of 14 days, from 10 to 15% of the mercury in the dust from the fabric is evaporated at room temperature. There is no difference in mercury content if the dust from the ESP is treated the same. There is a significant difference in chlorine content between the two ashes. Ash from the ESP has a chlorine content of about 15%, whilst the ash from the fabric filter contains 35% chlorine according to the analyses.

5. Conclusions

Mercury in the flue gas from waste incineration is mainly present in the vapour phase at temperatures down to 140 °C. Only a small portion of the mercury is metallic Hg^0. Most of it is oxidized, and is present as gaseous salts. $HgCl_2$ is one probable form since its high vapour pressure permits its existence at these gas temperatures.

The oxidized mercury is effectively attached to fly ash during filtration in, for example, fabric filters. No similar effect has been observed when lime is added to the flue gas.

By injecting fly ash and lime before a fabric filter, a high degree of collection can be achieved, both for acidic gases, primarily hydrochloric acid, and mercury in the flue gases. Reducing the flue gas temperature in the economizer to 140 °C helps to limit the lime consumption necessary to obtain the desired removal of hydrochloric acid. It also increases the energy which can be won from the burnt waste.

Our results, however, show that a reduction in temperature does not improve the attachment of mercury to the dust. A temperature reduction does however increase the retention time of the flue gases, which it can be assumed will facilitate the practical operation of a plant. Up to 90% of the mercury can become attached to the dust. By optimizing the operation and with efficient dust removal it is therefore possible to limit mercury emissions to less than 0.3 g per tonne on incinerated waste.

References

Bergström, J. (1983a), Emissions from Coal Firing and Oil Firing. *KHM Technical Report 56*. The Swedish State Power Board, Vällingby, Sweden.

Bergström, J. (1983b), Separation of Mercury in Electrostatic Filters and by Flue Gas Desulphurization. *KHM Technical Report 86*. The Swedish State Power Board, Vällingby, Sewden.

Bergström, J. (1985a), Mercury Separation in Flue Gas from SYSAV. Energy from Waste Plant. *Publication 85:3*. The Swedish Association of Public Cleansing and Solid Waste Management, Malmö, Sweden.

Bergström, J. (August 1985b), Mercury Separation Gärstadverket. Test with Pilot Plant. *Report MKS-85/69*. Environmental Consultants at Studsvik AB, Sweden.

Bergström, J. & Lundqvist, J. (1983), Operational Studies at the SYSAV Energy from Waste Plant in Malmö, Sweden. *Publication 84:7*. The Swedish Association of Public Cleansing and Solid Waste Management, Malmö, Sweden.

Bergström, J. & Lundqvist, J. (1985), *Operational Studies at Four Energy from Waste Plants in Sweden* (in press). The Swedish Association of Public Cleansing and Solid Waste Management, Malmö, Sweden.

Lindqvist, O. (1986), Fluxes of mercury in the Swedish environment: contributions from waste incineration. *Waste Management & Research*, 4, 35–44.

Lindqvist, O., Jernelöv, A., Johansson, K. & Rodhe, H. (1984), Mercury in the Swedish Environment; Global and Local Sources. *Report SNV PM 1816*. Distributed by National Swedish Environmental Protection Board, Box 1302, S-171 25 Solna, Sweden.

Lundqvist, J. (1984a), Operational Studies at the Avesta Energy from Waste Plant. *Publication 84:4*. The Swedish Association of Public Cleansing and Solid Waste Management, Malmö, Sweden.

Lundqvist, J. (1984b), Operational Studies at the UKAB Energy from Waste Plant in Uppsala. *Publication 84:1*. The Swedish Association of Public Cleansing and Solid Waste Management, Malmö, Sweden.

Lundqvist, J. (1984c), Operational Studies at the Linköping Energy from Waste Plant in Linköping. The Swedish Association of Public Cleansing and Solid Waste Management, Malmö, Sweden.

Moberg, P. O., Westermark, M. & Noläng, B. (1983), Migration of Trace Elements in Flue Gas Desulphurization. *KHM Technical Report 28*. The Swedish State Power Board, Vällingby, Sweden.

Shendrikar, A. & Ensor, D. S. (1986), Critical review: measurement of mercury combustion aerosols in emissions from stationary sources, *Waste Management & Research*, 4, 75–93.

Westergärd, B. (1986), Mercury from Hogdalen incineration plant in Stockholm 1972–1985, Waste Management & Research, 4, 21.

THE SPECIFIC ROLE OF CADMIUM AND MERCURY IN MUNICIPAL SOLID WASTE INCINERATION*

H. Vogg†, H. Braun†, M. Metzger† and J. Schneider†

(*Received 17 September 1985, revised 8 October 1985*)

Requirements with respect to reducing the emission of pollutants, in particular dust constituents such as heavy metals, especially cadmium and mercury are imposed on processes of municipal solid waste incineration. In the process of incineration, cadmium is volatilized as cadmium chloride to a considerable extent. In a series of *in situ* measurements it has been demonstrated that 99% of this cadmium condenses on dust particles and can be removed together with fly ash. The cadmium concentration in clean flue gas dusts amounts to about 2000 μg g^{-1}. Therefore dust emission values should not be higher than 20–30 mg dust Nm^{-3}. The ultimate disposal of filter ash increasingly poses difficulties on account of the mobility of cadmium.

More than 80% of all mercury is released into the gas phase. The optimization of the various flue gas purification techniques depends on information about the mercury species occurring at the boiler outlet. In order to clarify the speciation the condensation and solubility behaviour of samples is referred to. In the crude gas mercury (II)-chloride and, to a lesser extent, mercury (I)-chloride are present. The occurrence of metallic mercury can be excluded. The mechanism underlying mercury removal by the dry sorption and wet scrubbing techniques is clarified. Recommendations are given for improving the removal efficiency.

Key Words—Cadmium, mercury, chloride, heavy metals, municipal solid waste, incineration, speciation, vapourization, condensation, emission, Clean Air Regulation, Federal Republic of Germany.

1. The so-called "Heavy Metal Problem"

Increasing environmental consciousness in recent years has produced the effect that, with respect to municipal solid waste incineration, not only are drastic reductions in HCl, SO$_2$ and CO emissions and dust generation required, but likewise the dust constituents, especially heavy metals and organic pollutants, and also emissions of gaseous heavy metals and organic substances, have become subjects of interest. A growing number of signs of soil contaminations, which in many cases cannot be caused by other mechanisms than emissions and their depositions, prove that the requirement to reduce the emissions is justified.

However, in public debates about emissions from refuse incineration plants, the heavy metal problem is mostly discussed very globally, leaving out the fact that in various emission systems individual heavy metals can occur at greatly differing individual concentrations and hence with varying importance. Problems connected with heavy metal emissions in a smelting process are basically different from problems of coal combustion and the latter, in turn, cannot be compared with the problems encountered in refuse

---

*Presented at the ISWA Specialized Seminar *Incinerator Emissions of Heavy Metals and Particulates*, Copenhagen, 18–19 September 1985.

†Nuclear Research Center Karlsruhe, Laboratory for Isotope Technology, Post Box 3640, D-7500 Karlsruhe, F.R.G.

Waste Management & Research (1986) **4**, 65–74

TABLE 1

Heavy metal constituents of municipal refuse (values are approximate)

	Amount in refuse (g tonne^{-1})
Zn	3000
Pb	1500
Cu	100
Ni	100
Sb	50
Cd	20
Hg	5

TABLE 2

Heavy metal enrichment in clean flue gas dust

	In refuse (g tonne^{-1})	In clean flue gas dust (μg gv^{-1})	Enrichment factor
Ni	100	100	1
Cu	1000	3000	3
Pb	1500	30 000	20
Zn	3200	80 000	25
Sb	50	3000	60
Cd	20	2000	100
Hg	5	(3000)	600

incineration. There are some few elements specific to each process which due to their concentrations in the offgas play a crucial role with regard to emission.

The release of various heavy metals in refuse incineration does not depend so much in the concentrations in the refuse itself, but much more on the chemical mechanism acting at high temperature which, in combination with non-metallic components present, determines the transfer into the crude gas. Table 1 shows the concentrations of some important heavy metals present in municipal solid waste.

The fact that the elements cadmium and mercury, present in their relatively low amounts, actually represent the critical elements becomes evident only when one compares their initial concentrations with those in the clean flue gas dusts emitted and determines the enrichments implicit in these values (Table 2). The value in parentheses entered in Table 2 for mercury in clean gas flue dust has been found by mere computation incorporating just formally, for better comparability, the dominating gaseous mercury amounts (see section 3) into the considerations related to dusts consitituents. The highest enrichments are obtained for mercury and cadmium. They amount to 600 for mercury, to 100 for cadmium (Vogg 1984).

The particular role of mercury and cadmium becomes even more obvious if one compares the concentrations of the individual heavy metals present in clean flue gas dust with those in natural soils, as has been done in Table 3. Again, mercury and cadmium surprise by their extremely high comparison factors. This holds also for the element antimony, whose ecological importance actually has not yet been reasonably proved; therefore, it will not be considered here in more detail. On the other hand, there is no

TABLE 3

Comparison of heavy metal concentrations

	Clean flue gas dust (ppm)	Natural soils (ppm)	Comparison factor
As	100	2	50
Cd	2000	0.1	20 000
Cr	200	100	2
Cu	3000	50	60
Hg	(3000)	0.05	60 000
Ni	100	50	2
Pb	30 000	10	3000
Sb	3000	0.1	30 000
Sn	4000	2	2000
Tl	150	0.5	300
V	100	100	1
Zn	80 000	80	1000

doubt that mercury and cadmium belong to the hazard category I, and therefore they deserve the greatest attention both on account of the emission concentration and on account of their hazard potential.

It appears from Table 3 that other heavy metals are much less important. Therefore, the conclusion should be that with respect to refuse incineration one should speak less of a heavy metal problem but, more precisely, of a specific role and particular importance of the two elements cadmium and mercury. This is the reason why these two elements will be treated in more detail in the following sections.

2. Cadmium

2.1. *Volatilization*

It is known that cadmium, being a constituent of refuses, gets volatilized to a considerable extent during incineration and is carried away with the offgas. By oxidation to Cd^{2+} in the presence of HCl, cadmium chloride is formed as the main product. It has not been clarified why, under the given conditions of incineration at about 800–1000°C, volatilization does not proceed largely in quantitative terms, or which are the underlying parameters. We have found in our own experiments (Schneider 1984), which, however, have been performed so far in only one selected incineration plant, that about 30% of the cadmium content remains in the slag, whereas 70% occurred in the offgas (Fig. 1). We deem important the elucidation of these relationships, mainly because further cadmium depletion in the slag would imply that the latter could be recycled more easily and without restrictions, e.g. for use in road construction. In order to attain this goal, one has to study intensively the cadmium transport as a function of the conditions of incineration. Work directed to this goal is under way in Karlsruhe.

In recent years the question has been repeatedly discussed whether at least some of the volatilized cadmium is capable of passing through the process filters installed, e.g. electrostatic filters, because it occurs as gaseous species and is thus capable of reaching the ambient air. We were able to show in a number of *in situ* measurements performed at a large scale incineration plant that 99% of the cadmium occurs as a condensate in dust particles, a finding that had been expected from the known vapour pressure plot of

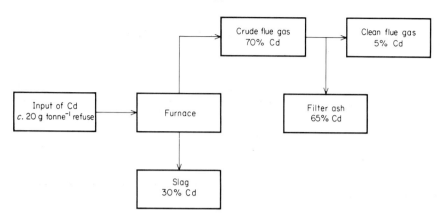

Fig. 1. Cadmium mass balance in waste incinerators.

cadmium chloride. Publications indicating different results and elevated gaseous portions are normally the result of a poor or insufficient efficiency of the filters used in testing. In our measurements we used plane filters made of quartz with a removal efficiency > 99% for particles > 0.6 μm (Braun *et al.* 1983).

2.2. Emission–deposition

Although it can be safely assumed meanwhile that cadmium is emitted as particles, great attention must nevertheless be paid to the amounts emitted. In the Federal Republic of Germany strict rules for cadmium deposition must be observed in conformity with the amended Clean Air Regulation, the numerical values being 5 μg cadmium m^{-2} day^{-1}. Compared with the present deposition rate of 1 μg cadmium m^{-2} day^{-1} in rural areas, a value reported by several authors (Nürnberg *et al.* 1982) and confirmed by us in comprehensive measurements, an only relatively narrow concentration range is obtained. In agreement with investigations conducted in Switzerland (Brunner & Zobrist) we have found—for the least favourable point of impact of the offgas plume from a refuse incineration plant—that observing the deposition limit value indicated before with a dust emission of 100 mg Nm^{-3} is very difficult. This might only be possible by construction of a stack of a height exceeding by far the normally required height. In this context the reader is referred once more to the cadmium concentrations in clean gas dust of several thousand ppm (see Table 3). The presently recommended reduction in dust emission from 100 to 50 mg Nm^{-3} should therefore be actively supported under the aspect of avoiding exposure to cadmium. One should pay attention to the fact, however, that with the grains of the particles emitted getting finer cadmium emission due to its enrichment in the finest particles decreases at a subproportional rate only (see also Greenberg *et al.* 1978, Lorber 1986). Still further reductions to 20 to 30 mg dust Nm^{-3} therefore do not seem unreasonable.

2.3. Filter dust

The specific role played by cadmium is not at all restricted to emission via the air path. About 90% of the cadmium transported with the offgas is removed from the process as fly ash via dust filters, with the ultimate disposal of these filter ashes posing growing difficulties. One of the main reasons is the high mobility of cadmium in these products

TABLE 4
Leaching behaviour of fly ash products

	Normal fly ash		Fly ash + lime reaction product	
	Leaching with H_2O (pH = 10) (%)	Leaching with H_2SO_4 (pH = 4) (%)	Leaching with H_2O (pH = 12) (%)	Leaching with H_2SO_4 (pH = 4) (%)
Cd	n.d.*	85	n.d.	90
Cu	n.d.	10	1	20
Pb	n.d.	5	40	10
Sb	1	3	0.1	5
Zn	n.d.	50	5	70

*n.d. = Non detectable.

in cases where water leaching, e.g. in case of deposition on a dumping site, cannot be definitely ruled out. Because of excess alkalinity of the flue dusts, no doubt mobilization of cadmium starts only after very long periods of time, i.e. when the environmental medium has become slightly acid due to the acid rain presently prevailing. But under these conditions cadmium is then nearly quantitatively soluble. This fact has been shown by us in laboratory scale experiments (see Table 4) (Vogg 1984).

Even if an extrapolation of results from the laboratory scale to the practical conditions prevailing on a dumping site is not possible, one should still proceed with the greatest care. Crack formations in a dumped body and water streams along these cracks could have caused an undesired release of cadmium at a very early stage already. Therefore, when fly ashes are transferred to a dumping site, careful inspections of the percolation waters must be prescribed, among others in account of the problems arising from cadmium.

3. Mercury

In recent years discussions have intensified about the mercury contents in our municipal solid wastes and about the behaviour of mercury deposited on a dumping site and mercury subjected to thermal treatment. Waste incineration in the Federal Republic of Germany now causes an estimated emission of 20 tonnes of mercury per year, an amount which corresponds to the annual mercury emissions from coal fired power stations. (Braun *et al.* 1984). By efforts expressly directed to collection and recycling, above all of mercury batteries, the attempt is being made to relieve refuse incineration plants at the input side already. However, as this will probably cause a reduction to only about 50% of all mercury waste arisings, also the means offered by technology must be fully utilized with a view to reducing mercury emissions. This will be treated in the following sections.

3.1. *Behaviour during incineration*

Obviously, the incineration of pure mercury will not be dealt with here, but incineration of about 5 ppm mercury (see Table 1) in a mixture of waste materials comprising the whole periodic system of the elements is considered. It is self-evident that a multitude of interactions are possible. Accordingly, it is difficult to interpret the mechanism responsible for the reactions. Difficulties are already encountered when a balance is to be established of the mercury streams which branch in the refuse incineration process

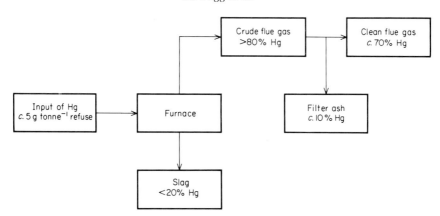

Fig. 2. Mercury mass balance in waste incinerators.

(Fig. 2). They attain a degree of inaccuracy hardly amenable to estimation in the representative testing of the slag material produced and in the subsequent analysis based on it. Non-destructive analytical methods, such as the highly sensitive neutron activation analysis, have proved to be indispensable for obtaining correct analytical results. Notwithstanding the difficulties before, results available now suggest that more than 80% of all mercury is released into the gas phase. (Braun *et al.* 1983). Further investigations will show why any measurable mercury residual concentrations will remain in the slag and whether this might constitute an indication of the quality of the whole incineration system.

So far the question of which chemical mercury compounds are present in the flue gas stream after incineration has not yet been answered unambiguously. The boundary condition to be included in the consideration is that the flue gases, on their way from the furnace to the boiler outlet, pass a zone characterized by a temperature drop from about 1000°C to about 250°C within a few seconds. In order to be able to formulate the question more precisely, it would be of particular importance to determine which mercury species occur at the boiler outlet, because the optimization of the various flue gas purification methods presently applied with a view to reducing mercury emissions depends on this knowledge. Also the composition of the offgas medium as a whole and the type of chemical reactions which may take place are factors of crucial importance. In this context, special attention should be paid to the high halogen concentrations which, on account of a chlorine concentration of 0.6–0.7% in the original refuse, attain in the offgas mean values of about 1000 mg HCl m^{-3} as a result of incineration.

Information reflecting actual conditions is obtained if one performs tests at the boiler outlet in the crude gas at temperatures between 220 and 250°C and compares the behaviour of mercury during testing with the results obtained in laboratory scale model investigations (Braun *et al.* 1986). During sampling it must be strictly guaranteed that no temperature decrease takes place at all because otherwise the conditions would change fundamentally. A number of our own measurements performed at two large-scale refuse incineration plants show that at temperatures between 200 and 230°C about 80% of the mercury occurs in the gaseous state, whereas about 20% is deposited on fly ash and entrained.

In order to clarify the speciation above, the condensation and solubility behaviour of the samples collected can be used (Braun *et al.* 1986). It was found that, in all experiments carried out under the conditions mentioned before, more than 95% of the

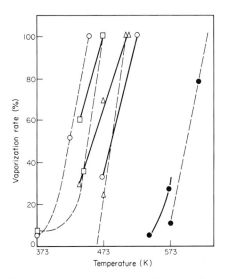

Fig. 3. Vaporization rate ($\Delta Hg/t$, where time, t, is measured in hours) of mercury and its compounds. ○, $HgCl_2$; □, $Hg^{(0)}$; △, Hg_2Cl_2; ●, HgS; – – –, pure substance; ——, substance in fly ash.

gaseous mercury fraction could be easily condensed. Consequently, the presence of metallic mercury can be excluded because laboratory tests have clearly confirmed that metallic mercury is poorly removed by condensation.

On the basis of these results, and by interpretation of the findings described earlier, it can be concluded that in the crude gas which has left the boiler outlet, mercury(II)-halogenides and, to a lesser extent, mercury(I)-halogenides (predominantly chlorides) must be expected to occur. The observed division of mercury into the gas phase and the ash fraction can thus be explained satisfactorily. Depending on the temperature, more or less mercury(II)-chloride is adsorbed on the fly ash and, following reduction to mercury(I)-chloride, bound there (Braun *et al.* 1986).

This thesis is in good agreement with the vaporization rates measured by us for various mercury substances as a function of the temperatures (Fig. 3). The relatively large difference between pure $HgCl_2$ and $HgCl_2$ in fly ash is evident.

3.2. *Removal through dry sorption methods*

In refuse incineration the flue gas dry sorption methods are characterized by an operation producing no waste water. An additional important point is that fly ashes and reaction products can be removed from the offgas through filtration at temperatures well below 200°C. At several plants this led, among other methods, to actual use of fabric filters. As a matter of fact, it can be assumed from Fig. 3 that at temperatures of 150°C mercury(II)-chlorides can be largely transformed into a solid form which can be removed by filtration. Consequently, a clear reduction in mercury emissions can be expected to result from the dry sorption methods carried out at lowered temperatures as follows (Braun *et al.* 1986):

(1) addition of lime or lime milk,
(2) decrease of temperature to 150°C,
(3) adsorption (and reduction) of mercury (II), and
(4) advantageous use of fabric filters,

giving a yield of > 80%. But it should be mentioned in this context that lower temperatures may cause problems in process engineering, e.g. due to filter plugging.

In order to be able to guarantee the emission limit value imposed for mercury of 100 μg Nm^{-3}, attention must be paid not only to the chemical mechanisms but also to the dynamic equilibria. The latter will probably be attained rarely. Longer gas residence times in the reaction spaces should therefore be another goal.

3.3. *Removal by wet scrubbing methods*

Assuming the existence of mercury(II)-chlorides in the crude gas, mercury removal in a wet scrubber should not pose a particular problem. Also, in laboratory scale experiments, it can be shown that mercury halogenides can be conveniently and very effectively eliminated from the gas phase through condensation. By contrast, mercury(0) calls for low temperatures and long residence times.

If mercury(II) is to be removed in a scrubber, special attention, however, must be paid to the following (Braun *et al.* 1986). The scrubbing solution represents a reducing agent, probably on account of the interaction with SO$_2$ present in the offgas at concentrations of 300–400 mg Nm^{-3}. This can be proved in a direct manner by the discolouration of potassium permanganate solution. With increasing pH we were able to show, in laboratory investigations, that mercury(II) can be reduced to mercury(I) which, through disproportionation, can further react to become mercury(II) and mercury(0). The mercury(0) thus formed follows the offgas and is discharged from the system. The reduction of the bivalent mercury can, however, be prevented by higher chloride concentrations and/or by a strongly acid scrubbing solution.

From measurements downstream of the demister we could demonstrate the presence of mercury(0). We found a mercury(II):mercury(0) ratio of about 1:1. We interpret this as a direct sign that the reduction reaction actually occurs. Until now, details of this reaction have not been well understood, especially with regard to part of the system the reaction mainly takes place in. A wet scrubbing system is a very complex liquid/gas phase reaction system which is not in equilibrium, with largely differing gas compositions and varying droplet contents on the scrubber head compared to its outlet. Also not well understood is what happens on the way to the demister, where very small droplets could have a chance to react with the SO$_2$.

In order to prevent this deleterious reaction we recommend high acid and/or high

TABLE 5

Mercury removal by wet scrubbing methods

Easy and quantitative condensation of Hg (II)-chlorides
Undesired secondary reductions by, for example SO$_2$:

$$2\ \mathrm{Hg}^{2+} \rightarrow 2\ \mathrm{Hg}^+ \quad \begin{matrix} \nearrow \mathrm{Hg}^{(0)} \\ \searrow \mathrm{Hg}^{2+}_2 \end{matrix}$$

Dependence of temperature, (H)$^+$ and (Cl)$^-$
Recommendations:
    pH < 3, (Cl)$^-$ > 0.1 M
    Temperature < 60°C
    Addition of oxidizing agents
    Yield > 80%

chloride concentrations, and, if possible, lower temperatures. By adding an oxidant the influences described above could be probably also counteracted. If one considers these findings, the yield of emission reduction for mercury would be much better than 80% (Table 5).

4. Conclusions

In incineration processes it is necessary to take specific counter-measures against the emission of the two toxic heavy metals, cadmium and mercury, present in municipal refuses.

In the case of cadmium extensive dust removal measures will suffice. Clean flue gas dust values of 20–30 mg Nm^{-3} are the goal. It must be noted that this implies shifting the problems connected with pollutants from the air into the solid. Better disposal strategies must be found for the solid material.

In the case of mercury it has been shown that mercury halogenides are predominant whereas mercury(0) is present only in insignificant amounts. Thus, mercury(II)-chloride with lower mercury(I)-chloride clearly dominates, the latter produced by adsorption and reduction on the fly ash.

Reductions of the flue gas temperatures well below 200°C, in connection with dry sorption methods, implys a decrease in mercury emissions. Adsorption, condensation and reduction processes play a role.

Wet scrubbing methods are very effective in mercury removal. However, measures must be taken also in this case in order to avoid mercury losses which are caused by reduction of mercury(II), e.g. with SO_2. Higher proton and chloride concentrations can prevent this undesired reaction. Reductions in temperature below 65°C as well as addition of an oxiding agent would be advantageous.

References

Braun, H., Maul, S. & Vogg, H. (1983), Heavy metals in the gas phase—selected examples for emission and environmental impact measurements. *Proc. Int. Conf. Heavy Metals in the Environment*, Heidelberg, Vol. 1, p. 155.

Braun, H., Vogg, H., Halbritter, G., Bräutigam, K. R. & Katzer, H. (1984), Comparison of the stack emissions from waste incineration facilities and coal fired heating power stations. *Proc. Recycling International*, Berlin, p. 73.

Braun, H., Metzger, M. & Vogg, H. (1986), Zur Problematik der Quecksilber-Abscheidung aus Rauchgasen von Müllverbrennungsanlagen (Mercury removal from flue gases of refuse incinerators), *Müll und Abfall*, 18, 62.

Brunner, P. H. & Zobrist, J. (1983), Die Müllverbrennung als Quelle von Metallen in der Umwelt (Waste incineration as a source of metals in the environment), *Müll and Abfall*, 15, 221.

Greenberg, R. R., Foller, W. H. & Gordon, G. E. (1978), Composition and size distributions of particles released in refuse incineration, *Environmental Science and Technology*, 12, 566.

Lorber, K. E. (1986), Monitoring of heavy metals by energy dispersive X-ray fluorescence spectrometry (EDXRF), *Waste Management & Research*, 4, 3–13.

Nürnberg, H. W., Valenta, P. & Nguyen, V. D. (1982). Wet deposition of toxic metals from the atmosphere in the Federal Republic of Germany. In *Deposition of Atmospheric Pollution* H. W. Georgii & J. Panrath, eds, p. 143. Dordrecht, Boston.

Schneider, J. (1984), *Beprobung des Schlacke-und Flugaschestromes im Müllheizkraftwerk cöppingen* (Determination of the Mass Balances for Slag and Fly Ashes in the Göppingen Refuse Incineration Plant), Internal KfK Report. Kernforschüngscentrüm Karlsruhe.

Vogg, H. (1984), Verhalten von (Schwer)-Metallen bei der Verbrennung kommunaler Abfälle (Behaviour of (Heavy)-Metals in the Incineration of Municipal Refuses), *Chem.-Ing.-Tech.*, 56, 740.

CRITICAL REVIEW: MEASUREMENT OF MERCURY COMBUSTION AEROSOLS IN EMISSIONS FROM STATIONARY SOURCES*

Arun D. Shendrikar† and D. S. Ensor‡

(*Received 17 September 1985*)

This review attempts to critically evaluate mercury aerosol emissions due to toxic and hazardous waste incineration. Since the literature surveyed indicated that sufficient information does not exist on this subject the technical discussion deals primarily with the emissions of mercury due to fossil fuel (e.g. coal) combustion.

Sampling methods commonly used to evaluate mercury emissions from utility stacks are discussed. The limitations of such methods are pointed out, and attempts by the authors and others to improve collection efficiency are also mentioned. The problems of sample instability are mentioned, and data on mercury size-dependent emissions are included. Commonly used analytical methods for mercury quantification are discussed and their limitations pointed out. Detection limits of some of the ideal analytical methods are also tabulated. Conclusions and recommendations for future work in the area of mercury emissions due to refuse incineration are also given.

Key words—Mercury emissions, collection substrates, stack sampling, U.S. EPA Method 5 sampling train, sample storage stability, adsorption patterns of mercury, analytical methods, mercury aerosol generation, U.S.A.

1. Introduction

1.1. *Review scope*

Although the primary objective of this review was to evaluate the emission of mercury aerosols due to the incineration of toxic and hazardous wastes, the literature surveyed indicated that there is not sufficient information on this subject to enable one to discuss in detail the magnitude of the problem, assess the impact of control technology, draw conclusions or recommend a control approach to the mercury emission problem. Therefore, the technical discussion included here deals with the emission of trace elements (primarily mercury), due to the combustion of fossil fuels, their impacts on the environment and the associated health hazards. The intent here is that this technical information, with slight modifications, may be directly applicable to trace element emission problems due to toxic and hazardous wastes incineration.

1.2. *Background basis*

In recent years there has been growing concern about the presence of toxic metals in our environment (Berry & Wallace 1974; Magee 1976; Smith 1980). Their presence in air is essentially due to (a) dust storms; (b) volcanic eruptions; (c) evaporation of ocean spray;

---

*Presented at the ISWA Specialized Seminar *Incinerator Emissions of Heavy Metals and Particulates*, Copenhagen, 18–19 September 1985.

†Compuchem Laboratories, Inc., P.O. Box 12652, Research Triangle Park, North Carolina 27709, U.S.A.

‡Center For Aerosol Technology, Chemical Engineering Unit, Research Triangle Institute, Research Triangle Park, North Carolina 27709, U.S.A.

Waste Management & Research (1986) **4**, 75–93

(d) forest fires and, most importantly, (e) man's activity on this planet. The anthropogenic trace element sources are the smelting of ores, chemical processes and, primarily, the combustion/incineration of fossil fuels (e.g. coal, oil, oil shale, etc.).

The combustion of fossil materials results in the atmospheric emissions of sulphur oxides, nitrogen oxides, carbon oxides, halogens, organic pollutants, and inorganic elements and their compounds. The organic and inorganic compounds include both gas phase and particulate matter emissions. The major gaseous pollutants, e.g. SO_x, NO_x, have been studied extensively, and thus a voluminous literature exists on the chemistry and control of these species. The emission of organic pollutants (e.g. polynuclear aromatic compounds) may be limited by the highly efficient combustion conditions.

The control of particulate matter emissions has been of concern for many years, but importance has been placed only on the visible stack emissions from the combustion facilities. To meet environmental regulatory demands for increasingly stringent control of particulate matter emissions, most of the facilities are equipped with particulate control devices such as electrostatic percipitators (ESP) with wide range design temperatures, fabric filters and wet scrubbers. Although the control devices often exhibit high particulate mass collection efficiencies, the collection efficiency for fine particles containing enriched levels of toxic metals such as Be, Cr, Ni, As, Se, Cd, Sn, Pb and Hg (Council on Environmental Quality 1971; Schroeder 1971) and elements in the gas phase is reported to be not high enough (Kaakinen *et al.* 1975; Bolton *et al.* 1973) in terms of environmental pollution and human health hazards. Additionally, each of these above-mentioned particulate control devices has a unique particle size-dependent removal efficiency. This removal efficiency, coupled with the enrichment of the fine particles with respect to certain toxic metals, offers intriguing possibilities as far as enrichments by control devices are concerned (Klein *et al.* 1975a,b; Natusch *et al.* 1974) because the minimum collection efficiency coincides with the maximum enrichments. In addition, wet scrubbing often uses recycled water; thus, water soluble elements are enriched in the water phase and may be introduced into the flue gas (Maddalone *et al.* 1981; Ondov *et al.* 1979).

1.3. *Trace element emissions*

In utility boilers fossil fuels are commonly subjected to high temperature combustion, and this process releases inorganic minerals in the form of fly ash particles. Most of the fly ash particles are retained within the plant hoppers; however, some are emitted in the form of fine particulate matter and vapours. These particles are generally referred to as "combustion aerosols".

The potential impact of fossil fuel combustion, in terms of the combustion aerosol emissions that can contribute to environmental pollution, is significant. At an estimated rate of coal combustion of 700×10^9 kg year^{-1} in utility boilers in the U.S.A. (Smith 1980), and an assumed 10% average ash content of coal and 80% carryover as fly ash, the yield of uncontrolled fly ash emissions would be approximately 56×10^9 kg year^{-1}. If such emissions are controlled by the use of a particulate control device operating at 98% efficiency, even then the particulate matter emissions would amount to 1.0×10^9 kg. For a trace element present in fossil fuel at a level of 1 ppm and assuming a 98% collection efficiency of the control device, the stack emissions would be about 1000 kg year^{-1}. If this element is mercury, where the collection efficiency of the control device is poor (Diehl *et al.* 1972; Billing & Matson 1972), and 98% of the coal-bound mercury is emitted into the atmosphere, then the 1 ppm component would result in stack emissions of 55,000 kg year^{-1}.

It is therefore understandable that the emission of combustion aerosols in the form of fine particles and vapours has been of regulatory concern, particularly as such fine particles often are found to contain high concentrations of toxic metals (Natusch *et al.* 1974; Linton *et al.* 1976) and by virtue of their aerodynamic diameters, can be efficiently deposited in the pulmonary alveoli (Task Group of Lung Dynamics 1966). In the past, attempts have been made to investigate the mechanisms of formation of these submicron size particles during coal combustion with the view of developing a control strategy (Flagen & Friedlander 1976; Sarofim *et al.* 1977; Neville *et al.* 1980; Desrosiers *et al.* 1979). Results of these studies indicate that the mechanisms of aerosol formation are a complex mixture of physical and chemical processes and among other things, depend on combustion conditions (Kaakinen 1974). The physical characterization of collected samples indicates that the stack emitted fine-fly ash particles range from submicron to 100 microns in aerodynamic diameters, and the size distribution is typically bimodal in nature (McElroy 1982).

Bimodal aerosol particles are considered to be formed by two distinctly different processes. The larger particles are predominantly mineral residue remaining after the combustion of fossil fuel particles. The smaller particles are believed to represent that portion of the fossil fuel combustion material which exists in the gaseous and/or liquid state under boiler conditions but converts into solid particles during condensation caused by the drop in the temperature of stack gases as they pass through the heat transfer sections and gas cleaning equipment (Flagan and Friedlander 1976). Because of different modes of formation, the chemical composition of the two modes are different. The larger particles are predominantly oxides of elements such as Al, Si, Fe, Na, Mg, K, etc.; smaller particles, representing only a small fraction of the total mass emitted, are primarily condensed volatile trace elements such as As, Se, Sb, Cd, Ni, Zn, Hg, etc., or their compounds. The overall environmental impact of trace element emissions, including mercury, is of concern because they are emitted as fine particles and vapours, which intensify their potential adverse health effects.

The general discussion above clearly indicates that the emission of toxic trace elements, including mercury, due to fossil fuel combustion is an environmental and human health hazard concern. The rest of this review includes a discussion of sampling and measurement of mercury and its compounds in utility boiler flue gas. The size-dependent mercury emissions due to coal combustion from the popularly used control devices are considered. Mercury data from various control devices are included. Most of the discussion relates to experiences in sampling the processes associated with coal combustion; however, it is believed that this experience and technical discussion may offer some guidance to other applications and combustion processes where mercury emissions occur—for example waste incineration, oil shale retorting, tar sands, etc.

2. Sampling for mercury combustion aerosols in process streams

2.1. *Introduction*

The release of mercury vapour during combustion is a well recognized fact, with estimates of the fractions of the feed coal mercury discharges ranging from 90 to 97% (Billing & Matson 1972; Anderson & Smith 1977). Mercury's unique behaviour appears to be intimately related to the special physical, chemical and toxicological features of this heavy metal. Its vapour pressure is substantial, even at room temperature, and it is relatively easily volatilized. This is one of the reasons that mercury is found everywhere, including ambient air, work area atmospheres, natural waters etc. Because of its toxic properties, emissions of mercury need to be monitored in fossil fuel combustion.

2.2. *Sampling for volatile mercury*

Sampling to quantify mercury and other trace element levels in a gas stream is similar to determining particulate loading of the flue gas in a utility stack. The problems encountered, and the sampling methods used for obtaining representative samples of such point sources, are common to both particulate and metal sampling. The differences and special considerations related to mercury/trace metal sampling in the gaseous streams are sample contamination, sample alteration, equipment selection and properties of trace elements with respect to sampling systems. Most of the commonly used methods for sampling trace elements were developed and used for particulate mass sampling in gaseous streams. In practice, particulate mass samples are collected using well-established sampling methods, and the samples collected are subsequently analysed for trace elements of interest.

Prior to 1970 the scientific literature contained relatively little information on stack sampling for trace elements (Cuffe & Gerstle 1967). In the early 1970s there was a sudden upward surge in the number of studies of this type. For example, in 1972 two reports appeared on mass balances of mercury which indicated that 90% of the mercury that entered via coal was measured leaving the stack (Billing & Matson 1972; Diehl *et al.* 1972). In these studies EPA Method 5 sampling trains (U.S. EPA 1971) that included impingers containing chemical solutions were used to collect and retain mercury and other volatile trace elements from stack gases. One of the first detailed studies describing mass balances of 50 trace elements, including mercury, on a cyclone furnace, was carried out by Bolton *et al.* (1973). For sampling this point source, a modified EPA Method 5 train was used with eight impingers to collect all volatile trace elements. Although the results of this study showed poor mass balances for mercury and selenium, numerous other trace elements showed excellent mass balances (Bolton *et al.* 1973). Other studies (Cato & Venezia 1976; Harrison *et al.* 1978; Ensor *et al.* 1979) of mass balances of mercury and other volatile trace elements around a particulate control device include the use of an EPA Method 5 train with the basic train modified to hold up to 10 impingers.

The high sampling volume version of EPA Method 5 is called the Source Assessment Sampling System (SASS). A similar sampling device can also be used to determine the levels of mercury in the stack gases. The SASS train, like EPA Method 5, also contains impingers with chemical solutions to collect mercury vapour. In both types of sampling trains, mercury vapours are collected in impingers which contain an oxidizing medium specifically used for the collection of this element. A literature search indicates that investigators in the field have used a variety of chemical solutions with the view of optimizing the mercury collection efficiency. Such attempts were based on reports (Billing & Matson 1975; Anderson & Smith 1977; Lindberg 1980; Klein *et al.* 1975*a,b*) which indicated the lack of good mercury material balances during coal combustion, probably because of the use of inefficient mercury collection media. Some of the popularly used mercury collection substrates are listed in Table 1 (Shendrikar *et al.* 1984*b*).

In spite of a number of available media consisting of metals, sorbents and absorbing solutions, poor mercury collection efficiencies have been reported during stationary source sampling (Ensor *et al.* 1981). This inefficiency probably contributed to the poor mercury mass balances achieved in studies of coal-fired power plants (Caban & Chapman 1972; Diehl *et al.* 1972). Ensor *et al.* (1981) have slightly modified the commercially

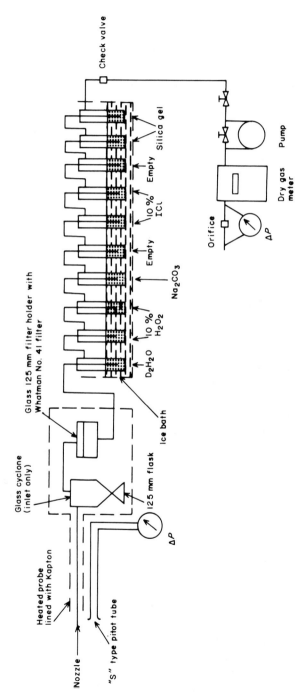

Fig. 1. Modified U.S. EPA method trace element sampling train (Ensor *et al.* 1981).

available EPA Method 5 train and sampled utility stacks: their sampling assembly used is shown in Fig. 1. The modification involved the use of 10 impingers to increase the collection efficiency of volatile trace elements including mercury. Sample recovery was facilitated by lining the probe with Kapton (Flegal *et al.* 1975). To avoid sample contamination, the entire train was made of Pyrex glass, and between the fifth and sixth impingers a side stream to a silver wool collector was used to collect elemental mercury from the flue gas (Wroblewski *et al.* 1974). Two impingers containing an iodine monochloride solution (250 ml in each) were used to specifically collect mercury. The sampling problem with this modified Method 5 train, as indicated by Ensor *et al.* (1981), was with the silver wool collector. It was found to be the source of serious leaks, and the mercury data obtained were erratic and difficult to interpret. As a result, the silver wool mercury collector was replaced by an impinger that contained iodized activated charcoal with multiple layers of silver wool over it (Murthy 1975; Moffitt & Kupel 1970). The results (discussed elsewhere) showed that this sampling system was also inefficient for mercury collection from stack gases.

Several investigators have attempted to use other sampling approaches for mercury. For example, Lindberg (1980) has collected vapour mercury samples in a power plant plume by using activated charcoal absorption traps and Teflon membrane filters for particulate mercury. Laboratory evaluation studies of the efficiency indicated that activated charcoal traps were efficient for mercury collection (Lindberg 1981). However, Shendrikar (1981) pointed out that such efficiency studies need to be carried out in the actual field environment to increase the validity of the results. Dumarey *et al.* (1981) reported the determination of mercury emissions from a municipal incinerator. Here the sampling system was an oxidant impinger containing $K_2Cr_2O_7/20\%$ HNO_3 with a fritted glass candle for better dispersion. On the back side of the impinger, they used a Tenax GC trap to remove organics contained in the stack gases followed by gold-coated sea sand absorber (Dumarey *et al.* 1979). A collection efficiency of 99% of mercury was reported (Dumarey *et al.* 1981) in the 4% $K_2Cr_2O_7/20\%$ HNO_3 solution, and complete absorption could be obtained by the use of a gold absorber placed after the absorption impinger. Selective absorption tube systems have also been used by some investigators to determine levels of mercury and its organic compounds in the air (Braman & Johnson 1974; Trujillo & Campell 1975; Johnson & Braman 1974; Fitzgerald & Gill 1979). Such sampling methods, although appearing to function efficiently in the ambient air environment, have not yet been applied to stack sampling. An attractive approach to continuously monitoring mercury emission in a stack has been recently attempted, by Hodgson *et al.* (1982; 1984) and Fox (1985) using the Zeeman Atomic Absorption method.

The poor collection efficiency of volatile mercury and its compounds during the high volume sampling of flue gas has been of concern for some time and, consequently, investigators have focused on identifying collection substrates that would result in optimum collection efficiency. In general, media selection considerations have been reagent purity, possible interferences during mercury quantification, collection efficiency for high volume sampling, reagent stability, cost and compatibility with other impingers in the sampling train assembly. A parameter that appears to have been given less attention is the methodology for testing the efficiency of these collection media. The analytical accuracy of "Standard" sources of elemental mercury vapour used in past investigations does not appear to be adequate. For the purpose of monitoring and developing control technology, it is also important that accurate and precise methods for sampling and analysing source emissions of mercury are available. Shendrikar *et al.* (1983) have recently evaluated the collection efficiency of various trapping media with known and stable laboratory generated mercury atmospheres.

To date, very little work appears to have been performed on the mercury speciation in the combustion sources (Shendrikar & Ensor 1984). Although sufficient evidence does not exist, some work (Lindberg 1981; Hodgson 1982, 1984) indicates the presence of organic mercury compounds in the flue gases. See also papers in this Seminar by Bergström, Lindqvist, Reimann and Vogg *et al.* (1986). More quantitative studies are needed in this area particularly because many organo-mercurial compounds are known to be more toxic than elemental mercury (D'ltri, 1982).

Attempts have been made to sample particulate mercury in the stack gases from coal combustion. In fact, the particulate matter collected in the front half (includes nozzel, probe, and filter) of the EPA Method 5 train or SASS train is commonly analysed for mercury (Ensor *et al.* 1980, 1981; Smith 1980). Present particulate matter emissions standards are based on total mass and do not differentiate with regards to chemical composition or size. However, as discussed earlier, fine particles of a less than 10 μm diameter have been considered potentially hazardous to health, particularly because of the enrichment of toxic metals (U.S. EPA 1977). Furthermore, fine particles can contribute to visibility degradation. The U.S. EPA has recently announced that it is considering promulgation of a size dependent inhalable particle standard in the 1980s (Frederick 1980). Therefore, mercury size-dependent emission data from stationary sources are desirable.

The various sampling approaches that have been used to obtain size-segregated mercury particle samples in the stack are cascade impactors, low pressure impactors, cyclones, cascade cyclones, etc. For impactor sampling, collection discs are covered with peelable Kapton film, 0.0127 mm thick. The Kapton is coated with Apiezon-L grease, which provides a base for sample collection and its retention on the impactor stage. An impactor sampling procedure for trace elements including mercury is described by Markowski *et al.* (1980).

3. Sample storage

Emission evaluation studies generally involve sampling the utility stacks and other associated point sources. All such samples are generally collected and recovered in the field and transported to the laboratory for chemical analysis. The scope of the programme is such that there is a considerable time lapse between sample collection and its further utilization for chemical analysis. The literature searched indicates that there is very little known about the storage stability/instability of such solid, liquid and flue gas samples. This information is considered important to provide a valid evaluation of the environmental effects of emissions due to fossil fuel combustion and also to provide some inputs for developing a control strategy.

Relevant studies to investigate integrity changes during storage of solid, liquid and flue gas samples from combustion sources indicate that workers in the field seem to have paid virtually no attention to this problem. Fisher *et al.* (1976), while examining micro-crystalline structures in fly ash samples, observed extensive growth on the surfaces of fly ash particles after a 4-month storage period in closed containers at ambient temperatures. This growth must be considered in terms of physical and chemical changes in fly ash particles with respect to time. Their report appears to be the first observation that indicates the instability of fly ash samples during storage. However, this evidence does not seem to have been followed up by the authors or by other investigators in the field; therefore, the magnitude of this work and its significance apparently remains unknown. Hulett & Weinberger (1980) have also demonstrated the formation of crystal phases in some fly ash particles. The formation of these crystal phases clearly indicates a mechanism for migration of species in fly ash and, in turn, the instability of fly ash particles with respect to time and storage.

In related areas Shendrikar *et al.* (1984*b*) have recently investigated adsorption characteristics of EPA Method 5 liquid samples from a full-scale power plant test. The losses of mercury and other volatile trace elements such as As, Se, Sb, Cd and Zn on the polyethylene containers (commonly used for field samples recovery and storage) were measured by adding radiotracers to the selected impinger solutions and measuring the amounts adsorbed onto the container walls over a period of 100 days. The media investigated were double-distilled water, 10% solutions of H_2O_2, Na_2CO_3 and iodine monochloride.

4. Chemical analysis

4.1. *Sample preparation*

Mercury emission evaluation studies result in solid and liquid samples which must be prepared before mercury levels can be quantified in them. Preparation of samples for chemical analysis is another important step that needs consideration; preferably, sample preparation should be minimal and, when required, care should be exercised to see that (1) the sample preparation approach is compatible with the analytical method being used; (2) the preparation method does not introduce contaminants or alter the sample chemistry; (3) losses of metal of interest do not occur; and (4) the sample preparation approach is simple, quick and efficient.

4.2. *Mercury analysis methods*

There are a number of analytical methods available for mercury analysis in samples of all types including ones with complex matrices. For example, there is the classical dithizone extraction method, where mercury is extracted by dithizone in chloroform from a strongly acidified solution. A mercury–dithizonate complex is orange in colour and has a maximum absorption at about 490 nm in chloroform. This method was extensively used in the 1940s and 1950s. Although dithizone analysis can be carried on with rather inexpensive equipment, available in all analytical laboratories, the method is time consuming, labour intensive, requires relatively large sample sizes (2–10 g) and shows low sensitivity compared to modern methods. The reported sensitivity is about 0.20 μg mercury in a 10 g sample, with a precision of 4–5%.

Shendrikar & Ensor (1981) have evaluated the applicability of four analytical methods in terms of precision and accuracy for samples from combustion sources. The methods included neutron activation analysis (NAA), proton-induced X-ray emission (PIXE), inductively coupled plasma (ICP) and atomic absorption spectrometer (AAS). The accuracy of the four methods for mercury in a NBS-SRM* coal sample was measured. The AAS cold vapour method showed -38% recovery of mercury while NAA showed -91% deviation from the reported NBS value. The other two methods could not even detect mercury.

For a number of reasons including sensitivity selectivity, availability, reliability and cost of analysis, ultra violet (UV) and atomic absorption spectrometric (AAS) methods have been by far the most popular instrumental techniques for the analysis of mercury

---

*NBS-SRM = National Bureau of Standards—Standard Reference Preparation.

in a wide variety of sample types. These methods are based on the fact that elemental mercury vapour has a strong absorption line at 253.63 nm in the UV region of the electromagnetic spectrum. Consequently, instruments using this principle of detection respond to that portion of the sample in which mercury exisits in the elemental state. To be detected, compounds of mercury need to be converted to elemental mercury vapour. This can be achieved by the addition of reducing agents, such as stannous chloride or sodium borohydride, to the sample solution before quantification.

Several AAS techniques have been developed over the years, and these have found a wide variety of applications in determining mercury in samples of all types: most of them involve cold-vapour techniques. Their sensitivity is better than 0.05 μg l^{-1}.

Atomic fluorescence spectrometry (AFS) involves the measurement of resonance emissions at a wavelength of 253.63 nm. It is reported to be more sensitive than AAS (Subber *et al.* 1974).

5. Results and discussion

Most of the data presented here are from authors' laboratory; however, for discussion and evaluation of mercury emission problems from stationary sources, results of other workers in the field are also considered.

5.1. *Mercury collection*

The mercury collection substrates used by Ensor *et al.* (1981) and a variety of other metal sorbants and absorption solutions (see Table 1) have been utilized to sample for mercury in stack gases and in the air. Such media have been used after their laboratory evaluation for optimum mercury collection efficiencies. In spite of this, poor mercury sampling efficiency during the field samplings has been reported. This may be due to the following.

(1) Sampling environment contains chemical components, which have not been simulated in the laboratory, that may poison the mercury collection substrate.
(2) Sampling environment contains mercury compounds other than those for which collection efficiency studies in the laboratory were performed.
(3) Incomplete recovery of mercury and/or its compounds from the collection substrate.
(4) Problems during analytical quantification of collected samples.
(5) High sampling rates and/or inefficient dispersion that results in inefficient collection and retention of mercury.
(6) Instability of mercury sampled solution with respect to storage time.

The problem of sampling efficiency needs to be resolved because, if it is not, mercury stack emission data can not be valid. Recently, McQuaker & Sandberg (1982) have used a sampling system with three Greenburg–Smith impingers in a series that contained an acidic KMNO$_4$ solution and silica gel. The field measurements with this system have shown greater than 99% mercury collection efficiency. Recent studies by Ensor *et al.* (1981) and others (Hodgson *et al.* 1982, 1984; Lindberg 1980) reportedly indicated the presence of organic mercury compounds in stack gases.

Shendrikar *et al.* (1983) have generated stable and known mercury atmospheres based upon the saturation of air with mercury vapours at a fixed temperature and evaluated the collection efficiencies of the popularly used media, in the SASS train impinger assembly (Table 1). Their experimental work included a three impinger assembly, an SASS system and sampling rates of between 1.5–3.0 l s^{-1}. Performance evaluations of the

TABLE 1

Popularly used mercury collection media

Mercury collection into a solution
  Potassium permanganate in sulphuric acid
  Potassium permanganate in nitric acid
  Iodine monochloride
  Iodine/potassium iodide
  Bromine, hypobromide
  Carbonate-phosphate
  Ethyl alcohol
  99% isopropyl alcohol
  Sodium borohydride
  Acidic hydrogen peroxide
  Acidic potassium dichromate
  Ammonium persulfate
  Silver-catalysed ammonium persulfate
  Hydrogen peroxide in ammonium hydroxide
  Acidic hydrogen peroxide with silver nitrate
  Nitric acid

Mercury collection by a solid
  Activated carbon/charcoal
  Activated carbon/charcoal treated with acid or base
  Activated charcoal/mineral wool impregnated with:
    Iodine
    Ferric Chloride
    Palladium Chloride
    Cadmium Sulphide
  Silica gel or alumina coated with gold chloride
  Hopcalite
  Paper impregnated with:
    Potassium Iodide
    Copper Iodide
    Selenium
    Selenium Sulphide

Mercury amalgamation on a metal surface
  Silver-gauze, wool, wire, thin film, silvered Chromosorb P
  Gold-foil, wire, chips, thin film
  Platinum
  Palladium
  Copper
  Zinc
  Tin
  Lead
  Bismuth

---

system indicated that the 10% hydrogen peroxide and 0.2 M ammonium persulfate solutions collected 20 and 27% respectively, of the mercury.

Shendrikar *et al.* (1983) pointed out that the 20% collection efficiency of the hydrogen peroxide impingers must be considered as a significant finding, particularly because during SASS or EPA Method 5 sampling such oxidative impingers are generally ahead of impingers specifically used for mercury collection. The results of this study show that hydrogen peroxide impingers also need to be analysed to obtain accurate and total mercury concentrations in the flue gas. Both 0.2 M ammonium persulfate with 0.025 M

TABLE 2
Summary of mercury collection efficiency of various media*

Medium	No. of runs	Average sampling rate ($1\ s^{-1}$)	Average collection efficiency
10% Hydrogen peroxide	4†	2.00	20.9
Acidified 10% hydrogen peroxide	1	1.85	18.2
0.2 M Ammonium persulphate	2†	1.75	26.8
Freshly prepared 0.2 M ammonium persulphate + 0.025 M silver nitrate	4‡	1.88	>99.0
Freshly prepared 0.2 M ammonium persulphate + 0.025 M silver nitrate	1§	2.04	73.3
Aged 0.2 M ammonium persulphate + 0.025 M silver nitrate¶	2†	1.76	80.1
1.5% Potassium permaganate in 10% sulphuric acid‖	2†	2.20	>99.0
1.5% Potassium permagnate in 10% sulphuric acid	1§	2.47	94.4

*A three impinger system was used unless otherwise specified. Sampling times in most cases were 60 min. Room temperature was in the range of 20–25°C and data on efficiency are based on relative absorbance readings at the inlet and outlet of the impingers.
†Includes one run at low mercury levels.
‡Includes two runs at low mercury levels.
§Only one impinger containing 250 ml of medium was used.
¶Aged for 48 h in the refrigerator.
‖Sampling times less than 60 min.

silver nitrate, and 1.5% acidified potassium permanganate solutions, showed a mercury collection efficiency better than 99%. However, the former medium needs to be prepared freshly, since aging by 48 h reduces its efficiency to 80% in a three-impinger SASS train assembly. The results of these findings are summarized in Table 2.

5.2. *Storage stability of flue gas mercury samples*

As pointed out earlier, there is not that much information on the storage stability of flue gas particulate matter samples with respect to time, and a systematic and detailed study is needed in this area so that health hazard potentials of combustion emissions can be validly extrapolated. Using EPA Method 5 impinger samples from a field test, Shendrikar et al. (1984a) have studied the adsorption pattern of mercury (see Fig. 2) and other elements such As, Se, Sb, Cd, Zn, etc.

As can be seen from Fig. 2, mercury shows significant losses from all media except iodine monochloride. These losses are minimum values since mercury loss due to evaporation was also observed. This loss, representing approximately 10%, was discovered when radioactive Hg^{203} was seen in the γ-ray spectrum of containers holding another group of samples (As, Sb, Cd, and Zn) in the laboratory. Further investigation showed that Hg^{203} was present in the "Saran Wrap" covering the Hg^{203} spiked impinger solutions of double-distilled water and Na_2CO_3. It was concluded (Shendrikar et al. 1984b) that mercury was reduced in the double-distilled and Na_2CO_3 solutions to elemental mercury which then passed as a vapour through the "Saran Wrap" and

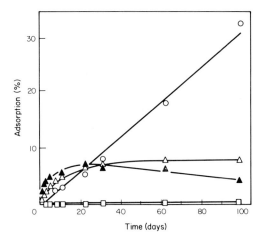

Fig. 2. Adsorption loss patterns of mercury from four storage media (Shendrikar *et al.* 1984*a*). ○, H_2O_2; △, Na_2CO_3; □, ICl; ▲, double distilled H_2O.

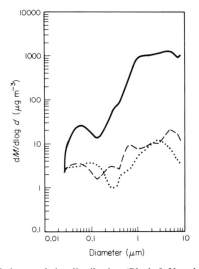

Fig. 3. Scrubber inlet mass and elemental size distribution (Black & Veatch 1982*b*). ——, Mass/1000; ---, Se; ......, mercury. Penetration (P_t) = $dM/d\log d$.

contaminated the other stored sample solutions. To estimate such types of loss, the total Hg^{203} activity in similar solutions and containers as those under study was monitored. A loss of about 10% was found in double-distilled water and the Na_2CO_3 solution during the first 24 h of storage, and there were no subsequent losses. Such evaporative mercury losses were not observed from the hydrogen peroxide and iodine monochloride solutions.

During this experimental work, aliquots of each of four types of impinger solutions were spiked with the same radiotracers, freeze dried in the containers of the same type and stored for 100 days. After this period, each of the samples was thawed, transferred to another container and their radioactivity was measured. No measurable loss of mercury or any other element was found in these freeze dried samples. Matsunaga *et al.* (1979) found that the mercury solutions can be stabilized if acidified with 0.2 M H_2SO_4

and more than 3% NaCl is added; no change of mercury concentration was observed for at least 60 days.

5.4. *Size dependent mercury emissions*

The concentration of mercury in emissions from industrial processes depends on the mechanisms of formation within the combustion area and the equipment installed to control particulate and gaseous emissions. The examples reported in this paper will be limited to results from coal-fired boilers in the electric utility industry. The particle size distribution leaving the boiler, as well as the emissions entering the atmosphere, will be shown to illustrate the importance of emission control. The total mass, Hg and Se are reported in the figures. Selenium is an example of a volatile element which may provide insights into the behaviour of mercury.

5.4.1. *Size distribution data*

The particle size distribution data were taken with a low pressure drop cascade impactor with peelable Kapton substrates as described by Ensor *et al.* (1981). A typical distribution for fly ash from the combustion of sub-bitumous low-sulphur coal is shown in Figure 3. The distribution is biomodal because the small mode is formed by condensing material, and the large mode is the fused residue of the mineral ash in the coal (for more details see Flagen & Friedlander 1976). The distribution has been normalized to the incremental logarithm of the particle diameter to eliminate instrumentation biases. The distribution of Hg and Se as a function of particle diameter generally follows the mass distribution with some enrichment for submicron particles. The in-stack samples were obtained within the flue gas at a temperature of 143 °C.

5.4.2. *Control technology*

The control technology used to control emissions includes wet scrubbers, electrostatic precipitators and fabric filters. Each type of control equipment modifies the emission in its own way. Wet scrubbers rapidly cool the gas to about 30 °C and then contact the flue gas with water to remove particles and gases. Scrubbers are designed to either remove gases or particles. The temperature drop can be quite large (150 °C) and the pressure drop for a high efficiency particle scrubber can be high (50 cm H_2O). Electrostatic precipitation involves charging the particles with a corona discharge, collecting the particles on grounded vertical plates and then cleaning the plates (by rapping) at frequent intervals. Usually the temperature drop is small (10 °C) as is the pressure drop (10 cm H_2O). Fabric filtration uses sets of glass fabric bags, about 0.3 m in diameter and 10 m high, to act as a support for collected ash which removes the suspended ash in the flue gas. The temperature drop is small (10 °C) and the pressure drop is moderate (18 cm H_2O).

5.4.3. *Scrubbing*

The particle dependent penetration for two types of scrubbers are shown in Figs 4 and 5. Particle size dependent penetration is given by the following:

$$P_t(d) = (dM/dlog\ d)_{out}/(dM/dlog\ d)_{in},$$

where P_t is the fractional penetration through the control device of particle with diameter d (M = mass).

A. D. Shendrikar & D. S. Ensor

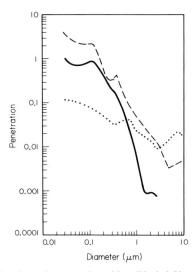

Fig. 4. Size-dependent penetration through a venturi scrubber (Black & Veatch 1982*b*). ——, Mass/1000; ---. Se; ......, mercury.

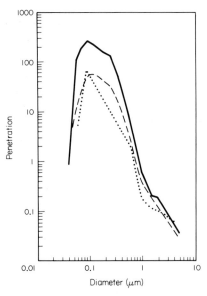

Fig. 5. Size-dependent penetration (fractional) through a turbulent contact scrubber (Black & Veatch 1982*a*). ——, Mass; ---, Se; ......, mercury.

If the fractional penetration is greater than 1.0, particles are being generated in the scrubber.

The penetration results in Figure 4 are for a venturi scrubber designed to remove both particulate matter and SO_2. The pressure drop through the scrubber was 43 cm H_2O and the liquid to gas ratio was 3.4×10^{-3} m^3 m^{-3} (Black & Veach, 1982*a,b*). The solid phase particles tended to follow the efficiency of removal observed for the total mass. For this particular study the inlet concentration of mercury was not determined, preventing determination of collection efficiency of both particles and gases.

TABLE 3

Comparison of collection efficiencies (penetration) of Se, and total mass for an electrostatic precipitator mercury, and a fabric filter (Ensor *et al.* 1981)

Source	Inlet concentration			Outlet concentration			Penetration (fractional)		
	Mass $(g\ m^{-3})$	Se $(\mu g\ m^{-3})$	Hg $(\mu g\ m^{-3})$	Mass $(g\ m^{-3})$	Se $(ug\ m^{-3})$	Hg $(ug\ m^{-3})$	Mass	Se	Hg
Electrostatic precipitation	5.72	41.06	5.5	0.0408	1.17	2.2	0.0071	0.0284	0.40
Fabric filter	1.09	13.08	0.0007	0.0041	0.204	0.00023	0.0038	0.016	0.33

The penetration in Figure 5 is for a turbulent contact absorber designed primarily for removal of SO_2. The contact between slurry and flue gas is accomplished in a chamber containing small plastic balls of about 2.5 cm in diameter. As shown, significant particle. generation was observed in the scrubber under the conditions of the test. The submicron particles are probably formed by the evaporation of droplets of scrubbing slurry because of the presence of water soluble elements. In addition, rapid cooling of the flue gas will also cause the condensation of vapour to form submicron particles. These submicron particles are poorly collected in the scrubber. The mechanisms have not been identified, however, similar results have been reported by Ondov *et al.* (1982) and Ensor *et al.* (1975). The penetration of particles (mercury and Se) through dry collectors is shown in Table 3.

The behaviour of volatile trace elements appears to be similar in fabric filters and electrostatic precipitators. The overall penetration for both mercury and Se is much higher than overall mass. It appears that some of the vapour Hg° may be collected with low efficiency in these high mass efficiency control devices. This is surprising because it is generally believed that Hg° would not be collected at all (see, however, Reimann 1986). However, considering the analytical difficulties, this conclusion should be verified with additional data. Selenium showed evidence of condensation because the particle size dependent penetration was much greater than for mass in both the electrostatic precipitator and fabric filter.

6. Conclusions and recommendations for further work

Although this review does not discuss the problem of mercury emissions due to toxic and hazardous waste incineration, it is considered that the technical information included here from coal combustion processes will offer some guidance to performing the field work in this new, developing area. Mercury is a common pollutant, toxic in nature, invariably found in almost all types of emissions due to incineration/combustion. As pointed out in this review, the existing particulate control technology, at least for coal combustion or oil-shale retorting, is ineffective in controlling the emission of mercury, and this may increase environmental pollution and human health hazards. Elemental mercury is toxic but organic mercury compounds are more toxic, and hence, greater attention must be directed to this problem.

There are several areas to the problem of mercury emissions where research efforts are still needed, and two of these include the following.

(1) Future developments in particulate control technology should also consider the

chemical behaviour of mercury and other trace elements due to combustion/incineration in addition to physical and engineering principles. It is only then that we may be able to achieve the "total control" of particulate emissions. After all, emitted particulate matter from control devices is essentially an aggregate of trace elements and their compounds. It may also contain some organics that can survive high temperature combustion or can be formed due to high temperature combustion.

(2) The task of emission evaluation efforts always needs to be adequately supported by efficient sampling methods so that data produced are scientifically valid. As pointed out in this review, such methods for mercury determination essentially do not exist, with only a few reported exceptions. Therefore, efforts need to be directed towards establishing and developing efficient and simple sampling methods.

It is pointed out here that laboratory substrate collection efficiency studies are no substitute for actual field evaluations. One just cannot account for all the chemical components present in the stack gases that may or may not effect the substrate collection efficiency or inefficiency during the laboratory experimental work.

Sampling that would permit the continuous monitoring of mercury emissions appears to be an attractive approach. The Zeeman Atomic Absorption technique seems to offer this advantage, as evidenced by the recent work of Hodgson *et al.* (1982; 1984) and Fox (1985), at least during oil shale retorting. A good material balance of mercury was obtained by Fox using the Zeeman Atomic Absorption Method.

Mercury speciation investigations need to be applied to particulate mass to determine how much vaporous elemental mercury and mercury inorganic/organic compounds are collected in the particulates on the filter or impactor stages. Care should also be exercised to ensure that no elemental mercury is lost due to vaporization during such sample storage, as this would create negative bias on mercury results.

References

Anderson, W. L. & Smith, K. E. (1977), Dynamics of Mercury at Coal-fired Power Plant and Adjacent Cooling Lakes, *Environmental Science and Technology, 11*, 75.

Berry, W. L. & Wallace, A. (1974), Trace Elements in the Environment: their Role and Potential Toxicity as Related to Fossil Fuels. A Preliminary Study, *UCLA-112-946*. Laboratory of Nuclear Medicine and Radiation Biology, California University, Los Angeles, U.S.A.

Bergström, J. (1986), Mercury behaviour in flue gases, *Waste Management & Research, 4*, 57–64.

Billing, C. E. & Matson, W. R. (1972), Mercury emissions from coal combustion, *Science, 176*, 1232.

Black and Veatch Consulting Engineers (1982*a*), Full-scale Scrubber Characterization of Conesville Unit 5, *EPRI Final Report CS-2525* Palo Alto, California.

Black and Veatch Consulting Engineers (1982*b*), Full-scale Scrubber Characterization of Colstrip Unit 2, *EPRI Final Report CS-2764* Palo Alto, California.

Bolton, R. L., Van Hook, Y., Fulkerson, F. C., Lyon, E., Anderson, A. W., Carter, J. A. & Emery, J. F. (1973), Trace Element Measurements at the Coal-fired Allen Steam Plant, *ORNL.NSF-EP-43*. Oak Ridge National Laboratory, Oak Ridge, Tennessee, U.S.A.

Braman, R. S. & Johnson, D. L. (1974), Selective absorption tubes and emission technique for determination of ambient forms of Mercury in air, *Environmental Science and Technology, 8*, 996.

Caban, R. & Chapman, T. W. (1972), Losses of mercury from chloride plants. A review of a pollution problem, *AICHE, 13*, 892.

Cato, G. A. & Venezia (1976), Trace element and organic emissions from industrial boilers. *69th Air Pollution Control Association Annual Meeting*, Portland, Oregon, U.S.A., 27 June.

Council on Environmental Quality (1971), *Toxic Substances*. GPO, Washington, D.C.

Cuffe, G. T. & Gerstle, R. W. (1967), Emissions from Coal-fired Power Plants: a Comprehensive Summary, *Public Health Service Publication, No. 999-AP-35*, Cincinnati, Ohio.

Desrosiers, R. E., Rehl, J. H. Ulrich, G. D. & Chu, A. S. (1979), Submicron fly ash formation in coal-fired boilers. *Proc. 17th Symposium on Combustion*, Waterloo, Canada, August 1979, 1395–1403.

Diehl, R. C., Hattman, E. A., Schultz, H. & Haren, R. T. (1972), Fate of Mercury in the Combustion of Coal, *Bureau of Mines, Report PB-210226*.

D'ltri, F. M. (1982), *The Environmental Mercury Problem*. Chemical Rubber Company Press, Cleveland, Ohio 44129, U.S.A.

Dumarey, R., Heindryckx, R. & Dams, R. (1981), Determination of mercury emissions from a municipal incinerator. *Environmental Science and Technology*, 15, 206.

Dumarey, R., Heindryckx, R., Dams, R. & Hoste J. (1979), Determination of mercury compounds in air with a Coleman Mercury Analyzer System, *Analytica Chimica Acta*, 107, 159.

Ensor, D. S., Jackson, B. S., Calvert, S., Lake, C., Wallon, D. V., Nilan, R. E., Campbell, K. S., Cahill, T. A. & Flocchini, R. G. (1975), Evaluation of a Particulate Scrubber on a Coal-fired Utility Boiler, *EPA-600/2-074*, NTIS PB249-562/AS, Research Triangle Park, NC 27709.

Ensor, D. S., Cowen, S., Hooper, R. & Markowski, G. R. (1979), Evaluation of the George Neal No. 3 Electrostatic Precipitator, *RP NO 780–1*. Electric Power Research Institute.

Ensor, D. S., Markowski, G. R., Legg, R., Cowen, S. J., Murphy, M. & Shendrikar, A. D. (1980), *Evaluation of Electrostatic Precipitator Performance at San Juan*. Unit No. 3, Electric Power Research Institute. Contract No. RP-780-1-2.

Ensor, D. S. Cowen, S. J., Shendrikar, A. D., Markowski, G. R. & Woftinden, G. J. (1981), *Kramer Station Fabric Filter Evaluation*. Electric Power Research Institute CS-1669, Project 1130-1.

Federick, E. (1980), *Technical Basis for Size-dependent Particulate Standard*. Air Pollution Control Association, Pittsburg, Pennsylvania, U.S.A.

Fisher, G. L., Chang, D. P. Y. & Brummer, M. (1976), Fly ash collected from the electrostatic precipitators-microcrystalline structures and the mystery of spheres, *Science*, 192, 553.

Fitzgerald, W. F. & Jill, G. A. (1979), Subnanogram determination of mercury by two-stage gold amalgamation and gas phase detection applied to atmospheric analysis, *Analytical Chemistry*, 51, 1714.

Flagan, R. C. & Friedlander, S. K. (1976), Particle formation in pulverized coal combustion. *82nd Meeting of AICHE*, Atlantic City, New Jersey, 29 August to 1 September 1976.

Flegal, C. A., Starkovich, J. A., Maddalone, R. F., Kraft, M. L., Zee, C. A. & Lin, C. (1975), *Procedures for Process Measurements of Trace Inorganic Materials*. TRW System Inc., EPA Contract 68-02-1393, July, Research Triangle Park NC 27709.

Fox, J. P. (1985), Distribution of mercury during simulated in-situ oil shale retorting, *Environmental Science and Technology*, 19, 316.

Harrison, P. R., Saunders, W. & Hillestad, W. (1978), *Evaluation of the George Neal No. 3 Cold-side Electrostatic Precipitator*. Electric Power Research Institute, Contract No. TPS-77-756 Palo Alto, California.

Hodgson, A. T., Pollard, M. J., Harris, G. J., Girvin, D. C., Fox, J. P. & Brown, N. J. (1982), Mercury Mass Distribution During Laboratory and Simulated *in-situ* Oil Shale Retorting, *Report LBL-12908*. Lawrence Berkeley Laboratory, Berkeley, California U.S.A.

Hodgson, A. T., Pollard, M. J. & Brown, N. J. (1984), Mercury emissions from a modified *in-situ* oil shale retort, *Atmospheric Environment*, 18, 247–253.

Hulett, L. D. & Weinberger, A. J. (1980), Some etching studies of the micro-structures and composition of large alumino silicate particles in fly ash from coal-burning process plants, *Environmental Science and Technology*, 14, 965–970.

Johnson, d. & Braman, R. S. (1974), Distribution of atmospheric mercury species near ground level, *Analytical Chemistry*, 8, 1003.

Kaakinen, J. W., Jorden, R. M., Lawasani, M. H. & West, R. F. (1975), Trace-element beavior in a coal-fired power plant, *Environmental Science and Technology*, 9, 862.

Kaakinen, J. W. (1974), Trace element in a pulverized coal-fired power plant. Ph.D. Dissertation, University of Colorado, Boulder, Colorado.

Klein, D. H., Andren, A. W., Carter, J. A., Emery, J. F., Feldman, C., Fulkerson, W., Lyon, W. S., Ogle, J. C., Talme, Y., Van Hook, R. I. & Bolton, N. E. (1975a), Pathways of thirty-seven trace elements through coal-fired power plant, *Environmental Science and Technology*, 9, 973.

Klein, D. H., Andren, A. W. & Bolton, N. E. (1975b), Trace element discharge from coal combustion for power production, *Water, Air and Soil Pollution*, 5, 71.

Lindberg, S. E. (1980), Mercury partitioning in a power plant plume and its influence on atmospheric removal mechanisms, *Atmospheric Environment*, *14*, 227.

Lindberg, S. E. (1981), Mercury partitioning in a power plant plume and its influence on atmospheric removal mechanisms, Editorial Discussion, *Atmospheric Environment*, *15*, 632.

Lindquist, O. (1986), Fluxes of mercury in the Swedish environment: contributions from waste incineration, *Waste Management & Research*, *4*, 35–44.

Linton, R. W., Lob, A., Natusch, D. F. S., Evans, Jr. G. A. & Williams, P. (1976), Surface predominance of trace elements in airborne particles, *Science*, *191*, 852–854.

McElroy, M. W., Carr, R. C., Ensor, D. S. & Markowski, G. R. (1982), Size-distribution of fine particles from coal combustion, *Science*, *215*, 13.

McQuaker, N. R. & Sandberg, D. K. (1982), The determination of mercury source emissions in the presence of high levels of SO_2, *Air Pollution Control Association*, *32*, 634–636.

Maddalone, R. F., Jackson, B. & Yu, C. (1981), *Scrubber-Generated Particulate Matter-literature Survey*. Electric Power Research Institute CS-1739, Project 982-11.

Magee, E. M. (1976), Evaluation of Pollution Control in Fossil Fuel Conversion Processes. *Report PB 255-842*. U.S. Environmental Protection Agency, Research Triangle Park, North Carolina 27709, U.S.A.

Markowski, G. R., Ensor, D. S., Drehsen, M. & Shendrikar, A. D. (1980), *Fine Particulate Sampling Analysis and Data Reduction Procedures Manual—Low Pressure Impactor and Electrical Aerosol Analyzer*. Electric Power Research Institute, Contract No. 1822-020 and RP-1130-1.

Matsunaga, K., Konishi, S. & Nishimura, M. (1979), Possible errors caused prior to measurement of mercury in natural waters—with special reference to sea water, *Environmental Science and Technology*, *13*, 63–65.

Moffitt, Jr. A. E. & Kupel, R. E. (1970), A rapid method employing impregnated charcoal and atomic absorption spectrometry for the determination of mercury in atmospheric, biological, and aquatic samples, *Atomic Absorption Newsletter*, *9*, 113.

Murthy, J. (1975), Determination of mercury in coals by peroxide digestion and coal vapor atomic absorption spectrometry, *Atomic Absorption Newsletter*, *14*, 151.

Natusch, D. F. S., Wallace, J. R. & Evans, Jr. G. A. (1974), Toxic trace-elements preferential concentration in respirable particles, *Science*, *193*, 202.

Neville, M. R., Quann, J., Haynes, B. S. & Sarofim, A. F. (1980), Vaporization and condensation of mineral matter during pulverized coal combustion. *19th Symposium on Combustion*, Air Pollution Control Association, Waterloo, Canada, 19 August.

Ondov, J. M. & Biermann, A. H. (1980), Effects of particle control devices on atmospheric emissions of minor and trace elements from coal combustion. In *Proceedings of the Second Symposium on the Transfer and Utilization of Particulate Control Technology*, Vol. IV (E. P. VendiHi, J.A. Armstrong & M. Durham, Eds) EPA-600/9-80-039d, September 1980, pp. 454–485. EPA, Research Triangle Park, NC 27709.

Ondov, J. M., Ragaini, R. C. & Biermann, A. H. (1979), Elemental emissions from a coal-fired power plant—comparison of a venturi wet scrubber system with a cold-side electrostatic precipitator, *Environmental Science and Technology*, *13*, 598.

Reimann, D. O. (1986), Mercury output from garbage incineration, *Waste Management & Research*, *4*, 45–56.

Sarofim, A. F., Howard, J. B. & Padia, A. (1977), The physical transformation of the mineral matter in pulverized coal under simulated conditions, *Combustion Science and Technology*, *16*, 187.

Schroeder, H. (1971), Metals in the air, *Environment*, *13*, 18.

Schendrikar, A. D. (1981), Editorial discussion: mercury positioning in a power plant plume and, its influence on atmospheric removal mechanisms, *Atmospheric Environment*, *15*, 631.

Shendrikar, A. D. & Ensor, D. S. (1984), Mercury emission from a modified in-situ oil shale retort, Editorial Discussion, *Atmospheric Environment*, *18*, 2559–2563.

Shendrikar, A. D., Damle, A., Gutknecht, W. F. & Briden, F. (1983), Collection efficiency of mercury trapping, media for SASS train impinger system. In *The Proceedings of APCA Speciality Conference on Measurement of Non-criteria Toxic Contaminants in Air*, 22–24 March, Chicago, Illinois, U.S.A., pp. 386–403.

Shendrikar, A. D., Damle, A. & Gutknecht, W. F. (1984a), Collection Efficiency Evaluation of Mercury-trapping Media for the SASS Train Impinger System, *EPA-600/7-84-089*. Research Triangle Park, North Carolina 27709, U.S.A.

Shendrikar, A. D., Filby, R., Markowski, G. R. & Ensor, D. S. (1984b), Trace element loss onto polyethylene container walls from impinger solutions from flue gas sampling, *Air Pollution Control Association*, *34*, 233–236.

Smith, R. D. (1980), The trace element chemistry of coal during combustion and the emissions from coal-fired power plants, *Progress in Energy Combustion Science*, 6, 53–114.

Subber, S. W., Fihn, S. D. & West, C. D. (1974), Simplified apparatus for the flameless atomic fluorescence determination of Hg, *American Laboratory*, 6, 38–40.

Task Group of Lung Dynamics (1966), *Health Physics*, *12*, 173.

Trujillo, P. & Campbell, E. E. (1975), Development of a multi-stage air sampler for mercury, *Analytical Chemistry*, 47, 1629.

U.S. EPA (1971), Standards of performance for new stationary sources, *Federal Register*, *36*, (234), 23245.

U.S. EPA (1977), Control Strategy Preparation Manual for Particulate Matter. *EPA-450/2-77-023*. Research Triangle Park, North Carolina 27709, U.S.A.

Vogg, H., Braun, H., Metzger, M. & Schneider, J. (1986), The specific role of cadmium and mercury in municipal solid waste incineration, *Waste Management & Research*, *4*, 45–74.

Wroblewski, S., Spittler, T. M. & Harrison, P. R. (1974), Mercury concentration in the atmosphere in Chicago. A new ultra sensitive method employing amalgamation, *Air Pollution Control Association*, *24*, 778–781.

ANALYSIS OF INORGANIC POLLUTANTS EMITTED BY THE CITY OF PARIS GARBAGE INCINERATION PLANTS*

J. Gounon† and A. Milhau‡

(*Received 17 September 1985, revised 11 November 1985*)

The City of Paris has to eliminate 2 million tons of household garbage each year, mainly by incineration with heat recovery, and while doing so wishes to participate fully in the international struggle against acid rain and heavy metal pollution. The City has decided to determine precisely the atmospheric effluent emanating from present industrial plants, and to this effect a comprehensive monitoring campaign was undertaken. The analysis, unique in France because of the exhaustive nature and size of the facilities deployed for the purpose, covered many parameters.

The results are that (1) the HCl gas concentration in smoke, about 1000 mg m^{-3}, contributing almost one-half of the fallout, was observed at a rate of 10 μg m^{-3} at 5 km from the plant; and (2) the total heavy metals concentration in a modern plant is about 4 mg m^{-3} but, excluding Zn, less than 2 mg m^{-3}. Analyses are given for each components Pb, Cd, Zn, Cr, Cu, Ni, Ba, Co, Ag and Hg.

Key Words—Incineration, air pollution, heavy metals, mercury, cadmium, lead, hydrogen chloride, sampling gear, standard measurement methods.

Mots clés—Incinération, pollution atmosphérique, métaux lourds, mercure, cadmium, Pb, acide chlorhydrique, jauges de mesures, normes, méthodes de mesures.

1. Introduction

The city of Paris is surrounded by some sixty *communes* totalling 4.5 million inhabitants who together generate 2,000,000 tons of household garbage each year. The main method of treating it for over half a century has been incineration with heat recovery. This is done in three large plants located on the outskirts of the city, at Saint-Ouen, Issay-les-Moulineaux and Ivry.

The plants at Ivry and Issy-les-Moulineaux, built during the Sixties, were when first commissioned among the most efficient of their kind in regard to both thermal performance and purification of gaseous effluent. Ivry is equipped with electrostatic precipitators (ESP) which are over 99% efficient, the emissions are sent into the atmosphere through a 100 m high smokestack at an ejection speed of 25–30 m s^{-1}. It is true that at the time, the question of atmospheric pollution control consisted mainly in dispersing the pollutants. In contrast, the Saint-Ouen plant commissioned in 1954 is only equipped with cyclone and rudimentary water scrubbing. It is now totally obsolete and is in the course of reconstruction (Gounon 1984).

In the compass of this project, the City of Paris, aided by the Air Quality Agency, decided to be extremely vigilant in the matter of pollution control by setting very low

---

*Presented at the ISWA Specialized Seminar *Incinerator Emissions of Heavy Metals and Particulates*, Copenhagen, 18–19 September 1985.

†Chief Engineer, Ville de Paris, Direction de la Propreté, Section du Traitment des Ordures Ménagères, 57 Boulevard de Sébastopol, 75001 Paris, France.

‡Agency for the Quality of Air.

Waste Managment & Research (1986) **4**, 95–104

effluent pollution thresholds. This requires that the pollutants be collected at the source as efficiently as possible, and not dispersed into the atmosphere as before. But before taking any such decision, it was necessary to determine precisely the degree of pollution generated by current incineration plants, estimated in absolute values as well as in relative values with respect to other sources of pollution.

In the course of 1984 a very exhaustive series of measurements were performed on the three plants and their surroundings, in close liaison with the operator, EDF-TIRU, and having recourse to the best known French laboratories in that respect, namely the Musém National d'Hsistoire Naturelle, the Laboratoire National d'Essais (LNE), and the National Institute of Applied Chemical Research (IRCHA). The analyses bore on the nature and amounts of flyash, on insoluble particulate fallout, the presence of heavy metals, dioxine (Gonnord *et al.* 1985) and hydrocarbons, as well as the acidity of emissions. This paper deals only with dust, hydrochloric acid and heavy metals.

For an eventual comparison to be effected between the test results, Table 1 gives the main technical particulars on the incineration plants in Paris city.

TABLE 1

Particulars of incineration plants with heat recovery in the City of Paris (all gas volumes are in normalized m³)

	Saint-Ouen	Issy	Ivry
Commissioned	1954	1965	1969
Capacity (tons h^{-1})	4 × 12.5	4 × 20	2 × 50
Average thermal efficiency (%)	58	66.5	73.5
Unburnt ratio in clinker (%)	5.9	4.3	2.9
Smoke purification	Scrubbing	ESP*	ESP
Stacks			
Number	2	2	1
Height (m)	60	80	100
Gas discharge speed (m s^{-1})	4–8	20	30
Mean capacity per gas furnace (m^3 h^{-1})	75,000	150,000	250,000
Flyash content in smoke (mg m^{-3})	412	73	52
HCl content at 7% CO_2 (mg m^{-3})	568	1049	1095
$SO_2 + SO_3$ content at 7% CO_2 (mg m^{-3})	218	124	168
NO_x content at 7% CO_2 (mg m^{-3})	202	167	143

*ESP, electrostatic precipitation.

2. Main measurement methods applied

2.1. *Analysis of hydrogen chloride*

The sample effluent is filtered inside the stack through a quartz filter, then passes through a series of scrubbers with sintered rods containing an appropriate solution in which the pollutants required are collected and subsequently titrated with mercuric nitrate.

2.2. *Measurement of dust and heavy metal particulates on emission*

2.2.1. *Procedure*

This measurement was effected with a French Pitot tube. Dust samples were obtained by means of Environment S.A. sampling gear, type MPM 80, in accordance with the

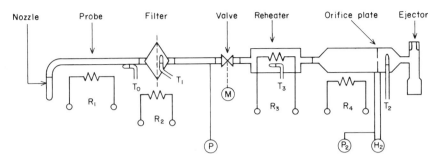

Fig. 1. Probe for measuring particulate and heavy metal samples (Norme NF × 44052 1978).

provisions of French standard Norme NF X 44.052 1978. Fractions of heavy metals and metalloids collected on the filters were obtained after previously dissolving the samples in a concentrated nitric acid solution. The analyses were made by atomic absorption spectrometry, with and without flame, and by plasma emission spectrometry.

2.2.2. *Particulars of dust sampling gear*

It is known that the type of instrumentation used may result in greatly differing measurement data. For instance, the shape of the tube nozzle alone may occasion errors of several tens of percent. Figure 1 shows the main particulars of the instrumentation approved in France for official tests, which differs somewhat in its design and construction from that used in most other countries (Milhau 1975) in the following manner.

(a) The sampling nozzles have a very slim profile and a large input diameter (greater than 8 mm). The combination of these two conditions ensures minimum disturbance in the flow by the nozzle.

(b) The dust is filtered through a plain filter located at the end of the probe outside the duct.

(c) Powerful heating helps eliminate condensation in the instrument, and it keeps the filter holder and the orifice plate at the desired temperature.

(d) The pressure across the orifice plate may be selected and held constant by means of a motor operated valve, M, compensating the increased pressure loss across the filter during the sampling.

(e) Flow measurement is performed by means of a diaphragm giving instant reading and adjustment.

2.3. *Measurement of heavy metals in gas form*

In France, there is no standard method for measuring heavy metals in the gas phase. At the Issy-les-Moulineaux plant, the method consists in removing a suitable fraction of the gas, say around 10% of the main sampling flow, downstream from the sampling filter which is kept at the temperature of the smokestack. The bypass flow goes through a condenser and a set of scrubbers. The condensate collected is analysed using the methods described earlier. The method has proved highly satisfactory for all of the metals except, perhaps, mercury. The very low values found for this metal, compared with results usually found, lead one to think that a considerable fraction of mercury had been held back in the sintered stainless steel holder of the sampling filter.

This method could not be used at the Saint-Ouen plant on account of the heavy dust content in the gas which leads to excessively rapid fouling of the filters in the sampling gear. The measuring train used for measuring heavy metals in gaseous form in that plant was identical to that used for measuring HCl. Here again, the major uncertainties are related to the mercury values.

2.4. *Measuring the environment*

The measurement of fallout by deposition has now become normal practice.

In the compass of this survey an effort was made to measure the HCl gas and particulate concentrations in the environment. A preliminary survey using various methods of sampling and analysis was performed by the National Testing Laboratory (LNE) and led to the following conclusions and choices.

The use of filter media for capturing inorganic chlorides present in the ambient air is of interest since it allows the taking of samples on the site irrespective of any handling problems while keeping the samples as aqueous solutions. It is necessary to use a dry filter upstream of the impregnated filters to separate out the particulate chlorides from the gaseous chlorides.

3. Flyash emissions

3.1. *During emission*

Chemical analyses of fly ash from IVRY are given in Table 2. The TRCHA tests performed at Issy-les-Moulineaux made it possible to check that the efficiency of the two-field Lurgui ESP filter was 98.75%, and that 85.9% of the flyash was collected by field 1. Altogether, the flyash content in the smoke after dedusting came to some 50–75 mg m^{-3}.

TABLE 2

Physical and chemical analysis of flyash from the Ivry incineration plant

	Percentage
Granular composition	
<0.08 mm	3.2
0.08 to <0.5 mm	83.8
0.5 to <4 mm	12.0
>4 mm	1.0
Chemical composition	
Ignition loss at 1000°C	15.17
SiO_2	30.72
Al_2O_3	17.03
CaO	17.00
Fe_2O_3	1.49
TiO_2	1.60
MnO	0.12
MgO	2.10
SO_3	5.20
Na_2O	4.05
K_2O	3.33
BaO	0.27
ZnO	1.92

3.2. *On the ground*

The concentration of insoluble particulates collected on the ground by the rainfall collector method, at distances of 500–3500 m around the considered sites, are summarized on Table 3 and shown in Fig. 2 for St-Ouen. It is of course difficult to separate from among the particules those stemming from other activities.

TABLE 3

Comparative fallout in the form of insoluble particulates and water-soluble Cl^{-1} at the Issy and Saint-Ouen incineration plants (values are annual means for 1983 and 1984)

Measuring station	Distance from plant (m)	Direction of down-sweeping winds (degrees)	Insoluble particulates ($g \, m^{-2} \, month^{-1}$)	Cl^{-} ($g \, m^{-2} \, month^{-1}$)
Issy				
1	500	240	10.8	0.678
2	500	20	10.8	0.225
3	700	280	5.6	0.590
4	1400	100	7.0	0.170
5	1500	100	10.0	0.167
St Ouen				
1	800	320	3.09	0.206
2	1000	300	1.95	0.160
3	1200	40	1.85	0.113
4	2500	200	2.02	0.153
5	2600	100	1.69	0.123
6	3300	340	2.6	0.184
7	3500	220	1.55	0.152

4. Hydrochloric acid emissions

4.1. *On emission*

At Saint-Ouen the HCl measurements made on emission comprised two sets of analyses in the course of 2 weeks: one in winter, the other in summer. Each week, four samplings of 2 h were taken per day for 5 days at four measuring points (upstream and downstream of the scrubbers).

The hydrochloric acid gas concentration emitted in the atmosphere was medium high and varied with the weather, from 198 to 746 mg m^{-3}. The mass flow rate of 113 kg h^{-1} was estimated by assuming that the volume flow rate of effluent upstream and downstream of the scrubber were identical.

4.2. *Acidity of air*

Extensive environmental measurements were performed around the sites of the Ivry and Saint-Ouen plants to try to detect a possible link between the air acidity and the emissions from the considered plants. The data relating to Saint-Ouen are shown in Table 3, in which the annual means of dust give 1–3 g m^{-2} month^{-1}, with very wide monthly fluctuations.

The drawback of the anlaysis is that it does not take into account any isolated pollution peaks that might occur over short periods. Despite this, the equipment may be

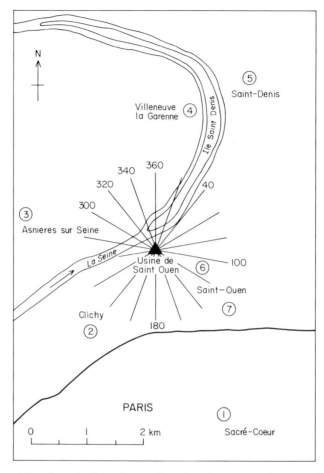

Fig. 2. Particulate fallout from the Saint-Ouen incineration plant measured at ground level at seven sites (circled in figure): (1) 3 g m² month⁻¹; (2) 2 g m² month⁻¹; (3) 1.85 g m² month⁻¹; (4) 2 g m² month⁻¹; (5) 1.7 g m² month⁻¹; (6) 2.6 g m² month⁻¹; (7) 1.6 g m² month⁻¹.

installed over a long period (3–5 years) at a reasonable cost, thus enabling one to project into the future the impact of a proposed plant. The analyses were supplemented by five sampling stations spread geographically around the Ivry plant over a radius of 2400–6500 m.

The results in strong acids, in chloride particulates and hydrochloric acid were collected and compared during two control periods for each sampling station. The mean measurements remained between 11.1 and 14.4 μg m⁻³ of total chlorides inclusive, giving a particulate chloride/gaseous chloride ratio generally greater than 1.0 (see Fig. 3). As a rule, a similarity was observed in the fluctuation of inorganic chloride content and of strong acids. The chloride content was less than 20% of the total gas pollution.

5. Pollution by heavy metals

The measurement of heavy metals is still developing in France and there are certain operational problems which are mentioned later. Current measurements relate only to emissions, and not to deposits.

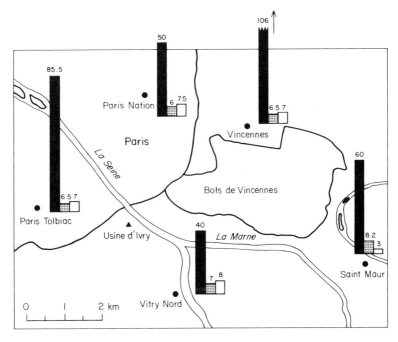

Fig. 3. Chloride and strong acid levels in the region of the Ivry incineration plant. Histogram values are in $\mu g\ m^{-3}$: ■, SO_2; ▦, gaseous chlorine; ▢, chloride particulate.

5.1. *Issy*

At Issy the analyses of the flyash showed the following main results (see Table 4).

(1) The heavy metal concentrations in the flyash collected by fields 1 and 2 of the dedusters were comparable.

(2) The concentration of mercury and cadmium in flyash collected by field 2 was about twice as high as the flyash collected by field 1.

The measured concentrations of heavy metals present in the gaseous effluent from Issy appear low compared with the usual published results. Irrespective of the nature of the incinerated products, which must affect the production of heavy metals, the validity of the measurements could perhaps be reconsidered.

5.2. *Saint-Ouen*

The Saint-Ouen plant has bad deduster, thus the situation was more difficult. The on-line sampling of dust and of the volatile fraction was disturbed, first on account of the high dust content, and second on account of the clogging power of the particles. In addition, because of the poor access to the chimney stack, measurement could be effected only at a height of 25 m.

Lastly, it should be noted that the fluctuation in the flow during the sampling, from 167,000–190,000 $Nm^3\ h^{-1}$ from one day to another, and gas velocities, varying from 4.4 to 7 m s^{-1}, did not permit any significant deduction about the concentration gradient in the measuring section.

The mean gas temperature during the test varied between 147 and 162°C.

TABLE 4

Concentrations of heavy metals in the flyash inlet, inside, and outlet of electrostatic precipitator (ESP) at the Issy incineration plant

Point of measurement	Ag	Cd	Co	Cr	Cu	Ni	Ba	Hg	Pb	Zn
17 October 1984										
Inlet ESP (mg g^{-1})	0.09	0.12	0.06	0.55	2.20	0.33	0.16	0.001	4.00	11.80
Inside ESP										
Field 1 (mg g^{-1})	0.13	0.52	0.03	0.35	1.45	0.08	0.096	0.004	9.40	23.10
Field 2 (mg g^{-1})	0.13	1.19	0.03	0.26	2.30	0.07	0.074	0.007	20.25	42.20
Outlet ESP (mg m^{-3})	0.015	0.10	0.007	0.28	0.13	0.02	0.086	0.006	1.68	2.07
18 October 1984										
Inlet ESP (mg g^{-1})	0.18	0.18	0.07	0.76	4.30	0.54	0.10	0.001	6.50	27.80
Inside ESP										
Field 1 (mg g^{-1})	0.36	1.18	0.04	0.77	3.75	0.02	0.06	0.003	26.90	64.25
Field 2 (mg g^{-1})	0.16	1.47	0.02	0.30	3.10	0.06	0.08	0.008	31.30	57.65
Outlet ESP (mg m^{-3})	0.018	0.06	0.007	0.09	0.13	0.01	0.055	0.008	1.94	2.27

TABLE 5

Concentrations of main pollutants emitted into the atmosphere by the Saint-Ouen incineration plant (mg m^{-3} at 7% CO_2) after gas has passed through the scrubbers

	Chimney No.	
	12	34
Average gas flow (m^3 h^{-1})	170,000	180,000
Average gas temperature (°C)	150	160
Solid pollutants		
Total particles	677	797
Pb	56.17	50.03
Zn	54.33	42.80
Cu	5.20	3.14
Ba	2.04	2.29
Cd	1.50	1.23
Cr	0.58	0.74
Hg	0.32	0.74
Ni	0.25	0.26
Ag	0.16	0.25
As	0.07	0.09
Co	<0.02	<0.02
Be	<0.01	<0.01
Gas pollutants		
HCl	421	638
NO	263	304
SO$_2$	254	312
Solid and gas pollutants		
Hg	0.642	0.826
Pb	56.85	50.83
Cd	1.48	1.25

The results are given in Table 5. The following concentrations of total lead, mercury and cadmium were found on 12 and 14 March 1985: Pb, 43.2 mg Nm^{-3}, mainly as solids; Hg, 0.58 mg Nm^{-3}, half as solids, half as gases; Cd = 1.11 mg Nm^{-3}, mainly as solids.

These figures are extremely high, and one must look at the obsolescence of the plant, 30% overcapacity of the furnaces, and the rudimentary design of smoke scrubber for an answer. It should also be stressed that the presence of a considerable amount of dust in the gas was certainly instrumental in falsifying the measurements, and in any case makes it impossible to validly compare these results with others.

6. Conclusion

The several forms of atmospheric pollution ascribable to large capacity incineration plants are now fully appreciated in France, thanks to a series of unprecedented analyses conducted during 1984 which are still under way. The outcome varies depending on the pollutants involved, as follows.

(1) With fine dust, two-field ESP gives good results, with emissions thresholds of around 50 mg mg m^{-3}. As against that, the particulates contain heavy metals at the rate of 25–30 g kg^{-1}, plus fallout on the ground reaching 2–3 g m^{-2} month^{-1}.

(2) Hydrochloric acid is a considerable source of pollution, even though it accounts for only a few percent of total acidity in the air. The unscrubbed emissions of smoke amount to around 1000 mg m^{-3}, contributing almost one-half of the fallout on the

ground, observed at a rate of 10 μg m^{-3}. Given this result, the city of Paris has decided to embark on a process of removing chlorides from smoke, setting the tailings threshold at 100 mg m^{-3}.

(3) The heavy metals, some of which are very volatile, are much more difficult to assess reliably. It would seem that the following mean values may be obtained in the compass of the city of Paris: on the Issy site, 4 mg m^{-3} (7% CO_2); on the Saint-Ouen site 50 mg m^{-3} (7% CO_2).

Although not all the measurements may be deemed entirely reliable, and comparison with data from other countries clash against the difficulty of interpreting the actual measuring methods used, it seems clear that ancient facilities operating at over-capacity, like the Saint-Ouen plant, are a considerable source of pollution. In this connection it is essential that those concerned agree on a standard measuring method which would help determine with certainty whether it is tolerable to continue operating certain facilities inadequately equipped with smoke purification systems. As regards the city of Paris, it has opted to start construction of a new incineration plant complying with the most stringent emissions thresholds which modern technology can aspire to today.

References

Gounon, J. (1984), Considerations of environmental criteria for the construction of an incineration plant at Saint-Ouen, France. *ISWA International Congress*, Philadelphia, U.S.A., 13 September.

Gonnord, M.F., Karasek, F.W. & Finet, C. (1985), Formation de dioxines et de chlorobenzènes à partir de PCV dans un incinération de déchets urbains (Formation of polychlorinated dibenzoparadioxin from polyvinyl chloride in municipal incinerators), *Revue technique et sciences municipales*, 5, 211–216.

Milhau, A. (1975), Mesure des émissions de poussière dans les conduits (Measurement of particulates in chimney pipes) *Journée Tirage et dispersion des Fumées*, May, épuisé.

Norme, N.F. × 44052 (1978), Prélèvement de poussière dans une veine gazeuse (Sampling of particulates in a gas stream), Edié par L'Afnor, Juillet 1978, Tour Europe Cedex 7 92080, Paris la Defense, France.

THE FLUX OF METALS THROUGH MUNICIPAL SOLID WASTE INCINERATORS*

Paul H. Brunner† and Hermann Mönch†

(*Received 30 August 1985*)

In two full scale municipal solid waste incinerators, M and B, the transfer of metals and non-metals from waste to slag, to electrostatic precipitator (ESP) dust, and to flue gas was investigated. If the input of an element into the furnace M is taken as 100%, the following partitioning was observed: carbon, slag 1.6%, ESP-dust 0.4%, flue gas 98%; sulphur 34, 26, 40; fluorine 34, 39, 27; chlorine 13, 20, 67; iron 99, 1, 0.02; copper 89, 10, 1; zinc 51, 45, 4; lead 58, 37, 5; cadmium 12, 76, 12; mercury 4, 24, 72. The comparison of incinerators M, B and others indicates that the fate of metals during combustion, gas cooling and gas cleaning is determined by the composition of the municipal waste, the properties of the individual metals, and the operating conditions of the incinerator. In order to improve waste incineration, it is necessary to understand better the physical–chemical processes taking place in an incinerator, and to apply this knowledge to the construction and operating of such a plant.

Key Words—Waste incineration, heavy metal, emission, slag, electrostatic precipitation (ESP), flue gas, waste composition, incineration parameter, Switzerland.

1. Introduction

Waste treatment is one of several processes in the cycling of elements (Fig. 1). Because the anthropogenic utilization of materials has increased considerably in this century, the contribution of waste management to the load of the environment with metals and non-metals became more important. Today the global natural fluxes of some elements, e.g. cadmium, are exceeded by anthropogenic fluxes (Stumm 1977; Baccini 1984). In order to prevent the rise in concentrations of metals in the major sinks "soil" and "sediment" it is necessary to know the contribution of each process to these environmental loads.

Modern waste management consists of a combination of waste pretreatment (separate collection, sorting etc.), incineration with heat recovery and/or sanitary landfilling (Fig. 1). The amount of materials which have to be disposed of in water, air and soil can be calculated if the composition and the amount of waste to be treated, as well as the distribution coefficients of each element for a given treatment process, are known. In order to decrease the dissipative material fluxes to the environment, an improved understanding of the basic mechanisms of the treatment processes is needed, so that distribution coefficients as well as educt specifications (e.g. criteria for "combustible materials") can be optimized.

In this work, we focus on the flux of metals and non-metals through municipal waste incinerators. Furthermore, we investigate the possibilities for controlling this flux to improve it with respect to the goal of incineration, namely immobilization and concentra-

---

*ISWA Specialized Seminar *Incinerator Emissions of Heavy Metals and Particulates,* Copenhagen, 18–19 September 1985.

†Swiss Federal Institute for Water Resources and Water Pollution Control, CH-8600 Dübendorf, Switzerland.

Waste Management & Research (1986) **4**, 105–119

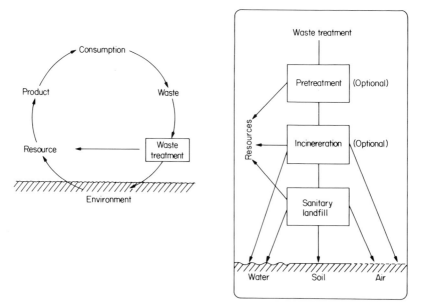

Fig. 1. The position of solid waste treatment in the global cycling of materials. The total flux of materials to the environment can be decreased by increasing the recycling rate, by decreasing resource exploitation, or by improving waste treatment in a way which yields more inert, ore-like materials in deposits excluded from the hydrological cycle.

tion of heavy metals and complete oxidation of organic carbon. In combination with research on the fate of elements in a sanitary landfill, it will become possible in future to model the total flux of elements from the generation of a waste material to the final disposal in water, soil or air.

1.1. *Objectives*

The objective of this work was to determine material balances for several elements in different municipal waste incinerators by measuring element concentrations in all products of incineration. The elements chosen were comprised of non-metals such as carbon, fluorine, sulphur and chlorine, and metals such as iron, copper, zinc, cadmium, mercury and lead. The rationale for this selection was to follow elements which are representative for a group of similar elements; for example, the physical–chemical behaviour of iron is typical for a lithophilic metal and can be applied to other lithophilics like cobalt, manganese or chromium. The thermal reaction pattern of cadmium is characteristic for volatile elements such as antimony, zinc, lead and thallium.

A second goal was to examine if the material balance of an incinerator is changed by varying combustion conditions. Since it was outside the scope of this work to manipulate existing municipal incinerators, the difference in element balances and operating parameters of several incinerators was used to examine the influence of such parameters on element distribution.

1.2. *Procedure*

To determine elemental balances, the massflows of slag, dust from electrostatic pre-

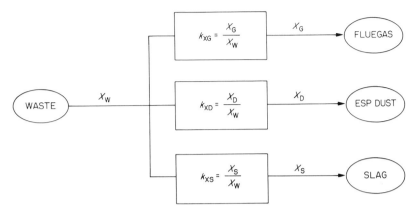

Fig. 2. The partition of an element, X, in a waste material, W, during incineration on slag, S, electrostatic precipitator dust, D, and flue gas, G. The distribution coefficients are defined as $X_{product}/X_{educt}$. X is given as a flux value, e.g. 2 kg Zn h^{-1}; $k_{XG} + k_{XD} + k_{XS} = 1$.

cipitators (ESP) and flue gas were measured in two full scale municipal solid waste incinerators. Samples were taken from slag, dust and flue gas and were analysed for carbon, chlorine, sulphur, fluorine, iron, copper, zinc, cadmium, mercury and lead. The results were used to calculate the partition coefficients, k_{XY} (Fig. 2), where X indicates the element (carbon, chlorine, etc.) and Y the product (slag, dust or flue gas).

The influence of combustion parameters on element partitioning was checked by the interpretation of the difference of the two incinerators as well as by evaluating investigations into the performance of additional incinerators. The incinerators examined are located in Switzerland.

2. Experimental

2.1. Incinerator and waste materials

Two similar incinerators, B and M, were investigated (Fig. 3, Table 1). Both consist of grate-type furnaces and ESP. Incinerator B is equipped with a boiler, while the off-gas of incinerator M is cooled by water injection and air/air heat-exchangers. The furnace temperature is maintained at *c*. 900 °C in B and M. In both plants, ESP dust and slag are combined in a water quench and are not treated separately.

Solid municipal waste was applied as the sole fuel for incineration. In the case of incinerator M, the waste is derived from a slightly more rural area than in B. The waste was fed to the furnace as received without pretreatment, and there was no selection of special ingredients when filling the hopper. It is therefore possible, and likely, that the feed used for the examination of plant M is not identical with the one used in B.

The waste material fed to the furnaces was weighed by a calibrated crane balance but not analysed. The chemical composition was calculated using the data from the products of incineration, assuming that, for the 10 elements examined, the mass of an element in the waste feed equals the sum of the masses of this element in slag, ESP dust and flue gas. To determine the water content of the waste, a water balance was attempted taking all sources of water into account.

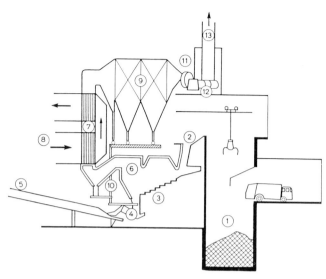

Fig. 3. Municipal solid waste incinerator M. Incinerator B is of the same type but includes a boiler for steam generation. 1, Bunker; 2, feeding hopper; 3, grate; 4, slag discharge; 5, conveyor belt to slag treatment; 6, combustion chamber; 7, heat-exchanger (M, air/air; B, boiler); 8, cooling air (M only); 9, electrostatic precipitator; 10, dust collecting main; 11, suction fan; 12, flue gas measuring point; 13, stack.

TABLE 1

Incinerator parameters

	Incinerator B	Incinerator M
Capacity (nominal, tonne h^{-1})	2×4	2×4
Fluegas		
Temperature (°C)	240–260	240–245
Specific volume (m^3 tonne^{-1} at		
101 kPa, O °C)	10,500	13,000
CO$_2$ (%)	4.2	4.0
H$_2$O (%)	7.9–9.3	6.6–9.0

2.2. Sampling and analysis of incinerator slag

For this investigation, the incinerator was slightly modified. The water quench for the slag discharge was operated in such a way that no effluent from the quench was produced; this was achieved by keeping a constant level on the quench and replacing only water which was taken up by the slag or which evaporated into the furnace.

The entire mass of slag was collected and weighed as received. For sampling, the slag was separated from large pieces of iron, crushed, and sieved (Fig. 4). The oversize material (*c.* 20%) was weighed but not analysed, it was assumed to consist mainly of iron. From the pretreated slag, three composite samples of *c.* 5 kg were taken each hour for 8 consecutive hours. In the laboratory, the samples were dried at 105 °C for 24 h and pulverized in a ball mill (2 h). For elemental analysis the samples were sieved by a 0.5 mm sieve and stored at 20 °C. The oversize material (*c.* 3%) was assumed to be of iron. For balance calculations, all fractions of slag were taken into account.

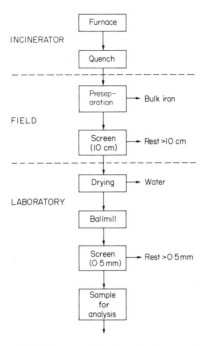

Fig. 4. Sampling and treatment of the incinerator slag. To calculate mass balances, all fractions were taken into account, and it was assumed that bulky iron and rests consist mainly of iron.

The concentrations of the elements in the pre-treated slag samples were analysed as follows.

Total carbon (TC) was determined gravimetrically by combustion of the sample at 800–1000 °C in pure oxygen and absorption of the resulting carbon dioxide on sodium hydroxide asbestos. To differentiate between organic carbon and carbonates, concentrated hydrochloric acid was added to a sample and the evolving CO_2 was measured as for TC.

Fluorine was determined by an ion-sensitive electrode after the sample had been digested in sodium peroxide and glycerin according to Wurzschmitt (BUS 1984). The same method with a different electrode was used to measure *chlorine*. To measure total *sulphur*, the sample was reduced in a hot suspension of phosphorus in the presence of I^- ions. The resulting sulphide was analysed by the iodometric method. Refluxing hot Aqua Regia was used to digest the samplers for *metal* determinations. The concentrations of iron, copper, zinc, cadmium and lead were analysed by Atomic Absorption Spectrometry (AAS) (cadmium: flameless by the graphite tube). For the determination of *mercury*, the sample was digested (Aqua Regia) and analysed by cold flameless AAS.

All elements were measured with the addition of five standards in order to exclude effects of the different matrices.

2.3. *Sampling and analysis of ESP dust*

For this investigation the incinerators were slightly modified in a way that made it possible to collect dry ESP dust separately without slag. The total amount of dust was collected in a barrel and weighed every 30 min. A composite sample of *c*. 3 kg dust was taken every 30 min, when the barrel was emptied. The samples were sealed in polyethylene bags and stored at −20 °C.

In the laboratory, the samples were dried (24 h at 105 °C) and pulverized in an agate mortar for 15 min. The resulting powdered dust completely passed a 200 μm screen and was used for element analysis. To determine mercury, samples were analysed immediately after collection and were not dried.

The concentrations of carbon, fluorine, sulphur and chlorine, and iron, copper, zinc, cadmium, mercury and lead were measured as described in Section 2.2.

2.4. *Sampling and analysis of flue gas*

The flue gas was sampled according to the regulations set by the Swiss Federal Environmental Protection Agency (BUS 1983). The following parameters were measured: gas velocity (Prandtl- and pitot tube), gas temperature (thermometer, thermocouples), gas pressure (barometer, manometer and micromanometer), carbon dioxide, carbon monoxide and nitrogen monoxide (non-dispersive infrared (NDIR, Binos of Leybold-Heraeus), oxygen (paramagnetism, Sybron-Taylor), moisture (psychrometry, Stroehlein), hydrochloric acid, hydrofluoric acid and sulphur dioxide (absorption in 0.1 N sodium hydroxide), gaseous heavy metals (sorption in 0.1 N sodium hydroxide), mercury (sorption in 10% sulphuric acid with 1% potassium permanganate), total particulates (iso-kinetic sampling on quartz wool, VDI 2066, 1979).

The elements in the samples were analysed as follows: hydrochloric and hydrofluoric acids were determined by ion chromatography (IC) with ion-sensitive electrodes; and sulphur dioxide with IC and precipitation as barium sulphate and gravimetry. Gaseous heavy metals were measured by AAS and inductively coupled plasma spectrometry (ICP-ESA). Mercury was measured after reduction of the permanganate with flameless AAS. Total particulates were dried, weighed, and dissolved in perchloric acid/nitric acid. Particulate metals were measured in this solution by ICP and AAS. Total sulphur and chlorine were analysed with IC after pyrolytic digestion.

3. Results and discussion

In the following, the mass and element balance of incinerator M are presented. The results of incinerator B, in as far as they are of any difference to incinerator M, are given later.

3.1. *Mass balance*

The mass balance (Fig. 5) was generated by using the mass of input and output, data on the inorganic material in slag and ESP dust, data on carbon in flue gas, slag and ESP dust, and by assuming that the organic fraction of the waste contains mainly cellulosic material. It appears that the material fed to the incinerator contained less moisture than average municipal solid waste (see Table 2).

3.2. *Elemental balances*

The partitions of non-metals and metals by the incineration of wastes are displayed in Figs 6 and 7. These figures have been computed from the mass balance (Fig. 5) and the concentrations given in Table 3.

The partitioning is a function of the physical–chemical properties of the elements.

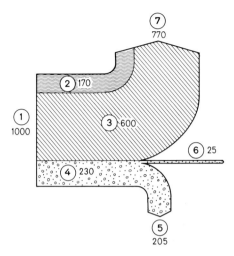

Fig. 5. Mass balance of incinerator M (g kg⁻¹) waste. 1, Waste; 2, water; 3, organic matter; 4, inorganic matter; 5, slag; 6, electrostatic precipitator dust; 7, flue gas.

TABLE 2
Composition of input waste

Composition	Incinerator M* (g kg⁻¹)	Average composition (BUS 1984) (g kg⁻¹)
Water	170	300
Organic matter	600	450
Inorganic matter	230	250

*Calculated from electrostatic precipitator dust, slag and flue gas.

Carbon, which readily forms gaseous oxides, is mainly transferred to the flue gas in the form of carbon dioxide. The remaining carbon in the ESP dust (0.4%) and in the slag (1.6%) contains a few carbonates only (10% and 30%, respectively), the more important part of it consists of unoxidized organic carbon.

The second most volatile element measured proved to be mercury, which is a typical atmophilic metal with a high vapour pressure and low boiling point of 356.6 °C. During incineration, mercury may be transformed to mercuric chloride and possibly to mercurious sulphate (SVA 1979). Since all these species are highly volatile, it is not surprising to find about threequarters of the mercury input in the flue gas. A considerable amount (24%) was measured in the ESP dust.

Another atmophilic metal is cadmium. Like mercury, this metal (b.p. 765 °C) is vaporized by incineration. During the cooling of the off-gases it is recondensed, deposited on the fly ash particles and collected in the electrostatic precipitator. Due to the fact that the volatile metals are concentrated on small submicron particles (Greenberg et al. 1978) and existing ESP are not optimized to collect particles smaller than 2 μm, a considerable amount of cadmium is released to the atmosphere (gaseous cadmium was not detectable). Metals with a lower vapour pressure such as lead and zinc are retained better in the slag and are less concentrated in the ESP dust.

P. H. Brunner & H. Mönch

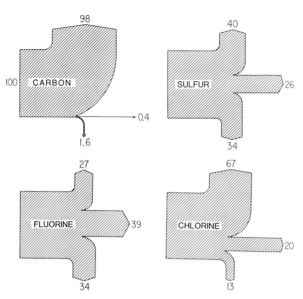

Fig. 6. The partitioning of nonmetals by municipal solid waste incineration. ↑, Flue gas; →, electrostatic precipitator dust; ↓, slag.

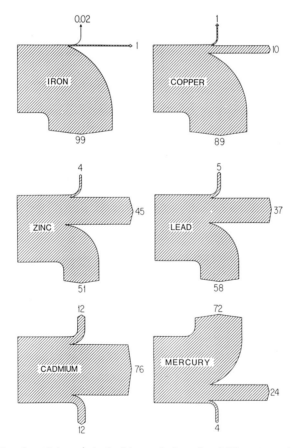

Fig. 7. The partitioning of metals by muncipal solid waste incineration. ↑, Flue gas; →, electrostatic precipitator dust; ↓, slag.

TABLE 3

Concentrations of metals and non-metals in the products of incineration of solid wastes of incinerator M. Gas volumes corrected to normal conditions

Product	C_{tot} (g kg^{-1})	C_{carb} (g kg^{-1})	F (mg kg^{-1})	S (g kg^{-1})	Cl (g kg^{-1})	Fe* (g kg^{-1})	Cu* (g kg^{-1})	Zn* (g kg^{-1})	Cd (mg kg^{-1})	Hg (mg kg^{-1})	Pb* (g kg^{-1})
Slag											
Mean	15	4.5	180	3.4	3.3	230	0.91	3.5	3.8	0.11	0.89
S.D.	3	0.6	24	0.5	0.8	40	0.27	0.9	1.2	0.08	0.22
Min	10	3.5	130	2.7	2.4	190	0.63	1.8	1.9	0.04	0.43
Max	19	5.4	250	4.8	5.3	320	1.41	5.5	6	0.32	1.23
ESP† dust											
Mean	44	4.9	2000	28	54	30	1.1	32	260	8	6.2
S.D.	6	1.5	560	6	7	4	0.31	20	30	4.1	0.5
Min	30	3.3	1500	19	43	24	0.75	15	210	3.0	5.5
Max	49	7.8	3100	36	64	38	1.8	77	310	15	7.2
Flue gas‡ (moist 0 °C 101 kPa)											
Mean	20	n.d.	3	0.08	0.4	1.8	0.2	5.2	0.08	0.05	1.4
S.D.	1	n.d.	1.3	0.013	0.1	2	0.14	2.4	0.04	0.06	0.6
Min	18	n.d.	2	0.011	0.2	0.3	0.1	1.6	0.02	0.001	0.5
Max	22	n.d.	6	0.1	0.5	6	0.5	8	0.12	0.18	2.1
Flue gas dust, Mean	n.d.	n.d.	n.d.	10	120	10	2.5	98	1700	n.d.	25

*Units for flue gas, mg m^{-3}.
†ESP, electrostatic precipitator.
‡Units for flue gas g (or mg) m^{-3}.
§n.d. = Not determined.

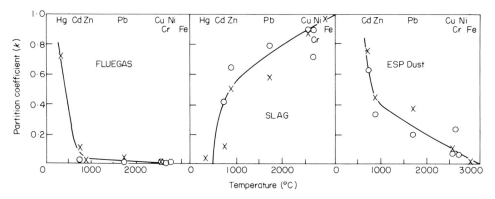

Fig. 8. The dependence of the partitioning of the metals on the their volatility. The partition coefficient, k_{slag}, equals 1.0 if a metal is transferred completely to the slag, and 0 if it is absent in this product. ×, Incinerator M; ○, incinerator B; ESP; electrostatic precipitator.

The lithophilic iron is completely trapped in the slag, the amounts released by the flue gas and ESP dust are $\leqslant 1\%$ of the input. The slightly more volatile copper shows a similar behaviour. An important fraction of iron and copper in the flue gas is found in the gaseous state.

In Fig. 8, the partitioning of the investigated metals is plotted versus their boiling points. Even if it is not the metal in the elementary state but rather an oxidized species which results from combustion, this graph can be used as a general guideline to estimate whether a metal is transferred to slag, ESP dust or the atmosphere.

The speciation of the metals, and therefore the behaviour of the metals during incineration, is strongly influenced by the presence of compounds of chlorine, sulphur, carbon, nitrogen, fluorine and others during combustion and gas cooling. The partitioning of sulphur, chlorine and fluorine, as given in Fig. 6, yields large amounts of sulphur oxides and hydrochloric and hydrofluoric acids in the off-gases. In this reactive mixture of metals, non-metals and water at high temperatures, many complex reactions take place most of which are not yet understood. The high concentration of chlorine species leads to metal chlorides, which often are more volatile than the elemental metal, and which always are highly soluble in water. It can also lead to chlorinated aromatic compounds.

From an environmental point of view, the incineration of waste materials should be directed towards complete mineralisation, concentration of toxic metals in one product and production of compounds of low solubility such as oxides or silicates. In the next section, the possibility of reaching these goals by varying incineration conditions is discussed.

3.3. Combustion parameters

In Table 4, the differences in elemental distributions of incinerator M and B are summarized. In incinerator M, the waste is very thoroughly oxidized yielding a slag with a low carbon content and an effective transfer of atmophilic metals to the combustion off-gas with low residual metal concentrations in the slag. In incinerator B, the combustion is less effective and yields an average slag with a higher loss on ignition and a larger concentration of atmophilic metals. Incinerator B is equipped with an "oversized" ESP with a very high collection efficiency, resulting in low $k_{flue\ gas}$ values, while incinerator M

TABLE 4

k-Values and concentrations of three metals in slag, electrostatic precipitator dust and flue gas for incinerators M (18 samples on 1 day) and B (54 samples on 3 days)

| | Incinerator M | | | Incinerator B | | |
| | | Concentration (g kg^{-1}) | | | Concentration (g kg^{-1}) | |
Products metal	k	Mean	S.D.	k	Mean	S.D.
Municipal solid waste*						
Zn	—	2.0	1.5	—	1.1	0.5
Cd	—	0.009	0.002	—	0.012	0.006
Pb	—	0.4	0.1	—	0.6	0.4
Slag						
Zn	0.5	3.5	0.9	0.7	4.2	1.0
Cd	0.1	0.004	0.001	0.4	0.030	0.015
Pb	0.6	0.9	0.2	0.8	2.6	0.9
ESP† dust						
Zn	0.5	32	20	0.4	20	3.5
Cd	0.8	0.26	0.03	0.6	0.35	0.20
Pb	0.4	6.2	0.5	0.2	6.0	1.7
Flue gas						
Zn	0.04	—	—	0.01	—	—
Cd	0.1	—	—	0.02	—	—
Pb	0.05	—	—	0.01	—	—
Loss on ignition of slag (g kg^{-1})		10			50	
Flue gas particulates (mg m^{-3})		110			12	

*Concentrations calculated from the products of incineration.
†ESP, electrostatic precipitator.

TABLE 5

Flue gas concentrations from two different fuels

| | Concentration in flue gas particulates | |
	Waste C$_1$	Waste C$_2$
Cu (g kg^{-1})	4	8
Zn (g kg^{-1})	33	76
Cd (g kg^{-1})	0.8	1.3
Pb (g kg^{-1})	18	26
Total particulates (mg m^{-3})	160	145
Relative calorific value	1	1.5
Throughput (tonne h^{-1})	5.5	3.6
$T_{furnace}$ (°C)	706	726
$T_{stack\ gas}$ (°C)	176	174

shows higher flue gas particulates and $k_{flue\ gas}$ values due to the less effective electrofilter (c.f. Section 3.4).

The difference in the partitioning of the metals in the two incinerators M and B led to the hypothesis that by changing incinerator parameters, the partitioning could be varied considerably. This was checked in incinerators C and D. In incinerator C, two

TABLE 6
Composition of electrostatic precipitator dust under different
operating conditions

	Concentration in electrostatic precipitator dust (g kg^{-1})	
	Furnace D$_1$	Furnace D$_2$
Cu	1.6	1.8
Zn	38	57
Cd	0.7	1.1
Pb	54	99
Cr	1.3	1.2

waste materials were burned which were of similar composition but had a different calorific value. Except for the throughput, the combustion parameters were kept constant and equal for both fuels. The fuel with the higher calorific value when incinerated produced double the concentrations of the metals copper, zinc, cadmium and lead in the flue gas particulates compared to the lower energy fuel (see Table 5). Possibly the higher energy content of waste C$_2$ caused higher evaporation rates of metals on the grate followed by an increased condensation on available nuclei. Grate temperatures were not measured.

In incinerator D, the same type of waste was combusted in two different furnaces with different operating conditions (control of grate temperature, pressure loss on the grate, distribution of underfire air) but the same gas cleaning equipment (Vaccani, pers. comm., 1980). Again there were significant differences in the concentrations of the atmophilic metals zinc, cadmium, and lead in the particulate of the two furnaces (see Table 6).

From the experience gained by the investigations of incinerators M, B, C, and D it can be concluded that it is possible to control incineration so that certain elements are concentrated in a specific product of incineration. The few investigations described in this work are not designed to answer the question how to control incineration to reach a specified objective. To achieve this, more research into the combustion processes is required.

3.4. *Waste parmeters*

The partitioning of an element by waste incineration is not only determined by the physical–chemical behaviour of this element and the combustion parameters but also by the composition of the waste material. In this work, the composition was calculated from the products of incineration (Table 7), and compared to the composition as measured by direct solid waste sampling and analysis.

Except for mercury, the concentrations determined by the two methods are of the same order of magnitude (the values of mercury for incinerator M may be influenced by a well-functioning battery collection system).

The municipal waste burned in incinerator M had a very low water content of 170 g kg^{-1}. This yielded a dry combustion off-gas with 6.6–6.9 vol. % moisture. The ESP, which is supposed to operate at 12–14 vol. % H$_2$O, did not work at its optimum efficiency and emitted more particulates (175 mg Nm^{-3}, 11% O$_2$) than it was designed for. When the moisture in the off-gas increased to 7.5–9.0 vol. % H$_2$O, the particulates dropped to an average of 62 mg Nm^{-3}. Considering the fact that the humidity in municipal waste is

TABLE 7

Chemical composition of municipal solid wastes determined by the analysis of incineration products compared to direct waste analysis

	C (g kg^{-1})	F (mg kg^{-1})	S (g kg^{-1})	Cl (g kg^{-1})	Fe (g kg^{-1})	Cu (mg kg^{-1})	Zn (g kg^{-1})	Cd (mg kg^{-1})	Hg (mg kg^{-1})	Pb (g kg^{-1})
Incinerator M	270 ± 50	140 ± 59	2.7 ± 0.5	6.9 ± 1.7	67 ± 36	200 ± 70	2.0 ± 1.5	8.7 ± 1.9	0.83 ± 0.81	0.43 ± 0.13
Incinerator B	n.d.*	n.d.	n.d.	n.d.	n.d.	460 ± 190	1.1 ± 0.5	12 ± 5.6	2	0.57 ± 0.43
Direct analysis of municipal waste samples (EAWAG 1982)	250	n.d.	5	7	n.d.	240–600	0.4 ± 1.6	3–15	5	0.5–1.2

*n.d. = Not determined.

mainly controlled by garbage from kitchen and gardening, it becomes obvious that the separate collection of such materials for composting might influence incineration of the remaining municipal waste in an unexpected way. The incineration of (dry) refuse-derived fuel (RDF) might yield similar moisture problems.

Another property of the waste which is important for the partitioning of the elements is the concentration of halogens, in particular, of chlorine. During incineration, metals may be transformed to halides which in general have higher vapour pressures than the oxides or elements, and are readily soluble in water. Therefore, a high concentration of chlorine-containing waste materials (e.g. polyvinylchloride) can increase the emission of volatile metal chlorides like $CdCl_2$, $ZnCl_2$ and $HgCl_2$, and can increase the water-soluble fractions of such metals in a scrubber system.

The two parameters "moisture" and "halogenes" have been chosen as simple examples which have to be supplemented with many additional properties of waste materials, e.g. content in silicates (formation of insoluble slag) or sulphur (formation of submicronic sulphate particles). These examples serve to illustrate that it becomes necessary to investigate the incineration process as a whole before individual measurements of waste management such as separate collection of single waste materials or RDF-pretreatments are introduced.

4. Summary and conclusion

Municipal solid waste incinerators can be of local and regional significance as a source of metals in the environment (Keller & Brunner 1983; Brunner & Zobrist 1983). In order to investigate the transfer of metals by waste incineration, the partitioning of iron, copper, zinc, cadmium, mercury and lead, as well as carbon, fluorine, sulphur and chlorine, was examined in two full-scale municipal incinerators. The results indicate, that the fate of metals during combustion, gas cooling, and gas cleaning is determined by the composition of the municipal waste, the physical–chemical behaviour of the individual metals, and the operating conditions of the incinerator.

Besides volume reduction and energy recovery, the goal of modern waste incineration must include the complete mineralization of carbonaceous materials and the concentration of metals in a nonsoluble form (Baccini & Brunner 1985). This investigation has shown that it may be possible to reach these objectives. If the importance of incineration as a valuable means to utilize municipal waste shall increase, it is necessary to improve the physical–chemical understanding of the complex processes taking place in a municipal solid waste incinerator, and to apply this knowledge to the operation of such a plant.

Acknowledgements

We thank the operators of the incineration plants who helped us during sample collection (R. Schweiss, K. Helfer) and we appreciate the technical assistance of R. Figi and M. Krähenbühl. The flue gas was sampled and analysed by Schweizerische Aluminium AG, CH-8212 Neuhausen (H. Lüdin) and Eidg. Materialprüfungsanstalt, CH-8600 Dübendorf (R. Müller).

References

Baccini, P. (1984), Conclusions and outlook. In *Metal Ions in Biological Systems* (H. Sigel, Ed.), p. 353–361. Marcel Dekker Inc., New York.

Baccini, P. & Brunner, P. H. (1985), Behandlung und Endlagerung von Reststoffen aus Kehricht-verbrennungsanlagen (Treatment and Storage of Products of Waste Incineration), *Gas-Wasser-Abwasser*, *65*, 403–409.

Brunner, P. H. & Zobrist, J. (1983), Die Müllverbrennung als Quelle von Metallen in der Umwelt (Solid Waste Incineration as a Source of Metals in the Environment), *Müll und Abfall*, *9*, 221–227.

BUS (1983), *Empfehlungen über die Emissionsmessungen von Luftfremdstoffen bei stationären Anlagen* (Guidelines for the Measurement of Air Pollution of Stationary Sources), Bundesamt für Umweltschutz, Bern.

BUS (1984), *Abfallerhebungen 1982/83* (Waste Analysis 1982/83), Bundesamt für Umweltschutz, Bern.

EAWAG (1982), Unpublished results, Swiss Federal Institute for Water Resources and Water Pollution Control, CH-8600 Dübendorf, Switzerland.

Greenberg, R. R., Gordon, G. E. & Zoller, W. H. (1981), Composition of Particles Emitted from Nicosia Incinerator, *Environmental Science and Technology*, *12*, 1329–1332.

Greenberg, R. R., Zoller, W. H. & Gordon, G. E. (1978), Composition and Particle Size in Refuse Incineration, *Environmental Science and Technology*, *12*, 566–573.

Keller, L. & Brunner, P. H. (1983), Waste Related Cadmium Cycle in Switzerland, *Ecotoxicology and Environmental Safety*, *7*, 141–150.

Stumm, W., Ed. (1977), *Global Chemical Cycles and their Alteration by Men*. Dahlem Conferences, Berlin.

SVA (1979), *The Behaviour of Spent Dry Batteries in Domestic Waste During Incineration*. Stitchting Verwijdering Avfallstoffen, NC-Amersfoort.

VDI (1979), *Verein Deutscher Ingenieure: VDI 2066. Messen von Partikeln. Staubmessungen in strömenden Gasen. Gravimetrische Bestimmung der Staubbeladung* (Assoziation of German Engineers, VDI-guidlines: Measurement of particles. Measurement of dust in moving gases. Gravimetrical determination of the dust load). VDI-Kommission Reinhaltung der Luft, VDI-Verlag GmbH, Düsseldorf 1975, 1979.

SEMINAR SUMMARY
INCINERATOR EMISSIONS OF HEAVY METALS
AND PARTICULATES*

Jens Aage Hansen†

(*Received 18 November 1985, revised 2 December 1985*)

1. Background and scope

It was the intention of this specialized seminar to present recent developments and experimental statistical or theoretical results regarding emission of particles and heavy metals from municipal solid waste incinerators.

The limited scope was to secure a qualified, in-depth discussion and achieve two results: firstly, a state-of-the-art assessment on emissions of heavy metals and particulates, as well as their correlation to plant operation; secondly, a realistic base of data to be used for environmental and health risk analysis, and formulation of operational strategies and procedures for emission control on a statistical basis.

The attendance was pre-limited to 60 particpants, including authors and organizers. The programme is shown in the Annex.

2. Proceedings

Each participant received a conference document that included all written contributions for the seminar. Papers that were intended for journal publication and which have since passed through refereeing and editing are found in this issue of WMR.

3. Summary of discussions

Based on discussions during the seminar and a short evaluatory session immediately after a summary is made here of some essential issues and considerations. The assistance of authors, programme committee members and the editor of WMR is greatly appreciated. However, the responsibility for any mistake or bias in the summary lies with the rapporteur.

3.1. *Inorganic emissions from MSW incinerators*

Emission of certain inorganic elements and compounds from incineration of municipal solid waste (MSW) can be significant. Table 1 supports this statement by drawing a comparison between emission per unit of energy *produced* by burning of coal and MSW. The first two lines of the table refer to an assessment of Danish emissions in 1984. Although MSW flue gas cleaning was predominantly by electrostatic precipitation (ESP)

---

*ISWA Specialized Seminar, Eigtveds Pakhus, Copenhagen, September 18–19 1985.
†Environmental Engineering Laboratory, University of Aalborg, Sohngardsholmsvej 57, 9000 Aalborg, Denmark.
Waste Management & Research (1986) **4**, 121–125

TABLE 1

Emission factors (g GJ^{-1})*

	Dust	HCl	SO$_2$	Cd	Hg
Coal, Denmark 1984	60	15	800	0.008	0.007
MSW, Denmark 1984	270	400	370	0.19	0.21
MSW, Typical of ESP only	50	400	370	0.08	0.21
MSW, Additional cleaning (seminar reporting)	5	30	100	4×10^{-5}	0.01

*MSW = Municipal solid waste; ESP = electrostatic precipitator.

the numbers are nevertheless strongly influenced by the use of cyclones only—or even no flue gas cleaning at all—at a number of smaller plants.

Through all-over installation of ESP the general emission number may appear as shown in the third line of the Table 1. The effect is seen on particulates and heavy metals such as cadmium.

The seminar gave evidence that acid gas absorption, e.g. by use of lime in combination with ESP or fabric filters, can reduce significantly emissions of particulates and heavy metals. Line four of Table 1 indicates this; background data are found in the proceedings. Acid emissions can be reduced by both wet scrubbing and dry sorption or combinations thereof; the numbers given in line four of Table 1 are indicative only of an order of magnitude. Research and further experiments are still needed to devise optimal technology combinations to remove both acid gases, particulates and heavy metals.

It is, however, a major conclusion of the seminar that reduction of emissions of inorganics from MSW incineration seems feasible by use of available technology to levels required for protection of the environment. The present general situation in MSW incineration is far from the potential expressed in line four of Table 1. A situation typical of transition from lines two to three is more likely to exist in most countries.

The discussions on emission data gave rise to the following recommendations.

(1) Longer periods of observation at several full-scale plants are necessary to substantiate the so far scanty evidence of good and steady performance of incineration and flue gas cleaning.

(2) More plants have to be built, operated and equipped for low inorganic emissions in order to verify the practical feasibility of generally reduced emissions from MSW incineration.

(3) Reduction by flue gas cleaning should be considered in combination with reduced levels of contaminants in the MSW fuel; e.g. through separation before incineration or substitution in the goods consumed (clean technology).

3.2. *Processes and chemistry*

The seminar produced emission data related to various makes of furnace and flue gas cleaning equipment. However, levels and variability of emission were normally not mated with specific information on combustion processes, mode of operation or waste inflow. The chemistry of incineration, including heating and gasification of waste and cooling of residuals, was poorly documented. For example, phase shifts for heavy metals in relation to temperature, redox, residence time and presence of particulates were not dealt with. For mercury, see below.

The need for more "pyrochemistry" was expressed, both in terms of basic research and in studies of operation and performance of existing plants. The obvious reasons are that the MSW incineration process needs to be improved and that data cannot be transferred from one installation to another before such basic knowledge exists.

3.3. *Mercury*

Mercury is vaporized during incineration and exhausted in an oxidized state, predominantly as $HgCl_2$. Mercury can be removed before emission; e.g. by wet scrubbing or dry filtration of fly ashes, with or without lime reaction products, in fabric filters at temperatures below 150 °C. Removal to levels below 15 μg m^{-3} were reported.

3.4. *Control*

Control applies to plant operation, incinerator (including furnace, afterburner, boiler and flue gas cleaner) processes and emissions (including stack gases, fly ashes and bottom slags and ashes).

There is a general need for continuous monitoring rather than intermittent observations. To facilitate such development new monitoring equipment must be installed—and computer equipment used to process data and efficiently use the information for improved control.

Referring to the relatively poor understanding of MSW incineration processes, a staged development has to be foreseen, in terms of choice of control parameters, equipment for monitoring and interpretation of digital data by computerized techniques. Training of operators to administer already acquired knowledge and to co-operate in establishing new information at existing facilities is deemed to be of high importance.

3.5. *Statistics and correlations*

A preliminary report of an attempt to determine size classes of fractionated particulates was inconclusive and more data is required. A presentation of the proper use of statistics for the control of highly variable emissions drew much attention and led to useful discussions.

A first step to be taken is therefore to establish data that are more comprehensive (e.g. over time), more consistent (e.g. simultaneous observations of incineration processes and emission data) and representative of the phenomenon to be studied. Transferability of correlations must be carefully considered before making analogies from one plant to another. Several authors agreed that statistics deserve more attention in their future work.

3.6. *Emission criteria*

The variation of emission criteria between countries was demonstrated. Examples were shown for the Lombardian region of Italy, Switzerland and Federal Republic of Germany. It was also noted that a trend is seen towards still lower legally permissible concentrations of certain heavy metals, particulates, and acid gases.

During the discussion of emission criteria the principle of "best technical means" or "lowest technically possible emission" were mentioned. These are, however, totally dependant on economical means and, therefore, not favourable to a rational design procedure. Also, the "risk assessment" procedure was mentioned, but generally there is a difficulty in defining an "acceptable risk", which is a prerequisite for use of the method.

The lesson of the seminar is that it is now technically feasible to remove particulates and heavy metals (and acid gases) to a desired level of emission. There is, therefore, an obvious need to establish a procedure whereby environmentally acceptable emission criteria be developed; either individually for each plant or generally for MSW incinerators.

3.7. *General*

The seminar was limited in scope and attendance according to the concepts laid down by the organization and programme committees. This "specialization" possibly enhanced the lively and very pointedly discussions to which substantial contributions were made by both speakers and other participants.

The duration of the seminar was 2 days only. While maintaining the degree of specialization it may be adequate for other seminars to consider durations of 2–4 days, depending on the amount of information to be delivered and discussed.

Annex

Programme

Opening addresses

Significance of Waste Incineration, by Per B. Suhr, Danish Agency of Environmental Protection, Denmark.

Scope of Seminar, by Jens Aage Hanssen, University of Aalborg, Denmark.

Novel technology and methodology in sampling and analyses

Monitoring of Heavy Metals by Energy Dispersive X-ray Fluorescence, by K. E. Lorber, Technical University of Berlin, West Berlin.

Heavy Metals and Particulates, a Statistical Study of Fractionated Samples, by Steffen Lauritzen, University of Aalborg, Denmark.

Emissions related to furnace operation and cleaning technology

Heavy Metal Emissions from Fläkt Dry Scrubbing Systems for Waste Incinerators, by Kurt Carlsson, Fläkt Industri, Sweden.

Design and Operations of the Pinella County Florida Electrostatic Precipitator, by Ian Peacy, JPC Consultants, Illinois, U.S.A.

Incinerator Emissions of Heavy Metals and Particulates, by Bengt Westergaard, Energi Production AB, Stockholm, Sweden.

Performance of Electrostatic Precipitators, by H. Hoegh Petersen, F. L. Smidth & Co., F.R.G.

Mercury chemistry and emission

Flows and Transformation of Mercury in the Environment, by Oliver Lindquist, University of Göteborg, Sweden.

Mercury and its Treatment in Gas and Dust of Garbage Incineration, by Dieter O. Reimann, Bamberg, Denmark.

Mercury in Air and Flow Gases, by Jan Bergström, Studsvik AB, Sweden.

The Specific Role of Cadmium and Mercury in the Incineration of Municipal Refuses, by H. Vogg, Kernforschungszentrum, Karlsruhe, F.R.G.

Measurement of Mercury Combustion Aerosols in Emissions from Stationary Sources, by Arun Shendrikar, Compuchem Laboratories, North Carolina, U.S.A.

Mass balances and total emissions of metals

Analysis of Inorganic Pollutants Emitted into the Atmosphere by Garbage Incineration Plants, by Jacques Gounon, City of Paris, France.

Mass Balances of Elements for Solid Waste Incineration, by Paul H. Brunner, EAWAG, Switzerland.

Strategies for limited and controlled emission

Statistical Principles for Emission Control, by Steffen Lauritzen, University of Aalborg, Denmark.

Conclusions and recommendations

Final Plenary Discussion and Conclusions. Introduction by Jens Aage Hansen, University of Aalborg, Denmark.

Programme committee

Jan Bergström, MKS Studsvik Energiteknik AB, Nyköping, Sweden. Bo Drougge, Swedish Environmental Protection Board. M. Lange, Umweltbundesamt, West Berlin. Jens Aage Hansen (chairman), University of Aalborg, Denmark. G. Hovsenius, Teknik & Milijöanalys, Sweden. Jan Hult, The Swedish Association of Public Cleansing and Solid Waste Management. Steffen Lauritzen, University of Aalborg, Denmark. Hans Mosbaek, Technical University of Denmark. Jens Erik Petterson, Norwegian State Pollution Control. Per B. Suhr, Danish Agency of Environmental Protection. David Sussman, U.S. Environmental Protection Agency.

Sponsoring organizations

Danish Agency of Environmental Protection*. Danish Committee for Solid Wastes (DAKOFA). ELMIA, Sweden. Pollution Foundation of 1972, Denmark*. International Solid Wastes Association (ISWA). Norwegian Ministry of the Environment*. Swedish Association of Public Cleansing and Solid Waste Management. Swedish Environmental Protection Board*. Swedish Power & Heating Producers' Joint Committee on Environmental Questions*. U.S. Environmental Protection Agency (U.S. EPA).

Organizing committee

Jens Aage Hansen, Jan Hult, Hans Mosbaek.

*Provided financial support.

IMPACT ON HEALTH OF CHLORINATED DIOXINS AND OTHER TRACE ORGANIC EMISSIONS*

Ulf G. Ahlborg† and Katarina Victorin†

(Received December 1986)

The potential health effects of incineration of municipal solid waste (MSW) have been studied by the Swedish National Institute of Environmental Medicine.

The greatest concern for health effects relates to the emission of PCDDs and PCDFs ("dioxins"). MSW incineration is presently estimated to be a large source for the emission of these compounds into ambient air. Based upon animal experiments, and by applying safety factors in the range 200–1000, a highest tolerable daily intake (TDI) has been estimated to be 1–5 pg kg^{-1} of TCDD for humans. This TDI-value has been extended to cover all the congeners of PCDDs and PCDFs by the application of the concept of "TCDD-equivalents" (Eadon *et al.*, 1983). The high concentrations found in human breast milk and fish indicate that the TDI value may be exceeded, especially among breast-milk fed babies. If the emission can be reduced to the proposed Swedish limit value of 0.1 ng m^{-3}n TCDD-equivalents, or less, the contribution from this source will be lowered. MSW incineration can be considered acceptable when the following aspects are taken into account: the risk estimation for TDI is conservative; there is no indication that man belongs to the most sensitive species although infants may be particularly sensitive; available studies indicate that the concept of TCDD-equivalents used overestimates the effect of mixtures of PCDDs and PCDFs; present levels in fish and human milk reflect the cumulative effect of many years of emission. Besides PCDDs and PCDFs, MSW incineration also gives rise to relatively high emissions of PAH, chlorinated PAH, phenols, benzenes and mutagenic substances under less well controlled combustion conditions. The emission of organic compounds is generally dependent on the combustion efficiency. If the combustion process is optimized and advanced flue-gas cleaning is applied so that the emission of TCDD-equivalents does not exceed 0.1 ng m^{-3}, the emission of other organics probably will not cause significant health hazards.

Key Words—Dioxin, emissions, PCDD/PCDF, incineration, municipal solid waste, health, mutagens, PAH, chlorinated aromatics.

1. Introduction

Reports on high levels of potentially harmful chlorinated dioxins and dibenzofurans in fish and human milk caused the Swedish Environmental Protection Board to issue a moratorium to allow the building of new or expanded MSW incinerators. A governmental committee was called upon to study the whole issue. The National Institute of Environmental Medicine was subsequently asked to perform a study on the potential health effects of municipal solid waste, (MSW) incineration. The present report summarizes the findings from that study with regard to organic compounds.

---

* Presented at the ISWA–WHO–DAKOFA specialized seminar on *Emissions of Trace Organics from Municipal Solid Waste Incinerators*, Copenhagen, 20–22 January 1987.

† National Institute of Environmental Medicine, Unit of Toxicology, P.O. Box 60208, S-104 01 Stockholm, Sweden.

Waste Management & Research (1987) **5**, 203–224

TABLE 1

Levels of various pollutants in flue gas from MSW incineration with present and future techniques and estimated maximum total annual emissions based on incineration of 1.4 Mt. Gas volumes are normalized to 10% CO_2 (dry) at standard conditions

Compound	Levels in flue gas per normal m³		Annual emission	
	Present	Future	Present	Future
Particulates	50 mg	20 mg	420 t	170 t
HCl	1000 mg	100–200 mg	8400 t	840 t
TCDD equiv. (Eadon 1983)	10–100 ng	0.1–2 ng	90 g*	9 g†
PAH	1–100 µg	0.01–1 µg	840 kg	8.4 kg
Chlorinated benzenes (monochlorobenzene not included)	10–70 µg	1–20 µg	590 kg	170 kg
Chlorinated phenols (monochlorophenol not included)	1–100 µg	1–20 µg	840 kg	170 kg
Phthalates	25–1000 µg	25–1000 µg	1000 kg	1000 kg
CO	500–1000 mg	100 mg	8400 t	840 t

* Using the emission value of 10 ng m⁻³. May well be 2–3 times higher.
† Using the emission value of 1 ng m⁻³.

2. Background

During 1985, 24 different MSW incinerators were in use in Sweden with a total of 1.4 Mt y⁻¹ of incinerated material. More than 70% of the total waste was incinerated at the five largest installations. Permission has been granted for the incineration of 1.8 Mt y⁻¹ of MSW. Expansion by a further 0.4 Mt y⁻¹ is expected in the near future, resulting in an incineration capacity of about 70% of the MSW in Sweden.

Based on measurements of concentrations of various compounds in the flue gas at present and after technically possible changes of the plants (Table 1), the maximal contribution to ambient air levels around incinerators of various sizes and techniques were calculated (Table 2). The technique used at present involves combustion in a well-functioning plant with good combustion efficiency and effective smoke gas cleaning using electrostatic filters, etc. Future technique means the expected emissions, once the combustion is optimized, and smoke-gas cleaning is supplemented with treatment in advanced dry, semi-dry or wet systems. Values are supplied by the Swedish Environment Protection Board; see also Olie *et al.* (1983).

The data presented in Tables 1 and 2 were subsequently used for the estimation of possible effects on health and on the environment. Besides the evaluations of the compounds occurring in the tables, the emission of mutagenic material from MSW incinerators will be discussed.

3. Chlorinated dibenzo-*p*-dioxins and dibenzofurans (PCDDs and PCDFs)

PCDDs and PCDFs constitute a group of chemicals that have been shown to occur ubiquitously in the environment. They do not occur naturally, nor are they produced as commercial products. The PCDDs and PCDFs are two series of almost planar

TABLE 2

Calculated maximal contribution to ambient air levels around various types of MSW incinerators (yearly average)

Compound (ng m^{-3})	8 MW	40 MW		120 MW	
		Present	Future	Present	Future
TCDD equiv. (Eadon)	70×10^{-6}	40×10^{-6}	33×10^{-6}	8×10^{-6}	7×10^{-6}
PAH	0.1	0.1	0.002	0.1	0.001
Benzo(a)pyrene*	0.7×10^{-5}	8×10^{-5}	20×10^{-5}	6×10^{-5}	13×10^{-5}
Chlorobenzenes*	0.1	0.02	0.03	0.01	0.03
Chlorophenoles*	0.08	0.08	0.16	0.07	0.1
Phthalates*	0	1	1	1	1

* The same concentration in flue gas for both present and future techniques was assumed for these calculations.

tricyclic aromatic compounds with very similar chemical properties. There are 75 congeners of PCDDs and 135 congeners of PCDFs. The toxic and biological properties of the different congeners probably have a common mode of action, the potency, however, is varied. The most well-known and well-studied congener is the 2,3,7,8-tetrachloro-dibenzo-*p*-dioxin, which will be referred to in this following report as TCDD, and this paper is mainly a review of the toxicology of TCDD with data on other PCDDs and PCDFs when available.

TCDD is one of the most toxic man-made chemicals. It is environmentally persistent and accumulates in biological systems. The toxic effects of TCDD may be delayed and are markedly accumulative upon repeated exposure and, when the exposure period is prolonged, even low daily doses of TCDD will eventually result in a certain degree of toxicity, which means that TCDD is an extremely hazardous chemical.

3.1. Animal data

3.1.1. Kinetics

Absorption of TCDD in the gastrointestinal tract is about 50–80% in several species. If TCDD is adsorbed on particulate matter such as activated carbon, absorption can be very much decreased. Uptake via skin contact has been reported. Distribution occurs to tissues high in lipid content and the liver is a major storage site in many species. Unchanged TCDD can be eliminated in feces or milk, while polar metabolites are excreted in the urine and feces. Available data indicate that the metabolites are less toxic.

Many studies have been performed on the elimination of TCDD in various species indicating great species variations, thus whole-body half-life times are in the order of 22–42 days in the guinea-pig, 22–31 days in the rat, and 10–12 days in the hamster. The reported half life in humans is five years (see section 3.2.1.).

3.1.2. Acute toxicity

TCDD is extremely toxic to all animals species tested. The oral LD$_{50}$ is in the μg kg^{-1} range. Acute toxicity in animals following dermal exposure has not been studied,

TABLE 3
Structure–activity relationships for some PCDDs

Chlorination of PCDDs	AHH-induction potencies (nM)*	Receptorbinding avidities (nM)†	LD$_{50}$ guinea-pig (μg kg^{-1} body weight)‡
2,8	Inactive		> 300,000
2,3,7	1100	1.9	29
2,3,7,8	0.4	0.27	2
1,3,7,8	89	1.7	
1,2,3,8	610		
1,2,3,7,8	5.4	0.42	3.1
1,2,4,7,8	> 120,000§		1125
1,2,3,4,7,8	7.6		72.5
1,2,3,6,7,8	31	0.57	70–100
1,2,3,7,8,9	46	1.4	60–100
1,2,3,4,6,7,8	130		> 600
1,2,3,4,6,7,9	3700		
1,2,3,4,6,7,8,9	19,000		

* Estimated concentration needed to produce 50% maximum enzyme induction in the rat hepatoma cell line H-4-II-E (Bradlaw et al. 1980).

† Estimated concentration needed to displace 50% of ^{3}H-TCDD bound to liver cytosol receptor from C57Bl/6J mice (Poland et al. 1976).

‡ McConnell et al., 1978.

§ Calculative value.

extensively, but lethal effects have been observed in rabbits following the application of TCDD to the abdominal skin. No inhalation studies have been reported to date.

One of the interesting features of TCDD toxicity is the pronounced species difference in sensitivity. Oral LD$_{50}$ varies from 0.6 μg kg^{-1} in guinea-pigs, the most sensitive species, to 5000 μg kg^{-1} in Syrian Golden hamster. Also different strains within the same species show pronounced differences, e.g. oral LD$_{50}$ for Sherman rats has been reported to be in the range 13–43 μg kg^{-1}, whilst the corresponding values for Han/Wistar rats are over 3000 μg kg^{-1} (Pohjanvirta & Tuomisto 1986). This large variation in sensitivity to TCDD (and also to related compounds) has so far not been explained by differences in metabolic rate, clearance time, body burden of compounds or by macromolecular adduct formation.

The toxicity of the various congeners of PCDDs and PCDFs vary with regard to their toxic potency and the structure–activity relationship, as illustrated in Table 3. In general, the highest toxicity is displaced by the congeners possessing chlorine substitution in positions 2, 3, 7 and 8 with the tetrachloro congeners being the most toxic, followed, in decreasing order, by the penta-, hexa- and hepta-chlorinated congeners. These are popularly referred to as "the dirty dozen". The toxicity of the octachlorinated congeners is comparatively low. The AHH induction and receptors binding values for PCDF follow a similar pattern (Bandiera et al. 1984).

The histopathological changes found in different species and tissues after single or repeated dosage with TCDD are displayed in Table 4 which illustrates some of the still unexplained species differences. It is also notable that almost all the pathological changes affect epithelial tissues.

Several other PCDDs and PCDFs cause signs and symptoms similar to those of TCDD, but there is a wide variation with regard to potency. Many have been tested in short-term studies both in vivo and in vitro.

TABLE 4

Histopathological changes caused by TCDD (adapted from Poland & Knutson 1982)*

	Monkey	Guinea-pig	Cow	Rat	Mouse	Rabbit	Chicken	Hamster
Hyper- and/or meta-plasia								
Gastric mucosa	+ +	0	+	0	0	−	−	0
Intestinal mucosa	+						−	+ +
Urinary tract	+ + ·	+ +	+ +	0	0	−	−	−
Gall duct and bladder	+ +	−	+	−	+ +	−	−	−
Lung alveoli	+ +	−	+	+ +	0	+ +	−	−
Skin	+ +	0	+	0	0	+ +	−	0
Hypoplasia, atrophy or necrosis								
Thymus	+	+	+	+	+	−	+	+
Bone marrow	+	+	−	−	+	−	+	−
Testicles	+	+	−	+	+	−	+	−
Other findings								
Liver lesions	0	0	0	+ +	+	+ +	+	0
Oedema	+	0	−	0	+	−	+ +	+

* 0, No change or very minor change; −, not reported in the literature; +, pronounced change; + +, very pronounced change.

3.1.3. *Reproduction effects*
TCDD has been shown to produce fetotoxic and teratogenic effects in rats and mice. In rats, malformations, predominantly in the form of kidney malformations, have been observed at doses above 0.5 μg kg^{-1}. A no-effect level (NOEL), or possibly a lowest-effect level (LOEL), of 1 ng kg^{-1} body weight per day for reproduction effects in rats has been discussed (Murray *et al.* 1979, Nisbet & Paxton 1982).

3.1.4. *Immunotoxicological effects*
Lymphoid organs, primarily thymus but also spleen and lymph nodes, are affected by TCDD over a wide range of doses in various species. A variety of endpoints have been studied, the most sensitive being cytotoxic T-cell generation in response to allogeneic antigens as demonstrated in mice (Clark *et al.* 1981, 1983). The response was apparent after four i.p. injections (given at intervals of one week) of 1 ng kg^{-1} body weight. At this dose, no effects were seen on delayed hypersensitivity, antibody response, thymus cellularity or enzyme induction.

3.1.5. *Genotoxic effects*
Early studies indicated a mutagenic response to TCDD (Hussain *et al.* 1972, Seiler 1972) but several later studies failed to detect such an effect (Gilbert *et al.* 1980, Geiger & Neal 1981, Mortelmans *et al.* 1984). Several PCDFs have also given negative results when tested for mutagenicity (Schoeny 1982). However, TCDD was shown to give a positive response in an *in vitro* suspension test and in an *in vivo* intrasangineous host mediated assay (both with yeast as detector organism) (Bronzetti *et al.* 1983) and on mouse lymphoma cells (Rogers *et al.* 1982).

3.1.6. *Carcinogenicity*

Several studies on the carcinogenicity of TCDD and related compounds have been made. TCDD has been shown to be carcinogenic after oral administration to rats (van Miller *et al.* 1977, Kociba *et al.* 1978, NIH 1982*a*) and mice (Toth *et al.* 1979, NIH 1982*a*). A mixture of 1,2,3,6,7,8- and 1,2,3,7,8,9-hexa-CDD also showed carcinogenic effects after oral administration to rats and mice (NIH 1980). A dermal study in mice (NIH 1982*b*) demonstrated a carcinogenic response to TCDD in females but not in males. However, the latter study has been criticized because no maximal tolerated dose was used and the number of animals in the exposed groups was too small. Unsubstituted dioxin and 2,7-dichlorodibenzo-*p*-dioxin did not show carcinogenic properties (NCI 1979*a,b*).

In the study by Kociba *et al.* (1978), groups of male and female Sprague-Dawley rats were fed 0.1, 0.01 and 0.001 μg TCDD kg^{-1} body weight for two years. This corresponds to levels in the feed of 2193, 208 and 22 ppt (ng kg^{-1}), respectively. Tumours caused by the ingestion of TCDD were confined to the liver, lungs, hard palate/nasal turbinates and the tongue. In the female rats that had received doses of 0.1 and 0.01 μg kg^{-1}, a statistically significant increase of neoplastic nodules (hyperplastic nodules, hepatomas) of the liver was noted, and in the rats that had received 0.1 μg TCDD kg^{-1} body weight, a statistically significant increase of hepatocellular carcinomas was also noted. An increased incidence of squamous cell carcinomas of the hard palate and nasal turbinates was seen in both male and female rats receiving 0.1 μg TCDD kg^{-1} body weight, whilst the incidence of squamous cell carminoma of the lungs at this dose showed an increase in females only.

3.1.7. *Carcinogenic promotion*

As mentioned earlier, some data indicate possibly weak initiating properties of the PCDDs and PCDFs, but other data indicate that the compounds may act as epigenetic carcinogens or as promoters.

Pitot *et al.* (1980) found TCDD to be a potent promoter in rat liver after initiation with diethylnitrosamine, whilst Berry *et al.* (1978) did not record any promoting effect in a two-stage system of mouse-skin tumorogenesis. In the latter study, it was also found that TCDD acted as a potent inhibitor of PAH-induced skin tumour initiation which has also been supported in studies by Cohen *et al.* (1979) and DiGiovanni *et al.* (1979, 1980).

3.1.8. *Mechanisms of action*

The induction of drug metabolizing enzyme systems has been suggested as one major mechanism of toxic action (see Tables 3 and 4). The induction is believed to be mediated through a cytosolic receptor protein. The results of several studies of TCDD and different congeners indicate that the binding affinity and the potency to induce microsomal mono-oxygenases correlate fairly well with the toxicity *in vivo*. However, neither the levels of the receptor nor the differences with regard to enzyme induction can explain the large variation in sensitivity between species. The amount of cytosolic receptor protein is thus about the same in the liver of guinea-pigs, rats, mice, rabbits and hamsters, although the acute toxicity varies by a factor of more than 1000. Furthermore, the LD$_{50}$ dose of TCDD in chicken embryos, C^{3}H/HeN-mice and SD-rats varies more than 100 fold, although the dose that causes half maximal induction of aryl hydrocarbon hydrolylase is about the same for different species. It has been suggested that the receptor is a necessary, but not the only, factor determining the toxicity of the compound. The toxicity seems to depend on a continuous onset of an endogeneous cellular regulating system, the nature of which is not known. Several other reported effects of TCDD on vital physiological mechanisms could very well be of importance in explaining the toxicity and the variation between species. Such effects are interactions with the vitamin A turnover (Thunberg *et al.* 1979, 1980, Thunberg & Håkansson 1983, Håkansson & Ahlborg 1985), effects on the function of plasmamembranes and their build up (Brewster *et al.* 1982, Matsumura *et al.* 1984), and effects on the formation of keratin and cell-differentiation (Knutson & Poland 1980, 1984, Gierthy & Crane 1984, Puhvel *et al.* 1984, Rice & Cline 1984). All these physiological processes are characterized by being equilibrium processes that occur in all cells in the organism. Depending on the cell system, the balance may be in a different state; in this regard there are also differences between both species and sexes.

3.2. *Human data*

3.2.1. *Kinetics*
Only one controlled study in humans has been done. After oral intake of 1.14 ng kg^{-1} of H^3-TCDD, elimination was followed for 25 days. During the first three days 11.5% was eliminated in feces indicating an almost complete uptake from the gut. Over the first days some activity was noted in the urine but was later below the detection limit (0.01% of the dose/day). The half-life was determined to be in the order of five years (Poiger & Schlatter 1986).

No systematic toxicokinetic data exist on the elimination of other PCDDs and PCDFs in man. However, from the analysis performed on both human fat and human mother's milk it is obvious that only PCDDs and PCDFs containing at least four chlorine atoms in symmetrical lateral position (i.e. positions 2, 3, 7 and 8) are retained at measureable levels. Octa-CDD, octa-CDF, tetra-CDD and tetra-CDF, 1,2,3,7,8-penta-CDD and 2,3,4,7,8-penta-CDF, three isomers of hexa-CDDs and the three isomers of hexa-CDFs and 1,2,3,4,6,7,8-hepta-CDD and -CDF have been identified and quantified in human mother's milk.

3.2.2. *Toxicity*
Effects on human health have been reported only for TCDD and, in most cases, from mixed exposures and mainly in connection with occupational exposure or in industrial accidents (Holmstedt 1980). Several acute clinical effects have been noted, whilst chronic effects have not been demonstrated except for persistent chloracne.

In 1968 and 1979 two outbreaks of poisoning occurred in Japan and Taiwan, respectively, People were poisoned by rise oil contaminated with PCBs, PCDFs, and PCQs (polychlorinated quarterphenyls). Besides chloracne, various other clinical effects were noted, but the data from the intoxication episodes do not allow any reliable quantitative conclusions to be drawn on the dose–response relationship. Data on other exposed general populations are scarce. One example, however, is the Seveso episode, in Italy, 1976. In 1984 an international steering group, appointed by the Italian authorities, concluded that "it is obvious that no clear-cut adverse adverse health effects attributable to TCDD, besides chloracne, have been observed".

A total of 193 persons had displayed symptoms of chloracne, but in 1984 only 20 presented active symptoms. Exposure to TCDD soil levels of 270–1200 μg m^{-2} for 15–20 days clearly caused an enhanced incidence of chloracne. An increase in urinary glucaric acid levels, indicating an increased microsomal enzyme activity as compared

TABLE 5

Some approaches to estimating relative toxicities of PCDDs and PCDFs (modified from Bellin & Barnes 1985)

Compound	Method*			
	1	2	3	4
Cl 1–2	—	—	—	—
Cl 3	—	—	0.001	—
2,3,7,8-TCDD	1	1	1	1
Other TCDDs	—	0.01	0.01	0.01
2,3,7,8-penta CDDs	1	0.2	0.1	0.1
Other penta-CDDs	—	0.002	0.1	0.1
2,3,7,8-hexa-CDDs	0.033	0.04	0.1	0.1
Other hexa-CDDs	—	0.004	0.1	0.1
2,3,7,8-hepta CDDs	—	0.001	0.01	0.01
Other hepta-CDDs	—	0.00001	0.01	0.01
Octa-CDD	—	—	—	—
2,3,7,8-tetra-CDF	0.33	0.1	0.1	0.1
Other tetra-CDFs	—	0.001	0.1	0.1
2,3,7,8-penta-CDFs	0.33	0.1	0.2	0.1
Other penta-CDFs	—	0.001	0.2	0.1
2,3,7,8-hexa-CDFs	0.01	0.01	0.1	0.1
Other hexa-CDFs	—	0.0001	0.1	0.1
Hepta-CDFs	—	0.001	0.01	—
Other hepta-CDFs	—	0.00001	—	—
Octa-CDF	—	—	—	—

 * 1, Eadon *et al.* (1983); 2, Bellin & Barnes (1985); 3, Denmark (1984); 4, Swiss Federal Office for Environmental Protection (1982).

to non-exposed children, was found in exposed children up to three years after exposure (Ideo *et al.* 1982). No chloracne or disturbance of biochemical functions were seen when the exposure had been limited to soil with TCDD-levels at or below 30–70 μg m^{-2} (Regione Lombardia 1984). From the data available to date, it has been speculated that chloracne is the most sensitive indication of human exposure to PCDDs and PCDFs.

3.2.3. Carcinogenicity
Several follow-up studies have been made on workers exposed to TCDD or TCDD-contaminated chemicals. Although some statistically significant differences can be found between exposed and control workers, there is a lack of uniformity between the different studies which might indicate that exposure to other compounds may have interfered. One study on workers exposed to TCDD after an accident (Thiess *et al.* 1982) reports a cancer incidence higher than expected which cannot be explained as a mere chance event. However, the small size of the cohort and the small number of deaths from any particular cause does not permit any definite conclusions concerning the carcinogenic effect of exposure to be drawn.

TABLE 6

TCDD equivalents (pg g^{-1}, ppt) in aquatic species (raw data from Nygren *et al.* 1986)

Sample	Method 1 (Eadon *et al.* 1983)	Method 2 (Bellin & Barnes 1985)	Method 3 (Denmark 1984)
Seal	100	30	41
Herring	3.5	1.2	1.9
Cod liver	8.1	2.7	4.1
Salmon	78	24	33

3.3. *Risk evaluations*

All available information from animal studies demonstrates the extreme toxicity of TCDD and several other PCDDs and PCDFs. There are, however, considerable species differences and also potency differences between the different congeners. No good quantitative information is available on the doses of TCDD or other PCDDs and PCDFs that are toxic to man, but the symptoms and signs of toxic exposure in man are similar. Follow-up studies of groups of occupationally or accidentally exposed men gave the overall impression that man does not belong amongst the most sensitive species. Despite all the studies conducted on animals, no definite information is available on the no-observed-effect levels in rodents or primates for long-term exposure. The carcinogenic effects of TCDD and hexa-CDDs in animal studies, and the fact that certain morphological alterations were induced by feeding rats levels of TCDD as low as 1 ng kg^{-1} for two years would suggest that long-term exposure, even at concentrations below or at the detection limit of the analytical procedures presently available, could present a certain risk to the population.

The data available on human exposure do not allow any risk assessment to be performed and so animal data are used. Several risk evaluations on TCDD have been performed in various countries. Some of these have applied one of the long-term oncogenic rate studies (Kociba *et al.* 1978) as the basis. Using these data, various extrapolations have been made to determine the "virtually safe dose", i.e. a dose that would give one extra case of cancer in 1 million humans in an average lifetime (Kimbrough *et al.* 1984). The studies on the mutagenicity and carcinogenicity indicate that TCDD is not a genotoxic compound and a few reports have given some evidence to that effect, but these are not convincing when compared to the reports stating the contrary opinion. On the other hand, TCDD has been shown to be strongly positive as a promoter in a two-stage precarcinogenesis study (Pitot *et al.* 1980). It has been argued that the straight forward mathematical extrapolation from animal studies should, therefore, not be used. Certain other risk evaluations have instead used the no-observed-effect level (NOEL) or lowest-observed-effect level (LOEL) from long-term or reproduction studies of about 0.005 pg TCDD kg^{-1} body weight and applied "safety factors" of 200 to 1000 (Denmark 1984, Umveltsbundesamt 1985). Regardless of the approach used, these evaluations have ended up with suggested "tolerable daily intake" for humans in the range 1–5 pg TCDD kg^{-1} body weight. This range has been accepted as a basis for the present discussion.

3.3.1. *The concept of TCDD equivalents*

Together with TCDD, several other PCDDs and PCDFs occur in the environment. There is reason to believe that these may be additive to TCDD in effect. It is thus necessary to evaluate the risk for all these congeners when they appear together. Several attempts at such estimates have been made. The approaches used related the toxicity of the various PCDDs and PCDFs to that of TCDD, and expressed the toxicity in what has been called "TCDD-equivalents". The bases used for comparison included enzyme induction potency (Swiss Federal Office for Environmental Protection 1982, Denmark 1984), acute toxicity (Eadon *et al.* 1983), carcinogenic potency (Bellin & Barnes 1985) and various different parameters (Grant 1977, Commoner 1984, Ontario Ministry of the Environment 1985). The conversion factors of some of these approaches are given in Table 5. This type of approach obviously has two levels of uncertainty: (i) in the evaluation of TCDD in itself, and (ii) in the determination of the fractional value given to each congener. Despite these uncertainties, the approach has its merits as an interim procedure, and has consequently been used for evaluating and comparing the toxicity of environmental samples (see Mukerjee & Cleverly and Commoner *et al.* in this issue).

3.3.2. *Food*

Although there is still little data on the importance of aquatic organisms in the uptake of TCCD, indications are that their importance is significant (Nygren *et al.* 1986, see Table 6). From the data in Table 6 it is quite clear that an intake of 100 g of herring, salmon or cod liver would cause excessive intake even in adults when compared to the suggested tolerable intake 1–5 pg kg^{-1} body weight when calculated as TCDD-equivalents.

Dairy products may also be an important source of exposure. The elimination of TCDD in cows' milk and cream has been studied in cows exposed to the phenoxyacetic acid 2,4,5-T with a known content of TCDD at levels in the diet corresponding to 5–500 ppt. The elimination was 10–20% at dietary levels of 15 and 50 ppt, respectively. The levels in the milk were 3 and 10 ppt, respectively (Jensen & Hummel 1982). Rappe *et al.* (1985) have reported on levels of PCDDs and PCDFs in milk from cows that have been grazing at various distances from incinerator plants in Switzerland. All the milk samples analysed showed the presence of some PCDFs or PCDDs but still higher levels were found in milk taken from cows grazing in the vicinity of the incinerator. All the identified isomers belonged to the group with chlorine in positions 2, 3, 7 and 8. It is thus apparent that diary products may be an important source of human exposure to this group of compounds. However, much further analysis will be necessary before the health implication of this exposure can be determined.

3.3.3. *Human mother's milk*

To date only a few samples of human mother's milk have been analysed for the occurrence of PCDDs and PCDFs using a complete isomer-specific analysis (Rappe 1985, Nygren *et al.* 1986). These data reveal common levels of TCDD at or slightly above 1 ppt (pg g^{-1}) on fat basis. Assuming a daily intake of 850 ml of milk in a baby with a body weight of 5 kg, this would result in a daily intake of TCDD of 5–10 pg kg^{-1} depending on the fat content of the milk. The calculation would thus indicate that the human-milk levels of TCFDD alone are such that, at least in industrialized countries, the tolerable daily intake could be approached or exceeded.

As shown in Table 7, several congeners other than TCDD are present in milk. The table gives a detailed conversion for one sample of mother's milk and shows that the different calculation methods give sums of TCDD equivalents in the same range, regardless of the different bases of the calculations. In Table 8, which displays the

TABLE 7

Levels of PCDDs and PCDFs in human mother's milk and TCDD equivalents using different methods (analytical data from Rappe 1985)

Isomer	Level (pg g⁻¹ fat)	Method*			
		1	2	3	4
PCDDs					
2,3,7,8-TCDD	1	1	1	1	1
2,3,7,8-PeCDDs	3.6	3.6	0.72	0.36	0.36
2,3,7,8-HxCDDs	24	7.2	0.96	2.4	2.4
2,3,7,8-HpCDDs	38	0	0.038	0.38	0.38
OCDD	225	0	0	0	0
PCDFs					
2,3,7,8-TCDF	3.6	1.188	0.36	0.36	0.36
2,3,7,8-TCDFs	11	3.63	1.1	2.2	1.1
2,3,7,8-HxCDFs	6.1	0.061	0.061	0.61	0.61
HpCDFs	4.4	0	0.0044	0.044	0
OCDF	11	0	0	0	0
SUM TCDD equivalents		16.68	4.24	7.35	6.21
Fat level	2.2				
Levels in milk (pg)		366.94	93.28	161.79	136.62
Intake for a 5-kg Baby (pg kg⁻¹ body weight day⁻¹)		62.38	15.86	27.50	23.23

* 1, Eadon *et al.* (1983); 2, Bellin & Barnes (1985); 3, Denmark (1984); 4, Swiss Federal Office for Environmental Protection (1982).

summarized data for the nine samples of human mother's milk that first became available, only three of these methods have been applied. From the data it is quite apparent that, based on presently possible risk evaluations, all samples would implicate an intake that considerably exceeds the calculated tolerable daily intakes that have been discussed in various countries.

Recently, additional data have been reported from a German study (Fuerst *et al.* 1985) in which analysis of 53 different samples of human mother's milk showed levels of TCDD comparable to those reported by Rappe (1985). However, the detection level for TCDD was 5 pg g⁻¹ fat, the levels of TCDD reported by Rappe being below this figure. Thus, no comparative calculations of the TCDD equivalent content of these milk samples can be performed. Several studies indicating similar or higher levels in many industrialized countries are in process (see Commoner *et al.* in this issue).

3.4. *Impact of MSW incineration*

The TCDD equivalents discussed below for present-day emissions are given with no correction for losses in sampling and do not take into consideration whether the analyses have been performed utilizing "state of the art" techniques. The values have been calculated by the Swedish Environment Protection Board and assume that the present-day average emission is 10 ng TCDD equivalents Nm⁻³. Naturally, these assumptions introduce certain errors, but the evaluation is still valid. The values for future emissions do not involve these assumptions.

TABLE 8

Daily intake of TCDD equivalents from human mother's milk (based on analytical data from Rappe 1985) and calculated for a 5-kg baby consuming 850 ml milk per day

Milk sample (fat level, %)	Daily intake (pg kg^{-1})*		
	Method 1	Method 2	Method 3
Sweden 1 (2.2)	38	16	28
2 (2.5)	93	37	68
3 (4.3)	160	54	90
4 (1.8)	26	12	21
Germany 1 (4.6)	160	55	85
2 (4.6)	220	83	130
3 (2.7)	190	67	100
4 (2.5)	140	54	84
5 (2.5)	110	40	58

* 1, Eadon *et al.* (1983); 2, Bellin & Barnes (1985); 3, Denmark (1984).

Obviously there are also other sources of environmental contamination of PCDDs and PCDFs. The total emission of these compounds in Sweden has been estimated to be 200–300 g y^{-1}. MSW incineration contributes with about 90 g annually. The anticipated technical changes to the incinerators are expected to reduce these emissions to below 10 g y^{-1}. The total annual emission may then be calculated to be in the range 100–200 g y^{-1}.

During recent years, several modifications have been made to existing incinerators. It is thus probable that the earlier contributions from MSW incineration were considerably higher than the present 90 g y^{-1} level.

In addition to these figures, there is the TCDD content of contaminated soot and ash. This will not be discussed further, as it is assumed that this material will be handled and stored in such a way that emission to the environment can be minimized.

3.4.1. *Evaluation*

The risk assessment of the contribution of PCDDs and PCDFs from MSW incineration is rather complicated. The uncertainty with regard to different sources is considerable, and the number of measurements on known sources is limited. Furthermore, the toxicological assessment is inaccurate. This is true for the estimated tolerable daily intake of 1–5 pg kg^{-1} body weight, as well as the use of the concept of TCDD equivalents.

It is apparent from the above discussion that emissions from MSW incinerators do not cause ambient air concentrations of significance to human health. However, the emitted PCDDs and PCDFs have a considerable stability in the environment and undergo significant bioaccumulation. This means that food will be the most important exposure route for man. The few analytical data available so far indicate that fish and marine species may be an important source. Dairy products are other sources, but the sparse data do not allow any estimations of the significance of these sources. For other types of food there are no available data.

All in all, the available analytical data on fish indicate that the tolerable daily intake may be exceeded at single intakes, depending on the species consumed.

The most disturbing problem, however, is the occurrence of PCDDs and PCDFs in human milk. The measured levels of TCDD alone are such that a baby may consume amounts of TCDD that approach or exceed the tolerable daily intake. If the intake is calculated on the basis of TCDD equivalents, the excess intake will be more pronounced. However, due to the uncertainty of such an assessment, this should not be used as an argument against breast feeding. The positive significance of breast feeding is judged to be of higher value than the potential risk involved with the exposure to the contaminants in the milk. This is in agreement with the conclusion of a WHO working group meeting on organochlorines in human breast milk (WHO 1985).

The results of the Swedish study indicates that the contribution to the environment of PCDDs and PCDFs from MSW incineration can be reduced to a comparatively insignificant level when compared to other possible sources. Continuous emissions at or below the level that can be achieved by using the best technology available could then be regarded as acceptable from an environmental point of view when the following aspects are taken into account:

(1) The risk assessment leading to a tolerable intake in the range 1–5 pg kg^{-1} body weight is conservative. A safety factor of 200–1000 has been applied to the LOEL and the NOEL in long-term animal studies.

(2) Available studies indicate that the concept of TCDD equivalents overestimates the effects of a mixture of PCDDs and PCDFs.

(3) There is a pronounced species variation in sensitivity and there is no indication that man is among the most sensitive species. However, there is good reason to believe that infants may be particularly sensitive to these types of compounds (e.g. effects on tissue differentiation and vitamin-A homeostasis).

(4) The suggested action plan for MSW incinerators will reduce their contribution of TCDD. Corresponding action must be taken with respect to other sources.

(5) The present levels of PCDDs and PCDFs in fish and human milk reflects the cumulative effect of many years of emissions. There are reasons to believe that the emissions were higher in earlier years. However, the long half-life of TCDD, and probably also several other PCDDs and PCDFs, means that the environmental levels will only be slowly affected by a decreased emission.

4. Polycyclic aromatic hydrocarbons (PAHs)

4.1. Background

PAHs are formed in combustion processes, especially during impaired combustion efficiency. The primary health risk connected with PAHs is cancer (NCR 1983). The best known PAH is benzo(a)pyrene (B(a)P) which has been used as an index when evaluating lung-cancer risk connected with air pollution in gas works, coke ovens and general air pollution in urban areas (Pike 1983). From the different epidemiological studies the estimated excess lifetime cancer risk is 2–6 × 10^{-4} per ng m^{-3} of B(a)P. Lung-cancer risk from urban air pollution has been estimated to be in the order of 5–10 cases per 100,000 males per year. For Sweden this would mean around 100 cases each year (out of the total number of 2200) (KI 1978, Holmberg & Ahlborg 1983, Cancer Committee 1984).

During recent years, combined chemical analysis and mutagenicity testing of combustion emissions and ambient air has shown that compounds other than pure PAHs make up a large part of the mutagenic activity. An important part is probably PAH-derivatives, for example, those strongly mutagenic nitro-PAHs found in diesel emissions. Chlorinated PAHs are found in waste incineration emissions, which seem to be a specific source of these compounds compared to other types of combustion plants.

4.2. *Impact of MSW incineration*

The emission of PAH may be very high from waste incineration plants if the combustion efficiency is not properly controlled. In well-controlled plants the emission has been judged to be of the same order, or somewhat higher than that from combustion of peat or coal in the same type of plant, but 10–100 times higher than from combustion of oil.

The contribution of PAH and benzo(a)pyrene from MSW incineration to ambient air would, however, only cause a very small excess cancer risk (2×10^{-4} cases per year per 100,000 inhabitants), using the risk factor mentioned above (Pike 1983). There is almost no information available on the health effects of chlorinated PAHs. Chlorination of pyrene has been shown to give mutagenic products (Colmsjö *et al.* 1984). Due to the relatively large emission of chlorinated PAHs from waste incineration, and the concern about long-term effects of other chlorinated hydrocarbons, their emission should not be neglected.

5. Chlorinated benzenes

5.1. *Background*

Chlorinated benzenes have become widely spread environmental pollutants due to their slow biodegradability and their tendency to bioaccumulation. Mono-, di- and tri-chlorobenzene are mostly found in air and water, whilst the less volatile tetra-, penta- and hexa-chlorobenzenes are found more frequently in food and soil. Chlorobenzenes have also been detected in human adipose tissue and mother's milk. The toxicity of chlorobenzenes seems to increase with an increasing degree of chlorination. Target organs in animal toxicity tests are liver and kidney and, at higher doses, the nervous system. The chlorinated benzenes are not mutagenic on Salmonella in the Ames test. Dichlorobenzene caused DNA damage in bacteria, yeast and plants as well as in lymphocytes in exposed humans and hexachlorobenzene was mutagenic, in yeast. Hexachlorobenzene has been shown to be carcinogenic in several studies, mainly causing liver tumours. The U.S. EPA (1985) estimated the human lifetime cancer risk to be $4.9 \times 10^{-4} \ \mu g^{-1} \ m^{-3}$ of hexachlorobenzene in air and $4.9 \times 10^{-5} \ \mu g \ l^{-1}$ in drinking water.

5.2. *Impact of MSW incineration*

The emission of chlorinated benzenes from combustion sources is rather specific for waste incineration, although they may be formed in wood combustion (Rudling *et al.* 1980). They have not been found in coal- or oil-combustion emissions or in automobile exhausts. Some Swedish measurements in ambient air point to concentrations of the same order of magnitude in both urban and rural areas of slightly below 0.1 ng m^{-3}. American measurements point to much higher values (order of magnitude μg m^{-3}) (EPA 1985).

Hexachlorobenzene is the most important chlorinated benzene from an environmental and health point of view, because of its low biodegradability, high bioaccumulation tendency and its toxicity. It has been suggested that municipal waste incineration is the dominant emission source of hexachlorobenzene in Switzerland (Muller 1982), and this might also apply to Sweden.

The maximum contribution of chlorobenzenes to ambient air from MSW incineration was calculated to be 0.1 ng m^{-3} (Table 2), which is of the same order as the background concentration. This concentration is far below the amount giving rise to health effects, even if a safety factor of 1000 is applied. Human cancer risk from hexachlorobenzene, estimated by EPA (1985), implies a lifetime risk of 1×10^{-5} at constant inhalation of 20 ng m^{-3}. The contribution to air concentrations from waste incineration is lower than this value, which might be regarded as a low-risk level. However, the intake of hexachlorobenzene by inhalation is not the only route. At present there is no basis on which to estimate the normal intake of hexachlorobenzene through water and food and the contribution from waste incineration. With regard to the bioaccumulation and carcinogenicity of hexachlorobenzene, a conservative judgement is that the emissions should be reduced as far as possible.

6. Chlorinated phenols

6.1. *Background*

The most widely used chlorophenols are tri-, tetra- and penta-chlorophenol. The chlorinated phenols have become widespread environmental pollutants, mainly due to the use of pentachlorophenol as a fungicide in wood preservation. Mono- and di-chlorophenol are also formed in chlorination of water. Unlike the chlorinated benzenes, chlorinated phenols are not bioaccumulated to the same degree and are cleared faster from the organism after intake.

The mechanism of acute toxicity of chlorinated phenols is the uncoupling of the oxidative phosphorylation in cell mitochondria. This effect, as well as general toxicity, increases with increasing degree of chlorination. Almost all sub-chronic or chronic toxicological studies have been done using pentachlorophenol. The evaluation of these studies is complicated by the fact that technical grade pentachlorophenols are usually contaminated with trace amounts of highly toxic polychlorinated dibenzo-furans and -dioxins. A value of 3 μg kg^{-1} day^{-1} has been recommended by WHO (1984) as the highest acceptable daily intake (ADI) of pentachlorophenol for humans.

The chlorophenols are not mutagenic on Salmonella in the Ames test, but 2,4,6-trichlorophenol and pentachlorophenol were mutagenic in yeast. Cancer tests have been performed with negative results in skin-application tests on mice using chlorophenols. However, 2,4,6-trichlorophenol is carcinogenic after oral administration (lymphoma and leukemia in male rats and liver tumours in mice). Some studies have also shown chlorophenols to be tumour promoters (Kauppinen 1984, Exon 1984). By extrapolation of the results with 2,4,6-trichlorophenol the lifetime human cancer risk 1×10^{-5} (low-risk level) has been estimated to be caused by 10 μg l^{-1} in drinking water, corresponding to an intake of 20 μg day^{-1} (WHO, 1984).

6.2. *Impact of MSW incineration*

Chlorinated phenols are emitted from the combustion of wood but not from combustion of coal or oil. Some attempts have been made to compare the emission from municipal waste incineration to other known emission sources in Sweden, which seem to indicate that the waste incineration is a relatively small source. One typical paper mill emits around 100 times more chlorophenols to water than one waste incineration plant to air. The estimated total emission of chlorophenols of 840 kg year^{-1} (Table 1) can be also be compared with the annual use of pentachlorophenol as fungicide of 50 t in Sweden in 1976.

The maximum contribution to ambient air from MSW incineration has been calculated to be 0.16 ng m^{-3} (Table 2). Assuming 100% uptake through the lungs, this would mean an uptake of 4 ng day^{-1} (0.06 ng kg^{-1} for a 70-kg person). Compared to the recommended ADI value of 3 μg kg^{-1}, this contribution is very small. Comparing what might be considered a low-risk level for carcinogenic effects, 20 μg day^{-1} of 2,4,6-trichlorophenol, the contribution is also very small.

Even though the contribution of intake via food and water is not known, we regard the emission of chlorophenols from waste incineration as posing no health hazard. However, their presence in the combustion process may be an important precursor to the formation of chlorinated dibenzo-furans and -dioxins.

7. Phthalates

Phthalic acid esters are widely used as plasticizers especially in PVC, of which diethylhexylphthalate (DEHP) is the most common. DEHP has caused liver tumours in rats and mice after long-term administration of very high doses. It has been discussed that this might be an indirect effect from peroxisome induction in liver cells, which releases H_2O_2 and other reactive products, because DEHP shows only slight or no genotoxic effects in mutagenicity tests and does not bind to DNA *in vivo* (Thomas and Thomas, 1984; Turnbull and Rodricks, 1985; Jäckh *et al*, 1984). Phthalates are widely distributed in the environment. High amounts of PVC material ends up in the waste incineration plant. The phthalates are not chemically bound to PVC and are consequently released during heating. Therefore, high amounts of phthalates are released during start-up conditions of waste incineration. It has been shown in Swedish measurements that the amount of phthalates decreases, due to decomposition, when the combustion efficiency increases (Moström *et al.* 1985).

The emission of phthalates from MSW incineration in Sweden has been estimated to be approximately 9 t y^{-1} (Table 1), which is relatively low compared to the 200 y^{-1} estimated total emission from industry. One single PVC working plant may emit 10 t y^{-1} (Nilsson 1983).

The air-quality calculations (Table 2) give the highest contribution of phthalates to ambient air from a waste incineration plant to be around 1 ng m^{-3}. This contribution is regarded as negligible compared to the much larger normal intake via food. It is also small compared to the background contamination of ambient air which, according to Ganning *et al.* (1984), is as high as 0.4–3 μg m^{-3} over the open sea.

8. Mutagenic acitivity

8.1. *Background*

Emission of carcinogens from combustion may imply a long-term health risk even at low doses. The most important carcinogenic compounds have not yet been identified in combustion emissions. During recent years, a short-term mutagenicity test, the Ames

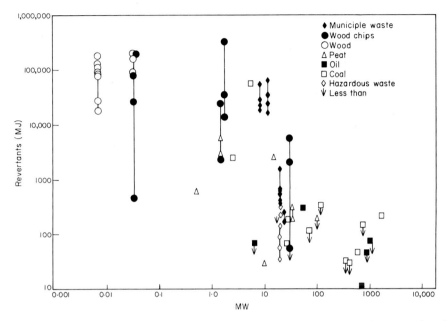

Fig. 1. Mutagenic activity in emissions from different Swedish combustion sources. The mutagenic activity is expressed as revertants per magajoule of fuel and compared to the size of the plant.

Salmonella assay, has been applied to smoke gas condensates to detect mutagenic and potentially carcinogenic activity. The results of such a test can be used, for example, to compare different emission control devices, especially together with chemical analysis. Mutagenic activity in emissions from the same kind of combustion source can also be used as a rough measure of carcinogenic activity, especially if combined with data on emission of PAHs or other organic substances. However, comparisons between different kinds of combustion sources may be misleading. For example, automobile exhausts contain highly mutagenic, but not necessarily strongly carcinogenic, nitro-PAHs, and waste incineration emissions contain strongly carcinogenic chlorinated dibenzodioxins that are not mutagenic (Holmberg & Ahlborg 1983, Victorin & Ahlborg 1985).

8.2. *Impact of MSW incineration*

The emissions from four different MSW incineration plants have been collected and tested in the Ames assay. Extracts from particles, condensate and XAD columns were combined and tested with the Salmonella strains TA 98 and TA 100, with and without metabolic activation. Figure 1 shows the results with the Salmonella strain giving the highest response together with results from other types of combustion sources. All samples have been collected and tested in principally the same manner and most of these results have been presented in several Swedish reports (see Victorin & Ahlborg 1985).

These mutagenicity studies have shown that MSW incineration may give rise to a relatively high emission of mutagenic activity under less well-controlled combustion efficiency conditions, thereby probably affecting the content of mutagenic and potentially carcinogenic compounds in the surrounding ambient air. Consequently, efforts should be made to reduce the emission of mutagenic activity to levels that could be attainable in waste incineration, as well as in incineration of other fuels.

9. Conclusions

Of the various organic compounds emitted from MSW incineration, the chlorinated dioxins and dibenzofurans are of the greatest concern from the public health point of view. Efforts must be made to reduce these emissions. Alarmingly high concentrations have been found in human breast milk and environmental samples. With combustion optimization and application of advanced flue-gas cleaning techniques the emission may be reduced to 0.1 ng m^{-3} (TCDD equivalents, Eadon *et al.* 1983). With this emission level, MSW incineration would probably be only a minor source to the environmental contamination and can be considered acceptable as there is no indication that humans belong to the most sensitive species. The recommended tolerable daily intake of 1–5 pg kg^{-1} body weight of TCDD probably provides a sufficient margin of safety.

The presence of other chlorinated organic compounds in emissions from MSW combustion has also been documented. Among the chlorobenzenes, hexachlorobenzene is the most important, from an environmental and health point of view, due to its low biodegradability, high bioaccumulation tendency and its toxicity. MSW is probably an important emission source for hexachlorobenzene, and these emissions should be reduced as far as possible. Emission of chlorophenols from well-functioning plants is regarded as posing no health hazard. The present knowledge of health effects of chlorinated PAHs does not allow a risk estimation to be made.

Other types of chlorinated organic compounds have not been analysed in the Swedish investigations. However, the combination of optimized combustion and advanced flue-gas cleaning, resulting in emissions of less than 0.1 ng m^{-3} TCDD equivalents, will probably prevent emissions of other halogenated organic compounds of public-health significance. This statement is probably valid also for other organic emissions such as PAH, phthalates and mutagenic substances. Generally these emissions are high with the technology commonly used at present for MSW combustion as compared to other fuels.

Acknowledgements

This work was supported by grants from the Swedish Environmental Protection Board (No. 5311236-3).

References

Bandiera, S., Sawyer, T., Romkes, M., Zmudzka, B., Safe, L., Mason, G., Keys, B. & Safe, S. (1984), Polychlorinated dibenzofurans (PCDFs): effects of structure on binding to the 2,3,7,8-CDD cytosolic receptor protein, AHH induction and toxicity, *Toxicology*, *32*, 131–144.

Bellin, J. S. & Barnes, (1985), Health hazard assessment for chlorinated dioxins and dibenzofurans other than 2,3,7,8-TCDD *US EPA Draft*. Update 1985.

Berry, D. L., DiGiovanni, J., Juchau, M. R., Bracken, W. M., Gleason, G. L. & Slaga, T. J. (1978), Lack of tumor-promoting ability of certain environmental chemicals in a two-stage mouse skin tumorigenesis assay, *Research Communications in Chemical Pathology and Pharmacology*, *20*, 101.

Bradlaw, J. A., Garthoff, L. N., Hurley, N. E. & Firestone, D. (1980), Comparative induction of aryl hydrocarbon hydroxylase *in vitro* by analogues of dibenzo-*p*-dioxin, *Food and Cosmetic Toxicology*, *18*, 627–635.

Brewster, D. W., Madhukar, B. V. & Matsumura, F. (1982), Influence of 2,3,7,8-TCDD on the protein composition of the plasma membrane of hepatic cells from the rat, *Biochemical and Biophysical Research Communications*, *107*, 68–74.

Bronzetti, G., Bauer, C., Corsi, C., Del Caratore, R., Nieri, R. & Paolini, M. (1983), Mutagenicity study of TCDD and ashes from urban incinerator *in vitro* and *in vivo* using yeast D7 strain, *Chemosphere*, *12*, 549–553.

Cancer Committee (1984), *Report from the Swedish Governmental Cancer Committee*, SOU 1984, p. 67 (in Swedish with English summary).

Clark, D. A. Gauldie, J., Szewczuk, M. R. & Sweeney, G. (1981), Enhanced suppressor cell activity as a mechanism of immunosuppression by 2,3,7,8-tetrachlorodibenzo-*p*-dioxin (41275), *Proceedings of the Society for Experimental Biology and Medicine*, *168*, 290–299.

Clark, D. A., Sweeney, G., Safe, S., Hancock, E., Kilburn, D. G. & Gauldie, J. (1983), Cellular and genetic basis for suppression of cytotoxic T-cell generation by halo-aromatic hydrocarbons, *Immunopharmacology*, *6*, 143–153.

Cohen, G. M., Bracken, W. M., Iyer, R. P., Berry, D. L., Skelkirk, J. K. & Slaga, T. J. (1979), Anti-carcinogenic effects of 2,3,7,8-tetrachlorodibenzo-*p*-dioxin on benzo(a)pyrene and 7,12-dimethylbenz(a)anthracene tumor initiation and its relationship to DNA binding, *Cancer Research*, *39*, 4027–4033.

Colmsjö, A., Rannug, A. & Rannug, U. (1984), Some chloro-derivatives of polynuclear aromatic hydrocarbons are potent mutagens in Salmonella typhimurium, *Mutation Research*, *135*, 21–29.

Commoner, B. (1984), Environmental and economic analysis of alternative municipal solid waste disposal technologies. I. An assessment of the risks due to emissions of chlorinated dioxins and dibenzofurans from proposed New York City incinerators. May 1.

Denmark (1984), *Dannelse og Spredning av Dioxiner Isaer i Forbindelse Med Affaldsforbraending* (*Formation and Emission of Dioxins Especially in Connection with Waste Incineration*). Miljöstyrelsen, Strandgade 29, 1401 Copenhagen (in Danish).

DiGiovanni, J., Berry D. L., Juchau, M. R. & Slaga, T. J. (1979), 2,3,7,8-Tetrachlorodibenzo-*p*-dioxin: potent anticarcinogenic activity in CD-1 mice, *Biochemical and Biophysical Research Communications*, *86*, 577–584.

DiGiovanni, J., Berry, D. L., Gleason, G. L., Kishore, G. S. & Slaga, T. J. (1980), Time-dependent inhibition by 2,3,7,8-tetrachlorodibenzo-*p*-dioxin of skin tumorogenesis with polycyclic hydrocarbons, *Cancer Research*, *40*, 1580–1587.

Eadon, G., Aldous, K., Hilker, D., O'Keefe, P. & Smith R. (1983), Chemical data on air samples from the Binghampton State Office Building. Memo from Center for Laboratories and Research, New York State Department of Health, Albany, NY 12201, 7 July 1983.

EPA (1985), *Health Assessment Document for Chlorinated Benzenes*, U.S. Environmental Protection Agency, Washington DC.

Exon, J. (1984), A review of chlorinated phenols, *Veterinary and Human Toxicology*, *26*, 508–521.

Fuerst, P., Meemken, H.-A. & Groebel, W. (1985), *Bericht Ueber die Untersuchung von Frauenmilch auf Polychlorinierte Dibenzo-dioxine und -furane 1984/85* (*Report on an Investigation of Contents of Polychlorinated Dibenzo-dioxin and -furan in mother's milk 1984/85*), Chem. Landesuntersuchuns Amt Nordrhein-Westfalen, 400, Muenster, Sperlich Strasse 19, B.R.D.

Ganning, A. E., Brunk, U. & Dallner, G. (1984), Phthalate esters and their effects on the liver, *Hepatology*, *4*, 541–547.

Geiger, L. E. & Neal, R. A. (1981), Mutagenicity testing of 2,3,7,8-tetrachlorodibenzo-*p*-dioxin in hiptidine auxotrophs of Salmonella typhimurium, *Toxicology and Applied Pharmacology*, *59*, 125–129.

Gierthy, J. P. & Crane, D. (1984), Reversible inhibition of *in vitro* epithelial cell proliferation by 2,3,7,8-tetrachlorobenzo-*p*-dioxin, *Toxicology and Applied Pharmacology*, *74*, 91–98.

Gilbert, P., Saint-Ruf, G., Poncelet, F. & Mercier, M. (1980), Genetic effects of chlorinated anilines and azobenzenes on Salmonella typhimurium, *Archives of Environmental Contamination and Toxicology*, *9*, 553–541.

Grant, D. L. (1977), *Proceedings of 12th Annual Workshop on Pesticide Residues Analysis*. Winnipeg, Canada, p. 251.

Håkansson, H. & Ahlborg, U. G. (1985), The effect of 2,3,7,8-tetrachlorodibenzo-*p*-dioxin (TCDD) on the uptake, distribution and excretion of a single dose of 11,12-3H-retinylacetate and on the vitamin A status in the rat, *Journal of Nutrition*, *115*, 759–771.

Holmberg, B. & Ahlborg, U. G. (eds) (1983), Consensus report, Mutagenicity and carcinogenicity of car exhausts and coal combustion emission, *Environmental Health Perspectives*, *47*, 1–130.

Holmstedt, B. (1980), Review article: prolegomena to Seveso, *Archives of Toxicology*, *44*, 211–230.

Hussain, S., Ehrenberg, L., Lofroth, G. & Gejvall, T. (1972), Mutagenic effects of TCDD on bacterial systems, *Ambio*, *1*, 32–33.

Ideo, G., Bellati, G., Bellobuono, A., Mocarelli, P., Marocchi, A. & Brambilla, P. (1982), Increased urinary D-glucaric acid excretion by children living in an area polluted with tetra-chlorodibenzo-*p*-dioxin (TCDD), *Clinical Chemical Acta*, *120*, 273–283.

Jäckh, R., Rhodes, C., Grasso, P., Carter, J. T. (1984), Genotoxicity studies on di-(2-ethylhexyl)phthalate and adipate, and toxicity studies on di(2-ethylhexyl)phthalate in the rat and Marmoset, *Food Chemistry and Toxicology 22*, 151–155.

Jensen, D. S. & Hummel, R. A. (1982), Secretion of TCDD in milk and cream following the feeding of TCDD on lactating cows, *Bulletin of Environmental Contamination and Toxicology*, *29*, 440–446.

Kauppinen, T. (1984), *Chlorophenols. Nordic Expert Group for Documentation of Occupational Exposure Limits*, Arbete och Hälsa 1984:46, the Swedish Worker Protection Board (in Swedish with English summary).

KI (1978), Air pollution and cancer: risk assessment methodology and epidemiological evidence, Report of a task group, *Environmental Health Perspectives*, *22*, 1–12.

Kimbrough, R. D., Falk, H. & Stehr, P. (1984), Health implications of 2,3,7,8-tetrachlorodibenzo-*p*-dioxin (TCDD) contamination of residential soil, *Journal of Toxicology and Environmental Health*, *14*, 47–93.

Knutson, J. C. & Poland, A. (1980), Keratinization of mouse teratoma cell line XB produced by 2,3,7,8-tetrachlorodibenzo-*p*-dioxin: an *in vitro* model of toxicity, *Cell*, *22*, 27–36.

Knutson, J. C. & Poland, A. (1984), 2,3,7,8-Tetrachlorodibenzo-*p*-dioxin: examination of biochemical effects involved in the proliferation and differentiation of XB cells, *Journal of Cell Physiology*, *121*, 143–151.

Kociba, R. J., Keyes, D. G., Beyer, J. E., Carreon, R. M., Wade, C. E., Dittenber, D., Kalnins, R., Frauson, L., Park, C. N., Barnard, S., Hummel, R. & Humiston, C. G. (1978), Results of a two-year chronic toxicity and oncogenicity study of 2,3,7,8-tetrachlorodibenzo-*p*-dioxin (TCDD) in rats, *Toxicology and Applied Pharmacology*, *46*, 279–303.

Matsumura, F., Brewster, D. W., Madhukar, B. V. & Bombick, D. W. (1984), Alteration of rat hepatic plasma membrane functions, by 2,3,7,8-tetrachlorodibenzo-*p*-dioxin (TCDD), *Archives of Environmental Contamination and Toxicology*, *13*, 509–515.

McConnell, E. E., Moore, J. A., Haseman, J. K. & Harris, M. W. (1978), The comparative toxicity of chlorinated dibenzo-*o*-dioxins in mice and guinea-pigs, *Toxicology and Applied Pharmacology*, *44*, 334–356.

Mortelmans, K., Haworth, S., Speck, W. & Zeiger, E. (1984), Mutagenicity testing of agent orange components and related chemicals, *Toxicology and Applied Pharmacology*, *75*, 137–146.

Moström, R., Dahlgren, O. & Sandström, G. (1985), *Flue Gas Measurements and Analysis Performed at the Incineration Plant Ålidhem in Umeå, Sweden*, Report no. 210, *The Subthermal Engineering Research Institute*, Stockholm (in Swedish).

Muller, M. D. (1982), Hexachlorobenzol in der Schweiz—Ausmass und Hintergrunde der Umweltkontamination, *Chimia*, *36*, 436–445.

Murray, F. J., Smith, F. A., Nitscke, K. D., Humiston, C. G., Kociba, R. J. & Schwetz, B. A. (1979), Three-generation reproduction study of rats given 2,3,7,8-tetrachlorodibenzo-*p*-dioxin (TCDD) in the diet, *Toxicology and Applied Pharmacology*, *50*, 241–252.

NCI (1979a), Bioassay of dibenzo-*p*-dioxin for possible carcinogenicity, *NCI Carcinogen Tech. Rep. Cer. 122*.

NCI (1979b), Bioassay of 2,7-dichlorodibenzo-*p*-dioxin (DCDD), *NCI Carcinogen Tech. Rep. Cer. 123*.

NIH (1980), Bioassay of 1,2,3,6,7,8- and 1,2,3,7,8,9-hexachlorodibenzo-*p*-dioxin for possible carcinogenicity (gavage). *D.H.H.S. Publications No. (NIH) 8-1754*.

NIH (1982a), Carcinogenesis bioassay of 2,3,7,8-tetrachlorodibenzo-*p*-dioxin (CAS No. 1746-01-6) in Osborne-Mendel rats and B6C3F$_1$ mice (gavage study), *NTP Technical Report Series, No. 209*.

NIH (1982b), Carcinogenesis bioassay of 2,3,7,8-tetrachlorodibenzo-*p*-dioxin (CAS No. 1746-01-6) in Swiss-Webster mice (dermal study), *NTP Technical Report Series, No. 201*.

Nilsson, R. (1983), *Report from the Swedish Environmental Protection Board on Phthalates* (In Swedish). Swedish Environmental Protection Board, Stockholm.

Nisbet, I.C.T. & Paxton, M. B. (1982), Statistical aspects of three-generation studies of the reproductive toxicity of TCDD and 2,4,5-T, *American Statistician*, 36, 290–298.

NRC (1983), *Polycyclic Aromatic Hydrocarbons: Evaluation of Sources and Effects*, National Research Council, Washington DC, U.S.A.

Nygren, M., Rappe, C., Lindström, G., Hansson, M., Bergqvist, P.-A., Marklund, S., Domellöf, L., Hardell, L. & Olsson, M. (1986), Identification of 2,3,7,8-substituted polychlorinated dioxins (PCDDs) and dibenzofurans (PCDFs) in environmental and human samples. In *Chlorinated dioxins and Dibenzofurans in Perspective* (Rappe, C., Choudhary, G. & Keith, L., eds), pp. 17–34. Lewis Publ. Inc., Chelsea, MI, U.S.A.

Ontario Ministry of the Environment (1985), Polychlorinated dibenzo-*p*-dioxins (PCDDs) and polychlorinated dibenzofurans (PCDFs), *Scientific Criteria Document for Standard Development No. 4-84*.

Pike, M. (1983), Human-cancer risk assessment. Appendix C. In *Polycyclic Aromatic Hydrocarbons: Evaluation of Sources and Effects*, National Research Council, Washington DC, U.S.A.

Pitot, H. C., Goldsworthy, T., Campbell, H. A. & Poland, A. (1980), Quantitative evaluation of the promotion by 2,3,7,8-tetrachlorodibenzo-*p*-dioxin of hepatocarcinogenesis from diethylnitrosamine, *Cancer Research*, 40, 3616–3620.

Pohjanvirta, R. & Tuomisto, J. (1986), Han/Wistar Rats are exceptionally resistant to TCDD. II. *Archives of Toxicology*, in press.

Poiger, H. & Schlatter, C. (1986), Pharmacokinetics of 2,3,7,8-TCDD in man, Proceedings from Dioxin-85, Bayreuth, *Chemosphere*, 15, 1489–1494.

Poland, A. & Knutson, J. C. (1982), 2,3,7,8-Tetrachlorodibenzo-*p*-dioxin and related halogenated aromatic hydrocarbons: examination of the mechanism of toxicity, *Annual Reviews of Pharmacology and Toxicology*, 22, 517–554.

Poland, A., Glover, E. & Kende, A. S. (1976), Stereospecific, high affinity binding of 2,3,7,8-tetrachlorodibenzo-*p*-dioxin by hepatic cytosol. Evidence that the binding species is receptor for induction of aryl hydrocarbon hydroxylase, *Journal of Biological Chemistry*, 251, 4936–4946.

Puhvel, S. M., Ertl, D. C. & Lynberg, C. A. (1984), Increased epidermal transglutaminase activity following 2,3,7,8-tetrachlorodibenzo-*p*-dioxin: *in vivo* and *in vitro* studies with mouse skin, *Toxicology and Applied Pharmacology*, 73, 42–47.

Rappe, C. (1985), Problems in analysis of PCDDs and PCDFs and the presence of these compounds in human milk. Paper presented at the WHO Consultation on Organohalogen Compounds in Human Milk and Related Hazards, Bilthoven, The Netherlands, 9–11 January.

Rappe, C., Nygren, M., Lindström, G., Buser, H. R., Blaser, O. & Wuthrich, C. (1985), Polychlorinated dibenzofurans (PCDFs) and dibenzo-*p*-dioxins (PCDDs) in cow milk from various locations in Switzerland (to be published).

Regione Lombardia (1984), Final Report and Recommendations of the International Steering Committee, 6th Meeting, Milano, 19–21 February 1984, pp. 1–17.

Rice, R. H. & Cline, P. R. (1984), Opposing effects of 2,3,7,8-tetrachlorodibenzo-*p*-dioxin and hydrocortisone on growth and differentiation of cultured malignant human keratinocytes, *Carcinogenesis*, 5, 367–371.

Rogers, A. M., Andersen, M. E. & Back, K. C. (1982), Mutagenicity of 2,3,7,8-tetrachlorodibenzo-*p*-dioxin and perfluoro-*n*-decanoic acid in L5178Y mouse-lymphoma cells, *Mutation Research*, 105, 445–449.

Rudling, L., Ahling, B. & Löfroth, G. (1980), Chemical and biological characterization of emissions from combustion of wood and wood-chips in a small central heating furnace and from combustion of wood in closed fireplace stoves, *SNV PM 1331*, Swedish Environment Protection Board (in Swedish with English summary).

Schoeny, R. (1982), Mutagenicity testing of chlorinated biphenyls and chlorinated dibenzofurans, *Mutation Research*, 10, 45.

Seiler, J. P. (1972), *A Survey on the Mutagenicity of Various Pesticides*, Swiss Federal Research Station for Arboriculture, Viticulture and Horticulture, CH-8820 Wädenswill, Switzerland.

Swiss Federal Office for Environmental Protection (1982), *Umweltungsbelastung durch Dioxine* (*Environmental Pollution Due to Dioxins and Furans from Chemical Rubbish Incineration Plant*), Schriften veighe Umweltschutz, No. 5, Bundesamt Fur Umweltschutz, Bern.

Thiess, A. M., Frantzel-Beyme, R. & Link, R. (1982), Mortality study of persons exposed to dioxin in a trichlorophenol-process accident that occurred in the BASF AG on November 17, 1953, *American Journal of Industrial Medicine* 179–189.

Thomas J. A., Thomas M. J. (1984). Biological effects of di-(2-ethylhexyl) phthalate and other phthalic acid esters. CRC Crit Rev. Toxicol *13*, 283–317.

Thunberg, T. & Håkansson, H. (1983), Vitamin A (retinol) status in the Gunn rat: the effect of 2,3,7,8-tetrachlorodibenzo-*p*-dioxin, *Archives of Toxicology*, *53*, 225–233.

Thunberg, T., Ahlborg, U. G. & Johnsson, H. (1979), Vitamin A (retinol) status in the rat after a single oral dose of 2,3,7,8-tetrachlorodibenzo-*p*-dioxin, *Archives of Toxicology*, *42*, 265–274.

Thunberg, T., Ahlborg, U. G., Håkansson, H., Krantz, C. & Monier, M. (1980), Effect of 2,3,7,8-tetrachlorodibenzo-*p*-dioxin on the hepatic storage of retinol in rats with different dietary supplies of vitamin A (retinol), *Archives of Toxicology*, *45*, 273–285.

Toth, K., Somfai-Relle, S., Sugar, J. & Bence, J. (1979), Carcinogenicity testing of herbicide 2,4,5-trichlorophenoxyethanol containing dioxin and of pure dioxin in Swiss mice, *Nature*, *278*, 548–549.

Turnbull, D. & Rodricks, J. V. (1985), Assessment of possible carcinogenic risk to humans resulting from exposure to di(2-ethylhexyl)phthalate (DEHP), *Journal of the American College of Toxicology*, *4*, (2), 111–145.

Umweltsbundesamt (1985), *Sachstand Dioxine—Stand November 1984*, Berichte 5/85, Erich Schmidt Verlag, Berlin.

van Miller, J. P., Marlor, R. J. & Allen, J. R. (1976), Tissue distribution and excretion of tritiated tetrachlorodibenzo-*p*-dioxin in non-human primates and rats, *Food and Cosmetic Toxicology*, *14*, 31–34.

Victorin, K. & Ahlborg, U. (1985), Carcinogenic and mutagenic compounds from energy generations—health effects. In *Mutagens and Carcinogens from the Production and Use of Energy*, Report No. 800901-11 to the Nordic Council of Ministers, MIL-2.

WHO (1984), *Guidelines for Drinking Water Quality*, WHO, Geneva.

WHO (1985), *Organohalogen Compounds in Human Milk and Related Hazards.* Report on a WHO consultation, Bilthoven 9–11 January 1985. European Regional Programme on Chemical Safety.

SOURCES AND RELATIVE IMPORTANCE OF PCDD AND PCDF EMISSIONS*

Christoffer Rappe, Rolf Andersson, Pers-Anders Bergqvist, Christina Brohede, Marianne Hansson, Lars-Owe Kjeller, Gunilla Lindström, Stellan Marklund, Martin Nygren, Stephen E. Swanson, Mats Tysklind and Karin Wiberg ‡

(*Received January 1987, revised March 1987*)

Polychlorinated dioxins (PCDD) and dibenzofurans (PCDF) have been identified in technical products and pesticides, most of which are not very widely used today. Other sources are incinerators of various types like MSW incinerators, hazardous waste incinerators and industrial incinerators. PCDDs and PCDFs have also been identified in exhausts from cars running on leaded gasoline with halogenated additives. Background levels of PCDDs and PCDFs have been identified in fish and other aquatic organisms from the Great Lakes and the Baltic Sea, and also in human adipose tissue samples from U.S.A., Canada, Sweden, Japan and Vietnam as well as in samples of breast milk from Sweden, Denmark, West Germany, the Netherlands, Yugoslavia and Vietnam. The isomeric pattern in all these biological samples is very similar. The relative importance of different sources to the general background is difficult to estimate although the contribution of direct inhalation from point sources like MSW incinerators is small.

Key Words—PCDDs, PCDFs, municipal incinerators, automobile exhausts, paper mills, environmental samples, adipose tissue, human milk.

1. Introduction

Polychlorinated dibenzo-*p*-dioxins (PCDDs) and polychlorinated dibenzofurans (PCDFs) are two series of tricyclic, almost planar, aromatic compounds that exhibit similar physical, chemical, and biological properties. These compounds, the subject of much concern in recent years, have been involved in a number of incidents: the chemical plant accident in Séveso, Italy, in 1976; the herbicide spraying program in Vietnam in the late 1960s; the Yusho disease in Japan in 1968 and Yu-cheng disease in Taiwan in 1979; the poisonings at horse arenas in Missouri, U.S.A., in 1971 and in Times Beach, MO, U.S.A., in 1982–83; and in the Love Canal incident in Niagara Falls, NY, U.S.A.

The chemical structures and numbering of these hazardous compounds are given in Fig. 1. The number of chlorine atoms in these compounds can vary between one and eight to produce up to 75 PCDD and 135 PCDF positional isomers.

2. Sources of PCDDs and PCDFs

2.1. *Commercial and technical products*

During the 1960s and 1970s most of the interest was focused on the PCDD and PCDF contamination in technical products like 2,4,5-T and other chlorophenoxy acids, penta-

---

* Presented at the ISWA–WHO–DAKOFA specialized seminar, *Emissions of Trace Organics from Municipal Solid Waste Incinerators*, Copenhagen, 20–22 January 1987.
‡ Department of Organic Chemistry, University of Umeå, S-901 87 Umeå, Sweden.
Waste Management & Research (1987) 5, 225–237

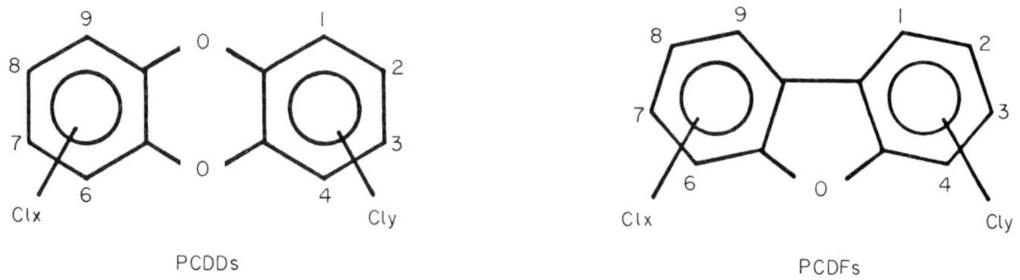

Fig. 1. Formulae for PCDDs and PCDFs.

chlorophenol and other chlorinated phenols, and PCB. Levels were found to vary batchwise, but the analyses were mostly non-isomer specific. The major contaminant in 2,4,5-T was 2,3,7,8-tetra-CDD, normally in the lower ppm range or less. In general, technical pentachlorophenols were found to be the most contaminated products, levels were reported in the range of 1000 ppm, mainly for octa-CDD, but also for a multitude of lower chlorinated congeners (Rappe 1984).

In many industrialized countries, the use of products contaminated by PCDDs and PCDFs has been significantly reduced. For instance 2,4,5-T, earlier a major herbicide in most countries, is now only produced and used in New Zealand and PCB is being phased-out as dielectric fluid in transformers and capacitors in most countries during the 1980s.

2.2. Municipal incinerators

In 1977–78 Olie *et al.* (1977) and Buser & Bosshardt (1978) reported that a series of PCDDs and PCDFs could be found in fly ash samples collected in the electrostatic precipitator of municipal solid waste (MSW) incinerators. Buser & Bosshardt (1978) studied fly ash from a MSW incinerator and from an industrial heating facility, both located in Switzerland. In the former, the total level of PCDDs was reported to be 0.2 ppm and 0.1 ppm for PCDFs. In the industrial incinerator, the levels were 0.6 ppm and 0.3 ppm, respectively. Since then a great number of reports from Europe, U.S.A., Canada, and Asia have confirmed the original findings. However, for many years interest was focused on the analysis of fly ash samples and not on the analysis of the total emissions, due to sampling problems.

Most of the analyses of samples from incinerators have been made using non-validated and non-isomer-specific sampling and analytical methods. Recent studies show the presence of a multitude of PCDD and PCDF congeners, in fact all isomers seem to be present. Moreover, a striking similarity in the isomeric pattern of PCDDs and PCDFs was found between samples from different incinerators (see Rappe *et al.* 1985, Marklund *et al.* 1986).

Various models have been used to convert a multitude of levels of more or less toxic PCDDs and PCDFs into a more simple expression like "TCDD equivalents" or "toxic equivalents" (see Bellin & Barnes 1985). In Sweden, and in this report, the approach discussed by Eadon *et al.* (1983) has been used.

Emissions from MSW incinerators operating under good conditions are in the range 1–100 ng TCDD equivalents m^{-3} resulting in total annual emissions of 1–100 g of TCDD equivalents from a normal size MSW incinerator (50,000–200,000 t y^{-1}) (see WHO 1986 and Suess in this issue).

Chlorine, organic chlorine compounds or inorganic chlorides are possible chlorine sources for the formation of PCDDs and PCDFs as well as other chloroaromatic compounds formed during combustion. Churney *et al.* (unpublished) have studied the chlorine content in the MSW, and they report that the major chlorine source is plastic material like PVC and bleached and unbleached paper.

Direct evidence for the conversion of PVC to PCDDs and PCDFs has recently been reported by Marklund *et al.* (1986) who found that laboratory pyrolysis of PVC results in the formation of PCDDs and PCDFs, mainly hexa- and hepta-CDDs and tetra- to hepta-CDFs. In many cases the isomeric patterns seem to be similar to those found in emissions from MSW incinerators.

Analyses reported from 1986 by Swedish laboratories and others have followed the proposed Nordic Standards (see Jansson & Bergvall and Rappe *et al.*, in this issue). The improved method employs ^{13}C-labelled spiking compounds to correct for losses during sampling and analyses.

2.3. *Hazardous waste incinerators*

Hazardous waste incinerators have also been the object of public concern especially those where PCB is being burned. However, available data indicate that emissions from such incinerators operating under good conditions are of the same magnitude as emissions from MSW incinerators. The isomeric patterns of PCDDs and PCDFs are similar to those reported from MSW incinerators (Rappe *et al.* 1984, Marklund *et al.* 1986).

2.4. *Industrial processes*

In a recent report, Marklund *et al.* (1986) identified industrial processes like copper smelters and electrical arcing furnaces in steel mills as sources of environmental contamination of PCDDs and PCDFs. The copper smelter used scrap copper containing PVC-coated wires and cords. In the steel mill, a high portion of the alloys or stainless steel was recycled. This recycled material was contaminated by PVC or polychlorinated paraffins. Very little data has been reported, but emissions from these sources seem to be of the same magnitude as emissions from MSW incinerators. However, due to a larger number of units, the total emissions from these industrial processes could exceed the emissions from MSW incinerators.

2.5. *Automobiles*

Ballschmiter *et al.* (1986) identified a series of PCDDs and PCDFs in used motor oil from automobiles. These authors also reported on a similarity in the isomeric pattern of the PCDFs found in this matrix and in samples from MSW incinerators. Ballschmiter *et al.* (1986) suggest chlorinated additives in the motor oil or in the gasoline as possible sources for the PCDDs and PCDFs, but no quantitative data is given (amount of PCDDs and PCDFs per km). Also very recently Marklund *et al.* (1987) reported on a study where real car exhausts were analysed for PCDDs and PCDFs. The test cars were collected in two groups: (1) cars equipped with a catalytic converter using unleaded gasoline with no halogenated scavengers, and (2) cars with no catalytic converter using leaded gasoline (0.15 g L^{-1}) and a dichloroethane scavenger (0.1 g L^{1}). Before test runs the motor oil was exchanged in all cars.

No PCDDs or PCDFs could be identified in the cars using the unleaded gasoline, while the emission average from the cars running on leaded gasoline was found to be 30–540 pg km^{-1} of TCDD equivalents (Eadon). It was assumed that the chlorinated scavenger (dichloroethane) was the precursor to the PCDDs and PCDFs formed. It was also estimated that the total amount of PCDDs and PCDFs from cars in Sweden using leaded gasoline with halogenated scavengers is in the range 10–100 g TCDD equivalents per year (see Commoner *et al.* in this issue).

Rappe *et al.* (1987) also reported an extremely close similarity between the isomeric patterns of the tetra- and penta-CDFs found in automobile exhausts and in emissions from MSW incinerators and steel mills (Fig. 2).

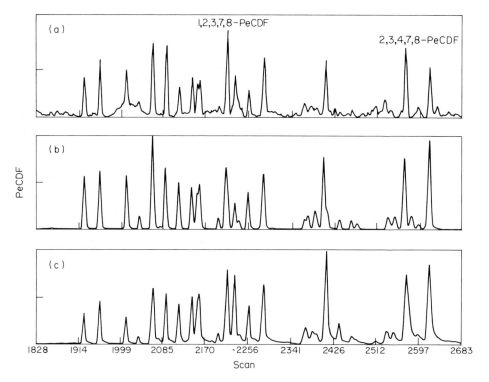

Fig. 2. Fragmentograms of penta-CDFs in samples from: (a) car exhausts, (b) an MSW incinerator, and (c) dust from a baghouse in a steel mill.

A mixture of dichloro- and dibromo-ethane is most frequently used as scavenger for the leaded gasoline. This mixture can produce the fully chlorinated and the fully brominated PCDDs and PCDFs as well as the mixed chloro/bromo compounds, where, theoretically, 5020 different congeners exist. The brominated and mixed chloro/bromo congeners have not been studied toxicologically, but it seems quite plausible to assume that they have the same toxicological properties as the chlorinated compounds.

2.6. *Burning of coal, peat and wood*

The emissions of PCDDs and PCDFs from coal-fired power plants (Kimble & Gross 1980) wood stoves (Nestrick & Lamparski 1982) and peat burning (Marklund *et al.*

1986) seem to be very low when calculated per m^3 flue gas. However, the very high flow rates and large number of units could make a significant total contribution.

3. Levels of PCDDs and PCDFs in environmental samples

3.1. *Air and particulate content*

Due to sampling and analytical problems, very few data are available on the levels of PCDDs and PCDFs in normal urban air. Samples of air particulates from Washington DC, and St Louis, MO, U.S.A. have been analysed by Crummett *et al.* (1985) and Czuczwa & Hites (1986). Crummett *et al.* (1985) report on isomer-specific analyses for tetra-CDDs and hexa-CDDs while Czuczwa & Hites (1986) only report a congener profile and do not discuss any specific isomers. In both studies, octa-CDD was found to be a major constituent, reported in levels of 150–200 ppb. The level of 2,3,7,8-tetra-CDD was 5–50 ppt and of 2,3,7,8-tetra-CDF was 100–380 ppt.

Recently, Oehme *et al.* (1986) reported on a study where urban air was investigated by high-volume sampling of 1000 m^3 of air using a glass fibre filter and polyurethane foam as collection media. Measurable amounts of a large number of PCDDs and PCDFs were found in cities and industrialized regions, while the levels in remote areas were lower. The highest levels were on the order of 5–10 pg m^{-3} for the sum of all PCDDs and PCDFs. In suburban areas the levels were lower by a factor of 5–10.

Recent studies by Rappe & Kjeller (1987) indicate that pg or sub pg m^{-3} levels of a variety of PCDDs and PCDFs can be found in air sampled in an industrialized area. The isomeric patterns found in these samples were very similar to those found in samples from MSW and industrial incinerators, car exhausts and also in new sediments. The levels found downwind from a MSW incinerator and the levels in a traffic tunnel were about the same.

3.2. *Soil and sediments*

A great number of analyses have been performed on soil and sediment samples, especially from "hot spots" where levels of PCDDs and PCDFs (mainly 2,3,7,8-tetra-CDD) as high as ppm have been reported, e.g. Seveso, Times Beach and Love Canal. In a few studies, background levels of PCDDs in soil and sediment samples are reported. However, in most of these studies, non-validated and non-isomer-specific analytical methods are used. These studies indicate background levels in the low ppt range, but in general no specific isomers are reported.

Recently Rappe & Kjeller (1987) reported that new sediments from the archipelago of Stockholm, Sweden, contain ppt or sub-ppt levels of a variety of PCDD and PCDF isomers. The isomeric profiles found in these sediments are very similar to those found in samples from MSW and industrial incinerators and car exhausts.

3.3. *Aquatic organisms*

In the late 1970s and early 1980s analytical methods were developed to determine 2,3,7,8-tetra-CDD as well as the other 2,3,7,8-substituted PCDDs in biological samples. Due to the high toxicity of these compounds, the detection levels should be in the order of pg g^{-1} (ppt) or lower. Such analyses are complicated and expensive and, up to now, only a limited number of analyses have been reported, mainly from U.S.A., Canada and Sweden.

Harless & Lewis (1982) reported on levels ranging from 4–695 ppt of 2,3,7,8-tetra-CDD in the edible portion of various fishes from Saginaw Bay, U.S.A., The highest concentrations were detected in bottom-feeding catfish and carp. In this study, 36 samples were analysed and 26 of these were reported to have detectable amounts (> 5–10 ppt) of 2,3,7,8-tetra-CDD with 10 samples containing concentrations greater than 40 ppt.

Rappe *et al.* (1981) identified a series of tetra- to octa-CDFs in fat samples of a snapping turtle from the Hudson River and gray seal from the Baltic Sea. The total levels of PCDFs in these samples were 3 ng g^{-1} and 40 pg g^{-1}, respectively. In both samples the major PCDFs were the most toxic isomers, i.e. 2,3,7,8-tetra-, 2,3,4,7,8-penta- and 1,2,3,4,7,8- and 1,2,3,6,7,8-hexa-CDF.

Fish and other aquatic animals from the Great Lakes have been analysed and the data indicate low background levels (1–300 ppt) of a series of PCDDs and PCDFs. Norstrom *et al.* (1982) have analysed pooled samples of herring gull eggs collected in 1983 from various parts of the Great Lakes. In all samples, 2,3,7,8-tetra-CDD was found in levels ranging from 9 to 90 pg g^{-1}. In another study, Stalling *et al.* (1983) were unable to identify measurable levels of tetra-CDDs and other PCDDs in fish samples from Lake Superior (the detection level was 2–5 pg g^{-1}). The difference in these two studies could be explained by the migration of the herring gulls during the winter. On the other hand, a series of PCDFs could be identified in the Lake Superior fish samples (15–40 ppt), indicating more widespread background levels for the PCDFs than for the PCDDs. Stalling *et al.* (1983) also reported on the analysis of fish samples from Lakes Michigan, Huron and Ontario. Total levels of PCDFs were found to be 12–290 ppt. The toxic 2,3,7,8-substituted PCDDs and PCDFs were present in all samples, the highest levels being found in samples from Lake Huron, Lake Ontario and Tittabawasee River. The residue pattern found in the fish and locally high levels suggest a strong influence of point-source discharges.

The Baltic Sea is another system which is of interest because it is a system without any known point sources. Nygren *et al.* (1986) have reported on low levels of a series of 2,3,7,8-substituted PCDDs and PCDFs in single samples of herring, salmon, guillemot and seal fat from the Baltic Sea. More recently, Rappe *et al.* (1987) have analysed other samples, two samples of salmon and two samples of pooled herring muscle, one from the Baltic Sea and the other from the Gulf of Bothnia (see Table 1). As expected, the levels in the salmon muscle are much higher than the levels found in the herrings, but unexpectedly, the levels in the herring sample from the Gulf of Bothnia (Luleå) were about the same as levels found in the sample from the Baltic Sea (Karlskrona).

An interesting observation is that, in the majority of the aquatic samples, only the toxic 2,3,7,8-substituted congeners are found. However, crustaceans seem to be an exception from this general behaviour. Norstrom *et al.* (unpublished) reported that crab hepatopancreas from the Canadian Pacific Coast contain other congeners, e.g. 1,2,4,7,8-penta-CDD and 1,2,3,6,7,9-/1,2,3,6,8,9-hexa-CDD. Consequently, crustaceans are good signal organisms for studying sources of environmental pollutants.

Samples of hepatopancreas from crustaceans have been collected at different locations along the Swedish West Coast and analysed by Rappe *et al.* (1987). The crab samples from the locations Grebbestad and Idefjord should represent background levels, while Väröfjord represents a potential point source from a pulp mill using chlorine in its bleaching processes. The results are given in Table 2.

TABLE 1

Levels of PCDDs and PCDFs in fish samples from the Baltic Sea (pg g^{-1})

	Salmon Ume River 1985	Salmon Ume River 1985	Herring Karlskrona 1983	Herring Luleå 1983
2,3,7,8-Tetra-CDF	29	12	5.5	3.0
2,3,7,8-Tetra-CDD	1.9	1.3	<0.3	<0.6
1,2,3,7,8-/1,2,3,4,8-Penta-CDF	6.9	3.3	1.4	0.9
2,3,4,7,8-Penta-CDF	49.0	23.0	6.8	8.8
1,2,3,7,8-Penta-CDD	8.8	4.3	1.1	4.7
1,2,3,4,7,8-/1,2,3,4,7,9-Hexa-CDF	1.1	0.7	0.4	0.3
1,2,3,6,7,8-Hexa-CDF	1.3	0.8	0.4	0.3
1,2,3,7,8,9-Hexa-CDF	ND	ND	0.4	0.2
2,3,4,6,7,8-Hexa-CDF	1.1	0.6	0.4	0.2
1,2,3,4,7,8-Hexa-CDD	ND	0.4	0.2	ND
1,2,3,6,8,9-Hexa-CDD	4.6	2.3	ND	8.1
1,2,3,7,8,9-Hexa-CDD	ND	ND	ND	ND
Total hepta-CDFs	ND	2.7	0.8	ND
Total hepta-CDDs	ND	ND	ND	ND
OCDF	ND	1.0	ND	ND
OCDD	ND	ND	ND	ND

ND < 0.1 pg g^{-1}.

Rappe *et al.* (1987) found low background levels of a series PCDDs and PCDFs in all samples. In addition, the sample from the Väröfjord also contained much higher levels of some congeners, especially 2,3,7,8-tetra-CDF and 2,3,7,8-tetra-CDD (see Table 2). This is an indication that paper mills could be a potential source of highly toxic PCDDs and PCDFs. This was the first report in which such a correlation has been made. For this reason Rappe *et al.* (1987) also analysed two sediment samples, one collected in the sedimentation lagoon in the pulp mill and the other in a nearby river mouth (see Table 2). The PCDDs and PCDFs in these two samples are also quite different, the sample from the pulp-mill lagoon contains high levels of 2,3,7,8-tetra-CDF and 2,3,7,8-tetra-CDD. There is good correlation to the crab samples.

3.4. Terrestrial animals

Nygren *et al.* (1986) analysed bovine samples (fat, liver and milk) and identified the same 2,3,7,8-substituted PCDDs and PCDFs as were found in the aquatic samples. However, the levels were lower and normally close to the detection limit. This indicates that the background levels are higher in the aquatic environment that in the terrestrial environment, which is in agreement with earlier experience for compounds such as DDT and PCB.

Rappe *et al.* (unpublished) have analysed six samples of cow milk from various locations in Switzerland for PCDDs and PCDFs. In all samples, 2,3,7,8-substituted PCDDs and PCDFs were found at levels of pg L^{-1}, however the levels were higher in samples collected in the vicinity of incinerators than in commercial milk samples.

TABLE 2

Levels of PCDDs and PCDFs (pg g^{-1}) in samples of crab hepatopancreas and sediments from the Swedish West Coast

	Crab hepatopancreas			Sediments	
	Idefjorden	Grebbestad	Väröfjorden	Värö Mill	Mouth of R. Viskan
2,3,7,8-Tetra-CDF	31	47	590	890	1.6
Total tetra-CDFs	90	114	800	1600	24
2,3,7,8-Tetra-CDD	17	17	170	120	0.2
Total tetra-CDDs	17	17	170	230	6.4
1,2,3,7,8-Penta-CDF*	6.0	7·6	45	15	1.3
2,3,4,7,8-Penta-CDF	44	50	130	13	1.7
Total penta-CDFs	130	150	490	130	30
1,2,3,7,8-Penta-CDD	13	11	28	15	0.9
Total penta-CDDs	86	76	270	170	13
1,2,3,4,7,8-Hexa-CDF†	12	16	50	1.7	1.9
1,2,3,6,7,8-Hexa-CDF	3	5	10	0.8	1.2
1,2,3,7,8,9-Hexa-CDF	3	3	11	2.0	2.0
2,3,4,6,7,8-Hexa-CDF	16	18	63	1.5	1.6
Total hexa-CDFs	70	88	280	17	44
1,2,3,4,7,8-Hexa-CDD	8	5	14	3.1	1.6
1,2,3,6,7,8-Hexa-CDD	26	18	71	21	10
1,2,3,7,8,9-Hexa-CDD	3	4	7	8.8	4.3
Total hexa-CDDs	154	170	465	92	64
Total hepta-CDFs	23	28	90	16	300
Total hepta-CDDs	32	30	85	31	190
Octa-CDF	<1	<1	<2	19	330
Octa-CDD	<1	<1	<2	87	900

* Not separated from 1,2,3,4,8-penta-CDF.
† Not separated from 1,2,3,4,7,9-hexa-CDF.

4. Levels of PCDDs and PCDFs in human samples

4.1. *Adipose tissue*

The TCDD exposure of soldiers and the general population during the military use of phenoxy herbicides during the Vietnam war has been a subject of much concern among the veterans in the United States, Australia and New Zealand and for the people in Vietnam.

Gross *et al.* (1984) reported on a study where 30 coded samples of adipose tissue from Vietnam veterans were analysed for TCDD. The TCDD levels found for two of the three heavily exposed men were 99 pg g^{-1} and 63 pg g^{-1}, which is higher than for the other Vietnam veterans or for the controls, all of whom were below 15 pg g^{-1}. Only one isomer of tetra-CDDs was found, and it was assumed that this was the 2,3,7,8-isomer. The data in this study has also been discussed by Young *et al.* (1983) who concluded that the levels do not correlate well with known exposure data or with health status.

Rappe *et al.* (1984) reported on a whole series of 2,3,7,8-substituted PCDDs and PCDFs in samples of adipose tissue from Northern Sweden. A series of reports presented during the period 1984–86 confirm these observations and it is clearly shown

TABLE 3

Levels of PCDDs and PCDFs in human adipose tissue (ppt on net weight)

Isomer	Sweden $n = 31$	U.S.A. (NY)* $n = 8$	Canada* $n = 46$	Japan* $n = 13$	N. Vietnam* $n = 9$	S. Vietnam* $n = 15$	F.R.G. $n = 4$
2,3,7,8-TCDD	3	7.2	6.4	9	<2	18	150
1,2,3,7,8-PeCDD	10	11.1	10	15	<2	9.1	19.2
1,2,3,6,7,8-HxCDD	15	95.9	87	70	5.6	57	77
1,2,3,7,8,9-HxCDD	4	NA	NA	12	NA	NA	9.4
1,2,3,4,6,7,8 HpCDD	97	164	135	77	17	121	56
OCDD	414	707	850	230	52	900	267
2,3,7,8-TCDF	3.9	NA	NA	9	NA	NA	0.9
2,3,4,7,8-PeCDF	54	14.3	15	25	7.2	12	44
1,2,3,4,7,8-HxCDF	6	NA	NA	15	NA	NA	10.0
1,2,3,6,7,8-HxCDF	5	31.3	16	14	7.7	33	6.7
2,3,4,6,7,8-HxCDF	2	NA	NA	8	NA	NA	3.8
1,2,3,4,6,7,8-HpCDF	11	16.5	30	NA	4.2	17	19.5
OCDF	4	NA	NA	NA	NA	NA	<1

* Mean values of positives. Levels below the detection level not included.
ND, not detected (<1.0 pg g^{-1}).
NA, not analysed.

that there is a background of 2,3,7,8-substituted PCDDs and PCDFs in the general population in the industrialized part of the world.

The Swedish study included 31 persons, of these 18 were exposed to phenoxy esters and 13 were non-exposed. The group contained 17 cancer patients and 14 non-cancer patients. The subgroups were matched against each other. No difference in the levels, patterns and ranges could be found between these subgroups, see Nygren *et al.* (1986). The mean values of the PCDDs and PCDFs found in these 31 persons are given in Table 3 (first column).

Schecter *et al.* (1986*a*) reported on mean levels of PCDDs and PCDFs in 46 samples of adipose tissue collected in Canada and in eight samples from the United States (see Table 3). The Canadian samples originated from people who had died accidentally in 1976 from such causes as car accidents, drownings, trauma and suicide. These samples, including all ages and both sexes, originated from all over the country. The U.S. samples consisted of both biopsy and autopsy samples taken in 1983–84 from New York State residents in the course of normal medical procedures.

Ono *et al.* (1986) reported on the levels of PCDDs and PCDFs in 13 adipose tissue samples obtained from cancer patients in Japan (see Table 3). The origin of the samples is not further discussed. Schecter *et al.* (1986*b*) also report on levels of PCDDs and PCDFs in samples of adipose tissue collected in South and North Vietnam (see Table 3).

It is interesting to note the similarity in isomers present, the levels, isomeric pattern and congener profiles in all these samples collected from the general population in industrialized countries on three continents (see Table 3). The profile of the PCDD isomers shows increasing levels with increasing number of chlorine atoms, the level of OCDD is 400–900 pg g^{-1}. On the other hand, the profile of PCDFs show a maximum for 2,3,4,7,8-penta- or 1,2,3,6,7,8-hexa-CDF. The difference in levels found between samples from South and North Vietnam can be explained by spraying during the war in the 1960s and by the difference in industrial activities between the two parts of the country.

Rappe *et al.* (1987) also reported on the analyses of four samples of adipose tissue taken from German workers exposed to TCDD in the early 1950s. Despite the fact that these workers were exposed more than 30 years before collecting the samples, levels as high as >200 pg g^{-1} and a mean value of 150 pg g^{-1} of 2,3,7,8-TCDD could be identified, but the levels of all the other PCDDs and PCDFs seemed to be in the normal range (see Table 3, last column). Some or all of these workers are still suffering from chloracne.

These high levels found in the exposed German workers indicate a very slow excretion rate or metabolism of TCCD in humans. This indicates a dramatic difference between man and rodents, in the latter the half-life of TCDD is reported to be in the range of a few weeks (see also Mukerjee & Cleverly in this issue).

4.2. *Human milk*

Rappe *et al.* (1984) reported on the analyses of five samples of human milk from volunteers in the F.R.G. Low levels of a series of 2,3,7,8-substituted PCDDs and PCDFs were found in these samples (see Table 4). In January 1985, Rappe reported on the results of four samples from the Umeå region in northern Sweden (Table 4).

Fuerst *et al.* (1986) have reported on the analyses of 53 samples of human milk from Rheinland—Westfalia in F.R.G. The results from this investigation are collected in

TABLE 4
Levels of PCDDs and PCDFs found in human milk (ppt on fat weight)

	Sweden $n = 4$	F.R.G. $n = 5$	F.R.G. $n = 53$	Vietnam $n = 1*$	Denmark $n = 1*$	Netherlands $n = 3*$	Yugoslavia $n = 2*$
2,3,7,8-TCDD	0.6	1.9	ND	<0.5	NA	9.7	<1.0
1,2,3,7,8-PeCDD	6.5	12.9	11.0	7.0	31	44	5.5
1,2,3,4,7,8-HxCDD	2.5	4.6	8.6	ND	13	25	3.5
1,2,3,6,7,8-HxCDD	19	17.3	32.9	50	97	251	15
1,2,3,7,8,9-HxCDD	6.3	1.6	6.4	24	32	23	ND
1,2,3,4,6,7,8-HpCDD	59.5	72.8	48.8	150	174	130	28
OCDD	302	434	143	754	328	744	106
2,3,7,8-TCDF	4.2	5.4	1.7	9.4	4.0	2.8	<1.0
1,2,3,7,8-PeCDF	<1	<1	2.0	<1	4.5	ND	ND
2,3,4,7,8-PeCDF	21.3	36.4	21.1	21	31	79	25
1,2,3,4,7,8-HxCDF	4.7	11.4	8.3	15.0	13	8.9	3.7
1,2,3,6,7,8-HxCDF	3.4	10.2	6.9	11.0	52	10.3	3.6
2,3,4,6,7,8-HxCDF	1.4	4.3	3.2	4.2	11	6.4	1.3
1,2,3,4,6,7,8-HpCDF	7.4	9.2	7.4	23.0	46	39	ND
OCDF	3.2	2.4	27.0	46.0	ND	ND	ND

* Pooled samples.
ND, not detected.
NA, not analyzed.

Table 4 together with the results of a few new analyses of human milk from Denmark, Yugoslavia, the Netherlands and Vietnam (Rappe *et al.* 1987).

A comparison between the isomers present, the levels, isomeric pattern and congener profiles found in human milk (Table 4) and adipose tissue (Table 3) shows a remarkable similarity.

At a WHO Consultation in 1985 it was assumed that MSW incinerators constitute the major source to environmental contamination by PCDDs and PCDFs, and consequently to the levels of PCDDs and PCDFs found in human milk. An interesting comparison could be made between Sweden, having 25–30 MSW incinerators, and Yugoslavia which does not have an incinerator. Despite this difference, the PCDD and PCDF levels found in the human milk samples from these two countries are comparable, indicating that other sources might contribute significantly to the background levels of PCDDs and PCDFs, e.g. car exhausts.

5. Conclusions

Available data, although from very few countries, indicate a general low background for 2,3,7,8-substituted PCDDs and PCDFs in the environment, especially for aquatic organisms and also in the general population.

In most biological samples only the most toxic PCDD and PCDF isomers were found (see Tables 1–4). In addition, two Cl_7 and two Cl_8 congeners were also found. An exception from this general behaviour is in crustaceans, where a multitude of isomers could be identified.

A poor correlation was observed between the isomeric distribution found in environmental or human samples and the respective potential sources. This indicates a combination of sources, e.g. incineration and technical products in addition to environmental and biological degradation. Of special interest here is the observation of 1,2,3,7,8-penta-CDD in all biological samples. This isomer is found in all samples from incinerators and car exhausts and also in low levels in a few technical pentachlorophenol formulations analysed in this laboratory from the U.S. and also from German producers, see Hagenmeyer & Berchtold (1986).

As mentioned above, all incineration processes involving organochlorine compounds, including MSW incinerators, steel mills and automobile exhausts, generate PCDDs and PCDFs with very similar isomeric patterns and congener profiles. Analysis of air, particulate and sediment samples show that these environmental samples contain typical incineration patterns and profiles. However, pattern recognition analyses cannot separate the contribution from various incineration sources. This can only be done

TABLE 5

Exposure of TCDD equivalents (Eadon 1983) for a 55-kg person or a 5-kg baby (Rappe *et al.* 1986)

Exposure	pg kg^{-1} Body weight day^{-1}
Inhalation	0.02
Milk (1 l day^{-1})	0.5–5
Salmon (100 g $week^{-1}$)	20
Breast milk (850 ml day^{-1})	20–200

after a careful mapping of the quantities of PCDDs and PCDFs produced by various sources, primarily incineration processes.

Rappe *et al.* (1986) discuss the human exposure from various sources, e.g. inhalation downwind from a MSW incinerator, consumption of fish and bovine milk and also the exposure of a nursing baby (see Table 5).

From Table 5 it is clear that the inhalation exposure is marginal compared to the exposure via food, especially fish and other foodstuffs from the aquatic food web. However, a correlation between incinerators of various kinds and the environmental levels of PCDDs and PCDFs seems quite likely, and consequently all such emissions should be controlled and minimized.

References

Ballschmiter, K., Buchert, H., Niemczyk, R., Munder, A. & Swerev, M. (1986), Automobile exhausts versus municipal-waste incineration as source of the polychloro-dibenzodioxins (PCDD) and -furans (PCDF) found in the environment, *Chemosphere, 15*, 901–915.

Bellin, J. S. & Barnes, D. G. (1985), Health hazard assessment for chlorinated dioxins and dibenzofurans other than 2,3,7,8-TCDD, *Toxicology and Industrial Health, 1*, 235–248.

Buser, H. R. & Bosshardt, H.-P. (1978), Polychlorierte Dibenzo-*p*-dioxine, Dibenzofurane und Benzole in der Asche Kommunaler und industrieller Verbrennungsanlagen (Polychlorinated dibenzo-*p*-dioxins and dibenzofurans in ashes from municipal and industrial incinerators), *Mitt. Geb. Lebensmitt. Hygiene, 69*, 191–199.

Crummett, W. B., Nestrick, T. J. & Lamparski, L. L. (1985), Analytical methodology for the determination of PCDDs in environmental samples: an overview and critique. In *Dioxins in the Environment* (M. A. Kamrin & P. W. Rodgers, Eds), pp. 57–83. Hemisphere Publishing, Washington.

Czuczwa, J. M. & Hites, R. A. (1986), Airborne dioxins and dibenzofurans: sources and fates, *Environmental Science and Technology, 20*, 195–200.

Eadon, G., Aldous, K., Hilker, D., O'Keefe, P. & Smith, R. (1983), Chemical data on air samples from the Binghampton State Office Building. Memo from Center for Laboratories and Research, NY State Department of Health, Albany, NY 12201, 7/7/83.

Fuerst, P., Meemkin, H.-A. & Grobel, W. (1986), Determination of polychlorinated dibenzo-dioxins and dibenzofurans in human milk, *Chemosphere, 15*, 1977–1980.

Gross, M. L., Lay Jr, J. O., Lyon, P. A., Lippstreu, D., Kangas, N., Harless, R. L., Taylor, S. E. & Dupuy Jr, A. E. (1984), 2,3,7,8-Tetrachlorodibenzo-*p*-dioxin levels in adipose tissue of Vietnam veterans, *Environmental Research, 33*, 261–268.

Hagenmeyer, H. & Berchtold, A. (1986), Analysis of waste from production of Na-pentachloro-phenolate for polychlorinated dibenzodioxins (PCDD) and dibenzofurans (PCDF), *Chemosphere, 15*, 1991–1994.

Harless, R. L. & Lewis, R. G. (1982), Quantitative determination of 2,3,7,8-tetrachlorodibenzo-*p*-dioxin residues by gas chromatography/mass spectrometry. In *Chlorinated Dioxins and Related Compounds. Impact on the Environment* (O. Hutzinger, R. W. Frei, E. Merian & F. Pocchiari, Eds.), pp. 25–36. Pergamon Press, Oxford.

Kimble, B. J. & Gross, M. L. (1980), Tetrachlorodibenzo-*p*-dioxin quantification in stack-collected coal fly ash, *Science, 207*, 59–61.

Marklund, S., Kjeller, L.-O, Hansson, M., Tysklind, M., Rappe, C., Ryan, C., Collazo, H. & Dougherty, R. (1986), Determination of PCDDs and PCDFs in incineration samples and pyrolytic products. In *Chlorinated Dioxins and Dibenzofurans in Perspective* (C. Rappe, G. Choudhary & L. Keith, Eds), pp. 79–92. Lewis Publishers, Chelsea, MI, U.S.A.

Marklund, S., Rappe, C., Tysklind, M. & Egebäck, K.-E. (1987), Identification of polychlorinated dibenzofurans and dioxins in exhausts from cars run on leaded gasoline, *Chemosphere, 16*, 29–36.

Nestrick, T. J. & Lamparski, L. L. (1982), Isomer-specific determination of chlorinated dioxins for assessment of formation and potential environmetal emission from wood combustion, *Analytical Chemistry, 54*, 2292–2299.

Norstrom, R. J., Hallett, D. J., Simon, M. & Mulvihill, M. J. (1982), Analysis of Great Lakes herring gull eggs for tetrachlorodibenzo-*p*-dioxins. In *Chlorinated Dioxins and Related*

Compounds. Impact on the Environment (O. Hutzinger, R. W. Frei, E. Merian & F. Pocchiari, Eds), pp. 173–181. Pergamon Press, Oxford.

Nygren, M., Rappe, C., Lindström, G., Hansson, M., Bergqvist, P.-A., Marklund, S., Domellöf, L., Hardell, L. & Olsson, M. (1986), Identification of 2,3,7,8-substituted polychlorinated dioxins and dibenzofurans in environmental and human samples. In *Chlorinated Dioxins and Dibenzofurans in Perspective* (C. Rappe, G. Choudhary, & L. Keith, Eds), pp. 17–34. Lewis Publishers, Chelsea, MI, U.S.A.

Oehme, M., Manø, S., Mikaelsen, A. & Kirschmer, P. (1986), Quantitative method for the determination of femtogram amounts of polychlorinated dibenzo-*p*-dioxins and dibenzofurans in outdoor air, *Chemosphere, 15*, 607–617.

Olie, K., Vermeulen, P. L. & Hutzinger, O. (1977), Chlorodibenzo-*p*-dioxins and chlorodibenzofurans are trace components of fly ash and flue gas of some municipal incinerators in the Netherlands, *Chemosphere, 8*, 455–459.

Ono, M., Wakimoto, T., Tatsukawa, R. & Masuda, Y. (1986), Polychlorinated dibenzo-*p*-dioxins and dibenzofurans in human adipose tissues of Japan, *Chemosphere, 15*, 1629–1634.

Rappe, C. (1984), Analysis of polychlorinated dioxins and furans, *Environmental Science and Technology, 18*, 78A–90A.

Rappe, C. (1985), Problems in analysis of PCDDs and PCDFs and presence of these compounds in human milk. Organohalogen compounds in human milk and related hazards. In *Report on a WHO consultation.* WHO Regional Office for Europe, Copenhagen, Denmark, IPC/-CEH 501/m 05.

Rappe, C. & Kjeller, L.-O. (1987), PCDDs and PCDFs in environmental samples. Air, particulate, sediments and soil, *Chemosphere*, in press.

Rappe, C., Buser, H. R., Stalling, D., Smith, L. M., Dougherty, R. C. (1981), Identification of polychlorinated dibenzofurans in environmental samples, *Nature, 292*, 524–526.

Rappe, C., Bergqvist, P.-A., Hansson, M., Kjeller, L.-O., Lindström, G, Marklund, S. & Nygren, M. (1984), Chemistry and analysis of polychlorinated dioxins and dibenzofurans in biological samples. Banbury Report 18. *Biological Mechanisms of Dioxin Action*, pp. 17–24. Cold Spring Harbor Laboratory.

Rappe, C., Marklund, S., Kjeller, L.-O., Bergqvist, P.-A. & Hansson, M. (1985), Composition of polychlorinated dibenzofurans (PCDF) formed in PCB fires. In *Chlorinated Dioxins and Dibenzofurans in the Total Environment. II* (L. H. Keith, C. Rappe & G. Choudhary, Eds), pp. 401–424. Butterworths, Boston.

Rappe, C., Marklund, S., Kjeller, L.-D. & Tysklind, M. (1986), PCDDs and PCDFs in emission from various incinerators, *Chemosphere, 15*, 1213–1217.

Rappe, C., Andersson, R., Bergqvist, P.-A., Brohede, C., Hansson, M., Kjeller, L.-O, Lindström, G., Marklund, S., Nygren, M., Swanson, S. E., Tysklind, M. & Wiberg, K. (1987), Overview of environmental fate of chlorinated dioxins and dibenzofurans. Sources, levels and isomeric pattern in various matrices, *Chemosphere*, in press.

Schecter, A., Ryan, J. J. & Gitlitz, G. (1986*a*), Chlorinated dioxin and dibenzofuran levels in human adipose tissues from exposed and control population. In *Chlorinated Dioxins and Dibenzofurans in Perspective* (C. Rappe, G. Choudhary & L. Keith, Eds), pp. 51–65. Lewis Publishers, Chelsea, MI, U.S.A.

Schechter, A., Ryan, J. J., Gross, M., Weerasinghe, N. C. A. & Constable, J. (1986*b*), Chlorinated dioxins and dibenzofurans in human tissues from Vietnam, 1983–84, p. 35–50. In *Chlorinated Dioxins and Dibenzofurans in Perspective* (C. Rappe, G. Choudhary, L. Keith, Eds), pp. 35–50. Lewis Publishers, Chelsea, MI, U.S.A.

Stalling, D. L., Smith, L. M., Petty, J. D., Hogan, J. W., Johnson, J. L., Rappe, C. & Buser, H. R. (1983), Residues of polychlorinated dibenzo-*p*-dioxins and dibenzofurans in Laurentian Great Lakes fish. In *Human and Environmental Risks of Chlorinated Dioxins and Related Compounds* (R. E. Tucker, A. L. Young, A. P. Gray, Eds), pp. 221–240. Plenum Press, New York.

WHO (1985), Organohalogen compounds in human milk and related hazards. Report on a WHO consultation, WHO Regional Office for Europe, Copenhagen, Denmark. IPC/CEH 501/m 05.

WHO (1986), PCDD and PCDF emissions from incinerators for municipal sewage sludge and solid waste—evaluation of human exposure. WHO Regional Office for Europe, Copenhagen, Denmark, IPC/CEH 003/m 06.

Young, A. L., Kang, H. K. & Shepard, B. M. (1983), Chlorinated dioxins as herbicide contaminants, *Environmental Science and Technology, 17*, 530A–540A.

PROBLEMS ASSOCIATED WITH THE MEASUREMENT OF PCDD AND PCDF EMISSIONS FROM WASTE INCINERATION PLANTS*

**Hanspaul Hagenmaier †, Hermann Brunner †, Roland Haag †, Michael Kraft †
and K. Lützke ‡**

(*Received January 1987*)

Fly ash and stack gases from municipal waste and industrial incinerators in the F.R.G. have been analyzed for dioxins (PCDD and PCDF). Most of the currently used procedures of stack gas sampling for PCDD/PCDF have been compared and were found to be equally effective. Differences are found, however, in the recovery of surrogates added to the sampling train before sampling, which makes it difficult to validate the sampling procedure. The analysis for PCDD/PCDF in stack gas or fly ash samples from municipal waste incinerators can no longer be considered an analytical problem. Thirty samples of stack gas from a single (old) municipal waste incinerator showed wide variation in PCDD/PCDF emission, indicating that single measurements are not useful in characterizing a plant for average PCDD/PCDF emission. It will be extremely difficult to correlate plant operating conditions to PCDD/PCDF stack gas emissions or PCDD/PCDF fly ash concentrations, because the effects produced by changing conditions are obscured by the variations which occur in PCDD/PCDF concentrations during steady conditions. The variations found under steady conditions can be explained by the proposed mechanisms of PCDD/PCDF formation and decomposition at low temperatures catalyzed by fly ash. Incineration of hospital waste and pyrolytic reclamation of copper in cables and aluminium produced significant emission of PCDD/PCDF. A major non-combustion source of higher chlorinated PCDD/PCDF (tetra- to octa-isomers) is pentachlorophenol, a widespread preservative which contributes to the PCDD/PCDF concentrations found, for example, in sewage sludge, river sediments and house dust.

Key Words—Dioxins, PCDD, PCDF, formation, decomposition, sources, municipal incinerators, metal reclamation, pentachlorophenol, sampling methods, analysis, variability.

1. Introduction

Dioxins, polychlorinated dibenzo-*p*-dioxins (PCDDs) and polychlorinated dibenzo-furans (PCDFs) were detected in the fly ash and stack gas of every municipal waste incineration plant tested to date. For various reasons there is concern that at least some isomers of the 75 PCDDs and 135 PCDFs are a general health risk (see Ahlborg & Victorin and also Mukerjee & Cleverly in this issue). For a reasonable calculation of this risk, the sources of these compounds, their distribution in the environment, and their fate must be known as accurately as possible.

The initial sampling procedure for flue gases used in this work was that described by

---

* Presented at the ISWA–WHO–DAKOFA specialized seminar, *Emission of Trace Organics from Municipal Solid Waste Incinerators*, Copenhagen, 20–22 January 1987.
† Institute of Organic Chemistry, University of Tübingen, D-7400 Tübingen, F.R.G.
‡ Rheinisch-Westfälischer TÜV, D-4300 Essen, F.R.G.
Waste Management & Research (1987) **5**, 239–250

Nottrodt *et al.* (1984), which is similar to the Nordic Method described by Jansson & Bergvall (in this issue). Fly-ash samples (5–25 g) were treated with 1 N HCl and air dried before Soxhlet-extraction with toluene. Prior to the extraction, 10 different ^{13}C-labelled isomers (one for each congener class) were added to the sample. Concentrations were determined by isotope dilution mass spectrometry. Analytical errors were much lower than sample-to-sample variations. PCDD/PCDF analyses of fly-ash and stack-gas samples if carried out with the neccessary quality control and quality assurance, can be considered as more or less routine analytical procedures.

2. PCDD/PCDF emissions of municipal waste incinerators

A typical municipal incinerator in Germany produces (for each tonne of waste burned) 300 kg bottom ash (slag) in 1000 l of water, 30 kg fly ash, and 5000 m³ of stack gas containing 0.15 kg fly ash. According to the few investigations which have been carried out, PCDD and PCDF can be detected in the bottom ash of municipal waste incinerators, but the concentrations are low compared to fly ash.

Minimum, average and maximum values for the sum of PCDD/PCDF isomers of the same degree of chlorination, and for the 2,3,7,8-substituted tetra- to hepta-CDD/CDF from 52 fly-ash analyses of 10 different municipal waste incinerators in Germany, are presented in Table 1. There is a range of more than two decades between minimum and maximum values (Hagenmaier 1985).

As PCDD/PCDF concentrations in fly ash have, in the past, frequently been used to characterize municipal waste incinerators with respect to their general PCDD/PCDF levels, it is of importance to know how representative single (or a few) measurements are for a particular plant, operating under "normal" conditions. We have studied this problem from various viewpoints. First, data was gathered on the concentration range of PCDD/PCDF in fly ash samples collected over a period of several months from two plants. The results are given in Table 2. It can be seen that, under normal operating conditions, concentrations of PCDD and PCDF in fly ash samples from a single plant vary by a factor of more than 10. It can be assumed that the analysis of a greater number of samples would broaden the observed concentration range. It might be argued that the reported variations in concentrations are, at least in part, due to the uncertainty of the analytical procedure itself. Therefore several laboratory investigations concerning quality control and quality assurance of PCDD/PCDF analyses were carried out. Standard deviations for the total analysis, starting with the extraction of the fly-ash samples, were less than 20% of the mean, which is far lower than the variations in concentrations reported in Tables 1 and 2.

In early 1985, the authors investigated a waste incinerator regarding the possibility of lowering the PCDD/PCDF concentrations in fly ash by changing the operating conditions; two important observations were made. The variations obtained in PCDD/PCDF concentrations were in the same range as the variations observed under constant operating conditions, and the changes in PCDD/PCDF concentrations observed by varying the operating conditions were not reproducible. From these results it was concluded, at that time, that PCDD/PCDF analyses of fly-ash samples are not suitable for investigating the influence of operating conditions on PCDD/PCDF formation and destruction in a waste incinerator (Hagenmaier 1985). The reason for these findings remained obscure until a better insight into the mechanisms of formation and decomposition of PCDD/PCDF in waste incineration facilities was obtained from recent investigations.

TABLE 1

Summary of PCDD/PCDF analyses of 52 fly ash samples from 10 municipal waste incinerators (ng g^{-1}); most of the samples were collected over a period of several days (Hagenmaier 1985)

	Minimum	Average	Maximum		Minimum	Average	Maximum
Tetra-CDDs	0.1	11	67	2,3,7,8-T$_4$CDD	0.11	0.6	2.3
Penta-CDDs	0.3	34	201	1,2,3,7,8-P$_5$CDD	0.11	3.3	11
Hexa-CDDs	0.4	50	253	1,2,3,4,7,8-H$_6$CDD	0.04	3.9	15
Hepta-CDDs	0.3	57	260	1,2,3,6,7,8-H$_6$CDD	0.07	7.2	30
Octa-CDD	0.2	65	365	1,2,3,7,8,9-H$_6$CDD	0.02	5.5	24
Sum PCDDs	1.3	210	861	1,2,3,4,6,7,8-H$_7$CDD	0.2	49.9	129
Tetra-CDFs	0.7	72	477	2,3,7,8-T$_4$CDF	0.03	4.6	28
Penta-CDFs	0.8	95	494	1,2,3,7,8-P$_5$CDF	0.14	9.4	29
Hexa-CDFs	0.3	82	404	2,3,4,7,8-P$_5$CDF	0.12	11.0	34
Hepta-CDFs	0.1	56	386	1,2,3,4,7,8-H$_6$CDF	0.09	13.5	46
Octa-CDF	0.02	13	174	1,2,3,6,7,8-H$_6$CDF	0.09	14.5	44
Sum-PCDFs	1.9	275	1660	1,2,3,7,8,9-H$_6$CDF	0.01	0.8	3
				2,3,4,6,7,8-H$_6$CDF	0.10	10.5	39
				1,2,3,4,6,7,8-H$_7$CDF	0.08	76.5	294
				1,2,3,4,7,8,9-H$_7$CDF	0.02	3.0	13

TABLE 2

Range of PCDD/PCDF concentrations in fly ash of two different municipal waste incineration plants (ng g^{-1}); samples (10 at each plant) were taken during a period of several months

	Plant A				Plant B		
	Minimum	Average	Maximum		Minimum	Average	Maximum
2,3,7,8-TCDD	0.12	0.80	2.3	2,3,7,8-TCDD	0.10	0.30	0.82
Tetra-CDDs	2	10.3	27	Tetra-CDDs	5	12.5	
Penta-CDDs	5	30.6	77	Penta-CDDs	14	40	33
Hexa-CDDs	7	53.2	127	Hexa-CDDs	22	62	125
Hepta-CDDs	8	82.5	187	Hepta-CDDs	13	51.3	200
Octa-CDD	13	156.2	365	Octa-CDD	6	27	128
Total PCDDs	35	332.8	785	Total PCDDs	69	192.8	67
							546
Tetra-CDFs	11	46.8	98	Tetra-CDFs	21	58.7	137
Penta-CDFs	25	133.8	260	Penta-CDFs	19	62.4	137
Hexa-CDFs	27	180.9	380	Hexa-CDFs	16	39.9	69
Hepta-CDFs	14	151.8	386	Hepta-CDFs	5	16.6	30
Octa-CDF	1	34	133	Octa-CDF	1	3.35	9
Total PCDFs	78	547.3	1228	Total PCDFs	67.2	180.95	364

Vogg and Stieglitz (1986, see also this issue) reported a ten-fold increase in PCDD/PCDF concentrations when fly ash from municipal waste incinerators was treated for two hours in an air stream at 300°C. Their explanation that "predioxins" and "prefurans" present in the fly ash were converted at this temperature into PCDD/PCDF was not acceptable from thermodynamic and thermokinetic considerations. In the present study, when fly ash samples from municipal waste incinerators were heated for two hours at 280°C in an open tube, or in a tube sealed under atmospheric pressure (conditions which we now refer to as "oxygen deficiency"), an overall decrease in PCDD/ PCDF concentrations was observed of about 90%. This decrease is, however, not evenly distributed over the various degrees of chlorination. While the concentrations of the higher chlorinated PCDD/PCDF decreased dramatically, the decrease in penta-CDD/CDF was much less pronounced and tetra-CDD concentrations were increased. In particular, concentrations of 2,3,7,8-TCDD increased significantly in all three samples of fly ash studied. As, for example, octa-CDD is thermally stable at a temperature of 280°C, the authors' explanation for this result was that fly ash shows a catalytic effect in the destruction of PCDD and PCDF. The concomitant decrease in higher chlorinated PCDD/PCDF and increase in tetra-CDD, is due to a catalytic dechlorination/hydrogenation reaction (Hagenmaier *et al.* 1986, 1986/1987). When the same fly ash samples were treated in a stream of oxygen at 300°C (conditions which we now refer to as "oxygen surplus"), the approximately ten-fold increase in PCDD/PCDF concentrations, first described by Vogg and Stieglitz (1986), was obtained. It is proposed that this formation of PCDD/PCDF is by a fly-ash catalyzed *de novo* synthesis, starting with the formation of chlorine from copper and/or other metal chlorides in a manner similar to the process for chlorine production described by Deacon in 1862 (Hagenmaier *et al.* 1986, 1986/1987). In the meantime, we have tested more than 80 fly-ash samples from municipal and hospital waste incinerators and all showed the catalytic effects described above for "oxygen deficient" and "oxygen surplus" conditions at 300°C.

One might ask whether these results from laboratory experiments which were done at a more or less fixed temperature of about 300°C have any relevance to actual processes in waste incinerators. In this respect a recent report by Loeffler (1986) is of particular interest. Loeffler found that only 1% of the PCDD present at the electrofilter exit could be detected at the boiler entrance. Obviously most of the PCDD and PCDF were formed in this incinerator between the boiler entrance and the electrofilter exit, most probably by the mechanism (*de novo* synthesis catalyzed by fly ash) discussed above. Fly ash is deposited on electrofilters and various other parts of an incinerator in the temperature range 200–400°C for an undetermined time, and it is therefore unknown which of the above described catalytic effects are involved and to what extent. In any case the "history" of fly ash sampled for analytical purposes has to date never been recorded, either with respect to overall residence time at certain temperatures, or with respect to exposure time to "oxygen surplus" or "oxygen deficient" conditions. Therefore, it must be taken into consideration that PCDD/PCDF concentrations determined in fly-ash samples are not necessarily identical to those of fly-ash particles at the moment of precipitation on the filter.

From the present findings it is obvious that the interdependence of PCDD/PCDF concentrations in fly-ash samples and the operating conditions of a waste incinerator is not straight forward. It is for this reason that it will be difficult, if not impossible, to corrleate PCDD/PCDF concentrations of fly-ash samples with operating parameters.

Parameters like furnace temperature, chlorine content of the waste, chlorine/sulfur ratio in the waste (Griffin 1986), primary and secondary air supply, etc., will of course have an influence on the PCDD/PCDF concentrations of fly ash. For example, temperature changes in the furnace will change the temperature gradients in the total waste incinerator and the flue-gas composition. This and the other parameters will influence catalytic formation of chlorine and, therefore, the dioxin formation at various parts of the incinerator. Whilst the analysis of fly-ash samples for PCDD/PCDF has made considerable progress in the last four years with respect to the quality of analytical results and can no longer be regarded as a serious problem. There remain, however, a series of open questions with regard to the interpretation of these analytical results.

2.1. *PCDD/PCDF emission in stack gas*

2.2.1. *Problems associated with sampling*

Several procedures have been described for sampling stack gas of waste combustion plants for PCDD/PCDF. There have been discussions on whether comparable results are obtained by different sampling methods and on how accurately the measured values correspond to the actual PCDD/PCDF concentrations in the stack gas. In Germany, at the present time, a sampling method is recommended, which was first described by Nottrodt *et al.* (1984), consisting of a heated filter, condenser and an absorption train filled with ethoxyethanol. In the following discussion this method will be referred to as "standard train". Because there have been (unpublished) reports that parallel sampling by different sampling procedures resulted in PCDD/PCDF concentrations differing by a factor of 10–50, we have carried out, in the last two years, studies comparing the "standard train" and other sampling methods by parallel sampling. Two reports with detailed results of this study have been completed and only the most important data from these reports and some unpublished data will be discussed (Hagenmaier *et al.* 1985*a*,*b*, 1986*c*).

The following sampling procedures were compared with the "standard train":

dilution method (VDI 1985),
EPA modified method 5 (ASME-method, Velzy 1986),
XAD-2 sampling cartridge alone,
XAD-2 modified standard train,
PUFP-method (Brenner *et al.* 1984).

The most important conclusion of this study was that comparable results were obtained with all sampling procedures. Deviations by a factor of 2 were not considered significant, as not enough measurements were made to compare the data on a statistical basis.

Despite the fact that the results obtained with various sampling techniques are comparable, there still remains an important question of sampling for PCDD/PCDF, especially if one considers the mechanisms of PCDD/PCDF formation and destruction discussed above, or the observations made by Rghei & Eiceman (1982, 1985). The question is whether what is analyzed as PCDD/PCDF in the final sample, was actually present in the stack gas, or whether formation and/or decomposition reactions also play a role under sampling conditions.

Whilst it is difficult to formulate an experimental test for a *de novo* synthesis of PCDD/PCDF during sampling, it is possible, at least theoretically, to follow the decomposition and/or dechlorination/hydrogenation of PCDD/PCDF during the sampling procedure by the introduction of ^{13}C-labelled PCDD isomers into the sampling train. A number of sampling experiments were done using ^{13}C-labelled spikes and the results obtained for the standard train are shown in Table 3. The losses of the ^{13}C-labelled compounds were consistently rather high (over 80%). The low recoveries may have been due to several reasons. One possibility would be that the ^{13}C-labelled

TABLE 3

Recoveries (%) of ^{13}C-labelled PCDD added to the filter of the standard sampling train before stack gas sampling was started. Recoveries are calculated for the sampling step only. Losses during the clean-up procedure are corrected (before clean-up ^{13}C-1,2,3,4-TCDD was added to the samples and its recovery set to 100%)

Sampling No.	1	2	3	4	5	6	7	Average
^{13}C-2,3,7,8-TCDD								
Filter	2.9	4.2	6.3	7.6	3.7	5.8	4.4	6.0
Condensate	3.4	3.3	0.8	0.2	1.7	<0.2	2.7	1.8
Impinger	17.2	16.9	6.2	5.4	3.4	4.1	7.6	9.7
Total	23.5	24.4	13.3	13.2	8.8	9.9	14.7	15.4
^{13}C-1,2,3,7,8-Penta-CDD								
Filter	3.2	6.9	10.5	6.0	3.8	12.3	1.9	6.4
Condensate	4.0	3.3	0.2	<0.2	1.6	0.2	3.0	1.8
Impinger	11.0	12.2	4.8	<0.2	3.6	0.2	8.6	5.8
Total	18.2	22.4	15.5	6.0	9.0	12.7	13.7	13.9
^{13}C-octa-CDD								
Filter	1.3	10.4	20.9	8.1	11.2	26.2	7.4	12.2
Condensate	2.8	<0.2	<0.2	<0.2	<0.2	<0.2	<0.2	0.4
Impinger	14.0	12.6	4.5	4.7	3.3	6.8	4.9	7.3
Total	18.1	23.0	25.4	12.8	14.5	33.0	12.3	19.9

compounds added to the filter of the standard train are lost by catalytic dechlorination/ hydrogenation reactions at filter temperatures of about 140°C. To test this possibility, filters were spiked with 1 μg of ^{13}C-octa-CDD. In two experiments, 20% and 30% of the ^{13}C-octa-CDD were recovered and no trace of ^{13}C-labelled tetra- to hepta-CDD could be detected. It must, therefore, be assumed that dechlorination/hydrogenation is not the reason for the losses of ^{13}C-labelled compounds during sampling. Other possibilities for the losses are decomposition by other mechanisms, irreversible adsorption on glass, etc., or insufficient retainment of the spikes in the sampling train compared to the stack gas constituents. It is difficult to distinguish experimentally between these possibilities.

In recent experiments, recoveries of ^{13}C-labelled spikes and PCDD/PCDF stack gas concentrations obtained by parallel sampling with the standard train and the dilution method were compared. The dilution method is distinguished from other methods by the temperature at which the sampling of the PCDD/PCDF takes place (below 50°C). The results are summarized in Table 4. Again low recoveries were obtained for the ^{13}C-labelled PCDD in the standard train. In three out of four samplings, ^{13}C-octa-CDD could not be recovered at all. The recoveries obtained with the dilution method were, however, satisfactory when in addition to the paraffin impregnated filter, an adsorption trap was used. In the authors' opinion it would not make much sense to correct the values shown in Table 4 for the losses in ^{13}C-labelled spikes. The values obtained using the two sampling methods would not compare any better, particularly if all data are compared and not only the tetra- and octa-CDD values.

The results do, however, allow two very important conclusions to be made. The PCDD/PCDF emission concentrations obtained with the dilution method, where the ^{13}C-labelled spikes were recovered to over 50%, were not significantly different from

TABLE 4

Comparison of recoveries of ^{13}C-labelled PCDD added to the filter of the standard train (A) and the dilution train (B), respectively, and the corresponding emission concentration measured in parallel sampling experiments.

Sampling No.	Tetra-CDD (ng Nm^{-3})		Recovery of ^{13}C-1,2,3,4-TCDD (%)		Octa-CDD (ng Nm^{-3})		Recovery of ^{13}C-Octa-CDD (%)	
	A	B	A	B	A	B	A	B
1	1.6	3.9	37	97	14	53	<1	40
2	4.3	5.1	33	66	10	46	17	58
3	2.7	4.6	30	80	12	55	<1	64
4	7.7	6.3	32	103	16	37	<1	44

those obtained with the standard train, where recovery of the ^{13}C-labelled spikes was 0–37%. This means that the standard train does not allow the results to be corrected for losses of the ^{13}C-labelled spikes during sampling. On the other hand, it can be concluded from the distribution of the ^{13}C-labelled spikes, and from the unlabelled compounds sampled from the stack gas in the sampling train (both standard train and dilution method), that the ^{13}C-labelled spikes added to the filter behave differently during sampling than as stack-gas constituents. These results should be taken into consideration for future designs of sampling trains if ^{13}C-labelled spikes are to be used as an aid in validating the sampling of stack gas for PCDD/PCDF. Such a validation procedure is obviously desirable, especially if the emission of PCDD/PCDF in the stack-gas of waste incineration facilities is limited by government regulations. In recent sampling experiments with the dilution method, recoveries of both ^{13}-C labelled tetra-CDD and octa-CDD of close to 100% could be obtained, which means that this sampling procedure could be used as a reference method in future comparisons of sampling procedures.

Attempts have been made to distinguish between particle-bound PCDD/PCDF and gaseous PCDD/PCDF in the stack gas by analyzing various fractions of the sampling train separately. It was demonstrated that the distribution of PCDD/PCDF between collected dust particles, condensate and absorption train is dependent to a large degree on the experimental set-up. When two standard trains were tested in parallel sampling, one operating with a temperature of about 90°C in the filter housing, and the other one operating at 140°C, a significant difference for the PCDD/PCDF distribution in the two trains was found, while there was no difference in the total PCDD/PCDF concentration (Hagenmaier *et al.* 1986c). It is concluded from this experimental result that, with current sampling techniques, it is not possible to distinguish between particle-bound and gaseous PCDD/PCDF in the stack gas, and that there is no need to analyze various fractions of a sampling train separately, except when testing the efficiency of sampling-train compoenents in trapping PCDD/PCDF.

2.1.2. *Results of PCDD/PCDF determinations in stack gas*
In the course of this study on sampling techniques extensive emission measurements were made on the stack gas of one municipal waste incinerator. Table 5 shows the results of 30 stack gas samplings taken in the summer and fall of 1985. It can be seen that there is an extremely wide variation of PCDD/PCDF emission concentrations

TABLE 5

PCDD/PCDF analyses of 30 stack gas samples collected during June and October 1985 at a municipal waste incinerator (ng m^{-3})

	Minimum	Average	Maximum		Minimum	Average	Maximum
Tetra-CDDs	10	44	428	2,3,7,8-T$_4$CDD	0.18	0.60	4.8
Penta-CDDs	18	73	607	1,2,3,7,8-P$_5$CDD	0.9	6.0	54
Hexa-CDDs	14	69	452	1,2,3,4,7,8-H$_6$CDD	0.7	4.2	29
Hepta-CDDs	10	61	394	1,2,3,6,7,8-H$_6$CDD	1.3	6.7	43
Octa-CDD	5	34	186	1,2,3,7,8,9-H$_6$CDD	0.9	4.8	28
Sum PCDDs	60	280	2069	1,2,3,4,6,7,8-H$_7$CDD	5.5	31.4	201
Tetra-CDFs	47	397	4793	2,3,7,8-T$_4$CDF	0.8	9.9	121
Penta-CDFs	47	356	3693	1,2,3,7,8-P$_5$CDF	4.2	25.2	257
Hexa-CDFs	20	168	1376	2,3,4,7,8-P$_5$CDF	3.4	30.2	310
Hepta-CDFs	6	67	488	1,2,3,4,7,8-H$_6$CDF	2.4	19.6	159
Octa-CDFs	1	7	38	1,2,3,6,7,8-H$_6$CDF	3.4	19.9	163
Sum PCDFs	140	995	10347	1,2,3,7,8,9-H$_6$CDF	0.1	1.0	7
				2,3,4,6,7,8-H$_6$CDF	1.6	14.6	124
				1,2,3,4,6,7,8-H$_7$CDF	4.2	47.9	355
				1,2,3,4,7,8,9-H$_7$CDF	0.3	3.7	25

under "normal" operating conditions. Operation was not specifically optimized at any sampling period. The plant had particulate emission of 30–100 mg m^{-3}, and apart from the electrostatic filter no other stack gas cleaning devices were installed. This particular incinerator has been in operation for more than 20 years. Despite the rather high average PCDD/PCDF emission concentrations, no tetra- or penta-CDD/CDF could be detected in soil samples down-wind of this incinerator.

PCDD/PCDF measurements were done on the stack gas of five other municipal waste incinerators. The number of samples taken was no more than eight over a period of two years for any incinerator. Again a rather broad range of emission concentrations was found for each plant, although the range is much smaller than those given in Table 5. Consistently low emissions were observed when additional gas cleaning devices (quasi dry scrubbers, etc.) and efficient particulate filters were installed. Low particulate emissions (<5 mg m^{-3}) coincided with consistently low PCDD/PCDF emission concentrations.

3. PCDD/PCDF emissions from other thermal waste treatment facilities

3.1. *PCDD/PCDF measurements at hospital waste burning facilities*

PCDD/PCDF analyses of ash and stack gas from hospital waste incinerators showed average PCDD/PCDF concentrations which were considerably higher than those reported in Table 1 for fly ash from municipal waste incinerators. Whether this is due to a lower catalytic effect in dechlorination/hydrogenation of these samples, or due to a higher chlorine content of the hospital waste (this waste contains more plastic material than the average municipal waste) has not been determined. Average stack-gas concentrations of PCDD/PCDF at the hospital waste incinerators were in the same range as the concentrations reported in Table 5 for a municipal waste incinerator.

Investigations were also carried out at facilities for incineration of sewage sludge, at metal reclamation plants and cement factories. Three incineration facilities for sewage sludge were investigated. Concentrations of PCDD/PCDF in fly ash were below 2 ppb. 2,3,7,8-TCDD could not be detected. No PCDD/PCDF could be detected in stack gas from these facilities.

Four metal reclamation plants were tested, three of which were for pyrolyzing cables, and one of which was for recycling aluminum. PCDD/PCDF concentrations were in the range of the maximum values of municipal waste incinerators. Stack gas concentrations were also very high. Down-wind of two of the metal reclamation plants (100–300 m from the plant) soil and grass samples were analyzed and all PCDD/PCDF isomers, with characteristic distribution pattern of waste incinerator stack gas, were found in these samples, including 2,3,7,8-TCDD (maximum value 103 ppt). Grass samples analyzed half a year after shut down of one of the facilities did not contain any PCDD/PCDF, despite the fact that the soil sample concentrations were unaltered.

At one plant, only PVC-coated cables were pyrolyzed, and fly-ash and stack-gas sampling was carried out. PCDD/PCDF isomer distribution patterns were identical to those found at other waste incineration plants and concentrations were also in the same range.

No PCDD/PCDF could be detected in fly ash samples from three cement factories, burning used tires.

4. Other sources for PCD/PCDF

Wilson (1986) and Eltzer & Hites (1986) have recently exchanged views on a publication by Czuczwa & Hites (1986) entitled "Airborne Dioxins and Dibenzofurans: Sources and Fates". Whilst Wilson suggests that the ultimate source of PCDD/PCDF found in human adipose tissue has not yet been found, Eltzer & Hites conlude that "combustion is the only source of sufficient size and ubiquity to account for the PCDD and PCDF in human adipose tissue". It has been shown here that there are indeed numerous combustion sources emitting PCDD/PCDF. Recently Marklund *et al.* (1987) have shown that motor vehicles might be another combustion source for PCDD/PCDF emission. The fundamental question is, however, how much do these sources contribute to the human body burden of PCDD/PCDF, and does the ubiquitous occurrence of PCDD/PCDF in river and lake sediments, sewage sludge and soil originate indeed mainly or exclusively from combustion sources? (See Commoner *et al.* in this issue.)

According to investigations (Hagenmaier *et al.* 1986*b*) of river sediments and sewage sludge samples, the major source of higher chlorinated PCDD/PCDF (hexa- to octa-CDD/CDF) found in every sample analyzed (more than 50 samples each) is due to the widespread use of pentachlorophenol (and possibly other chlorophenols). Pentachlorophenol contains these higher chlorinated PCDD/PCDF in comparatively high concentrations as side products. An important marker for this source is the 1,2,3,4,6,8,9-hepta-CDF, which is present in all pentachlorophenol samples tested, at about the same concentration as 1,2,3,4,6,7,8-hepta-CDF, while the isomer distribution for the hepta-CDF isomers from combustion sources is quite different. It can be calculated that the input of PCDD/PCDF into the environment by pentachlorophenol and sodiumpentachlorophenate by far exceeds the input by combustion sources (at least in Germany).

It could be demonstrated (Hagenmaier 1986*a*, Hagenmaier & Brunner 1986/1987*a*) that sodium-pentachlorophenate can contain 2,3,7,8-TCDD as well as 1,2,3,7,8-penta-CDD (an isomer postulated by Rappe *et al.* (1986) as a marker of combustion sources) and, therefore, it might well be possible that the major source of the 2,3,7,8-substituted PCDD/PCDF found in human tissue are the PCDD/PCDF introduced into the environment by the widespread use of pentachlorophenol. The ambient air concentrations of PCDD/PCDF determined so far (Kirschmer 1986) are extremly low compared to indoor concentrations (Eckrich 1986). Hexa- to octa-CDD/CDF were found in every house-dust sample analyzed (Hagenmaier 1987) whether wood preservers containing pentachlorophenol had been applied or not. Besides the point sources of combustion plants, the pentchlorophenol source of PCDD/PCDF should be considered if future human exposure to PCDD/PCDF is to be minimized. Considering how many millions of dollars and D-Mark have already been invested in investigating the possibilities of minimizing PCDD/PCDF emission from municipal waste incinerators, it would cost very little to eliminate one of the major sources of current PCDD/PCDF emission: pentachlorophenol. This could be done, however, only by a worldwide ban of the chemical or, if it can indeed not be replaced, by applying stringent regulations on its high-purity production and the necessary waste disposal. Whether other major sources of ubiquitous PCDD/PCDF emissions exist, besides the two discussed here (combustion and pentachlorophenol), is an open question.

5. Conclusion

Considerable effort has been made in this laboratory to compare various sampling technqiues for polychlorinated dibenzo-*p*-dioxins (PCDD) and dibenzofurans (PCDF). Virtually all currently used procedures of stack gas sampling for PCDD/PCDF have been compared and were found to be equally effective. Procedures for clean-up of samples and quantitation of GC/MS results were further advanced, and it is concluded that the analysis for PCDD/PCDF in the stack gas or fly-ash samples from municipal waste incinerators can no longer be considered an analytical problem. Single measurements are not useful in characterizing a plant for average PCDD/PCDF emission. Multiple sampling of stack gas from a single municipal waste incinerator showed a wide variation in PCDD/PCDF emission. It is postulated that it will not be possible to correlate plant operating conditions with PCDD/PCDF stack-gas emissions or with PCDD/PCDF fly-ash concentrations, because the effects obtained by changing the conditions are obscured by variations in PCDD/PCDF concentrations observed during steady conditions.

Mechanisms of formation and decomposition of PCDD/PCDF catalyzed by fly ash are reported, and these must be taken into consideration in future attempts to minimize PCDD/PCDF emissions from waste incinerators. There are a large number of (small) waste incineration facilities other than municipal solid waste incinerators in the Federal Republic of Germany which emit PCDD/PCDF. A major non-combustion source of higher chlorinated PCDD/PCDF (tetra- to octa-isomers) is pentachlorophenol, a widely used preservative, which contributes to the concentrations found, for example, in river sediments, sewage sludge and house dust.

Acknowledgements

This work was supported in part by the Ministerium für Ernährung, Landwirtschaft, Umwelt und Forsten, Baden-Württemberg and the Umweltbundesamt, Berlin. The skilful technical assistance of Achim Gulde is acknowledged.

References

Brenner, K. S., Mäder, H., Steverle, H., Heinrich, G. & Womann, H. (1984), Dioxin analysis in stack emissions and in the wash water circuit during high-temperature incineration of chlorine-containing industrial wastes, *Bulletin of Environmental Contamination and Toxicology*, *33*, 153.

Czuczwa, J. M. & Hites, R. A. (1986), Airbourne dioxins and dibenzofurans: sources and fates, *Environmental Science and Technology*, *20*, 195.

Eckrich, W. (1986), "Dioxine", VDI-kommission reinhaltung der luft, International Symposium on Dioxins and Related Compounds, Fukuoka 1986, *Chemosphere* (in press).

Eltzer, B. D. & Hites, R. A. (1986), Airbourne dioxins and dibenzofurans: sources and fates (reply), *Environmental Science and Technology*, *20*, 1185.

Griffin, R. D. (1985/1986), A new theory of dioxin formation in municipal solid waste combustion, *Chemosphere*, *15*, 1987.

Hagenmaier, H. (1985), *Dioxinanalysen an Abfallverbrennungsanlagen* (Dioxin Analyses at Municipal Waste Incinerators). EF-Verlag Berlin: Müllverbrennung und Umwelt.

Hagenmaier, H. (1986), Neue Aspekte über die Bildung und Zerstörung von Dioxinen bei der Abfallverbrennung (New apsects of Dioxin formation and decomposition in waste incineration), *5th International Recycling Congress 1986, Berlin*, Messen und Analysieren, EF-Verlag, Berlin.

Hagenmaier, H. (1986a), Determination of 2,3,7,8-tetrachlorodibenzo-*p*-dioxin in commercial chlorophenols and related compounds, *Fresenius' Zeitschrift fur analytische Chemie*, *325*, 603.

Hagenmaier, H. (1987), Abschlußbericht zum Forschungvorhaben, *Umweltbelastung mit Dioxinen* (Environmental Dioxin Loads), an das Ministerium für Ernährung, Landwirtschaft, Umwelt und Forsten, Baden-Württemberg.

Hagenmaier, H. & Brunner, H. (1986/1987a), Isomer-specific analysis of pentachlorophenol and sodium pentachlorophenate for 2,3,7,8-substituted PCDD and PCDF at sub-ppb levels, International Symposium on Dioxins and Related Compounds, Fukuoka 1986, *Chemosphere* (in press).

Hagenmaier, H., Jäger, W., Mayer U., Vater, B., Siegel, D., Rhom, G., Walenda, R., Lützke, K., Rentel, G. & Kraft, M. (1985a), *Vergleichende Untersuchungen von Probenahmetechniken für PCDD and PCDF in Abgas von Müllverbrennungsanlagen* (Comparative Studies of Sampling Techniques for PCDD and PCDF in Flue Gas from Municipal Waste Incinerators), Umweltbundesamt Berlin, Bericht No. 143 03793/1, Teil I.

Hagenmaier, H., Kraft, M., Jäger, W., Mayer, U., Lützke, K. & Siegel, D. (1985b), Comparison of various sampling methods for PCDDs and PCDFs in stack gas, *Chemosphere*, *15*, 1187.

Hagenmaier, H., Brunner, H., Haag, R. & Berchtold, A. (1986b), PCDD and PCDF in sewage sludge, river and lake sediments from southwest Germany, *Chemosphere*, *15*, 1421.

Hagenmaier, H., Kraft, M., Jäger, W., Mayer, U. & Vater, B. (1986c), *Vergleichende Untersuchungen für PCDD und PCDF in Abgas von Müllverbrennungsanlagen* (Comparative Studies of PCDD and PCDF in Flue Gas from Municipal Waste Incinerators), Umweltbundesamt Berlin, Bericht No. 143 0792/1, Teil II.

Hagenmaier, H., Kraft, M., Brunner, H. & Haag, R. (1986/1987), Catalytic effects of fly ash from waste incineration facilities on the formation and decomposition of polychlorinated dibenzo-*p*-dioxins and polychlorinated dibenzofurans, International Symposium on Dioxins and Related Compounds, Fukuoka 1986, *Environmental Science and Technology*, to be published.

Kirschmer, P. (1986), *Dioxine*, VDI-Kommission Reinhaltung der Luft Band 3.

Löffler, H. (1986), Messungen von Dioxin—und Dibenzofuranemissionen an der MVA Flötzensteig (Wein)—Emissionen und Bilanzen (Measurement of PCDD and PCDF at the incinerator in Flötzensteig (Vienna)—emissions and balances), 5th International Recycling Congress 1986, *Berlin Messen und Analysieren*, p. 227, EF-Verlag, Berlin.

Marklund, S., Rappe, C., Tysklind, M. & Egebäck, K.-E. (1987), Identification of polychlorinated dibenzofurans and dioxins in exhausts from cars run on leaded gasoline, *Chemosphere*, *16*, 29–36.

Nottrodt, A., Sladek, K. D., Zoller, W., Buchert, H., Class, Th., Krämer, W., Kohnle, S., Magg, H., Mayer, P., Schäfer, W., Swerew, M. & Ballschmitter, K. (1984), Emissions of polychlorinated dibenzodioxins and polychlorinated dibenzofurans from waste incineration plants, *Müll und Abfall*, *16*, 313.

Rappe, C., Marklund, S., Kjeller, L. O. & Tysklind, M. (1986), PCDD and PCDF emissions from various incinerators, *Chemosphere*, *15*, 1213–1217.

Rghei, H. O. & Eiceman, G. A. (1982), Adsorption and thermal reactions of 1,2,3,4-tetrachloro-dibenzo-*p*-dioxin on fly ash from a municipal incinerator, *Chemosphere*, *11*, 569.

Rghei, H. O. & Eiceman, G. A. (1985), Effect of matrix on heterogenous phase chlorine substitution reactions for dibenzo-*p*-dioxin and hydrogen chloride in air, *Chemosphere*, *15*, 165–171.

Velzy, C. O. (1986), ASME standard sampling and analysis methods for dioxins/furans, *Chemosphere*, *15*, 1179.

VDI-Richtlinie 3873 (1985), Messen von Emissionen. Messen von PAH an genehmigungspflichtigen Anlagen. Gaschromatographische Bestimmung. Verdünnungsmethode. (Measurement of PAH for Licensing of Plants, Gas chromatographic Determination. Dilution Method, Vorentwurf Mai 1985.

Vogg, H. & Stieglitz, L. (1986), Thermal behaviour of PCDD/PCDF in fly ash from municipal incinerators, *International Symposium on Dioxins and Related Compounds, Bayreuth 1985, Chemosphere*, *15*, 1373.

Wilson, J. D. (1986), Comment on "Airborne Dioxins and Dibenzofurans: Sources and Fates" *Environmental Science and Technology*, *20*, 1185.

RECOMMENDED METHODOLOGY FOR MEASUREMENTS OF PCDD AND PCDF IN THE NORDIC COUNTRIES *

Bo Jansson ‡ and Gunnar Bergvall ‡

(*Received February 1987*)

In April 1986 the Nordic Council of Ministers recommended that the Nordic countries use a specific method for measurements of polychlorinated dibenzo-*p*-dioxins (PCDD) and dibenzofurans (PCDF) in flue gas emissions from waste combustion. The recommended protocol, which will be re-evaluated in a years time, includes the following.

A one week registration period during which the plant is studied by continuous registration of a number of operating and emission parameters. The sampling period is included in this time.

A sampling procedure based on a heated filter followed by a condenser, a bottle for the condensate and an adsorbent column. Before the sampling, at least two labelled PCDD are added to the filter.

No specified analytical procedure. A labelled PCDF is added before the clean-up procedure and an injection standard before the final analysis. The laboratory is free to use any method that gives at least 25% recovery of the sampling standards and 50% recovery of the clean-up standard.

Reporting requirements include homologue specific results for PCDD and PCDF containing four to eight chlorine atoms as well as isomer-specific results for the "dirty dozen". The results should be compensated for incomplete recoveries and the factors used should be reported.

Key Words—Dioxin, analysis, incinerator emissions, municipal solid waste.

1. Background

Polychlorinated dibenzo-*p*-dioxins (PCDD or Dioxins) and dibenzofurans (PCDF) have been found in environmental samples at levels that may cause effects. It is essential to find and limit the sources of these toxic substances. One of the known sources is waste incineration but, when this was studied in Sweden, difficulties in comparing results from different laboratories were realized. To minimize this problem, a standardized procedure was recommended for the measurement of PCDD and PCDF. In April 1986, this protocol was also recommended by the Nordic Council of Ministers for use in all Nordic countries. It was also suggested that the method should be re-evaluated after about one year. A full-text copy of the recommended method in Swedish can be obtained from the authors.

2. Recommended method

The recommended method contains the minimum demands that the measurements must fulfill and is not a detailed manual for the procedure.

* Presented at the ISWA–WHO–DAKOFA specialized seminar, *Emission of Trace Organics from Municipal Solid Waste Incinerators*, Copenhagen, 20–22 January 1987.
‡ The National Environmental Protection Board, Box 1302, S-171 25 Solna, Sweden.
Waste Management & Research (1987) **5**, 251–255

2.1. *Description of the plant operation*

The emission of PCDD and PCDF is believed to be a function of the plant operation. It is thus essential to verify that the sampling period represents normal operation of the plant. It is necessary therefore, to have information on the operation conditions over a longer period of time (registration period) than the sampling period.

2.1.1. *Registration period*

The registration period must be at least one week, and during this time the plant is studied continuously via a number of operating and emission parameters (see below). The parameters studied are registered as 1–15 minute mean values. The mean-value times are chosen with respect to the variability of each parameter. The registration period includes the sampling period.

Data obtained during the registration period are also compared with older data in the plant operation record, especially the waste load and the composition of incinerated waste.

2.1.2. *Operating parameters*

The following operating parameters are registered continuously during the registration period: heat production, flow of primary air, flow of secondary air, furnace temperature, flue gas temperature before and after the boiler, oxygen concentration before the boiler, and carbon dioxide concentration before and after the boiler. When plant instruments are used these must be carefully calibrated before the registration period. The position of the temperature sensor in relation to the combustion zone must be specified carefully.

2.1.3. *Emission parameters*

The following emission parameters are registered continuously during the registration period: concentration of dust (particulates), hydrogen chloride, sulfur dioxide, carbon monoxide and carbon dioxide, and the temperature of the emitted flue gas. When plant instruments are used, these must be carefully calibrated before the registration period.

2.1.4. *Waste composition and amount*

It is not possible to determine the detailed composition of the incinerated waste. The waste should, however, be of normal composition for the plant studied if nothing else is specified. The sampling personnel must observe the waste being loaded during the sampling period to ensure a normal composition. The amount of waste incinerated during the registration period is also measured.

2.1.5. *Plant load record*

The plant load defined as the amount incinerated and the energy produced should be normal during the sampling period. This can be controlled by comparison with the plant operating data.

An alternative method to determine the load is to use a combustion diagram. The load is then calculated according to DIN 1942. If the measurements are made to study any extraordinary conditions, these must be specified in the report.

2.2. *Sampling*

2.2.1. *Sampling equipment*
The isokinetic sampling train includes a glass-fiber filter held at $160 \pm 15°C$, followed by a condenser which takes the temperature down to at least 20°C. The condensate is collected in a bottle and the gas passes an adsorbent column containing at least 5 g XAD-2 m^{-3} gas sampled. Known amounts of at least two internal standards ($^{13}C_{12}$-2,3,7,8-TCDD and $^{13}C_{12}$C-OCDD) must be added to the filter (filter spike) before sampling.

2.2.2. *Sampling procedure*
The sampling should be isokinetic and performed at several points in the sampling plane. The sampling time must not be shorter than three hours.

 The sampling equipment must be tested for leaks before and after sampling. Leak flows greater than 4% of the sampling flow cannot be accepted.

 Each sample series must include a sampling blank which is obtained by assembling the equipment and then letting it stand for an ordinary sampling period without pumping.

2.3. *Analysis*

2.3.1. *Laboratory blank*
One laboratory blank has to be analyzed for each series of up to 10 samples. This blank is passed through the whole analytical procedure.

2.3.2. *Addition of internal standards*
Special internal standards have to be added to the sample before it is extracted in the laboratory. This procedure differentiates between sampling and laboratory losses of the labelled compounds. The addition of a known amount of $^{13}C_{12}$-2,3,7,8-TCDF to the filter is suggested for this purpose. Other labelled PCDDs and/or PCDFs may also be added to filter, condensate or adsorbent to verify extraction efficiencies. A special internal standard must be added just before the final analysis so that the recovery of the other internal standards can be calculated.

2.3.3. *Extraction and clean-up*
The methodology for analysis of PCDD and PCDF is still in the development phase and, therefore, no specific methods are given in this protocol. The laboratory is free to use any method that will give at least 25% recovery of the internal standards added before the sampling and at least 50% of the internal standards added before the extraction.

 There are no methods available that disclose the distribution between adsorbed and vapor phases of a compound in the emission. The analysis can, therefore, be performed on the combined extracts from filter, condensate and adsorbent.

2.3.4. *Mass spectrometric analysis*
If multiple-ion detection is used, at least two mass numbers for each homologue group must be measured. The abundance ratio between these must be within $\pm 10\%$ of the theoretical value.

2.4. Reporting requirements

2.4.1. Plant and process description

The best way to describe the measurement is to include a drawing (with the sampling points marked) of the plant in the report. The operation and emissions are described with the above mentioned parameters. All conditions at the plant that can influence the interpretation of the results are also described in the report. This includes design of emission control equipment, the use of pre-heated air, etc. Calibration of plant instruments is also described. The combustion efficiency (FE) is given as

$$FE = 100([CO_2] - [CO])/[CO_2].$$

2.4.2. Analytical results

The results of the PCDD and PCDF analysis are reported as concentrations of individual congeners with four to six chlorine atoms and the positions 2, 3, 7 and 8 chlorinated (isomer-specific analysis of "the dirty dozen"). Furthermore, the sums of tetra-, penta-, hexa-, hepta- and octa-chlorinated dioxins and furans are reported (homologue specific analysis). The results must be corrected for incomplete recoveries. Compounds containing four and five chlorine atoms are recalculated according to the recovery of $^{13}C_{12}$-2,3,7,8-TCDD, and compounds containing seven or eight chlorine atoms according to the recovery of $^{13}C_{12}$-OCDD. The average of the two recoveries is used for the hexachlorinated compounds. The recoveries of all internal standards are also reported. The detection limits are given for the compounds that cannot be detected.

The recommended unit for PCDD and PCDF concentrations is nanogram per cubic meter dry gas at 10% carbon dioxide (ng m_{norm}^{-3} dg 10% CO_2). If some sort of "TCDD equivalents" are calculated, the factors must be given.

Results that do not fulfill the requirements in this recommendation can be reported only if the divergence(s) is carefully specified.

All methods used must be described (possibly with references). Divergence(s) from the methods referred to must be described, as must any, unusual observations made during the work. Primary data must be available at least one year after the results are reported.

3. Experiences

The recommended method has now been in use for some time and the use of labelled internal standards provides a possibility for evaluating how useful the method is. This technique guarantees that the reported results are not too low, but the only way to avoid results which are too high is probably by intercalibration between tests.

Two laboratories were compared in a measurement where they tried to take parallel samples in a stack. The results were comparable, at least for the twelve most toxic congeners.

The general experience of using internal standards in the sampling is that the compounds added to the filter seem to evaporate to a greater extent than the native compounds in the sample. This may be explained by the longer residence time of the internal standards in the hot zone and by a stronger adsorption of the native compounds to particles.

Low recoveries of the internal standards added before the sampling have also sometimes been observed. This problem may be due to aerosol formation in the condenser and this problem will be investigated.

In summary, it can be concluded that the recommended method has improved the results from PCDD and PCDF measurements in flue gas samples. It has also made comparisons of results from different sources possible. However, in its present version, the method is not perfect and must be re-evaluated when more experience has been gathered.

References

Bergvall, G. & Jansson, B. (1986), *Recommended Method for Dioxin Measurements in Flue Gas at MSW Incinerators*, Statens Naturvårdsverk, Stockholm, Sweden 1986-02-19 (in Swedish).

PCDD AND PCDF EMISSIONS AND POSSIBLE HEALTH EFFECTS: REPORT ON A WHO WORKING GROUP*

Michael J. Suess †

(*Received November 1986, revised February 1987*)

An international group of experts, convened by the WHO Regional Office for Europe, discussed the health risks of PCDD and PCDF emissions from the incineration of municipal sewage sludge (MSS) and municipal solid waste (MSW) at a meeting in Naples, Italy, held 17–21 March 1986. A detailed analysis of emission data has shown that old and badly operated incinerators will emit up to many thousand ng Nm^{-3} of PCDD and PCDF, while most modern, highly controlled and carefully operated plants will emit them at a very low level. It is still not known what contribution municipal incinerator emissions make to the overall environmental load and, consequently, human exposure. For modern incineration plants this contribution was estimated to be in the range of about a tenth to a few percent of the total background daily body burden [assumed to be 1–5 pg of 2,3,7,8-TCDD (dioxin) equivalents per kilogram bodyweight and day]. The Working Group nevertheless recommended that efforts should be made to reduce further the PCDD and PCDF emissions from municipal incinerators.

Key Words—Municipal incinerators, municipal solid waste, municipal sewage sludge, PCDD, PCDF, TCDD, dioxin, health effects, human exposure.

1. Introduction

Emissions from municipal solid waste (MSW) and municipal sewage sludge (MSS) incinerators have long aroused concern. In the late 1970s and early 1980s, poly-chlorinated dibenzo-*para*-dioxins and dibenzofurans (PCDD and PCDF) were reported in fly ash from MSW incinerators. The general public, being aware of the high toxicity of these compounds, has shown much concern about the incineration of MSW and MSS. Therefore, there has been a need to develop a better understanding of the emission levels and potential public health effects of PCDD and PCDF from municipal incinerators.

Consequently, and at the request of the Italian authorities, the WHO Regional Office for Europe convened a working group in Naples, 17–21 March 1986, to review the issue of emissions of PCDD and PCDF from incineration of MSS, MSW, or both together, and the possible health effects.

The discussion focused on: (i) the influence of the composition of the material being incinerated and the main features of the incineration process (temperature, mixing, retention of combustion products, oxygen, and the managerial aspects) on the quality and quantity of PCDD and PCDF emissions; (ii) the environmental pathways of emitted PCDD and PCDF as related to human exposure; (iii) the relative importance

* Presented at the ISWA–WHO–DAKOFA specialized seminar, *Emissions of Trace Organics from Municipal Solid Waste Incinerators*, Copenhagen, 20–22 January 1987. The views expressed in this paper are those of the author and the WHO group of experts and do not necessarily represent the decisions or the stated policy of the World Health Organization. See also WHO Environmental Health Series No. 17 (1987).

† Regional Officer for Environmental Health Hazards, WHO Regional Office for Europe, Scherfigsvej 8, 2100 Copenhagen, Denmark.

Waste Management & Research (1987) **5**, 257–268

of incineration of MSS and MSW as compared to other sources of human exposure to PCDD and PCDF; and (iv) the public health significance of emissions of PCDD and PCDF during incineration of MSS and MSW.

2. Incineration

The primary function of an incinerator is to burn waste to an inert residue. The solid waste combustion process is rather complex. The waste is heated by contact with hot combustion gases or with preheated air, and by radiation from the furnace walls. Drying occurs in a temperature range of 50–150°C. At higher temperatures, volatile matter is formed by complicated thermal decomposition reactions. This volatile matter is generally combustible and, after ignition, gives rise to flames. The remaining material is further degassed and burns much more slowly as a char.

The combustion of the waste proceeds without supplementary fuel when the heat value is at least 5000 kJ kg^{-1}. This occurs when the waste has not more than 60% ash, not more than 50% moisture and not less than 25% combustible matter. Rotating drum incinerators, fluidized beds and multiple-hearth ovens have been used for sludge incineration. Sludge may also be burnt in municipal waste incinerators in conjunction with other MSW if it is properly prepared (dried and reduced in size) prior to intro-duction into the furnace. A modern incinerator is designed to achieve substantially complete combustion of the volatile matter distilling from the waste. This objective is achieved by providing adequate residence time, post-combustion temperature and turbulent mixing. When this objective is achieved, the concentration level of carbon monoxide remains consistently below 0.1% (by volume). The occurrence of incomplete combustion can be detected by monitoring the flue gas for CO, and O_2 or CO_2. It can be corrected by suitable control of the loading rate, the operating temperature, the draft and the distribution of primary and secondary air.

3. Formation of PCDD and PCDF

A much publicized problem in waste incineration is the emission of extremely small amounts of chlorinated polycyclic aromatic compounds, such as PCDD and PCDF (Dioxins). While their origin is not entirely clear, they appear, at least partially, as a result of complex thermal synthesis reactions during periods of poor combustion. Because of their high thermal stability, they can only be destroyed after adequate residence times at relatively high temperatures. The high sensitivity of presently avail-able analytical techniques means that the occurrence of PCDD and PCDF and other polychlorinated compounds (such as chlorobenzenes, chlorophenols and PCB) at extremely low trace levels in emissions from MSW incinerators is generally to be expected.

Three basic theories have been proposed for the occurrence of PCDD and PCDF in the emissions from municipal incinerators:

(i) PCDD and PCDF occur as trace constituents in the waste itself, and a portion simply passes through the incinerator process without transformation;

(ii) PCDD and PCDF are produced during the incineration process, or in the boiler, from precursors such as PCB, pentachlorphenols and chlorinated benzenes;

(iii) PCDD and PCDF are synthesized from materials not directly related to these compounds, e.g. petroleum products, chlorinated hydrocarbons, inorganic chloride ions and plastics.

With respect to the first theory, some analysis of MSW has been performed to determine the presence and quantity of PCDD and PCDF in the waste. However, it is generally agreed that there is little reason to expect PCDD and PCDF in the waste to be a significant source of these compounds in emissions from MSW incinerators. Furthermore, if they did occur in the waste, normal temperatures of combustion and gas retention times (e.g. about 900°C and 1–2 s) would indicate nearly complete destruction in the combustion process. PCDD and PCDF have also been reported to occur in sewage sludge samples (Lamparski 1984). The limited data of this and other studies indicate that MSS could be a minor source for introducing PCDD and PCDF into the combustion process.

In the second case, precursors of PCDD and PCDF compounds may be introduced into the incinerator as components of MSW. If these substances are heated to temperatures below destruction levels, PCDD and PCDF may be formed. Laboratory studies have shown that pyrolysis and combustion of a variety of precursors can lead to PCDD and PCDF emissions (Jansson & Sundström 1979).

The third formation mechanism, a synthesis of PCDD and PCDF from unrelated chemicals under specific incinerator operating conditions, has been proposed on the basis of results from certain laboratory-scale tests (e.g. Liberti *et al.* 1983). Also, it has been recently reported that chloroaliphatic compounds, such as PVC, saran and hexachloroethane, can also be converted to PCDD and PCDF by pyrolytic reaction (Marklund *et al.* 1987).

In terms of basic chemistry, HCl and carbon, in the presence of oxygen, alone can form dioxins. HCl and carbon react at 900°C to give tetrachloromethane, which can form chlorinated aromatic compounds (Ballschmiter *et al.* 1983). However, it is not yet known how far these possible reaction pathways are realized in the actual combustion of MSW. Another study (Zoller & Ballschmiter 1986), using only 2,3,4- and 3,4,5-trichlorophenol as starting materials, has shown that nearly all tri- through octa-chlorodibenzodioxins and dibenzofurans can be formed at 440°C. There are good reasons to assume that the ratio and availability of oxygen in the flames govern the possible pathways (Ballschmiter *et al.* 1983). Investigations of fly ash from coal burning plants, which were practically free of dioxins and furans, seem to support this assumption.

4. Emission levels

Data on emissions of PCDD and PCDF from tests on MSW incinerators range between a few and several thousand ng m^{-3} at 10% CO_2 (Table 1). The plants in Hamilton, ON, Canada, and Hampton, VA, U.S.A., have relatively high emissions. Both of these plants are known to have experienced operational problems at the time of testing. The plant in Hamilton was recently closed for retrofitting, to improve combustion conditions.

The plants tested in Belgium, the old plant in the Federal Republic of Germany and the plants in the Netherlands are not considered to be representative of the most modern, highly controlled MSW incineration plants, and the results for the PCDD and PCDF emission tests at these installations are higher than at the more modern and highly controlled installations, such as the plants in Sweden, Prince Edward Island, Canada, Chicago NW, IL, U.S.A., and Westchester RESCO, NY, U.S.A. The extremely low emissions from the pilot plant tests in Canada, using acid gas control equipment, should also be noted as well as the high emissions from the Swedish plant during start-up.

TABLE 1

Range of emissions of PCDD and PCDF (ng m^{-3} at 10% CO_2) in different MSW incinerators

Incinerator plant	PCDD	PCDF
Belgium (Detré *et al.* 1985)		
Incinerator I	3900	4600
Incinerator II	840	2900
Canada (Environment Canada 1985)		
Hamilton, ON (range)	1100–7200	3000–10 000
Prince Edward Island (range)	60–190	100–210
Acid gas control (average, pilot plant)	1	2
Federal Republic of Germany		
Hagenmaier (range, old plant)	130–610	300–2400
Netherlands (Olie *et al.* 1982)		
Average (tests from 9 plants)	1500	1300
Sweden (Marklund *et al.* 1987)		
Start-up	1300	1700
U.S.A.		
Hampton, VA (range, Hahn 1985)	500–3800	1600–16 000
Chicago NW, IL (range, Hahn 1985)	30–40	170–180
Westchester RESCO, NY (range, (NYSBTAS 1986)	15–30	50–80

Table 2 presents the results of tests considered at the meeting, expressing a range of estimated isomer-specific emissions for those isomers of major concern under different operating conditions. In column 1 are tabulated emissions that the Working Group considered to be achievable in the most modern, most highly controlled and carefully operated plants in use at the present time. Such results do not reflect what is felt to be achievable by use of acid gas cleaning equipment; use of such equipment should result in much lower values (probably at least one order of magnitude lower). The results given in column 1 would not be representative of emissions that might be expected from such plants during start-up or under occasional upset conditions. The Working Group considered the emission levels listed in column 2 to be indicative of the higher limit of emissions from modern MSW incinerators. Such plants might experience such emissions during start-up or under occasional upset conditions. Consequently, the majority of the available concentration data falls between columns 1 and 2. Some of the data reviewed has shown that the value in column 2 should not be considered as an absolute maximum. However, most existing plants, if carefully operated, will have PCDD and PCDF emissions in the range between the values listed in columns 1 and 2.

The highest values for MSW incinerators (column 3) were obtained by multiplying the values in column 2 by a factor of 5. The data in column 3 is equal to or greater than the highest emission data that were reported to the Working Group from all tests and under all circumstances. Generally, these emission levels are associated with irregular or unstable operating conditions, high moisture content of the MSW, low combustion or afterburner temperatures, less than adequate technologies, etc.

The Working Group was aware of both lower and higher emission levels than those

TABLE 2

Estimated range of emissions from MSW and MSS combustion for exposure evaluation

Isomers	Emissions from MSW Combustion (ng m^{-3}, dry, at 10% CO$_2$)		
	1 Achievable with modern plants with no acid gas cleaning	2 Maximum from average operation	3 High emissions
2,3,7,8–T4CDD	0.1	1.5	7.5
1,2,3,7,8–P5CDD	0.3	14	70
1,2,3,4,7,8–H6CDD	0.2	31	155
1,2,3,6,7,8–H6CDD	0.6	56	280
1,2,3,7,8,9–H6CDD	0.4	20	100
2,3,7,8–T4CDF	0.9	10	50
1,2,3,7,8/1,2,3,4,8–P5CDF	2.3	52	260
2,3,4,7,8–P5CDF	2.0	40	200
1,2,3,4,7,8/1,2,3,4,7,9–H6CDF	1.1	48	240
1,2,3,6,7,8–H6CDF	1.3	40	200
1,2,3,7,8,9–H6CDF	0.06	52	260
2,3,4,6,7,8–H6CDF	2.0	36	180

included in Table 2. However, it was felt that the values included in this Table are likely to be representative of emissions from today's facilities.

No formal publications were available on dioxin and furan emissions from MSS incineration. A number of recent studies in the U.S.A., F.R.G., and Belgium were said to have shown very low to undetectable dioxin emission from different types of sludge incinerators.

Emission levels to be used in assessing health hazards from MSS incineration are the same as the levels considered achievable in the most modern, highly controlled and carefully operated MSW incinerators, given in column 1. This was considered by the Working Group to be a conservative estimate of emissions from this type of incinerator. On the basis of the limited information available, projected emissions from MSS incinerators are generally lower than those from MSW incinerator plants, and frequently down to non-detectable levels. Results of tests from fluidized-bed MSS incinerators have consistently indicated little or no detectable emissions of PCDD and PCDF. Thus, total mass emissions from the incineration of MSS from a particular area should be at least one to two orders of magnitude lower than emissions from the incineration of MSW from the same area. This is due to the consistently lower emission concentrations and the fact that (in the U.S.A.) production of MSW is of the order of 1 kg per day per person, while production of sewage solids is approximately 0.1 kg day^{-1} of dry solids per person.

5. Environmental pathways

PCDD and PCDF emitted from incinerators are often found in the environment adsorbed onto particulate matter such as dust, fly ash, sediments and/or soil, and may also contaminate water bodies and plants. Photodegradation is likely to be one factor affecting the ultimate fate of PCDD and PCDF, and the effectiveness of ultraviolet light in degrading these compounds in the presence of a hydrogen donor is well established (e.g. Hutzinger *et al.* 1973). In view of their lipophilic nature, persistent PCDD and PCDF have a potential for accumulating in the food chain (e.g. Pocchiari *et al.* 1986).

As far as the aquatic environment is concerned, PCDD and PCDF are more frequently found at measurable levels in sediment than in water. PCDD and PCDF are strongly adsorbed onto most soils where they are expected to be relatively immobile (Wipf *et al.* 1982). Transport of PCDD and PCDF from soil to the atmosphere may take place via contaminated airborne dust particles, and to surface waters via water-borne eroded soil.

Contamination of aerial parts of plants may take place through the settling of contaminated airborne particles and through volatilization of PCDD and PCDF from soil (Pocchiari *et al.* 1986). As far as the transfer from soil to vegetation is concerned, PCDD and PCDF tend to be adsorbed onto the external surfaces, but no bio-concentration has been observed (Kenaga & Norris 1983).

Soil contamination can lead to the contamination of animal feed as a consequence of plant contamination. The direct ingestion by animals of contaminated soil is also an important route for their contamination (Dean & Suess 1985).

6. Health effects

A number of comprehensive reviews dealing with health effects of PCDD and PCDF are available (e.g. Kimbrough 1980, Coulston & Pocchiari 1983, Tucker *et al.* 1983, Bellin & Barnes 1985, Umweltbundesamt 1985). Several risk evaluations have been performed in various countries on 2,3,7,8-tetrachlorodibenzodioxin (TCDD, dioxin), the PCDD of greatest known toxicological concern. It is, however, a minor component of emissions from incinerators. As the available data on human exposure do not allow any risk assessment to be performed, animal data must be used for this purpose. From a limited number of animal studies it is known that isomers other than 2,3,7,8-TCDD are also likely to be of toxicological concern. Therefore, the Working Group believes that the consideration of the hazard of PCDD and PCDF emissions from combustion sources cannot be limited to 2,3,7,8-TCDD alone. Yet, although no data are available for PCDD and PCDF mixtures, it is to be expected that exposure to complex PCDD and PCDF mixtures may elicit responses different from those observed with individual chemicals.

Occupational exposure to 2,3,7,8-TCDD during production of certain chemicals has been summarized in the literature (e.g. Kimbrough 1980). Industrial accidents have also occurred (e.g. Suskind & Hertzberg 1984), resulting in heavy contamination of factories with 2,3,7,8-TCDD, and workers who have probably received heavy exposure. However, in none of these episodes have any measurements been made of the human exposure to 2,3,7,8-TCDD. Workers, such as applicators of herbicides, were also exposed to mixtures of chemicals which included PCDD and PCDF. Occasionally, members of the general population have been exposed to levels of 2,3,7,8-TCDD along with other chemicals which resulted in some adverse effects (e.g. Pocchiari *et al.* 1986).

These occupational exposures are considered to be much higher than those of the general population, who may get contaminated from the presence of these chemicals in the environment. Recently, chemical analyses have been developed to the extent that low concentrations of PCDD and PCDF can now be measured in human adipose tissue and milk. So far, results have been published on several hundred adipose tissue samples from a few countries (Canada, Japan, Sweden, U.S.A., Vietnam) and more than 100 human milk samples (Denmark, F.R.G., Sweden, U.S.A.). The levels for different isomers have ranged from non-detectable to low parts per trillion (for tetra-CDD) up to around 1000 ppt (for octa-CDD) on a fat basis (e.g. Rappe *et al.* 1986). As a matter of fact, no information is presently available in the literature on the human health effects resulting from exposure to PCDD and PCDF emissions from MSW or MSS incineration. Yet, the incidence and severity of the health effects observed after incidents of heavy occupational exposure might be considered an upper limit for the estimate of health effects in the general population from PCDD and PCDF emissions from municipal incinerators. (See Ahlborg & Victorin and Rappe *et al.* in this issue).

7. Human exposure

In order to assess the impact of PCDD and PCDF emissions from MSW to MSS incineration on a local general population, one would have to examine the potential contribution of such emissions to the overall background daily dose. Emission exposures can be direct, through inhalation, dermal absorption and ingestion, and indirect, through contribution to the environmental load and eventual exposure to man from food.

7.1. *Direct exposure contribution*

Inhalation is the most important route of direct exposure. To estimate concentrations of PCDD and PCDF in the ambient air, certain assumptions must be made with respect to dilution factors, ground-level concentrations, breathing rate and human body weight. In the absence of valid isomer-specific air sample data, dispersion models have been used to generate plausible estimates of air concentrations to which people might be exposed (e.g. Olie *et al.* 1982). These models, reflecting local climatological conditions, take measured mass emission rates from the stack and calculate ground-level concentrations at various points around the stack. Attention is usually focused on the point of maximum average annual ground-level concentration. Different models and different local conditions give rise to different dilution factors.

For the purpose of a calculated example, the following parameters are assumed: a conservative dilution factor (F_d) of 10^{-5} (although values of the order of 10^{-4} are not uncommon), a human total air intake (I_a) (or breathing rate) of 20 m^3 day^{-1} (which represents a relatively high level of physical activity, some apply lower values such as 10 m^3 day^{-1}), and a standard adult bodyweight (W_b) of 70 kg (although 60 kg is often used). The 'worst case' calculated daily inhalation dose could then be derived. This 'worst case' includes other assumptions, such as continuous lifetime exposure at the point of maximum average annual ground-level concentration, no degradation or redistribution of PCDD and PCDF between stack and ground, and inhalation, retention and absorption of 100% of the particle-bound PCDD and PCDF. (These are very conservative assumptions, possibly by as much as 100-fold.) Accordingly, a Worst Case Daily Inhalation Dose (D_i) could be derived:

$$D_i = 1000 \times T_e \times F_d \times I_a \times W_b^{-1}$$

where T_e is the total 2,3,7,8-TCDD (dioxin) equivalents emitted from the stack and expressed as ng m^{-3}. D_i is expressed as picograms of 2,3,7,8-TCDD equivalents per kilogram bodyweight and day (pg[TCDD] kg^{-1} day^{-1}).

From the levels of PCDD and PCDF likely to be found in emissions from modern properly operated incineration plants of MSW and MSS (Table 2, columns 1 and 4), D_i is calculated to be about 0.002 pg[TCDD] kg^{-1} day^{-1}. Quite clearly, this could make only a very minor contribution to the normally assumed total background daily body burden of 1–5 pg[TCDD] kg^{-1} day^{-1}. However, a rather small contribution is calculated, equal to about 0.07 pg[TCDD] kg^{-1} day^{-1}, when the higher emission levels from the most modern MSW incineration plants (Table 2, column 2) are to be considered. The worst-case hypothesis, concerning the levels of PCDD and PCDF emissions from incinerators with irregular operating conditions, high moisture content in the waste, low combustion or afterburner temperatures and poor technologies (Table 2, column 3), would result in an inhalation dose of about 0.3 pg[TCDD] kg^{-1} day^{-1}. At the extreme, this could represent as much as 30% of the total daily body burden, but 6% would be more realistic.

As stated previously, these doses are considered to be gross overestimates, making it unlikely that the direct inhalation contribution of emissions from modern well-run MSW and MSS incineration plants would make a significant contribution to the apparent background daily intake of PCDD and PCDF.

7.2. _Indirect exposure contribution_

A study in Switzerland reported a correlation between levels of PCDD and PCDF in cow milk and exposure to emissions of MSS incinerators (Rappe _et al._ 1986). Therefore, this potential route of exposure should be carefully considered in any specific local situation.

Recent studies have revealed a level of contamination of human milk by PCDD and PCDF (Nygren _et al._ 1985). The extent of the contribution of MSW and MSS combustion to these levels cannot be assessed at the present time. (WHO/EURO is presently involved in a separate assessment of the significance of these findings.)

A large body of data has been gathered on the levels of PCDD and PCDF in fish. However, the contribution of MSW and MSS combustion to the accumulation of PCDD and PCDF in fish remains unknown.

No evidence exists for the direct contamination of drinking water. An extensive survey of drinking water supplies in Ontario revealed only two positive results at extremely low levels (0.015 ppt) of octa-CDD. This contamination was believed to be the result of chemical contamination and not combustion of waste.

Hence, an estimate of the indirect contribution of MSW and MSS incineration to the background daily dose cannot be made at this time. It should be recognized that certain population groups (e.g. persons consuming milk produced solely at farms in the immediate neighbourhood of municipal incinerators, and those eating large quantities of fish) may receive relatively higher exposure.

7.3. _Exposure from other sources_

There is a wide range of other combustion sources which contribute to the overall environmental load of PCDD and PCDF (see Hagenmaier in this issue). The inventory in any one region or country will determine the total environmental loading and will affect the absolute rank order of sources of these compounds.

Given the uncertainty about the number and magnitude of sources which contribute PCDD and PCDF to the environment, it is currently not possible to assess accurately the portion of the environmental load of PCDD and PCDF due to MSW and MSS combustion. However, the greater the extent to which new major sources are discovered, the lower the relative contribution from MSW and MSS. Nevertheless, further direct action should be taken toward achieving the minimal attainable emissions from all known sources, including MSW and MSS incinerators.

8. Conclusions and recommendations

The Working Group reached the following conclusions and recommendations:

8.1. *Conclusions*

(1) The level of PCDD (dioxin) and PCDF emissions from municipal solid waste (MSW) incinerators vary widely and factors causing these variations are not yet thoroughly understood. However, tests on modern, well-run municipal sewage sludge (MSS) and/or MSW incinerators generally emit consistently lower levels of PCDD and PCDF than older, and/or poorly maintained and poorly operated incinerators.

(2) Available data suggest that high temperature, adequate retention time, high turbulence and excess oxygen (together, reflecting good combustion conditions) are likely to result in low PCDD and PCDF emissions.

(3) 2,3,7,8-TCDD (dioxin), which is generally considered to be the most toxic of the PCDD and PCDF compounds, is only a minor component of the overall emissions of MSS and/or MSW incinerators.

(4) The limited data presently available on the level of PCDD and PCDF emissions from MSS incinerators suggest that these levels are significantly lower than those for MSW incinerators. Results from testing of fluidized-bed incinerators indicate PCDD and PCDF emissions at or below detection limits.

(5) Available data indicate that the application of appropriate acid-gas control facilities is likely to reduce PCDD and PCDF emissions significantly to below the lowest levels considered in the present analysis.

(6) Inhalation of emissions from well-operated MSS and/or MSW incinerators appears to contribute only a small fraction to the apparent overall daily intake of PCDD and PCDF, including people living in the maximum emission zone.

(7) The contribution of MSS and/or MSW incinerators through indirect exposure routes (e.g. food chain) to the overall human exposure from PCDD and PCDF cannot be determined at present. However, it appears that in particular situations a significant contribution could be made through these routes.

(8) The relationship between the levels of PCDD and PCDF, detected in environmental and human specimens, and the many potentially contributing environmental sources is not well understood.

(9) Some data indicate the presence of PCDD and PCDF in certain geographical areas in both biotic and abiotic specimens. However, significant differences exist between their profiles as detected in the environment (e.g. in soil and sediments), and observed in living organisms.

(10) Available limited data on the relatively uniform levels of PCDD and PCDF in human adipose tissue suggest the presence of a background influence.

(11) No information is presently available in the literature on the human health effects resulting from PCDD and PCDF emissions from MSS or MSW combustion. Also unknown is the degree of human exposure from such emissions. Yet, based on

information related to workers' exposure to very high concentrations, it can be deduced that the severity of emissions from incinerators remains below that concentration.

8.2. *Recommendations*

(1) Selection of appropriate incineration technology should be made with due regard to the area of origination, quantity and quality of the waste.

(2) A better, more comprehensive scientific data base should be developed with which to refine criteria for the selection of operating conditions of incinerators, in order to control PCDD and PCDF emissions more adequately.

(3) Evaluation of PCDD and PCDF emissions should be based on a series of measurements of emission levels from incinerators, and the recording of corresponding operating conditions.

(4) Additional studies should be done to validate sampling techniques and analytical methods for the measurement of PCDD and PCDF emissions from incinerators.

(5) The installation of afterburners should be considered if the nature and/or composition of a waste or the operation of an incinerator indicate that there may be a problem in maintaining adequate temperatures and other operating conditions.

(6) The construction of small incinerators should be discouraged when adequate and properly trained personnel cannot be provided on a cost-effective basis.

(7) When MSS incineration is being considered, recognition and account should be given to the physical and chemical characteristics which differentiate MSS from MSW.

(8) MSS should be properly prepared prior to incineration to ensure its proper combustion, alone or in combination with MSW.

(9) Additional monitoring should be conducted to determine the range of human body burdens of PCDD and PCDF in the general population.

(10) Studies should be carried out to evaluate the relative importance of incinerators as sources of PCDD and PCDF in the human body.

(11) Surveys should be done to identify any group with potentially high exposures to PCDD and PCDF from incinerators, to enable the evaluation of possible health effects.

(12) Additional studies should be performed to clarify better environmental pathways and health impact of PCDD and PCDF from incinerators.

(13) The health and environmental impact of incinerators on the local environment should be evaluated on a case-by-case basis.

(14) Because of the very limited data on human body burdens of PCDD and PCDF from MSS and/or MSW incinerators and other sources, the uncertainties inherent in the concept of the toxic equivalency of different PCDD and PCDF isomers and homologues, and the wide range in present calculated emissions, the evaluation of human exposure (referred to in the Working Group's report) should be reviewed as more information and a clearer base of understanding develop.

Acknowledgement

The final complete report on the WHO Working Group will be issued later in 1987. This paper is a condensed version of this report.

References

Ballschmiter, K., Zoller, W., Scholz, Ch. & Nottsadt, A. (1983), Occurrence and absence of polychlorodibenzofurans and polychlorodibenzodioxins in fly ash from municipal incinerators, *Chemosphere, 12,* 585–594.

Bellin, J. S. & Barnes, D. (Eds) (1985), *Health Hazard Assessment for Chlorinated Dioxins and Dibenzorurans other than 2,3,7,8-TCDD.* U.S. Environmental Protection Agency, Washington, DC.

Coulston, F. A. & Pocchiari, F. (Eds) (1983), *Accidental Exposures to Dioxins: Human Health Aspects.* Academic Press, London.

Dean, R. B. & Suess, M. J. (Eds) (1985), The risk to health of chemicals in sewage sludge applied to land, (A World Health Organization report), *Waste Management & Research, 3,* 251–278.

DeFré, R. (1986), Dioxin levels in the emissions of Belgian municipal incinerators, *Chemosphere, 15,* 1255–1260.

Environment Canada (1985), *The National Incinerator Testing and Evaluation Program: Two-stage Combustion (Prince Edward Island). Vol. IV. Detailed Results.* Environment Canada, Report EPS3/UP/4.

Hahn, J. L. (1985), *Trace Metal, Acid Gas and Dioxin Emissions Data Collected at Refuse Energy Recovery Facilities in the U.S., Japan and Europe: Testing Methods, Results and Emission Factors.* EPRI Conference on Energy from Waste, Madison, Wis.

Hutzinger, O., Safe, S., Wentzell, B. R. & Gejvall, T. (1973), Photochemical degradation of di- and octa-chlorodibenzofuran, *Environmental Health Perspectives, 5,* 267–271.

Jansson, B. & Sundström, G. (1979), Formation of polychlorinated dibenzo-*p*-dioxins during combustion of chlorophenol formulations, *Science of the Total Environment, 10,* 209–217.

Kenaga, E. E. & Norris, L. A. (1983), Environmental toxicity of TCDD. In *Human and Environmental Risks of Chlorinated Dioxins and Related Compounds* (R. E. Tucker, A. L. Young, & A. P. Gray, Eds), pp. 277–299. Plenum Press, New York.

Kimbrough, R. D. (Ed) (1980), *Halogenated Biphenyls, Terphenyls, Naphthalenes, Dibenzodioxins and Related Products.* Elsevier, Amsterdam.

Lamparski, L. L. (1984), Presence of chlorodibenzodioxins in a sealed 1933 sample of dried municipal sewage sludge, *Chemosphere, 13,* 361–365.

Liberti, A., Goretti, G. & Russo, M. V. (1983), PCDD and PCDF formation in the combustion of vegetable wastes, *Chemosphere, 12,* 661–663.

Marklund, S., Kjeller, L.-O., Hansson, M., Tysklind, M., Rappe, C., Ryan, C., Collazo, H. & Dougherty, R. (1986), Determination of PCDDs and PCDFs in incineration samples and pyrolytic products. In *Chlorinated Dioxins and Dibenzofurans in Perspective* (C. Rappe, G. Choudhary & L. H. Keith, Eds), pp. 79–92. Lewis Publishers, Inc., Chelsea, MI, U.S.A.

Nygren, M., Rappe, C., Lindstrom, G., Hansson, M., Bergqvist, P.-A., Marklund, S., Domellof, L., Hardeli, L. & Olsson, M. (1986), Identification of 2,3,7,8-substituted polychlorinated dioxins and dibenzofurans in environmental and human samples. In *Chlorinated Dioxins and Dibenzofurans in Perspective* (C. Rappe, G. Choudhary & L. H. Keith, Eds), pp. 15–34. Lewis Publishers, Inc., Chelsea, MI, U.S.A.

NYSBTAS (1986), *Preliminary Report on Westchester RESCO RRF, 8 January 1986.* New York State Bureau of Toxic Air Sampling, Division of Air Resources, Albany, NY, U.S.A.

Olie, K. *et al.* (1982), Polychlorinated dibenzo-p-dioxins and related compounds in incinerator effluents. In Chlorinated Dioxins and Related Compounds: Impact on the Environment (O. Hutzinger *et al.*, Eds). Pergamon series on environmental science. Vol. 5, pp. 227–244. Pergamon Press, Oxford.

Olie, K., Berg, M. V. D. & Hutzinger, O. (1983), Formation and fate of PCDD and PCDF from combustion processes, *Chemosphere, 12,* 627–636.

Pocchiari, F., Cattabeni, F., Della Pozta, G., Fortunati, V., Silano, V. & Zapponi, G. (1986), Assessment of exposure to 2,3,7,8-tetrachlorodibenzo-*p*-dioxin (TCDD) in the Seveso area, *Chemosphere, 15,* 1851–1865.

Rappe, C., Nygren, M., Lindström, G. & Hansson, M. (1986), Dioxins and dibenzofurans in biological samples of European origin, *Chemosphere,* in press.

Suskind, R. R. & Hertzberg, V. S. (1984), Human health effects of 2,4,5-T and its toxic contaminants, *Journal of the American Medical Association, 251,* 2372–2380.

Tucker, R. E., Young, A. L. & Gray, A. P. (Eds) (1983), *Human and Environmental Risks of Chlorinated Dioxins and Related Compounds*. Plenum Press, New York.

Umweltbundesamt (1985), *Sachstand Dioxine – Stand November 1984* [State of the art on dioxin – status of November 1987], Berichte 5/85. Erich Schmidt Verlag, Berlin (West).

Wipf, H. K., Frei, R. W., Mesian, E. & Pocchiari, F. (1982), TCDD-levels in soil and plant samples from the Seveso area. In *Chlorinated Dioxins and Related Compounds: Impact on the Environment* (O. Hutzinger, *et al.*, Eds), pp. 115–126. Pergamon Press, Oxford.

Zoller, W. & Ballschmiter, K. (1986), Formation of polychlorinated dibenzodioxins and dibenzo-furans by heating chlorophenols and chlorophenates at various temperatures, *Zeitschrift für Analitische Chemie, 323*, 19–23.

RISK FROM EXPOSURE TO POLYCHLORINATED DIBENZO-p-DIOXINS AND DIBENZOFURANS EMITTED FROM MUNICIPAL INCINERATORS*

Debdas Mukerjee† and David H. Cleverly‡

(*Received December 1986, revised March 1986*)

Incineration of wastes seems to be one of the major sources of PCDDs and PCDFs (dioxins). Their prevalence and extreme stability in the environment, bioavailability and bioaccumulation in the biota and human adipose tissues and breast milk are of much concern. 2,3,7,8-TCDD is one of the most toxic chemicals known and has been found to have teratogenic and carcinogenic activities in animals. Exposure to TCDD can result in chloracne, general weakness, drastic weight loss, hyperpigmentation of skin, hirsutism, porphyria cutanea tarda, liver damage, changes in activities of various liver enzymatic levels, abnormal lipid metabolism, abnormalities of the endocrine and immune systems, and possible teratogenic effects in humans. Moreover, chronic bioassay data indicate that TCDD is one of the most potent carcinogens known. It promotes liver and skin carcinogeneses, and is an initiator for various target organs in rodent test systems. There is only a limited number of human epi-studies on carcinogenic outcome as a result of exposure to TCDD in isolated population.

According to the classification system of the International Agency for Research on Cancer (IARC), the qualitative evidence for carcinogenicity of TCDD is considered to be "sufficient" in animals and "inadequate" in humans. Consequently, this chemical has been placed in IARC's 2B category. A modification of the multistage model is utilized for extrapolating high-dose, two-year animal cancer bioassay data to estimate human cancer risk for long-term, low-dose human exposure. The upper limit of incremental cancer risk is 3.3×10^{-5} for a continuous lifetime exposure to 1 pg m^{-3} of TCDD in ambient air. With the exception of 2,3,7,8-TCDD and a mixture of 1,2,3,6,7,8- and 1,2,3,7,8,9-HxCDDs, the chronic toxicity data on the rest of the 75 PCDD and 135 PCDF congeners are badly deficient. In the absence of chronic bioassay data on other PCDDs and PCDFs, several TCDD equivalent approaches have been proposed for risk assessment on other congeners or mixtures. This paper compares the various approaches.

Key Words—Dioxins, TCDD, TCDF, municipal incineration, health risk, isomer equivalents.

1. Introduction

Polychlorinated dibenzo-p-dioxins (PCDDs) and dibenzofurans (PCDFs) enter the environment as unwanted trace impurities in products derived from chlorinated phenols; 2,4,5-trichlorophenoxyacetic formulations, commercial mixtures of polychlorinated biphenyls, polychlorinated naphthalenes and through diverse combustion processes. PCDFs are also produced by overheated polychlorinated biphenyls in mal-

* Presented at the ISWA–WHO–DAKOFA specialized seminar, *Emission of Trace Organics from Municipal Solid Waste Incinerators*, Copenhagen, 20–22 January 1987.

† U.S. Environmental Protection Agency, Environmental Criteria and Assessment Office, Cincinnati, OH 45268, U.S.A.

‡ U.S. Environmental Protection Agency, Office of Air Quality Planning and Standards, Research Triangle Park, NC 27711, U.S.A.

Waste Management & Research (1987) **5**, 269–283

functioned transformers or capacitors. No known biogenic source, or any commercial use of PCDDs/PCDFs has yet been discovered. Municipal. industrial and other incinerators combusting organic materials and chlorinated compounds appear to be one of the major sources of PCDDs and PCDFs in the environment. The chlorinated-benzenes, -biphenyls and -phenols, which are present in high concentrations in emissions from waste incinerators, act either individually or in combination as precursors or intermediates of PCDDs and PCDFs. Tri- through octa-chlorinated homologous groups of PCDDs/PCDFs in stack emissions of municipal and industrial waste incinerators have been measured. A dilemma arises with respect to risk assessment as to how to evaluate the total PCDD and PCDF emissions in terms of toxicity when not every compound has yet been tested and is possibly not toxicologically equipotent.

PCDDs/PCDFs are highly lipophilic compounds and can easily bioaccumulate in fish, turtles, seals, terrestrial animals and even humans. Residues of these compounds have been detected in human adipose tissues and mothers' milk. Human exposure can occur via ingestion of fish from contaminated water bodies, contaminated meat or milk, or through inhalation or dermal contact. Human exposure has also occurred through occupational and accidental exposure to chemicals contaminated with PCDDs/PCDFs. 1,2,3,7,8-PeCDD has not been confirmed as a widespread contaminant in any commercial products but is always present in the emissions from waste incinerators. Detection of PCDD/PCDF residues, especially 1,2,3,7,8-PeCDD in mothers' milk indicate that the major source of exposure to these populations is occurring from municipal waste incinerator emissions (Rappe *et al.* 1984, Buser & Rappe 1984). Consequently, considerable concern has arisen over the public health impact of emissions of PCDDs/PCDFs from waste incinerators (see also Rappe *et al.* in this issue).

2. Toxicity of PCDDs and PCDFs

PCDDs/PCDFs (Dioxins) are members of a group of widely distributed and environmentally persistent compounds of which the 2,3,7,8-tetrachloro-dibenzo-p-dioxin (2,3,7,8-TCDD) isomer is one of the most toxic, teratogenic and carcinogenic chemicals known. The single oral dose, LD_{50}, of 2,3,7,8-TCDD in male guinea-pigs is 0.6 μg kg^{-1} (Schewtz *et al.* 1973). There are only limited LD_{50} data on other PCDD/PCDF congeners. The LD_{50} values of seven PCDD congeners and three PCDF congeners in guinea-pigs are higher than 2,3,7,8-TCDD (Table 1). (Compare with Ahlborg & Victorin, Table 3, in this issue.)

TABLE 1

Estimated single oral LD_{50} for PCDDs and PCDFs in guinea-pigs

Congeners	LD_{50} (μg kg^{-1})	Reference
2,3,7-TriCDD	29	McConnell *et al.* 1978
2,3,7,8-TCDD	0.6	Schewtz *et al.* 1973
1,2,3,7,8-PeCDD	3.1	McConnell *et al.* 1978
1,2,4,7,8-PeCDD	1125	McConnell *et al.* 1978
1,2,3,4,7,8-HxCDD	72.5	McConnell *et al.* 1978
1,2,3,6,7,8-HxCDD	70–100	McConnell *et al.* 1978
1,2,3,7,8,9-HxCDD	60–100	McConnell *et al.* 1978
1,2,3,4,6,7,8-HpCDD	>600	McConnell *et al.* 1978
2,3,7,8-TCDF	5–10	Moore *et al.* 1979
2,3,4,7,8-PeCDF	<10	McKinney & McConnell 1981
2,3,4,6,7,8-HxCDF	120	McKinney & McConnell 1981

2.1. *Mechanism of toxicity*

A number of reviews and comparative studies (Kimbrough 1974, Allen *et al.* 1979, McConnell & Moore 1979, Taylor 1979) clearly indicate that PCDDs and PCDFs elicit similar toxic and biological responses. They differ only in the degree of such responses. The exceptionally high and broad spectrum of 2,3,7,8-TCDD toxicity and other toxic congeners of PCDDs and PCDFs seem to be due to their distinctive mechanism of toxicity. Studies with genetically-inbred animals have demonstrated the role of aromatic hydrocarbon (Ah) regulatory gene (termed "Ah complex") and its gene product, the Ah cytosolic receptor protein (Nebert 1980, Nebert & Jansen 1979, Poland 1984), in their toxicity. Most of the toxic PCDDs and PCDFs elicit similar signs and symptoms of toxic effects in susceptible species that contain the Ah receptor protein (Carlstedt-Duke 1979, Carlstedt-Duke *et al.* 1979, 1981, Okey 1983, Mason & Okey 1982). The Ah-receptor protein interacts with TCDD and the resultant TCDD:Ah-receptor complex translocates into the nucleus, binds with DNA and activates specific mRNA (Carlstedt-Duke *et al.* 1981). Receptor binding is associated with the induction of aryl hydrocarbon hydroxylase (AHH) (Nebert 1980, Tukey *et al.* 1982).

2.2. *Structural activity relationship of PCDDs and PCDFs*

Recently, considerable interest has been generated on the effects of structure on the toxic and biological activity of PCDDs and PCDFs. Using the dextran charcoal receptor assay and ^{3}H-2,3,7,8-TCDD as the competing ligand, the relative binding affinities of 23 PCDD and PCDF congeners were first revealed by Poland *et al.* (1976). A correlation between the toxicity of PCDD congeners in guinea-pigs and mice (McConnell *et al.* 1978) and their AHH induction potencies in chick embryo and rat hepatoma H-4-II-E cells in culture and their binding affinities for mouse heptatic cytosolic receptor protein has been demonstrated (Poland *et al.* 1976, 1979, Bradlaw & Casterline 1979, Bradlaw *et al.* 1980). Structure–activity relationships have been reported for the PCDFs (Poland *et al.* 1979, Poland & Knutson 1982) and, like the PCDDs, there is some correlation among the toxicity of several individual PCDFs (Yoshihara *et al.* 1981), e.g. their binding affinities to male Wistar rat hepatic Ah-receptor site and AHH induction potencies in rat H-4-II-E hepatoma cells in culture (Bandiera *et al.* 1984*a*). The activity of the PCDD/PCDF ligand:Ah-receptor bond is a function of the geometric configuration of the compounds. Congeners with a chlorine substitution pattern at the four lateral positions (positions 2, 3, 7 and 8) and at least one vacant ring periposition (positions 1, 4, 6 and 9) of the molecule, have the greatest affinity for the Ah-receptor and the maximum inducibility of AHH activity. Additional chlorine substitution at positions 1, 4, 6 or 9 decreases AHH activity, and removal of one or more of the laterally attached chlorine atoms diminishes activity even further. One of the initial events of pathways in the mechanism of the biological activities of PCDDs/PCDFs seems to be stereospecific recognition and binding of these compounds by the Ah-receptor (Poland *et al.* 1979). Receptor binding assays and AHH induction assays have been established as useful indicators of the potency of individual PCDD/PCDF congeners relative to 2,3,7,8-TCDD (termed "TCDD equivalents"), as well as estimating the total potency of PCDD/PCDF as a complex mixture of the compounds. The utility of the TCDD equivalents approaches are supported by the apparent correlation of AHH induction and various *in vitro* biological activities with toxicity.

3. Health risk assessment of 2,3,7,8-TCDD

The rationale for assessment of public health risk from exposure to 2,3,7,8-TCDD has been discussed (Mukerjee *et al.* 1986, U.S. EPA 1985). Exposure to 2,3,7,8-TCDD can result in chloroacne and associated dermal abnormalities, thymic atrophy, severe body-weight loss, immunotoxicity, porphyria and other toxic effects.

From animal bioassay data (van Miller *et al.* 1977, Toth *et al.* 1979, Kociba *et al.* 1979, NTP 1980*a*) it can be concluded that 2,3,7,8-TCDD is an animal carcinogen. This bioassay data also indicate that 2,3,7,8-TCDD acts as an initiator for cancer of organs other than liver and skin. Observations by Pitot *et al.* (1980) and Poland *et al.* (1982) demonstrate its promotion action in liver and skin carcinogenesis in animals.

Epidemiologic observations by Hardell & Sandstrom (1979), Hardell & Ericksson (1981), Hardell *et al.* (1981), Eriksson *et al.* (1979, 1981), and Lynge (1985) supported by observations by Puntoni *et al.* (1986). Sarma & Jacobs (1981), Moses & Selikoff (1981), Bishop & Jones (1981) and Hoar *et al.* (1986) indicate that 2,3,7,8-TCDD is probably carcinogenic for humans and that exposure to it increases the incidence of soft tissue sarcoma and non-Hodgkin's lymphoma.

Using the available carcinogenic data on 2,3,7,8-TCDD from the study by Kociba *et al.* (1979), the cancer risk from exposure to 2,3,7,8-TCDD can be estimated by applying the modified multistage cancer model by Crump & Watson (1979). This model assumes that a cancer risk can be estimated for any dose of population exposure. Using this model, the slope of the dose–response relationship from the data of Kociba *et al.* (1979) was estimated and the 95% upper-limit carcinogenic potency for 2,3,7,8-TCDD was determined for humans to be 1.56×10^5 (mg/kg/day)$^{-1}$ (U.S. EPA 1985). The cancer risk for continuous lifetime 70-year exposure to an ambient air concentration of 1 pg m^{-3} of air of 2,3,7,8-TCDD has been estimated to be 3.3×10^{-5} (U.S. EPA 1985). In this estimation it was assumed that the breathing rate is 20 m^3 day^{-1} for an adult (70 kg man) and that 75% of the inhaled material will be absorbed. The linearized multistage model leads to a plausible upper-limit to the risk. This risk may not reflect the exact prediction of the risk. The range of risks is defined by the upper and lower limits and the lower limit may be as low as zero. The best or most probable estimates of risk can only be predicted when human data are utilized for assessing the risk and when exposures are in the dose range of the data. Consequently, U.S. EPA Cancer Risk Assessment Guidelines preclude the use of the statistical lower-bound estimate when extrapolating animal dose-response to a prediction of a likely response in human. The upperbound risk is used in order to err on the side of the protection of the public health.

Using the animal bioassay data on a mixture of 1,2,3,6,7,8- and 1,2,3,7,8,9-HxCDD (NTP 1980*b*), the potency for HxCDD has been estimated as 6.2×10^3 (mg/kg/day)$^{-1}$ and lifetime cancer risk for an ambient concentration of 1 pg m^{-3} of a mixture of 1,2,3,6,7,8- and 1,2,3,7,8,9-HxCDD to be 1.3×10^{-6} (U.S. EPA 1985).

4. TCDD equivalents approaches for risk assessment of total PCDDs and PCDFs

Except for 2,3,7,8-TCDD and a mixture of 1,2,3,6,7,8- and 1,2,3,7,8,9-HxCDD, there are no long-term chronic toxicity data for PCDD/PCDF congeners. Because of their prevalence in the environment, it is possible that other PCDD/PCDF congeners may add to the toxic burden caused by 2,3,7,8-TCDD. In the absence of any long-term chronic toxicity data, several schemes have been devised (in evaluating the exposure from classes of PCDD and PCDF emissions from municipal waste incinerators) to derive the toxic equivalents (TCDD equivalents) based on AHH induction, Ah-receptor binding assays and other *in vitro* biological activities.

4.1. *Swiss approach*

The Swiss Federal Office for Environmental Protection (1982) devised a potency weighting system based on AHH induction to convert total tetrachlorinated through octachlorinated dioxins and furans into TCDD equivalents in the emissions of a municipal waste incinerator to facilitate risk assessment of exposure to all the reported chlorinated dioxin and furan homologues. When applied to emissions from a municipal waste combustor it seemed that the "2,3,7,8-TCDD equivalents" of the mixture of chlorinated dioxins and furans were approximately 60 times the actual amount of 2,3,7,8-TCDD measured in the emissions.

4.2. *Dutch approach*

Olie *et al.* (1983) devised a toxic equivalency method based on AHH induction to evaluate the magnitude of chlorinated dioxin and furan emissions from a municipal incinerator in The Netherlands. In this analysis, the TCDD equivalents were estimated to be 80 times the actual amount of 2,3,7,8-TCDD measured. Bioanalysis of fly ash collected from the electrostatic precipitor hopper to a municipal incinerator, as measured by the dose-dependent displacement of ^{3}H-2,3,7,8-TCDD bound to the Ah-receptor by the active congeners in the fly ash extract, showed the mixture of PCDDs and PCDFs to be at least 45 times more active than the concentration of 2,3,7,8-TCDD present by analysis.

4.3. *New York State approach, Eadon equivalents*

In an incident in which PCDD/PCDF contaminated soot emanating from a PCB-HCB transformer fire spread throughout the State office building in Binghamton, New York, the New York State Health Department applied an *in vitro* keratinization assay to soot extracts to evaluate dioxin-like biological activity. XB epithelial cells (derived from cloned mouse teratoma cells) exhibit a dose-dependent keratinization response to TCDD exposure when co-cultured with irradiated 3T3 cells (Eadon *et al.* 1983, Gierthy *et al.* 1984). Incubation of the soot extract with PCDD/PCDF congeners showed a correlation (0.89) between keratinization activity and the relative total dibenzofurans and dibenzodioxins present. The assay is apparently sensitive to only the most toxic compounds of the PCDDs and PCDFs and, therefore, provides a dose–response method of relating the potency of the extract to the inducible potency of 2,3,7,8-TCDD. By this method it was shown that 2,3,7,8-TCDF has about $1/20 \times$ the keratinization potential of 2,3,7,8-TCDD, and other PCDF isomers have even lower activity. The dibenzofurans and PCDDs without substitution at any of the four lateral positions were sufficiently inactive to warrant little concern based upon comparison of the keratin-ization ability of 2,3-, 2,7-, 1,6-, 1,3,6,8-, 1,3,7,8- and 2,3,7-chlorodibenzodioxins to 2,3,7,8-TCDD. It was observed in the assay that the majority of biologically active isomers were members of the tetra- and penta-chlorinated homologues. The assay per-mitted the researchers to develop a scale of biological activity of various congeners relative to the keratinization potential of 2,3,7,8-TCDD (Eadon equivalents).

4.4. *U.S. EPAs interim approach*

Many compounds of PCDD and PCDF have been compared to the potency of 2,3,7,8-TCDD utilizing *in vitro* biological activity assays, e.g. AHH enzyme activity in rat hepatoma cells and chick embryo liver, ALA synthetase in chick embryo liver, and keratinization of XB/3T3 mouse teratoma cells. These have been reviewed by Kociba & Cabey (1985). From these enzyme-induction and cell-transformation assays it is possible to predict the toxic potency of 2,3,7,8-substituted congeners of these compounds, relative to the known potency of 2,3,7,8-TCDD. Bellin & Barnes (1987) and Barnes *et al.* (1986) incorporated this information into a calculation of TCDD equivalents, for using the scheme in hazard assessment of dioxin-contaminated waste and/or commercial products contaminated with a complex mixture of dioxin and furan compounds. Basically, TCDD equivalents are calculated using a Relative Potency Factor (RPF) or Toxic Equivalence Factor (TEF) derived from the various assays. When the isomer-specific concentration or homologue concentration of PCDD/PCDF are multiplied by the TEF the product is a concentration of TCDD equivalents that may be regarded as equipotent to 2,3,7,8-TCDD. Table 2 shows the RPF to be used when specific analyses of isomers are quantified.

TABLE 2

Comparison of the U.S. EPA (Bellin & Barnes 1987) and the method proposed by Safe (1986) to estimating relative toxicity of PCDDs and PCDFs

Congeners	U.S. EPA (Barnes & Barnes 1987)	Safe (1986)
Mono- to tri-	0	0
	0	0
2,3,7,8-TCDD	1	1
Other TCDDs	0.01	0.001
2,3,7,8-PeCDDs	0.5	0.01
Other PeCDDs	0.005	0.006
2,3,7,8-HxCDDs	0.04	0.03
Other HxCDDs	0.0004	—
2,3,7,8-HpCDDs	0.001	—
Other HpCDDs	0.0001	—
OCDD	0	0.0002
2,3,7,8-TCDFs	0.1	0.2
Other TCDFs	0.001	0.004
2,3,7,8-PeCDFs	0.1	0.3
Other PeCDFs	0.001	0.01
2,3,7,8-HxCDFs	0.01	0.2
Other HxCDFs	0.0001	—
2,3,7,8-HpCDFs	0.001	—
Other HpCDFs	0.00001	—
OCDF	0	—

4.5. *Ontario province, Canada approach*

The Ministry of Labor of the Ontario Government, Canada (1982) has developed a risk assessment guideline for complex mixtures of compounds of dioxins and furans in water, air and soil samples. The guidelines involve the utilization of Toxic Equivalent Factors (TEFs) based on AHH induction in rat hepatoma cells, *in vitro*. In their evaluation of airborne emissions of PCDDs/PCDFs they assume (based on experience in source testing) that 2,3,7,8-TCDD is 5–6% of total tetra-CDD emissions. Thus, when using the TEFs they first subtract the estimated 2,3,7,8-TCDD from the tetra-CDD homologue.

4.6. *Approach proposed by Safe* (*1986*)

Mason *et al.* (1985) correlated the *in vitro* AHH-inducing potency of PCDFs with the thymic atrophy or body-weight loss caused by each congener in rodents. Although this is an obvious oversimplification of the problem, it may be accepted as a good model when a rapid indication of the potential toxicity of new congeners is needed.

Bradlaw and Casterline (1979), working with rat hepatoma cell culture (as a rapid screen test for detecting minute (pg) amounts of certain classes of compounds, e.g. PCDFs, PCDDs and PCBs), found that AHH activity was induced by PCDF containing at least three or four lateral ring positions substituted by chlorine atoms in the ring positions 2, 3, 7 and 8; congeners with two or less chlorine atoms in the lateral positions showed no inductive effect up to a dose of 5 or 10 mg kg^{-1} body weight.

The quantitative *in vitro* data reported by Bandiera *et al.* (1984b) and Mason *et al.* (1985) demonstrate the relationship between the different PCDDs and PCDFs in their AHH and EROD-inducing potency. Bandiera *et al.* (1984b) showed that the AHH inductive ratios of the 2,3,4/1,3,8, 2,6,7/1,3,8, and 2,3,4,6/1,2,4,8 pairs of PCDF isomers were 1, 2, 8, 7 and 9, respectively.

The $-\log EC_{50}$ values for *in vitro* AHH inducing potencies versus the $-\log ED_{50}$ values for body-weight loss and thymic atrophy for a series of PCDF congeners have been plotted (Safe 1986). Statistical analysis of the plots showed an excellent correlation, corroborated by the fact that the compounds tested differed widely in both *in vivo* and *in vitro* biological activities and toxic potencies. 2,3,7,8-TCDC was the most active AHH inducer *in vitro* and the most powerful and toxic congener *in vivo*. Comparison of this approach with that of the U.S. EPA (Table 2) indicate that these two approaches give more or less similar values.

4.7. *Swedish approach*

The current Swedish approach, using Eadon equivalents, to estimate the toxicity and health risk of dioxins is summarized by Ahlborg (in this issue) including a comparison of some of the existing equivalents.

5. Evaluation of TCDD equivalents approach for risk assessment

The aforementioned rank ordering of the potency of various PCDD/PCDF congeners based mostly on induction of enzyme activity or keratinization assays provides a means of estimating, albeit crudely, the toxicological significance of exposure to a complex array of these compounds. This is especially important in view of the fact that most of these compounds have not been asssayed for teratogenic, carcinogenic, or other chronic effects. Thus, these various methods of rank ordering potency in relation to 2,3,7,8-TCDD may provide a reasonable means even though not fully supported by scientific data to assess the risk of cancer to populations exposed to chronic and dispersive emissions of PCDDs/PCDFs from stationary combustion sources. This is important to regulators who need to estimate a hazard now, without having to wait perhaps several years for the results of animal bioassays. Various schemes utilizing the notion of toxic equivalency to 2,3,7,8-TCDD are based primarily on microsomal mono-oxygenase activity.

Co-administration of a non-toxic or non-inducing dose of 2,3,7,8-TCDF can decrease the AHH induction and immunotoxicity of 2,3,7,8-TCDD (Rizzardini *et al.* 1983). A molecule with low toxicity but high affinity for the Ah-receptor may possibly offer protection against the toxicity of 2,3,7,8-TCDD. Furthermore, age and sex-related decreases in the mixed function oxidase (MFO) activity is associated with increased 2,3,7,8-TCDD lethality (Beatty *et al.* 1978). This suggests that reduced MFO activites may enhance 2,3,7,8-TCDD toxicity.

The major shortcomings of utilizing the microsomal mono-oxygenase activity assays in risk assessment to airborne emissions of chlorinated dioxins and dibenzofurans are:

(1) enzyme induction has not been directly linked with carcinogenicity, or any other chronic toxicologic endpoint;
(2) elucidation of specific intranuclear events leading to transcription of specific mRNAs, and translation of mRNAs into enzyme induction remains unknown;
(3) the ultimate biochemical lesion of the proposed mechanism of toxicity is unknown;
(4) the concentration of the Ah-receptor in various human tissues has not been fully investigated, nor has a toxic response in humans been correlated with enzyme induction. Hypothyroidism, observed in animals exposed to 2,3,7,8-TCDD is possibly involved in the manifestations of a spectrum of pathological conditions (Bastomsky 1977). The partial protection from 2,3,7,8-TCDD induced wasting syndrome and immunotoxicity as a result of thyroidectomy (Rozman *et al.* 1984, Pazdernik & Rozman 1985) seems not to be mediated through any change in the liver Ah-receptor regulated processes (Henry & Gasiewicz 1986);
(5) photolysis of higher chlorinated PCDDs/PCDFs can result in ultimate dechlorination of the molecule (Choudhury & Hutzinger 1982). However, there is some possibility of highly toxic 2,3,7,8-TCDD formation due to photolysis of 2,3,4,7,8,9- and 1,2,3,7,8,9-HxCDDs (Buser 1979) if these compounds are emitted from the incinerators.

These shortcomings suggest that using TCDD equivalent approaches for risk assessments may result in underestimation of risk.

Lack of complete elucidation should not, however, preclude the regulator from developing risk assessment methodologies based on AHH induction or receptor-binding assays as a reasonable means of estimating the hazard of exposure to a complex mixture of PCDDs/PCDFs from emissions of stationary combustion sources. The responsibility of the regulator is to manage risk to the exposed population even before all the scientific information is available. Thus toxic equivalency schemes can be used as an interim basis of assessing risk to the exposed population residing near emitters of PCDDs and PCDFs.

6. Risk assessment of PCDD/PCDF emissions from selected U.S. incinerators

6.1. *Earlier approach*

In 1981 the U.S. Environmental Protection Agency issued a report evaluating the health risks associated with exposure to emissions of a homologous mixture of tetra-chlorinated dibenzo-*p*-dioxins (TCDD) from five municipal solid waste heat recovery incinerators of various size and design (U.S. EPA 1981). Specific speciation of only one congener, 2,3,7,8-TCDD, was accomplished leaving risk assessors with the dilemma of how to evaluate risk of perhaps 21 other toxic dioxin compounds comprising the class of TCDD. Of the five facilities sampled, only one (Chicago, NW) provided speciation data of 2,3,7,8-TCDD with sufficient analytical confidence to compare with

TABLE 3

Comparison of 2,3,7,8-TCDD toxic equivalency methods in determining risk from population exposure to CDD/CDF emissions from a heat recovery massburn MWC operating in Westchester, New York*

Compound	Conc.†	EPA TEFs	NY TEFs	Ontario Canada	Swiss TEFs	EPA TE	NY TE	Can. TE	Swiss TE
2,3,7,8-TCDD	3.65	1	1	1	1	3.65	3.65	3.65	3.65
Other TCDD	33.00	0.01	0	0.01	0.01	0.33	0	0.33	0.33
1,2,3,7,8-PeCDD	9.38	0.5	1	0.1	0.1	4.69	9.38	0.94	0.94
Other PeCDD	27.17	0.005	0	0.001	0.1	0.14	0	0.03	2.72
1,2,3,4,7,8-HxCDD	4.47	0.04	0.03	0.1	0.1	0.18	0.13	0.45	0.45
1,2,3,6,7,8-HxCDD	0.14	0.04	0.03	0.1	0.1	0.01	0.00	0.01	0.01
1,2,3,7,8,9-HxCDD	1.55	0.04	0.03	0.1	0.1	0.06	0.05	0.02	0.16
Other HxCDD	43.91	0.0004	0	0.001	0.01	0.02	0	0.04	0.44
Total HpCDD	71.77	0.001	0	0.01	0.01	0.07	0	0.72	0.72
Total OCDD	115.4	0	0	0.0001	0	0	0	0.01	0
2,3,7,8-TCDF	27.89	0.1	0.33	0.5	0.1	2.8	9.2	14.0	2.79
Other TCDF	358.7	0.001	0	0.005	0.1	0.36	0	1.8	35.9
1,2,3,7,8-PcDCF	51.2	0.1	0.33	0.5	0.1	5.12	16.9	25.6	5.12
2,3,4,7,8-PcCDF	30.2	0.1	0.33	0.5	0.1	3.02	10.0	15	3.02
Other PcCDF	145.2	0.001	0	0.005	0.1	0.15	0	0.73	14.5
1,2,3,4,7,8-HxCDF	19.0	0.01	0.01	0.1	0.1	0.19	0.19	1.9	1.9
1,2,3,7,8,9-HxCDF	1.01	0.01	0.01	0.1	0.1	0.01	0.01	0.1	0.1
2,3,4,6,7,8-HxCDF	5.29	0.01	0.01	0.1	0.1	0.05	0.05	0.53	0.53
Other HxCDF	248.5	0.001	0	0.001	0.1	0.25	0	0.25	24.9
Total HpCDF	135.9	0.001	0	0.01	0	0.14	0	1.36	0
Total OCDF	4.98	0	0	0.0001	0	0	0	0	0

	EPA	NY	Can.	Swiss
Total ground-level concentration of 2,3,7,8-TCDD Equivalents (10^{-15} gm m^{-3})	21.24	49.6	67.5	98.2

	EPA	NY	Can.	Swiss
Maximum individual lifetime cancer risk (10^{-6})	1	2	2	3

* *Description of the incinerator:* Heat Recovery Massburn waterwall MWC: capacity, 2000 tonne day^{-1}; operating temperature, 900°C; steam generated, 228,202 kg h^{-1}.

† Maximum ground-level concentration of specific CDDs/CDFs in femtograms m^{-3} of air.

TABLE 4

Comparison of 2,3,7,8-TCDD toxic equivalency methodologies in determining maximum individual lifetime risk from exposure to CDDs/CDFs in the emissions of a non-heat recovery massburn municipal waste combustor operating in Philadelphia, Pennsylvania*

Compound	Emissions (μg s^{-1})	EPQ TEFs	NY TEFs	Can. TEFs	Swiss TEFs	EPA TE	NY TE	Can. TE	Swiss TE
2,3,7,8-TCDD	0.14	1	1	1	1	0.14	0.14	0.14	0.14
Other TCDD	4.26	0.01	0	0.01	0.01	0.043	0	0.04	0.04
1,2,3,7,8-PeCDD	1.10	0.5	1	0.1	0.1	0.55	1.1	0.11	0.11
Other PeCDD	8.90	0.005	0	0.001	0.1	0.045	0	0.01	0.89
1,2,3,4,7,8-HxCDD	2.50	0.04	0.03	0.1	0.1	0.1	0.08	0.25	0.25
1,2,3,7,8,9-HxCDD	2.50	0.04	0.03	0.1	0.1	0.1	0.08	0.25	0.25
1,2,3,6,7,8-HxCDD	2.50	0.04	0.03	0.1	0.1	0.1	0.08	0.25	0.25
Other HxCDD	10.50	0.0004	0	0.001	0.01	0.004	0	0.01	0.11
1,2,3,4,6,7,8-HpCDD	3.30	0.001	0	0.01	0.01	0.003	0	0.03	0.03
Other HpCDD	3.00	0.00001	0	0.0001	0.01	†	0	0	0.03
2,3,7,8-TCDF	0.35	0.1	0.33	0.5	0.1	0.035	0.12	0.18	0.04
Other TCDF	6.55	0.001	0	0.005	0.1	0.007	0	0.03	0.66
1,2,3,7,8-PcCDF	0.39	0.1	0.33	0.5	0.1	0.039	0.13	0.20	0.04
2,3,4,7,8-PeCDF	0.52	0.1	0.33	0.5	0.1	0.052	0.17	0.26	0.05
Other PcCDF	9.09	0.001	0	0.005	0.1	0.009	0	0.05	0.91
1,2,3,4,7,8-HxCDF	2.50	0.01	0.01	0.1	0.1	0.025	0.03	0.25	0.25
1,2,3,7,8,9-HxCDF	1.38	0.01	0.01	0.1	0.1	0.013	0.01	0.14	0.14
1,2,3,6,7,8-HxCDF	0.25	0.01	0.01	0.1	0.1	0.003	0.003	0.03	0.03
2,3,4,6,7,8-HxCDF	1.38	0.01	0.01	0.1	0.1	0.013	0.01	0.14	0.14
Other HxCDF	12.49	0.0001	0	0.001	0.1	0.001	0	0.01	2.35
1,2,3,4,6,7,8-HpCDF	4.40	0.001	0	0.01	0.1	0.004	0	0.04	0.44
1,2,3,4,7,8,9-HpCDF	0.35	0.001	0	0.01	0.1	†	0	0.004	0.04
Other HpCDF	1.50	0.00001	0	0.0001	0.1	†	0	†	0.15
OCDD	2.5	0	0	0.0001	0	0	0	†	0
OCDF	0.50	0	0	0.0001	0	0	0	†	0
2,3,7,8-TCDD equivalent emissions (μg g^{-1})						1.29	2	2.4	6.2
2,3,7,8-TCDD equivalent ground-level concentration pg m^{-3}						1.2	1.6	2.0	5.1
Maximum individual lifetime cancer risk (10^{-6})						40	50	70	170

* Description of the incinerator: refractory lined massburner municipal incinerator; no heat recovery; capacity, 682.5 tonne day^{-1}; maximum operating temperature, 1100°C.

† Measurements of emissions were too low to result in toxic equivalent emissions.

the abundance of TCDD. At the Chicago plant, 2,3,7,8-TCDD constituted about 7% of the total tetrachlorinated dioxin emissions (Haile & Stanley 1983). The agency, in undertaking a risk assessment, assumed that all the TCDDs were as carcinogenic as the 2,3,7,8-TCDD congener and, therefore, the emission of a mixture of TCDD compounds was 14 times more potent than the actual concentration of 2,3,7,8-TCDD present in stack emissions (Barnes 1983). Thus, the agency reduced the analysis of perhaps as many as 22 separate compounds of tetrachlorine-substituted dioxin to an equivalent toxicity of 2,3,7,8-TCDD. The maximum annual average ground-level concentration of total TCDD was 0.092 pg m^{-3} and this was treated as total 2,3,7,8-

TCDD. Applying the unit risk factor for 2,3,7,8-TCDD to the linearized multi-stage model of the toxic equivalents concentration indicated an upper bound individual risk of cancer to be 8×10^{-6}.

The agency used an identical procedure in evaluating the risks from TCDD exposure in emissions in the Hampton, Virginia incinerator (Cook 1983). The maximum annual ground-level concentration of total TCDD was found to be 0.51 pg m^{-3}. Using the same risk model, the upper limit individual risk of cancer of exposure to the 2,3,7,8-TCDD toxic equivalents was determined to be 4.6×10^{-5}. Thus, the emission of 2,3,7,8-TCDD toxic equivalents from the Hampton, Virginia incinerator produced an individual lifetime risk of cancer approximately six times greater than emissions from the Chicago, NW incinerator.

6.2. *Current approach*

Regulatory authorities in Sweden, Denmark, Norway, The Netherlands, Switzerland, West Germany, Canada and the U.S.A. have recognized the utility of "TCDD equivalents" risk-assessment procedures in generating probabilistic estimates of public health risk posed by the mixtures of PCDD/PCDF compounds characteristic of incinerator emissions. Of particular interest to the community of environmental managers is whether agreement exists among the wide variety of toxic equivalency procedures in terms of predicting carcinogenic risk to the population exposed to incinerator emissions. To investigate this question we have selected the PCDD/PCDF emissions measured at a modern energy recovery municipal waste combustor to serve as an example of the risk prediction resulting from application of the various toxic equivalency procedures. Tables 3 and 4 show the comparative results of various procedures when specific isomers of PCDD/PCDF have been quantified in the emission. Table 5 makes the comparison when only homologue data are available. As can be seen in Table 3 all the various procedures predict a 10^{-6} maximum lifetime risk to individuals exposed continuously for 70 years to the predicted maximum ground-level concentra-

TABLE 5

Comparison of toxic equivalency methodologies where only homologue data are available: CDD/CDF emissions from a heat-recovery massburn MWC in Westchester, New York

Compound	Conc. (fg m^{-3})	EPA TEFs	NY TEFs	Ontario Canada	Swiss TEFs	EPA TE	NY TE	Can. TE	Swiss TE
2,3,7,8-TCDD	3.65	1	1	1	1	3.65	3.65	3.65	3.65
Other TCDD	33.00	0.01	0	0.01	0.01	0.33	0	0.33	0.33
Total PeCDD	36.55	0.5	1	0.1	0.1	18.3	36.55	3.66	3.66
Total HxCDD	50.07	0.04	0.03	0.1	0.1	2.0	1.5	5.00	5.00
Total HpCDD	71.77	0.001	0	0.01	0.01	0.7	0	0.72	0.72
OCDD	115.4	0	0	0.0001	0	0	0	0.01	0
Total TCDF	386.6	0.1	0.33	0.5	0.1	38.7	127.58	193.3	38.66
Total PeCDF	226.6	0.1	0.33	0.5	0.1	22.7	74.78	113.3	22.66
Total HxCDF	233.8	0.01	0.01	0.1	0.1	2.34	2.34	23.38	23.38
Total HpCDF	135.9	0.001	0	0.01	0.1	0.14	0	1.36	13.59
OCDF	4.98	0	0	0.0001	0	0	0	0.00	0
Total 2,3,7,8-TCDD equivalents						88.23	246.4	344.7	111.65
Maximum individual lifetime risk (10^{-6})						3	8	11	4

tion of 2,3,7,8-TCDD equivalents. The procedures differ from the prediction of the U.S. EPA by a factor of 2–3. However, given the uncertainties inherent in predicting the public health risk, there is generally good agreement in estimating risk. As can be seen in Table 5, the toxic equivalency procedures do predict high risk associated with the same incinerator emissions when only homologue data are used. This increase in risk is on a range of three-fold for the EPA procedure and up to five-fold for the Canadian procedure. However, one should not conclude that isomer-specific data gives more precise measure of health risk than homologue data, because there may be additional halogenated isomers manifesting similar toxicity that are not considered in the risk-assessment procedures. For example, tri- or di-chlorinated PCDDs/PCDFs may be tested in whole animals and be shown to elicit a similar toxic response as 2,3,7,8-TCDD. Likewise, the mechanism of toxicity for this family of compounds has yet to be elucidated fully.

7. Conclusions

Various estimates of health risks from emissions from municipal incinerators are compared and the reasoning behind the current U.S. EPA methods for evaluating such risks are described. One should not be intellectually seduced into believing that these methodologies are truly accurate in their prediction of risk. Much more needs to be discovered concerning the macromolecular pathways of carcinogenesis, teratogenesis and other chronic diseases associated with these compounds before more scientifically reliable statements of risk can be made. Until we are more knowledgeable in this matter, a concept of TCDD equivalency is at best considered as a predictive tool for risk managers to evaluate the atmospheric emissions of PCDD/PCDF mixtures for combustion sources.

Acknowledgements

We are grateful to Ms Eleanor J. Read for computer assistance and Ms Carol Haynes for editorial assistance.

References

Allen, J. R., Barsotti, D. A., Lambrecht, L. K. & van Miller, J. P. (1979), Reproductive effects of halogenated aromatic hydrocarbons on non-human primates, *Annals of the New York Academy of Science*, 320, 419–425.

Bandiera, S., Sawyer, T., Romkes, M., Zmukda, B., Safe, L., Mason, G., Keys, B. & Safe, S. (1984a), Polychlorinated dibenzofurans (PCDFs): Effects of structure on binding to the 2,3,7,8-TCDD cytosolic receptor protein, AHH induction and toxicity, *Toxicology*, 32, 131–144.

Bandiera, S., Farrell, K., Mason, G., Kelley, M., Romkes, M., Bannister, R. & Safe, S. (1984b), Comparitive toxicities of the polychlorinated dibenzofuran (PCDF) and biphenyl (PCB) mixtures which persist in Yusho victims, *Chemosphere*, 13, 507–512.

Barnes, D. (1983), *Dioxin Production from the Combustion of Biomass and Wastes*. Presented at the Institute of Gas Technology, Chicago, IL, Symposium: Energy from Biomass and Wastes, Lake Buena Vista, FL, pp. 291–327.

Barnes, D., Bellin, J. & Cleverly, D. (1986), Interim procedures for estimating risks associated with exposures to mixtures of chlorinated dibenzodioxins and dibenzofurans (CDDs and CDFs), *Chemosphere*, 15, 1895–1903.

Bastomsky, C. H. (1977), Enhanced thyroxine metabolism and high uptake goiters in rats after a single dose of 2,3,7,8-tetrachlorodibenzo-p-dioxin, *Endocrinology*, 101, 292–296.

Beatty, P. W., Vaugh, W. K. & Neal, R. A. (1978), Effect of alteration of rat hepatic mixed-function oxidase (MFO) activity of the toxicity of 2,3,7,8-tetrachlorodibenzo-p-dioxin (TCDD), *Toxicology & Applied Pharmacology, 45*, 513–519.

Bellin, J. S. & Barnes, D. G. (1987), Interim procedures for estimating risks associated with exposures to mixtures of chlorinated dibenzo-p-dioxins and dibenzofurans, *EPA/625/3-87/ 012.*

Bishop, C. M. & Jones, A. H. (1981), Non-Hodgkin's lymphoma of the scalp in workers exposed to dioxins, *Lancet, 2* (8242), 369.

Bradlaw, J. A. & Casterline Jr, J. L. (1979), Induction of enzyme activity in cell culture. A rapid screen for detection of planar polychlorinated organic compounds, *Journal of the Association of Official Analytical Chemistry, 62*, 904–906.

Bradlaw, J. A., Garthoff, L. H., Hurley, N. E. & Firestone, D. (1980), Comparative induction of aryl hydrocarbon hydroxylase activity *in vitro* by analogues of dibenzo-p-dioxin, *Food and Cosmetics Toxicology, 18*, 627–635.

Buser, H. R. (1979), Formation and identification of tetra- and pentachlorodibenzo-p-dioxins from photolysis of two isomeric hexachlorodibenzo-p-dioxins, *Chemosphere, 8*, 251–254.

Buser, H. R. & Rappe, C. (1984), Isomer-specific separation of 2,3,7,8-substituted poly-chlorinated dibenzo-p-dioxins by high resolution gas chromatography/mass spectrometry, *Analytical Chemistry, 56*, 442.

Carlstedt-Duke, J. M. (1979), Tissue distribution of the receptor for 2,3,7,8-tetrahclorodibenzo-p-dioxin and its endocrine independence, *Cancer Research, 39(11)*, 4653–4656.

Carlstedt-Duke, J. M., Elfstrom, G., Hogberg, B. & Gustafsson, J.-A. (1979), Ontogency of the rat hepatic receptor for 2,3,7,8-tetrachlorodibenzo-p-dioxin and its endocrine independence, *Cancer Research, 39(11)*, 4653–4656.

Carlstedt-Duke, J. M., Harnemo, U. B., Hogberg, B. & Gustafsson, J.-A. (1981), Interaction of the hepatic receptor protein for 2,3,7,8-tetrachlorodibenzo-p-dioxin with DNA, *Biochimica et Biophysica Acta, 672, 131–141.*

Choudhury, G. G. & Hutzinger, O. (1982), Photochemical formation and degradation of poly-chlorinated dibenzofurans and dibenzo-p-dioxins, *Residue Reviews, 84*, 113–161.

Cook, M. (1983), *TCDD Emissions for Municipal Waste Combustors*, Memorandum, 16 December 1983.

Crump, K. S. & Watson, W. W. (1979), Global 79: a Fortran program to extrapolate dichotomons animal carcinogenicity data to low dose. NIEHS Contract No. I-ES-2123.

Eadon, G., Aldous, K., Hilker, D., O'Keefe, P. & Smith, R. (1983), Chemical data on air samples from the Binghampton State Office Building. Memo from Center for Laboratory and Research, NY State Dept. Health, Albany, NY 12201, July 1983.

Eriksson, M., Hardell, L., Berg, N. O., Moller, T. & Axelson, O. (1979), *Case-control Study on Malignant Mesenchymal Tumors of the Soft-Tissue and Exposure to Chemical Substances. Lakartidningen, 76*, 3872–3875 (translation).

Eriksson, M., Hardell, L., Berg, N. O., Moller, T. & Axelson, O. (1981), Soft-tissue sarcomas and exposure to chemical substances: a case-referent study, *British Journal of Industrial Medicine, 38*, 27–33.

Gierthy, J. F., Grane, D. & Frenkel, G. D. (1984), Application of an *in vitro* keratinization assay to extracts of soot from a fire and a polychlorinated biphenyl-containing transformer, *Fundamental and Applied Toxicology, 74*, 91–98.

Haile, C. & Stanley, J. (1983), *Pilot Study of Information of Specific Compounds from Combustion Sources*. EPA-560/5-83-004.

Hardell, L. & Ericksson, M. (1981), Soft-tissue sarcomas, phenoxy herbicides, and chlorinated phenols, *Lancet, 2*, 8240.

Hardell, L. & Sandstrom, A. (1979), Case-control study: soft-tissue sarcoma and exposure to phenoxyacetic acids or chlorophenols, *British Journal of Cancer, 39*, 711–717.

Hardell, L., Ericksson, M., Lenner, P. & Lundgren, E. (1981) Malignant lymphoma and exposure to chemicals, especially organic solvents, chlorophenols and phenoxy acids: a case-control study, *British Journal of Cancer, 43*, 169–176.

Henry, E. C. & Gasiewicz, T. A. (1986), Effects of thyroidectomy on the Ah receptor and enzyme inducibility by 2,3,7,8-tetrachlorodibenzo-p-dioxin in the rat liver, *Chemical and Biological Interactions, 59*, 29–42.

Hoar, S. K., Blair, A., Holmes, F. F. (1986), Agricultural herbicide use and risk of lymphoma and soft-tissue sarcoma, *Journal of the American Medical Association, 256*, 1141–1147.

Kimbrough, R. D. (1974), The toxicity of polychlorinated polycyclic compounds and related compounds, *CRC Critical Reviews on Toxicology*, 2, 445–489.

Kociba, R. J. & Cabey, O. (1985), Comparative toxicity and biological activity of chlorinated dibenzo-*p*-dioxins and furans relative to 2,3,7,8-tetrachlorodibenzo-*p*-dioxin (TCDD), *Chemosphere*, 14, 649–660.

Kociba, R. J., Keyes, D. G., Beyer, J. E., Carreon, R. M. & Gehring, P. J. (1979), Long-term toxicological studies of 2,3,7,8-tetrachlorodibenzo-*p*-dioxin (TCDD) in laboratory animals, *Annals of the New York Academy of Science*, 320, 397–404.

Lynge, E. (1985), A follow-up study of cancer incidence among workers in manufacture of phenoxy herbicides in Denmark, *British Journal of Cancer*, 52, 259–270.

Mason, G., Sawyer, T., Keys, B., Bandiera, S., Romkes, M., Piskorska-Pliszczynska, J., Zmudzka, B. & Safe, S. (1985), Polychlorinated dibenzofurans (PcDFs): correlation between *in vivo* and *in vitro* structure–activity relationships, *Toxicology*, 37, 1–2.

Mason, M. E. & Okey, A. B. (1982), Cystolic and nuclear binding of 2,3,7,8-tetrachlorodibenzo-*p*-dioxin to the Ah-receptor in entra-hepatic tissues of rats and mice, *European Journal of Biochemistry*, 123, 209–215.

McConnell, E. E. & Moore, J. A. (1979), Toxicopathology characteristics of the halogenated aromatics, *Annals of the New York Academy of Sciences*, 320, 138–150.

McConnell, E. E., Moore, J. A., Haseman, J. K. & Harris, M. W. (1978), The comparative toxicity of chlorinated dibenzo-*o*-dioxins in mice and guinea-pigs, *Toxicology and Applied Pharmacology*, 44, 335–356.

McKinney, J. D. & McConnell, E. (1981), Structural specificity and dioxin receptor. In *Chlorinated Dioxins and Related Compounds. Impact on the Environment* (O. Hutzinger, R. W. Frei, E. Merian & F. Pocchiari, Eds), p. 367. Oxford: Pergamon Press.

Moore, J. A., McConnell, E. E., Dalgard, D. W. & Harris, M. W. (1979), Comparative toxicity of three halogenated dibenzofurans in guinea-pigs, mice and rhesus monkeys, *Annals of the New York Academy of Science*, 320, 151–163.

Moses, M. & Selikoff, I. J. (1981), Soft-tissue sarcomas, phenoxy herbicides and chlorinated phenols, *Lancet*, 1 (*8234*), 1370.

Mukerjee, D., Stara, J. F. & Schaum, J. L. (1986), Rationale for assessment of risk from exposure to 2,3,7,8-TCDD, *Chemosphere*, 15, 1805–1813.

NTP (National Toxicology Program) (1980*a*), *Bioassay of 2,3,7,8-Tetrachlorodibenzo-*p*-dioxin for Possible Carcinogenicity (Gavage Study)*, DHHS Publ. No. (NIH) 82-1765, Carcinogenesis Testing Program, NCI, NIH, Bethesda, MD, and NTP, RTP, Box 12233, NC.

NTP (National Toxicology Program) (1980*b*), *Bioassay of 1,2,3,6,7,8- and 1,2,3,7,8,9-Hexachlorodibenzo-*p*-dioxins (Gavage) for Possible Carcinogenicity*, DHHS Publ. No. (NIH) 80-1754, Carcinogenesis Testing Program, NCI, NIH, Bethesda, MD, and NTP, RTP, Box 12233, NC.

Nebert, D. W. (1980), The Ah locus. A gene with possible importance in cancer predictability, *Archives of Toxicology (Supplement 3)*, 195–207.

Nebert, D. W. & Jensen, N. M. (1979), The Ah locus: genetic regulation of the metabolism of carcinogens, drugs, and other environmental chemicals by cytochrome P-450 mediated monoxygenases, *CRC Critical Reviews of Biochemistry*, 6, 401–437.

Okey, A. B. (1983), The Ah receptor: a specific site for action of chlorinated dioxins. In *Human and Environmental Risks of Chlorinated Dioxins and Related Compounds* (R. E. Tucker, A. L. Young & A. P. Gray, Eds), pp. 423–440. Plenum Press, New York.

Olie, K., Lustenhouwer, J. W. A. & Hutzinger, O. (1983), Formation and fate of PCDD and PCDF from combustion processes, *Chemosphere*, 12, 627–636.

Ontario Government (1982), *Chlorinated Dioxins and Chlorinated Dibenzofurans. Ambient Air Guidelines*. Health Studies Services, Ministry of Labor, 16 December.

Parkinson, A. & Safe, S. H. (1981), Aryl hydrocarbon hydroxylase induction and its relationship to the toxicity of halogenated aryl hydrocarbons, *Toxicology and Environmental Chemistry Research*, 4, 1–46.

Pazdernik, T. L. & Rozman, K. K. (1985), Effect of thyroidectomy and thyroxine on 2,3,7,8-tetrachlorodibenzo-*p*-dioxin induced immunotoxicity, *Life Science*, 36, 695–703.

Pitot, H. C., Goldsworthy, T. & Poland, A. (1980), Promotion by 2,3,7,8-tetrachlorodibenzo-*p*-dioxin of hepatocarcinogenesis from diethylnitrosamine, *Cancer Research*, 40, 3616–3620.

Poland, A. P. (1984), Reflection on the mechanism of action of halogenated aromatic hydrocarbons. In *Biological Mechanisms of Dioxin Action, Banbury Report 18* (A. Poland & R.

D. Kimbrough, Eds), pp. 109–117. Cold Spring Harbor Laboratory.

Poland, A. & Knutson, J. C. (1982), 2,3,7,8-Tetrachlorodibenzo-*p*-dioxin and related halogenated aromatic hydrocarbons: examination of the mechanism of toxicity, *Annual Review of Pharmacology and Toxicology*, *22*, 517–554.

Poland, A., Glover, E., Kende, A. S. (1976), Stereospecific, high affinity binding of 2,3,7,8-tetrachlorodibenzo-*p*-dioxin by hepatic cytosol. Evidence that the binding species is receptor for induction of aryl hydrocarbon hydroxylase, *Journal of Biological Chemistry*, *251*, 4936–4946.

Poland, A., Greenlee, W. F. & Kende, A. S. (1979), Studies on the mechanisms of action of the chlorinated dibenzo-*p*-dioxins and related compounds, *Annals of the New York Academy of Sciences*, *320*, 214–230.

Poland, A., Palen, D. & Glover, E. (1982), Tumor promotion by TCDD in skin of HRS/J mice, *Nature*, *300*, 271–273.

Puntoni, R., Merlo, F., Fini, A., Meazza, L. & Santi, L. (1986), Soft tissue sarcoma in seveso, *Lancet*, *2*, 525.

Rappe, C., Berggvist, P.-A., Hansson, M., Kjeller, L.-O., Lindstrom, G., Marklund, S. & Nygren, M. (1984), Chemistry and analysis of polychlorinated dioxins and dibenzofurans in biological samples. In *Biological Mechanisms of Dioxin Action, Banbury Report 18* (A. Poland & R. D. Kimbrough, Eds), pp. 17–25. Cold Spring Harbor Laboratory.

Rizzardini, M., Ramano, M., Tursi, F., Salmona, M., Vecchi, A., Sironi, M., Gizzi, F., Benfenati, E., Garattini, S. & Fanelli, R. (1983), Toxicological evaluation of urban waste emissions, *Chemosphere*, *12*, 559–564.

Rozman, K., Rozman, T. & Greim, H. (1984), Effect of thyroidectomy and thyroxine on 2,3,7,8-tetrachlorodibenzo-*p*-dioxin (TCDD) induced toxicity, *Toxicology and Applied Pharmacology*, *72*, 311–376.

Safe, S. H. (1986), Comparative toxicology and mechanism of action of polychlorinated dibenzo-*p*-dioxins and dibenzofurans, *Annual Review of Pharmacology and Toxicology*, *26*, 371–399.

Sarma, P. R. & Jacobs, J. (1981), Thoracic soft-tissue sarcoma in Vietnam veterans exposed to agent orange, *Lancet*, *306* (*18*), 1109.

Sawyer, T. & Safe, S., *In vitro* AHH induction by polychlorinated biphenyl and dibenzofuran mixtures: additive effects, *Chemosphere*, *14*, 79–84.

Schewtz, B.A., Norris, J. M., Sparchu, G. L., Rowe, V. K., Gehring, P. J., Emerson, J. L. & Gerbig, C. G. (1973), Toxicology of chlorinated dibenzo-*p*-dioxins, *Environmental Health Perspectives*, *5*, 87–89.

Swiss Federal Office for Environmental Protection (Bundesamt Für Umweltschutz, Bern) (1982), *Environmental Pollution Due to Dioxins and Furans from Chemical Rubbish Incineration Plant*. Schriften veighe Umweltschutz, No. 5.

Taylor, J. S. (1979), Environmental chloroacne: update and overview, *Annals of the New York Academy of Science*, *320*, 295–307.

Toth, K., Samfai-Pelle, S., Sugar, J. & Bence, J. (1979), Carcinogenicity testing of herbicide 2,4,5-trichlorophenoxyethanol containing dioxin and of pure dioxin in Swiss mice, *Nature*, *278*, 548–549.

Tukey, R. H., Hannah, R. R., Negishi, M., Nebert, D. W. & Eisen, H. J. (1982), The Ah locus: correlation of intranuclear appearance of inducer–receptor complex with induction of cytochrome P_1-450 mRNA, *Cell*, *31*, 275–284.

U.S. Environmental Protection Agency, OSW, OPTS (1981), *Interim Evaluation of Health Risks Associated with Emissions of Tetrachlorinated Dioxins from Municipal Waste Resource Recovery Facilities*. November, Washington, DC.

U.S. Environmental Protection Agency (1985), *Health Assessment Document for Polychlorinated Dibenzo-*p*-dioxins*. EPA/600/8-84/014F. Final Report. NTIS PB86-122546.

van Miller, J. P., Lalich, J. J. & Allen, J. R. (1977), Increased incidence of neoplasms in rats exposed to low levels of 2,3,7,8-tetrachlorodibenzo-*o*-dioxin, *Chemosphere*, *6*, 625–632.

Yoshihara, S., Nagata, K., Yoshimura, H., Kuroki, H. & Masuda, Y. (1981), Inductive effect on hepatic enzymes and acute toxicity of individual polychlorinated dibenzofuran congeners in rats, *Toxicology and Applied Pharmacology*, *59*, 580 588.

RECENT FINDINGS ON THE FORMATION AND DECOMPOSITION OF PCDD/PCDF IN MUNICIPAL SOLID WASTE INCINERATION*

H. Vogg†, M. Metzger† and L. Stieglitz†

(*Received November 1986*)

The thermal formation of PCDD/PCDF in fly ashes of refuse incineration plants preferably in the low-temperature region of the boiler at 300°C is fully confirmed. Important parameters for the reaction of formation are the oxygen content and the water vapor in the offgas. Elemental carbon in the fly ash acts as an adsorbent to the precursor compounds. The oxidation of carbon may serve as a basis for the mechanism of PCDD/PCDF formation. Both reactions proceed by the Deacon process scheme. The catalytic action of $CuCl_2$ can be counteracted by the addition of NH_3.

Key Words—Dioxins, furans, fly ash, boiler ash, formation, decomposition, characterization, carbon oxidation, mechanisms, Deacon process, ammonia.

1. Introduction

At the Fifth International Dioxin Conference held in Bayreuth, Federal Republic of Germany in 1985, we reported the thermal behaviour of dioxins and furans in the fly ashes of municipal waste incineration (MWI) plants (Vogg & Stieglitz 1985). We were able to demonstrate, by treating electrostatic filter dust samples of a refuse incineration plant in a laboratory furnace purged by an air flow for two hours, that there is a drastic increase in all chlorination stages of dioxins and furans at a temperature of ca. 300°C. At temperatures > 500°C and with gas residence times in the range of minutes, however, almost quantitative decomposition was observed. We interpreted these findings as indications of a potential secondary mechanism of dioxin and furan formation in the low-temperature region of the boiler of an MWI plant. This report will present the continuation of our experiments and the most recent findings obtained.

1.1. *Temperature dependence of formation*

Our early investigations were conducted using relatively large temperature steps of 100°C, with a maximum level of formation arising at a temperature of 300°C. The position of that peak level has now been defined more accurately by experiments in the temperature range 200–400°C, using temperature steps of 50°C. The results are shown in Tables 1 and 2. The very low amounts volatilized at 300°C, which are not negligible at 350 and 400°C, were added to the contents in the solid. The Tables include data from Vogg & Stieglitz (1985) at 300°C as an indication of reproducibility.

---

*Presented at the ISWA–WHO–DAKOFA specialized seminar, *Emission of Trace Organics from Municipal Solid Waste Incinerators*, Copenhagen, 20–22 January 1987.

† Nuclear Research Center Karlsruhe, Post Box 3640, D-7500, Karlsruhe, F.R.G.

Waste Management & Research (1987) **5**, 285–294

TABLE 1

PCDD content (ng g^{-1}) of fly ash at different temperatures

| | Temperature (°C) | | | | | |
	200*	250	300	300*	350	400*
8CDD	90	147	483	640	200	15
7CDD	100	208	1103	1000	430	60
6CDD	65	217	1029	1640	550	110
5CDD	40	110	517	570	590	135
4CDD	15	26	188	65	220	50
PCDD	310	708	3320	3915	1990	370

* Data from Vogg & Stieglitz (1985).

TABLE 2

PCDF content (ng g^{-1}) of fly ash at different temperatures

| | Temperature (°C) | | | | | |
	200*	250	300	300*	350	400*
8CDF	12	74	171	218	72	12
7CDF	48	195	698	1030	428	112
6CDF	61	236	944	1255	680	260
5CDF	129	367	1256	1571	1010	687
4CDF	122	560	1379	507	1185	530
PCDF	372	1432	4448	4581	3375	1601

* Data from Vogg & Stieglitz (1985).

1.2. *Time dependence of formation*

In a separate series of experiments, in which the optimum temperature of formation of 300°C was retained, the length of treatment was varied. It was seen that the reaction is not complete after two hours, but that even higher dioxin and furan contents can be induced over a period of at least six hours (Stieglitz & Vogg 1986).

2. Flue gas atmospheres

2.1. *Investigation of fly ash*

The findings presented so far about the formation of dioxins and furans from fly ashes of refuse incineration plants were obtained by thermal treatment in a normal air atmosphere. It was therefore necessary to examine whether these effects would occur also under the realistic conditions of an MWI plant, i.e. with flue gas as the ambient medium. For this purpose, a laboratory-size tube furnace (useful volume, 0.42 l) was purged continuously with synthetic flue gas (gas residence time, 15 s). The gas contained 1000 mg of HCl, 300 mg of SO_2, 11% O_2, 150 g of H_2O (per std. m³). The fly ash sample was taken from the base material used for all earlier tests, but in this case, ground and then exposed to the gas at 300°C for two hours. The ash was analyzed for

PCDD and PCDF using ^{13}C-labelled PCDD as internal standard, as described by Stieglitz *et al.* (1985) and Vogg & Stieglitz (1985).

The results are summarized in the column headed M1 in Table 3. A parallel sample was exposed directly to the real flue gas of an MWI plant. For this purpose, a small amount of flue gas was taken out with a bypass line, filtered in an absolute filter, and the dust-free gas was passed through a tube containing the fly ash sample (gas residence time, 7 s). The other conditions were again two hours of treatment at 300°C. This test is shown as M14 in Table 3.

The control, WO, in Table 3, represents the untreated sample for comparison; W1 represents the sample treated in normal air (Vogg & Stieglitz 1985).

The results show that the formation of dioxins and furans in the fly ash of MWI plants at low temperatures (300°C) can also occur under realistic flue gas atmosphere conditions in plants operated on a technical scale. The necessary residence times are existent because fly ash deposits can persist for long periods on surfaces in the boiler area (see Defeche 1983). It still needs to be clarified why the levels were even higher than those found in experiments conducted in air. This is most probably due both to the different gas atmosphere and to the larger surface of the sample material produced by grinding.

TABLE 3

PCDD and PCDF content (ng g^{-1}) of fly ash after two hours at 300°C
in various gas mixtures

	Control W O	Air W 1	Acid gas M 1	Flue gas M 14
8CDD	120	640	480	709
7CDD	125	1000	1830	2550
6CDD	85	1640	2144	3452
5CDD	45	570	1473	1972
4CDD	20	65	270	292
PCDD	395	3915	6197	8975
8CDF	12	218	404	140
7CDF	48	1030	580	752
6CDF	56	1253	864	1313
5CDF	129	1570	1300	1950
4CDF	113	506	800	886
PCDF	358	4577	3948	5041

TABLE 4

Assay for dioxin in boiler ash (ng g^{-1} of ash)

	Pass 2/3	Pass 4
8CDD	0.6	265
7CDD	0.2	124
6CDD	0.1	105
5CDD	0.1	75
4CDD	0.1	25
PCDD	1.1	594

2.2. *Investigation of boiler ash*

The hypothesis proposed by Vogg & Stieglitz (1985) that, in the light of the findings made, the boiler of an MWI plant in connection with its fly ash deposits was the most likely site of dioxin and furan formation, needed to be verified experimentally. For this purpose, one dust sample was taken simultaneously from pass 2/3 and pass 4 of the boiler of an MWI plant in operation. The temperatures in pass 2/3 were between 800 and 400°C, and those in pass 4 between 400 and 220°C. Both samples were assayed for dioxins. The results are shown in Table 4.

The fact that only traces of dioxins were found in pass 2/3, whilst relatively high dioxin levels were found in pass 4 is, in our opinion, another indication, now verified experimentally, of dioxin formation taking place to a considerable extent through secondary reactions in the low-temperature field of the boiler.

2.3. *Dependence of dioxin and furan formation on O_2 content*

The test set-up described in Section 4 was used to determine the influence of oxygen on the formation of dioxin and furan. The findings are summarized in Table 5.

Column 1 in Table 5 shows the concentrations of untreated material; column 2 shows the result of a test conducted in a pure N_2 atmosphere without any further additions. Columns 3–6 refer to experiments with N_2 as carrier gas each with 1000 mg of HCl std. m^{-3}, 300 mg of SO_2 std. m^{-3} and, as the parameter to be studied, 1, 4 and 10 vol% O_2, respectively. Columns 5 and 6 differ in the experimental conditions only in that an additional 150 g of H_2O std. m^{-3} was added to the gas stream as water vapour.

In the absence of oxygen there is decomposition, especially of the more highly chlorinated dioxins and furans, at 300°C. This finding agrees with studies by Rghei & Eiceman (1982) and also explains and confirms the experiments described by Hagenmaier *et al.* (1986*a*, and this issue). In the latter experiments, the experimental conditions selected produced an inert gas atmosphere. However, already at 1% O_2 a slight increase in the PCDD/PCDF concentrations relative to the initial material could be

TABLE 5

Influence of oxygen on the formation of PCDD/PCDF on fly ash after two hours at 300 °C
(ng g^{-1} ash)

	(1) Untreated	(2) N_2	(3) 1%O_2	(4) 4%O_2	(5) 10%O_2	(6) 10%O_2 (+H_2O)
8CDD	146	5	187	1707	4879	292
7CDD	125	9	202	1071	2479	1898
6CDD	92	17	229	603	1150	4501
5CDD	34	26	87	125	174	2765
4CDD	16	19	33	31	26	1899
PCDD	423	76	738	3537	8708	11 355
8CDF	16	1	54	455	1065	55
7CDF	74	4	146	554	1068	706
6CDF	96	9	229	466	819	1873
5CDF	197	28	456	593	892	4992
4CDF	175	47	340	401	517	3967
PCDF	558	89	1225	2469	4361	11 593

observed. Further increases in the O_2 content made the concentrations rise drastically with an especially pronounced formation of hexa- to octa-chlorinated congeners.

The fact that the new formation of dioxins and furans also involves additional chlorination of aromatic structures can be demonstrated by evaluating the mean degree of chlorination. It increases for dioxins from 6.85 (column 1) to 7.38 (column 5), and for furans from 5.21 to 6.29.

Comparisons of the results in columns 5 and 6 show another surprising feature. The presence of water vapour obviously plays an important role with respect to the composition of the reaction product. Whilst, in the "dry" experiments, the formation of more highly chlorinated dioxins dominates, the "moist" experiments produce a peak in the range of hexachloro-isomers, which is associated with a clearly increased formation of penta- and tetra-chloro-isomers. This finding is in good agreement with the results in Table 3, where the acid gas and the flue gas atmospheres both contained water vapour.

The average chlorine content for dioxins in column 6 is 5.65 and for furans 4.96, i.e. in both cases the average content is below that of the untreated material. Consequently, in the presence of water, the new formation of dioxins and furans is accompanied by a dechlorination leading to a congener pattern which corresponds quite well to that reported by Hagenmaier (1986a, and this issue).

The results in Table 5 show that it is not only the O_2 concentration which has a major influence on the reaction mechanism, but also the presence of H_2O.

3. Components of fly ash

The possibility of dioxins and furans forming in the fly ash of MWI plants preferably at 300°C raises the question of the reaction partners and also of the reaction mechanisms involved. Fly ash as the carrier of those substances and their precursor compounds, respectively, must be included in these considerations.

3.1. Carbon in fly ash

In our experiments we were always struck by the fact that fly ashes acquired brighter (lighter) colours after treatment for several hours in the air stream above a temperature of ca. 300°C. The interesting feature about this discovery was that this change did not occur on the surface of the sample material exposed to the air stream, but rather came from inside the fly ash bed. We were soon able to establish a connection between this finding and the content of elemental carbon in the fly ash, which required us to take a closer look at the behaviour of carbon in the temperature treatment of fly ash.

The rules for waste incineration emphasize the significance of achieving good burnout of the slag, while obviously attaching less importance to attaining a specific quality of fly ash. This may be associated with the use of slag in road construction, the dry mass of which may have a maximum ignition loss of 5% at 550°C. Fly ash, as a residue to be disposed of, is not covered by any rules. For the offgas, however, the observation of CO limits is required; in the F.R.G., TA Luft, the new Technical Provisions on Air Pollution Control, gives a limit of 100 mg of CO std. m^{-3} as well as an upper limit for organic C of 20 mg std. m^{-3}.

In our opinion, the content of elemental carbon in the fly ash would be an excellent additional yardstick by which to judge the quality of the combustion process, and could be used for its characterization. However, it must be borne in mind that assaying for elemental carbon in the fly ash of an MWI plant (e.g. by measuring ignition losses) is not unambiguous, as it is complicated by water bound to different extents in the basic matrix and by its release. Metzger (1987) therefore developed a method using the reduction capability of the carbon contained in the fly ash to make it available for simple, direct, titration in a redox system with cerium(IV). For details, reference is made to the original literature (see also Brunner in this issue).

3.2. On the mechanism of carbon oxidation in fly ash

An obvious explanation of the brightening of the fly ash during temperature treatment is carbon oxidation. That this assumption is correct is shown by the carbon contents in fly ashes A, B and C, both untreated and treated for two hours at 350°C, which are listed in Table 6, as determined by the method developed by Metzger (1987).

Surprisingly enough, further experiments indicated, both in qualitative optical and in quantitative terms through cerium(IV) titration, that this carbon oxidation in fly ashes leached in an acid medium (pH = 3) does not occur in the range of temperatures which we had investigated. This implies that acid soluble fly ash components must play an essential role in the oxidation process. Artificial doping might provide more information on this hypothesis.

MnO_2, $AgNO_3$, $CuCl_2$, $CuSO_4$, KCl, NaCl, $CaCl_2$, $MgCl_2$ and $FeCl_3$ were studied as additives either singly, in various concentrations, or in selected combinations. The most effective additives were found to be $CuCl_2$ and, in combination with copper, KCl and other alkali and alkaline earth chlorides. The latter probably act as suppliers of HCl (Balarew 1926) for an intermediate reformation of $CuCl_2$ from the copper residue of the extracted fly ash material (only some 5% of the copper contained in the fly ash can be leached at pH = 3) and as a preliminary stage of the formation of Cl_2.

Carbon oxidation consequently seems to take place in a reaction analogous to the Deacon process. The catalytic action of $CuCl_2$,

$$2CuCl_2 \rightarrow 2CuCl + Cl_2,$$

and oxidation of HCl (e.g. from KCl) with airborne oxygen,

$$2HCl + 1/2O_2 \rightarrow H_2O + Cl_2,$$

causes the formation of chlorine (Griffin 1985). As a result of the high reactivity of carbon, oxidation occurs on the surface (oxychlorination).

3.3. On the Mechanism of dioxin and furan formation

The production of a molecule of dioxin or furan in the fly ash probably proceeds by the same basic pattern as the carbon oxidation: HCl is formed from chlorophenols, polychlorobiphenyl ethers, chlorobenzenes, etc. Subsequently, there is oxidation catalyzed by $CuCl_2$, of HCl with airborne oxygen to produce chlorine, the intermediate products being dioxins and furans, respectively, e.g.

$$\text{2-chlorophenol} + 1/2O_2 \xrightarrow{CuCl_2} \text{dioxin} + Cl_2.$$

A reaction pathway proceeding via the Deacon reaction is also postulated (Hagenmaier 1986b). However, in contrast to the opinion of Hagenmaier, we feel that it is less the HCl available from the gas atmosphere, but rather the HCl released from the fly ash matrix, which determines the chlorine-forming reaction. Either the aromatic structures present as precursors or the newly produced dioxin/furan molecules are further chlor-

TABLE 6
Reduction capacity and carbon content of fly ash

Fly ash	Reduction capacity mg Ce g^{-1} of fly ash		Carbon content (%)	
	Original	350°C, 2 h	Original	350°C, 2 h
A	1200	440	4.3	1.6
B	430	270	1.5	1.0
C	500	290	1.8	1.0

TABLE 7
PCDD/PCDF content of fly ash samples (A–C) in (ng g^{-1}) after oxidation in air at 300°C for various treatment times (h)

	A				B			C		
	0	2	8	22	0	2	8	0	2	8
8CDD	120	640	1083	507	163	280	349	23	341	81
7CDD	125	1000	2981	569	49	360	577	18	535	199
6CDD	85	1640	3516	628	24	810	647	13	377	344
5CDD	45	570	1485	214	10	170	291	6	180	236
4CDD	20	65	790	138	3	50	209	5	29	218
PCDD	395	3915	9855	2054	249	1670	2073	65	1462	1078
8CDF	12	218	346	143	43	74	91	3	240	38
7CDF	48	1030	3637	700	63	234	643	11	524	403
6CDF	56	1253	5010	915	27	248	814	14	446	734
5CDF	129	1570	6947	836	20	243	1226	29	506	1516
4CDF	113	506	3431	662	4	177	730	14	222	1096
PCDF	358	4577	19 371	3256	157	976	3504	71	1938	3787
C (%)	4.3				1.5			1.8		
Cl (%)	6.2				2.6			2.9		
H$_2$O (%)	2.5				1.5			1.6		
Cu (μg g^{-1})	1190				1060			780		

inated. The result is a relative preference of isomers chlorinated in *ortho-* and *para*-positions (Stieglitz & Vogg 1986). The presence of water results in an accompanying dechlorination process. The question whether water is directly involved in the mechanism of PCDD/PCDF formation should be investigated.

3.4. *Comparison of various fly ashes*

The quantities of dioxins and furans formed depend on a number of parameters, as is shown in Table 7 by comparing three fly ashes of very different origins. The treatment times selected were 2, 8, and 22 h, respectively, always at 300°C in air.

The results obtained are interesting, not only because they generally confirm the thermal formation of PCCD/PCDF, but also because they convey other important information. Thus, it is seen that fly ash sample C, with clearly the lowest initial value, loses this advantage after thermal treatment, building up concentrations comparable to those of B. With longer treatment times, the PCDD/PCDF content again decreases, which is probably associated with the fact that carbon oxidation has come to an end. In fly ash C, this effect begins earlier than in A. Dioxins and furans behave differently in this respect. Decomposition seems to begin with dechlorination, but as it continues, a destruction of oxygen bridges also occurs. Perhaps even polymerization reactions should be considered (Boyd & Mortland 1985). Whether these findings can be confirmed for the real conditions of an MWI plant needs to be determined from the long-term experiments which we plan to conduct in a flue gas atmosphere.

The characteristic data of fly ashes A–C listed in Table 7 indicate that high carbon contents, and probably also high chloride concentrations, in the fly ash favour the formation of PCDD/PCDF. Elemental carbon, in this respect, is not only a measure of the quality of the combustion process, but also acts as a sorbent to the precursor compounds. Further experiments are needed to indicate the extent to which differences in the copper and water contents of fly ash also play a role. Technical process parameters, such as the temperature field of the boiler, the amounts of fly ash deposits on the boiler tubes and, consequently, especially the residence times of fly ashes in the preferred zones of formation in the boiler, will have to be considered to a greater extent than previously.

3.5. *Measures against the formation of dioxin and furan*

The secondary formation of dioxins/furans in low-temperature zones of an MWI plant does not change the fact that primary measures, especially improved combustion conditions, can also counteract the production of dioxin. This does not necessarily imply high temperatures. Improved turbulences and longer residence times of the combustion gases in the core region of the furnace, or larger afterburning zones are quite efficient in promoting the destruction of aromatic compounds in the refuse. However, more attention should be devoted to improved cleaning techniques for the boiler, e.g. by using ultrasonic air blasting. It is to be expected that this will allow clearly lower dioxin levels to be achieved.

The catalytic action of metal halides, especially of $CuCl_2$, which has been found to play an important role in the mechanism of dioxin formation, constitutes another possibility of influencing conditions by trying to synthetically poison or remove the catalyst. It was thought that ammonia was promising, and also feasible, in this respect. The result of a test conducted for this purpose is shown in Table 8. One test, M1, using synthetic flue gas (cf. Table 3) is compared with another test, M3, which additionally contained 300 mg of NH_3 std. m^{-3} in the flue gas. The reduction of catalytic activity is evident. This may open up the possibility for stopping, or at least suppressing, the formation of dioxin/furan by adding ammonia, e.g. to the economizer of an MWI boiler.

This fact also explains the very small amount of dioxin found in pyrolysis processes. The presence of considerable amounts of NH_3 in the pyrolysis gas and the oxygen-deficient atmosphere might be a reason. In further technical experiments to be conducted in the near future, we plan to study the influence of NH_3.

4. Summary of the most important findings

(a) The formation of PCDD/PCDF in the fly ashes of refuse incineration found to occur preferably at 300°C was fully confirmed.

TABLE 8

Influence of ammonia in the formation of PCDD/PCDF (ng g^{-1} fly ash) in the acid gas mixture of Table 3 (300°C for two hours)

	M 1 Acid gas	M 3 (M1 plus 300 mg NH$_3$ m^{-3})
8CDD	480	93
7CDD	1830	230
6CDD	2144	311
5CDD	1473	220
4CDD	270	60
PCDD	6197	914
8CDF	404	18
7CDF	580	88
6CDF	864	157
5CDF	1300	287
4CDF	800	169
PCDF	3948	719

(b) The major parameters associated with the reaction of formation are the oxygen content and the water vapour fraction in the offgas.

(c) Additional important facts were found to indicate that the formation of PCDD/PCDF occurs preferably in the low-temperature region of an incineration plant.

(d) Elemental carbon in the fly ash probably acts as an important adsorbent to the precursor compounds; its concentration level can be used as a first measure in evaluation.

(e) The oxidation of carbon in the fly ash may serve as a basis for the mechanism of PCDD/PCDF formation. Both reactions proceed by the Deacon process scheme, in which HCl is oxidized to Cl$_2$ with airborne oxygen.

(f) CuCl$_2$, especially in connection with alkali/alkaline earth chlorides in the fly ash, plays an important catalytic role.

(g) The catalytic action of CuCl$_2$ can be counteracted effectively by the addition of NH$_3$.

(h) Additional experiments are necessary to determine, in detail, all the parameters associated with the reactions of formation and decomposition. Unequivocal statements will be possible only after the residence times and the thermal history of a fly ash sample are known precisely and can be included in the assessment of mechanisms as important parameters.

Acknowledgements

The authors would like to thank Messrs P. Beck, P. Käse, K. Wiese and G. Zwick for their participation in the experiments and analyses, and for their careful work.

References

Balarew, D. (1926), Veränderungen auf der Oberfläche eines frisch zerriebenen kristallartigen Salzes (Changes at the surface of a freshly disrupted cristalline salt), *Zeitschrift für anorganische Chemie, 158,* 103.

Boyd, St. A. & Mortland, M. M. (1985), Dioxin radical formation and polymerization on Cu(II)smectite, *Nature, 316,* 532.

Defeche, J. (1983), Combustion, corrosion and fouling aspects of energy recovery from municipal waste, *Waste Management & Research, 1,* 17–30.

Griffin, R. D. (1985/1987), A New Theory of dioxin formation in municipal solid waste compounds, *5th International Symposium on Chlorinated Dioxins and Related Compounds,* 16–19 September 1985, Bayreuth, Germany, *Chemosphere, 15,* 1987.

Hagenmaier, P. *et al.* (1986*a*), Copper catalyzed dechlorination/hydrogenation of PCDD and PCDF, *6th International Symposium on Chlorinated Dioxins and Related Compounds,* 16–19 September 1986, Fukuoka, Japan, and VDI-Veranstaltung Dioxine, April 22, 1986, Essen.

Hagenmaier, P. *et al.* (1986*b*), Catalytic effects of fly ash waste incineration facilities on formation and decomposition of PCDD and PCDF, *6th International Symposium on Chlorinated Dioxins and Related Compounds,* 16–19 September 1986, Fukuoka, Japan.

Metzger, M. (1987), Determination of carbon in fly ashes from incineration processes, *Zeitschrift für Analytische Chemie,* in press.

Rghei, H. O. & Eiceman, G. A. (1982), Adsorption and thermal reactions of 1,2,3,4-tetrachlorodipenzo-*p*-dioxin on fly ash from a municipal incinerator, *Chemosphere, 11,* 569.

Stieglitz, L. & Vogg, H. (1986), On formation conditions of PCDD/PCDF in fly ash from municipal waste incinerators, 6th International Symposium on Chlorinated Dioxins and Related Compounds, 16–19 September 1986, Fukuoka, Japan, *Chemosphere,* in press.

Stieglitz L. *et al.* (1985/1986), Investigation of different treatment techniques for PCDD/PCDF in fly ash, 5th International Symposium on Chlorinated Dioxins and Related Compounds, 16–19 September 1985, Bayreuth, Germany, *Chemosphere, 15,* 1135.

Vogg, H. & Stieglitz, L. (1985/1986), Thermal behaviour of PCDD/PCDF in fly ash from municipal incinerators, 5th International Symposium on Chlorinated Dioxins and Related Compounds, 16–19 September 1985, Bayreuth, Germany, *Chemosphere, 15,* 1373.

VALIDATION OF SAMPLING AND ANALYSIS OF DIOXINS*

Christoffer Rappe ‡, Stellan Marklund ‡ and Mats Tysklind ‡

(*Received January 1987*)

During 1985 and 1986 the PCDD and PCDF emissions from MSW incinerators have been carefully studied in Sweden. The use of ^{13}C-labelled compounds shows that sampling and analysis should be validated by the use of such compounds. Corrections should be made for losses during sampling and analysis. Isomer-specific analytical methods should be used. Minor differences were found in isomeric patterns and congener profiles between different incinerators. Emission levels were found to vary greatly.

Key Words—PCDDs, PCDFs, MSW incinerators, validation, sampling, analysis, isomeric pattern, Sweden.

1. Introduction

On 13 February 1985, the Swedish EPA issued a moratorium on the construction of new MSW incinerators. On 11 June 1986, the same agency suggested that the moratorium be lifted and replaced by temporary guidelines. During 1985 and 1986 an extensive research program was carried out to investigate the emissions from various types of incinerators and to correlate these data with potential health risks. In this presentation we will discuss the technical experiences we have collected, especially those related to the validation problem in sampling and analyses.

2. Experimental

2.1. *Sampling*

In principle, the sampling guideline issued by the Swedish EPA (Bergvall & Jansson 1986) was followed (see Jansson & Bergvall in this issue). The sampling volume was 5–10 Nm³ and the following sub-samples were collected:

(a) particulate collected on a glass-fiber filter;
(b) condensate combined with washing solvent;
(c) cartridge of XAD-2 adsorbent.

Due to its superior solubility capacity, toluene is suggested as the solvent for washing of sampling equipment, following an acetone prewashing. Rappe *et al.* (1986) suggested that sampling and laboratory work should be validated by the use of ^{13}C-labelled surrogates, sampling "spikes" and clean-up "spikes". The greatest losses of the ^{13}C surrogates occurred on the filter and, consequently, it is suggested that the spiking

---

* Presented at the ISWA–WHO–DAKOFA specialized seminar, *Emissions of Trace Organics from Municipal Solid Waste Incinerators*, Copenhagen, 20–22 January 1987.
‡ Department of Organic Chemistry, University of Umeå, S-901 87 Umeå, Sweden.
Waste Management & Research (1987) **5**, 295–300

TABLE 1
Sampling and clean-up surrogates*

Sampling surrogates	Clean-up surrogates
^{13}C-2,3,7,8-Tetra-CDD	^{13}C-2,3,7,8-Tetra-CDF
^{13}C-1,2,3,7,8-Penta-CDD	^{13}C-1,2,3,6,7,8-Hexa-CDD
^{13}C-1,2,3,4,7,8-Hexa-CDD	^{13}C-1,2,3,4,6,7,8-Hepta-CDD
^{13}C-Octa-CDD	

* Internal standard: ^{13}C-1,2,3,7,8-Penta-CDF.

should be done preferentially on the filter (5–10 ng per congener). The ^{13}C-labelled surrogates used are given in Table 1.

2.2. *Analysis*

When received in the laboratory, the samples were fortified with other ^{13}C-labelled surrogates clean-up "spikes" (see Table 1). The amount added was normally 7.5 ng per congener and sample. After extraction, the samples were cleaned-up on a column which is essentially described and evaluated in Marklund *et al.* (1986). The final HR GC/MS analyses were performed on a quadrupole MS instrument operating in the EI and NCI (methane) modes.

3. Results

3.1. *Recovery of ^{13}C-labelled surrogates*

Small variations were found in the recovery of the clean-up spikes and, in general, the recovery was in the range 80–110% [see Fig. 1(a) for 2,3,7,8-tetra-CDF and Fig. 1(b) for 1,2,3,6,7,8-hexa-CDD]. On the other hand, much lower levels and larger variations were found for the recovery of the sampling spikes (see Fig. 2). In general, the recovery figures were found to decrease with a decreasing number of chlorine atoms (39–51%) indicating a possible relationship to the volatility of the different groups of congeners. Another interesting observation is that the only ^{13}C-labelled isomer identified was that originally added as sampling spike, even in cases where the recovery was extremely low. Chemical degradation or rearrangements during the sampling, therefore, does not seem likely.

Our experiences strongly indicate that sampling and clean-up should be validated by the use of ^{13}C-labelled surrogates. The majority of the available surrogates should be used to validate the sampling; only one or two ^{13}C spikes should be used to control the laboratory work. The most reliable results were obtained when the sub-samples were analyzed separately and the values obtained were corrected for recovery. The extent to which this compensation should be made is still being debated. The sampling spikes are present during the total sampling period, while, on average, the natural PCDD and PCDF molecule is present only during half of the sampling period.

3.2. *Isomeric pattern and congener profiles*

The pattern of individual isomers in the emissions was studied, e.g. tetra-CDDs and penta-CDFs. Using validated methods small variations were found in the pattern of

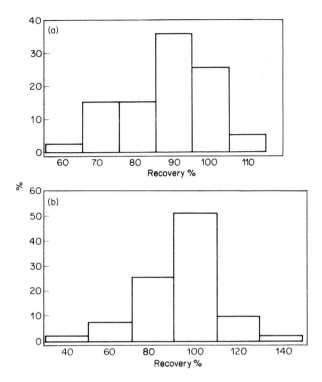

Fig. 1. Recovery of ¹³C-labelled surrogates added to validate clean-up. (a) ¹³C-TCDF clean-up spike: $n = 39$, mean $= 92$, SD $= 11$. (b) ¹³C-HxCDD clean-up spike: $n = 39$, mean $= 101$, SD $= 17$.

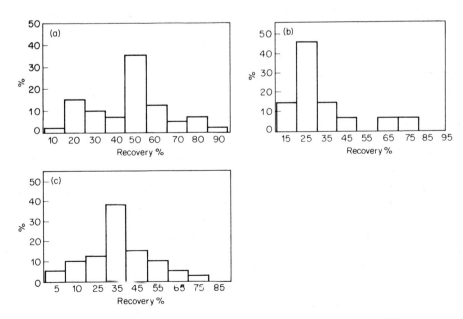

Fig. 2. Recovery of ¹³C-labelled surrogate added to validate sampling. (a) ¹³C-HxCDF sampling spike: $n = 39$, mean $= 51$, SD $= 20$. (b) ¹³C-TCDD sampling spike: $n = 13$, mean $= 39$, SD $= 19$. (c) ¹³C-PeCDD sampling spike: $n = 39$, mean $= 40$, SD $= 16$.

TABLE 2
Operation parameters used in the prediction model

CO_2	Temperature grate 1
CO	Temperature grate 2
NO	Temperature grate 3
SO_2	Post combustion zone 1 temperature
Smoke density	Post combustion zone 2 temperature
Feed rate	Post combustion zone 3 temperature
Heat production	Post combustion zone 4 temperature
Flue gas flow	Total air intake
Steam flow	Air intake: Location 1
Flue gas temperature	Air intake: Location 2
Combustion chamber temperature	Air intake: Location 3

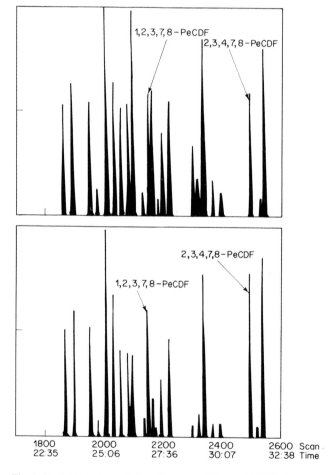

Fig. 3. Penta-CDFs in emissions from two different MSW incinerators.

individual groups of isomers and congeners between different incinerators (see Fig. 3) which shows the penta-CDFs from two different MSW incinerators giving high and low emissions levels. A typical pattern of the tetra-CDFs is given in Fig. 4 (upper curve). The GC column used was found to separate the 2,3,7,8- and 2,3,4,8-isomers. As

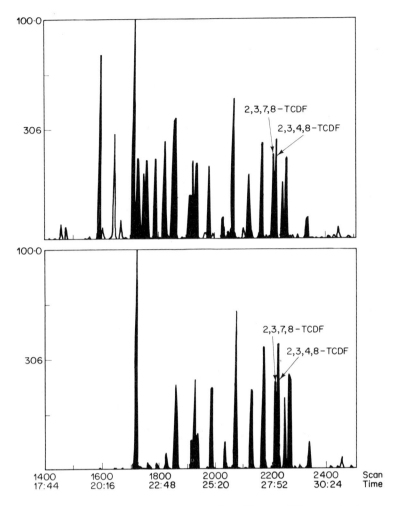

Fig. 4. Tetra-CDFs in the same extract cleaned by two different methods.

a part of a round-robin study, we also analyzed the same sample cleaned-up by another laboratory using the same GC/MS system (see Fig. 4, lower curve). Here it was found that several of the peaks seen earlier were lost during the clean-up as a consequence of too narrow elution windows in the clean-up column systems. The recovery of the ^{13}C-2,3,7,8-tetra-CDF was the same in both cases.

The congener profiles in the total emissions from three Swedish MSW incinerators were also studied. Although some variation was found in the emission levels, the congener profiles showed only a small variation (see Fig. 5). In the PCDF series, the highest emissions were found for the tetra- and penta-chlorinated congeners, and in the PCDD series, the highest values were found for the penta-CDDs.

3.3. *Emission levels*

The total emission levels of PCDDs and PCDFs were investigated and were found to vary greatly depending on the technology used, the actual combustion parameters (see

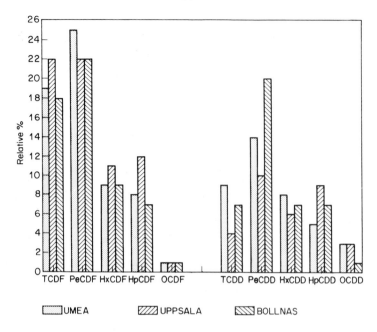

Fig. 5. Congener profiles of PCDDs and PCDFs in emissions from three Swedish MSW incinerators.

Table 2) and the cleaning equipment. The emission levels were in the range 0.5–100 mg of TCDD equivalents (Eadon 1983) m^{-3} dry gas, 10% CO_2.

References

Bergvall, G. & Jansson, B. (1986), Recommended method for dioxin measurements in flue gas at MSW incinerators. Statens Naturvårdsverk, Stockholm, Sweden 1986-02-19.

Eadon, G., Aldous, K., Hilker, P., O'Keefe, P. & Smith, R. (1983), Chemical data on air samples from the Birminghamton State Office Building. Memo from Center for Lab. Research, New York State Department of Health, Albany, NY 12201, 7/7/83.

Marklund, S., Kjeller, L.-O., Hansson, M., Tysklind, M., Rappe, C., Ryan, C., Collazo, H. & Dougherty, R. (1986), Determination of PCDDs and PCDFs in incineration samples and pyrolytic products. In *Chlorinated Dioxins and Dibenzofurans in Perspective* (C. Rappe, G. Chouldhary, & L. Keith, Eds) pp. 79–91. Lewis Publishers, Chelsea, MI, U.S.A.

Rappe, C., Marklund, S., Kjeller, L.-D. & Tysklind, M. (1986), PCDDs and PCDFs in emission from various incinerators, *Chemosphere*, **15**, 1213–1217.

CANADA'S NATIONAL INCINERATOR TESTING AND EVALUATION PROGRAM (NITEP) AIR POLLUTION CONTROL TECHNOLOGY ASSESSMENT*

R. Klicius,† D. J. Hay,† A. Finkelstein† and L. Marentette‡

(*Received January 1987, revised March 1987*)

In order to address the many concerns associated with emissions from municipal energy-from-waste facilities, Environment Canada established the National Incinerator Testing and Evaluation Program (NITEP). In recognition of the absence of a useful data base on incinerator emission control systems, Environment Canada, in co-operation with Flakt Canada, constructed a pilot plant to evaluate a dry scrubber system and a spray-dryer (wet-dry) system, each followed by a fabric filter (baghouse).

Extensive sampling was done before and after each reactor, as well as in the stack. All particulate material collected in the bottom of the scrubbers and the fabric filter were analysed and subjected to leaching tests to determine the suitability of subsequent disposal alternatives. All samples taken were analysed for dioxins, furans, other organic substances, metals and acid gases.

Many different operating conditions were tested to identify optimum removal efficiency for all pollutants of concern. The final results were very significant. Flue gas temperature was found to be an important operating variable for achieving high removal efficiency for many of the pollutants measured. Appropriate operating conditions were identified to obtain extremely high removal efficiencies for dioxins and furans ($>99\%$), other trace organics (up to 98%), heavy metals, including mercury, arsenic, lead ($>99\%$) and up to 97% for mercury. Excellent removal ($>95\%$) was also obtained for acid gases, i.e. HCl and SO_2.

Key words—Incinerators, dioxins, metals, acid gases, emission control, scrubber/ fabric filter, Canada.

1. Introduction

Environment Canada established the National Incinerator Testing and Evaluation Program (NITEP) to address the environmental impact of energy-from-waste (EFW) facilities. This will be accomplished by determining the optimum design and operating conditions to minimize emissions. Three generic incinerator designs for municipal solid waste (MSW) were selected for detailed testing and evaluation: the two-stage modular design, the mass burning incinerator and the refuse-derived fuel (RDF) incinerator.

In addition to minimizing the generation of emissions at source (i.e. at the furnace), NITEP recognized that modern air emission control technologies can play an important role in reducing stack emissions. Accordingly, under the NITEP, Environment Canada, in co-operation with Flakt Canada Ltd., established an extensive test program to evaluate conclusively the capability of two control systems to remove particulate, acid

*Presented at the ISWA–WHO–DAKOFA specialized seminar, *Emission of Trace Organics from Municipal Solid Waste Incinerators*, Copenhagen, 20–22 January 1987.

† Environment Canada, Industrial Programs Branch, Urban Activities Division, Ottawa, Ontario, K1A OE7, Canada.

‡ Flakt Canada Ltd., 1400 Merivale Road, Ottawa, Ontario, Canada.

Waste Management & Research (1987) **5**, 301–310

gases, heavy metals, dioxins, furans and other organic compounds. In addition, the optimum operating conditions to minimize these contaminants were also of great interest.

In order to undertake this work, a large-scale pilot plant facility was constructed at the EFW plant in Quebec City owned by the Quebec Urban Community (CUQ) and operated by Montenay Inc.

2. Description of facilities tested

2.1. *Incinerator description*

The CUQ incinerator is a mass burning design, developed in the early 1970s to burn as-received refuse in a water wall furnace. There are four incinerators, each rated at 227 t day^{-1} with a common refuse storage pit and stack. Each incinerator consists of a vibrating feeder-hopper, feed chute, drying/burning/burn-out grates (Von-Roll design), refractory lined burning zone, water-walled, partially lined upper burning zone, a waste-heat recovery boiler with superheater and economizer (Dominion Bridge), a two-field electrostatic precipitator, an induced draught fan and a wet ash quench/removal system.

The incinerator receives municipal, commercial and suitable industrial solid waste. Each of the four units is capable of independent operation and is rated to produce 37,000 kg h^{-1} of steam when burning 227 t day^{-1} of refuse with a heating value of 13,950 kj kg^{-1}. All the steam generated is sold to Reed Paper Ltée at a guaranteed steady ($\pm 7\%$) flow and specified pressure range.

2.2. *Pilot plant description*

2.2.1. *General features*
The principal components of the pilot plant are shown in Fig. 1 and described below.

(1) A flue gas stream take-off duct (with eight nozzles) from the electrostatic pre-
    cipitator inlet of incinerator unit No. 3. The arrangement was employed to obtain
    a representative sample of flue gas to the pilot plant.

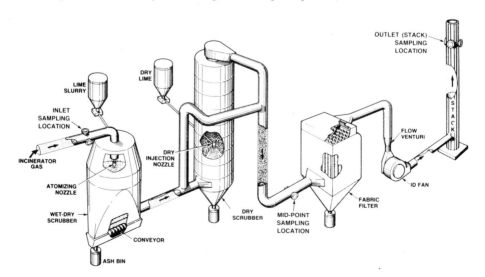

Fig. 1. Main equipment components of Flakt's pilot plant.

(2) A wet–dry scrubber, also used as a gas cooler, with slurry spray nozzle and bottom screw conveyor.

(3) A dry scrubber with a single dry lime injection nozzle and internal cyclone integral with the scrubber at the entrance.

(4) A pulse-jet fabric filter using high temperature Teflon bags as the filtering media with an air-to-cloth ratio of 4.4 ACFM per square foot. Instrumentation included a pulse pressure controller, as well as duration and timer controls.

(5) An induced draft fan with flow venturi.

(6) A stack.

Ancillary equipment included by-pass ducts across the dry scrubber and fabric filter, removable ash hopper drums on each of the three vessels, flue gas duct isolating dampers, ID-fan flow control damper, two lime slurry variable-speed pumps with associated mix tanks, agitators, controls and a venturi-eductor dry lime feed system with variable control and lime silo.

2.2.2. *Modes of pilot plant operation*
The pilot plant was operated in one of two modes.

(1) *Dry system.* The hot flue gas from the incinerator entered at about 255–270°C into the wet–dry scrubber (now in the role of a gas cooler) where it was cooled to the desired temperature with a water spray. It then entered the bottom of the dry scrubber tangentially into an internal cyclone. Dry hydrated lime was then air injected through a single nozzle counter current into the gas stream. The flue gas with entrained particulates and lime was then directed into the fabric filter dust collector.

(2) *Wet–dry system.* Hot flue gas from the incinerator entered the top of the wet–dry reactor at 255–270°C, where it was intimately mixed and cooled with a finely atomized lime slurry spray. The flue gas was then directed into the fabric filter dust collector.

For both systems, final removal of particulates, including lime, was accomplished with a fabric filter dust collector. Seventy-two bags arranged in 6 rows of 12 bags each were contained in a one-compartment design. The bag material was Teflon with Gortex scrim, which is chemically inert to acid gases and has a maximum operating temperature of 250°C. The bags were supported on cylindrical wire cages with particulate collection occurring on the outside of the bag.

The pilot plant process-control system was relatively uncomplicated. Temperature control was accomplished either by adjusting the rate of slurry into the wet–dry system, or by water spray into the dry system. Flue gas flow was controlled by adjusting the damper at the inlet of the induced draught fan. To ensure that constant flow was maintained during the tests, the pressure drop across a venturi upstream of the ID fan was monitored continuously.

3. Test program description

3.1. *Sampling locations*

Three sampling locations were selected to monitor the incinerator gases and to measure emissions (see Fig. 1). In addition, all material settling out in the bottom hoppers of the scrubbers and the fabric filter were collected for analysis.

3.2. *Quality assurance/quality control*

To ensure that the data was collected in a manner which would minimize any negative effects on data quality, an extensive third-party quality assurance/quality control programme (QA/QC) was set up. This programme component represented about 10% of the overall effort and was in addition to the internal QA/QC that is a routine part of all sampling programmes.

3.3. *Test phases*

As in previous NITEP tests, the project was divided into two parts. The first was a characterization phase to familiarize project staff with the facility and to assess, using conventional parameters, the effect of the various operating variables on system performance. The characterization-phase test results identified that flue gas temperature and the ratio of lime to acid gas were the key parameters influencing the removal efficiency of the pollutants measured.

Based on the first-phase results, six performance test conditions were selected for a more detailed assessment of all parameters of interest (organics, metals, acid gases and conventional gas parameters). Four conditions were tested for the dry system, for which the flue gas temperature at the fabric filter inlet was 110, 125, 140 and 209°C. Two conditions were selected for the wet–dry system, 140°C with recycle of ash, and 140°C with no recycle. Each condition was tested twice to assess repeatability of results.

For each of the performance test conditions selected, sampling and data collection were conducted for the parameters shown in Fig. 2. Ten manual sampling trains and

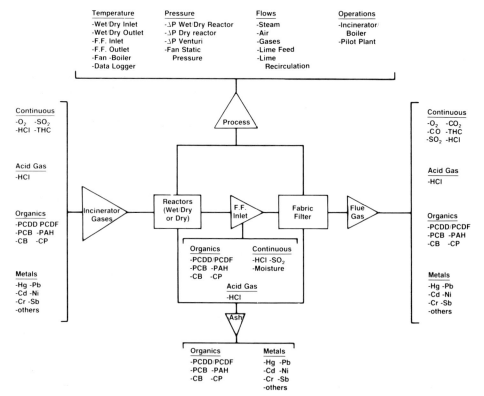

Fig. 2. Parameters measured during performance tests.

TABLE 1

Key operating conditions*

Incinerator	
Steam	32,000 kg h⁻¹
Gas at boiler outlet	280–300°C
Pilot plant	
Gas at pilot plant inlet	255–270°C
Lime Ca(OH)₂	3.4–3.8 kg h⁻¹
Δ P fabric filter	14–16 cm H₂O
Outlet gas flow	3600 m³ h⁻¹ for 200°C; 4100–4300 Sm³ h⁻¹ for 110, 125 and 140°C
CO	120–200 ppm (dry)
Oxygen	12–13% (dry)
Inlet particulate	6000–8000 mg m⁻³ at 8% O₂

*S, Standard dry-gas conditions (25°C and 101.325 kPa).

13 continuous gas monitors were operated simultaneously during these tests, requiring over 30 engineers and technicians. Protocols recognized in North America were used for sampling and analyses. The analytical protocol for trace organic compounds is detailed in EC (1987).

4. Summary of results

4.1. *Operating parameters*

The most significant operating parameters measured during the performance tests are summarized in Table 1. The incinerator was operated as it normally operates at a steam production rate of 31,000–34,000 kg h⁻¹. The average flow rate of the flue gas slip stream for the pilot plant was measured as 4000 Sm³ h⁻¹ (dry). The operating parameters for the pilot plant, such as fabric filter pressure drop, lime flow rate, and flue gas temperature after cooling, were carefully controlled at the selected conditions for each test.

TABLE 2

PCDD concentrations (ng Sm⁻³ at 8% O₂) (total tetra- to octa-homologues) in flue gas and efficiency of removal

	Dry system				Wet–dry system	
Operating condition	110°C	125°C	140°C	> 200°C	140°C	140°C + recycle
Inlet	580	1400	1300	1030	1100	1300
Mid-point	310	570	540	1140	840	1270
Outlet	0.2	ND	ND	6.1	ND	0.4
Efficiency (%)						
Inlet/mid-point	47	60	57	(11)	24	2
Overall	> 99.9	> 99.9	> 99.9	> 99.8	> 99.9	> 99.9

ND, not detected.

4.2. PCDD/PCDF

4.2.1. PCDD in flue gas streams

For the parameter of greatest concern, polychlorinated dibenzodioxins (PCDD), Table 2 summarizes the inlet, mid-point and outlet concentrations, total of tetra- to octa-homologues in particulate and gaseous forms and overall removal efficiencies. As is clearly evident, the greatest proportion of PCDD removal occurs across the fabric filter for both systems and under all temperature conditions tested.

Although the outlet concentration of PCDD was low for all operating conditions, there appeared to be some temperature effect at operating conditions below 140°C. Slightly higher removal efficiencies were observed at the lower temperatures.

The PCDD homologue distribution is similarly important and a typical example is shown in Fig. 3 for the dry system operating at 140°C. The bell shape of the distribution

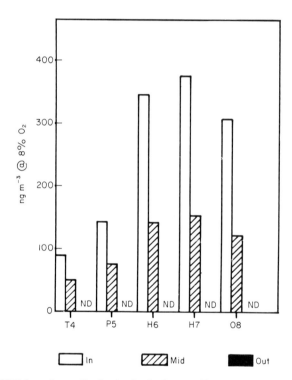

Fig. 3. Typical PCDD homologue distribution in the flue gas. Dry system at 140°C. ND, not detected.

curve is similar for all test conditions. The tetra-substituted homologues are the least prevalent with the 2,3,7,8-isomer being generally less than 0.5% of the total PCDD.

4.2.2. PCDF in flue gas streams

For total tetra- to octa-homologues of polychlorinated dibenzofurans (PCDF) in particulate and gaseous forms, the removal efficiencies were similarly high (over 99.3%) as for PCDD. Table 3 gives the average data for each performance test condition. Figure 4 shows a typical PCDF homologue distribution. It is interesting to note that, in the PCDF homologue distribution, there is a greater prevalence of the tetra-isomers.

TABLE 3

PCDF concentrations (ng Sm^{-3} at 8% O$_2$) (total tetra- to octa-homologues) in flue gas and efficiency of removal

	Dry system				Wet–dry system	
Operating condition	110°C	125°C	140°C	>200°C	140°C	140°C + recycle
Inlet	300	940	1000	560	660	850
Mid-point	270	440	630	490	690	1030
Outlet	2.3	ND	1.0	1.2	ND	0.9
Efficiency (%)						
Inlet/mid-point	11	54	37	13	−4	−21
Overall	99.3	>99.9	99.9	99.8	>99.9	99.9

ND, not detected.

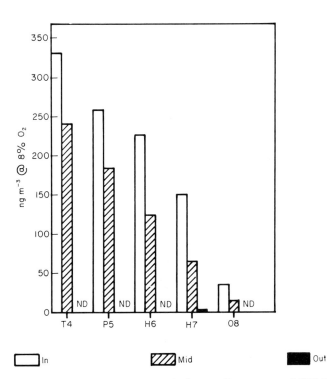

Fig. 4. Typical PCDF homologue distribution in the flue gas. Dry system at 140°C. ND, not detected.

4.2.3. *PCDD/PCDF in ashes*

Table 4 gives the concentration of PCDD (total tetra- to octa-homologues) measured in representative hopper ash samples from the three vessel hoppers. The concentrations are by far the greatest in the fabric filter ash. Similar results were obtained for PCDF in the hopper ashes. These results were expected because the fabric filter had the greatest impact on PCDD and PCDF removal. It is significant to note that the fabric filter ash was much finer in appearance than the scrubber ashes. The homologue distribution of PCDD and PCDF in the ash phase is essentially identical to that noted for the flue gas.

TABLE 4
PCDD (ng g^{-1}) concentration in ash (total tetra to octa-homologues)

Operating condition	Dry system				Wet–dry system	
	110°C	125°C	140°C	> 200°C	140°C	140°C + recycle
Wet–dry scrubber ash	13	14	6	6	6	12
Dry scrubber ash	160	64	94	31	NA	NA
Fabric filter ash	280	570	570	740	160	230

NA, not applicable.

4.3. Other organics

The removal efficiency for other organics, such as chlorobenzenes (CB), chlorophenols (CP), polychlorinated biphenyls (PCB) and polycyclic aromatic hydrocarbons (PAH), was also measured. Appropriate conditions were determined to achieve 80–99% removal. These results are reported in EC (1986a).

4.4. Metals

The removal efficiency for 27 metals was also determined. As reported in EC (1986a), metal removal exceeded 99.9% for all metals except mercury. The only notable exception occurs with mercury at the higher (200°C) temperature tested, at which there is no removal of mercury. However, it was determined that mercury removal can be significantly enhanced (up to 97% removal) by operating the system at a flue gas temperature below 140°C.

4.5. Acid gases

The ability of the two systems to reduce the emission of acid gases, hydrogen chloride (HCl) and sulphur dioxide (SO$_2$), was evaluated for several different operating conditions. Table 5 demonstrates the impact of operating conditions on acid gas removal. It is evident that temperature is a major factor in acid gas removal, which is consistent with observations for organics and metals. At the lower operating temperatures, the removal efficiencies are significantly higher than at the higher temperatures. In addition, the fabric filter played a key role in achieving high removal efficiency, especially for SO$_2$. This has important negative implications in the use of an electrostatic precipitator in lieu of a fabric filter. There appears to be no significant difference between the dry and wet–dry systems for removal of acid gases; however, the recycle condition (wet–dry mode) did show that less lime was required to achieve the same removal efficiency as without recycle. This is a significant finding because it shows the potential for reducing operating costs by reducing lime consumption.

5. Ash leaching

The substantial increase of pollutant concentrations in the fabric filter ashes generated an important interest in ash leachability. Accordingly, the ashes collected from each of the scrubbers and fabric filter were subjected to a series of leaching tests. These results are published in a separate report (EC 1986b).

TABLE 5

HCl and SO$_2$ concentrations (ppm) at 8% O$_2$, and collection efficiency (%)

Operating condition	Dry system				Wet–dry system	
Flue gas temp. at FF, inlet (°C)	110	125	140	> 200	140	140 + recycle
Stoichiometric ratio	1.16	1.03	1.04	1.49	1.19	1.10
Hydrogen chloride						
Inlet (ppm)	423	464	425	392	366	470
Mid-point (ppm)	15	69	129	196	149	152
Outlet (ppm)	7	9	29	91	29	42
Eff. to mid-point (%)	96	85	73	50	59	69
Eff. overall (%)	98	98	94	77	92	91
Sulphur dioxide						
Inlet (ppm)	119	118	99	117	106	106
Mid-point (ppm)	24	65	64	103	67	70
Outlet (ppm)	4	10	41	83	35	43
Eff. to mid-point (%)	80	45	35	11	37	35
Eff. overall (%)	96	92	58	29	67	60

6. Conclusions

The following key conclusions have been drawn from the extensive test data on the NITEP pilot plant system.

(1) Both the wet–dry system, using lime slurry, and the dry system, using powdered lime, followed by a fabric filter, are capable of high removal efficiency for all pollutants of concern, with no significant difference in removal efficiency by either system.

(2) Cooling of the flue gas temperature was a key operating parameter for effective removal of HCl, SO$_2$ and mercury for both systems.

(3) The removal efficiencies for PCDD and PCDF were very high, exceeding 99%. For most test runs, the concentrations of PCDD and PCDF after the control system approached the detection limits of the sampling and analytical methods employed.

(4) The highest PCDD and PCDF concentrations in the ashes occurred in the fabric filter ash and the lowest concentrations were found in the scrubber ashes. These results were anticipated based on the high removal efficiency of PCDD and PCDF across the fabric filter collector.

(5) Other trace organics, such as chlorobenzenes (CB), polychlorinated biphenyls (PCB), chlorophenols (CP) and polycyclic aromatic hydrocarbons (PAH) were also efficiently removed (80–99%) by both systems when operated under cooled flue gas conditions.

(6) Concentrations of trace organics in the various hopper ashes followed a similar pattern as for PCDD and PCDF, whereby the highest concentrations occurred in the fabric filter ash.

(7) Metal collection efficiencies generally exceeded 99.9% with both systems except for mercury, for which flue gas cooling was essential to maintain a high removal efficiency.

(8) Low emissions of acid gas can be accomplished either by increasing the ratio of lime to acid gas, or by cooling the flue gases. However, flue gas cooling is a more economical approach because increasing lime utilization is more costly.

(9) Ash recycle (i.e. fabric filter ash containing some residual unreacted lime) added to the fresh make-up lime was beneficial in providing the same SO_2 removal efficiency as the no-recycle condition. By recycling ash, less fresh lime was used, which reduces the operating costs.

(10) Two key independent variables tested were flue gas temperature control and the ratio of lime to acid gas concentration. Temperature was found to be the most significant variable in affecting removal efficiency.

References

EC (1987), Methodology for Organic Analysis—NITEP/FLAKT Project, *NITEP—Air Pollution Control Technology—Detailed Methodology 1987*, Attachment No. 6, Vol. III, Environment Canada, Analytical Services Division.

EC (1986a), *The National Incinerator Testing and Evaluation Program: Air Pollution Control Technology*, Report EPS 3/UP/2, Environment Canada, Ottawa, September 1986.

EC (1986b), *NITEP Phase II—Testing of the FLAKT Air Pollution Control Technology at the Quebec City Municipal Energy From Waste Facility, Assessment of Ash Contaminant Leachability*, Report IP 70, Environment Canada, Wastewater Technology Centre, Ottawa, December 1986.

OPTIMIZATION OF COMBUSTION CONDITIONS TO MINIMIZE DIOXIN EMISSIONS*

Floyd Hasselriis †

(*Received December 1986, revised February 1987*)

Polychlorinated dibenzo-*p*-dioxins (PCDD) and polychlorinated dibenzofurans (PCDF) may enter an incinerator with the waste, be created in poor combustion or form in post-combustion zones under certain conditions of temperature and oxygen. Tests of MSW burning plants show a wide range of emissions of PCDD and PCDF. Diagnostic tests show the relationship between combustion conditions and the emission of PCDD/DF before and after emission controls. Mixing effectiveness, tightness of control, moisture, furnace and post-furnace temperatures, and the use of lime and reduced temperatures for acid-gas control all have an effect on emissions of trace organics. Carbon monoxide (CO), oxygen, moisture and furnace temperature have been found to be closely related to PCDD/PCDF emissions. By control of temperature and/or oxygen, and the use of CO as an indicator, it is possible to find and maintain optimum combustion conditions so as to minimize dioxins and furans. Plants having acid-gas controls reduce emissions below those achieved by good combustion alone.

Key Words—municipal solid waste (MSW), dioxins, furans, combustion, optimization, control, moisture, temperature, carbon monoxide.

1. Introduction

Dioxins (polychlorinated dibenzo-*p*-dioxins, or PCDD) and furans (polychlorinated dibenzofurans, or PCDF) have been found to be ubiquitous in the environment. Combustion, especially of organics in the presence of chlorine in some form, has been found to be a significant source of these very toxic compounds (Hasselriis 1986*c*, and Rappe *et al.* and Vogg *et al.* in this issue).

In tests of fly-ash and stack emissions from plants burning municipal refuse, PCDDs and PCDFs were found. Although the quantities measured have varied by over three orders of magnitude, most contemporary plants have achieved emissions low enough to be acceptable on the basis of elaborate environmental impact studies (Hart 1984, and Bergvall in this issue). Some plants have had emissions so low that they were below the detection level.

The concern about dioxin and furan emissions from combustion processes caused great efforts to be made to determine how emissions of PCDD/PCDF could be controlled to acceptable levels. Research was undertaken in Europe, Canada and the United States where there was a desire to use combustion as a means of recovering useful energy and greatly reducing the need for placing wastes in landfills. In Sweden, a moratorium was declared on accepting permit applications for new plants until the results of research programs, already under way, had been studied. This extensive

---

* Presented at the ISWA–WHO–DAKOFA specialized seminar, *Emissions of Trace Organics from Municipal Solid Waste Incinerators*, Copenhagen, 20–22 January 1987.
† Gershman, Brickner and Bratton, Inc., 2735 Hartland Road, Falls Church, VA 22043, U.S.A.
Waste Management & Research (1987) **5**, 311–326

research has been reported (see Bergstrom & Warman in this issue) along with guide-lines for maintaining good combustion of MSW, and the recommendation that the moratorium on new permits be lifted (Aslander & Modig 1986).

2. Background

A substantial amount of data has been collected over the last few years on emissions of PCDD and PCDF from many plants. This data, plotted in various ways, shows striking relationships (Hasselriis 1982). Table 1 shows total PCDD and PCDF measurements ranging from over 10,000 to under 0.1 ng Nm^{-3}, a remarkable range. When these data are plotted graphically, lines of constant PCDF/PCDD show that this ratio ranges from 1 to over 10 for various plants (Hasselriis 1985). Correlations between dioxin and furan emissions from MSW burning and operating parameters, such as furnace tempe-rature, excess air (or excess oxygen), and carbon monoxide (CO), would be expected. Refuse moisture was also found to have a strong correlation with dioxin emissions (NITEP, 1985). This would not be surprising because moisture and excess air (or oxygen concentration) are the main factors determining flame temperature (Hasselriis 1984, 1985). With high moisture, both temperature and oxygen concentrations tend to fall, resulting in less effective combustion. Moisture can also be expected to influence the chemical reactions. Some data indicate that refuse moisture may have a significant influence on the PCDF/PCDD ratio: the Des Carriere data (Boisjoly 1984) shows a different furan/dioxin ratio in November than in March.

Multivariate statistical analysis of eight North American incinerators (Bauer et al. 1986) showed three major factor groups by pattern recognition. Stack temperature explained 83% of the variance in the five homologs of PCDD in the major factor, moisture and gas flow explained 75% of the variance of the second factor, and oxygen, CO and the octachlorodioxin explained 87% of the variance of the third factor. These findings, which develop purely from statistical analysis of data, provide a potentially useful insight, although they provide no information on the technical basis.

In another approach to multivariate analysis using data from tests at Umea (49 variables), it was found that the TCDD-equivalent could be predicted with a correlation coefficient of 80–98% (Tysklind et al.). The procedure used in data analysis included not only pattern recognition and multiple regression but also partial least-squares modeling which made prediction possible (Wold et al. 1983). The variables included nine temperatures, CO, CO_2, the acid gases, chlorinated compounds and dioxins, and heavy metals (see also Rappe et al. in this issue).

The destruction of PCDD and PCDF is primarily a function of exposure tempera-ture, oxygen concentration and, to a lesser extent, of time. The temperature required to reach a given destruction efficiency increases rapidly as the oxygen concentration is reduced toward the pyrolysis temperature (Duvall & Rubey 1977, Hasselriis 1984).

On the basis of laboratory data and chemical kinetics, it would be expected that, with the normal amount of oxygen available in a conventional incinerator, a tempera-ture of about 800°C would reduce PCDD to parts per trillion (10^{-9}) levels. If this destruction is not achieved in an actual furnace, non-ideal conditions must be present. Among these are poor mixing of reactants, low temperatures caused by excess air, and low oxygen concentration. Only tests of full-scale incinerators can show how design and operating conditions affect destruction efficiency.

In the combustion of fossil fuels it is well known that carbon monoxide (CO) is an effective indicator of good combustion. However, it is also generally found that, while

TABLE 1
PCDD, PCDF and carbon monoxide emitted by various plants

Plant location		PCDD	PCDF	Total	CO (ppm)	Temp. (°C)
		Stack emissions (ng Nm^{-3})				
Hampton, VA	Max.	13,000	24,000	37,000	1000	
	Min.	670	3700	3670		
Hamilton, Ont.	Max.	1700	7000	8700	480	738
	Min.	1300	4000	5300	300	764
Chicago, IL	Max.	61	490	551	+70	
Albany,	Avg.	300	88	388	200	
PEI, ONT	Max.*	123	156	279	40	788
	Min.	64	100	164	14	1038
Stapelfeld, WG	Max.	40	120	160		
	Min.	20	90	110		
Peekskill, NY	Avg.	18	40	58	30	
Pittsfield, MA	Ph.I	76	270	346	140	677
	Ph.II	55	144	200	144	700
	Ph.II	8	17	25	30	760
	Ph.II	0.7	5	5.7	9	843
	Ph.II	0.8	10	10.8	7	843
	Ph.II	14	36	50	5	980
	Ph.II	28	39	67	14	980
	Ph.I	24	38	62	16	1010
Wurzburg, WG	Max.	36	54	90	40	
	Min.	12	10	22	31	
Tulsa, OK	Avg.	19	19	36	16	
Neustadt, F.R.G.	In†	80	95	175		
	Out	5	9	14		
Marion, OR	Max.	1.5	2.0	3.5	17	
	Min.	0.8	1.0	1.8	14	
Quebec, Ont.	In‡	1030	560	1590	160	
	Out	0.4	0.9	1.3	170	
Montreal, Q§	March	0.75	0.54	1.2		
	Nov.	0.01	0.02	0.03		

* Lowest and highest practical furance temperatures.
† In and out of dry lime scrubber (Hay *et al.* 1986).
‡ In and out of wet scrubber (TUV 1984).
§ Lime fed with the MSW (Boisjoly 1984).

reducing excess combustion air reduces CO, an increase in CO takes place at some point. While, theoretically, the reduction in CO would continue as temperature increases, due to reduced excess air and oxygen, as the oxygen concentration decreases, the probability of pockets deprived of oxygen increases, and effective mixing becomes more important. Thus an optimum oxygen concentration is found corresponding to minimum CO. Improvements in distribution of the air to the fuel and better mixing

may shift the low point of the CO curve to lower oxygen levels. Operation in the range
of minimum CO can be maintained by measurement and control of oxygen, or alter-
nately, of the corresponding temperature. If it can be shown that conditions which
result in minimum CO emissions also result in minimum dioxin emissions, then the use
of continuous monitoring of CO using newly available instrumentation will also serve
to assure minimum dioxin emissions.

The important questions to answer are, "what is (or are) the best combustion para-
meter(s) for use in finding and maintaining minimum CO emissions", and "do the
conditions which produce minimum CO emissions also produce minimum dioxin
emissions?" To find the relationship between design and operating parameters such as
temperature and oxygen on CO, dioxin and furan emissions, it is necessary to vary the
important parameters deliberately so that their effect can be evaluated. Normal
compliance tests are carried out under design conditions with adjustments which are
perceived to be optimum. Such tests do not provide information on what would have
happened if other adjustments had been made, nor indications as to how near or far
from optimum the operating conditions were. To obtain this information, diagnostic
tests over a wide range of conditions must be performed.

In order to confirm the relationship between CO and emissions of dioxins and furans
it is necessary to run difficult and extremely expensive tests, the cost of which cannot
generally be placed on the plant operator. Public financing of such tests has therefore
been necessary.

3. Research progams

To gain insight into the relationship between operating parameters and PCDD/PCDF
emissions, the Ontario Ministry of Environment sponsored a combustion testing
program at Hamilton, Ontario (Envirocon 1984), using diagnostic techniques to
identify the effects of changing operating parameters on dioxin emissions. A matrix of
13 tests was run, at low and high capacity, and with various settings of the overfire air
dampers, during which operating conditions and emissions data were determined. After
the stack samples were analysed, the results could be used to find relationships between
emissions and operating conditions. The analysis presented below shows that strong
correlations become evident when data from distinctly separate tests are analysed
(Hasselriis 1984, 1985, 1986a,b).

Environment Canada has carried out extensive diagnostic and analytical testing of a
starved-air two-chamber incinerator at Prince Edward Island (NITEP 1985). Data
analysis showed a weak trend with furnace temperature, and a strong correlation with
refuse moisture. In another program, a pilot scrubber attached to the Quebec City
incinerator was tested. Recently this water-wall incinerator was extensively tested after
physical modifications were made to the furnace, and computer controls installed
(NITEP 1986, Hay et al. 1986). These programs have shown that good combustion
and reduced gas temperatures, separately or together, can reduce PCDD-PCDF emissions to levels approaching or below the detection limit (see Klicius et al. in this issue).

The New State State Department of Environmental Conservation (NYSDEC) has
tested five different plants, including two refractory and one water-wall incinerator, and
two RDF-burning stokers, to measure trace organic and heavy metal emissions
(NYSDEC 1986). The Phase I tests did not include diagnostic testing to elucidate
relationships between operating parameters and emissions.

New York State Energy Research and Development Authority (NYSERDA) and the

American Society of Mechanical Engineers (ASME) sponsored testing of an excess-air refractory incinerator with flue gas recirculation at Pittsfield, MA. This test program was designed to find the effects of combustion variables as well as the influence of the composition of waste burned. Household refuse, paper and cardboard (PVC-free and with added PVC), and MSW with added vinyl chloride (PVC), were burned during tests sampling gases entering and leaving the boiler. Additional tests were run with higher moisture (Visalli 1986, 1987).

4. Diagnostic correlations

To obtain sufficient sample to measure the emissions of dioxins and furans at trace levels, it is necessary to operate the incinerator for many hours in order to exceed the detection limit of these trace organics. During these lengthy periods (which in general must exceed four hours), it is necessary to maintain operating conditions as nearly constant as possible so that the deviations of parameters from the mean value will be relatively small, and the differences due to changed parameters result in significantly different results. By running a series of tests wherein operating parameters are varied systematically, the effect of these variations can be discerned. The major variables in such a test matrix may include changes in load, furnace temperature, combustion air distribution, oxygen concentration and the composition and moisture content of the waste.

The data for the 13 runs at Hamilton are shown in Figs 1 and 2, showing PCDD versus temperature and CO. The points 12, 13, 19 and 24 represent normal operation with overfire dampers shut. Points 11 and 17 had the damper on the back jets half

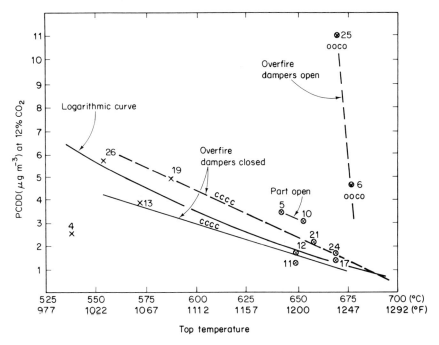

Fig. 1. Hamilton data: total dioxins (PCDD) versus furnace temperature. All test data points are shown, with lines marked to show various damper settings (Envirocon 1984).

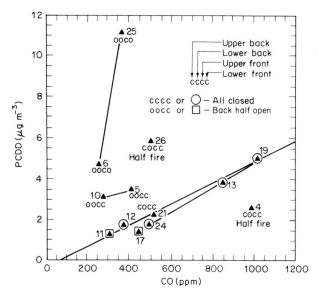

Fig. 2. Hamilton data: carbon monoxide versus total dioxins (PCDD), indicating a linear relationship pointing toward zero. This data appears to be a mirror image of the points in Fig. 1.

open. These data fall into a low fire group and high fire group. A line connecting the half-fire and the high-fire groups would represent the operating or performance curve of this plant, with underfire air held essentially constant, as was their practice. The two graphs appear to be mirror images.

Two runs were performed with all dampers open (ooco—points 6–25). Lines connecting these two different tests show a much steeper trend than, for instance, points 5 and 10 which had both front dampers closed. These trends are repeated on all the graphs relating temperature, CO and PCDD.

The trends were drawn as straight lines for lack of a better basis for connecting pairs of data. Although it could be anticipated that PCDD and CO would exhibit a logarithmic relationship with temperature, this could not be confirmed until more data from other plants became available.

The data from the four runs representing normal operation of this plant, and the data from all 13 runs, have been analysed by using multiple regression analysis (Hasselriis, unpublished). The results are shown in Table 2. A correlation factor of 1.00 was found between PCDD and overfire air, underfire air, lower furnace temperature, and the moisture, carbon monoxide and chlorophenol measured in the stack gases. Moisture showed a negative correlation: this means higher moisture produced lower dioxins. PCDF showed a factor of 0.97, oxygen 0.95, and polychlorinated biphenols (PCB) 0.78. Chlorobenzenes showed 0.05, or no relationship at all. When data from all 13 runs is analysed, including the various experimental settings, these coefficients fall into the 0.55 to 0.75 range, indicating poorer correlations.

4.1. Relationship between furnace temperature and PCDD/PCDF

As data from more plants became available, it was possible to investigate the broad relationship between PCDD and furnace temperature shown in Fig. 3 (Hasselriis 1985).

TABLE 2
Correlation matrix analysis of Hamilton, Ontario tests

Variable	Coefficient of correlation with PCDD emissions	
	4 Runs at normal damper settings	All 13 runs at various overfire damper settings
Carbon monoxide	1.00	0.55
Lower furnace temperature	−1.00	−0.81
Underfire air flow	−1.00	−0.19
Overfire air flow	1.00	0.19
Moisture in stack gas	−1.00	−0.92
Moisture in refuse fuel	1.00	0.57
Particulate	−1.00	−0.65
Chlorophenol	1.00	0.65
PCDF	0.97	0.65
Oxygen in stack gas	0.95	0.65
Feed chute air flow	−0.95	−0.21
Steam flow	−0.93	−0.75
Excess air	0.92	0.74
Temperature at top of furance	−0.90	−0.68
Polychlorinated biphenyl (PCB)	0.78	0.55
Temperature in upper furance	−0.45	−0.18
Total air flow	−0.21	−0.32
Chlorobenzene	−0.05	−0.17

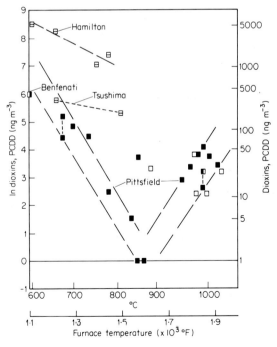

Fig. 3. Pittsfield data: total PCDD plotted versus furnace temperature. While curves drive toward zero, a sudden increase occurs above about 900 °C.

Dioxin levels found at excessively low temperatures reduced rapidly as temperatures were increased. When data from Hamilton, Benfenati, Tsushima and Pittsfield was entered onto this graph it became obvious that parameters other than temperature must account for the wide range of PCDD emissions reported corresponding to the same temperature: such as the distribution of underfire and overfire air, the effectiveness of mixing of the gases, and the relationship between refuse moisture and oxygen concentration.

A substantial increase in PCDD above a certain temperature was noted in the case of one of the Hampton tests, and also in the Benfenati data. In the case of Hampton, three other tests showed a decline with increasing temperature, but the 1983 set of five tests showed an increase. Inspection of operating conditions reveals that this series of tests was performed under overloaded conditions with oxygen ranging as low as 3% at times.

The Pittsfield data for MSW combustion, which was obtained from deliberately well-spaced tests, shows a deep dip to much lower PCDD, a rather narrow range of optimum conditions, and then a rapid increase in PCDD (Visalli 1987).

The Pittsfield data from tests at furnace temperatures below the optimum show that the dioxin and furan emissions follow a logarithmic relationship with temperature, that is, the data follows a straight line on semi-log paper (see Fig. 4). Taking the PCDD data for the low side of the minimum, obtained from tests at temperatures ranging from 1250 to 1550°F, regression analysis shows that an exponential equation represents a good fit. The sum of PCDD + PCDF was found to correlate somewhat better. Because the sum of PCDD + PCDF relates more closely to the Eadon toxic equivalent, it is preferable to redirect our attention to this summation, which results in the following equation:

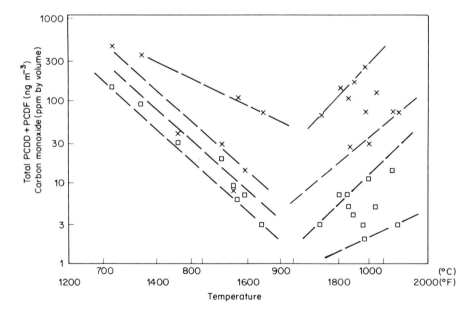

Fig. 4. Pittsfield data: total dioxins plus furans (PCDD + PCDF, ng m^{-3}), and carbon monoxide (CO, parts per million by volume) plotted versus secondary furnace temperature. A logarithmic scale is used to permit showing the wide range of data. Points are shown for duplicate tests with MSW, MSW plus PVC, PVC-free (paper and cardboard) with and without PVC addition, and high moisture. Trends are parallel up to about 1700°F, above which a rapid rise takes place. ×, PCDD + PCDF; □, carbon monoxide.

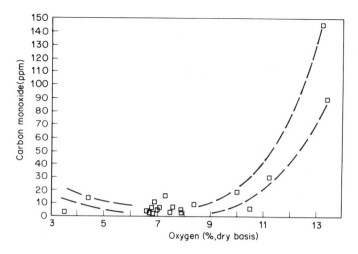

Fig. 5. Pittsfield data: carbon monoxide (parts per million by volume) plotted versus oxygen. Points are shown for duplicate tests with MSW, MSW plus PVC, and PVC-free (paper and cardboard) with and without PVC addition; and some with high moisture. Substantial increases are noted on either side of optimum oxygen range; shape of curve is similar to that for PCDD + PCDF.

$$PCDD + PCDF = Ae^{-T/B}.$$

Where PCDD + PCDF is in ng m^{-3}, T is in °C, $A = 5.2 \times 10^7$, and $B = 40.6$.

4.2. *CO versus temperature and oxygen concentration*

The results of the first phase of Pittsfield tests showed the effect of furnace temperature on CO, and even more important, the wide range of variation of CO which resulted from oscillations in combustion conditions. These oscillations were measured and recorded by computer for later analysis. The oscillations in CO and oxygen occurred while the furnace temperature was deliberately held constant and the MSW was ram-fed on a six-minute cycle, and were especially strong when efforts were made to maintain lower than normal operating temperatures (Visalli 1986). Oxygen and temperature were found to be mutually dependent, as expected. The minimum CO occurred at 8% oxygen, and an upward trend was noted as oxygen was reduced further.

4.3. *PCDD + PCDF versus CO, temperature and oxygen*

The Phase-II test was designed to space apart the operating temperatures, and to confirm the noted rise in CO at elevated tempertures (see Fig. 5). Data from the second phase of tests at Pittsfield (Fig. 4) shows that PCDD + PCDF and CO have similar relationships with temperature, which, on logarithmic paper appear to be linear and parallel, up to the optimum point. Figure 6 shows clearly that PCDD + PCDF has a similar relationship to oxygen as to CO. When the oxygen is varied outside of the range 7–9%, both CO and PCDD + PCDF increase. Duplicate tests were run to obtain better confidence in the data, and differences in conditions. The range of variation between data from the duplicate tests was generally quite similar.

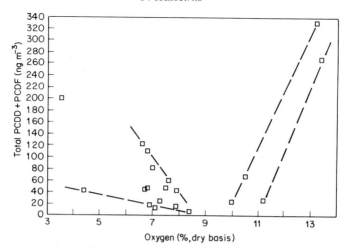

Fig. 6. Pittsfield data: total dioxins plus furans (PCDD + PCDF) plotted versus oxygen. Points are shown for duplicate tests with MSW, MSW plus PVC, and PVC-free (paper and cardboard) with and without PVC addition; and some with high moisture. Substantial increases are noted on either side of optimum oxygen range.

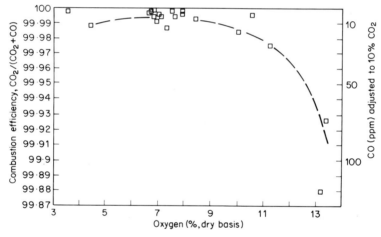

Fig. 7. Pittsfield data: combustion efficiency versus oxygen, measured before emission controls. Combustion efficiency is calculated according the definition used in the U.S.

4.4. Combustion efficiency versus oxygen

Combustion efficiency (CE), defined as carbon dioxide emitted divided by carbon dioxide plus carbon monoxide emitted, reflects the efficiency of carbon combustion. Figure 7 shows CE as a function of excess oxygen measured at the same point as the CO and CO_2, based on the Pittsfield tests. Efficiencies greater than 99.99% were achieved in the optimum range of operation.

5. Effect of emission controls on CO and PCDD + PCDF

Measurements of PCDD, PCDF, total PCDD/DF, carbon monoxide (CO) and, in some cases, temperature obtained from testing various plants were shown in Table 1.

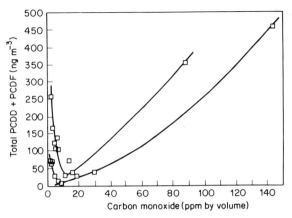

Fig. 8. Pittsfield data: total PCDD + PCDF plotted versus carbon monoxide (CO). While curves drive towards zero, a sudden increase occurs below about 15 ppmv.

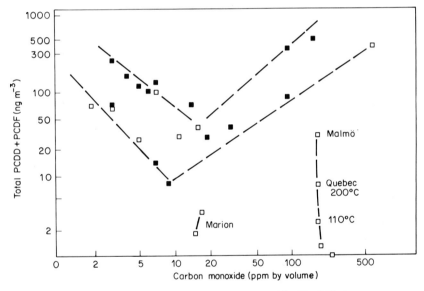

Fig. 9. Logarithmic plot of PCDD + PCDF versus carbon monoxide. Pittsfield data was measured after boiler, before emission controls. Data from Marion County, (Oregon), Quebec City (Canada), and Malmo (Sweden) is from stack measurements after lime scrubbers.

A fairly linear correlation of CO versus PCDD + PCDF is obtained, shown in Fig. 8, with a drastic rise at CO values less than about 15 ppm.

A logarithmic plot of PCDD + PCDF versus CO is shown in Fig. 9 in order to show the lower range. The minimum point and rise is shown in detail. Data from plants with ESP emission controls and stack temperatures exceeding 200°C are shown along with the Pittsfield data. Data from plants having scrubbers and stack temperatures under 200°C are included in Fig. 9 in the lower right-hand quadrant in order to show the completely different trends of emissions versus CO, and the influence of stack temperature. The Quebec and Marion County plants have different CO emissions, but the same range of low PCDD + PCDF emissions. For a given CO level, plants with scrubber/baghouses had much lower PCDD + PCDF emissions than those with ESPs operating at temperatures over 200°C.

6. Optimizing combustion with oxygen and CO measurements

From the above, it is clear that burning MSW in various types of furnaces seems to follow the same rules. For starved-air or excess air refractory, and massburn or RDF water-wall furnaces, there is an optimum range of oxygen and temperature which produces minimum CO and dioxins and furans.

Control of combustion of MSW by oxygen is now becoming common. The use of

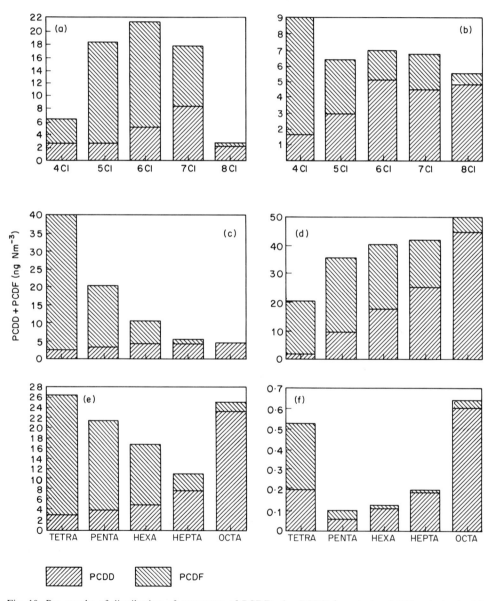

Fig. 10. Bar graphs of distribution of congeners of PCDD plus PCDF from tests of different plants: (a) Westchester, (b) Tulsa, (c) Cattaraugus, (d) Oneida County, (e) Wurzburg, (f) Marion County.

CO readings to find, and perhaps to maintain the optimum oxygen level is now possible, with sensitive and reasonably reliable CO-reading instruments. By this means, optimum combustion conditions can be maintained, assisted by computer-controlled grates and distribution of underfire and overfire air. When temperature can be reliably measured, it can take the place, at least temporarily, of oxygen measurements.

7. Congener patterns

It has been stated that there is a characteristic pattern to the distribution of congeners of PCDD/PCDF from refuse combustion, and that these patterns are found in the atmosphere and in lake sediments (Czuczwa & Hites 1986, see also Commoner *et al.* in this issue). Looking at data available today indicates that this matter is much more complex.

Plotting both PCDD and PCDF on the same graph reveals the tendency for the total to be fairly constant, with the ratio varying, as noted above. Figure 10 shows the distribution of the tetra, penta, hexa hepta and octa congeners of PCDD and PCDF. Figure 10 parts (a) and (b) are based on two large plants with electrostatic precipitators (ESPs): Westchester, NY (750 t day^{-1}) and Tulsa, OK (275 TPD units), which have similar water-wall plants with essentially the same stack temperature of about 235°C. Furans dominate at both plants with little octa isomer at Westchester and lower overall emission at Tulsa (note differences in scale). Figure 10 parts (c) and (d) are from tests of small refractory-walled incinerators with waste-heat boilers and ESPs. The emissions are essentially inverse with hepta and octa isomers lowest at Cattaragus and highest at Oneida, CO. Figure 10 parts (e) and (f) are from tests of two Martin plants with fabric filters, Wurzburg with dry injection, Marion, CO, with spray-dry scrubbers, showing similar patterns but an astonishing difference in the total quantity of emissions: total TCDD + TCDF of 26 versus 0.4 ng Nm^{-3}, a ratio of over 50. Note the different concentration scales.

8. Combustion versus post-combustion control

There are many explanations as to the source, formation and destruction of PCDD and PCDF. PCDD (but not PCDF) have been consistently found in the MSW. They can form or fail to be destroyed in combustion, and they can also be formed or destroyed in the fly-ash and ash deposits on tubes and collecting surfaces. The complex chemistry involved has been described (Drum 1986). Catalytic action by metals is an important factor: in the presence of copper, catalysis has been found to cause dechlorination/hydrogenation reactions with PCDD/PCDF and other chlorinated aromatic compounds at temperatures between 150 and 280°C, forming the toxic penta and hexa dioxins and furans from the octa form, in the presence of oxygen. At these temperatures, which are normal stack temperatures for plants with ESPs, and also the temperatures at which ash samples have been maintained during the collection of samples, PCDD and PCDF can also form from precursors (Stieglitz & Vogg 1986, Hagenmeier 1986, see also other papers in this issue).

Oxygen content strongly influences whether formation or decomposition of chlorinated compounds occurs: formation occurs in air, and decomposition occurs without oxygen. Apparently formation is inhibited and decomposition starts to occur at about 8% oxygen, which is the normal operating oxygen concentration for modern, well-controlled furnaces (Hagenmeier *et al.* 1986).

In addition, it has been found that temperatures under 140°C are sufficiently low to cause condensation of trace organics such as PCDD/PCDF onto particulate matter or onto filter cake, so that they can be collected and removed from the gases (NITEP 1986). This phenomenon has been demonstrated with both dry powder lime injection and spray-dry scrubbing (see Hasselriis 1986b).

The emissions listed in Table 1 were generally measured after the emission control devices. In the case of plants with ESPs it would be expected that no significant changes took place while passing swiftly through the ESP and ducting. On the other hand, a considerable amount of data show that the relatively high PCDD/PCDF in the gases entering a fabric filter, the concentrations exiting the filter are extremely low. The filter cake, retained for hours, provides time for reactions to take place, and the ability to absorb surges in concentration of not only acid gases but trace organics and metals.

The NITEP data showed that PCDDs at 1000 ng m^{-3} entering the scrubber/baghouse exiting at 140°C contained less than 1 ng m^{-3} or were below the detection limit. The PCDD/PCDF were collected with the fly ash. Under these conditions the PCDD were found to be about 570 ng g^{-1} of fabric filter ash, or 0.57 parts per million, which may be a level of concern when disposing of the fly ash. On the other hand, plants with good combustion controls have achieved PCDD levels of 16 ng m^{-3} or less, prior to ESP or other controls, or even to far below 1 ng m^{-3} (Boisjoly 1984). Results of recent tests by NITEP at Quebec City after optimization of combustion controls confirm this. When PCDD/PCDF and their precursors are reduced to such low levels, the concentrations of PCDD/PCDF on the fly ash is found to be correspondingly low, and would not be of concern. From this it is evident that it is preferable to destroy or to prevent formation of PCDD/PCDF rather than rely on the emission controls to capture them.

9. Summary

The relationships between combustion conditions and emissions of carbon monoxide and dioxins and furans have been greatly clarified as a result of diagnostic testing carried out at various full-scale MSW combustion facilities. With sufficient temperature, oxygen, mixing of reactants, and tight combustion control, stable operation under optimum conditions can be achieved, with combustion efficiencies exceeding 99.99%, equivalent to 10 ppm CO at 10% CO_2.

The optimum combustion conditions for minimizing carbon monoxide emissions are closely related to those which minimize dioxins and furans. These optimum conditions can be found by measuring CO, and maintained by controlling oxygen, temperature, or both within a limited range. Beyond this range, emissions of dioxins and furans are noted to increase substantially.

Factors other than furnace temperature and oxygen concentration have been found to affect substantially the minimum CO and dioxin emissions as measured after the boiler. Proper distribution of combustion air is a major factor.

The similarity of response of PCDD and PCDF and CO to variations in combustion parameters such as air distribution and mixing, furnace temperature, and excess oxygen makes it possible to use CO as a surrogate for emissions of trace organics such as dioxins and furans. Low CO corresponds to low trace organics.

The formation of dioxins and furans on particulates in the back passes of boilers is apparently reduced by providing efficient combustion. Even though emissions of dioxins and furans can be brought to extremely low levels (close to or below detection levels) by optimizing combustion conditions, even further reductions can be achieved by reducing gas temperatures well below 200°C so that reactions are arrested and organic pollutants are condensed and collected on particulates. The lower the emissions from combustion, the lower the concentrations on particulates.

Research on the relationship between combustion conditions and emissions of PCDD/PCDF has advanced to a point where the parameters are basically understood, and can be controlled sufficiently well to make it possible to maintain extremely low levels of PCDD/PCDF emissions. In addition, research has provided important new information and understanding of formation and destruction of PCDD/PCDF on fly ash in post-combustion regions, and their condensation and collection by emission control devices.

With this body of knowledge and understanding, and with the help of additional information from continuing research, the complex web of information regarding dioxins and furans is becoming unraveled, so that good combustion and minimum emissions of these and other toxic organics can be achieved. The use of temperature and/or oxygen control with CO monitoring and perhaps control is an important step ahead in providing operators with means to find and maintain the conditions necessary to minimize organic emissions. Additional reductions take place when acid gas controls are provided to reduce stack temperatures to 140°C or below.

References

Aslander, O. & Modig, S. (1986), *A Program for Action in Sweden to Limit Emissions of PCDDs and PCDFs from Waste-to-Energy Plants*, Dioxin 86 Symposium, Fukuoka, Japan, September 1986.

Bauer, K., Haile, C. & Hathaway, R. (1986), *Multivariate Statistical Analysis of Airbourne Emissions of PCDD and PCDF from Municipal Refuse Incinerators*, USEPA, Office of Air Quality, RTP, NC.

Boisjoly, L. (1984), *Measurement of Emissions of PCDD and PCDF from Des Carrieres Incinerator in Montreal*, Report EPS 5/UP/RQ/-1, Environment Canada, December 1984.

Czuczwa, J. M. & Hites, R. A. (1986), Airbourne dioxins and dibenzofurans: sources and fates, *Environmental Science and Technology*, 20(2), 195–200.

Drum, D. (1986), *Chemistry of Municipal Solid Waste Incineration*, APCA, Minneapolis, MN, June 1986.

Duvall, D. S. & Rubey, W. S. (1977), *Laboratory Evaluation of High Temperature Destruction of Polychlorinated Biphenyls and Related Compounds*, University of Dayton Research Institute, USEPA, MERL, Cincinnati, OH, December 1977.

Envirocon (1984), *Report on Combustion Testing Program at the SWARU plant, Hamilton-Wentworth*, ARB-43-ETGRD, Ontario Ministry of the Environment, January 1984.

Hagenmaier, H., Brunner, H., Haag, R. & Kraft, (1986), 6th International Symposium on Chlorinated Dioxins, Fukuoka, Japan, September 1986.

Hart, F. C. Associates (1984), *Assessment of Potential Public Health Impacts Associates with Predicted Emissions of PCDD and PCDF from Brooklyn Navy Yard Resource Recovery Facility*, New York City Dept. of Sanitation, August 1984.

Hasselriis, F. (1982), *Variability of Composition of Municipal Solid Waste and Emissions from its Combustion*, ASME Solid Waste Processing Conference, Miami, FL.

Hasselriis, F. (1984), *Variability of Municipal Solid Waste and Emissions from its Combustion*, ASME SWPD Conference, Orlando, FL, June 1984.

Hasselriis, F. (1985), *Relationship Between Municipal Refuse Combustion Conditions and Trace Organic Emissions*, 78th Annual Meeting of APCA, Detroit, June 1985.

Hasselriis, F. (1986a), *Minimizing Trace Organic Emissions from Combustion of Municipal Wastes by the Use of Carbon Monoxide Monitors*, 1986, ASME SWPD Conference, Denver, June, 1986.

Hasselriis, F. (1986*b*), *Minimizing Refuse Combustion Emissions by Combustion Control, Alkaline Reagents, Condensation and Particulate Removal*, Synergy/Power Symposium on Energy from Solid Wastes, Washington, October, 1986.

Hasselriis, F. (1986*c*), *Effects of Burning Municipal Waste on Environment and Health*, ASME/IEEE Power Generation Conference, Portland, OR, October, 1986.

Hay, D. J., Finkelstein, A. & Klicius, R. (1986), *The National Incinerator Testing and Evaluation Program: An assessment of (A) Two-stage Incineration and (B) Pilot-scale Emission Control*, APCA Annual Meeting, Minneapolis, MN, June 1986.

NITEP (1985), *National Incinerator Testing and Evaluation Program: Two-stage Combustion (Prince Edward Island)*, ESP 3/UP/1, 1985, Environment Canada, Ottawa, Ontario.

NITEP (1986), *Air Pollution Control Technology*, Report EPS 3/UP/2, September 1986, Environment Canada, Ottawa, Ontario.

NYSDEC (1986), *Emission Source Test Report—Preliminary Report on Westchester Resource Recovery Facility*, NYSDEC Division of Air Resources, Albany, NY, January 1986. Additional reports for other facilities tested.

Stieglitz, L. & Vogg, H. (1986), *On Formation Conditions of PCDD/PCDF in Flyash from Municipal Waste Incinerators*, 6th International Symposium on Chlorinated Dioxins, September 1986.

TUV (1984), *Tests of Uncontrolled and Clean Gas and Discharged Salts of a MSW Incinerator for PCDD/PCDF*, Hamburg, F.R.G.

Tysklind, M., Marklund, S. & Rappe C. (1986), *Experiences from the Swedish MSW Moratorium*, Dioxin 86 Symposium, Fukuoka, Japan, September 1986.

Visalli, J. (1986), *Pittsfield Incinerator Research Project, Status and Summary of Phase 1: Plant Charcterization and Performance Testing*, ASME 10th National Waste Processing Conference, Denver, CO, June 1986.

Visalli, J. (1987), *Results of the Combustion and Emissions Research Project at the Vicon Incineration Facility in Pittsfield, MA*, Midwest Research Institute, February 1987.

Wold, S. *et al.* (1983), Multivariate data analysis in chemistry, *Proceedings, NATO Advance Study Institute on Chemometrics*, Cosenza, Italy, September 1983.

THE ORIGIN AND HEALTH RISKS OF PCDD AND PCDF *

Barry Commoner,† Karen Shapiro and Thomas Webster

(*Received December 1986, revised May 1987*)

PCDD/PCDF are ubiquitous in the emissions of trash-burning incinerators. They are synthesized in the cooler parts of the incinerator, and emissions are not reduced by controlling combustion conditions. Estimates of maximum lifetime risks of PCDD/PCDF emissions range over two orders of magnitude from a minimum of one per million. This risk is greater than that which has triggered regulatory procedures against airborne carcinogens by U.S. EPA. Computations based on PCDD/PCDF in adipose tissue of a representative sample of the U.S. population indicate a national lifetime cancer risk of 330–1400 per million depending on the choice of equivalence methodology. In comparison, U.S. EPA has regulated environmental exposure to benzene based on a national lifetime cancer risk of 71.4. Because waste-burning incinerators contribute significantly to this risk, it is the authors' opinion that their PCDD/PCDF emissions should be reduced if U.S. EPA is to be consistent in its regulatory practice.

Key Words—municipal solid waste, incineration, dioxins, PCDD/PCDF, synthesis, risk.

1. Introduction

It is widely recognized that the method now used to dispose of more than 90% of the municipal solid waste (MSW) in the United States—deposition in landfills—is unacceptable and must be replaced. Landfills give rise to a number of serious environmental problems, and in many places their capacity is becoming rapidly depleted. The most popular alternative is an incinerator that burns unseparated MSW or a refuse-derived fuel prepared from it. This paper considers the environmental impact of such MSW incinerators, and concludes that, like landfills, the incinerators are also environmentally unacceptable.

The MSW incinerator is generally presented to a community faced with replacing its landfill as a "proven technology". In physical terms, this is a valid description. It has certainly been established that a mass-burn incinerator can destroy about 75–80% (by weight) of the MSW (leaving a residue that must be consigned to a landfill) at a high combustion efficiency and a reasonable thermodynamic efficiency. However, in environmental terms, the MSW incinerator is not a "proven technology". First, the design theory employed to control the incinerator's environmental impact turns out to be incorrect. Second, in actual practice the incinerators have generated cancer-inducing emissions which, judged by standards now employed by the U.S. EPA with respect to airborne carcinogens, are clearly unacceptable. The evidence which leads to these conclusions is presented below.

* Presented at the ISWA–WHO–DAKOFA specialized seminar, *Emission of Trace Organics from Municipal Solid Waste Incinerators*, Copenhagen, 20–22 January 1987.
† Center for the Biology of Natural Systems, Queens College (CUNY), Flushing, NY 11367, U.S.A.
Waste Management & Research (1987) **5**, 327–346

2. Incinerator PCDD/PCDF emissions

2.1. *Relationship to furnace temperature and combustion efficiency*

MSW incinerators were designed on the theory that a high furnace temperature and combustion efficiency would destroy toxic organic compounds in the fuel and thereby prevent hazardous emissions. However, actual tests of operating incinerators show that, despite this theoretical expectation, in practice MSW incinerators emit a variety of organic compounds, of which PCDDs and PCDFs (the family of 210 polychlorinated dibenzo-*p*-dioxins and polychlorinated dibenzofurans) are the most hazardous.

As test data have accumulated, it has become apparent that the rates of PCDD/PCDF emission from different incinerators vary widely, ranging over nearly two orders of magnitude. Efforts to explain such variations have frequently relied on the supposed effect of furnace temperature on emission rate. However, as can be seen from Table 1, there is no correlation between PCDD/PCDF emission rate and furnace temperature among MSW incinerators for which both values are available (compare Hasselriis Table 1 and Fig. 3 in this issue). For example, the lowest rate of emission was observed at the Chicago Northwest incinerator when it operated at 650°C (U.S. EPA, 1983). Yet, the Zaanstad incinerator, operating at 911°C, emitted PCDD/PCDF at a rate about ten times higher (Olie *et al.* 1982). Similarly, the Hampton incinerator has consistently emitted PCDD/PCDF at a rate nearly two orders of magnitude higher than the Chicago Northwest plant, although it operated at temperatures ranging from 550 to 868°C (Haile *et al.* 1984). In this connection, the test of an Albany, New York, RDF incinerator in which an auxiliary gas burner had been installed as a means of enhancing PCDD/PCDF destruction is particularly revealing (NYS DEC 1985). The results showed that about twice as much PCDD/PCDF was emitted with the burner on than with the burner off (570 vs. 310 ng m^{-3}).

The foregoing data may of course be influenced by the possible effect of incinerator

TABLE 1

Total PCDD/PCDF (Cl$_4$–Cl$_8$ congeners) emission rates and furnace temperatures of different incinerators*

Incinerator	PCDD + PCDF emission rate (ng m^{-3})	Furnace temperature (°C)	Pollution control device
Chicago, Northwest	180†	650	ESP
Eskjo, Sweden	555	700	Not given
Como, Italy	722	994	ESP
Zaanstad, Netherlands		911	ESP
Tsushima, Japan	2713		
Test 1	2047	800	
Test 2	7001	510–815	Baghouse
Hamilton, Canada	11,575	700	ESP
Hampton, Virginia			
EPA test (1984)	12,620	771–868	
Tiernan test (1983)	9647	550	ESP

* See Commoner *et al.* (1985*a*) for references regarding sources of data (see also Hasselriis and Klicius *et al.* in this issue).

† Excludes Cl$_5$ congeners (not reported).

design, fuel composition, and other variables among different plants. However, in two cases data are available which describe the effects of different operating temperatures and combustion conditions on PCDD/PCDF emissions from a single incinerator. In the tests conducted at the Hamilton and Hampton incinerators, the number of observations (13 and 5, respectively) are sufficient to warrant regression analyses that test the relationship between the rate of PCDD/PCDF emission and combustion conditions. The results are shown in Table 2 (see Commoner *et al.* 1985*a*, for details). Regression analysis of the Hamilton data yields a linear correlation coefficient (*r*) of −0.05 for the relation between top furnace temperature and the rate of PCDD emission. For the relation between top furnace temperature and the rate of PCDF emission, *r* is 0.26. Neither correlation is significant at the 95% confidence level. The corresponding correlation coefficients derived from the Hampton data are 0.2 for PCDD and 0.18 for PCDF, which are also non-significant at the 95% confidence level (see Dean, this issue, section 4.4.).

One response to such data, which contradict the assumption that elevated furnace temperatures will destroy PCDD/PCDF, has been the suggestion that destruction is more closely related to combustion efficiency than to furnace temperature. Values of combustion efficiency can be computed from the Hamilton and Hampton data and their correlation with the rate of PCDD/PCDF emissions can be determined by regression analysis. As shown in Table 2, the correlation coefficient at Hamilton is −0.14 for PCDD and 0.06 for PCDF; at Hampton the values are −0.02 for PCDD and −0.07 for PCDF. None of these values are statistically significant at the 95% confidence level. Appropriately, the report of the Hamilton tests reaches the operational conclusion that:

> The lack of positive trends between dioxin and furan concentrations [in the emitted flue gas] and parameters examined, including furnace top temperature, overfire air port flow, total air, THC [total hydrocarbon] and CO concentrations, suggests that none of these parameters can be used as the single parameter to minimize dioxin and furan emissions. (Envirocon 1984).

In sum, the available data regarding the relationship between the rate of PCDD/PCDF emissions and either furnace temperature or combustion efficiency contradict the widely held view that these substances can be destroyed and emissions reduced by operating an incinerator at a sufficiently high temperature and/or combustion efficiency (compare with Hasselriis Section 4.4. and with Bergstrom & Warman in this issue).

TABLE 2

Correlation coefficient (*r*)* = rates of PCDD and PCDF emissions with combustion conditions for Hampton and Hamilton incinerators†

Incinerator	Emission	Combustion efficiency	Percent CO	Furnace temperature
Hampton	PCDD	−0.02	−0.21	0.20
	PCDF	−0.07	−0.16	0.18
Hamilton	PCDD	−0.14	−0.02	−0.05
	PCDF	0.06	−0.26	0.26

* Significant levels of *r*: Hampton, 0.88 (*N* = 5); Hamilton, 0.55 (*N* = 13).
† See Commoner *et al.* (1985*a*) for details.

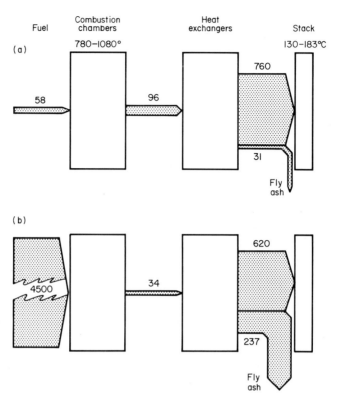

Fig. 1. Diagrammatic presentation of mass balance from the test of the Prince Edward Island incinerator described in Environment Canada (1985). The data confirm that PCDD and PCDF are synthesized between the point of entry of the flue gas into the heat exchanger and the stack. (a) Furans, (b) dioxins. All data are in $\mu g \ h^{-1}$.

2.2. PCDD/PCDF formation in incinerators

Because the actual test data on incinerator emissions contradict the expectations from the conventional theory of incinerator operation (i.e. that hazardous emissions of organic compounds such as PCDD/PCDF can be prevented by effectively destroying them in the furnace), we at CBNS (Center for the Biology of Natural Systems) have re-examined the evidence and have developed a new theory (Commoner et al. 1984). According to our theory, the rate of PCDD/PCDF emission reflects the actual *synthesis* of these compounds in the incinerator system rather than the degree of destruction of pre-existing PCDD/PCDF in the furnace. This conclusion is based on the following considerations (see Vogg et al. and Hagenmaier et al. in this issue).

First, it is known from the work of Olie et al. (1983) that PCDDs and PCDFs are readily formed when lignin is burned in the presence of HCl. This suggests that, in such a process, phenolic compounds, which are readily derived from lignin, can be chlorinated and dimerized to form PCDDs and PCDFs. Important additional evidence regarding the chlorination reactions is provided by the experiments of Eiceman & Rghei (1982, Rghei & Eiceman 1984), which demonstrate that both unchlorinated dibenzodioxin and 1,2,3,4-TCDD can be readily chlorinated by HCl at temperatures ranging up to 250°C if they are adsorbed on fly ash. Adsorbtion of phenolic precursors would be expected to occur only at temperatures below ca. 400°C. This observation and the theoretical improbability of purely gas-phase reactions among phenolic derivatives and sources of chlorine (Shaub 1984) indicate that at least these final stages in the production of PCDDs and PCDFs take place in association with fly ash particles in those sectors of the incinerator system where temperatures are likely to be about 250—300°C (Commoner *et al.* 1984).

Chlorine is present in a number of MSW components, either as an organo-chlorine compound such as PVC, or in an inorganic form, such as NaCl. An incinerator test shows that combustion of PVC yields HCl quantitatively (Kaiser & Carotti 1972). Other experiments indicate that NaCl can react with SiO_2 at combustion temperatures to produce HCl (Uchida *et al.* 1983).

These considerations suggest that PCDD/PCDF synthesis involves phenolic precursors derived from lignin, and HCl derived from chlorinated organic compounds, which combine through some, as yet unidentified, dimerization and chlorination reactions, at least some of them occurring on the surface of fly ash. Because these reactions take place in the cooler parts of the incinerator system which are downstream of the furnace, PCDD/PCDF emissions are not affected by the destructive influence of the high temperatures that occur in the incinerator furnace.

The theory of dioxin synthesis has now been confirmed by two recent tests. In a test of an incinerator at Prince Edward Island, Canada, it was found (see Fig. 1) that although almost no PCDD or PCDF left the incinerator furnace, considerable amounts occurred at the base of the stack (Environment Canada 1985). This confirms that PCDDs and PCDFs are literally synthesized in the incinerator system after the flue gas leaves the furnace, and that the process occurs at temperatures consistent with the theory. As can be seen from Fig. 1, this test also confirms that PCDD *can* be destroyed in the incinerator, provided it is present in the fuel. Vogg (in this issue) has also shown that PCDD/PCDF synthesis occurs on the surface of fly ash at the predicted low temperatures (Vogg & Stieglitz 1985). Fly ash taken from an incinerator precipitator was treated at temperatures between 120—600°C. Very large amounts of PCDD/PCDF were produced, especially at temperatures of 250—350°C.

It seems evident, therefore, that MSW incineration must be regarded as a process that synthesizes PCDD/PCDF on fly ash. Therefore, there is no basis for the conventional view that PCDD/PCDF emissions can be controlled by proper furnace conditions alone. This means that if an incinerator based on the conventional design theory is built, it is impossible, at this time, to predict how much PCDD/PCDF will be emitted or how combustion efficiency or furnace temperature should be regulated in order to reduce the emissions. Building such an incinerator therefore involves a serious technological risk.

This conclusion has important implications for the effort to control PCDD/PCDF emissions. First, it calls into question the approach, often taken in regulatory proposals, which cites high furnace temperature and combustion efficiency as a means of reducing PCDD/PCDF emissions (see Magagni & Boschi in this issue). Second, this conclusion conditions the strategy of reducing emissions by trapping them in a control device. The synthesis theory suggests that a primary requirement for such a device is that it must be located at a position downstream from the zone of synthesis. In practice, this means that the gas stream must be cooled to the temperature range which enhances PCDD/PCDF synthesis (200–300°C) *before* it enters the control device. It is possible that the observation of relatively low PCDD/PCDF emissions from certain incinerators may result from the fortuitous occurrence of the proper relationship between the zone of synthesis and the location of the control device. In this connection it is significant to note that the apparent success of the Quebec pilot plant in controlling PCDD/PCDF emissions depends on cooling the gas in a scrubber before it enters the baghouse (Hay *et al.* 1986).

While the synthesis theory may lead to improved incinerator control systems by specifying the relation between flue gas temperature and the control device, we do not yet have reports of successful application to a full-scale system. It should be noted that the Quebec experiment was conducted on a flue gas stream representing the combustion of only 20 tpd of MSW. Serious scale-up problems remain to be solved before this success can be regarded as indicative of comparable results in a full-scale incinerator. It is our opinion that the MSW incinerator cannot be regarded at this time as a "proven technology", suitable for adoption by a community that wishes to avoid the risks of experimenting with such a costly investment (compare with Bergstrom & Warman in this issue).

3. The health effects of incinerator PCDD/PCDF emissions

3.1. *Incinerator cancer risk assessments*

Until now it has appeared that the most serious health effect due to incinerator PCDD/PCDF emissions is the risk of an increased incidence of cancer. However, Hoffman *et al.* (1986) have indicated that there is also a risk of suppression of the immune system, i.e. the system that protects the body from a variety of diseases, including cancer. It was found that people exposed to dioxin-contaminated soil in Missouri exhibited a significant reduction in their cellular immune system. It will be important to assess this risk from incinerator emissions as well.

At present, incinerator health-risk assessments relate only to PCDD/PCDF and toxic metals in the emissions, based on their effect on cancer incidence. In recent months a relatively consistent picture of the PCDD/PCDF-induced cancer risk from MSW incinerators—which was previously a subject of a good deal of disagreement—has begun to emerge. As shown in Table 3 (Commoner *et al.* 1986a), risk assessments made by various state agencies and consulting firms, as well as by CBNS, now agree that the maximum lifetime cancer risk from MSW incinerators is 1–160 per million, even if the assumed PCDD/PCDF emissions are at the low rate determined in the test of the Chicago Northwest incinerator. However, because many operating incinerators emit much higher levels of PCDD/PCDF, the actual risks may be 25–50 times higher than those shown in Table 3.

Also shown in Table 3 are the cancer risks determined from tests of two operating incinerators in New York State. The cancer risks determined by the New York State Department of Health are 1–2 per million for the Peekskill incinerator and 11–20 per million for the Niagara Falls incinerator. However, when the risk is recalculated using revised estimates of PCDD/PCDF dosage of the exposed population, the cancer risks due to the emissions from these incinerators are 17 and 270 per million, respectively (Commoner *et al.* 1986a).

The significance of such risks has become clearer as a result of certain governmental decisions. In announcing the result of the Niagara Falls test, the New York State Departments of Health and Environmental Conservation ". . . recommended steps be taken immediately to reduce levels of dioxins and furans being emitted in Niagara Falls, because of health concerns . . ." (NYS DEC 1986). This implies that an 11–20 per million lifetime cancer risk is unacceptable. Although no U.S. Federal PCDD/PCDF standards have yet been established, recent actions by EPA regarding

TABLE 3

Incinerator cancer risk assessments (additional cases per million people exposed to maximum PCDD/PCDF concentration over 70-year lifetime)

Location	Author	Risk assessment
Proposed incinerators*		
Brooklyn, NY	Hart	5.9
Brooklyn, NY	CBNS	29
Newark, NJ	Camp, Dresser & McKee	1
San Diego, CA	HDR	10
Rutland, VT	Department of Health	12–29
Detroit, MI	Department of Natural Resources	2–31
Detroit, MI	CBNS	160
Los Angeles, CA	CBNS	22
Palm Beach, FL	CBNS	10
Minneapolis, MN	CBNS	9
Operating incinerators		
Niagara Falls, NY	Department of Health	11–20
Niagara Falls, NY	CBNS	270
Peekskill, NY	Department of Health	1–2
Peekskill, NY	CBNS	17

* These risk assessments are based on an assumed PCDD/PCDF stack concentration equivalent to that measured at the Chicago Northwest incinerator.

the regulation of airborne carcinogens under Section 112 of the Clean Air Act and Section 4(f) of the Toxic Substances Control Act (U.S. Public Law 1970) suggest a standard more stringent than that of New York. EPA uses the maximum lifetime risk of cancer in part to determine whether or not to begin regulatory proceedings against airborne carcinogens. As shown in Table 4, EPA has begun proceedings to regulate a carcinogen (methylene chloride) with a maximum lifetime cancer risk as low as 0.83 per million. All of the risk assessments for existing and proposed incinerators are in excess of this value, some of them considerably so. This comparison indicates that PCDD/PCDF emissions from trash-burning incinerators are likely to be subject to EPA regulation, requiring that they be reduced so that the resultant cancer risk is no more than about one per million.

3.2. *PCDD/PCDF in human adipose tissue*

A second way of assessing the significance of the incinerator cancer risk relative to national regulatory practice can be derived from recent data on the amount of PCDD/PCDF which the general U.S. population has absorbed from past environmental exposure. Data on the PCDD/PCDF content of human adipose tissue is available for Canada (Ryan *et al.* 1985), northern Europe (Rappe 1984), for New York State (Schecter *et al.* 1985), and for the U.S. from the recent EPA survey (Stanley *et al.* 1985). Comparable data for North and South Vietnamese samples are available from studies reported by Schecter *et al.* (1986).

It is possible to estimate the PCDD/PCDF dosages which lead to the observed adipose tissue levels (Commoner *et al.* 1985*b*). We assume that the uptake and elimination of PCDD/PCDF are adequately described by first-order kinetics, based on experiments in animals and humans (Fries *et al.* 1975, Poiger & Schlatter 1985).

TABLE 4

U.S. EPA cancer risk assessments and regulatory actions taken on airborne organic carcinogens

| | Cancer risk per million | | |
	Maximum lifetime (70-year) risk*	National average lifetime (70-year) risk†	EPA action
Benzene	154	71.4	Regulatory standard established (6/6/84)
Carbon tetrachloride	154	13.3	Assessment (U.S. EPA, 8/13/85)
Chloroform	77	4.9	Intend to List (U.S. EPA, 9/27/85)
Ethylene dichloride	18	12.6	Intend to List (U.S. EPA, 10/16/85)
Formaldehyde	206	58.1	Under extended assessment
Methyl chloride	0.46	<0.7	No information
Methylene chloride	0.83	0.7	Listed‡ (U.S. EPA, 10/17/85)
Perchloroethylene	18.8	7.0	Intend to List (U.S. EPA, 12/28/85)
Trichloroethylene	25.9	5.6	Intend to List (date NA)
Vinyledene chloride§	830	0.02	No regulatory action (U.S. EPA, 8/13/85)

* Data from Hunt et al. (1985a). Table 9 (two or more valid quarters) except for ethylene dichloride and formaldehyde, which, according to Hunt, are erroneously reported there. For these compounds, values are the maximum reported in Table 7(a and b), which are accurate.

† Data from Hunt et al. (1985b), Table 6.

‡ Initiation of comprehensive regulatory investigation as required under Section 4(f) of the Toxic Substances Control Act.

§ Data from EPA Decision Not to Control Vinyledene Chloride and Solicitation of Information (U.S. EPA 1985c). Decision based on inadequate evidence of carcinogenicity and small population exposure.

Assuming steady-state concentrations in lipid (about 13% of body weight, Heilbrunn 1943), we estimate absorbed dosages in humans using a 4.95 year half-life for all 2,3,7,8-substituted PCDD isomers, and 1.8 years for 2,3,7,8-PCDF isomers (Poiger & Schlatter 1985, Gorski et al. 1984). These are converted to 2,3,7,8-TCDD equivalents and multiplied by the U.S. EPA's upper-bound cancer potency for 2,3,7,8-TCDD (U.S. EPA 1985a) to calculate lifetime risk The results assume that the dosages computed from 1982 tissue concentrations are equal to the average lifetime dose.

We estimate the maximum additional lifetime cancer risk due to the 2,3,7,8-TCDD present in adipose tissue to be 48 per million in the U.S. The risk for all PCDD/PCDF isomers is 330–1400 per million, depending on the equivalence methodology used, U.S. EPA (1985a) or California (Stephen 1986).

It has been shown that, in humans, the PCDD/PCDF concentration in the lipid of breast milk is approximately equivalent to that in adipose tissue lipid (see Rappe et al. in this issue). The adipose tissue data therefore enable us to compute the PCDD/PCDF dosage to infants that are breast-fed by mothers in the exposed population and hence to compute the resultant cancer risk (for methodological details see Commoner et al. 1985b). This computation reveals that an infant consuming milk from a mother with adipose levels equal to those determined for the U.S. population by the EPA survey is exposed to enough PCDD/PCDF to account for a lifetime risk of 23–64 per million in only one year of breast feeding.

The foregoing results indicate that current exposure of the U.S. population to PCDD/PCDF is unacceptable and should be reduced. This is evident from recent EPA regulatory action. Under the provisions of Section 112 of the Clean Air Act and Section

TABLE 5

Potential chlorinated dioxin and dibenzofuran source categories in California*

Source category	Estimate of relative emissions† in California
Point sources	
Municipal waste incinerators and RDF boilers	High
Commercial waste oil burners	Unknown
Hazardous waste incinerators	Low
Industrial boilers cofiring wastes	Unknown
Wire reclamation incinerators	Unknown
Sewage sludge incinerators	Unknown
Wood/bark boilers	High‡
Black liquor boilers	Unknown
PCP sludge incinerators	High
Cement kilns cofiring wastes	Low
Hospital incinerators	Unknown
Sawmills§	High‡
Area sources	
Mobile sources	Unknown
Wood stove/fireplaces	Unknown
Forest fire/agricultural burning	Unknown

* Source: Table I-2 (CARB 1986) California Air Resources Board "Report to the Scientific Review Panel on Chlorinated Dioxins and Dibenzofurans", Feb. 1986.

† This is a qualitative assessment of the expected emissions relative to the other source categories listed.

‡ Estimate is high when burning wood treated with chlorophenol, otherwise these are rated as low.

§ Most sawmills have the capability to incinerate some or all the woodwaste produced at the facility. A wood/bark boiler may be used at a sawmill to incinerate process wastes. This source category may overlap other source categories listed in the table.

4(f) of the Toxic Substances Control Act, EPA has begun regulatory proceedings against a series of airborne carcinogens. The chief criteria for such action are estimates of: (a) the maximum lifetime (70-year) cancer risk, and (b) the national average lifetime cancer risk. Since it is based on the widespread sampling used in the EPA survey, it can be assumed that the cancer risk represents the national average lifetime cancer risk to the U.S. population due to the uptake of PCDD/PCDF, if the dosage characteristics of the population sampled in 1982 were to continue. When compared with recent EPA actions on airborne carcinogens (see Table 4), it is evident that the PCDD/PCDF exposure qualifies for regulatory action. The national average cancer risk for PCDD/PCDF (330 per million)—which, it should be noted, is computed according to EPA equivalence methodology—is considerably greater than even the highest risk from the airborne carcinogens which EPA has begun to regulate. According to the EPA Office of Air Quality Planning and Standards, the highest national average cancer risk for airborne carcinogens is that of benzene, a substance which is now subject to a regulatory standard. The national average lifetime cancer risk for benzene is 71.4 per million, clearly less than that for PCDD/PCDF. It follows that the exposure of the general population to PCDD/PCDF should be regulated and action taken to reduce it. Failure to take this action (which is now under consideration by EPA) would be grossly inconsistent with previous EPA action on benzene and other airborne carcinogens.

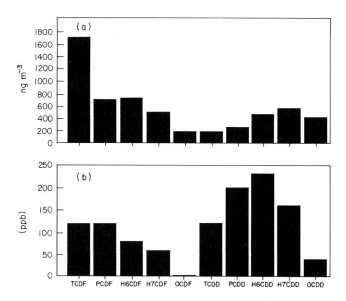

Fig. 2. PCDD/PCDF homologue patterns of combustion sources. (a) MSW incineration (Ontario Ministry of the Environment 1985, Commoner *et al.* 1986*b*). (b) Industrial (chemical) waste incineration (Czuczwa & Hites 1986).

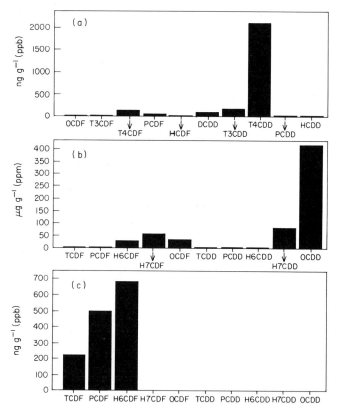

Fig. 3. PCDD/PCDF homologue patterns of chemical sources. (a) Agent Orange (Rappe *et al.* 1978). (b) PCP (Ontario Ministry of the Environment 1985). (c) PCBs (Ontario Ministry of the Environment 1985). Note that the homologues of (a) are different from those of (b) and (c).

Measurements of PCDD and PCDF in five samples of breast milk obtained from South Vietnam in 1973 allow a direct computation of risk from breast-feeding without calculating milk concentrations from adipose tissue levels (Schecter *et al.* 1986). A South Vietnamese infant breast feeding for one year on milk contaminated at the levels measured in 1973 absorbed a dose of 310 pg kg^{-1} day^{-1} of 2,3,7,8-TCDD, or a total of as much as 340 pg^{-1} kg^{-1} day^{-1} of 2,3,7,8-TCDD equivalents. This is far higher than the acceptable daily intake of 1–10 pg kg^{-1} day^{-1} recommended by several government agencies. The upper-bound lifetime cancer risk associated with one year of breast feeding, without subsequent exposure, is 49–54 per million.

4. The sources of adipose tissue PCDD/PCDF

Regulatory action presupposes the identification of the sources that are chiefly responsible for the environmental PCDD/PCDF levels and which, if regulated, would significantly reduce these levels. The main environmental sources of PCDD/PCDF are listed in Table 5. The sources differ considerably in the relative proportions of the different PCDD and PCDF homologues and isomers which they contain (see Figs 2 and 3 and Rappe *et al.* in this issue); in their route of entry into the environment, and in the amounts released to the environment annually. According to several assessments in California, Canada and Denmark, combustion of municipal solid waste and industrial wastes are the major sources of environmental PCDD/PCDF (Californian Air Resources Board 1986, Environment Canada 1983, Danish National Environmental Protection Agency 1984).

Nevertheless, there is a good deal of uncertainty about this conclusion, for it is based only on estimated emissions. The adipose tissue data are, of course, evidence of the acquisition of PCDD/PCDF by the population from some general source(s) in the environment, and it is useful to examine the relation between these data and the various potential sources in order to evaluate directly their relative contributions to PCDD/PCDF uptake.

4.1. *The significance of the Vietnam data*

North Vietnam represents an environment relatively unaffected by PCDD/PCDF sources that are associated with modern industrial activities. Unlike South Vietnam, North Vietnam was not sprayed with Agent Orange (which was heavily contaminated with PCDD); it presumably uses little or no chlorinated organic chemicals, or burns waste or wood containing such chemicals. In contrast, South Vietnam was heavily sprayed with PCDD-contaminated Agent Orange and may have been exposed to other chlorinated organic chemicals (such as pentachlorophenol) introduced during French occupation of that area.

The distribution patterns of PCDD and PCDF homologues in adipose tissue from North and South Vietnam and the United States are compared in Fig. 4. It is immediately evident that the levels in North Vietnam are about an order of magnitude below those found in either South Vietnam or the United States (note differences in scale). This indicates that those proposed sources of PCDD/PCDF that are common to all three countries—for example, combustion processes such as forest fires and domestic burning of untreated wood—do not contribute significantly to the elevated levels in South Vietnam or the United States. This contradicts the "trace chemistry of fire hypothesis" proposed by Dow chemists (Bumb *et al.* 1980), i.e. that all combustion

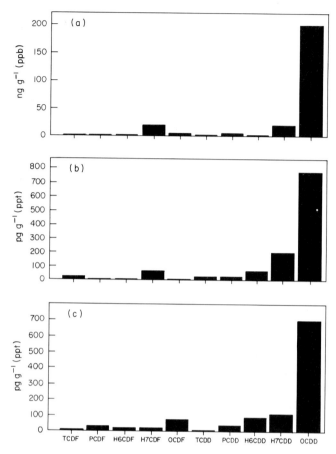

Fig. 4. PCDD/PCDF homologue patterns of human adipose tissue. (a) North Vietnam 1984 (Schecter *et al.* 1986). (b) South Vietnam 1984 (Schecter *et al.* 1986). (c) United States 1982 (Stanley *et al.* 1985).

processes contribute to environmental PCDD/PCDF, a view that would lead to the conclusion that forest fires are a major contributor.

The PCDD/PCDF adipose tissue levels in South Vietnam are about 60% above those in the United States. With one important exception, the isomer patterns are also generally similar. In the South Vietnam homologue pattern, the relative concentration of 2,3,7,8-TCDD is considerably higher than it is in the United States, by a factor of 3.5. This is indicative of the prominence of exposure to Agent Orange—in which 2,3,7,8-TCDD predominates (see Fig. 3)—in the population of South Vietnam. This conclusion is reinforced by measurements of breast milk made from five samples collected in 1973 in South Vietnam (Schecter *et al.* 1986). Only three isomers were detected: 2,3,7,8-TCDD at 100 ppt, 2,3,4,7,8-PeCDF at 10 ppt, and OCDD at 170 ppt. (These values refer to concentrations in milk lipid, averaged by setting non-detection equal to zero.) Assuming that milk lipid concentrations reflect adipose tissue concentrations, comparison of the 1973 and 1984 data should indicate changes in environmental exposure over that time. The concentration of 2,3,7,8-TCDD in adipose tissue collected in 1984 was 22.3 ppt, a 78% reduction from the 1973 value. Over that period the concentrations of the other isomers increased. This result is consistent with the initial exposure of the South Vietnamese population to Agent Orange, metabolic conversion and excretion of

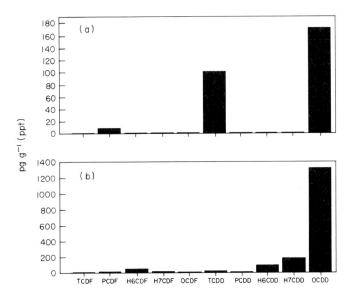

Fig. 5. Comparison of 1973 breast milk lipid (a) and 1984 adipose tissue (b) levels of PCDD and PCDF from South Vietnam (from Schecter *et al.* 1986).

2,3,7,8-TCDD with a half-life of about five years, and subsequent exposure to other sources of PCDD and PCDF relatively low in 2,3,7,8-TCDD but containing other isomers (see Fig. 5).

Apart from the foregoing differences, there is a general resemblance between the relative levels of the different PCDD and PCDF homologues in all three countries, except for the unique presence of TCDF and OCDF in the U.S. adipose tissue, which is unexplained. As we show below, the U.S. pattern is probably derived from combustion of chlorine-containing fuels, followed by the preferential degradation of the less-chlorinated homologues in the atmosphere. This suggests that exposure in South Vietnam is due to similar combustion sources, with 2,3,7,8-TCDD from Agent Orange superimposed. Such a combustion source might be the burning of lumber and brush contaminated with Agent Orange; wood burned with 2,4,5-T (an ingredient of Agent Orange) yields an array of PCDDs and PCDFs in its combustion products (Ahling & Lindskog 1977). It is possible that the low levels of exposure reflected in adipose tissue in North Vietnam may result from such combustion products drifting northward from South Vietnam.

4.2. *The sources of PCDD/PCDF in the U.S. environment*

In the United States, exposure of the general population to PCDD/PCDF may originate in two generic types of sources: (a) PCDD/PCDF-contaminated chemicals that enter the food chain from waste effluents or agricultural sprays; (b) PCDD/PCDF-contaminated particles (such as fly ash) created by combustion of chlorine-containing fuels, disseminated into the atmosphere and thence into the food chain or ingested or inhaled directly. From a Canadian survey (Sheffield 1985*a,b*), it appears that the major chemical sources are the wood preservative, pentachlorophenol, the herbicides 2,4-D and 2,4,5,-T, and PCBs. The homologue composition of these sources relative to the homologue pattern in adipose tissue tends to minimize their possible contribution to the PCDD/PCDF found in adipose tissue (see Fig. 3, and Rappe *et al.* in this issue). In the United States, adipose tissue contains each of the 10 tetra–octa PCDD and PCDF homologues, which, with the exception of the HxCDDs (unspecified in the EPA analyses) are represented almost exlusively by those isomers which are chlorinated in the 2, 3, 7 and 8 positions. Hence, a chemical source that contributes to the adipose tissue levels must contain at least these particular isomers. However, PCDFs and the higher-chlorinated PCDDs are essentially absent from 2,4-D and 2,4,5-T; pentachloro-phenol is lacking in the less (4- and 5-) chlorinated PCDDs and PCDFs; PCDDs are almost absent from PCBs. It would appear, therefore, that no one of these chemical sources can, by itself, account for the homologue pattern observed in adipose tissue. Exposure to mixtures of these sources might account for the adipose tissue content, but this is unlikely given the fact that the sources of these chemicals tend to be localized, while the sources affecting adipose tissue must be generally distributed in the environment.

It would appear, therefore, that the sources responsible for the PCDD/PCDF in U.S. adipose tissue originate in the combustion of chlorine-containing fuels. This conclusion is confirmed by observations of the PCDD/PCDF content of dated sedimentary layers in the Great Lakes (Czuczwa *et al.* 1984*a*,*b*). Little or no PCDD/PCDF is detected in sediments laid down before 1930–40, ruling out significant contributions from any earlier sources to the rising concentrations found in later years (e.g. forest fires, wood and coal burning). This confirms the conclusion derived from the low PCDD/PCDF levels in North Vietnam. Czuczwa & Hites (1986) also show that the homologue pattern in current sediments (with the exception of a Lake Ontario sample apparently affected by a local source) is significantly correlated with the pattern found in airborne urban particulates, both of which differ from the pattern found in chemical sources such as pentachlorophenol. Because certain lake sediments which exhibit this general pattern can be shown to be exclusively derived from deposits of atmospheric particulates, which include combustion products. Czuczwa & Hites conclude that:

> These results imply that PCDD and PCDF are transported through the atmosphere—suggesting that combustion is the source of these compounds (Czuczwa & Hites 1986).

The homologue pattern in U.S. adipose tissue resembles the pattern of both the lake sediments and atmospheric particulates. This is suggested by Fig. 6 which compares the homologue patterns for air particulates from Washington DC, an example of a current sediment (from Lake Michigan), and for U.S. adipose tissue from the EPA survey. This comparison is only suggestive, because PCDD/PCDF associated with atmospheric particulates will be subject to differential degradation once taken into the body.

As is evident from a comparison of Figs 2 and 6, the homologue patterns of the lake sediments and of atmospheric particulates are very different from the patterns in emissions from the combustion of both MSW and chemical waste. (The latter have considerably higher proportions of the less-chlorinated PCDDs and PCDFs.) Czuczwa & Hites (1986) suggest that, after the combustion products enter the atmosphere, the less-chlorinated homologues are preferentially subject to photochemical decomposition. Hence, with time, airborne particulates originating in combustion emissions exhibit the OCDD-rich pattern found in atmospheric particulates. These relationships suggest, therefore, that the PCDD/PCDF in lake sediments are derived from atmospheric particulates, which in turn represent the degraded products of combustion of MSW and industrial waste.

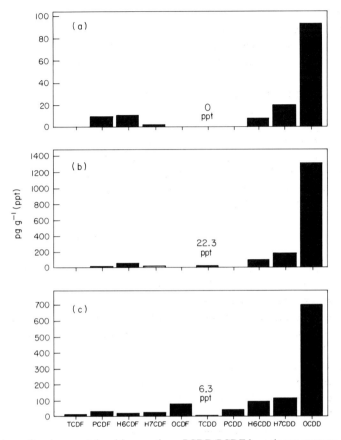

Fig. 6. Comparison of environmental and human tissue PCDD/PCDF homologue patterns. (a) Air particulates, Washington DC. (b) Sediment, Lake Michigan. Data taken from Czuczwa & Hites (1986). (c) Adipose tissue, U.S. population. Data taken from Stanley *et al.* (1985).

One of the noteworthy features of the lake sediment data is that PCDD/PCDF concentrations rise to a peak between 1970 and 1977 and thereafter decline probably because of new environmental regulations. This is most evident in Czuczwa & Hites' (1986) analysis of two locations in Lake Erie where the average PCDD/PCDF content decreased by about 30% between 1977 and 1983. If the airborne particulates that comprise the lake sediments are also the chief source of the PCDD/PCDF in adipose tissue, then this recent decline should be reflected in the adipose tissue PCDD/PCDF concentrations. For example, adipose tissue samples taken at different times might be expected to reflect the changing PCDD/PCDF concentration in the lake sediments. Adipose tissue samples in Canada and the United States have been taken in 1972, 1976, 1980, 1982 and 1983–84. Unfortunately it is difficult to compare them because, in most cases, the numbers of samples are small and taken from limited locations. Nevertheless, the values do appear to have declined slightly in recent years, possibly in response to decreasing concentrations of PCDD/PCDF in atmospheric particulates (Ryan *et al.* 1985, Schecter *et al.* 1985, Stanley *et al.* 1985).

Another way to examine the relation between the recent decline in the concentration of PCDD/PCDF in both the lake sediments and adipose tissue is to examine the latter as a function of the donor's age. The EPA survey of samples taken in 1982 provides separate data on the adipose tissue concentrations of three age groups: 0–14 years, 15–

44 years, and 45 + years. The concentration of PCDD relative to the oldest group are, respectively, 0.54, 0.96, and 1.0. The PCDFs do not exhibit this pattern; the values are relatively low and exhibit no common behavior among the several age groups. This may reflect the relatively low half-life of the furans, which would tend to reduce the differential effect of time of exposure. Qualitatively, these relationships conform with the expected effect of the decline in the PCDD/PCDF concentration of atmospheric particulates, as reflected in the lake sediments. Individuals up to 14 years old in 1982 will have received most of their environmental PCDD/PCDF exposure since 1975–76, when the exposure declined, and therefore should have lower adipose tissue concentrations than older donors.

To test this relationship more precisely, we modelled adipose tissue concentrations of PCDD assuming that human exposure paralleled the levels in Lake Erie sediments (Czuczwa & Hites 1986). Concentrations for different age groups were estimated using this time-varying proxy for dose and the differential equation describing first-order kinetics. The results were converted to fractions of the concentration found in the 45 + age group. For the 15—44 year age group, the actual value was 0.96 and the computed value is 0.99. For the 0—14 age group, the actual value was 0.54 and the computed value was 0.66. The variation in PCDD/PCDF concentration with age may thus be due to a time-varying environmental load. (It could also be explained by a non-linear model and changes in body-fat content with age.) This supports the view that the PCDD/PCDF in both lake sediments and adipose tissue are ultimately derived from the same source, atmospheric particulates produced by the combustion of chlorine-containing fuels.

Some effort has been made to quantify the relative contributions of various combustion processes to the environmental levels of PCDD/PCDF. Certain of potential sources listed by Sheffield (1985*a*,*b*) can be eliminated on the grounds that they were present before 1930–40, when (based on lake sediment data) there was no atmospheric PCDD/PCDF, for example, forest fires and coal, oil and gas combustion. The remaining significant sources are municipal solid waste (MSW) incineration, sewage sludge incineration, and combustion of chlorophenol-treated wood. According to Sheffield's data, combustion of municipal solid waste appears to be the largest contributor (with forest fires excluded, for the reason cited above). A similar but qualitative evaluation has been made for California by the California Air Resources Board (California Air Resources Board 1986).

The contribution from incinerators that burn hazardous chemical waste is not considered in the Sheffield report (such facilities are absent in Canada). The California report designates this source as "low" with respect to relative PCDD/PCDF emissions. This conclusion is suggested by the fact that about 15 million tons of MSW and about 0.44 milllion tons of chemical waste were incinerated in the United States in 1981 (Chemical Manufacturers Assn 1986), and that the average emission rate of PCDD and PCDF from MSW incinerators appears to be considerably greater than the typical emission rates from chemical incinerators (Cleverly 1986). In sum, it is likely that the contribution of chemical waste combustion to the environment, relative to that of MSW combustion, is very small.

Recently Marklund *et al.* have studied the emissions from automobiles provided with unleaded gasoline to which 0.15 g l^{-1} of tetraethyl lead and 0.1 g l^{-1} of dichloroethane (DCE, a scavenger that is used in commercial leaded gasoline) were added (Marklund *et al.* 1987). Significant concentrations of PCDDs and PCDFs were found in these emissions; none were detected in the emissions of automobiles using the unleaded fuel, which does not contain DCE. Based on this observation, the authors conclude that emissions from cars using leaded gasoline represent a significant contribution to environmental PCDD/PCDF.

However, the fuel was compounded specially for these tests and does not have the composition of commercial leaded gasoline, which contains a mixture of both DCE and dibromoethane (DBE). Muller *et al.* (1986) studied the emissions from a car using Swiss premium leaded gasoline containing both DCE and DBE and found, contrary to Marklund's results, that PCDDs or PCDFs were not detectable in the emissions Instead, a considerable number of brominated benzenes and phenols were found, together with smaller concentrations of brominated benzofurans and bromo-chlorophenols.

Thus, it appears that the amounts of PCDD and PCDF measured in automotive emissions by Marklund *et al.* may be a consequence of the absence of DBE in the experimentally compounded fuel used in their tests. Their results are therefore not representative of the emissions of automobiles run on commercial leaded gasoline. Although additional experimentation is needed to resolve this issue, clearly the present data do not support the conclusion that emissions from automobiles using normal, commercial leaded gasoline contribute significantly to environmental PCDD/PCDF.

Finally, it is possible to estimate the emissions of PCDD and PCDF from incineration of MSW and automobiles in the United States, based on the following assumptions, for 1974 (nearly the peak of PCDD/PCDF levels in Great Lake sediments), when 65,800 tpd of MSW was incinerated in the United States (Alvarez 1980):

(1) Only three incinerators, operating in 1974, with ESP or minimal emission control, could be identified from Beychok's standardized database (Beychok 1986), and a reference on incinerator construction (U.S. EPA 1979): Stuttgart, F.R.G.; Hamilton, Ontario; Chicago, Illinois. Their upper and lower PCDD/PCDF emissions rates are: Chicago, 1.9 mg t^{-1}; Hamilton, 260 mg t^{-1}. These values include only emissions from tetra- and penta-chlorinated dioxins and furans, so that they are comparable to the emissions reported by Marklund for automobiles, which include only these homologues.

(2) We assume that total emissions from automotive vehicles in the United States in 1974 are equal to the rate reported by Marklund *et al.* multiplied by the number of vehicle miles traveled by passenger automobiles in that year (U.S. Dept. of Commerce 1984).

Based on these estimates, automobile emissions in the United States in 1974 might have acounted for 2.3 to 31 kg year^{-1} of tetra- and penta-PCDD and PCDF. However, in view of Muller and Buser's results, the true value is probably much lower. In comparison, MSW incineration probably emitted between 46 and 6300 kg year^{-1}. It would appear from these considerations that PCDD/PCDF in the emissions of MSW incinerators made a major contribution to environmental PCDD/PCDF, and hence to their levels in adipose tissue.

This conclusion emphasizes the trend in MSW combustion. Alvarez has established that the total capacity of operating MSW incinerators in the United States declined from 65,800 t day^{-1} in 1974 to 33,200 t day^{-1} in 1979 (Alvarez 1980). (Most incinerators were in violation of the new environmental regulations and many were closed down.) Since the late 1970s, increasing numbers of newly designed "resource recovery" plants (MSW incinerators that recover useful heat) have been constructed. According to a survey by Combustion Engineering Inc. in 1986 for the U.S. Conference of Mayors, about 20,000 t day^{-1} was incinerated in the United States, which—given the present rapid rate of authorization and construction of "resource recovery" incinerators—is predicted to rise to about 73,000 t day^{-1} by 1989.

5. Conclusions

Based on the average adipose tissue concentration determined by the EPA survey, and assuming a constant chronic dose, the average lifetime cancer risk for the U.S. population due to PCDD/PCDF exposure is as much as 330–1400 per million, depending on the methodology used to estimate the relative cancer-enhancing effect of different isomers. PCDD/PCDF emissions from waste-burning incinerators are a major contributor to environmental exposure to these substances. Hence, the present PCDD/PCDF emissions from MSW incinerators must be significantly reduced if the cancer risk to the U.S. population is to be brought to a level consistent with EPA regulatory practice.

References

Ahling, B. & Lindskog, A. (1977), Formation of polychlorinated dibenzo-*p*-dioxins and dibenzofurans during combustion of 2,4,5-T formulation, *Chemosphere, 8*, 461.

Alvarez, R. J. (1980), *Status of Incineration and Generation of Energy from Thermal Processing of MSW*, presented at National Waste Processing Conference, ASME, Washington DC, 11–14 May.

Beychok, M. R.(1986). A data base of dioxin and furan emissions from municipal refuse incinerators, *Atmospheric Environment* (in press).

Bumb, R. R., Crummett, W. B., Cutie, S. S., Gledhill, J. R., Hummell, R. H. Kagel, R. O., Lamparski, L. L., Luoma, E. V., Miller, D. L., Nestrick, T. J., Shadoffy, L. A., Stehl, R. H. & Woods, J. S. (1980), Trace chemistries of fire: a source of chlorinated dioxins, *Science, 210*, 385.

California Air Resources Board (1986), *Report to the Scientific Review Panel on Chlorinated Dioxins and Dibenzofurans*, February.

Chemical Manufacturers Assn and Engineering Science Inc. (1986), *Results of the 1984 CMA Hazardous Waste Survey*, January.

Cleverly, D. (1986), personal communication, May.

Commoner, B., McNamara, M., Shapiro, K. & Webster, T. (1984), *Environmental and Economic Analysis of Alternative Municipal Solid Waste Disposal Technologies. II. The origins of chlorinated Dioxins and Dibenzofurans Emitted by Incinerators that Burn Unseparated Municipal Solid Waste, and an Assessment of Methods of Controlling them*, CBNS, Queens College, Flushing, NY, 1 December.

Commoner, B., Webster, T., Shapiro, K. & McNamara, M. (1985*a*), *The Origins and Methods of Controlling Polychlorinated Dibenzo-p-Dioxin and Dibenzofuran Emissions from MSW Incinerators*, presented at 78th Annual Meeting of the Air Pollution Control Association, Detroit, MI, 16–21 June.

Commoner, B., Webster, T. & Shapiro, K. (1985*b*), *Environmental Levels and Health Effects of PCDDs and PCDFs*, presented at the Fifth International Symposium on Chlorinated Dioxins and Related Compounds, Bayreuth, F.R.G., 16–19 September.

Commoner, B., Isaacson, J., Shapiro, K. & Webster, T. (1986*a*), *A Re-evaluation of the New York State Department of Health's Health Impact Evaluation of the Westchester and Occidental incinerators*, CBNS, Queens College, Flushing, NY. Jan. 28.

Commoner, B., Shapiro, K. & Webster, T. (1986*b*), *Risk assessment of the health effects of polychlorinated dibenzo-p-dioxin [PCDD] and dibenzofuran [PCDF] emissions from the proposed Hennepin County trash-burning incinerator*, January 17.

Czuczwa, J. M. & Hites, R. A. (1986), *Airborne dioxins and dibenzofurans: sources and fates*, *Environmental Science and Technology, 20*(2), 195.

Czuczwa, J. & Hites, R. A. (1984*a*), Environmental fate of combustion generated polychlorinated dioxins and furans, *Environmental Science and Technology, 18*(6), 444–450.

Czuczwa, J. McVeety, B. D. & Hites, R. A. (1984*b*), Polychlorinated dibenzo-*p*-dioxins and dibenzofurans in sediments from Siskiwit Lake, Isle Royale, *Science, 226*, 568–569.

Danish National Environmental Protection Agency (1984), *Formation and Dispersion of Dioxins, Particularly in Connection with Combustion of Refuse*, December.

Eiceman, G. A. & Rghei, H. O. (1982), Chlorination reactions of 1,2,3,4-tetrachlorodibenzo-*p*-dioxin on fly ash with HCl in air, *Chemosphere, 11*, 822.

Envirocon Ltd. (1984), *Report on Combustion Testing Program at the SWARU Plant, Hamilton-Wentworth*, prepared for Ontario Ministry of the Environment Air Resources Branch, Report No. ARB-43-84-ETRD, January.

Environment Canada, Health and Welfare Canada (1983), *Report of the Joint Health and Welfare Canada/Environment Canada Expert Advisory Committee on Dioxins*, Ottawa, November.

Environment Canada (1985), The national incinerator testing and evaluation program: two-stage combustion (Prince Edward Island), September.

Fries, G. F. & Marrow, G. S. (1975), Retention and excretion of 2,3,7,8-tetrachlorodibenzo-*p*-dioxin by rats, *Journal of Agriculture and Food Chemistry, 23*(2), 265–269.

Gorski, T., Konopka, L. & Brodzki, M. (1984), Persistence of some polychlorinated dibenzo-*p*-dioxins and polychlorinated dibenzofurans of pentachlorophenol in human adipose tissue, *Rocznik Pzh., 35*(4), 297–301.

Haile, C. L., Blair, R. B., Lucas, R. M. & Walker, T. (1984), *Assessment of Emissions of Specific Compounds from a Resource Recovery Municipal Refuse Incinerator*, Task 61, Final Report, prepared by Midwest Research Institute for EPA. EPA Contract No. 68-01-5915, 22 May.

Hay, D. J., Finkelstein, A., Klicius, R. & Marentette, L. (1986), *The National Incinerator Testing and Evaluation Program: An Assessment of (A) Two-stage incineration; (B) Pilot scale emission Control*, prepared for presentation at APCA Annual Meeting, June.

Heilbrunn, L. V. (1943), *An Outline of General Physiology*. W. B. Saunders, Philadelphia.

Hoffman, R. E., Stehr-Green, P. A., Webb. K. B., Evans, R. G., Knutsen, A. P., Schramm, W. F., Staake, J. L., Gibson, B. B. & Steinberg, K. K. (1986), Health effects of long-term exposure to 2,3,7,8-tetrachlorodibenzo-*p*-dioxin, *Journal of the American Medical Association, 255*(15), 2031.

Hunt, W., Faoro, R. B., Curran, T. C. & Montz, J. (1985*a*), *Estimated Cancer Incidence Rates for Selected Toxic Air Pollutants Using Ambient Air Pollution Data*, U.S. EPA Office of Air and Radiation, Office of Air Quality Planning and Standards, Monitoring and Data Analysis Division.

Hunt, W., Faoro, R. B. & Haemisegger, E. (1985*b*), *Future Air Toxic Monitoring Needs*, ASQC Quality Congress Transcript, Baltimore, MD.

Kaiser, E. & Carotti, A. (1972), Municipal incineration of refuse with 2 percent and 4 percent additions of four plastics: polyethylene, polyurethane, polystyrene and polyvinyl chloride, *Proceedings of the 1972 National Incinerator Conference*, ASME, New York, p. 230, June.

Marklund, S., Rappe, C., Tysklind, M. & Egebeck, K.-E. (1987), Identification of poly-chlorintated dibenzofurans and dioxins in exhausts from cars run on leaded gasoline, *Chemosphere* (in press)

Muller, M. D., Buser, H.-R. (1986), Halogenated aromatic compounds in automotive emissions from leaded gasoline additives, *Environmental Science Technology 20* (11) 1151–1157.

NYS DEC (1985), New York State Department of Environmental Conservation, Division of Air Resources, *Preliminary Report on Sheridan Ave. RDF Plant, "Answers"*, 28 January.

NYS DEC (1986) New York State Department of Environmental Conservation, News Release, 24 January.

Olie, K., Lustenhouwer, J. W. A. & Hutzinger, O. (1982), Polychlorinated dibenzo-*p*-dioxins and related compounds in incinerator effluents. In *Chlorinated Dioxins and Related Compounds—Impact on the Environment* (O. Hutzinger *et al.*, Eds), pp. 227–244. New York: Pergamon Press.

Olie, K., Van Den Berg, M. & Hutzinger, O. (1983), Formation and fate of PCDD and PCDF from combustion processes, *Chemosphere, 12*(4/5), 627.

Ontario Ministry of the Environment (1985), Scientific criteria document for standard development No. 4-84: Polychlorinated dibenzo-*p*-dioxins (PCDDs) and polychlorinated dibenzofurans (PCDFs), September.

Poiger, H. & Schlatter, C. (1985), *Pharmokinetics of 2,3,7,8-TCDD in man*, presented at the Fifth International Symposium on Chlorinated Dioxins and Related Compounds, Bayreuth, F.R.G., 16–19 September.

Rappe, C. (1984), *Problems in Analysis of PCDDs and PCDFs and Presence of these Compounds in Human Milk*, World Health Organization Regional Office for Europe, December.

Rappe, C., Buser, H. R. & Bosshardt, H. P. (1978), Identification and quantification of polychlorinated dibenzo-*p*-dioxins (PCDDs) and dibenzofurans (PCDFs) in 2,4,5-T-ester formulations and herbicide orange, *Chemosphere, 5*, 431.

Rghei, H. O. & Eiceman, G. A. (1984), Adsorption and chlorination of dibenzo-*p*-dioxin and 1-chlorodibenzo-*p*-dioxin on fly ash from municipal incinerators, *Chemosphere, 13*(3), 421.

Ryan, J., Lizotte, R. & Lau, B. P.-Y. (1985), Chlorinated dibenzo-*p*-dioxins and dibenzofurans in Canadian human adipose tissue, *Chemosphere, 14*(6/7), 697–706.

Schecter, A., Ryan, J. J., Lizotte, R., Sun, W.-F., Miller, L., Gitlitz, G. & Bogdasarian, M. (1985), Chlorinated dibenzodioxins and dibenzofurans in human adipose tissue from exposed and control New York State patients, *Chemosphere, 14*(6/7), 933–937.

Schecter, A., Weerasinghe, N. C. A., Gross, M., Gasiewicz, T., Constable, J. D. & Ryan, J. J. (1986), Human Tissue Levels of Dioxin and Furan Isomers in Potentially Exposed and Control Patients up to 15 Years after Cessation of 2,3,7,8-TCDD Environmental Contamination, presented at American Chemical Society National Meeting, Symposium on Solving Hazardous Waste Problems, New York, 15 April.

Shaub, W. M. (1984), *Technical Issue Concerned with PCDD and PCDF Formation and Destruction in MSW Fired Incinerators*, prepared for P. Casowitz, New York City Department of Sanitation.

Sheffield, A. (1985a), Polychlorinated dibenzo-*p*-dioxins (PCDDs) and polychlorinated dibenzofurans (PCDFs): Sources and releases, *Environment Canada Report*, EPS 5/H1/2, July.

Sheffield, A. (1985b), Sources and releases of PCDDs and PCDFs to the Canadian environment, *Chemosphere, 14*(6/7), 811–814.

Stanley, J. S., Boggess, K. E., Onstot, J. & Sack, T. M. (1985), *PCDDs and PCDFs in Human Adipose Tissue from the EPA FY82 NHATS Repository*, presented at the Fifth International Symposium on Chlorinated Dioxins and Related Compounds, Bayreuth, F.R.G., 16–19 September.

Stephen, R. (1986), California Department of Health Services, personal communication, 27 January.

Uchida, S., Kamo, H., Kubota, H. & Kanaya, K. (1983), Reaction kinetics of formation of HCl in municipal refuse incinerators, *Industrial Eng. Chem. Process Des. Dev.*, 22(1), 144.

U.S. Conference of Mayors (1986), *City Currents*. Washington, DC, March.

U.S. Department of Commerce (1984), *Statistical Abstract of the United States*, Bureau of the Census, 104th Edition.

U.S. EPA (1979), Refuse-fired energy systems in Europe: an evaluation of design practices, Office of Water & Waste Management, SW 771, November.

U.S. EPA (1983), *Comprehensive Assessment of the Specific Compounds Present in Combustion Processes. I. Pilot Studies of Emissions Variability*, EPA-560, Office of Toxic Substances, Washington DC, June 1983.

U.S. EPA (1985a), Chlorinated Dioxins Work Group, *Interim Procedures for Estimating Risks Associated with Exposures to Mixtures of Chlorinated Dibenzodioxins and Dibenzofurans (CDDs and CDFs)*, 21 November.

U.S. EPA (1985b), Assessment of carbon tetrachloride as a potentially toxic air pollutant, *Federal Register, 50*(156), 32621–7.

U.S. EPA (1985c), Air pollution control; decision not to regulate vinyledene chloride and solicitation of information, *Federal Register, 50*(156), 32632–4.

U.S. EPA (1985d), Intent to list chloroform as a hazardous air pollutant, *Federal Register, 50*(188), 39626–9.

U.S. EPA (1985e), Assessment of ethylene dichloride (EDC) as a potentially toxic air pollutant, *Federal Register, 50*(200), 41994–8.

U.S. EPA (1985f), Methylene chloride; initiation of regulatory investigation, *Federal Register, 50*(201), 42037–47.

U.S. EPA (1985g), Intent to list perchloro ethylene, *Federal Register*, 28 December.

U.S. Public Law 91–604 (1970), *National Emission Standards for Hazardous Air Pollutants*, Section 112(a) and (b), in *U.S. Statutes at Large*, Vol. 84, Part 2, p. 1685, December 31.

Vogg, H. & Stieglitz, L. (1985), *Thermal Behavior of PCDD in Fly Ash from Municipal Incinerators*, presented at the Fifth International Symposium on Chlorinated Dioxins and Related Compounds, Bayreuth, F.R.G., 16–19 September.

EMISSION OF TRACE ORGANICS FROM MUNICIPAL SOLID WASTE INCINERATORS—RATIONALE OF NATIONAL GUIDELINES IN THE FEDERAL REPUBLIC OF GERMANY *

L. Barniske †

(*Received January 1987*)

In the Federal Republic of Germany a working party has developed recommendations for dealing with the dioxin problems posed by waste incineration. According to these recommendations limit values for dioxin emissions are neither necessary nor practical. However, from the point of view of preventive environmental protection, dioxin emissions should be further reduced as far as is possible with present-day technology. The TA Luft (Technical Instructions for Maintaining Air Quality) contains stipulations and advice on this. The most significant of the solid residues from waste incinerators are the filter ashes as they have a high dioxin content. The working party of Länder (states) has compiled a catalogue of recommendations for the disposal of filter ashes. The transport of solid residues from solid waste incinerators is controlled under the Abfallgesetz (Waste Act) and regulations passed in connection with this act and under the Gefahrgutverordnung Strasse—GGVS (Regulation on the transport of dangerous freight by road). The latter stipulates at what level of dioxin certain transport conditions must be respected. The new Gefahrstoffverordnung—GefStoffV (Regulation on dangerous substances) prohibits substances containing dioxin in concentrations above a certain level from being placed on the market. It does not apply to residues from solid waste incinerators.

Key Words—Dioxin emissions, waste incineration, Federal Republic of Germany, AbfG (Waste Act), BImSchG (Federal Air Quality Control Act), TA Luft (Technical Instructions for Maintaining Air Quality), GGVS (Regulation on the transport by road of dangerous freight), GefStoffV (Regulation on dangerous substances).

1. Introduction

Since the beginning of the 1980s, solid waste incineration plants have been under discussion in the Federal Republic of Germany as being a source of trace emissions for highly toxic organic pollutants. Included in this category of substances are polychlorinated dibenzodioxins (PCDDs) and polychlorinated dibenzofurans (PCDFs) including their precursors as well as polychlorinated biphenyls (PCBs) and terphenyls (PCTs). All these substances are grouped together and referred to as Dioxins in the public discussion.

In 1984, at the request of the conference of environment ministers, a special working party was set up at the Federal Ministry of the Interior to look at whether it was practical, or even necessary, to set limit values for emissions of dioxins in the flue gases of solid waste incinerators.

The working party came to the following conclusions:

* Presented at the ISWA–WHO–DAKOFA specialized seminar, *Emission of Trace Organics from Municipal Solid Waste Incinerators*, Copenhagen, 20–22 January 1987.

† Umweltbundesamt, Bismarckplatz 1, D 1000 Berlin 33, F.R.G.

Waste Management & Research (1987) **5**, 347–354

(a) no significant risk of harm being caused to the population can be ascertained from dioxin emissions from solid waste incinerators which are operated in-line with state-of-the-art technological developments;

(b) it is, therefore not, necessary to lay down emission limit values for dioxins in order to avert risks. It is not possible to measure emissions continually. Limit values for monitoring purposes would also not be practicable as it would not be possible to take the continual emission measurements which would be necessary to monitor these limit values. The high costs (in terms of time, money and administration) which would be necessary to make a representative evaluation on the basis of individual measurements (spot checks) taken within a continual monitoring programme do not seem justified. As it is expected that dioxin emissions will be minimized as a result of improved flue gas burnout, the obvious solution is to analyse the burnout level of the flue gas by means of the relatively simple, continual monitoring of operational parameters and indicative compounds;

(c) as part of a policy of prevention, dioxin emissions from solid waste incinerators should continue to be reduced as far as is possible in line with the latest technological developments. The Technical Instructions for Maintaining Air Quality (TA Luft) are designed to reflect the present state of knowledge (compare Bergwall in this issue).

2. Technical instructions for maintaining air quality

Two laws apply to the incineration of waste: the Waste Act (AbfG), and the Federal Air Quality Control Act (BImSchG). The latter lays down the most important obligations on the operator of a solid waste incineration plant. It stipulates that plants are to be constructed and operated in such a way that:

(a) no harmful effects to the environment nor any other risks can occur which could prove disadvantageous and of nuisance to the general public and people living in the immediate vicinity;

(b) precautions are taken to prevent harm to the environment, in particular by measures to limit emissions to levels which correspond to the best available technology;

(c) residues are avoided and that any which do occur are recycled properly and in a way which causes no harm. Where it is neither possible to avoid nor recycle residues, or at least this cannot be reasonably expected, the waste must be disposed of in a way which does not pose any threat to the well-being of the general public; and

(d) any heat generated, which is not passed on to third parties, is used on site in so far as the type and location of the plant makes this technically possible and feasible.

Numerous references in the Federal Air Quality Control Act to "harmful effects on the environment" can only be seen as very general legal prescriptions. It was necessary therefore to issue concrete administrative regulations. To cover the subject in question in this paper the Technical Instructions for Maintaining Air Quality (TA Luft) was passed (last version in February 1986). TA Luft contains, amongst other things, general prescriptions concerning the maintenance of air purity including air quality requirements and fundamental requirements for, and general restrictions on, emissions. The most important requirements which concern the reduction of dioxin emissions are those which apply to the operation of waste incinerators but also those concerning restriction of emissions of particulate matter, carbon monoxide and organic pollutants (Appendix 1). The new TA Luft reflects the results of the enquiry carried out by the working party of the Federal Ministry of the Interior which was mentioned at the beginning of this paper.

2.1. *General requirements for auxiliary and secondary combustion*

Solid waste incinerators must be fitted with a secondary combustion chamber either in the furnace itself or behind it. In this secondary combustion chamber the flue gas must have a temperature of at least 800°C after the final air-supply opening. In addition, an adequate retention time of the flue gases in the secondary combustion chamber must be ensured, as must an oxygen content of at least 6% by volume.

If waste containing polychlorinated aromatic hydrocarbons, such as PCBs or PCPs, in levels higher than is usual in household or similar waste is incinerated, a temperature of at least 1200°C is necessary. Other technology may be used in conjunction with lower secondary combustion temperatures if it can be proved that higher emission levels do not occur. The waste must not be introduced into the incinerator until the minimum temperature has been reached by firing additional fuel or operating auxiliary burners. When the plant is shut down the auxiliary burners must be put into operation to maintain the minimum temperature until there is no more waste in the combustion chamber.

2.2. *Restriction of carbon monoxide*

The carbon monoxide (CO) levels emitted in the flue gas must not exceed 100 mg m^{-3} which corresponds to 99.992% combustion efficiency (see Bergstrøm this issue). This reduction of permitted CO from the previous level of 1000 mg m^{-3} ensures improved combustion and, consequently, the emissions of uncombusted organic pollutants are reduced. Due to the indicator function of CO, there is an additional requirement that the auxiliary burners must be put into operation within five minutes when 80% of the emission limit value is reached or exceeded.

2.3. *Restriction of organic pollutants*

In order to keep the monitoring efforts within reasonable limits the regulations which previously applied have been simplified such that now only an overall emission limit for the total carbon for each plant of 20 mg m^{-3} applies. This means that the usual determination and restriction of emissions of individual pollutants is no longer necessary.

There is a requirement to minimize the emissions of pollutants which have a particularly low level of degradability or which are highly toxic and, due to their composition, can have extremely harmful effects on the environment (e.g. dioxins, PCBs, etc.). This requirement states that these emissions must be restricted as far as possible within the limits of what is feasible. As well as flue gas treatment, measures must be taken relating to the process itself as well as measures which effect the properties of the material used and the process products. This material is usually hazardous waste which is incinerated in special hazardous waste incinerators.

The requirements to limit emissions of carcinogenic chemicals must also be observed. The main chemicals in this category which are of significance in waste incinerators are those such as the polycyclic aromatic hydrocarbons (PAH) benzo(a)pyrene and dibenz-(a,h)anthracene. The emission limit value for organics has a similar function to that for

CO as the reduction of the total carbon in the flue gases means a reduction in the content of organics.

2.4. *Limitation of particulate matter emissions*

The reduction of the limit value for particulate matter emissions from 100 mg m^{-3} to 30 mg m^{-3} also has the effect of reducing the emissions of organic pollutants, in particular dioxins, as the majority of these substances settle down in dust particles.

3. Regulations for the treatment and deposition of solid residues

Solid residues generated in waste incinerators which cannot be recycled in a proper and harmless way must be deposited as waste (residues). The solid residues from waste incineration fall into the categories incinerator bottom ash, boiler ash, filter dust and solid residues from the pollutant gas precipitation process (Appendix 2) and are increasingly difficult to recycle or deposit harmlessly in that order.

When evaluating the risk potential of dioxin traces in the individual categories of residues it is important to bear in mind the accumulation effects in the chain bottom ash/filter dust/particulate matter from the treated gas, which depend mainly on the composition and structure of the solid residues (grain structure, grain surfaces). This was taken into account during the consultations of the Working Party mentioned at the beginning of this paper. The Working Party reached agreements on the following points concerning the disposal of residues from waste incineration processes.

(a) The residues (filter dusts, bottom ash) can, if certain precautions are taken, be deposited or, in the case of bottom ash, recycled into other products without any problem to the environment.

(b) At the present time in the F.R.G., between 7.5 and 8 million tonnes of household and similar waste are incinerated per year. In this process between 250 and 300 thousand tonnes of filter dust and almost 2 million tonnes of bottom ash are formed.

(c) Throughout the F.R.G., Länder (states) programmes have begun in almost all waste incineration plants to measure dioxin in the residues. In some cases they have already been completed. According to the information provided by the Länder programmes, recent measurements have shown 2,3,7,8-TCDD concentration levels in filter dusts of less than 0.05 μg kg^{-1} ppb rising to 1.2 (ppb). In most cases, the level was less than 0.2 ppb. Concentration levels for the total content of TCDD are in the order of 1 ppb.

(d) The low dioxin levels determined in the fly ash means that they can, according to present knowledge, be deposited without any risk. No scientific justification can be found for establishing limit values for dioxin in deposited fly ash. The safety depends mainly on the observation of certain depositing conditions. Variations in dioxin content, to the extent that they have been determined, in the generally very low concentrations in fly ash should have no effect on safety if the deposition is carried out properly. There is, therefore, no scientific connection between the adherence to limit values in the area of a few ppb and safe depositing.

(e) When bottom ash was investigated, the dioxin levels were always below or, in a few cases, on the border of the detection level. Whenever concentration levels could be detected they were clearly lower than in the fly ash (by up to a factor of 100). Bottom ash can still be recycled (e.g. used for building paths or car parks). The fact that any dioxin present is bound in a coarse-grained glass-like matrix, which prevents any leaching, also speaks in favour of the safety of recycling. Bottom ash which is to be recycled must be separated from filter dusts.

The recommendations issued in April 1984 by the joint working party of the Länder on waste disposal which were updated in June 1986 are of particular importance for the depositing of fly ash from waste incinerators:

> Filter dust from household waste incineration plants can be deposited if the following precautions are observed at the landfills:
>
> (a) Filter dusts must be deposited in landfills which have a base seal. Leachate must be treated in an appropriate way.
>
> (b) When filling the landfill, care must be taken to ensure that the dusts are not blown away nor washed away by rain. To do this it is necessary to dampen, condition or package the filter dusts.
>
> (c) The landfill should be built up and operated in such a way that it is not possible for the filter dusts to come into contact with leachate which contains oils or solvents.
>
> (d) When the landfill or section of the landfill is full it must be protected against matter being blown away, against erosion and leaching by covering the surface with a suitable material which is at least 30 cm thick. An exception may be made if the filter dusts have been packaged or solidified as described in the next paragraph.
>
> (e) An additional safety precaution (barrier) which can be considered to minimize the leaching out of salts is to solidify the filter dusts with suitable materials. The competent authority makes a decision on such a safety measure in each individual case.
>
> (f) Bottom ashes which are not recycled are suitable due to their cement-like properties to be deposited in conjunction with filter dust.

The depositing of filter dusts in underground landfills is to be recommended wherever landfills of this kind with sufficient storage capacity exist. Given the small dioxin concentrations in filter dusts, a general requirement that they be deposited underground could not be justified.

4. Regulations on the transport of solid residues

Another aspect of the dioxin problem, apart from its treatment and disposal, is posed by the transport of residues containing dioxin. The discussion of the transport of filter dust from waste incinerators shows this clearly.

There are numerous regulations covering this area; the most comprehensive ones are to be found in the Waste Act and the regulations issued with it, although they are general in form and make no direct reference to the special case of dioxin. Apart from this, the act on the transport of dangerous freight provides the basis for special regulations specific to the individual means of transport (road, rail, waterways). In the wake of the transport of the "Seveso" barrels of poisonous waste which caused such a public stir, the transport of 2,3,7,8-TCDD in any concentration whatsoever (with the exception of licensed pesticides and wood preservatives) was banned within the framework of the above-mentioned regulations. It was, therefore, only possible to transport waste containing dioxin, including filter dusts from waste incinerators, if a special permit was obtained which imposed certain conditions. This regulation caused considerable problems in the disposal of filter dusts, sometimes leading to waste incinerators being taken out of operation. Due to this problem, a new version of the regulation concerning the transport of dangerous freight by road (GGVS) was passed. It contains limit values for dioxin concentrations at which certain transport conditions must be adhered to or at which transport is prohibited. These stipulations prescribe that:

Chemicals with a concentration of 2,3,7,8-TCDD greater than 10 ppb.	Transport prohibited, exception granted imposing certain conditions.
Chemicals with a concentration of 2,3,7,8-TCDD greater than 2 ppb less than 10 ppb.	Transport permit and special packaging required.
Chemicals with a concentration of 2,3,7,8-TCDD up to 2 ppb.	Transport permit required.

This regulation (GGVS) contains no comparable limit value prescriptions for furans.

As the concentration of 2,3,7,8-TCDD in filter ashes from waste incinerators is usually considerably lower than 2 ppb (see Appendix 3), no further requirements need be met for the transport of these residues apart from the normal transport permit. For reasons of general environmental protection, suitable precautions must be taken to prevent any dust from blowing away.

5. Regulations concerning the placing on the market of substances containing dioxins

The Chemikaliengesetz (Chemicals Act) offers the possibility of countering potential dangers which could be caused by dioxin with bans and restrictions for certain chemicals. The GefStoffV (Regulation on dangerous chemicals) which was issued in conjunction with this act contains strict prescriptions which prohibit the placing on the market of chemicals, preparations and products containing dioxin if they contain a total of more than 5 ppb of: 2,3,7,8-TCDD, 1,2,3,7,8-penta-CDD, 1,2,3,6,7,8-hexa-CDD, 1,2,3,7,8,9-hexa-CDD, 1,2,3,4,7,8-hexa-CDD, 2,3,7,8-TCDF, 2,3,4,7,8-penta-CDF, or 1,2,3,6,7,8-hexa-CDF. This also applies if the content of 2,3,7,8-TCDD exceeds 2 ppb. This ban does not apply if the chemical compound is passed on as an intermediary product, for disposal or for research and analysis purposes. The regulation on dangerous substances is therefore only of minor significance for the disposal of filter ashes from waste incinerators. It should simply be pointed out here that the limit value of 2 ppb for 2,3,7,8-TCDD is the maximum concentration laid down in both the regulation on dangerous freight and the regulation on dangerous substances, and that special safety measures are not deemed necessary below this concentration.

Bibliography

AbfG (1986), *Gesetz über die Vermeidung und Entsorgung von Abfällen* (*Act on Avoidance and Disposal of Waste*) of 27 August 1986 (BGBl, I, p. 1410) (Abfallgesetz – AbfG).
BImSchG (1986), *Gesetz zum Schutz vor schädlichen Umwelteinwirkungen durch Luftver-unreinigungen, Geräusche, Erschütterungen und ähnliche Vorgänge* (*Act on the Protection from Harmful Effects on the Environment Caused by Air Pollution, Noise, Vibrations and Similar Phenomena*) of 15 March 1974 (BGBl, I, p. 721, corrected p. 1193); last amended with paragraph 34 of the *Erstes Rechtsbereinigungsgesetz* of 24 April 1986 (BGBl, I, p. 560) (Bundesimmissionsschutzgesetz—BImSchG) (Federal Air Quality Control Act).
TA Luft (1986), *Technische Anleitung zur Reinhaltung der Luft,* (*Technical Instructions for Maintaining Air Quality*). First general administrative regulation issued in connection with the *Bundesimmissionsschutzgesetz,* of 27 February 1986 (GMBl, p. 95, corrected p. 202)
Gesetz über die Beförderung gefährlicher Güter (1975) (*Act on the Transport of Dangerous Freight*) of 6 August 1975 (BGBl, I, p. 2121)
GGVS (1985), *Verordnung über die innerstaatliche und grenzüberschreitende Beförderung gefähr-licher Güter auf Straßen* (*Regulation on National and International Transport of Dangerous Freight by Road*) of 22 July 1985 (BGBl, I, p. 1550) (Gefahrgutverordnung Straße—GGVS) (Regulation on dangerous freight).

Chemikaliengesetz (1980), (Chemicals Act) of 16 September 1980 (BGB1, I, p. 1718).

GefStoffV (1986), *Gefahrstoff-Verordnung* (*Regulation on dangerous substances*) of 26 August 1986 (BGB1, I, p. 1470) (GefStoffV).

Dioxin (1984). Report compiled by the working party set up at the Federal Ministry of the Interior, *Dioxin in Müllverbrennungsanlagen* (*Dioxin in Waste Incinerators*). Publication of the Bavarian Staatsministerium für Landesentwicklung und Umweltfragen (Ministry for Regional Development and Environmental Issues) of 27 November 1984.

Umweltbundesamt (1985). *Sachstand Dioxine* (*Dioxin Situation*), Berichte 5/83. Series of reports published by the Umweltbundesamt (Federal Environmental Agency). Published by Erich Schmidt, Berlin.

Appendix 1

Emission values (mg m^{-3}) for incineration plants for household waste and similar material

Pollutants	Measured values*		TA Luft limit values	
	Untreated gas	Treated gas	1974 Version†	Update of 1986‡
Hydrochloric acid	700–900	50–900	100	50
Hydrofluoric acid	3–9	0.5–9	5	2
Sulphur dioxide	200–300	70–300	—	100
Oxides of nitrogen	200–300	150–300	—	500
Carbon monoxide	50–600	50–600	1000	100
Organics given as total carbon	<20	<20	—	20
Particulate matter	2000–10,000	20–100	100	30
Particular substances contained in particulate matter				
Class I, e.g. Cd, Hg		<0.01–0.1	20	0.2
Class II, e.g. Ni, Co		<0.01–1.3	50	1
Class III, e.g. Cu, Pb		<0.2−2	75	5

* According to results gained from measurements taken in waste incinerators in Bavaria (different degrees of flue gas treatment).
† Based on 11% O_2 (damp flue gas).
‡ Based on 11% O_2 (dry flue gas).

Appendix 2

Solid residues from waste incinerators

Residue	Volume generated (dry) (kg tonne^{-1} waste)
Bottom ash (residue on grates or which has fallen through grates, fly ash from boiler drafts)	250–350
Filter dust from flue gas treatment process	10–40
Residues from gaseous pollutant treatment process	
Wet treatment process	5–12
Dry treatment process without particulate matter	10–40
Dry treatment process with particulate matter	30–70

L. Barniske

Appendix 3

PCDD and PCDF concentrations in filter ash (μg kg^{-1}, ppb) from waste incineration plants (measurements in the F.R.G. 1983–85)

	Dioxins		Furans		No. of measurements analysed/number of measuring institutes involved
	2,3,7,8-TCDD	TCDD	2,3,7,8-TCDF	TCDF	
Older plants (built before 1975)	<0.01–2.2 0.5*	<0.01–42 8.7*	<0.01–1.2 0.2*	<0.01–176 38*	26/6
Newer plants (built after 1975)	<0.01–0.8 0.17*	<0.01–17.3 2.7*	<0.01–0.8 0.3*	<0.01–72 19*	13/5

* Average value.

TOTAL ORGANIC CARBON EMISSIONS FROM MUNICIPAL INCINERATORS*

Paul H. Brunner,‡ Markus D. Müller,§ Stephen R. McDow‡ and Hermann Moench‡

(*Received December 1986, revised March 1987*)

Total carbon (TC), carbonate carbon (CC) and total organic carbon (TOC) were determined in bottom ash, filter dust and flue gas of Swiss municipal solid waste (MSW) incinerators. The highest TOC load was found in the bottom ash (2–3 g kg^{-1} MSW), followed by the filter dust (0.1–1.0 g kg^{-1} MSW) and the flue gas (0.05–0.3 g kg^{-1} MSW). The composition and behaviour of the bulk of TOC in these products is not yet known. In order to minimize the risk of leaching organic substances as well as metals due to biological, chemical and physical reactions of the products of incineration in a landfill, it is suggested the incineration process be optimized towards complete combustion.

Key Words—waste incineration, emission, TOC, organic carbon, bottom ash, filter dust, flue gas, sampling, combustion.

1. Introduction

The objectives of municipal solid waste (MSW) incineration have changed over the past decades. Initially the goal was the reduction of the volume of waste materials in order to minimize the mass to be landfilled. Then, the recovery of energy from refuse became increasingly important. Today, the new priorities must be the complete combustion of the organic materials, and the immobilization and concentration of the resulting inorganic material. The reason for these new priorities is the increasing knowledge of the potentially harmful reactions of organic substances derived from the products of MSW incineration in landfills and in the atmosphere. Historically the first discussion on organic matter in incineration products concerned the bottom ash, and was an attempt to qualify the combustion process by setting a standard for the "loss on ignition" of the bottom ash (Lauer 1971). This early work was followed by studies which focused on volatile organic carbon (Salo *et al.* 1975) and on polynuclear aromatic hydrocarbons (Davies *et al.* 1976). In 1977, when the first paper on the existence of chlorinated dioxins in the emissions of a MSW incinerator was published by Olie *et al.* (1977), the analysis of organic substances produced by MSW combustion became increasingly important. Most of this work concentrated on the measurement of chlorinated dioxins and furans and did not take account of the more abundant (but less toxic) organic substances in gas, filter dust and bottom ash. Today, the nature and concentration of certain trace substances in the products of MSW incineration are much better known than the more abundant organic components. Because the organic matrix compounds can determine the behaviour and fate of the trace organic substances, and

* Presented at the ISWA–WHO–DAKOFA specialized seminar, *Emission of Trace Organics from Municipal Solid Waste Incinerators*, Copenhagen, 20–22 January 1987.

‡ Swiss Federal Institute for Water Resources and Water Pollution Control, EAWAG, CH-8600 Dübendorf, Switzerland.

§ Swiss Federal Research Station, CH-8820 Wädenswil, Switzerland.

Waste Management & Research (1987) **5**, 355–365

because the emission and/or leaching of the organic matrix itself can pose a threat to the environment, it seems appropriate to elucidate the nature and composition of this matrix. A first step towards such an exploration would be to determine the total organic carbon (TOC) content in the bottom ash, filter dust and flue gas. For this work, TOC is defined as the difference between total carbon (TC) and carbonate carbon (CC) and consists of elemental and organic carbon. In a following step, the organic substances, which make up the bulk of this TOC, must be identified. The information gained by this procedure is expected to be a useful tool in optimizing total incineration towards complete combustion.

The goals of the work presented in this paper were:

(1) to determine TOC in bottom ash and filter materials from MSW incinerators by methods which are state of the art;

(2) to sample and analyze TOC in the stack gas. For lack of a standard method (Johnson 1986), a new method had to be developed;

(3) to differentiate between particulate, condensable, sorbable and volatile organic carbon in the stack gas; and

(4) to estimate the TOC load from the stack of a MSW incinerator for the assessment of total TOC in bottom ash, filter dust and flue gas as a source of organic carbon in the environment.

2. Experimental

2.1. *Bottom ash*

Thirty samples were taken from three Swiss MSW incinerators on four sampling days. Bottom ash free of fly ash and filter dust was sampled for 9 h. The water quench for the slag discharge was operated in such a way that no effluent from the quench was produced. The entire mass of ash was collected and weighed as received. For sampling, the ash was separated from large pieces of iron, crushed and sieved, and treated according to Brunner & Moench (1986) until a particle size <0.5 mm was achieved. Dried samples were analyzed for TC using a Carlo Erba C-N-S-Analyzer 1500. The CC was measured after acidification with perchloric acid by a carbon dioxide colourimeter of Colourmetrics Incorporated. TOC was calculated as the difference between TC and CC. The results were corrected for the material which was rejected during sieving operations, assuming that rejects contain no carbon. In contrast to this assumption, it happens that large items of high carbon content, which cannot be pulverized to d_p <0.5 mm, are contained in the ash (rootstocks, rolls of plastic foil, lump of epoxiresins, etc.). Therefore, TOC measured by this method is a minimum value.

2.2. *Filter dust*

Filter-dust samples from electrostatic precipitations (ESP) and from fabric filters were collected in four MSW incinerators. The entire mass of filter dust was collected in fractions of ~30 kg for 9 h. Each fraction was homogenized and 3-kg samples were transferred to the laboratory. The samples were dried (24 h at 105°C) and pulverized in an agate mortar for 15 min. The resulting dust, which completely passed a 200-μm screen, was used to determine TC, CC and TOC according to section 2.1. In addition, individual compounds were determined in one sample of raw, untreated but homogenized filter dust as follows: for chlorinated benzenes, the dust samples were digested in

1 N hydrochloric acid for 12 h, dried and extracted with toluene in a soxhlet apparatus (Lustenhouwer *et al.* 1980). The extract was analyzed by gas chromatography—ECD and GC/MS—and the chlorinated benzenes were identified and quantified according to standard chromatograms. The chlorinated phenols were analyzed by gas chromatography after methylation of the extract by diazomethane.

2.3. *Flue gas*

Flue gas was sampled in one MSW incinerator from a duct connecting the suction fan to the stack. The distance from the sampling port to the fan was 15 m, to the stack 5 m, and the diameter of the duct 1.45 m. The gas flow was measured by Prandtl and Pitot tubes and was found to average 14 m s^{-1}. Flue-gas samples were taken from the duct by a sampling train as shown in Fig. 1. During the sampling time of 2 h, 1.2 m^3 of gas were collected. The sampling train, which was designed for pseudo-isokinetic sampling (no simultaneous gas flow metering), consisted of the following parts:

(1) a particle filter (4-cm diameter, glass fibre filter Munktell 3-A-1/NM, collection efficiency for Dioctylphtalate particles with $d_p \simeq 0.3$ μm >99.998%) in an insulated and heated box at 180 ± 20°C;

(2) a condensate trap in an ice bath at −10°C;

(3) a two-stage sorption trap filled with Florisil (a Mg–Silicate) at ambient temperature;

(4) a gas pump and gas flow control, and a 40-l gas bag (Linde Plastigas for laboratory purpose).

The products of sampling were the following: particulate matter on the filter; water, acids and condensable organic substances in the condensation trap; adsorbed organic substances on the Florisil; and inorganic and organic gases in the gas bag. TOC on the filter and the Florisil was calculated from the difference between TC, as measured with the Carlo Erba C-N-S-Analyzer 1500, and CC, as measured with the colourimeter of Colourmetrics Inc. In the condensate, TC and CC were analyzed by a Dohrmann Carbon analyzer, CC after treatment with 10-N hydrochloric acid. In the gas bag, N_2, O_2 and CO_2 were determined with a Carlo Erba HR Gaschromatograph 5300 Mega series. It was not possible to determine TOC in the gas directly. It is assumed that after filtration, condensation and sorption of the flue gas, only volatile hydrocarbons reach the gas bag. Therefore, the volatile hydrocarbons from C_1 to C_6 were measured by a Carlo Erba G1 Gaschromatograph equipped with a micropacked 4-m glass column filled with Separon SDA and flame ionization detection. TOC was calculated from the concentrations of the individual constituents.

3. Results and discussion

The concentrations and loads of TOC, as measured in several Swiss incinerators, are given in Table 1. Although some of the flue gas values included in this table are of a preliminary nature and have to be confirmed by further studies, it can be clearly stated that all products of incineration contain considerable amounts of organic carbon, and that from a *quantitative* point of view, the highest load of TOC is caused by the ash, followed by filter dust and flue gas. Because the individual constituents of TOC in ash, filter dust and flue gas are relatively unknown, a *qualitative* comparison of the impor-

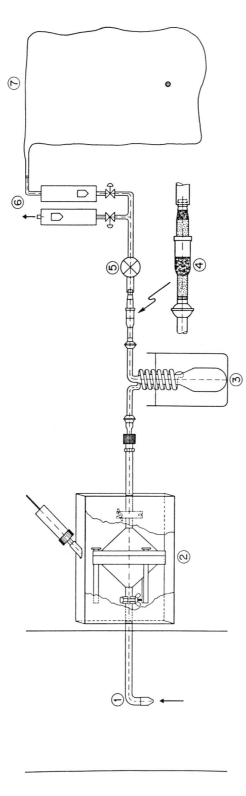

Fig. 1. Sampling train for the sampling of flue gas in MSW incinerators: 1, probe in stack; 2, insulated, heatable box with filter holder and filter; 3, condensator in NaCl/ice-bath; 4, adsorption by two fractions of florisil; 5, pump; 6, gas control and gas velocity meters; 7, gasbag. Probe 1 and filter holder 2 are made of stainless steel, condensator and adsorption tube are of pyrex glass.

TABLE 1

Range of TOC in bottom ash, filter dust and flue gas as measured in Swiss MSW incinerators

	Bottom ash	Filter dust	Flue gas (11% O_2)
TOC concentration (g kg^{-1})	10–14	10–40	
(g Nm^{-3})			0.01–0.06
TOC load (g kg^{-1} MSW)	2–3*	0.1–1.0†	0.05–0.3‡

* Assuming 250 kg ash per kg MSW incinerated.
† Assuming 2.5 kg filterdust per kg MSW incinerated.
‡ Assuming 6 Nm^3 flue gas per kg MSW incinerated.

tance of each product is difficult. The presence of halogenated dioxins and furans in flue gas and filter dust are important reasons for concentrating the analytical effort on these two products. Nevertheless, because the incompleteness of combustion of the ash is indicated by the high TOC content, the nature of the major individual organic compounds in the ash should be analyzed as well as in the filter dust and in the flue gas. It can be assumed that the TOC contained in the flue gas is being dispersed in the environment more widely than the TOC contained in ash and filter dust. This assumption is based on the high volatility of some of the TOC in the dissipating flue gas as well as on the small aerodynamic diameter of the flue gas particles bearing TOC, and the low mobility (low solubility in water, high affinity to surfaces) of a fraction of TOC in the solid ash and filter dust.

The fate and behaviour of the main part of TOC in the atmosphere and in the soil (landfill) is not yet known. To control the flux of organic substances from waste incineration to the environment, the processes which produce TOC, as well as the processes and substances which are responsible for the leaching and/or mobilization of such compounds, should be investigated. An interesting example for such a study would be a sanitary landfill where mixtures of slag and filter-dust are being disposed.

3.1. Bottom ash

Values for TC, CC, TOC (calculated as TC minus CC) from ash (slag) samples of three Swiss MSW incinerators are given in Table 2. Assuming that all carbon contained

TABLE 2

Concentration and load of TC, CC and TOC in ash from three Swiss municipal incinerators.

	TC		CC		TOC		
MSW incinerator	Conc. (g kg^{-1})	Load (g kg^{-1}) MSW	Conc. (g kg^{-1})	Load (g kg^{-1}) MSW	Conc. (g kg^{-1})	Load (g kg^{-1}) MSW	% TC
A	15 ± 3*	3.1	4.5 ± 0.6	0.9	10	2.4	70
B	19 ± 4	4.1	5.4†	1.2	14	3.0	72
C	18 ± 3	2.8	4.5	0.7	13	2.1	75

* Standard deviation of ⩾6 samples taken during 8 h.
† Value of a sample composed of ⩾6 samples taken during 8 h.

in the ash consists of cellulose ("worst case"), a maximum loss on ignition of the ash of 3–4% by weight can be calculated. For MSW incinerators, this value is small and indicates the comparatively high standard of the incinerators investigated.

The fraction of CC is surprisingly similar for the three incinerators and is only 25–30% of the TC. The more important fraction of the TC consists of organic carbon and equals 2–3 g of carbon per kg of MSW. Considering the average carbon concentration in Swiss MSW of 270 g kg^{-1} MSW (Brunner & Ernst 1986), this means that about 1% by weight of the carbon contained in the MSW is transferred to the ash. This figure is much higher than the conversion factors achieved in the combustion of wood, coal and fuel oil (0.1–0.01%).

The ash is usually used for landfilling or road and dam construction. The concentration of TOC in the leachates thereof has been observed in the range from 10–50 mg l^{-1} (Fichtel *et al.* 1983). Some of the organic carbon in the ash serves as a substrate for micro-organisms, which produce significant amounts of methane and carbon dioxide. The carbon dioxide may react with the metal hydroxides and subsequently lower the pH value of the deposit, favouring the mobilization and leaching of heavy metals in the ash. Thus, a deposit of ash has to be looked at as a chemical *and* biological reactor, where a complex mixture of elements and compounds react in a manner which few have investigated. In order to exclude biological reactions from the deposits of ash, it is suggested that the degree of combustion of the ash be improved by at least one order of magnitude.

The nature of the leachate of TOC from ash deposits has not yet been looked at. Although it can be assumed that most organic substances in the ash are lipophilic, well bound to surfaces and not easily leachable by water, the possibility of mobilization of trace organic compounds by carrier substances (small particles, abundant organic substances) should be taken into account.

3.2. *Filter dust*

Values for TC, CC and TOC (calculated from the difference between TC and CC) in filter-dust samples from four Swiss MSW incinerators are given in Table 3. It is interesting to note that the ranges of TC and TOC concentrations are higher for the filter dusts than for the ash. The carbonate fraction amounts to 10% of the TC and is

TABLE 3

Concentration and load of TC, CC and TOC in filter dust from four Swiss municipal incinerators.

MSW incinerator	TC Conc. (g kg^{-1})	TC Load (g kg^{-1}) MSW	CC Conc. (g kg^{-1})	CC Load (g kg^{-1}) MSW	TOC Conc. (g kg^{-1})	TOC Load (g kg^{-1}) MSW	% TC
A*	44 ± 6	1.1	4.9 ± 1.5	0.12	39	0.98	89
B†	11 ± 3	0.13	1.5	0.018	10	0.11	86
C*	26 ± 3	0.42	2.9	0.046	23	0.37	89
D*	24	0.48	2	0.04	22	0.44	92

* Electrostatic precipitator.
† Fabric filter.

smaller than for the slag samples. When the specific loads of carbon per kg of MSW combusted are calculated, comparatively large variations of one order of magnitude are noted between the different incinerators. This confirms the hypothesis that the design and operation of a MSW incinerator can be improved towards more complete mineralization of carbonaceous compounds in the offgas by existing technology.

Filter dusts are disposed of together with the ash in sanitary landfills, road constructions and dams, or separated from the ash in landfills and hazardous-waste sites. The fate of filter-dust borne TOC in these various disposal sites is not yet known. The presence of trace organic substances, like chlorinated dioxins, in filter dust, is well documented (Lustenhouwer *et al.* 1980, see Hasselriis and Rappe *et al.* in this issue). In order to assess the risk of leaching of organic substances from dust deposits, it is necessary to know the composition of the TOC. Available information, including the work presented here, does not account for more than 0.5% of the TOC in filter dust.

Our investigation into the more abundant organic compounds in filter dust samples yielded about 1 mg kg^{-1} chlorinated benzenes (trichlorobenzene $\simeq$ 10 μg kg^{-1}, tetrachlorobenzene $\simeq$ 200 μg kg^{-1}, pentachlorobenzene $\simeq$ 300 μg kg^{-1}, hexachlorobenzene $\simeq$ 400 μg kg^{-1}) and 0.5 mg kg^{-1} chlorinated phenols (2,4,6-trichlorophenol $\simeq$ 10 μg kg^{-1}, 2,3,4,6-tetrachlorophenols 250 μg kg^{-1}, pentachlorophenol 250 μg kg^{-1}). Chlorobromobenzenes and polycyclic aromatic hydrocarbons with methylated and chlorinated analogues were also detected. The values for total chlorinated benzenes and phenols are similar to the figures given by Lustenhouwer *et al.* (1980) and Paasivirta *et al.* (1985). The main question concerns the mobility of these subtances in a landfill: the compounds which are most likely to be leached from a deposit are chlorinated phenols. Their pK value ranges around the pH value of an aqueous suspension of the filter dust (pK of 2,4,6-trichlorophenol is 7.59, pK of higher chlorinated phenols is presumably lower). Therefore it cannot be excluded that some chlorinated phenols are being leached from dust deposits. Investigations into the behaviour and fate of organic substances in landfills of filter dusts are needed.

3.3. *Flue gas*

In contrast to the figures of carbon in ash and filter dust, which are based on established analytical methods and on many sampling campaigns from several incinerators, the values of carbon in flue gas presented in this paper have been analyzed by a method which is in its *status nascendi* and which has been applied to a single incinerator only. The incinerator examined (incinerator A in Tables 2–4) is one of the most investigated incinerators in Switzerland. This plant represents the performance of the average Swiss incinerators.

Because there is no standard procedure for sampling and analysis of TOC in MSW incinerators, a new method has been worked out (Fig. 1). This sampling train has not yet been tested and optimized sufficiently to serve as a "state-of-the-art" method to measure TOC. Nevertheless, it can serve as a tool to give a first estimate on the importance of TOC in flue gas. The main disadvantages of the procedure as used for this work are the breakthrough of TOC in the florisil at high loadings, and the limited analytical possibilities for measuring TOC in the gasbag at low concentrations. (When C_1 to C_7 hydrocarbons were analyzed, only ethylene and acetylene were detected.) The only initial problem in sampling and determination of TOC on the filter and the condensate were high background concentrations, which were overcome by sampling larger amounts of flue gas. The comparison of TC, CC and TOC in filter dust and flue gas

TABLE 4

Concentration of TC, CC and TOC in flue gas from a municipal incinerator for four sampling periods of 2 h

	Particle filter				Condensate			Adsorption*			Gasbag TOC	Total TOC
	TC	CC	TOC	TOC	TC	CC	TOC	TC	CC	TOC		
	(mg Nm^{-3}, 11% O$_2$)			%TC	(mg Nm^{-3}, 11% O$_2$)			(mg Nm^{-3}, 11% O$_2$)			(mg Nm^{-3}, 11% O$_2$)	(mg Nm^{-3}, 11% O$_2$)
I	7.6	0.9	6.7	87	20	4.4	16	8.6/1.0	2.6/1.0	6.0/0	<4	29
II	3.3	0.07	3.2	96	5.9	0.77	5.1	2.2/1.0	1.2/0.8	1.0/0	<4	9
III	3.1	0.16	2.9	92	15	3.9	11	7.3/1.9	0.31/0.41	6.9/1.4	32	55
IV	2.0	0.07	1.9	94	15	3.6	11	5.9/3.2	0.25/1.1	5.6/2.1	33	54
m̄ ± s	4 ± 2.5	0.3 + 0.4	3.7 ± 2.1	93	14 ± 5.9	3.2 ± 1.6	10.8 ± 4.5	6 ± 2.8 1.8 ± 1.0	1.1 ± 1.0 0.83 ± 0.3	4.9 ± 2.6 0.9 ± 1.1	18 ± 16	37

*Two figures are given for the two florisil adsorbents (cf. Fig. 1).

TABLE 5

Mean values and standard deviations of concentrations and loads of TOC in four fractions of flue gas from a MSW incinerator.

	TOC		
	(mg Nm^{-3}, 11% O$_2$)	(mg kg^{-1} MSW)	%
Particle filter	3.7 ± 2.1	22 ± 13	10
Condensate	10.8 ± 4.5	65 ± 21	29
Adsorption	4.9 ± 2.6	29 ± 16	13
Gasbag	18 ± 16	108 ± 96	48
Total flue gas	37 ± 17	224 ± 100	100

particulates (Tables 3 and 4) serves as a good check for the reliability of the TOC data on the filter: the fraction of TOC in the two materials was quite similar (89% and 93%, respectively).

Results from four sampling campaigns are given in Tables 4 and 5. The TOC content in the flue gas ranged from 9 to 55 mg Nm^{-3} at 11% O$_2$. Although most of the TOC was found in the gasbag, followed by the condensate, the order of magnitude of the TOC content in the four fractions is similar. Considering the nature of the TOC analyzed in the gasbag (ethylene and acetylene), it should still be possible to reduce TOC in the flue gas of incinerators by improving combustion conditions. Only 10% of the TOC measured in the flue gas was concentrated on particulate matter; the rest was gaseous at the filtration temperature of 180°C. The influence of the long sampling time of 2 h on the TOC on the filter was not assessed. If it is assumed that the ratio of particulate to non-particulate TOC is not changed to a large extent by possible reactions on the filter, it may be concluded that in MSW incinerators the emissions of TOC cannot be decreased significantly by improved filtration techniques (ESP or fabric filter). Condensation and wash-out by wet scrubbers or condensation and adsorption onto surfaces might remove TOC more efficiently from the flue gas of a municipal incinerator. Of course a better approach would be to reduce the amount of TOC in the untreated offgases by improving the process of combustion and, possibly, gas cooling.

For this work, a long sampling period was chosen. Thus, the results should be more representative than if short sampling periods were used which often yield large variations. Still, the differences between the four sampling campaigns are quite large. The ratio maximum value to minimum value is >8 for TOC in the gasbag, ∼7 for the adsorptions, ∼4 for the filters and ∼3 for the condensates. This indicates that the combustion in the furnace investigated is by no means a stationary process. It has to be kept in mind that municipal solid waste is the most difficult fuel with rapidly changing heating value, water content, density and elemental composition, and that the problem of the control of a combustion process without knowing the actual quality of the fuel has not yet been completely resolved.

As for the ash and filter dust, the composition of the TOC in the flue gas is not yet well characterized. As a first step towards its characterization, samples were analyzed for polyaromatic hydrocarbons (PAHs) over the molecular weight range from phenanthrene to coronene. The PAHs analyzed did not account for more than 1% of the TOC in the Florisil, the filter and the condensate. The highest loads were found in the Florisil, the most abundant single compound appeared to be phenanthrene, and no large molecular weight PAHs above pyrene were detected. The question of the more abundant compounds remains to be resolved (see also Oehme and Benested in this issue).

4. Conclusion

The method applied in this project to measure TOC in the stack of MSW incinerators is well suited to be further developed to a standard method, which is needed due to emission regulations in various countries. The TOC in the stack gas consists mostly of non-particulate carbon and is not removed by filtration techniques, but can be partly eliminated by condensation and wet scrubbing. Less than 10% of the TOC is amorphous or graphitic carbon, and most of the compounds in the TOC of the stack gas have not yet been identified.

Bottom ash contains at least one order of magnitude more organic carbon per kg MSW incinerated than filter dust and flue gas. About 1% of the carbon entering a MSW incinerator leaves the furnace as TOC with the bottom ash. The nature of the TOC in ash and filter dust remains to be analyzed. Preliminary investigations have shown that a significant fraction of carbon in the ash and dust consists of non-graphitic and non-amorphous carbon; during treatment with dichloromethane, up to 20% of the TOC in the filter dust and 45% of the TOC in the ash are extracted. When the solid products of incineration are used for landfilling, organic compounds may be leached and/or mineralized by micro-organisms. The CO_2 produced by this mineralization may account for the observed decrease in the pH value of landfill leachates with time (Brunner & Baccini, 1987).

It is suggested that the incineration of MSW be improved towards more complete combustion of the bottom ash, filter dust and flue gas. If the TOC content of the incineration products is lowered by one order of magnitude, the disposal of the residues from MSW incineration will pose fewer problems. The solution of these disposal problems, which implies new priorities for MSW incineration (Baccini & Brunner, 1985), is *a conditio sine qua non* in order to operate a MSW incinerator successfully. Thus, the maximum combustion efficiency should become a new objective and be of equal importance as maximum volume reduction and energy recovery.

Acknowledgements

The authors thank Mrs I. Farrenkothen, EMPA, for the analysis of the gasbag, Mrs H. Bolliger for the drawing of Fig. 1 and Mr K. Schweiss, MSW incinerator at Müllheim, for his substantial support of the sampling campaign.

References

Baccini, P. & Brunner, P. H. (1985), Behandlung und Endlagerung von Reststoffen aus KVAen (Treatment and Ultimate Disposal of Waste Products from MSW Incineration), *Gas-Wasser-Abwasser, 65*, 403–409.

Brunner, P. H. & Baccini, P. (1987), *The Generation of Hazardous Waste by MSW-Incineration Calls for New Concepts in Thermal Waste Treatment*, 2nd International Conference on New Frontiers for Hazardous Waste Management, 27–30 September, Pittsburgh, PA.

Brunner, P. H. & Ernst, W. R. (1986), Alternative methods for the analysis of municipal solid waste, *Waste Management & Research, 4*, 147–160.

Brunner, P. H. & Moench, H. (1986), The flux of metals through municipal solid waste incinerators, *Waste Management & Research, 4*, 105–119.

Davies, I. W., Harrison, R. M., Perry, R., Ratnayaka, D. & Wellings, R. A. (1976), Municipal incinerator as source of polynuclear aromatic hydrocarbon in the environment, *Environmental Science and Technology, 10*, 451–453.

Fichtel, K., Beck, W. & Giglberger, J. (1983), Auslaugeverhalten von Rückständen aus Abfallverbrennungsanlagen (The Leaching of Residues from MSW Incinerators), *Bayerisches Landesamt für Umweltschutz*, Heft 55.

Johnson, L. D. (1986), Detecting Waste Combustion Emissions, *Environmental Science and Technology, 20*, 223–227.

Lauer, H. (1971), Ausbrand und Volumenreduktion bei der Müllverbrennung (Slag quality and volume reduction of waste incineration). Ph.D. Dissertation, University of Stuttgart, Stuttgart, B.R.D.

Lustenhouwer, J. W. A., Olie, K. & Hutzinger, O. (1980), Chlorinated dibenzo-*p*-dioxins and related compounds in incinerator effluents: a review of measurements and mechanisms of formation, *Chemosphere, 9*(7–8), 501–522.

Olie, K., Vermeulen, P. L. & Hutzinger, O. (1977), Chlorodibenzo-*p*-dioxins and chlorodibenzofurans are trace components of fly ash and flue gas of some municipal incinerators in the Netherlands, *Chemosphere, 8*, 455–459.

Paasivirta, J., Heinola, K., Humppi, T., Karjalainen, A., Knuutinen, J., Mäntykoski, K., Paukku, R., Piilola, T., Surma-Aho, K., Tarhanen, J., Welling, L., Vihonen, H. & Särkkä, J. (1985), Polychlorinated phenols, guaiacols and catechols in environment, *Chemosphere, 14*, 469–492.

Salo, A. E., Oaks, W. L. & MacPhee, R. D. (1975), Measuring the organic carbon content of source emissions for air pollution control, *Journal of the Airpollution Control Association, 4*, 390–393.

STATISTICAL ASSESSMENT OF PCDD AND PCDF EMISSION DATA *

Lars Pallesen ‡

(*Received 12 March 1987*)

Real PCDD and PCDF emission data from a statistically planned measurement programme at Amagerforbrænding, Copenhagen, 1985 are analyzed. It is demonstrated how statistical analysis of variance can be used to break down the total variability in the data into interpretable components. Crossed and nested data structures are considered. Emission differences over time are significant, but less so than differences due to alternative sample taking methods, and even greater differences were found between laboratories.

Key Words—Statistical analysis, design of experiments, analysis of variance, dioxin emission, PCDD, PCDF.

1. Introduction

In 1985, a dioxin measurement programme was undertaken at "Amagerforbrænding" a 300,000 t y^{-1} incinerator in Copenhagen, Denmark. The project required a collaborative effort of a number of institutions and individuals which included Miljøstyrelsen, Teknologisk Institut, dk-Teknik, Kemikaliekontrollen, and Ångpanna Föreningen. The project results are documented in a paper by Grove (1987, see also in this issue). The present author served as statistical consultant to the project and, as such, advised on the statistical design and analysis of the measurement data. The present paper gives a statistically more detailed account of some of the statistical analysis.

The emphasis here is on general aspects of statistical analysis of dioxin data, which may be of interest when future measurement programmes are being planned, executed, analysed, and interpreted. Statistics plays an important role, both in the planning (design) and in the analysis of experiments. The latter is often done by an analysis of variance technique, the simpler forms of which are well known to most scientists and engineers. Besides the obvious point that more accurate measurements in greater number contain more information than fewer and less accurate ones, it is a less recognized fact that the information content of a data set is largely determined by the design of the experiment.

It is tempting, but incorrect, to imagine that, given the measurement precision, one data point supplies one piece of information and, therefore, the information content of a data set is determined by the number of measurements alone. This notion is akin to the cliché: "You get what you pay for". Luckily this previously widespread misconception is losing popularity among experimenters. In statistical terms, it is correct to say that one observation supplies one *degree of freedom*, but whether or not it contains information depends on what the experiment is asked to clarify, i.e. which effects or

---

* Based on a talk presented at the ISWA–WHO–DAKOFA specialized seminar, *Emission of Trace Organics from Municipal Solid Waste Incinerators*, Copenhagen, 20–22 January 1987.

‡ The Institute of Mathematical Statistics and Operations Research, The Technical University of Denmark, DK-2800 Lyngby, Denmark.

Waste Management & Research (1987) **5**, 367–379

parameters are to be estimated from the experimental data. It is one of the most exciting applications of statistical experimental design to make each observation do double duty—or even multiple duty—i.e. serve simultaneously in the estimation of more than one parameter. In doing so the amount of information to be extracted from a fixed number of measurements may increase dramatically.

A beneficial side effect of planning experiments is that the data often becomes straightforward to analyse, offering little opportunity for making gross errors in the interpretation. In contrast, unplanned happenstance data, may not only contain little or no information of interest, but the required statistical analysis may be cumbersome and yield ambiguous conclusions. This is not to say that only the simplest kinds of analysis are useful, in fact more complicated analysis of variance techniques can often yield very illuminating insights. However, any valid analysis can only extract actually existing information from the data, and this content is largely determined by design, and cannot be altered by the statistical analysis. It is not the purpose of this paper to present a structured summary of the topics of Statistical design and analysis of experiments (see, e.g., Hicks 1964, Box *et al.* 1978), rather it is hoped, that the following discussion and analysis of some real dioxin data from a full-scale incineration plant will demonstrate how statistics can be useful in these circumstances, where measurements are comparatively expensive and imprecise.

2. Data and design

The data analysed in this paper are taken from Grove (1987), with the kind permission of Miljøstyrelsen, The Danish Environmental Agency.

The main purpose of the first set of measurements (Table 1) was to determine the

TABLE 1
First data set *

Sample period	1		2		3		4		5		6	
Analysing lab.	K	K	K	K	U	K	K	U	K	K	K	K
Sample taker	ÅF	DK	ÅF	DK	ÅF	DK	ÅF	DK	ÅF	DK	ÅF	DK
Sum TCDD	0.4	1.9	0.5	1.7	60	2.4	0.4	53	0.3	0.7	1.0	2.0
Sum PeCDD	1.8	28	3.0	7.3	35	19	2.2	39	2.7	5.5	7.0	11
Sum HxCDD	2.5	24	2.6	7.3	55	19	4.2	120	3.8	5.1	4.7	6.0
Sum HpCDD	17	155	16	62	100	162	33	390	29	45	30	40
OCDD	7.4	55	7.3	28	—	68	14	—	14	21	12	17
Sum TCDF	4.9	26	7.8	18	—	23	5.2	—	5.8	9.0	13	13
Sum PeCDF	4.2	31	11	22	130	33	6.4	150	7.0	12	17	24
Sum HxCDF	3.5	31	11	28	110	38	6.9	150	8.0	14	18	19
Sum HpCDF	9.1	103	32	80	210	109	11	370	32	41	47	62
OCDF	3.8	19	6.4	18	66	23	7.2	340	6.6	7.0	6.7	6.7
Sum PCDD	29.1	264	29.4	106	250	270	53.8	622	50	77	55	76
Sum PCDF	25.5	210	68.2	166	516	226	36.7	1010	59	83	102	126
Sum PCDD + PCDF	54.6	474	97.6	272	766	496	90.5	1632	109	160	157	202

* Measured concentrations are in ng m^{-3} normal dry gas actual CO_2%.

natural emission variability under normal incineration conditions, and to estimate the measurement uncertainty. It was decided to take two parallel samples from each of six 3½-hour sampling periods, taken over a three-day period. The two parallel samples were taken using the somewhat different equipment of the two different sampletakers: dk-Teknik (DK) and Ångpanna Föreningen IPK (ÅF). *A priori*, it was judged, that the measurements would not be affected significantly by sampling techniques.

Each sample was analysed for the five dioxin groups (TCDD, PeCDD, HxCDD, HpCDD, OCDD) and for the five furan groups (TCDF, PeCDF, HxCDF, HpCDF, and OCDF). The analysis was carried out by Kemikaliekontrollen (K). Two of the 12 samples, one from each sampling equipment, were analysed in the laboratory at Umeå University, Sweden (U). Because these two laboratories (K and U) use essentially the same analysis technique, it was anticipated that no real difference should exist between their results.

This experimental design was a compromise between different *a priori* notions, practical considerations, and certain constraints. Limitations of this kind always exist when "real-world" experiments are being designed. The uncertainty about the outcome of the experiments, both motivate them and impede their planning. If the experiments hold no promise for surprise because their outcomes can be predicted with certainty, there is no reason for actually carrying out the experiments. On the other hand, an optimal experimental design rests on certain assumptions, which the experiments may prove wrong, rendering the design non-optimal. Accordingly, a sound experimental design may not be optimal under all circumstances, but should be good under a wide range of possible "true" circumstances. It should be able to answer the questions posed, but should also allow crucial assumptions to be checked. In the present situation, crucial assumptions are the equivalence of the sampling equipment, and of the results

TABLE 2

Second data set*

	Start up			Normal			Wet sludge added			High load
Sample period	2	3	4	5	6	7	8	9	10	11
Analysing lab.	K	K	U	U	K	U	U	U	K	K
Sum TCDD	38	23	30	2.8	7.5	<2.4	15	26	21	35
Sum PeCDD	90	99	73	42	32	8.9	35	121	56	35
Sum HxCDD	23	26	20	5.0	21	1.8	9	20	13	174
Sum HpCDD	44	74	12	3.81	16	1.4	4.9	11	11	502
OCDD	16	37	5	<0.8	65	0.8	1.5	3.7	16	135
Sum TCDF	347	193	135	118	62	19	52	73	100	137
Sum PeCDF	222	168	141	102	54	23	65	128	57	148
Sum HxCDF	128	172	52	19	38	6.6	26	39	35	173
Sum HpCDF	32	52	79	62	16	8	36	44	12	69
OCDF	12	19	—	—	12	—	—	—	4.6	33
Sum PCDD	210	260	140	54	242	15	66	182	143	882
Sum PCDF	742	604	407	301	182	56	180	276	208	559
Sum PCDD + pCDF	952	864	547	355	424	71	246	458	351	1441

* Measured concentrations in ng m^{-3} normal dry gas actual CO_2%.

from the different laboratories. A partial solution to the paradox that only after the experiment is carried out, can it be designed efficiently, is a sequential strategy, i.e. the full experimental budget should not be expended in one shot. This philosophy was adopted in the present case.

The second data set (Table 2) was planned after some preliminary analysis of the first data set. The main purpose of the second data set was to relate dioxin emission to the operating conditions. Measurements were therefore made under a number of different conditions: upstart, heavy load, normal conditions, wet sludge added (for details see Grove 1987). Parallel sampling was not done, because it was considered imperative that as many independent samples as possible be analysed.

Sampling was carried out during 10 periods, each lasting for about two hours, and was spread over a total period of four days, three of which were consecutive. Only one sample-taking procedure was used (DK). Two laboratories were used (K and U), however, one laboratory, K, had altered its analysis procedure in order to conform better to U. Each laboratory analysed five samples, Isomer-specific analysis of the so-called "dirty dozen" was also carried out (Table 3).

TABLE 3
Isomer-specific analysis of the "dirty dozen" from the second data set *

Sample period	Start up				Normal				Wet sludge added	High load
	2	3	4	5	6	7	8	9	10	11
Analysing lab.	K	K	U	U	K	U	U	K	K	K
2,3,7,8-TCDF	11.9	8.0	6.2	4.9	3.5	1.0	2.7	4.2	4.7	7.4
2,3,7,8-TCDD	0.9	LD (<0.1)	0.6	0.5	LD (<0.1)	LD (<0.1)	0.4	0.9	0.2	0.3
1,2,3,7,8-PeCDF	22.7	17.8	11.2	9.5	5.6	2.3	6.0	12.8	6.8	16.5
2,3,4,7,8-PeCDF	15.6	17.0	11.8	6.4	4.3	1.6	5.2	10.0	4.9	13.5
1,2,3,7,8-PeCDD	5.2	6.2	2.4	1.7	1.2	0.2	1.5	3.9	2.0	8.3
1,2,3,4,7,8-HxCDF	17.2	19.6	5.6	2.0	4.8	0.8	2.7	3.9	4.3	19.5
1,2,3,6,7,8-HxCDF	15.5	23.0	5.6	2.2	4.8	0.8	3.0	4.2	4.2	24.0
1,2,3,7,8,9-HxCDF	LD (<0.1)	3.4	4.2	1.1	LD (<0.1)	0.4	1.8	2.6	0.5	3.8
2,3,4,6,7,8-HxCDF	11.9	21.2	2.5	0.6	4.5	0.2	1.1	1.5	4.5	24.2
1,2,3,4,7,8-HxCDD	LD (<0.1)	1.2	1.5	0.5	0.7	0.2	0.7	1.4	0.4	4.3
1,2,3,6,7,8-HxCDD	LD (0.1)	2.3	1.9	LD (<0.1)	1.9	0.2	0.9	1.9	1.0	12.0
1,2,3,7,8,9-HxCDD	LD (0.1)	3.2	1.7	0.4	1.3	0.2	0.5	1.3	0.7	8.49
TCDD ekv. (Eadon)	23.1	21.2	13.0	9.6	5.7	1.9	6.6	14.0	7.8	22.4

* Measured concentrations in ng m^{-3} normal dry gas actual CO_2%. LD, limit of detection.

Again, the design was the result of compromise. Neither one of the laboratories could handle all the chemical analysis work within the set time limit, so two laboratories had to be used. It was hoped that any difference between laboratories would be eliminated giving 10 comparable observations; otherwise only two sets of five observations would be obtained.

3. Analysis of variance

Analysis of variance is a part of statistical theory which addresses the problem of assigning a total variance among the individual observations in a data set to a number of sources. The variance is measured as the sum of squares of the observations after adjustment for a general level, i.e. the general average of the observations, N in number, is subtracted from all observations. The total (adjusted) sum of squares is separated into contributions from a number of possible sources, which are specified by a (tentative) statistical model. In some situations this assignment is unique, in other situations a hierarchy among sources must be imposed to make the assignment unique, and in still other situations uniqueness cannot be induced even in this way. Clearly the first type of situation is the most desirable in data analysis, and the last one is the least desirable. In this context it is important to recognize, that the outcome of the experiment does not determine which type of situation occurs; this is predetermined by the design of the experiment.

The latter statement requires one qualification: a planned, but unobtained, data point (a missing value) will, not surprisingly, alter the situation. However, some designs are less affected by missing values than others. In any event, statistical considerations are all important before the data collection. Statistics is unreliable at best as a cure-all for analysis of ill-conceived experimental data.

In deciding whether a contemplated experimental design should be used, modified or discarded, one should look ahead. One should investigate which analysis the, as yet uncollected, data could support, if questions of interest can be answered clearly, and whether side issues and assumptions can be checked. This kind of exercise can be done more or less formally, and, more than anything, requires an understanding of how the analysis of variance works in practical terms. The study of "real-life" examples may serve well as a guide.

The analysis of variance model may be written in the general form:

$$Y_u = \mu_u + \varepsilon_u$$
$$u = 1, 2, \ldots N$$

where Y_u is the uth observation, N is the total number of observations, μ_u is the true response under the conditions for the uth experiment, and ε_u is the random disturbance, or error, assumed to be independently distributed according to a normal distribution with mean zero and constant variance, σ^2.

The true response, μ_u, may be specified by some expression which is linear in the parameters. Depending on the actual mathematical form for μ, special analysis of variance cases arise; textbook references on the analysis of variance are Rao (1965) and Searle (1971). In the statistical analysis given below, emphasis is placed on variance decomposition and interpretation rather than on model specification and estimation. The calculations below were carried out using the computer program package described in *SAS USER'S GUIDE: Statistics* (1982). The following names of variables are used:

L = Laboratory
  K = Kemikaliekontrollen, Denmark
  U = University of Umeå, Sweden

S = Sample taker
  ÅF = Ångpanna Föreningen
  DK = dk-Teknik

P = Period, i.e.
  P = 1, 2, 3, 4, 5, 6 for first data set (Table 1)
  P = 2, 3, 4, 5, 6, 7, 8, 9, 10, 11 for second data set (Tables 2 and 3)

DF = Dioxin/Furan

CL = Chlorination
  CL = 4 is tetrachloride (TCDD or TCDF)
  CL = 5 is pentachloride (PeCDD or PeCDF)
  CL = 6 is hexachloride (HxCDD or HxCDF)
  CL = 7 is heptachloride (HeCDD or HeCDF)

GROUP, i.e. clorination groups of dioxins and furans.

LNC = $\log_e$ C = $\log_e$ (measured concentration)

It was found to be useful to analyze the log measurements rather than the raw data; this makes the assumption of constant variance σ^2 for ε more realistic (see Dean in this issue).

3.1. *Analysis of periods 1, 2, 5 and 6 from first data set*

Four of the six periods in the first data set have parallel measurements of all five dioxin and five furan groups: $2 \times 10 \times 4 = 80$ measurements in total. The chemical analysis was carried out by one laboratory (K), and the parallel samples were taken by the two sample takers, DK and ÅF. With respect to the four factors P, S, DF, and CL, the data set is a completely balanced set with no repeats: each level combination of the four factors are represented once and only once. A geometric representation of

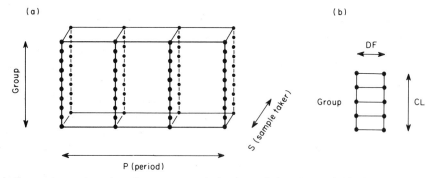

Fig. 1. Geometric representation of measurement design for periods 1, 2, 5 and 6 in data set 1. The factor group in (a) represent the 10 combinations of DF (dioxin/furan) and CL (clorination) shown in (b).

TABLE 4
Source of variance, first data set

Source of variation	Sum of squares SS	Degrees of freedom df	Mean square MS
DF	11.1309	(1)	11.1309
S	18.3423	(1)	18.3423
DF*S	0.2408	(1)	0.2408
P	1.9847	(3)	0.6616
DF*P	1.1749	(3)	0.3916
S*P	9.7071	(3)	3.2357
DF*S*P	0.0112	(3)	0.0037
CL	54.5564	(4)	13.6391
DF*CL = GROUP	22.7618	(4)	5.6905
S*CL	0.0895	(4)	0.0224
DF*S*CL	0.0826	(4)	0.02065
P*CL	1.4142	(12)	0.1179
DF*P*CL	0.8545	(12)	0.0712
S*P*CL	0.6229	(12)	0.0519
DF*S*P*CL	0.2305	(12)	0.0192

this design is shown in Fig. 1. The variance (sum of squares) among the 80 measurement can be separated in a unique fashion as shown in Table 4.

The sum of the sum of squares in the second column of Table 4 is 123.2043 = $\Sigma(Y_u - \bar{Y})^2$ = the adjusted total sum of squares. The individual terms in the sum of squares column, measure the variability due to their respective sources listed in the first column plus some random observation error (measurement error). The expected error contribution is the measurement variance, σ^2, multiplied by the degrees of freedom given in parentheses.

For example, the sum of square 18.3423 in the second row, measures the variation due to the different sampling techniques of the sample takers, plus an estimate of σ^2. If the sampling techniques really perform alike, then 18.3423 is just an estimate of σ^2. The sum of squares in the P row has a similar interpretation, it measures the variability due to different true emission levels during the four sampling periods, plus $3\sigma^2$. If the true emission is constant, so that observed fluctuations over time are really reflections of measurement error only, then 1.9847/3 = 0.6616 is an estimate of σ^2. This number is much lower than the possible estimate 18.3423 mentioned above, making it extremely unlikely, even at this point, that S has no effect. The S*P sum of squares, 9.7071, measures the interaction between S and P (plus σ^2).

An interaction can be interpreted as lack of additivity between the involved effects, here S and P. If the difference between the sampling techniques is constant from one period to the next, then the interaction is zero, otherwise it is non zero and similarly, for the other two-factor interactions. Three-factor interactions measure the constancy of two-factor interactions with respect to the third factor. For example, DF*S*P is inflated if the S*P interaction is different for the different values of DF, i.e. if S*P has a different magnitude for dioxins than for furans, or, equivalently, whether DF*S is different at different periods (P), or, equivalently, whether DF*P depends on S. The interpretation of other high (and higher) order interactions are explained along the same lines.

It is hard to imagine that, for example, DF*S*P*CL could have a sensible interpretation, the existence of non-negligible high-order interactions signifies a state of
disorder which makes mathematical modelling uninteresting. For practical purposes it
makes sense to consider the DF*S*P*CL sum of squares as a result of the modelling
error, and accordingly estimate σ^2 as the mean square $0.2305/12 = 0.0192$, listed in the
last column of Table 4. Compared to this mean square, the mean square of S*P*CL is
a factor 2.70 higher. However a formal F-test (with 12 and 12 degrees of freedom),
shows that the two mean squares are not significantly different. It may be induced,
therefore, that essentially no S*P*CL interaction exists, and that the associated sum of
squares can be regarded as error only.

Closer inspection of the magnitudes and the interpretations of the sum of squares in
Table 4 suggests the groupings shown in Table 5. The two factors DF and CL, including

TABLE 5

Analysis of variance, first data set

Source of variation	Sum of squares SS	Degrees of freedom df	Mean square MS	F-statistic (df, df)
General differences between levels of Dioxin/Furan groups (DF + CL + DF*CL)	88.4490	9	9.8277	
Level difference between sample takers, S	18.3423	1	18.3423	573 (1,27)
Level differences among sampling periods, P	1.9847	3	0.6616	20 (3,27)
Interaction between S and P, S*P	9.7071	3	3.2357	101.0 (3,27)
Interaction between S and Dioxin/ Furan groups (S*DF + S*CL + S*DF*CL)	0.4130	9	0.04588	1.43 (9,27)
Interaction between P and Dioxin/ Furan groups (P*DF + P*CL + P*DF*CL)	3.4435	27	0.12754	3.98 (27,27)
Residual (S*P*DF + S*P*CL + S*P*DF*CL)	0.8646	27	0.03202	
Corrected total	123.2043	79		

their mutual interaction DF*CL, may be regarded as one factor, GROUP, as illustrated in Fig. 1. Examination of the column of F-statistics, shows that the difference
between sample takers (S) is much more significant than the differences among periods
(P). Moreover, the interaction between S and P is more significant than P, i.e. the
difference between sample takers is not stable over time, but overshadows differences
in measured emission levels from one period to the next. Therefore, it makes no sense to
relate the measured emission to the operating conditions of the incinerator before this
uncertainty due to sampling equipment has been reduced greatly. The interaction between S and Dioxin/Furan groups is insignificant, showing that the two alternative
sampling procedures, do not have different relative sensitivity for the different groups.
However, the larger interaction between P and GROUP signifies that the composition
of the total emission does change somewhat from day to day. The residual mean

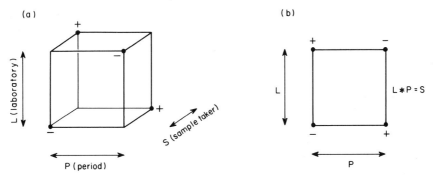

Fig. 2. Geometric representation of the measurement design for periods 3 and 4 in data set 1. The difference between the front and back measurements of the cube (a) provides an estimate of the S factor. It is seen from (b), however, that this contrast also reflects any interaction between L and P.

square of $0.03202 = 0.18^2$ can be interpreted as an estimated measurement error with a standard deviation of about 18%.

3.2. *Analysis of periods 3 and 4 from the first data set*

Parallel samples were also taken during periods 3 and 4 of the first data set, as described in Section 3.1. One sample from each period was analysed by the alternative laboratory, U, in a crossed fashion (see Table 1). This arrangement is illustrated geometrically in Fig. 2(a). The corners of the cube represent all possible combinations of P (period 3 or 4), of S (one sample taker or the other), and of L (one laboratory or the other). Conceivably, a vector of measurements (group concentrations) could be made in each corner which would give a full, two-level, factorial experiment in the factors P, S and L. Such an experimental design would clearly allow the effects of these three factors and their interactions to be assessed. This requires eight samples to be taken; two four-fold parallel sets.

In the present case, only four samples could be taken, and by design they were placed in the diagonal pattern shown in Fig. 2(a). This is a fractional factorial experiment, which also allows the factor effects to be estimated, but not independently of the interactions. If, for example, the cube is collapsed along the S dimension, Fig. 2(b) is produced. The effect of L is the difference between the average of the top and the bottom measurements, the effect of P is the difference between left and right, and the interaction is the effect of L at one level for P *minus* the L effect at the other P level (or *vice versa*). In any case, the P*L interaction is estimated as the difference between one set of diagonal measurements and the other. However, looking back at Fig. 2(a), it is seen that this difference *also* estimates the effect of S. Therefore, P*L and S are confounded. Similar confounding exists for the other interactions. This is the price to be paid for being able to assess three main factors in only four experimental runs.

Subjecting balanced data of this kind to an analysis of variance produces a decomposition of variance which is unique except for confounding. It is usually sensible to assume *a priori* that main effects are more important than two-factor interactions which, in turn, are more important than three-factor interactions, and so on. As it turned out, the situation was further complicated by the four missing values (see Table 1). Considering first only the complete groups, and treating dioxins and furans separately, the resulting variance decompositions are given in Tables 6 and 7.

For the Furans, the interaction sums of squares (P*CL, S*CL and L*CL) are not significantly different, and pooled together they provide an estimate of the measurement

TABLE 6

Dioxin variance components, 3rd and 4th period in first data set

Source of variation	Sum of squares SS	Degrees of freedom df
P + S*L	1.2706	(1)
S + P*L	5.7450	(1)
L + P*S	21.1783	(1)
CL	16.3333	(3)
P*CL + S*L*CL	0.4604	(3)
S*CL + P*L*CL	0.2326	(3)
L*CL + P*S*CL	4.9098	(3)

TABLE 7

Furan variance components, 3rd and 4th period in first data set

Source of variation	Sum of squares SS	Degrees of freedom df
P + S*L	1.0724	(1)
S + P*L	5.5930	(1)
L + P*S	19.6864	(1)
CL	1.8478	(3)
P*CL + S*L*CL	0.7779	(3)
S*CL + P*L*CL	0.2237	(3)
L*CL + P*S*CL	0.0910	(3)

error of $(0.7779 + 0.2237 + 0.0910)/(3 + 3 + 3) = 0.1214 = 0.35^2$, corresponding to a standard deviation of about 35%. The main effects of P and S are significant, as was found above in Section 3.1. However, L is even more significant which could, in principle, be due to the P*S interaction also found significant above, but the sum of square is much too large for this explanation (above S*P was less than S). Hence, on this data evidence, one is led to conclude that laboratory differences are even more pronounced than differences due to the sampling methods, and to period-to-period variation.

For dioxins (Table 6) essentially the same conclusions are drawn, except here the L*CL interaction is significant. This means that laboratory differences are not merely a level shift, but are group specific. In particular this makes it unreasonable to estimate the missing dioxin measurement, OCDD, and indeed to extend the analysis to incorporate the measured OCDD values.

An analysis of variance could of course be conducted on the combined Dioxin/Furan measurements. The dissimilarity of the L*CL interaction for the dioxins versus furans, make the three-factor interaction L*CL*CF large which diagnose the advantage of splitting the analysis, as was done above.

3.3. Analysis of the "dirty dozen" measurements, second data set

The data in Table 3 are measurements of the "dirty dozen" isomers found in the second data set samples. The data set is complete in the sense that there are no missing values, but some measurements were below the detection limit. For the present purpose it sufficed to use the detection limit as the measured value in these cases. Because parallel sampling was not used for the second data set, the structure of the experimental design is fundamentally different from before. Figure 3 shows geometrically how the factors ISOMER and P (period) are *crossed* much like before, but because each period only occurs once, the factor P becomes *nested* within L (laboratory). This is written P(L), and the (unique) variance decomposition is presented in Table 8.

The nested design implies that an observed difference between the laboratories (L) may, to some extent, be due to differences among periods. In other words, the significance of an L effect must be assessed against the variability among periods within laboratories P(L). This variability, as was seen in Sections 3.1. and 3.2., is much larger than the measurement error and, therefore, such nested experimental design does not allow for a very sensitive test of differences between laboratory levels. The pertinent F-statistic is $(13.81/1)/(59.58/8) = 1.85$, which is non-significant when referenced to an $F(1,8)$ distribution. On the other hand, differences between the laboratories in terms of relative sensitivity among the isomers, L*ISOMER, can be tested against the much smaller variance component ISOMER*P(L), which measures the (random) variability of the isomer distribution from period to period within a laboratory. The F-statistic here is $(15.34/11)/(41.74/88) = 2.94$, which is strongly significant when referenced to an $F(11,88)$ distribution.

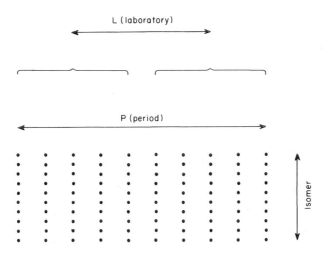

Fig. 3. Geometric representation of the isomer-specific measurement design for data set 2. The factors ISOMER and P (period) are crossed, while P is nested within L (laboratory).

TABLE 8

"Dirty dozen" variance components

Source of variation	Sum of squares SS	Degrees of freedom df
L	13.8123	(1)
ISOMER	144.2826	(11)
L*ISOMER	15.3402	(11)
P(L)	59.5783	(3)
ISOMER*P(L)	41.7401	(88)

In conclusion, there is solid evidence, that systematic deviations exist between the laboratories in their relative detection of the "dirty dozen" isomers. This is clearly of some concern when Eadon equivalents are to be calculated.

3.4. *Analysis of the second data set*

The second data set (Table 2) has the same nested structure as the "dirty dozen" data depicted in Fig. 3. Accordingly, the analysis of variance would consist of exactly the same elements as discussed in Section 3.3., had it not been for the five missing measurements: namely all OCDF values from one laboratory. Loosely speaking, had the missing values been scattered around the table, the analysis could still be performed using the available data. The computing involved would be many times that required for a complete data set, and the sums of squares would not be unique. The degree of non-uniqueness, and the difficulty of interpretation thereby induced would depend on the number of missing values and their location in the table, as well as the on the relative magnitudes of the variance components. An unbalanced experiment is more likely to suffer adversely because of missing values, than is a planned, balanced design which has become unbalanced because of missing values. In the present case, the complete absence of OCDF values from one laboratory makes it necessary first to analyse the data disregarding all OCDF values. If the L*GROUP interaction is small, then the laboratories can be considered equal in terms of measuring the various Dioxin/Furan groups, except possibly for a calibration constant common to all groups. The necessity for such a general level adjustment is assessed from the size of the L effect.

Table 9 contains the (unique) variance components. Proceeding as described in Section 3.3., the significance of L is tested by referring the *F*-statistic $(28.32/1)/(39.88/8) = 5.68$ to an $F(1,8)$ distribution; it is significant at the 5% level. The significance of L*GROUP is tested by referring the *F*-statistic $(21.01/8)/(17.94/64) = 9.37$ to an $F(8,64)$ distribution; the L*GROUP interaction is highly significant. The two laboratories cannot, therefore, be considered equivalent in their relative determinations of the various Dioxin/Furan groups and the missing values cannot be estimated meaningfully. In addition, it would make no sense to analyse the data set in Table 2 as a whole.

4. Conclusion

The data-collection program followed during the Amagerforbrænding investigation, 1985, produced both crossed and nested data. Statistical analysis of variance is a very

TABLE 9

Analysis of variance, second data set

Source of variation	Sum of squares SS	Degrees of freedom df
L	28.3208	1
GROUP	60.4166	8
L*GROUP	21.0139	8
P(L)	39.8778	8
G*P(L)	17.9434	64

useful tool for breaking down the total variability of such experimental data into interpretable components. For well-executed experiments, designed in a complete, balanced fashion, the break down into groups is unique, allowing clear conclusions to be drawn from data information. Due to experimental constraint and/or economy, fractional balanced designs can be used so that few experimental runs shed light on a relatively large number of main factors. The price is a predetermined confounding of main effects with interactions. Nested designs imply that the significance of certain effects can be tested with (usually) much less sensitivity than others. It was found that emission differences over time are significant, but less so than differences due to sample-taking methods, and even greater differences between laboratories were found. Unfortunately the two latter components cannot be compensated by some calibration constant, because the differences are of a more complex nature.

References

Box, G.E.P., Hunter, W. G. & Hunter, J. S. (1978), *Statistics for Experimenters*, Wiley, New York.

Grove, A. (1987), Dioxinmålinger på Amagerforbrænding; Dioxinemissionen i relation til fors-kellige driftsbetingelser (Dioxin measurement at Amager incinerator; the dioxin emission related to different working conditions), Arbejdsrapport fra Miljøstyrelsen No. 5, Ministry of the Environment.

Hicks, C. R. (1964), *Fundamental Concepts in the Design of Experiments*, Holt, Rinehart and Winston, New York.

Rao, C. R. (1965), *Linear Statistical Inference and Its Applications*, Wiley, New York.

Searle, S. R. (1971), *Linear Models*, Wiley, New York.

SAS Institute Inc. (1982), *SAS USER's GUIDE: Statistics*, Cary, NC, U.S.A.

THE IMPACT OF THE DIOXIN ISSUE ON RESOURCE RECOVERY IN THE UNITED STATES *

Norman Steisel †, Regina Morris ‡§ and Marjorie J. Clarke ‡

(*Received 12 March 1985*)

Alternative solutions to the solid waste disposal crisis include recycling and waste reduction and large-scale energy and materials recovery facilities (known as resource recovery and RDF, respectively). The discovery of dioxin and furan emissions from resource recovery plants has led to an intensive focus on the dioxin issue by the public, the regulators, and the builders of the plants. This paper discusses the issues concerning dioxin currently being debated by the scientific community, including dioxin and furan toxicity in animals (and extrapolation to humans), toxic equivalents, the processes of dioxin formation in resource recovery plants, the role of source separation of plastics and paper from refuse in mitigation of dioxin formation, and the roles of combustion-regulation and air-pollution control devices in the destruction and reduction of dioxin emissions. In addition, the steps that the New York City Sanitation Department has chosen for exploring the health risk of dioxin emissions (the Fred C. Hart Risk Assessment) and to reduce emissions of dioxins from its proposed resource recovery plants (both in terms of combustion regulation and control devices) are discussed.

Key Words—Resource recovery, energy recovery, dioxin (2,3,7,8-TCDD), municipal solid waste disposal, source separation, recycling, incineration, electrostatic precipitator, baghouse, scrubber, refuse-to-energy, combustion regulation, risk assessment, U.S.A.

1. A perspective on resource recovery in the U.S.A.

The solid waste disposal crisis, which arose as the result of landfills being filled to capacity and a shortage of land for new sites near expanding urban areas, has generated an increasing interest of cities throughout the United States and the world to invest in various types of resource recovery.

Waste reduction and recycling can help alleviate the crisis, but most experts agree that the total waste stream cannot feasibly be recycled, and thus, such methods must be supplemented by some other form of waste disposal. Mass burning, a technology perfected in Europe decades ago for energy recovery, is used in numerous plants now operating in the United States. Most of the mass burn plants create steam for district heating loops and for industrial processes; a few generate electricity. There are other plants which employ a variety of separation and Refuse-Derived Fuel (RDF) preparation technologies. Whilst many of the facilities in the U.S.A. will process only relatively small quantities of refuse (less than 500 tons per day), approximately 40% of the plants will process sewage sludge in addition to garbage. Some of the RDF facilities

* Prepared for: Elmia Waste Treatment 85, Fifth International Exhibition and Conferences on Waste Treatment, Recovery of Materials and Energy, Public Cleansing and Waste-Research. 23–27 September 1985, Elmia, Jöknöping, Sweden.
† Present address: Lazard Freres & Co., New York, NY 10020, U.S.A.
‡ City of New York, Department of Sanitation, NY 10013, U.S.A.
§ To whom all communication should be directed.
Waste Management & Research (1987) **5**, 381–394

will produce a number of usable products, including both pelletized and fluff refuse-derived fuel for different uses, ferrous metals, aluminium, chilled water, glass (colour sorted in some cases), methane gas, carbon monoxide, humus, compost, and corrugated and baled paper. Most plants have been constructed in urban centres and dispose of municipal waste, but some have been built on army and navy bases and on college campuses. The total investment involved in these plants is over $3.9 billion.

2. The U.S.A. debate on dioxin

In recent years, increasing attention has been focused on the issue of dioxin emissions from combustion processes. (The terms dioxins and furans refer in this paper to chlorinated products of which the 2,3,7,8-tetrachlorodibenzo-*p*-dioxin isomer is by far the most toxic.) Following the realization, in 1977, that waste incinerators were probably one source of toxic materials such as dioxins and dibenzofurans, tests were made on at least 41 such plants in nine countries including the U.S.A. and Canada. Without exception, some dioxin and furan cogeners were found in all the fly-ash and flue-gas samples taken where state-of-the-art analyses were made. However, the amounts found varied widely among the plants, even after allowance is made for variation in the solid waste firing rates. Furthermore, based on two extended tests, it was found that emission of dioxins and furans from a particular plant varies from time to time.

The dioxin issue has been raised by a number of community and environmental groups as a reason to oppose construction of resource-recovery plants in such U.S.A. cities as San Diego, California, Newark, New Jersey, and New York City, where eight plants are planned in the near future. In San Diego, for example, environmental groups have succeeded in negotiating a contract with the operator of the (as yet) unbuilt plant, in which the operator agrees to a large number of plant operating conditions and continuous monitoring of several combustion parameters and emission factors. Not only will the results of such continuous monitoring be displayed in the plant's control room, but also in the offices of the environmental regulatory agency. Environmental groups and other concerned citizens have been guaranteed access to this information. Thus, if the temperature in the furnace drops, or other combustion or emissions data indicate that dioxins might be forming in unacceptable quantities, this information will be available instantaneously to environmentalists and environmental regulatory authorities who can then order either improvements in plant operation or shut downs, as appropriate.

3. Dioxin/furan toxicity and health effects

Despite the influential voices of some community and environmental groups, conflicting opinions with the scientific community over the potential hazard of dioxin emissions have exacerbated confusion and concern in the residents of communities where new plants are being proposed. The scientific debate, concerning dioxin emissions mainly from mass burn resource recovery, centres on a number of issues which are listed below.

1. The relative toxicity of specific dioxins and furans, and the mix of these pollutants emitted in resource recovery plants, as compared with ambient levels contributed by other sources.
2. The health effects on humans from inhalation, ingestion and skin contact of various doses of dioxins and furans.

3. The process(es) of dioxin formation in resource recovery plants.
4. The role of source separation of plastics and paper from refuse, combustion-regulation and air-pollution control devices in the reduction of dioxin emissions.

To understand dioxin and furan toxicity, it is necessary to understand the differences in their molecular structure. Both dioxins and furans contain two benzene rings connected by oxygen. The substance widely referred to as 2,3,7,8-TCDD is the most toxic of a group of 75 chemically-similar materials, all referred to as polychlorinated dibenzo-*p*-dioxins. These materials differ from one another in the amount of chlorine they contain, its location in their structures, and in their toxicity. The polychlorinated dibenzofurans are quite similar to the dioxins and are frequently encountered with dioxins.

Dioxins and furans are not purposely manufactured. Certain dioxins are by-products, produced in the ppm range, when some wood preservatives and herbicides are manufactured. Dioxins and furans are also produced in trace amounts when wood, other plant materials, and a wide variety of natural and man-made organics are burned under certain conditions. They tend, therefore, to be produced when residential and other solid wastes are burned, unless precautions are taken to suppress their production. Their emission from a fire is favoured when the fire is not very hot, when the air supply and its control are inadequate to assure complete burning, and when careful provision is not made for burning the volatile combustibles which escape from the firebed with the gaseous products of combustion.

The chronic toxicity of the dioxins and furans to a variety of test animals has been examined. In these tests, sets of animals were given regular oral doses of a particular dioxin or furan over a period of time (up to two years). Lethal doses of dioxins varied considerably depending on the animal species tested. The cancer threshold rate for rats is given in two studies as 1–1.4 ng kg^{-1} body weight per day (Kociba *et al.* 1978, NCI 1980) and for mice in another study (Toth *et al.* 1979) as 1–30 ng kg^{-1} body weight per day. In many instances, the cancers affected the liver and lungs. Reproductive problems have been observed in rats and mice and changes in the immune system have been reported for mice.

It is impossible to extrapolate these results to estimate any possible effects of dioxins and furans on humans. However, data on accidental exposures to these materials can give some indication as to their toxicity to humans. Although long-term damage from accidental exposure to dioxin remains unproven, it has been known since the 1890s that chloracne in humans—an acne-like skin disfigurement which affects the face, neck and shoulders—is caused by skin contact with a wide variety of chlorinated polycyclic organic materials of which the dioxins and furans are examples. By the middle 1960s it had been determined that the factor in certain herbicides which causes chloracne in man is the most toxic of all the dioxins, namely the 2,3,7,8-tetrachloro-dibenzo-*p*-dioxin (TCDD). However, after chloracne is observed and the source of exposure is eliminated, it generally clears up in a few months and has always disappeared within two years.

The accumulating evidence from the accidents in which dioxin is known to have been involved, for example, in Nitro, West Virginia, U.S.A., and Seveso, Italy, clearly suggests that dioxin and furan exposure which is at least as severe as that in these accidents does not lead to higher than normal incidence of expected cancer, miscarriage, malformed children, or death among its victims. Furthermore, whilst the exposures have left many of the victims with temporary maladies including chloracne, liver problems, unusual hair growth, kidney problems, nervous disorders, and lack of drive and vigour, none of these difficulties has persisted. In fact, all of them seem to have disappeared within two years of the accidents. Those who are competent to judge these matters conclude with considerable confidence that humans have substantial tolerance for dioxins and furans when exposed to them topically or by inhalation.

Accidental exposure, however, only yields descriptive information of toxic effects and seldom reports information concerning levels of exposure that would provide dose–response data. In addition, industrial accidents generally involve exposure to more than one chemical. Thus information derived from human exposure cannot be readily translated to data for the establishment of emission standards. Nevertheless, clinical experience does provide qualitative descriptions of expected effects when man is exposed to large doses of TCDD.

In addition to the fact that no proven, accurate method has been developed to determine the toxicity in humans of resource recovery plant emissions of dioxin, it is also true that no means of accurately monitoring the level and type of dioxin emitted by a given resource recovery plant in an instantaneous manner has been devised. The public, then, must currently be satisfied with monitoring of surrogate combustion and emission parameters, which indicate, albeit imperfectly, the extent of dioxin emissions.

Another difficulty in determining the health effects of resource recovery plant dioxin emissions concerns their relative contribution to ambient dioxin levels because they are byproducts, produced in the ppm range, in the manufacture of some wood preservatives and herbicides. When these burn, in any fire, dioxins and furans may be given off as a result of incomplete combustion. Also when certain other natural and man-made organics are burned incompletely (i.e. wood, other plant materials), dioxin precursors can form and combine with any free chlorine present (from HCl, PVC or NaCl, for example). Thus forest fires, building fires, internal combustion engine emissions, cigarette smoke, and other products of incomplete combustion can contribute to an ambient level of dioxin and furan. As a result of this consideration, ambient levels of dioxin/furan and relative contributions to this level by these other sources, as well as resource recovery plants, is now being addressed by new studies in a number of cities. In Washington, DC and Montreal, tests of urban-air particulate content revealed significant ambient levels of dioxins and, at least in the case of Washington, this cannot be attributed to emissions of a resource recovery plant because none exists there. With respect to the Montreal data, compiled and analysed by R. C. Lao, Environment Canada (1985), unusually low levels of dioxins were found in the emissions of a resource recovery incinerator there, and studies are now being designed to determine the extent of automobile emissions as a source of dioxins found in ambient samples. If further research supports this possibility, then the incremental addition by resource recovery plants to ambient concentrations, and hence the degree of health hazard which can be attributed only to resource recovery, will be even harder to estimate—a further source of confusion to the public.

Despite the confusion with respect to human health risk from exposure to the resource recovery produced dioxin emissions, resulting from the paucity of usable and accurate data, governmental agencies have endeavoured to research this issue based on literature surveys (to fix a number for human dose response to dioxin) and limited sampling for resource recovery produced dioxin emissions. In the early 1980s, USEPA tested six resource recovery plants for dioxin emissions. The dioxin emissions were modelled to determine possible ambient dioxin concentrations, and the human health impacts from these figures were modelled to determine the number of cancers per million inhabitants based on the EPA Cancer Assessment Groups dinearized multi-stage extrapolation model. (This model takes into account the differences in the conditions of laboratory experiments on animals and the probable environmental exposure conditions which man faces.) Using this method, EPA found that the range of dioxins continually produced by five of the plants would not be hazardous to human health.

A new study by F. C. Hart Associates (Lipsky *et al.* 1985), commissioned by the City of New York, which assesses potential human health risk from a resource recovery plant to be built in Brooklyn, also concluded that emission levels from the plant (assumed to be similar to those emitted by the Chicago N.W. plant, one of the better-operated of the five plants tested and analysed by EPA, and to a plant in Zurich) would not pose a serious risk to human health because such emissions would only result in ambient concentrations of 0.0257 pg TCDD m^{-3} or 29% of the New York State guideline of 0.092 pg TCDD m^{-3}.

To provide an independent review of the Hart study, and to ensure its accuracy and impartiality, a nine-member panel of internationally renowned experts on resource recovery produced dioxin and its human health impacts, scrutinized the study. Most members concurred with the report's conservative methodology and its worst-case upper bound excess cancer risk of less than 5.9×10^{-6}. The conservative assumptions, on which this cancer risk figure was based, included the following:

(1) No credit was taken for the improvement in dioxin removal to be effected by the baghouse and scrubbers planned for the plant vs. the removal effected by the ESP-equipped Chicago and Zurich plants.

(2) No credit was taken for the effect of auxiliary burners and other combustion-control equipment effective in maximizing complete combustion, and hence destruction of organic compounds.

(3) Risks were calculated based on maximum 24 h a day exposure, over a 70-year lifetime at the point of maximum impact.

(4) Assessment of three potential pathways of exposure: inhalation of gaseous or particulate emissions, ingestion, and dermal absorption of dioxin-laden particulates deposited on indoor and outdoor surfaces.

(5) Application of a toxic equivalency multiplier (equal to 59) to account for potential toxic effects of all dioxin and furan compounds that may be present along with 2,3,7,8-TCDD. The multiplier is based on enzyme induction anlayses done by the Swiss and provides an estimate of the non-carcinogenic toxicity of the complex mixture of PCDDs and PCDFs compared with the concentration of 2,3,7,8-TCDD. This equivalency factor was also used to estimate carcinogenic equivalency as a worst-case assumption although such an application is speculative.

(6) No losses of PCDDs were assumed through volatilization, photolysis or other degradation processes, or via losses due to rainfall runoff.

(7) Indoor ambient air quality was assumed to equal outdoor air quality.

(8) The most conservative cancer-risk extrapolation model was used to estimate an upper bound to increased cancer risk.

(9) Conservative assumptions for bioavailability and rates of ingestion and dermal absorption were used to estimate worst-case daily uptake of PCDDs.

The Hart team also compared the Brooklyn Navy Yard emissions with standards set elsewhere which were based on different assumptions. For example, the guidelines developed in Ontario, Canada assumed that all of the dioxins are as toxic as the most toxic isomer (2,3,7,8-TCDD) and that all of the furans are assumed to be 1/50th as toxic as 2,3,7,8-TCDD. The acceptable human dose is calculated by taking the lowest dose that has produced any observable effects in laboratory animals and then dividing that dose by 1000 as a safety factor. This is similar to the approach followed by the Ontario Ministry of the Environment and the Netherlands in defining safe levels for dioxin exposure, although the Netherlands used a safety factor of 250 (RIPH 1982). The predicted maximum impact on ambient air quality for the Brooklyn Navy Yard plant would be of the order of 0.007% of the Netherlands acceptable daily intake guideline and would be 0.6% of the Ontario provisional guideline using conservative assumptions.

4. Dioxin control via source separation

In addition to the debate on the health effects and the toxicity of dioxins and furans, another issue in the scientific debate regarding dioxin from resource recovery plants is the mechanism(s) of dioxin formation in the furnace and elsewhere in the plant. Some groups maintain that because chlorine is required for the formation of chlorinated compounds such as dioxins and furans, reduction of chlorine in the waste stream going into a resource recovery plant, by removal of certain plastic products, may result in some reduction in the chlorinated organic compound mass emissions (CARB 1984). According to this theory, PCDDs and PCDFs are formed in the combustion plasma, the gas plume, or possibly in the stack or pollution control devices when specific thermal-degradation products arising from combustion of such non-chlorinated organics as lignin (the non-cellulose component of vegetable matter that makes up 20–30% of the dry weight of the woody tissues of plants) combine with chlorine. Lignin degrades at around 600 °C to produce predioxin molecular structures such as phenols. If temperatures and other oxidizing conditions in the combustion zone are not sufficiently high to destroy the organic precursors, then the opportunity would exist for the formation of dioxin and furan via the mechanism of chlorination of the phenols and their subsequent combination to yield PCDDs and PCDFs.

When discussing whether source-separation programs for removing plastic from refuse would accomplish the goal of reducing chlorine in the flue gas, and hence, dioxin emissions from resource recovery plants, it is useful to examine the results of a study of dioxin emissions done by Karasek in Paris (personal communication). It was reported that, when PVC pellets were fed at a rate of three times the normal PVC content of the raw refuse into a well-oxygenated waterwall resource recovery plant in Paris at a high temperature (950 °C), there were no differences in the fly-ash levels of PCDDs as compared to the combustion of normal refuse by this facility. Assuming that the Paris refuse contained significant quantities of lignin, the explanation for this result could be that the high temperature and well-oxygenated conditions in the furnace ensured complete combustion of the organics present, including any dioxin or furan precursors that may have been formed, so that the amount of chlorine in the flue gas would not have been critical to the production of the level of PCDDs observed.

Moreover, theoretical kinetic analysis by Dr Walter Shaub (personal communication) indicates that a reaction between HCl or Cl_2 and organic precursors under the conditions that exist in an incinerator, is unlikely in the existing time frame. Furthermore, PVC only accounts for about 50% of the chlorine content of municipal waste. Therefore, unless dioxin formation is sensitive to the concentration of chlorine, removal of PVC would not be expected to materially affect dioxin and furan emissions.

Given that there is no positive evidence that removing PVC would have any effect on dioxin emissions, it is necessary to know whether other sources of chlorine in waste would be available in sufficient quantities to combine with precursor organics to eventually form dioxins. Experiments on HCl formation in incinerators have shown that even when all of the plastic is removed from the waste prior to combustion, significant concentrations of HCl are still present in the flue gases (Nchida & Kamo 1983). Wood burning experiments have demonstrated that chlorophenols and chloro-benzenes, which can combine to form dioxins and furans, can be produced without the addition of HCl or PVC or Cl_2 during combustion, (Choudry *et al.* 1982, Olie *et al.* 1983). From this information, it seems likely that removal of plastics from waste would probably leave sufficient quantities of chlorine in the waste stream to form dioxins and furans. In addition to the probability that plastics separation would not affect the quantities of dioxin and furan emitted, and hence would not be a useful expenditure of resources, other statistics, such as those presented earlier, show that U.S.A. RDF and separation plants have a poor record of operation (60% of separation plants have closed vs. 17% of mass burn plants closed). Thus the hypothesis that separation of chlorine-containing PVC from the waste stream would reduce dioxin emissions has neither been validated scientifically, nor demonstrated technologically in the U.S.A.

Another issue under current discussion in the U.S.A. dioxin debate is whether dioxins and furans can be formed either in the pollution control devices or in the stack, which are well beyond the combustion zone in the furnace. According to this hypothesis, these compounds are formed by chlorination on the surfaces of fly-ash particles containing dioxin precursors, and are then desorbed into the vapour phase in the stack or control devices and released as emissions. A study by Rghei *et al.* (1982), in which 1,2,3,4-TCDD was vaporized over fly-ash at 100–300 °C, resulted in total adsorption by the fly-ash with no desorption taking place. Shaub's theoretical calculations would indicate dioxin would begin to desorb from fly-ash only when the temperature is raised above 400 °C. In a follow-up study by Eiceman & Rghei (1982), 1,2,3,4-TCDD adsorbed onto fly-ash reacted with HCl resulting in some higher chlorinated isomers of dioxin, but did not result in a net increase in dioxins. Only when the temperature was raised above 400 °C did some of the dioxin begin to desorb from the fly-ash and combine with chlorine from the HCl, resulting in some higher chlorinated isomers of dioxin, but not a net increase in dioxins. This mechanism would not contribute to formation of new dioxin under normal conditions because temperatures in the stack and pollution-control devices are normally well below 400 °C, but may increase the chlorination of the dioxins and furans already present.

5. Dioxin control via optimal combustion

Other aspects of the dioxin debate in the U.S.A. centre on the quantity of dioxins produced by resource recovery plants and on what degree the quantity of emissions varies with combustion conditions in the furnace and emissions control devices present. To date, the data available for such correlations is not extensive. This kind of in-formation is important to demonstrate the effects on combustion of low temperatures, wet refuse, insufficient or too much oxygen, and insufficient mixing or residence time. Only a few resource recovery plants around the world have been tested for dioxin emissions but, although for some of these temperature and/or oxygen conditions were also taken, the place in the furnace at which the temperature probe was placed was not uniform in all tests, and in almost all cases the temperature and other combustion conditions, when recorded at all, varied over the several hours during which dioxin sampling took place. These differences in sampling protocol make it difficult to make accurate correlations of dioxin emissions with causative factors. Since the quantity of dioxins emitted from a given resource recovery plant varies over time depending on the combustion factors mentioned, it is no surprise that dioxin emissions from resource recovery plants tested worldwide vary considerably. At this stage it is only possible to make generalizations about the correct set of operating conditions needed to minimize dioxin formation and/or emission, for the reasons given. Many in the scientific community agree that temperature is an important factor in dioxin formation and destruction in an incinerator, and that the formation temperature of dioxin is in the vicinity of 500 °C and a conservative, practical estimate of the destruction temperature is at least 900 °C. Destruction at these temperatures requires that the furnace is well oxygenated and that the residence time of the toxic gases at these conditions is at least 1 s.

However, temperature alone cannot be used as a reliable measure of combustion efficiency. First, temperature measured at a single point cannot tell us the spatial temperature distribution within the combustion zone or the temperature/residence profile of the incinerator. Second, in addition to high temperature, there must be a high degree of turbulence to ensure effective mixing within the combustion and the avoidance of cold spots, as for example, along the incinerator walls. Finally, there must be an adequate supply of oxygen to maximize the destruction of the organic compound of concern.

Oxygen is very important in the combustion of organic compounds: if oxygen content is that of air (ca. 20%), then the temperature required to extinguish many organic compounds (see, for example, the extinction curves for pentachlorobiphenyl illustrated in Fig. 1) is hundreds of degrees less than if there is no oxygen present (Hasselriis 1985). The combination of the overfire and underfire air provided also affects combustion, as insufficient air results in low oxygen or pyrolysis conditions, and too much air can lower the temperature in the combustion zone. Preliminary data taken from resource recovery plants seem to suggest that conditions optimal for small emissions of dioxin and furan are: temperatures above 900 °C, in the presence of 7–10% oxygen, or 50–100% excess air, and residence times of at least 1 s (Hasselriis, personal communication). To ensure the destruction of organics in flue gas, some of the newer resource recovery plants under design are incorporating auxiliary burners, devices which burn fossil fuel, when necessary, to keep the temperature in the combustion zone at a preset, minimum level. The auxiliary burners are used during start-up or with unusually wet or low BTU waste—under normal conditions the temperature is regulated by the control of the waste feed and combustion air.

As no device has yet been invented that will instantaneously measure and monitor dioxin and furan emissions in the flue gas of a resource recovery plant (sampling and analysis of dioxin usually requires many months), the current strategy adopted increasingly by plant designers, operators and by regulators at all levels, has been to utilize new microprocessor technology to monitor and control automatically certain combustion conditions, such as temperature and oxygen, as well as to monitor and control the production of other surrogate parameters, such as carbon monoxide, which have been shown to respond similarly to dioxin to changes in refuse composition and operating conditions.

The process of destruction of toxic organics is aided by means of superior furnace design, involving multi-stage combustion zones. If the unburned material which escapes

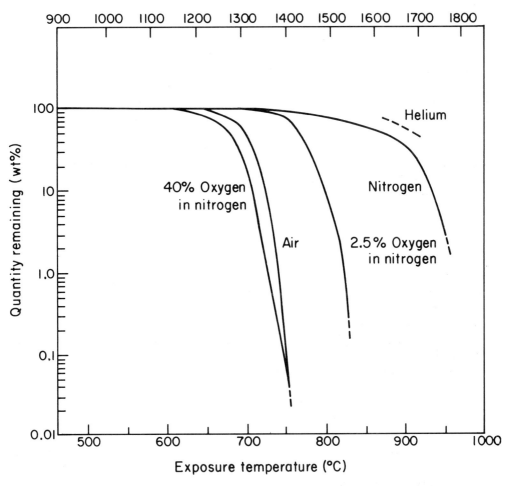

Fig. 1. Effect of oxygen concentration on destruction of pentachlorobiphenyl (Hasselriis 1985).

the primary combustion zone above the grate without passing through the flame is subsequently fed into, or through, a small, well-mixed and oxygenated chamber or narrowing in the furnace which is kept at high temperature, the increased opportunity for thermal destruction would likely result in far greater reductions in dioxin, furan and precursor emissions from the furnace. Although most scientists agree that combustion regulation can minimize emission of large amounts of toxic organics, the destruction of all dioxins and furans in resource recovery emissions cannot presently be assured by these means alone.

6. Dioxin control devices

It is postulated by a number of experts in the field that the capture of any toxic organics remaining in the flue gas after passage through the combustion zone in the furnace should be possible by means of air-pollution control devices such as electrostatic precipitators (ESPs) baghouses, and scrubbers. This theory is based on the hypothesis that particulate control can reduce dioxin and furan emissions and is characterized by the following assumptions.

(1) Dioxins and furans bind extremely tightly to fly-ash particles under normal conditions (theoretical experiments by Shaub, U.S. National Bureau of Standards and practical experiments confirm this).

(2) Many studies report that toxic organics tend to bind/coat preferentially to finer particles (< 1–2 μm in diameter).

(3) Such fine particles, when inhaled, are capable of penetrating the lungs to the alveoli, where acidic conditions exist and constant gas exchange with the bloodstream occurs.

(4) Because there are no cilia in the alveoli, there is no mechanism to remove fine particles coated with toxic organics from this pulmonary region, therefore, residence times for such particles are quite long.

(5) Thus, some scientists infer that there is a long-term possibility for insoluble compounds (dioxin and furan are examples) to enter the bloodstream via this mechanism (Natusch et al. 1974).

(6) For inhalation of those larger particles on which dioxin has adsorbed, and which cannot enter the alveoli due to their size, ciliar sweeping and mucous coughing mechanisms can result in ingestion of a fraction of the dioxin/furan entering the lungs.

Therefore, if dioxins and furans escape the combustion zone, there is the opportunity for them to condense/adsorb onto fly-ash particles in the flue gas as the gas enters the cooler regions of the boiler equipment. If the cooled gas is passed through the stages of an electrostatic precipitator (ESP), a device capable of removing particles by means of charging them and attracting them to collection plates, then those dioxins and furans on the surfaces of particles can be removed from the flue gas and toxic emissions will be reduced. However, ESPs are generally not capable of consistent particulate-removal efficiencies in the fine-particle range (< 2 μm, see Fig. 2) unless three or more stages of plates are used (increasing their expense considerably). In addition, ESP performance usually decreases dramatically with fluctuations in particle size, particle concentration and density in the gas, moisture and temperature, and resistivity of the fly-ash. For these reasons, ESPs have fallen out of favour in the U.S.A. as the unquestioned best means of particulate removal from resource recovery emissions.

Fabric filters, or baghouses, operate in a manner similar to a giant vacuum cleaner, drawing flue gas through woven or felted fabrics, on which fly-ash impacts and collects. The longer the baghouse is in operation, the thicker, is the ash caked on the fabric, and the better the filtering efficiency. After a certain period of time, the bagcake becomes too thick, the energy required to drive flue gas through the fabric increases, and the bag is cleaned and the cycle begins again. As experience increases with baghouses, or fabric filters, and further research and development into improved fabrics and baghouse design produces favorable results, and because baghouses have consistently demonstrated the capability of superior collection efficiencies (above 99% for all sizes of particles) despite fluctuating flue gas volumes, particulate concentrations and temperature excursions, the preference on the part of certain state regulatory agencies for new facilities to be designed to incorporate them is becoming increasingly prevalent. As a result of these factors, the current trend in the U.S.A. resource recovery industry has been moving towards their use in new plants. That baghouses are usually more efficient at particulate removal then ESPs (see Fig. 2) would mean that dioxin

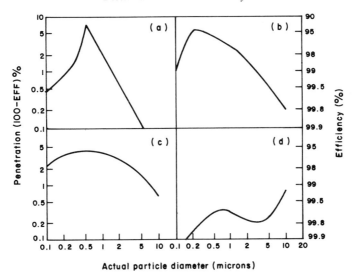

Fig. 2. Typical fractional efficiencies for existing collectors (EPRI 1978). Typical hot-side ESP (a); typical American cold-side ESP (b); typical European cold-side ESP (c); typical fabric filter (d).

removal efficiency would be higher under the above hypothesis if baghouses were used. This is due to three mechanisms: (1) removal of particles on which dioxins and furans have already formed; (2) the removal of particulates containing precursor compounds, thereby further limiting any potential formation of dioxin and furan after the control device; and (3) removal of particulate matter and thereby further reducing the available surface area for any potential formation reaction after the gas passes through the baghouse.

Another means of amplifying the efficiency of dioxin removal in a baghouse that is postulated by some scientists, is effected by passing the flue gas through a dry scrubber prior to the baghouse. Dry scrubbers, designed mainly to capture acid gases such as HCl, SO_2, HF and H_2SO_4 by means of injection of alkaline particles into the flue gas stream, may increase the ability of fly-ash particles containing dioxin to agglomerate, which would increase the likelihood of their collection in the baghouse and improve overall efficiency of this device. However more experimental data is required to test this hypothesis. Furthermore, since "dry" scrubbers involve the use of an alkaline slurry containing small amounts of water which would be evaporated, they decrease the temperature of flue gas and thereby increase the condensation of dioxin and furan vapours onto fly-ash particles prior to their collection in the baghouse and protecting the baghouse from fire-inducing hot cinders. Since the decrease in temperature has the ironic effect of decreasing the plume height from the stack, and this increases the ground-level concentrations of pollutants to above what they would have been without the temperature drop, some scientists have suggested that the introduction of water along with the dry lime be minimized. This may result in a design tradeoff between plume rise, acid removal efficiency, and scrubber economy.

As was mentioned earlier, at the advice of responsible environmental organizations, the first proposed resource recovery plant for New York City, to be located at the Brooklyn Navy Yard, will include many of the mitigation measures just outlined (baghouse, dry scrubber, auxiliary burners, combustion monitoring devices). As a result of their inclusion in the design, the projected dioxin emissions from the facility should be minimized. Even without taking credit for the increased efficiency to be afforded by the baghouse and dry scrubber, the dioxin emission predicted for the plant, as given in the Draft Environmental Impact Statement (DEIS), is well within the previous New York State guideline for RCDD (9.2×10^{-8} μg m^{-3}). Thus, given the conservatism incorporated in the DEIS emission figure, the Department of Sanitation feels confident that the risk to human health from the plant's dioxin emissions will be in the acceptable range.

7. Conclusions

Based on the information presented, it is clear that the scientific community is not in complete agreement on many aspects of the resource recovery dioxin debate. This is largely due to the paucity of usable data from operating resource recovery plants (i.e. complete combustion information and dioxin samples taken over periods of time during which combustion conditions are held constant) and, up until recently, lack of agreement on sampling and analysis protocol. Fortunately, the American Society of Mechanical Engineers (ASME) has recently developed a proposed protocol which was long awaited by the scientific community and which is now under review. If the new protocol is used universally, once it is finally accepted, then differences among sets of data due only to the use of non-uniform methods will be eliminated.

It is also fortunate that some new combustion research, pertaining to dioxin creation and destruction in operating resource recovery incinerators, is ongoing and in preparation by the Canadian government and a number of State governments. Scientists attempting to correlate dioxin emissions with combustion conditions have recognized that the kind of dioxin testing previously conducted on resource recovery plants, which was designed with the purpose of quantifying the dioxins produced in a given incinerator, but giving no indication as to the cause, is of little use in determining means of minimizing emissions, there has been, therefore, an impetus for the funding of new research designed to address these issues. Comprehensive research by the Canadian government has been conducted at a Tricil resource recovery plant at Prince Edward Island and will also be conducted over the next two years at the old incinerators in Quebec City (after retrofit) and Hamilton.

Also ongoing at present is research by the New York State Department of Environmental Conservation at six resource recovery plants of different design within the State of New York. Although some of the New York State program does not yet involve sufficient funding to conduct the kind of rigorous combustion research which is necessary to determine how to minimize dioxin/furan emissions, such funding is currently under consideration.

Of greater promise is the testing program of the ASME which was established for the purpose of conducting combustion research at a numbr of facilities, not only to ascertain combustion conditions that minimize dioxin emissions, but also to learn the effects of varying refuse composition (i.e. moisture and PVC content) on emissions of dioxin and similar toxic organics. A series of dioxin tests, funded by the states of New York, Florida, California, Massachusetts and others, will be run at a number of previously selected steady-state fuel composition and combustion conditions. Testing at the first site, a Vicon resource recovery plant in Pittsfield, Massachusetts, is planned to be undertaken in the summer and fall of 1985 with results available early in the following year. If these tests are successful and concrete evidence is obtained to substantiate the theory that combustion of refuse at high temperatures in the presence of oxygen, proper mixing and sufficient residence times will result in no or very little dioxin/furan emissions, despite changing feedstock composition, then the resource recovery industry will have made considerable progress in resolving the dioxin problem.

One additional type of research which will be helpful in determining how to minimize dioxin emissions, and which has been undertaken in Tsushima, Japan, involves testing which is designed to demonstrate the efficiency of various pollution control devices (baghouses, ESPs, scrubbers) in removing dioxin from the flue gas. (Such a test is soon to be completed on a scrubber–baghouse retrofitted facility in Quebec City. Preliminary results indicate excellent dioxin removal efficiencies.) To make the results of such a test a reliable indicator of removal efficiency, the combustion conditions would have to be strictly controlled to steady state both before and during the dioxin sampling, and dioxins would have to be sampled before and after each pollution control device. Undertaking this precaution would avoid such questionable results as those from Tsushima, where it appeared that the baghouse was manufacturing dioxins, because before and during the testing at Tshushima combustion conditions varied widely, resulting in inconclusive test results. The consultant has since withdrawn his draft report primarily because of these anomalies in the test protocol.

To facilitate the research proposed in this discussion as well as the optimal functioning of resource recovery plants in the future, funding the development of new equipment capable of detecting extremely minute dioxins instantaneously in a flue gas stream would be of great value.

In addition to conducting the research initiatives outlined above, in order to maximize the benefit to be derived from such programs a cooperative atmosphere should be fostered among interested parties, including resource recovery facility personnel, consultants (both involved in the research and not), governmental officials on all levels, professional societies, academics, and community groups. Only full disclosure of all test results and peer review will improve general understanding of the processes at work in dioxin formation, destruction and containment, and in turn, foster the public trust which is so important in siting, permitting and constructing resource recovery facilities.

References

CARB, California Air Resources Board 1984, *Air Pollution Control at Resource Recovery Facilities*, Final Goldenrod version, 24 May 1984.

Choudhry, G. G., Olie, K. & Hutzinger, O. (1982), Mechanisms in the thermal formation of chlorinated compounds including polychlorinated dibenzo-*p*-dioxins and polychlorodibenzofurans in urban incinerator emissions. In: *Chlorinated Dioxins and Related Compounds: Impact on the Environment*. Pergamon Press, New York.

EPRI (1978) Electric Power Research Institute, *Economics of Fabric Filters vs. Precipitators*. Denver, CO.

Eiceman, G. & Rghei, H. (1982), Chlorination reactions of 1,2,3,4-tetrachlorodibenzo-*p*-dioxin on fly ash with HCl in air, *Chemosphere, 11, 833–839.*

Hasselriis, F. (1985), Waste energy recovery, *1985 EST Yearbook*, McGraw Hill, New York.

Kociba, R. H. *et al.*, (1978) Results of a two-year, chronic toxicity and oncogenicity study of 2,3,7,8-TCDD in rats, *Toxicology and Applied Pharmacology, 46, 1279.*

Lao, R. C. (1985), Cleanup, Separation and Analytical Procedures for PCDD/PCDF contents and environmental samples: presented before the Division of Environmental Chemistry, *American Chemical Society Symposium on Chlorinated Dioxins and Dibenzofurans in the Total Environment III*, 29 April–3 May 1985, Miami, FL, U.S.A.

Lipsky, D., Boldt, K. R., Manto, M. S. & Robal, R. R. (1985), *Assessment of Potential Public Health Impacts Associated with Predicted Emissions of Polychlorinated Dibenzo-Dioxins and Polychlorinated Dibenzo-Furans from the Brooklyn Navy Yard Resource Recovery Facility.* F. C. Hart Assoc. Inc., New York.

NCI (1980), National Cancer Institute, Bioassay of 2,3,7,8-TCDD in rats, *DHHS No. NIH80-1765.*

Natusch, D. *et al.* (1974), Urban aerosol toxicity: the influence of particle size, *Science, 186, no. 4165.*

Nchida, S. & Kamo, H. (1983), Reaction kinetics of formation of HCl in municipal refuse incinerators, *Industrial Engineering Chemistry Process Des. Dev. 22,* 144–49.

Olie, K., Berg, Hutzinger, O. (1983), Formation and fate of PCDD and PCDF from combustion processes, *Chemosphere, 12 627–636.*

Rghei, H. O., *et al.* (1982), Adsorption and thermal reactions of 1,2,3,4-TCDD on fly ash from municipal incinerator, *Chemosphere, 11, 569–76.*

RIPH (1982), Royal Institute for Public Health, Bilthoven, The Netherlands. *Report DOC/LCM 300/292.*

Toth, K., *et al* (1979), Carginogenicity testing of the herbicide 2,4,5-trichlorophenoxy ethanol containing dioxin or of pure dioxin in Swiss mice, *Nature, 278, 548.*

REPORTS

All of the following Reports are based on papers presented at the ISWA–WHO–DAKOFA Specialized Seminar *Emissions of Trace Organics from Municipal Solid Waste Incinerators*, Copenhagen, 20–22 January 1987. References to authors in the Reports are all to papers in this issue of *Waste Management & Research*.

REPORT:
PRODUCTION AND CHARACTERIZATION OF TRACE ORGANIC EMISSIONS IN SWEDEN. By Jan G. T. Bergström and Kristofer Warman, Environmental Consultants at Studsvik, S-611 82 Nyköping, Sweden.

1. Introduction

During the last five years, significant progress has been made in many countries to improve the waste incineration process which, in all Swedish plants, is combined with energy production. The energy produced is used mostly for district heating. In Sweden, the DRAV project has underlined the importance of optimization of the combustion process (Bergvall 1985). During waste incineration, a very efficient oxidation of the organic substances takes place. The particle size of waste varies and there is a big difference in composition. Despite this, usually less than 2% of the organic matter in the waste leaves the furnace with the slag and fly ash (see Brunner *et al.* in this issue). More than 99.5% of the burnt waste is oxidized into carbon dioxide and water. The non-oxidized gases which leave the furnace along with the flue gas consist mainly of carbon monoxide and the same type of light hydrocarbons that occur with all incineration. Waste incineration is notable, in comparison with wood fuel firing, for its higher chlorine content. About 75% of the chlorine in the fuel occurs as HCl in flue gas. Less than 0.1% of the chlorine produces chlorinated aromatics. The reactions which form these organic micro-compounds are generally unknown.

Polychlorinated dibenzodioxins (PCDD) and dibenzofurans (PCDF) comprise only a small part of the chlorinated aromatics that are produced. Despite this, they attract a large amount of interest. Of a total of more than 200 possible PCDDs and PCDFs, authorities in Sweden have chosen to describe the emission by a weighted mean value of 12 isomers which are considered to be especially toxic according to a model developed by Eadon *et al.* (1983). The TCDD equivalents that are released with the flue gases from different incinerators amount to between 1 and 50 ng m^{-3} of flue gas (see Ahlborg & Victorin in this issue). Taking into consideration the uncertainty of the method of measurement, the differences are very small. The incineration conditions have a greater influence on the emission of many other organic trace compounds, such as polycyclic aromatic hydrocarbons (PAH), than on PCDD/PCDF (see Benested & Oehme in this issue).

PCDDs and PCDFs are present on dust particles and separated with the fly ash to a much higher degree than many other compounds formed during the combustion. The emission of PCDDs and PCDFs can effectively be reduced by an efficient flue gas cleaning system, however, flue gas cleaning does not reduce the quantity of pollutants fed with the wastes or formed in the incinerator. Flue gas cleaning prevents the

Waste Management & Research (1987) **5**, 395–435

spreading of certain pollutants with the flue gases. It is generally accepted that the pollutants are less harmful in solid or liquid products than as gases.

Most of the studies on waste incineration report only on the emission of pollutants and do not report pollutants adsorbed on the ashes. Therefore, it is difficult to use these studies to confirm if production of organic micro-pollutants, such as polyaromatic hydrocarbons, chlorobenzenes, chlorophenols, PCDDs and PCDFs, will be minimized by the same operational parameters. Very few of the reported studies of emissions of PCDDs and PCDFs are documented in such a way that they are comparable (Lindfors *et al.* 1985). This makes it even more difficult to deal with the pollutants of greatest concern.

We have carried out measurements on several municipal waste heating plants in Sweden during the last few years using the same sampling and analytical methods on each plant. In this paper we present a comprehensive evaluation of organic micro-pollutants from different combustion conditions and fuel compositions.

2. Sampling and analyses

2.1. *Furnace operation*

The operational studies carried out by DRAV followed a procedure for optimizing the combustion process (Bergström 1985). The experience from that study has been used for characterization of the firing conditions during the sampling period and the organic micro-compounds produced in the furnace and boiler.

The furnace load and heat input with the waste were calculated. Furnace temperature, flow and distribution of combustion air were measured. The amount of combustibles in slag and fly ash were checked during the test. Excess oxygen (O_2) from the boiler, carbon dioxide (CO_2) and carbon monoxide (CO) in the stack were recorded continuously. Operational parameters and the flue gas composition were stored in a computer, as average values for five minutes.

The combustion efficiency (CE) was calculated as a percentage:

$$CE = [1 \times (CO/CO_2)] \times 100$$

At 10% CO_2, the percentage CO is $10 - (CE/10)$. The CE describes a summarized final result of the entire combustion process in all parts of the furnace and the boiler. CE as function of excess oxygen in the combustion gas from a grate fired furnace will generate a curve of the type shown in Fig. 1. The CE and O_2 for each five minutes, presented according to the figure, show the combustion stability and oxidation rate during the sampling time. Chlorine content in waste is usually unknown but the concentration of chlorides is measured in the flue gas from the boiler.

2.2. *Sampling*

The sampling system for organic micro-compounds in the flue gas was developed by Studsvik to enable isokinetic sampling with all glass equipment. The Studsvik sampling train is given in Bergvall & Hult (1985) and in Oberg *et al.* (1985).

The interchangeable probe was extended into the oven module which was kept at 160°C during sampling. The oven contained a variable-range cyclone and a high-purity tissue quartz thimble filter. After leaving the filter, the flue gas was drawn through a high-efficiency cooler, a condensate collector, and an XAD-2 sorbent trap. The coolant

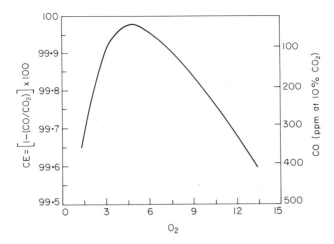

Fig. 1. Combustion efficiency as a function of the excess oxygen.

was maintained at a temperature below $-10°C$ so that the temperature of the gas entering the XAD-2 adsorbent bed did not exceed 5–10°C. At the end of the sampling run the probe and the cooler were washed with acetone; the residue was then treated as a part of the sample. The flue gas volumes were between 10 and 20 m^3 in each sample. The sampling and analytical procedure followed closely the Nordic Standard method described by Jansson & Bergvall in this issue.

2.3. *Sample treatment*

The samples were transported to the laboratory as soon as possible after collection. Internal standards were added to the samples before extraction. The sampling equipment fractionated the material into three parts: particles, condensate and matter adsorbed on XAD-2 resin. All three parts were extracted separately with appropriate solvents, and all three extracts were combined. Acidic components, e.g. phenols, were extracted with water at pH 12 and recovered by extraction at pH 1. The remaining neutral/basic fraction was analysed for chlorinated aromatic hydrocarbons. In both fractions the "total" amount of organic matter was determined by gas chromatography (GC)/FID and the peak area of all compounds eluting after *n*-nonane were compared with the peak areas of the internal standards. The results of the "total amount of organics RI > 900" were not adjusted by relative response factors for different compounds. Chlorinated benzenes were determined in the neutral/basic fraction by GC/ECD or by GC/single ion monitoring (SIM). In addition, PAH and PCB were determined by GC/SIM.

Dioxins and related compounds were determined after clean up on alumina according to Buser (1975). Fractions containing PCDD/PCDF were analysed by GC/SIM. At least two ions were monitored for each PCDD/PCDF isomer using the electron impact mode. The system separated all toxic isomers except 1,2,3,7,8-PnCDF/1,2,3,4,8-PnCDF and 1,2,3,4,7,8-HxCDF/1,2,3,4,7,9-HxCDF. Quantification was done by the internal standard method. The recoveries were calculated for the surrogates added to the samples. Conpensation was done for the isomers with the same number of chlorine atoms per molecule as the number of chlorine atoms in the spike.

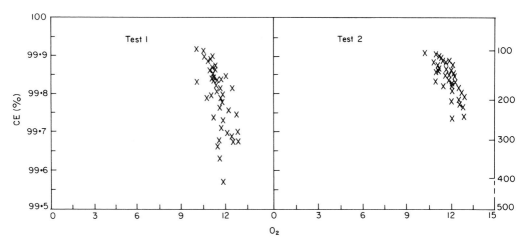

Fig. 2. CE and excess oxygen during sampling.

TABLE 1

Organic micro-pollutants in flue gas samples (μg/ standard m^3) corrected to 10% CO_2

	Test	
	1	2
CE	99.80	99.85
CE	99.64	99.78
Total organics (RI > 900)	140	100
Total PAH	1.3	0.5
Total chlorobenzenes	17	8.0
Hexachlorobenzene	5.3	2.6
Total chlorophenols	25	8.0
Pentachlorophenol	1.3	0.7
Total TCDD	1.9	0.9
2,3,7,8-TCDD	0.5	0.2
Total PeCDD	18	6.9
1,2,3,7,8-PeCDD	1.2	0.6
Total TCDF	38	15
2,3,7,8-TCDF	3.8	1.9
Total PeCDF	58	25
1,2,3,7,8-PeCDF	7.1	3.5
TCDD equivalents (Eadon)	7	4

3. Results

The test results from different plants show the same three factors to be of great importance when limiting the production of organic micro-compounds in the furnace and boiler. Combustion efficiency, CE, is the most important factor influencing the

TABLE 2

Influence of combustion efficiency on the production of TCDD-equivalents

Number of five-minute periods with CE < 99.9% during sampling	TCDD-equivalents (Eadon) ($ng\ m^{-3}$)
9	44
4	9
2	3
0	2

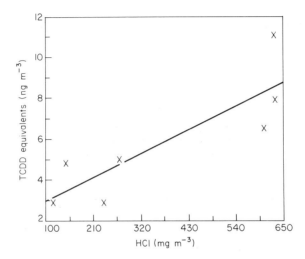

Fig. 3. TCDD equivalents related to the HCl concentration in the flue gas.

production of all kinds of aromatic compounds in the flue gas. Figure 2 shows the relationship between CE and oxygen concentration calculated as averages for five-minute periods. The results were obtained during the normal operation of an older waste heating plant in Sweden. This furnace was operated with a large excess of air. The organic micro-components found in the flue gas are given in Table 1.

The analyses presented in Table 1 show that test 2 gives lower concentrations of all components in the flue gas. The difference in CE average is not significant, but during test number 2 there was no five-minute period with CE lower than 99.78%. In the authors' opinion, the number of periods with CO peaks is very important. We consider CE ⩾ 99.9%, i.e. 100 ppm CO adjusted to 10% CO_2, to be a high combustion efficiency for ordinary grate fired units. During such operating conditions the frequency of CO peaks has a great influence on the production of aromatic compounds, including PCDD/PCDF. Table 2 shows the influence of CO peaks on the production of TCDD equivalents in another waste heating plant equipped with a high efficiency flue gas cleaning. The values in Table 2 represent PCDD/PCDF concentration after the boiler but before flue gas cleaning. After cleaning, the emission of TCDD equivalents with the flue gas was less than 0.1 ng m³ at 10% CO_2 in all four tests.

The results show a co-variation of different aromatic micropollutants produced in the furnace and the boiler. Seven tests in one waste heating plant show that combustion conditions which result in small amounts of PCDD/PCDFs also produce low concentrations of PAH and the chlorobenzenes. We assume that the chlorine content in the waste has been at a normal level for Swedish municipal solid waste. The chloride concentrations in the flue gas after the boilers have certainly been in the range 600–1000 mg m^{-3} sd at 10% CO_2 calculated as HCl.

In 1986 the opportunity arose to carry out a number of tests sponsored by the National Energy Administration at the waste heating plant in Borlänge. We were able to operate the furnace with constant load and different fuel mixtures. We used RDF and different amounts of added waste wood fuels to dilute the Cl in the RDF. The combustion efficiency was not quite the same during all the tests, but it was possible to demonstrate the effect of chlorine on dioxin production (Fig. 3, see also Öberg *et al.* 1985).

It was possible to make a good prediction of the chlorinated micro-pollutants present in the flue gas using the factors CE and HCl content. A third factor that was found to be important was excess air, measured as O_2, in the flue gas. However, because CE and O_2 content are highly correlated in the range 5–12% O_2, as shown in Figs 1 and 2 and elsewhere, either one could be used to predict the production of chlorinated aromatic pollutants.

The authors do not consider the increased oxygen concentration itself to be responsible for production of aromatic compounds in the furnace. The enhanced oxygen concentrations are the result of the increased excess air. As the heat input to the furnace was kept constant, the increased excess air results in reduced temperatures in the combustion zone.

4. Conclusions

It is possible to optimize the operating conditions in waste heating plants to minimize the production of organic micro-pollutants in the flue gas. Uniform treatment of operational parameters from the plant and repeatable sampling and analyses show three factors which must be considered when limiting the production of chlorinated aromatics: the chlorine content in the fuel, combustion efficiency, and the energy density (or temperature in the furnace). It is possible to use many different types of components in the combustion gases as indicators when optimizing the operational conditions and, therefore, it is not necessary to use those which are expensive to analyse. The emission with flue gas does not need to correspond to the changes in the combustion parameters if a high-efficiency flue gas cleaning system is installed at the plant.

References

J. Bergström, J. (1985), *Handledning för Optimerad Drift av Avfallsvärmeverk* (*Procedures for Optimal Operation of Waste Fueled Heating Plants*), Publication 85:12, The Swedish Association of Public Cleansing and Solid Waste Management, Malmö, Sweden, S-212 22 Malmö (in Swedish).

Bergvall, G. & Hult, J. (1985), *Technology, Economics and Environmental Effects of Solid Waste Treatment. Final report from the DRAV-project.* Publication 85:11, the Swedish Association of Public Cleansing and Solid Waste Management, Malmö, Sweden, S-212 22 Malmö (in Swedish).

Buser, H.-R. (1975), Analysis of polychlorinated dibenzo-*p*-dioxins and dibenzofurans in chlorinated phenols by mass fragmentography. *Journal of Chromatography*, *107*, 295–310.

Eadon, G., Aldons, K., Hilker, D., Keefe, P. O., & Smith, R. (1983), *Chemical Data on Air Samples from the Binghamton State Office Building*, Center for Laboratories and Research, New York State Department of Health, Albany, NY 12201, 7 July 1983.

Lindfors, L.-G., Solyom, P., Waltersen, E. & Eriksson, G. (1985), *Litteratursammanställning av Dioxinutsläpp Från Avfallsförbränning* (*Bibliography of Dioxin Emissions from Municipal Waste Incineration*), Publication 85:15, The Swedish Association of Public Cleansing and Solid Waste Management, Malmö, Sweden, S-212 22 Malmö (in Swedish).

Öberg, T., Aittola, J.-P. & Bergström, J. G. T. (1985), Chlorinated aromatics from the combustion of hazardous waste, *Chemosphere*, *14*, 215–221.

REPORT:
LEGISLATIVE ASPECTS OF EMISSION CONTROL. By Jack Bentley, Department of the Environment, London SW1 3PY, U.K.

The British system of air pollution control has been built up pragmatically in response to particular problems. It is therefore contained in a number of statutes, and the administrative arrangements are a blend of central direction and local discretion, based on the principle of "best practicable means".

Section 5 of the Health and Safety at Work, etc., Act, 1974, sets out the general duty on any person having control of any premises of a class specified in the Health and Safety (Emissions into Atmosphere) Regulations 1983 to use the *best practicable means* for preventing emissions to air of noxious or offensive substances, and for rendering any that are emitted harmless and inoffensive. The two aspects are not alternatives. The system recognizes that complete removal—through arrestment equipment or process modification—cannot always be guaranteed, but where there is necessary emission to the atmosphere, it must be adequately dispersed (by tall stacks) to render ground-level concentrations harmless and inoffensive. Reliance on dispersal alone is only permitted when there are no practical means of removing or further reducing emissions. It should be noted that the legal requirement to use the best practicable means does not depend on proof of need because of damage or potential damage.

The processes defined in the 1983 Regulations—some 3367, mostly in the heavy and chemical industries, at 2284 works at the end of 1985—are controlled in England and Wales by Her Majesty's Industrial Air Pollution Inspectorate, and in Scotland by Her Majesty's Industrial Pollution Inspectorate. The Inspectorates require that the operator of any scheduled process shall take the best practicable means to control *all* emissions—uncontained ones (e.g. from vent shafts, liquid effluent streams and stock piles) as well as those from the stacks. The operator must not only provide and efficiently maintain his abatement equipment and adequately design his process, but he must also ensure proper supervision and operation of the plant, and any other part which may give rise to emissions.

The Inspectorate issue a series of best-practicable-means notes for various scheduled processes, which set out the minimum requirements for new works which must be met by them on first registration. Detailed agreements based on these guidelines are then worked out for each scheduled process. Best-practicable-means notes contain details of emission limits which can be set in quantitative terms. These are *presumptive* in that operating within them is normally accepted by the Inspectorates as a presumptive indication that the best practicable means are being used. Conversely, failure to operate within them would indicate that the best practicable means are not being used. These presumptive limits are updated from time to time to take account of new technology or control methods, or of new information about the effect of emissions. The limits currently enforced are set each year in the Chief Industrial Air Pollution Inspector's annual report which is available from HMSO.

Where quantitative emission limits would be impracticable, e.g. for uncontained sources, the requirements of best practicable means may be framed as qualitative assessments or as operational procedures, process control conditions, working practices or design principle, as is most appropriate. It should be noted that the requirement is to use the best practicable means—the word "practicable" is very important. If there is no risk to public health, "practicable" is interpreted as having regard to local conditions and circumstances, to the financial implications and to the current state of technical knowledge. The words "financial implications" relate both to the direct capital and to revenue costs borne by the operator of the process. In deciding a requirement, the aim is to achieve a reasonable balance between the costs of prevention and/or dispersal and the benefits. Complete evaluation in monetary terms is seldom possible, and experience must be used in arriving at a decision. Each individual best-practicable-means agreement also takes account of technical knowledge on pollution control technology, and on the effect of substances on human health, flora and fauna, construction materials, property, agriculture, amenity, etc.

The best-practicable-means principle applies not only to the scheduled processes which, because they have significant potential for pollution or because they raise difficult technical problems of control, are the responsibility of the Inspectorates. The best-practicable-means system is also central to the control exercised on all other industrial processes by local authorities. For reasons of cost-effectiveness and direct accountability, it has long been the practice in the U.K. that, wherever possible, air pollution control should be exercised at the local level. Generally, local authorities control non-scheduled processes by the use of statutory nuisance and offensive trades powers in the Public Health Acts, which operate after nuisance has occurred. However, under the Clean Air Acts they have pro-active powers of prior control for combustion processes.

The Clean Air Acts require *inter alia* that new furnaces must be notified to the local authority, be capable of smokeless operation, generally be fitted with adequate grit and dust arrestment plant and that any associated chimney must be of adequate height to ensure proper dispersion. The local authority may also require the measurement of emissions of grit and dust from certain specified furnaces. There are various rights of appeal to the Secretary of State.

The U.K. concept of best practicable means has effectively been enshrined into E.C. legislation in a "framework" directive on air pollution from individual plants, which came into effect on 30 June 1987. Under the directive, new plants will be required to satisfy the authorities that the best available technology "not entailing excessive costs" will be used to reduce emissions, and that the plants will not give rise to significant air pollution. The directive also provides for the gradual adaptation of existing plants to the best available technology, taking into account each plant's technical characteristics, rate of use and remaining life, the nature and volume of polluting emissions and the costs of controlling them. The Council of the European Communities may, if necessary, fix emission limits for specific pollutants based on the best available technology not involving excessive costs, and taking account of the nature, quantities and harmfulness of the emissions concerned.

This report sets out the basic system of pollution control that has evolved since the industrial revolution, based on a partnership between central inspectorates and local authorities and the use of best practicable means to control emissions. It is a system that has operated well, and one that we will be seeking to build on, rather than overturn, in the consultation paper which reviews the legislation (to be issued shortly).

REPORT:
NEW EMISSION LIMITS FOR WASTE-TO-ENERGY PLANTS IN SWEDEN. By Gunnar Bergvall, National Environmental Protection Board, Box 1302, S-171 25 Solna, Sweden.

Background

At the beginning of 1984, it became clear in Sweden that waste incineration was a significant source of dioxin emissions (Dioxin is here used as a short form for polychlorinated dibenzo-*p*-dioxins and dibenzofurans). At that time, this was the only known important source of dioxin emissions. At about the same time, dioxins were identified in the environment. Measurements proved that dioxins were bioaccumulated in the food chain and could be found in, for example, fish and mother's milk. Somewhat later the first tentative values for acceptable daily intakes of dioxin were formulated in Sweden. The implications of these were that consumption of, for example, fish from the Baltic and also mother's milk, would give intakes larger than the acceptable daily intake.

At this point dioxins became the subject of widespread interest in the press and on television. As, at this time, waste incineration was the only known large source of dioxin emissions in Sweden, attention was concentrated on this source as regards the whole dioxin issue. The information given to the public was characterized by such headlines in the press as: "Stop incineration of waste", "The garbage will be our death", and "Too high dioxin levels in flue gas". This message was quickly picked up by the environmentally conscious Swedish public and led to numerous debates at both local and national levels.

In February 1985, the Environmental Protection Board decided on a moratorium on building further waste-to-energy plants in Sweden. The aim of the moratorium was to give time for an evaluation of the situation and to draw up a basis for future policies for waste-to-energy plants.

Furthermore, in May 1985, the Environmental Protection Board and the Energy Administration received a request from the Cabinet to review the current environmental and energy-related policies with regard to the incineration of waste.

Waste incineration in Sweden

At the present time there are 25 waste incineration plants in operation in Sweden. Of the 2.5×10^6 tonne of municipal waste produced yearly, 1.5×10^6 tonne or 60% is incinerated at present. All plants utilize the energy from waste incineration for producing hot water for district heating systems. The plants produce a total of 3.5 TWh of heat per annum, which accounts for some 9% of the total district heating production. On a local scale, the waste heat accounts for up to 35% of the district heating.

The waste-to-energy plants in Sweden are of a fairly modern design, and most of them were built after 1972. All plants are equipped with at least electrostatic precipitators (ESP) or bag house filters, giving dust emissions of between 2 and 80 mg m^{-3}, normal, 10% CO_2. It is estimated that by the beginning of the 1990s the waste-to-energy plants will be incinerating up to 70% of all municipal waste in Sweden.

The dioxin situation

Dioxin measurements have recently been carried out at 15 waste-to-energy plants in

Sweden using the recommended Nordic Standard (see Jansson in this issue). Flue gas emissions varied over a wide range from less than 5 to over 100 ng m^{-3} of Eadon TCDD equivalents per cubic meter with a median value between 10 and 20. The estimated total annual emission from waste-to-energy plants in Sweden is about 100 g. The iron and steel industry may emit about 50 g, and hospital incinerators about 30 g. Emissions from automobiles may be anywhere between 10 and 150 g. Dioxin emissions have also been identified from other sources such as pulp and paper industry, aluminium smelters, wire reclamation, and incineration of hazardous waste. The yearly emissions from these activities have been estimated to be in the order of 1–5 g.* Judging from this data, waste incineration plants seem to be responsible for about half the total dioxin emissions in Sweden (but see Hagenmaier *et al.* in this issue). The values quoted above are not corrected for sampling train losses and should only be used as an indication of relative emissions.

Effect of improved flue gas cleaning

Poorly controlled combustion conditions cause high emissions of a number of pollutants. Reductions of emissions down to the order of 5–10 ng TCDD (Eadon equivalents) m^{-3} can be reached by optimizing the incineration conditions in existing installations. These and the following values include the corrections for sampling train recoveries, which means that they are some 2–3 times higher than data for which sampling train losses were not taken into account.

The flue gas dioxin emissions can be reduced further by furnishing the plants with new advanced flue gas cleaning techniques. Both direct and indirect flue gas condensation (cooling) and dry scrubbing with lime are utilized in Sweden. Values below 0.1 ng TCDD (Eadon equivalents) have been reported from three full-scale dry lime plants. Pilot plants using condensation have been measured at 0.4 and less than 0.1 ng m^{-3}. Emissions from three other full-scale plants have not yet been measured. Flue gas cleaning systems show a very good effect on mercury and hydrogen chloride emissions and also on other organic substances of higher molecular weight.

The flue gas condensation systems are also interesting from an economic point of view, because waste-to-energy plants will then be capable of supplying 15–30% more energy to the district heating systems, provided there is a market for the extra energy produced.

The dioxin distribution in a waste-to-energy plant

Dioxin can be found not only in the flue gas but also in the fly ash and bottom ash that leave the incineration plant. Several studies of the relative importance of the different routes have been made. One example is from the new Uppsala plant (250,000 t year^{-1}) which is fitted with ESP. The corrected emissions of TCDD, 22 g year^{-1}, are about equal to the combined dioxin loadings of fly ash and bottom ash.

The fly ash contains much higher dioxin concentrations than the bottom ash. Extensive leaching of fly ashes with melted snow (to simulate natural conditions) did not produce any detectable dioxin concentration in the leachate (detection level 1–10 p l^{-1}). The conclusion is that with the landfill technique currently employed in Sweden,

---

* Swedish Association of Public Cleansing and Solid Waste Management (Svenska Rehållnings-verksföreningen), Compilation of Emission Data Regarding PCDDs and PCDFs from Swedish Waste-to-Energy Plants, Report, Malmö, 1986. 35 pp. (in Swedish).

the addition from fly ash in landfills cannot contribute significantly to the overall environmental load of dioxin.

Assessment of health risks

The assessment of health risks related to dioxin is particularly difficult (see Ahlborg in this issue). For dioxin, the risk evaluations are also complicated by the fact that direct exposure to air polluted by, for example, flue gases from waste combustion gives only low doses as compared to intake through foods. Having a fish dinner consisting of Baltic herring (which is not very high in dioxin if compared to some other fish data) gives a dioxin intake that is at least 100 times larger than that produced by breathing polluted air for a whole day in the location downstream from waste-to-energy plant where maximum ground concentrations occur. Due to bioaccumulation of dioxin which spread to the marine environment from many sources, the top levels of the ecosystems end up with fairly high dioxin loads. Consequently the herring contain much more dioxin than will be contained in the 20 m³ of air that you breathe in the course of a day. A tentative limit for an acceptable daily intake has been proposed in Sweden, set at 1–5 pg TCDD kg⁻¹ of body weight. This tentative limit is exceeded if, for example, fish from the Baltic is consumed. In this estimate the presence of the 12 most toxic isomers of PCDDs and PCDFs has been recognized by applying the TCDD-equivalent concept.

Of great concern are the levels of dioxin that have been measured in human mother's milk. The data indicates that nursing infants are exposed to levels which clearly exceed the tentative ADI value. The uncertainty in the risk assessment, however, is such that this fact should not be considered as an argument against the breast feeding of babies. Breast feeding provides many positive effects that are considered important to the healthy development of babies.

The findings emphasize that the present situation as regards dioxins is unsatisfactory from a health and environmental viewpoint. Even if the connection between emissions of dioxins from waste-to-energy plants and the levels of dioxins appearing in the environment is not very clear, the dioxin emissions from major sources should be significantly decreased.

Conclusions

The basic strategy in Sweden for handling environmental problems connected with the disposal of waste is to reduce the amounts of waste and to increase the recovery of materials from waste. Even if these measures have a high priority in Sweden, experience has shown that a rapid progress along these lines cannot be hoped for. When materials cannot be recovered, then at least the energy that they contain should be utilized.

For the future it is absolutely essential that pollution from waste-to-energy plants should be kept sufficiently low, so that the risks to human health and environment can be kept at an acceptable level even in a long perspective. Today, waste incineration adds to the large-scale pollution problems such as the acidification of soil and water and also the accumulation of heavy metals and certain organic compounds such as dioxins in the ecosystems. Current estimates suggest that waste incineration alone is responsible for about half the total dioxin emissions in Sweden. In Sweden, therefore, it has been judged essential to take additional vigorous steps if waste incineration is to be used for waste treatment and energy production in the future.

End of moratorium—new emission limits

In June 1986 the Swedish Environmental Protection Board and the Energy Administration presented a report to the Cabinet where current environmental and energy related policies on waste incineration were reviewed. At the same time the Environmental Protection Board decided to lift the moratorium and to introduce new emission limits for waste-to-energy plants. The limits, corrected to dry normal gas at 10% CO_2 are as set out below.

Hydrogen chloride: emissions should not exceed 100 mg m^{-3}, calculated as a monthly average.

Mercury: emissions should not, at inspection, exceed 0.08 mg m^{-3}. After appropriate product control measures have been imposed (i.e. organized collection of Hg batteries, etc.), it should be possible to decrease this value to 0.03 mg m^{-3}.

Particulate matter: emissions should not exceed 20 mg, calculated as a monthly average.

PCDDs and PCDFs: Emissions from existing incinerators should not, at inspection, exceed a limit of 0.5–2.0 ng m^{-3}. For new incinerators a limit of 0.1 ng m^{-3} should apply. Limits are given at TCDD-equivalents calculated by the Eadon model (see Ahlborg & Victorin in this issue) and measured using the Nordic recommendations (see Jansson & Bergvall in this issue) under normal working conditions. These limits will serve as guidelines during a given trial period for each facility. Definitive limits will be set after the trial period. A period of a couple of years will probably be necessary for testing and evaluation of the new incinerator designs/flue gas cleaning systems (compare with Barniske in this issue).

REPORT:
EMISSION OF DIOXINS FROM PILOT PLANT INCINERATION OF MSW IN DENMARK. By Arne Grove, Department of Chemical Technology, Technological Institute of Copenhagen, P.O. Box 141, DK-2630 Taastrup, Denmark.

Emission of polychlorinated dibenzo-*p*-dioxins (PCDD) and polychlorinated dibenzofurans (PCDF) has been studied in a pilot test programme at a 13 t h^{-1} MSW incinerator in Copenhagen. The methods used were similar to the now "Recommended methodology for measurements of PCDD and PCDF in the Nordic countries" (see Jansson & Bergvall this issue). The test programme included parallel sampling to provide information on standard deviations of sampling and analysis, and covered different operation conditions to provide information on emissions of dioxins. Data reduction was performed by conventional statistical tools assuming that the populations were normally distributed.

The number of samples analysed (12) was not sufficient to show significant correlations between the emission of PCDD and PCDF and the operating conditions. Graphical presentations suggest that emissions of dioxin and related compounds are low only at low CO and high CO_2 concentrations. Other operating parameters gave best results at intermediate conditions and, therefore, could not be linearly correlated with emissions. The problem now is to find the best set of parameters and for these parameters to find the windows within which the emission of dioxins can be reduced to a minimum. Recent studies in Denmark, Sweden, West Germany, Canada, U.S.A., and other countries indicate that it should be possible to find a common set of parameters that are sufficient to describe operation conditions during sampling (see other papers in this issue).

Further details of this pilot study are available in a report by A. Grove to Miljøstyrelsen, July 1986, *Dioxinmålinger på Amagerforbrænding 1985* (*Dioxin measurements at the Amager Incinerator, 1985*).

REPORT:
DIOXINS AND RELATED POLYCHLORINATED AND POLYCYCLIC AROMATIC HYDROCARBONS IN EMISSIONS FROM SMALL INCINERATORS IN NORWAY. By Ch. Benestad, Centre for Industrial Research, P.B. 350, N-0314 Oslo, Norway and M. Oehme, Norwegian Institute for Air Research, P.B. 64, N-2001 Lillestrøm, Norway.

The content of polychlorinated dibenzo-*p*-dioxins (PCDD) and dibenzofurans (PCDF) in the flue gases of small municipal incinerators in Norway is compared with the level of other polychlorinated compounds which might act as precursors. A reasonable correlation has been found between the presence of chlorinated benzenes and PCDD/PCDF. Furthermore, a large number of mainly apolar poly- and per-chlorinated as well as brominated substances were found in the emissions of a continuous municipal incinerator even at high temperatures ($\sim 1000°C$) when waste oil sludge was burned.

This study also showed that the polycyclic aromatic hydrocarbon (PAH) concentrations in the emissions from a poorly operated incinerator can be several orders of magnitude higher than for halogenated compounds (mg m^{-3} instead of ng–μg m^{-3}).

Six small incinerators with capacities of 0.4 to 7 t h^{-1}, four of which were batch operated, were sampled essentially according to Nordic Standards (see Jansson, this issue) and analysed for polyhalogenated compounds by high resolution GC/MS. A separate part of the sample was analysed for PAH and PAH derivatives by GC/FID and GC/MS. Some samples were prefractionated by high performance liquid chromatography (HPLC) before analysis of the most polar compounds.

A batch-operated 1 t h^{-1} incinerator (No. 4 in Table 1) which was emitting soot and high levels of CO above 1000 ppm was chosen for extensive analysis of substituted aromatic compounds because the highest PAH levels were found at this site.

TABLE 1

Concentration of polyhalogenated compounds and PAH in the emissions of small incinerators (all values adjusted to normal conditions at 10% O_2)

Incinerator No.	n	ng m^{-3}				μg m^{-3}
		ΣCLB	PCB	ΣPCDD/PCDF	2,3,7,8-TCDD EQ*	ΣPAH
1	3	160/179/540	<0.03/4.5/6.5	47/58/133	NA	13/51/210
2	1	3800	5.4	530	NA	3
3	3	34/42/46	<0.03	NA	NA	56/47
4	2	95/110	0.7/0.8	97/97	1.9/2.6	6000
5	3	730/860/2300	34/45/60	930/1100/1800	9/13/20	0.84/0.96
6	2	360	14	73/220	2.0/2.4	1.8/14

NA, not available.
* EQ, Eadon equivalents.

TABLE 2

Concentration levels of aromatic compounds in the emissions of incinerator 4 (values expressed in mg kg^{-1} waste are given in parentheses)

Classes of compounds	Filter	Condensate + XAD-2	Acetone rinse	Sum	
		μg Nm^3 flue gas at 10% O$_2$ (mg kg^{-1} waste)			
C2-alkylbenzenes	280	990		1270	(9)
C3-alkylbenzenes	30	2670	0.1	2700	(20)
Bicyclic aromatic compounds	50	2040		2090	(10)
PAH	2330	580	3850	6760	(50)
Indenes		570		570	(4)
Benzofuranes		210		210	(1)
Carbazoles		0.5		0.5	(0.004)
Thiophenes		100		100	(0.7)
Quinolines/isoquinolines		10	1	10	(0.07)
Benzaldehydes		6		6	(0.04)
bicyclic aldehydes		8	0.2	8	(0.06)
PAH-aldehydes		0.1		0.1	(0.0007)
Aliphatic ketones		10		10	(0.07)
Phenylketones		30		30	(0.2)
Bicyclic ketones		30		30	(0.2)
PAH-ketones		50	0.6	50	(0.3)
Phenols		20	1	20	(0.1)
Bicyclic alcohols		1		1	(0.007)
Methoxybenzenes		0.4		0.4	(0.003)
Methoxynaphthalenes		1		1	(0.007)
Phenylated carboxy-acids		60		60	(0.4)
Bicyclic carboxy-acids		0.3		0.3	(0.002)
Phthalates		9		9	(0.06)
Benzoates		1		1	(0.007)
Benzonitriles		40	5	50	(0.3)
Cyano-benzenes		6		6	(0.04)
Cyano-naphthalenes		15	6	20	(0.1)
Cyano-PAH		7	28	40	(0.3)
Cyano-indenes			4	4	(0.03)
Indenones			20	20	(0.1)
Nitroalkylbenzenes			2	2	(0.01
Nitroindenes			6	6	(0.04)

In addition to PAH, aromatic compounds identified under reducing conditions included alkylated benzenes, aromatic aldehydes, ketones and nitro compounds, and carbonylic- and cyano-PAHs. The quantitative results are summarized in Table 2. More than 57% of the parent PAH were found in the acetone rinse of the sampling train which indicated that wall adsorption is significant. Consequently, the rinsing of the sampling equipment is of high importance. The compounds identified correspond to about 80% of all organic material found in the HPLC fractions. About half the compounds were substituted or parent PAHs. Bicyclic substances represented about 15% of the total organic material. The quantity of aromatic ketones correspond to about 1%.

TABLE 3

Polyhalogenated compounds identified in the emission of incinerator No. 5.

Fraction 1
Chlorobenzenes, penta-, and hexa-chlorobenzene. Bromo-trichloro-, bromo-tetrachloro, and bromo-pentachloro-benzene. Tetrachloro-, pentachloro-, and hexachloro-naphthalene. Penta-chloro-, hexachloro-, heptachloro-, octachloro-, nonachloro-, and decachloro-biphenyl. Penta-chloro- and hexachlorohexahydro-naphthalene. Pentachloro- and hexachloropyrene/fluoranthene.

Fraction 3
Hexachloronaphthalenes. Hexachlorobenz-1,4-dioxin. Tetrachloropyrenes. Pentachloro- and hexachloro-fluorenones.

Fraction 4
Traces of compounds as found in Fraction 1.

Fraction 5
Polychlorinated dibenzo-*p*-dioxins and dibenzofurans. Hexachlorobenzofuran. Pentachloro- and hexachloro-naphthalenes. Tetrachloropyrene. Bromo-pentachlorobenzofuran.

Fraction 6
Mainly oxygenated cyclic chlorinated compound (difficult to identify due to insufficient mass spectrometric information). Tetrachloro- and pentachloro-benzonitrile. $C_8H_8OCl_5$. $C_7H_6OCl_5$ (acetophenone?).

Chlorinated benzenes (tri- to hexa-) (CLB), biphenyls (PCB) and PCDD/PCDF and PAH were quantified in the emission samples from all incinerators. The results are summarized in Table 1. Maximum values for the batch-wise operated incinerators (Nos 1–4) were normally obtained during the start-up period.

The sample extracts from incinerator 5 contained high concentrations of various polyhalogenated compounds. The occasional burning of waste motor oil sludge was found to be the major source for such compounds (brominated and monobromo-poly-chlorocompounds formed during combustion of fuel additives such as dibromoethane). Table 3 gives the details of a survey on the identified compounds. The results can be summarized as given below.

(a) Tri- to hexa-chlorobenzenes, PCDD/PCDF and perhaps chlorophenols (not quantified), were the most common compound groups.

(b) The concentration level of chlorinated PAHs decreased strongly with increasing number of ring systems. Polychlorinated naphthalenes are present at 3–4 times higher concentrations than PCB. Only traces of the latter were found in all samples. Other chlorinated PAHs such as fluoranthenes/pyrenes were only present at concentration levels below that of PCB.

(c) The highest concentrations of single compounds were found for the completely chlorinated species such as perchlorinated benzene, -benz-1,4-dioxin, and -ben-zofuran. Monobromopolychloro substances were also present.

(d) Non-chlorinated compounds such as parent PAH and aliphatic hydrocarbons were present at minor levels compared to the polyhalogenated representatives, in contrast with incinerator 4.

(e) Starved air incineration conditions which favour the formation of PAH obviously suppress production of PCDD/PCDF. Griffin (1987) postulated that the avail-ability of Cl_2 in the emissions is important for the formation of PCDD/PCDF.

The presence of reducing species such as SO_2 transforms Cl_2 to HCl which can undergo chlorination reactions only when an excess of O_2 is present. The results in Table 1 indicate that reductive combustion conditions (O_2 deficiency, high PAH emissions) also suppress the formation of PCDD/PCDF. Only moderate PCDD/PCDF emissions could be observed when high PAH amounts were present. There were no indications for a lower recovery of PCDD/PCDF due to a higher amount of soot present in these samples (see also Vogg in this issue).

(f) The total amount of polychlorinated benzenes (CLB) formed seems to correlate with the observed levels for PCDD/PCDF. However, more data must be collected before a proper statistical analysis can be carried out. Hexachlorobenzene (HCB) has been proposed previously as an indicator for the presence of PCDD. According to our data, a better correlation is obtained for the total quantity of CLB. This opens the possibility of substituting rather expensive PCDD/PCDF quantifications by CLB analysis in a routine surveillance programme, where often only low-cost parameters are controlled.

(g) Negative-ion chemical ionization mass spectrometry was very useful for obtaining information about mixed polyhalogenated compounds (presence of both Cl^- and Br^- in the mass spectrum).

Acknowledgements

This work was financially supported by the Royal Norwegian Council for Scientific and Industrial Research (Committee for Toxic Compounds in the Environment).

References

Benestad, Ch., Jebens, A. & Tveten, G. (1987), Emissions of organic Pollutants from waste incineration, *Chemosphere*, in press.

Griffin, R. D. (1985/1987), A new theory of dioxin formation in municipal solid waste combustion, 5th International Symposium on Chlorinated Dioxins and Related Compounds, 16–19 September 1985, Bayreuth, Germany, *Chemosphere*, *15*, 1987.

Oehme, M., Manø, S. & Kirschmer, P. (1986), Quantitative method for the determination of femtogram amounts of polychlorinated dibenzo-*p*-dioxins and dibenzofurans in outdoor air, *Chemosphere*, *15*, 607–617.

Oehme, M., Manø, S. and Mikalsen, A. (1987), Formation and presence of polyhalogenated compounds in the emissions of small- and large-scale municipal waste incinerators, *Chemosphere*, *16*, 143–153.

REPORT:
THE INFLUENCE OF PLANT DESIGN AND OPERATING PROCEDURES ON EMISSIONS OF PCDDs AND PCDFs IN ENGLAND. By M. J. Woodfield, B. Bushby, D. Scott and K. Webb, Warren Spring Laboratory, Stevenage, United Kingdom.

Every year in England and Wales between two and a half and three million tonnes of domestic, trade and industrial wastes are incinerated at 35 municipal waste incinerators, this amounts to about 10% of the country's annual arisings. These plants are of varying sophistication, most are over 10 years old and only four are equipped with energy-recovery systems. There was a large, but rather uncoordinated, programme of incineration-plant building in the 1960s and 1970s; several of the plants have subsequently been closed for various reasons, some technical, e.g. structural problems, and some because more economic methods, such as landfill, became available. Consequently, there is considerable scope for energy recovery and interest is being shown in the development of both waste-derived fuels and combined heat and power schemes based on refuse incineration. However, some difficulties are being encountered with both these developments as a result of uncertainties in the environmental consequences of emission of air pollutants from waste combustion, especially emissions of particulate material, metals, acid gases and products of incomplete combustion; the possibility of emissions of dioxin are viewed with particular concern. As a result, work has been carried out in Britain to assess emissions from incinerators, identify emission problems (where possible proposing remedial options), and examining technical options for future development.

The environmental significance of process emissions can be difficult to assess, especially when trace constituents such as dioxins are involved (see Rappe *et al.* in this issue). Consequently, the incinerator emission measurement programme is part of a wider study in which soil samples and ambient sampling are being carried out to establish background concentrations and identify/rank other potential sources. There is little data at present on the relative importance of alternative sources; many low-level small sources of dioxins may be more significant than a few large high-level sources such as incinerators. As a result, sampling and analytical resources are at a premium and must be targeted to best effect. Where possible, simplified procedures have had to be adopted and carried out to determine design factors or operating procedures likely to affect PCDD emissions. In view of this R&D requirement, emissions of 2,3,7,8-tetrachlorodibenzo-*p*-dioxin (Dioxin) (2378TCDD), total tetra-chlorodibenzo-*p*-dioxins (T(4)CDD), octachlorodibenzo-*p*-dioxin (OCDD), and total tetrachlorodibenzofurans (T(4)CDF) were used as indicators of the total PCDD/F emission rather than adopting the sophisticated toxic equivalence methods used by some workers (see Ahlborg & Victorin in this issue).

In-depth studies covering a wide range of emissions have been carried out on a substantial proportion of U.K. incinerators, but it would be very expensive to examine them all; it is important that plant assessment methods are developed which will reduce the need for expensive monitoring/analytical work. The analysis of past data has shown some evidence of relationships between easily/cheaply measured parameters and emissions of species which are costly to determine.

The organic emissions from refuse combustion are complex and difficult to characterize and little progress has been made in systematically establishing the degree of hazard presented by each component, either individually or synergistically, and, therefore, little effort has been made to rank them in order of importance. Present emphasis is on a limited number of specific compounds which are known to be toxic, such as PCDDs and polychlorinated biphenyls (PCBs). However, there is some evidence that other components, such as nitrated species, have demonstrable mutagenicity (Jantunen *et al.* 1986). Consequently we have endeavoured throughout to develop sampling and analytical methods which will collect whole samples of incinerator effluents which can be stored for subsequent analyses if and when other toxic compounds or groups of compounds have been identified.

Early work at WSL showed that incinerator emissions produced large quantities of artifacts in the collection media (XAD2 resin) used to sample the vapour phase component; therefore a form of sampling for vapour-phase components which is more consistent with our general goal of obtaining samples more representative of the emission as a whole was adopted. This condensation method underestimates the total vapour-phase emission but can still be used for ranking sources in order of importance. The more specific ASTMS method (1984) using a modified EPA MkV sample train— which utilizes XAD2 for vapour-phase collection—is increasingly being used to supplement our existing procedures due to concern over dioxin emissions to the exclusion of other considerations (see also Hagenmaier *et al.* in this issue).

Ideally the sampling work should reflect the variability of the process but this can be difficult with refuse incinerators where the feed composition changes with time, con- sequently all sampling was carried out over at least a three-day operational period and was carried out in duplicate, sampling times all exceeded three hours. In addition to sampling the flue gas, samples of grate residues, arrestment equipment ash, and quench water were taken simultaneously to evaluate the discharge rates of the various components throughout the system.

The stack sampling equipment is described in Woodfield (1984) and is somewhat similar to the SRI total inhalable particulate sampler (Smith 1982). Most of the particulate material is retained on a filter. Organic components are cooled and condensed heterogeneously before being appreciably diluted and collected on a glass fibre filter. While this system is not 100% efficient, it does collect a significant proportion of the gas-phase high molecular weight fraction and minimizes artifact formation due to acid attack.

The samples collected from combustion sources are composed of complex mixtures of components in mixed-phase matrices which require extraction into a suitable solvent. Many of the components in the extract will be present in much higher concentrations than the components of interest and will almost certainly interfere in analyses for trace species. Consequently, the samples must be subjected to a clean-up procedure to remove these potential interferences. There have been several useful articles reviewing the various approaches that have been used (see Rappe *et al.* and Hagenmaier *et al.* in this issue, also Crummet 1983).

Toluene was chosen as extraction solvent, as used by the American Society of Mechanical Engineers/EPA/Department of Energy as part of their analytical pro- cedures for stack effluent and residual combustion product samples (ASTMS 1984). The clean-up consisted of a one-step normal-phase HPLC fractionation based on the previous work of Tong *et al.* (1984). After concentration, the fraction obtained in the clean-up stage was analysed by GC/MS by exact mass matching of the most intense chlorine isotope peak of each compound. Spiking with radioactive isotopes to correct for losses was not used.

The 35 existing British municipal incinerators have capacities in the range 2–16 t h^{-1}. The 10 that were investigated have electrostatic precipitators (ESP) which reduced particulate emissions to between 245 and 3580 g t^{-1} of refuse and acid gases to about 5000 g t^{-1}. Emissions of dioxins (2378 isomer) were as low as 2.8 µg $^{-1}$ but varied widely. The Figure 1 shows the emissions of total tetrachlorinated dioxins as a function of type of grate and CO_2 concentration in the offgases. None of the incinerators reached the high CO_2 levels recommended in other papers (see Hasselriis in this issue).

Plant operation also varies considerably from plant to plant. As expected, the plants with heat recovery operate for lengthy periods between shutdowns, can justify high expenditure on maintenance, and generally have a high reliability. Those without heat recovery tend to be run for much shorter periods of time, most being shut down at weekends and several overnight; staffing and maintenance levels vary accordingly. All

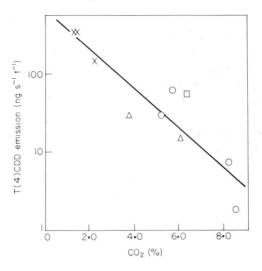

Fig. 1. Possible relationship between excess air and T(4)CDD emission. ×, Chain grates; △, Nichols type; ○, roller type; □, Martin type.

the plants are different, even those built by the same contractor and using similar grates, so generalizations should not be taken too far. Each of the plants investigated has its own particular characteristics, and emission patterns tended to reflect this. As indicated in Fig. 1, emissions vary by about 100 fold between plants. Emissions are not only a function of the refuse feed, combustion system and abatement equipment performance, but also depend on the operating procedures adopted throughout.

The plant with the lowest total dioxins emission used a roller grate system, and it was found that only roller grates were capable of raising the CO_2 content above 6%, possibly because better control could be exercised over smaller portions of the overall grate surface. However, it was noticeable that there was a large overlap between the values obtained for different grate types, indicating that local operational practices and/or refuse composition differences were probably an important factor. The plants with heat recovery tended to have lower dioxin levels in the residues but they had benefited from larger capital investment, ran for longer periods between shut downs, had greater staffing ratios and better maintenance; they also tended to try to achieve the best possible combustion in order to maximize energy recovery. It was observed that few of the plants had sufficient instrumentation to enable them to optimize combustion; some plants had oxygen measurement equipment, none had carbon monoxide monitors.

From the survey it was apparent that much could be achieved by combustion optimization, but an appreciable emission would remain even if this were carried out. Since a sizeable proportion of the PCDD/F is in the fly ash, the reduction of particulate emissions is especially important and, consequently, abatement equipment performance is a primary factor in the overall emission.

Both the results in Fig. 1 and those reported internationally indicate that if combustion is optimized on an efficient grate, quite low residual PCDD/F values can be achieved. However, poor particulate abatement can still lead to appreciable emissions and it is important that ESP performance should also be optimized. Figure 1 shows a possible relationship between the excess combustion air expressed as percentage CO_2

and the T(4)CDD emission per tonne of refuse burnt, this observation is based on limited data but, if validated, could prove a useful diagnostic aid (see Hasselriis in this issue). Karasek *et al.* (1986) have also demonstrated a similar relationship between excess air and dioxin content of EP ash on a large single unit.

The variability of the results from similar grate types indicated that local operational practices or variability in the feed were significant factors. It was observed that, with combustion optimization, quite low residual PCDD/F levels could be achieved, but due to a lack of suitable instrumentation many plants could not optimize their combustion. As there will invariably be some dioxin in fly ash, optimization of particulate abatement plant is also important, here again the use of instrumentation to indicate plant performance would be beneficial.

Acknowledgement

The authors are pleased to acknowledge the support of the Land Waste Division of the U.K. Department of the Environment who sponsored the work reported.

References

ASTMS (1984), DRAFT Analytical Procedures to Assay Stack Effluent Samples and Residual Combustion Products for Polychlorinated Dibenzo-*p*-dioxin (PCDD) and Polychlorinated Dibenzofurans (PCDF). Sponsored by the American Society of Mechanical Engineers. U.S. Environmental Protection Agency. See also Velzy, C. O. (1986), *Chemosphere*, *15*, 1179.

Crummett, W. B. (1983), Status of analytical systems for the determination of PCDDs and PCDFs, *Chemosphere*, *12*, 429–446.

Karasek, K. W., Gonnard, M. F. & Finet, C. (1986), Control of the Emission of Dioxins in the Emission of Fly Ash from Incinerators of Urban Waste. TSM-L'Eau.

Jantounen, M. J., Liimatainen, A., Ramdahl, T., Itkonen, A. (1986), Rapid changes in peat fly ash mutagenicity after release into the atmosphere, *Environmental Science and Technology*, *20*, 684–689.

Smith, W. B. *et al.* (1982), Sampling and Data Handling Methods for Inhalable Particulate Sampling. Southern Research Institute, 2000 Ninth Avenue, South Birmingham, AL 35255, NTIS PB 82-24987.

Tong, H. Y., Shore, D. L., Karasek, F. W., Helland, P. & Jellum, E. (1984), Identification of organic compounds obtained from incineration of municipal waste by HPLC fractionation and gas chromatography–Mass spectrometry, *Journal of Chromatography*, *285*, 423–441.

Woodfield, M. J. & Bushby, B. B. (1984), Interim Report on the Design and Development of a Sampling and Analytical Procedure for the Determination of Low Volatility Carbonaceous Material in Flue Gases. Warren Spring Laboratory, Stevenage, U.K.

REPORT:

EMISSION OF DIOXIN AND RELATED COMPOUNDS FROM ITALIAN MUNI-CIPAL WASTE INCINERATORS. By Aulo Magagni, Managing Director of Municipal Public Cleaning Company (A.M.N.I.U.P.), Padova, Italy, and Gieorgio Boschi, Head of Environmental Service (A.M.N.I.U.P.).

A recent Italian law leading to regulations which became effective in 1986 requires waste incinerators to be equipped with post-combustion chambers that will achieve the following minimum operating conditions:

free O_2 content of 6% in wet gas at exit of chamber;
gas velocity of 10 m s^{-1}, average at entrance to chamber;
contact time of 2 s; and
temperature of 950°C.

This regulation forced the closing of about 50 large and small incinerators leaving only four that met the requirements. The rationale behind the law was based on reports in the literature on the destruction of organic wastes and was not at that time supported by any experimental data from local incinerators.

Measurements on existing incinerators

The Italian National Research Council (CNR) recently carried out a study of 10 Italian incinerators that did not have post-combustion chambers and three that are now equipped with them (Ghezzi & Giuliano 1985, Giuliano 1984). Emissions of tetra-chlorodibenzo-*p*-dioxin (TCDD) are shown in Table 1. The post-combustion chamber

TABLE 1

Emissions of TCDD from Italian incinerators using ESP

| Code | Temperature (°C) | | TCDD (ng m^{-3}) |
	Combustion chamber	Post-combustion	
(A) Old incinerators without post-combustion			
1	973–1273	—	189
2	873–1023	—	19
3	1123–1323	—	71
4	773–1273	—	16
5	1123–1173	—	85
6	1048–1228	—	10
(B) Modern incinerators without post-combustion			
7	1173–1223	—	21
8	1173–1323	—	0.2
9	1073–1323	—	9
10	1123–1273	—	19
(C) Modern incinerators with post-combustion			
11	1073–1273	1223–1323	0.1–1.5
12	1073–1273	1223–1323	0.8
13	1123–1273	> 1223	1.2–21

alone does not appear to be sufficient to ensure low emissions of TCDD. Of the 10 incinerators without post-combustion chambers, four are of modern design and have electrostatic precipitators (ESP), as do the three fitted with post-combustion facilities as a result of this study. There is no significant difference between the emissions from the two types of modern incinerators. Two with post-combustion and one without are able to keep TCDD emission levels below 1 ng m^{-3}. None of the old-style incinerators were able to give levels below 10 ng m^{-3}.

A recent series of measurements of TCDD emissions were carried out in an incinerator fitted with post-combustion facilities followed by a wet–dry lime scrubber and an ESP (Benfenati *et al.* 1986). In this device a slurry of lime (milk of lime) is spray dried by the flue gases leaving solid lime particles with adsorbed pollutants which are removed in the ESP. The lime scrubber–ESP system removed less than half of the TCDD emitted from the post-combustion chamber, even though the ESP captured 98% of the particulates.

Acknowledgement

The help of Prof. Michele Guiliano of the Politecnic of Milan is gratefully acknowledged.

References

Benfenati, Pastorelli, Castelli, Fanelli, Carminati, Farneti & Lodi (1986), Studies on the tetra-
    chlorodibenzo-*p*-dioxin (TCDD) and tetrachlorodibenzofurans (TCDF) emitted from an
    urban incinerator, *Chemosphere, 15*, 557.
Ghezzi & Giuliano (1985), L'incenerimento ed i microinquinanti organoclorurati effetti della post-
    combustine (Incineration and organochlorinated micropollutants: post-combustion effects),
    Ingegneria Sanitaria, 14.
Giuliano (1984), L'emissioni di microinquinanti dai forni di incenerimento di rifiuti solidi urbani
    (Micropollutants emission from municipal solid wastes incinerator), *Ingegneria Sanitaria, 13*.

REPORT:
LIMITS TO STATISTICAL EVALUATION OF INCINERATOR EMISSIONS.
**By R. B. Dean, Editor Waste Management & Research, based on a talk presented at
the ISWA–WHO–DAKOFA specialized seminar,** *Emission of Trace Organics from
Municipal Solid Waste Incinerators*, **Copenhagen, 20–22 January 1987.**

1. Introduction

This Symposium has presented abundant data related to the emissions of Dioxin and
related substances from municipal solid waste (MSW) incinerators. There are many
apparent conflicts between different sets of this data and some attempts have been
made to interpret these disparate results. The present paper, most of which was
prepared after the Seminar presentations, endeavours to point out some of the reasons
for the wide range of values presented.

2. Sources of variability

An MSW incinerator is not a steady-state reactor. There are large fluctuations in all
the operating variables, both in time and space. The time fluctuations may be shorter
than 1 s and are apparent at every time scale up to the life of the equipment. Space
variations occur on every cross-section to the direction of flow and may only be damped
out when the gases reach the top of the incinerator stack. Fluctuations have their
origin in the raw material which, even on the scale of a truck load, varies according to
the economic level of the district where it was collected and on the time of year: does it
contain melon rinds or Christmas wrappings? The heterogeneity is even more apparent
on smaller scales. For example, Brunner *et al.* (1986) quote a value of 3 mg of mercury
per kg of MSW. This corresponds to 3 g, or about one small wrist watch battery per
ton of MSW. The component of first concern, from the point of view of combustion, is
water, because it has the greatest quenching effect and is high in fruit and vegetable
residues but low in fats and dry paper. Even more spectacular are explosions of paint
cans and flares of fast burning polystyrene foam blocks. The fire box of an operating
municipal incinerator provides a vivid example of heterogeneous behaviour with temperatures represented by colours from red to bright yellow.

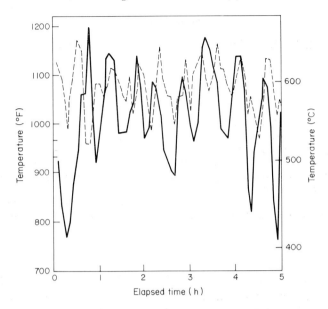

Fig. 1. Temperature fluctuations as a function of time when burning MSW or RDF. ———, Firing with unprocessed MSW; – – –, firing with processed RDF. Redrawn from a Buhler-Miag advertisement based on TVA (1985).

The high degree of inhomogeneity of solid waste fed to a mass-burning furnace can be discussed in terms of the limiting "open" length of the equipment in relation to the maximum "particle" length in the feed. If the feeding equipment is jammed by wastes then the "particle" length is comparable to the "open" length. Work in other fields has shown that unless the size of moving particles is less than a small fraction of the opening, the behaviour of the particles is erratic. In a furnace this leads to fluctuations in burning behaviour, even when there is no actual jamming.

2.1. *Temperature variations*

Inhomogeneities in feed are substantially reduced when refused-derived fuel (RDF) is burned because the scale length is less than 10 cm and much extraneous material has been removed. Nevertheless, temperature variations are still large. Figure 1 shows a plot of furnace temperatures comparing RDF and bulk MSW. The rise time of the measured temperature fluctuations is only a few minutes and is truly chaotic. Temperature measurements within a fire box also vary with position and differences of 100°C between simultaneous measurements at different spots are frequently mentioned in informal discussions, but more rarely in written reports. Temperatures are usually averaged over an arbitrary period of time and may also be averaged over position in the furnace. The average value will, of course, show lower fluctuation, but vital information about the variance of the measurements is discarded. The key point to remember is that thermal combustion reactions are predominantly exothermic and increase in rate exponentially with temperature. This means that most of the chemical reactions take place during the peaks of temperature. On the other hand, the spatial heterogeneity means that some puffs of gas could get right through the furnace without being heated as hot as the lowest temperature recorded during operation.

2.2. *Compositional variations*

The variations in composition of the gases is a result of the random composition of the fuel and the random turbulant motion in the fire box which is amplified at every turn or obstruction. Turbulance is a result of inertial flow of the gas. It is reduced by flow-through filters or other porous structures, but the accompanying fluctuations in composition may not be damped out. Flow through long pipes can also reduce both inertial and compositional fluctuations and, therefore, the top of the stack is the prefered place to get a representative flue gas sample.

3. Monitoring

An example of heterogeneous chemical production is shown in Bergstrom & Warman's Figure 2 (in this issue). Variations in carbon monoxide (CO) from flue gas samples taken at 5-min intervals exceed four-fold. These authors further show that Dioxin production is related not so much to average CO concentrations, as to the number of times CO exceeds an upper critical level, or when combustion efficiency drops below a lower critical level.

From a statistical point of view, this dependence on extreme values means that perhaps we should not average to smooth out fluctuations, but should instead use Poisson statistics that apply to random counts. Furthermore, if easily measurable events can be correlated with noxious emissions, then the cost of control can be reduced to a manageable range. It is unlikely that just one parameter can be found, but a combination of measures such as CO, which is a good indicator of complete combustion, particulates, which appear to carry much of the Dioxin emitted, and perhaps HCl, because its removal carries along so many other pollutants, may provide useful controls.

The use of classical statistical quality-control methods derived from the manufacturing industries, where continuous variables are used to monitor production, is probably inappropriate because of the chaotic nature of the process. The heterogeneous feed is in marked contrast to the uniformity of raw materials that is the aim of every factory manager. It would be more appropriate to count "alarms" or excursions of a variable that is easy to monitor and highly correlated with desired output. Quality-control programs based on counts have been developed for radiation monitoring and may perhaps be useful for furnace control.

Another problem with sampling from a furnace is hold-up. A slug of gas, for example from the explosion of a can of paint, will be spread out as it passes through the furnace so that some of it may take much longer than the average flow time through the furnace, which may be around 10 s. Furthermore, some of the solids may be held up for long periods on surfaces of ducts and be periodically released (see Vogg *et al.* in this issue). For example, Bergstrom (1986) found mercury emissions many hours after the solid waste fuel had been replaced by wood that was free from mercury.

4. Problems with non-normal data

4.1. *The log-normal distribution*

When the primary data are concentrations there are typically many small values and a few larger ones. The median or middle value is smaller than the average and the standard deviation may be large and comparable to the average. Such data cannot be described by a normal distribution because lower confidence limits become meaningless negative numbers. Calculations depend ultimately on normal distributions and there is a great temptation to try to use the tools one has and hope that the deviations from normality will not be too serious. An alternative is to convert the data to a form that is more nearly normal. A great number of workers have found, by trial, that the logarithms of data such as these are more nearly normal than the raw data. As pointed out by Dean (1981) and others, the log-normal distribution has just as strong a theoretical base as the normal distribution. From a chemists point of view, one can also say that, if the concentrations are log-normal, the chemical activities, such as pH, are normally distributed.

Modern computers and even desk calculators now make it easy to do log-normal statistics, usually (for the benefit of the machine) to the base of natural logarithms ($\log_e$). This editor refuses to publish graphs whose ordinates are in natural logarithms because few people can interpret the values at sight. When data are converted to logarithms for statistical analysis of variance, the assumption of constant variance between sets becomes much more realistic. A problem arises when some measurements are below the detection limit. One obviously cannot enter zero as a data point when converting to logs, and using the detection limit decreases the variance and increases the apparent significance of observed differences. The problem of such truncated data sets is discussed by Dean (1981). It is frequently sufficient to employ the detection limit as the measured value.

When data are converted to logarithms, the numerical values of the mean and standard deviation depend on the base of logarithms used. Such values should always be converted back to their antilogs. The average of the logs becomes the geometric mean (M_g) and the standard deviation (sd) becomes a Spread Factor (S) (Dean 1981). Many trace contaminants show S values of 2 or more. Two sd, which covers the 95% probability limits, corresponds to S^2 times or divided into M_g. If $S = 2$, this means that the confidence limits range from $\frac{1}{4}$ M_g to 4 M_g. The three sd limits, covering 99.74% probability, are correspondingly $\frac{1}{8}$ to 8 times the mean. If, however, $S = 4$, the corresponding factors (S^2 and S^3) are 16 and 64. Brunner *et al.* (in this issue, Table 4) reports a range of ratios up to more than eight-fold for four samples. Taking his total TOC, where the range is six-fold, one can calculate $M_g = 30$ mg m^{-3} and $S = 2.3$. Then, 95% probability limits are from 5.5 to 162 mg m^{-3}.

4.2. *Ranges and rejection of outliers*

As the range of Brunner's four values is only from 9 to 55, one might be tempted to reject a value of 162 because "something must have gone wrong". Before applying any test for rejection of outliers (such as the Q factor of Dean & Dixon 1954), one should first make sure that the population is within normal limits, i.e. that the test is applied to the logarithms of the data, if it is concentrations.

A common measure of the spread of data is the range. If the data are log-normal, then the ratio of the maximum to the minimum is the appropriate measure because it is directly related to the difference in the logs. Unfortunately the range is a relatively poor measure of the spread of the data. The ratio of the standard deviation to the range depends markedly on the number of observations, being, on aveage, 0.40 for six samples, only 0.33 for 10 samples, and falls to zero for an infinite number of samples. Therefore when quoting the range, the number of samples should also be quoted.

Especially when dealing with stochastic data, such as puff of CO and presumably other parameters, the rejection of any datum detracts from the confidence one has in the remainder. The only safe justification for rejection is if something went wrong which could have been detected before the data were examined. For example, any evidence that a sample was incorrectly handled should cause it to be rejected even though the value reported may be near the middle of the data points. Wild points are, after all, inherent in the fuel source: as has been pointed out, all of the mercury in one ton of waste may be in a single small battery, more likely there will be many tons free of this source followed by a container containing several batteries. In any case, the wild points are real but make it difficult to estimate averages. The geometric mean, which is close to the median or central value, is a low estimate of the average or the total emission, especially when S is large. At $S = 4$, the average is more than twice the geometric mean.

4.3. *Sources of error*

In the study of Dioxin emissions from one of Copenhagen's incinerators (see Pallesen, and Grove in this issue), the number of samples analysed (12) was not sufficient to show significant correlations between emissions and operating conditions when using conventional statistical tools. When the data were converted to logarithms, it was possible to do a classical analysis of variance. The results did not answer the questions that were asked when the experiment was designed, but they did provide valuable information regarding the problems that arise. The number of samples to be taken is always a primary consideration when analyses are expensive. Jansson & Bergvall (see this issue) have estimated that each analysis for Dioxin costs over $1200 and the collection of each sample may cost nearly as much again. Ideally one would like to run duplicate analyses, including the taking of duplicate, simultaneous samples to get a direct measure of variation. This was beyond the available budget but, by planning a balanced experimental design, it was possible to estimate the variation by classical analysis of variance.

It can be concluded that differences in data on emissions reflects not only differences in the actual emissions but, to an even larger extent, differences between sample-taking techniques and analytical laboratories. Until these differences can be resolved by careful quality control procedures, it will be difficult to set legal emission limits. Similar differences have been found by other workers reporting at this symposium.

4.4. *Correlation coefficients*

When a variable, such as CO, goes through a minimum or maximum, forming what Hasselriis (in this issue) calls a parabola, it is not possible to fit a straight line to the data. Using conventional statistics, even after normalizing by taking logs, correlation factors (r) will necessarily be small and non-significant. If there is enough data it may be possible to fit a second or higher degree curve with a high value of r. If the data fits closely to any smooth curve, the correlation is good even though the conventional statistical test for r shows no correlation. The smooth curve must not have too many arbitrary factors in its construction, because each factor detracts from the degrees of freedom available for interpretation.

Several examples of correlations that were not detected in the original reports have been presented in this symposium. For example, the Canadian data discussed by Klicius *et al.* (in this issue) found no linear correlation between furnace parameters and Dioxin emissions. Commoner *et al.* (in this issue) argue that the lack of correlation means that emissions cannot be controlled by adjusting furnace conditions. Hasselriis (in this issue) divides the data into two parts on either side of a minimum, in his Figure 4 this is at 900°C. The eight CO points lie quite close to a straight line. A calculation of *r* would show a high degree of correlation but, because at least one arbitrary assumption was made, i.e. to reject all points above 900°C, at least one degree of freedom has been lost. Roughly speaking this means that the sum of squares should be divided by six rather than seven.

When we look at the Dioxin (PCDD + PCDF) points in the same figure there is nothing to distinguish high points from low points and, although several sloping lines have been drawn, they are only suggestive. Assuming that the three points defining the top line are all from one condition of the furnace, we have still lost two degrees of freedom, one by deciding to exclude the points above 900°C and one by deciding to study this particular condition after inspecting the data. The result is that there is no confidence at all in the *r* value, based on these three points.

The problem of searching for significant results from a set of data including several possible factors is known as a fishing expedition. Suppose one were looking for cancer in subjects living downwind from an incinerator and taking for comparison either those living up wind or some other acceptable control group. Suppose there are 20 types of cancer reported and it is decided to accept data as significant if there is only a 5% chance that it is the same as the control. When a 5% or 1-in-20 choice is applied 20 times, there is a very good chance (64%) that at least one of the types of cancer will show a significant difference between test and control groups. Tukey (1978) suggested that when *N* multiple choices are made, the confidence limit is approximately *N* times the limit for only one choice. Therefore to have a 95% confidence in your result you must take 0.05/20 or the 0.0025 limit which is about 3 sd away from the average instead of 2 sd for a single choice. The use of 3 sd limits would also eliminate a lot of other errors of statistical interpretation, and would drastically reduce the number of results that get reported.

4.5. *Clumped data*

Another problem with calculations of correlation coefficients (*r*) comes when the data is clumped in two groups with little or no data in between. Thus, if emissions are measured at 300 and 400°C, with no data in between, as was done by Vogg *et al.* (see this issue), a very high value of *r* may be found. However, if normal furnace operation is at 350 ± 50°C and data are taken across the whole temperature range, although the slope will be nearly the same, the calculated value of *r* will be much less. The lesson is that confidence in statistical parameters depends critically on the data being normally distributed. If this is not the case there is little or no information in statistically calculated variables such as confidence limits, correlation coefficients, or *F* factors in analysis of variance.

The very large variance in normal incinerator operation, which has its origin in the raw materials and is compounded with intentional turbulance in the fire-box, means that a limited number of analyses of emissions can convey only a limited amount of useful information about what will happen in future operation. To get more information more analyses are required, but unfortunately the increase in confidence goes up only as the square root of the number of data points. To get one more significant figure, one hundred times as many samples are needed. A better method for making the measurements can increase the systematic accuracy, but without more measurements it is not possible to get a better estimate of the inherent variance.

The law of large numbers states that averages have a smaller variance than the original data, no matter what distribution the original data may have. Averages also tend to be more normal than the original population. One way to obtain averages at low cost is to pool samples, mix them well and analyse the mixture. This is an excellent way to find out what has been emitted, but it destroys most of the information about likely variations in future emissions. Because the original data are not normal, one cannot extrapolate from the variance of the averages of a few pooled samples to estimate the variance of the original samples.

5. Time required to make measurements

Some types of data require a long time to collect the sample. Dioxin emissions fall into this category. Approximately 3 h are required to collect enough sample for a chemical analysis. Such a long time corresponds to many loads of waste and averages out much of the information about the variance. In contrast, temperature measurements can be obtained in a time comparable to the time to burn a chunk of waste. Furthermore, temperature measurements are low in cost and individual measurements can provide information about the effect of various system modifications on the course of combustion. Figure 1 illustrates temperature variations in an incinerator when burning refuse-derived fuel (RDF) in contrast with bulk waste. The average temperature is nearly the same in both cases, but the extreme values and the variance is much greater when burning bulk waste.

It should be noted that temperatures measured every few minutes give good information about the fuel, but not much information about the fluctuations in temperature experienced by a particle as it passes through the flames, because the average time spent by air flowing through any part of the system is measured in seconds. Very high-speed temperature measurements can be made by special equipment and some idea of fluctuations can be seen by the presence of bright sparks in the hotter parts of the furnace. Therefore, temperature should be specified in terms of the response time of the temperature sensor as well as the maximum and minimum values observed.

6. Evaluation of toxicity data

Several authors at this symposium (Ahlborg & Victorin, Mukerjee & Cleverly and Commoner *et al.*) refer to upper limits of toxic risks. The upper limit, in an ideal case, would be the dose that would be not quite enough to have an effect on the most sensitive individual in the total population. In practice this cannot be determined exactly, if only because it is not considered ethical to conduct toxicity tests on humans. Where we do have toxicity information from accidental exposure the experiment was, by definition, not planned and actual exposures were not accurately measured.

In practice, toxicity is measured at a dose that produces effects in a significant number of test animals at at least two dose levels. Some assumption is then made about the relationship between response and dose and from this assumption the dose that will produce a specific low level of response is calculated. The result is the most probable dose that will cause an effect in a similar population of test animals. Like any other result calculated from concentrations it has a mean, which is the most probable value, and a spread factor that, in practice, is greater than 2. The cube of the spread factor would be about the upper one-in-a-thousand limit of confidence of the experimental data.

Additional factors are arbitrarily introduced. As the experiment was done on animals, and not on humans, and because different species show different response (see Ahlborg & Victorin Section 4.1.2., where the toxic dose of 2,3,7,8-TCDD (Dioxin) toward common laboratory test animals varies by a factor of nearly 10,000), a safety factor is introduced. In the case of Dioxin, an arbitrary safety factor of 200 or 1000 is included (Denmark 1984, Umveltsbundesamt 1985) even though there is evidence that humans are not especially sensitive to Dioxin (Ahlborg & Victorin, Section 4.2.). The result is a cumulative safety factor of at least 1600 (if $S = 2$) and which may be as great as one million.

It has become standard practice to quote only the maximum probable risk level including all the safety and uncertainty factors because this errs on the safe side (see Mukerjee & Cleverly, this issue, Section 3.). As safety and uncertainty factors differ markedly for different substances and even, as we have seen, for different official interpretations of the data, it is unacceptable to compare published maximum risk levels for different substances. It is necessary to refer to the original data and to the assumptions made regarding the dose–response curve.

A very important source of uncertainty lies in the assumption made regarding the appropriate dose–response curve. The simplest assumption is that the response is proportional to the dose in an all-or-none manner. For example, if 1 mg of a carcinogen produces cancer in 1.0% of the test animals, 0.1 mg should produce cancer in 0.1% of the animals and 0.1 μg should produce cancer in 1 out of one million animals. The chief advantage of this assumption is that it appears to have no arbitrary constants.

$$R = Kd$$

where K is determined by the data, R is the response (in this case cancer) and d is the dose. The equation could also be written:

$$R = Kd^n$$

where n is assumed to be one.

In one type of genetic effect which can lead to cancer, i.e. the effect of ionizing radiation, it has been shown that the effect on the genetic material is linearly proportional to dose. However, the carcinogenic effect, as opposed to the initial genetic effect, has not been shown to be linear and living systems have many ways of recovering from genetic damage. As stated by Rossi (1987) "The so-called linear hypothesis lacks any substantial justification in the case of radiation carcinogenesis and seems in fact most dubious in view of the complexity of the process."

An alternative hypothesis which may be more appropriate to carcinogenic chemicals is that there is a minimum threshold dose. This may occur if the chemical irritates the cells, finally causing more damage than can be corrected by the natural recovery systems and thus leading to cancer. The fact that many chemical carcinogens only produce cancer at the maximum tolerated dose (i.e. a higher dose would kill the test animal before it has time to develop cancer) suggests that there may well be a threshold dose. The exact value of the threshold is, however, very difficult to assess; Fig. 2, which is taken from the Layfield Report (redrawn from Johnstone 1987), illustrates this

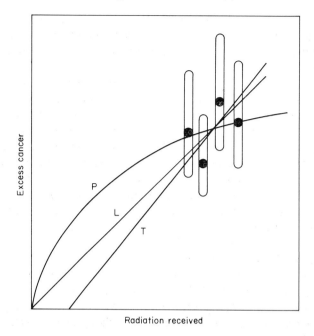

Fig. 2. Various extrapolations of excess cancer as a function of radiation. ●, Excess of cancer observed in four groups of people exposed to different absorbed doses of X-rays. The vertical error bars represent the range of uncertainty in the observations. Three assumptions are used to extrapolate these data to obtain a relationship between dose and rate of excess cancers at low doses. (1) The excess of cancer is proportional to the absorbed dose, as represented by the straight line, L. (2) There is a threshold dose below which there is no risk of radiation-induced cancer, as represented by the line T. (3) A relationship exists, represented by the curve P, which would fit excess cancers observed in workers at the Hanford atomic plant in the United States.

difficulty. Excess cancers as a result of X-ray exposure are the best evaluated human carcinogenic dose–response data available. Four different sets of data are shown with their average and range of uncertainty. Three curves based on three different assumptions, are seen to fit the data equally well. Curve L is the usual linear hypothesis. Curve T has a reasonable, but arbitrary, threshold. Curve P is a square-root type curve where the response is proportional to a fractional power of the dose; such a curve implies that very little radiation does most of the damage and larger amounts have little effect. Because it is not total cancers that are plotted (20% of the population of a developed country dies of cancer), but excess cancer above this background, it is hard to justify curve P. Curve P fits not only this data but has also been found to fit excess death curves of workers at the Hanford, U.S.A., radio nucleotide production factory. Obviously many other curves can be drawn through the four plotted averages and the origin. Like the T curve, these need not be smooth curves and it is not possible, on statistical grounds, to decide which one is the best fit.

Despite the large number of equally reasonable hypotheses, most officials charged with estimating carcinogenic risks assume some version of the linear hypothesis (see Mukerjee & Cleverly in this issue, Section 3.). The reason for this unanimity cannot lie in the data itself, nor does it lie in other physiological responses. Even such a simple non-biological system as a silver chloride crystal exposed to ionizing radiation followed by chemical development does not show a linear response. Low doses produce no response, above an effective threshold there is a nearly linear region followed by a saturation level where all crystals respond. This example from photography is admittedly over simplified, but even the most complicated theory of photographic chemistry is far less complicated than the simplest living cell. Why then should we expect a strictly linear response from whole animals?

A possible reason for the apparent unanimity among official toxicologists is that otherwise their conclusions would appear to be even more arbitrary and they would not have the support of their fellow officials (because each one would be defending his own special version). Another possible reason is that the linear response is certain to give numbers greater than zero. This is also a justification for quoting maximum risk rather than most likely risk; even though the most likely response is zero, the upper limit of the accepted risk is a number that someone can worry about.

Regardless of the reasons for the various assumptions which are made in an attempt to estimate toxic responses (especially cancer) at levels far below any possible experimental verification, it should be recognized that the necessary assumptions make it meaningless to compare upper limits determined for different substances under quite different conditions. Thus Commoner's assumption (in this issue) that the U.S. EPA uses the same set of arbitrary assumptions to evaluate carcinogenic risks from benzene and Dioxin is probably not justified. There is a great deal of information on toxic reactions to benzene and actually very little for Dioxin (see Ahlberg & Victoria or Mukerjee & Cleverly in this issue). Therefore it is likely that a much higher arbitrary safety factor will be used for Dioxin than for benzene.

Quoting an upper limit of expected risk combines the most likely value with an estimate of uncertainty. It would be more informative to quote both the most likely value and the uncertainty factor, including the arbitrary safety factor and the statistical uncertainty. The most likely value should be used in comparative evaluations because the upper limit is confounded by arbitrary uncertainty factors.

7. Conclusions

The lack of homogeneity in the feed (waste is probably the most unpredictable of all feeds to industrial processes) and the design of incinerators, which emphasizes turbulant motion of the gases, means that incinerators do not operate as steady-state reactors. Therefore quite extended collections of data are required to reach confident conclusions about incinerator emissions.

Many conventional statistical techniques based on normal distributions with low constant variances cannot be applied to data from incinerators without significant modifications. As a first step, the use of log-normal statistics makes the data more nearly normal. However, the rejection of some data because it looks unreasonable can hardly be justified.

Any report of a "maximum expected risk" from exposure to a toxic substance includes so many unstated confidence factors, some of which are completely arbitrary, that they provide little information on real risks. The data available are not, and probably never can be, good enough to estimate the low levels of risk currently believed to be politically acceptable.

References

Bergstrom, J. G. T. (1986), Mercury behavior in flue gases, *Waste Management & Research*, 4, 57–64.

Brunner, P. H. & Ernst, W. R. (1986), Alternative methods for the analysis of municipal solid waste, *Waste Management & Research*, *4*, 147–160.

Dean, R. B. (1981), Use of log-normal statistics in environmental monitoring. In *Chemistry in Water Reuse*, Vol. 1 (Cooper, W. J., Ed.), pp. 245–258. Ann Arbor Science Publishers, Ann Arbor, MI.

Dean, R. B. & Dixon, W. J. (1954), Simplified statistics for small numbers of observations, *Analytical Chemistry*, *23*, 636–638.

Denmark (1984), *Dannelse og Spredning av Dioxiner Isaer i Forbindelse med Affaldsforbraending* (Formation and emission of dioxins especially in connection with waste incineration), Miljöstyrelsen, Strandgade 29, 1401 Copenhagen (in Danish).

Grove, A. (1987), *Dioxinmålinger på Amagerforbrænding; Dioxin-Emission i Relation til Forskellige Driftsbetingelser* (Dioxin Measurement at Amager Incinerator; the Dioxin Emission Related to Different Working Conditions), Arbejdsrapport fra Miljøstyrelsen no. 5, Ministry of the Environment (in Danish).

Johnstone, B. (1987), Sizewell inquiry leaves question unanswered, *Nature*, *325*, 378.

Rossi, H. H. (1987), Rem overdose, *Nature*, *325*, 570.

Tukey, J. W. (1978), Thoughts on clinical trails, especially problems of multiplicity, *Science*, *198*, 679–684.

TVA (1985), *Sumner Co. Solid–Waste Energy Recovery Facility*, Vol. 2, *Performance*. Tennessee Valley Authority, Chattanooga TN.

Umweltsbundesamt (1985), *Sachstand Dioxine—Stand November 1984*, Berichte 5/85. Erich Schmidt Verlag, Berlin.

REPORT:

SEMINAR SUMMARY: EMISSIONS OF TRACE ORGANICS FROM MUNICIPAL SOLID WASTE INCINERATORS. By J. Aa. Hansen and R. B. Dean (Editors). (Based on material prepared by the following members of the symposium acting as a summary committee: L. Andersen, J. Bentley, J. Carlé, A. Grove, F. Hasselriis, P. Henschel, N. Olsen, L. Pallesen, C. Rappe, M. Suess & E. Yrjanheikki.)

1. Background and scope

ISWA specialized seminars were started in 1985 as one important step towards improved knowledge and communication between professionals at all levels of waste management. Results of academic research as well as practical operation are within the scope of such topically limited, specialized seminars.

The first specialized seminar in September 1985 was on Incinerator Emissions of Heavy Metals and Particulates. The proceedings were published in *Waste Management & Research*, **4**(1) 1986. These proceedings demonstrate clearly that a gap exists between emissions at most existing facilities (ordinary), and facilities which are equipped and operated to achieve low emissions of acid gases, particulates and heavy metals (modern); cf. Table 1. The conclusion reached in September 1985 was that the lower (average) emissions, referred to in Table 1 as "modern", are achievable by existing technology, given adequate installations, equipment, operation and training of personnel at each facility, and that the lower emissions would seem environmentally acceptable.

Dioxins and other trade organics were not included in the first seminar. Although removal of HCl was evaluated, there was no discussion of the role of chlorine/chloride in combination with organic compounds in various temperature regimes that will inadvertently establish themselves within incinerators from input of waste to outlet of bottom residuals or stack gases. Thereby, the need for the present seminar on Emission

TABLE 1

Typical emissions from MSW incinerators of particulates, acid gases and heavy metals in grams per GJ heat produced

Emission	Facility equipment and operation	
	Ordinary	Modern
Particulates	50	5
HCl	400	30
SO$_2$	370	100
Cd	0.18	0.00004
Hg	0.21	0.1

of Trace Organics from Municipal Solid Waste Incinerators became obvious, given the increased concern in recent years regarding organohalides in the environment.

The World Health Organization Regional Office for Europe, a co-organizer of this seminar, has extensive programmes on chemical safety and the control of environmental health hazards. It has published material dealing with various aspects of solid and hazardous waste and municipal sewage sludge, on the one hand, and on quality guidelines, health effects, sources and control technology of air pollutants, on the other hand. Of particular relevance is a chapter with guidelines for incineration in *Solid Waste Management—Selected Topics* (WHO, Copenhagen, 1985); sections on health effects, sources and control technology in *Ambient Air Pollutants from Industrial Sources* (Elsevier, Amsterdam, 1985), and *Air Quality Guidelines* (WHO, Copenhagen, in press).

On the basis of this common interest, cooperation between WHO/EURO and ISWA seemed relevant. DAKOFA, the Danish Solid Waste Committee and Danish national member of ISWA, became involved due to its own on-going work regarding incineration of solid waste, and was able to undertake the major part of secretarial work in preparing the seminar that took place in Copenhagen at WHO/EURO.

It has been the intention of the programme committee (cf. Annex) to make this specialized seminar complementary to the first one in September 1985. The result now is the two specialized issues of *Waste Management & Research*, i.e. **4**(1) and **5**(3), which together give a good technical and theoretical coverage regarding emission from municipal solid waste incinerators of particulates, acid gases, heavy metals and trace organics.

The seminar attendance was pre-limited to 100 participants, including authors and organizers. Details on programme, programme committee and organization can be found in the Annex.

The following views and comments are made solely by the group of persons named at the head of this summary. Neither the WHO nor ISWA or any of the institutions with which these persons are affiliated could be held responsible.

2. Overview and perspectives

Incineration is one possible technology of solid waste processing to reduce volume and weight of organic wastes. Depending on types of waste and stage of industrial

development other technologies may be more appropriate. Given limits to the degree
of recycling and conveniently located space for landfilling, it seems that incineration is
an attractive alternative for solid waste processing in many industrialized countries. In
some European countries more than 70% of municipal solid wastes is burned and the
heat is recovered.

It was made clear at the seminar that incineration of solid wastes is associated with
risks to the environment. Trace organics may be released, either through the stack in
gaseous or particulate form, or through the bottom of the incinerator and the gas
cleaning equipment as bottom ash (slag) and fly ash. These potential hazards must be
carefully controlled; i.e. sufficiently low stack emission must be achieved, and slag and
ash must be processed to the extent necessary for safe use or land-filling. The situation
regarding stack emissions may be summarized as shown in Table 2 based on emissions
reported at both specialized seminars.

TABLE 2

Typical emissions from MSW incinerators of particulates, acid gases, heavy metals and trace
organics* per m³ of gas at standard conditions

Emission item	Unit	Facility equipment and operation	
		Ordinary	Modern
CO	g	0.5–1	0.1
Particulates	mg	100	10
HCl	mg	700	50
SO$_2$	—	600	150
Cd	μg	300	0.07
Hg	—	350	16
PAH	μg	1–100	0.01–1
Cl-benzenes	—	10–70	1–20
Cl-phenols	—	1–100	1–20
Phthalates	—	25–1000	25–1000
2,3,7,8-TCDD-eq.†	ng	10–100	0.1–2

* Conversion from Table 1 is feasible by use of 1 GJ $\simeq$ 600 m³ normal dry gas, which implies 1 tonne
MSW $\simeq$ 10 GJ $\sim$ 6000 m³ normal dry gas.
    † Eadon methodology of accounting toxic PCDD & PCDF isomers (see Ahlborg & Victorin in this issue).

On several occasions the seminar stressed that MSW incineration is a significant
source of Dioxins (PCDDs and PCDFs) found in the environment. Several other
sources also exist, e.g. emission by automobiles, metal reclamation plants or widespread
use of chlorophenols (particularly pentachlorophenol). MSW incinerators can, however, be equipped and operated so as to achieve what seems to be acceptably low
PCDD emission levels with regard to health and the environment.

Results from the previous seminar on particulates, acid gases and heavy metals
showed that stack gases from MSW incinerators can be controlled efficiently by up-to-
date equipment and good operation. It is noteworthy that this implies multicomponent

choices in both hardware and software before satisfactory performance of the equipment and operation by the personnel be achieved. Training of personnel is a key issue if good operation is to be achieved. The seminar did not give conclusive observations on trace organics in slag and ashes (bottom residuals from both incinerator furnaces and gas cleaning equipment), because emphasis was on stack emissions. The issue of environmentally safe use or disposal of these residuals is, however, of great importance and leaves open the question of how to obtain "complete" destruction and thereby low emission of organics in both stack gases and ashes.

While several papers dealt with the destruction and formation of halogenated organics and the relationship between their ash and gas phases depending on temperature regimes, it is left for a future specialized seminar to provide the missing information. The possibility of a third seminar entitled "Treatment and disposal of solid residuals from MSW-incineration" was mentioned.

3. Sampling and analysis

3.1. *General*

Analysis of Dioxins is a very difficult and expensive operation costing about $1200–1500 (U.S.) per sample of flue gas emission. Early work was done on fly ash collected in ESP or bag filters for which analytical procedures are reasonably satisfactory. About 3 h are required to collect one sample of flue gas and there is great danger that the composition of the various isomers will change during collection especially if parts of the system are too hot. Labelled isotopes of specific samples are used to correct for losses during sampling. Losses can be as great as 75% and still be acceptable. Differences between laboratories analysing equivalent samples can be several-fold. Although attempts are being made to standardize methodology, it was generally agreed that differences of two-fold are not significant.

3.2. *Flue gas sampling equipment*

The majority of flue gas data is based on modifications of the U.S. EPA Method 5 Train for Organics' Sampling. The recommended Nordic methodology was presented by Jansson & Bergvall. Gases are filtered, cooled and organics are absorbed on a resin. Some organics are deposited on the walls of the equipment and some are adsorbed on the particulates. At least one labelled isotope is added to the filter before sampling begins. Other labelled isotopes are used to check for losses during the laboratory phase of the analyses. Present methods of gas sampling and analysis still leave much to be desired.

3.3. *Other trace organics*

The requirements stated for PCDD and PCDF also apply to other trace organics. The seminar did not discuss or provide a list of other trace organics to be included in a test programme. The following compounds are considered to be important and should, if possible, be incorporated in the programme:

hexachlorobenzene and lower chlorinated benzenes;
chlorophenols;
polychlorobiphenyls;

polynuclear aromatic hydrocarbons (PAH);

chlorinated PAH;

total organic chlorine;

brominated analogs of the above-mentioned compounds including chloro–bromo Dioxins.

3.4. *Reporting*

There is a need for more uniform presentation of data and a detailed description of conditions for sampling and analysis that make control of systematic errors possible.

PCDD/PCDF data should be stated as real numbers and be isomer specific for the toxic isomers. The toxic equivalent, e.g. expressed in terms of 2,3,7,8-TCDD, must be fully specified, if used.

Flue gas content should be reported at reference conditions, e.g. dry gas, normal state and 10% CO_2.

Description of sampling should always include: equipment, duration of sampling, sampling conditions, and deviations from sampling strategy and protocols.

Special attention should be given to the way that tracer isotopes are used.

For every sample the chain of custody should be identified.

The laboratory report should include a detailed description of the analytical conditions (GC/MS, GC and MS variables) as well as any deviation from the protocols.

4. Processes and performance

4.1. *Waste*

The importance of the chlorine content of the waste was discussed but no conclusion was made. Swedish investigations show that a ton of waste contains approximately 6–7 kg of chlorine, the majority of which is found in the stack emissions as HCl. PVC plastics account for only a part of the total chlorine. It was pointed out that the moisture content of the waste has a strong influence, especially as a parameter affecting furnace temperature. Incineration of special types of waste (e.g. hospital waste, burnables from metal scrapping) was mentioned as a possible source of high Dioxin (PCDD/PCDF) emission.

4.2. *Furnace conditions*

There is no doubt that high furnace temperatures will destroy organic compounds. Unfortunately the heterogeneous nature of the waste fuel means that average furnace temperatures give little informaton about cool spots. Grates that provide efficient burn out and post-combustion chambers that bring all of the gases up to temperature can destroy organics present in the waste. Fluidized-bed incinerators have shown promising results in preliminary trials. One of the most useful parameters related to Dioxin emissions is carbon monoxide (CO) which provides a direct indication of combustion efficiency.

Direct-reading CO meters are now available but are not yet easy to operate. Bergstrom & Warman found a positive correlation between the number of CO peaks and Dioxin levels. Furnace designs that minimize CO peaks are expected to destroy most organic emissions. Combustion efficiency, expressed as CE $= (CO_2 - CO)/CO_2$, is used by some authors as a measure of good furnace operation. Maintenance of high O_2 levels (near 10%) in the flue gas (which is directly related to CO_2) was also shown to correlate well with low CO, and hence with low Dioxin, emissions. Good instrumentation, automatic control of air and supplementary fuel to compensate for changes in the waste, and well-trained operators are all necessary for good performance. High emissions are expected during start up and shut down. Therefore continuously operated large furnaces should give better performance than small intermittent units.

4.3. *Synthesis of Dioxin after combustion*

There is no doubt that Dioxins can be formed in the furnace after the firebox or post combustion chamber as has been demonstrated by several authors. Fly ash deposits can synthesize Dioxins from chlorine that is produced by the Deacon process from HCl and O_2. However, a long time is required for this process and no evidence was presented to show how much of the fly ash deposits eventually reach the stack. This must depend on the techniques used to remove deposits from collecting surfaces. Vogg showed that the optimum synthesis temperature is 300°C and that synthesis on fly ash continues for several hours under exposure to various gases. He also showed that copper on fly ash acts as a catalyst for the post synthesis of Dioxins. He showed that the catalytic effect could be reduced by adding ammonia to the fly gas passing over the fly ash; this may have removed the copper as a volatile amine complex. Vogg suggests that black carbonaceous deposits on the fly ash are the source of Dioxin synthesis. Others felt that unburned aromatic compounds coming from the furnace are more likely precursors.

4.4. *Flue gas cleaning*

Most of the Dioxins appear to be adsorbed on the fly ash particles, at least at lower temperatures. As the smaller particles have the greater surface area per kg, they have more of the Dioxin. Therefore, just as with metals, flue gas cleaning systems that give good retention of particulates and operate at low temperatures give least emission. Electrostatic precipitators (ESP) have been shown to be less efficient than bag filters for removal of small particles.

The addition of lime to control acid gases also gives good reductions. Lime may be added dry to the furnace before the bag filter, or as a slurry which is spray dried in the flue gases. There are trade-offs between the quantity of lime required by the different techniques and the emission control. Analytical surrogates for Dioxin and other organic emissions would include particulates and acid gases (either HCl or SO_2) as well as some measures of complete combustion such as CO or O_2.

5. Emissions

5.1. *Stack emissions*

A Swedish study showed that emissions from one tonne of waste burned were about 5 kg HCl, 10^{-2} kg organic carbon and 3×10^{-3} kg chlorinated aromatics. This emission may be compared with 6×10^{-9} kg of Dioxin from a modern plant and up to 10^{-6} kg from a plant not designed to minimize emissions (see Table 2).

A Norwegian study (Oehme & Benestad) showed very high organic emissions from small incinerators which are usually operated batchwise. One incinerator operating with starved air had very high organic and PAH emissions but very little Dioxin. This can be explained as a result of no O_2 and hence no Cl_2 was formed under the reducing conditons in the furnace. Pyrolytic systems also have negligible Dioxin emissions. However, the combustion of waste oils or chlorinated insulation on copper wires showed high emissions, as did some studies of the incineration of hospital wastes (Rappe).

5.2. *Ash residues*

Concern has been expressed about the presence of Dioxins in ash residues. Very little is found in bottom ash (sometimes called slag although most incinerators are designed to operate below temperatures that will melt the ash and produce slag). Even the quantities found on fly ash from filter bags or ESPs is usually below the level limiting its transport in the Federal Republic of Germany (Barniske). In some areas it may still be rejected for landfills.

Bergvall (Sweden) found low leachability of Dioxins adsorbed on fly ash using melted snow. Other workers have shown higher extractability of Dioxin in waters of high organic content such as leachate from waste deposits. The problem of proper disposal of fly ash containing Dioxin needs further work.

6. Risk assessment

Risk assessment is a key issue in much on-going regulatory work in many countries. It is also a priority issue with several international organizations. Much work must be done before basic principles for assessing and comparing risk can be commonly agreed.

Two papers directly addressed the problem of health risks from Dioxin emissions. Other authors applied established risk assessments to their own situations. Although essentially all of the risk assessments depended on the same basic experiments, the conclusions regarding the health risk from incineration of municipal waste varied over several orders of magnitude.

6.1. *Risk equivalents*

Ahlborg presented a general review of the European approach to evaluating the health risk from Dioxin emissions. He explained the concept of TCDD equivalents (actually equivalent values of 2,3,7,8-TCDD that would have the same effect as the quantities of the isomers detected). In Sweden, the Eadon equivalent is most commonly used (although the original communication in which it appeared has not been published in the scientific literature).

All toxicity data are based on animal studies or on tissue or single-cell preparations. There is a dearth of whole-animal toxicity data for most of the isomers and most work has concentrated on 2,3,7,8-TCDD itself. Although all equivalent measures are arbitrary, they give results with no more variability than the analytical data itself.

Mukerjee presented the U.S. EPA approach which examined similar equivalent measures. The EPA attempts to calculate a maximum probable lifetime risk of cancer from exposure to Dioxin equivalents.

Both U.S. and European approaches include arbitrary factors to allow for the fact that actual toxicity or carcinogenicity measurements on humans are not available. There are, in addition, natural statistical fluctuations in the raw data. In effect these fluctuations multiply the maximum likely risk by an additional factor based on the uncertainty of the raw data. Different authorities apply different safety factors, e.g. Denmark 200, F.R.G. 1000. The result gives a very high level of safety, but it makes comparison of real risks from such standards impossible (see preceeding report in this issue by Dean).

6.2. *Risk from municipal incineration*

Different estimates of the contribution of municipal incineration to the overall levels of Dioxins in the environment led to widely different risk estimates. Many authorities had concluded that municipal incinerators have been the major source, although recent work has shown that pentachlorophenol (a widepread pesticide), paper mills, and perhaps automobiles have made comparable contributions. All agree that modern, well-run municipal sewage sludge (MSS) and/or municipal solid waste (MSW) incinerators generally emit consistently lower levels of PCDD and PCDF than older, and/or poorly maintained and poorly operated incinerators.

6.3. *World Health Organization*

Michael J. Suess presented a summary of a recent working group of the WHO Regional Office for Europe on PCDD and PCDF emissions (Naples, March 1986). The group concluded, among other things:

Inhalation of emissions from well-operated MSS and/or MSW incinerators appears to contribute only a small fraction to the apparent overall daily intake of PCDD and PCDF, including people living in the maximum emission zone.

The contribution of MSS and/or MSW incinerators through indirect exposure routes (e.g. food chain) to the overall human exposure from PCDD and PCDF cannot be determined at present. However, it appears that in particular situations a significant contribution could be made through these routes.

No information is presently available in the literature on the human health effects resulting from PCDD and PCDF emissions from MSS or MSW combustion. The degree of human exposure from such emissions is also unknown. Yet, based on information related to workers' exposure to very high concentration, it can be deduced that the severity of emissions from incinerators remain below that concentration.

The Working Group also recommmended that: the construction of small incinerators should be discouraged, when adequate and properly-trained personnel cannot be provided on a cost-effective basis.

6.4. *Center for the Biology of Natural Systems*

Barry Commoner of CBNS concluded that there is no consistent explanation for the fact that the rates of PCDD/PCDF emissions from different incinerators vary considerably and that there is no correlation between emissions and furnace temperature or combustion efficiency. He also emphasized that PCDD/PCDFs are synthesized in the cooler parts of the incinerator. Evidence from analyses of adipose tissue and breast milk together with the assumptions of linear excretion rates allow Commoner *et al.* to compute an estimate of the environmental exposure that must have produced these levels. Applying various estimates of maximum lifetime cancer risks Commoner *et al.*

show that the risk they computed is greater than the calculated risks that have led the U.S. EPA to initiate action against a number of common organic chemicals. Commoner concludes that PCDD/PCDF emissions from trash burning incinerators are a major contributor to environmental exposure of these chemicals. Hence the present PCDD/PCDF emission from MSW incinerators must be significantly reduced, if the cancer risk to the U.S. population is to be brought to a level consistent with EPA regulatory practice. He therefore concludes that "there appears to be a considerable and unavoidable risk in building MSW incinerators".

6.5. *Floyd Hasselriis U.S.A.*

Hasselriis presented much the same data on emissions as Commoner *et al.* and included more recent studies showing much lower values from new plants. He emphasized that several variables, particularly CO and Dioxin production, pass through a minimum with respect to O_2. He showed linear correlations when plotting data on one side of the minimum where the original study had reported no correlation. Bergstrom & Warman (Sweden) showed the same minimum with regard to CO and others also related the CO minimum to low Dioxin emissions.

Hasselriis further emphasized that gas cooling below 200°C and efficient acid gas and particulate removal will bring Dioxin emissions down to detection limits which are orders of magnitude below emissions from unregulated incinerators.

6.6. *Christoffer Rappe* et al., *Sweden*

A summary of available data, though from very few countries, indicated a generally low background for toxic Dioxins in the environment. The isomeric distribution indicated a combination of sources, e.g. incineration and technical products such as pentachlorophenol in addition to selective degradation of isomers. It is clear from the data that inhalation exposure is marginal compared to the exposure via food, especially fish and other foodstuffs from the aquatic food web. However, a correlation between incinerators of various kinds and the environmental levels of PCDDs and PCDFs seems quite likely. Consequently, all such emissions should be controlled and minimized.

7. National policies

A wide variety of national policies regarding control of Dioxin emissions were presented. Sweden, where a temporary ban on new incinerator construction had been imposed, now permits and encourages MSW incineration provided that measured Dioxin and other emissions are within specified limits (Bergvall). The F.R.G. recommends that limit values for Dioxin emissions are neither necessary nor practical. However, from the point of view of preventive environmental protection, Dioxin emissions should be further reduced as far as is possible with present-day technology (Barniske).

The U.K. depends on "best practicable means" for controlling all emissions. The Council of European Communities, while endorsing best available technology "not entailing excessive cost" may, if necessary, fix emission limits for specific pollutants that would apply to the U.K. and F.R.G. (Bentley).

8. Guidelines and monitoring programmes

The seminar presented various national approaches. Some important observations are given below. No priority is attached to the order of presentation.

A disparity of approaches and objectives was clearly demonstrated, which arises out of different legal frameworks and social systems. Quality objectives are frequently translated into emission standards.

The major thrust was towards protecting humans though some control systems gave consideration to general environmental protection.

Different critical paths were used. In some cases standards relate to stack emissions and in others to ground level values. Where standards are set they were in most cases, based on animal data. There is an essential interrelationship between individual standards.

There is a need for legislative requirements to be capable of practical and meaningful implementation. Standards or protocols cannot be absolute. They must take account of natural variability.

Where measurements are required there needs to be guidance on generally accepted methods of sampling and analysis.

An essential feature of any practical control system is recognition of the need for statistical methods in the design of protocols and in the analysis of monitoring data. There should be provision for feedback in iterative modification of sampling frequencies, protocols and standards.

9. Further investigations

A general need was felt for more studies concerning:

desirable design features;
optimal operation conditions;
(re)formation conditions in the cooler parts of the heat recovery boiler;
fly ash recirculation;
disposal of fly ash;
other sources of Dioxins in the environment and their formation; and
toxicity of Dioxin isomers containing bromine.

International collaboration in planning and implementing further studies was strongly recommended.

ANNEX

Programme

Introduction

J. Aa. Hansen, Professor, University of Aalborg, Denmark.

Opening address

J. I. Waddington, Director, Environmental Health Service, WHO/EURO, Copenhagen.

Overview

Impact on Health and Environment from Trace Organic Emissions, by U. G. Ahlborg & K. Victorin, The National Institute of Environmental Medicine, Stockholm, Sweden.

Sources of Relative Importance of PCDD and PCDF Emissions, by C. Rappe, University of Umeå, Sweden.

Formation and decomposition

Recent Findings on the Formation and Decomposition of PCDD/PCDF in Solid Waste Incineration, by H. Vogg et al., Kernforschungszentrum, Karlsruhe, F.R.G.

Sampling and analysis

Total Organic Carbon Emissions from Municipal Incinerators, by P. H. Brunner et al., EAWAG, Dubendorf, Switzerland.

Problems Associated with the Measurement of PCDD and PCDF Emissions from Waste Incineration Plants, by H. Hagenmaier et al., University of Tübingen, F.R.G.

Recommended Methodology for Measurements of PCDD and PCDF in the Nordic Countries, by B. Jansson & G. Bergvall, Statens Naturvårdsverk, Solna, Sweden.

Statistical Assessment of PCDD and PCDF Emissions Data by L. Pallesen, Technical University, Copenhagen, Denmark.

Validation of Sampling and Analysis, by C. Rappe, University of Umeå, Sweden.

Performance and emission

Production and Characterization of Trace Organic Emissions, by J. T. Bergström & K. Warman, Miljøkonsulterna, Nykoping, Sweden.

Emission of Dioxins from Incineration of MSW at Different Operating Conditions, by Arne Grove, Technological Institute, Copenhagen, Denmark.

Optimization of Combustion Conditions to Minimize Dioxin Emissions, by F. Hasselriis, Gershman, Brinker & Bratton, Washington, DC, U.S.A.

Identification of Polycyclic Aromatic and/or Polychlorinated Hydrocarbons in Emissions from Small Incinerators, by Ch. Benestad, Center for Industrial Research,

Oslo and M. Oehme, Norwegian Institute of Air Research, Lillestrom, Norway.

The Influence of Plant Design and Operating Procedures in Emissions of PCDDs and PCDFs, by M. J. Woodfield *et al.*, Warren Spring Laboratory, Stevenage, U.K.

Emission reduction

Canada's National Incinerator Testing and Evaluation Program (NITEP). Air Pollution Control Technology Assessment by R. Klicius *et al.*, Environment Canada, Ottawa, Canada.

Trace Organics Emission Following Post-Combustion and Lime-Scrubbing, by A. Magagni & B. Boschi, AMNIUP, Padova, Italy.

Risk assessment

The Origin and Health Risks of PCDD and PCDF, by B. Commoner *et al.*, Queens College, Flushing, NY, U.S.A.

PCDD and PCDF Emissions and Possible Human Exposure: Report on a WHO Working Group, by M. J. Suess, WHO/EURO, Copenhagen, Denmark.

Strategies for Assessing Risk from Exposure to Polychlorinated Dibenzo-*p*-dioxins and Dibenzofurans Emitted from Municipal Incinerators, by D. Mukerjee & D. H. Cleverly, U.S. EPA, Cincinnati, IL, U.S.A.

Rationale of national guidelines

New Emission Limits for Waste-to-energy Plants in Sweden, by G. Bergvall, Statens Naturvårdsvek, Solna, Sweden.

Air Pollution Control in Great Britain. Legislation and Administration. An Overview, by J. Bentley, Department of the Environment, London, U.K.

Emission of Trace Organics from Municipal Solid Waste Incineration in F.R.G. by L. Barniske, Umweltbundesamt, Berlin, F.R.G.

Design and interpretation of monitoring programmes

Design and Interpretation of Monitoring Programmes by H. Madsen & L. Pallesen, Technical University of Denmark, Copenhagen, Denmark.

Limits to Statistical Correlations of Data on Incinerator Emissions, by R. B. Dean, WMR, Copenhagen, Denmark.

Conclusions and recommendations

Final Plenary Discussion, by J. Bentley and J. Aa. Hansen.

Programme committee

J. Bentley, Department of the Environment, London, U.K.; J. Carle, The State Chemical Supervision Service, Copenhagen, Denmark; A. Grove, Technological Institute, Copenhagen, Denmark; J. Aa. Hansen, University of Aalborg, Denmark; P. Henschel, Federal Environmental Agency, Berlin (West); L. Pallesen, Technical University, Copenhagen, Denmark; C. Rappe, University of Umeå, Sweden; M. J.

Suess, WHO/EURO, Copenhagen, Denmark; P. Suhr, National Agency for Environmental Protection, Copenhagen, Denmark; S. Tarkowski, WHO/EURO, Copenhagen, Denmark; J. I. Waddington, WHO/EURO, Copenhagen, Denmark.

Organizing committee

J. Aa. Hansen, Arne Grove, Nils Olsen, M. J. Suess and E. Yrjänheikki.

Administrative secretaries

Kirsten Andersen, Aalborg University and Jeanne Møller, DAKOFA, Copenhagen.

Economy guaranteed

The Pollution Foundation of 1972, Denmark and Danish Committee of Solid Wastes (DAKOFA).

Scientific sponsorship

International Solid Wastes and Public Cleansing Association (ISWA), Paris. World Health Organization, Regional Office for Europe (WHO/EURO), Copenhagen. Danish Committee for Solid Wastes (DAKOFA), Copenhagen.